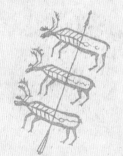

THROUGH INDIAN EYES

THROUGH INDIAN EYES

The Untold Story of Native American Peoples

THE READER'S DIGEST ASSOCIATION, INC.
Pleasantville, New York/Montreal

THROUGH INDIAN EYES

STAFF

Editorial

Project Editor
James J. Cassidy, Jr.

Editors
Bryce Walker (Chief)
Jill Maynard

Senior Associate Editor
Judith Cressy

Editorial Assistant
Louise DiBerardino

Art

Senior Art Editor
Larissa Lawrynenko

Associate Art Editors
Georgina Sculco
Susan Welt

Art Production Associate
Wendy Wong

Research

Project Research Editor
Pamela Kladzyk

Senior Research Editor
Christine Morgan

Research Editor
Kathleen Derzipilski

Picture Research Editors
Anita Dickhuth
Linda Patterson Eger
Sue Israel
Yvonne Silver

With special assistance from Associate Picture Editor Sybille Millard, Senior Staff Editors Alma E. Guinness and Edmund H. Harvey, Jr., Senior Research Editor Eileen Einfrank, Research Editors Sandra Streepey and Diane Zito, Senior Associate Art Editor Nancy Mace, and Associate Art Editor Colin Joh

CONTRIBUTORS

Consultants
A. Yvonne Beamer
Duane Champagne
Alvin M. Josephy, Jr.
Clara Sue Kidwell
Shepard Krech III
Peter Nabokov
Richard Nichols
A. LaVonne Brown Ruoff
Robert W. Venables
Edwin Wade

Writers
Colin Calloway
Albert L. Hurtado
Peter Iverson
Aldona Jonaitis
Philip Kopper
Jay Miller
Peter Nabokov
Joe S. Sando
Timothy Silver
Helen Hornbeck Tanner
Terry P. Wilson

Editors
John L. Cobbs
Charles Flowers
Joseph L. Gardner
Harvey B. Loomis

Designer
Barbara Marks

Researchers
Erin Davies
Jill McManus
Stephen Weinstein

Picture Researchers
Lucy Barber
Alice Lundoff
Sabra Moore

Copy Editor
Virginia Croft

Indexer
Vitrude DeSpain

READER'S DIGEST GENERAL BOOKS

Editor-in-Chief, Books and Home Entertainment
Barbara J. Morgan

Editor, U.S. General Books
Susan Wernert Lewis

Editorial Director
Jane Polley

Art Director
Evelyn Bauer

Research Director
Laurel A. Gilbride

Affinity Directors
Will Bradbury
Jim Dwyer
Joseph Gonzalez
Kaari Ward

Design Directors
Perri DeFino
Robert M.Grant
Joel Musler

Business Manager
Vidya Tejwani

Copy Chief
Edward W. Atkinson

Picture Editor
Marion Bodine

Senior Research Librarian
Jo Manning

The credits and acknowledgments that appear on pages 388–390 are hereby made a part of this copyright page.

Copyright © 1995 The Reader's Digest Association, Inc.
Copyright © 1995 The Reader's Digest Association (Canada) Ltd.
Copyright © 1995 Reader's Digest Association Far East Ltd.
Phillipine Copyright 1995 Reader's Digest Association Far East Ltd.

Library of Congress Cataloging in Publication Data
Through Indian eyes : the untold story of Native American peoples.
        p.   cm.
     Includes index.
     ISBN 0-89577-819-X
     1. Indians of North America—History. I. Reader's Digest Association.
 E77.T48   1995
 970.004'97—dc20   95-34273

CONTENTS

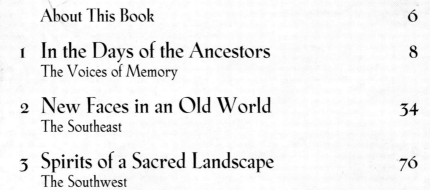
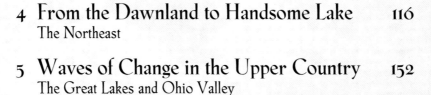
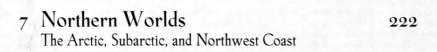

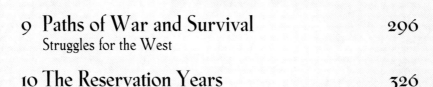

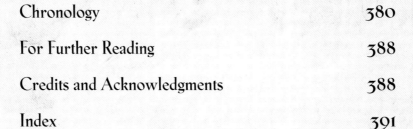

ABOUT THIS BOOK

History, it has been said, is written by the winners—a point that American history books have been proving for generations. The fact is that millions of people were already living in North America in 1491, and to their descendants the true story of the last 500 years is not told in those books.

> When a white army battles Indians and wins, it is called a great victory, but if they lose it is called a massacre.
>
> —*Chiksika, Shawnee*

THROUGH INDIAN EYES seeks to present American history as it was experienced by the Americans who were here first. They were a populace of enormous variety—500 or more societies north of the Rio Grande, as different from one another as Vikings were from Basques. They were sedentary in some places, perennially on the move in others. This group was generally peaceable, that one habitually aggressive. Here priestly elites ruled with absolute power; there village councils deliberated every issue until a consensus was reached.

For all their diversity, the first Americans had much in common. Foremost was a reverence for the harmony of the Creator's works, the web of relationships linking every human to every other thing in the natural world—plant or animal, rock or river, invisible spirit or thunderstorm. It was a world pervaded by traditions—handed down in daily rituals and seasonal celebrations, and in a wealth of stories told and retold by the old to the young, stories answering essential questions: Who are we? Where did we come from? Where have we traveled? How must we live?

> These stories were the libraries of our people. In each story, there was recorded some event of interest or importance. . . . A people enrich their minds who keep their history on the leaves of memory.
>
> —*Luther Standing Bear, Lakota*

The memories were nurtured through the ages, evolving as communities moved, subdivided, and recombined in response to famine or prosperity, commerce or warfare. Balances shifted, traditions renewed themselves. When the billowing sails of European ships lifted above the horizon, it seemed like another episode in the natural progression.

"Winter counts," as Plains people call them, are pictographic records on hide or cloth of each year's key event; below, a history of the Upper Yanktonai Dakota from 1785 to 1913.

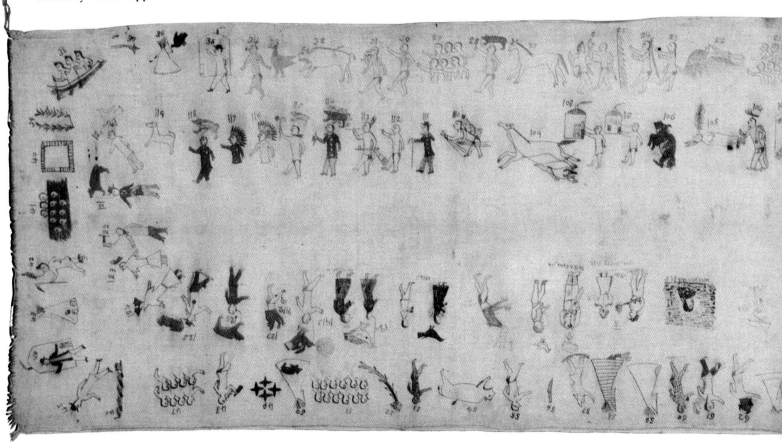

America's Indians (as they were soon called) dealt with the new realities as best they could. Some fought the whites, others formed alliances with them; some embraced white customs and values, others turned inward to traditional lifeways and religions. Most sought out their own middle ground in circumstances that were seldom predictable. Complex issues of personal and cultural identity continue to face native people across the continent, defying easy answers and familiar stereotypes. An ongoing debate over names typifies the feisty diversity of American Indian communities on the eve of the 21st century.

"I loathe the term 'Indian,'" says Lenore Keeshig-Tobias, an Ojibway, voicing an opinion shared by many. "'Indian' is a term used to sell things—souvenirs, cigars, cigarettes, gasoline, cars. . . . 'Indian' is a figment of the white man's imagination." A different view comes from Oren Lyons, historian, author, and elder of the Onondaga Nation. In 1993 Syracuse University sent Lyons a draft of an upcoming press release describing him as "the first native American to deliver the commencement address at Syracuse." Lyons asked that the phrase "the first native American" be changed to "the first American Indian," explaining that he considered anyone born in America to be a native American.

In this volume both of these terms are used, more or less interchangeably—much as they are used by native people every day. Similarly, readers will find variants of some tribal names—Ojibwa, Ojibway, Ojibwe, and Chippewa, for example, are all used today by separate bands of the people originally known as Anishinabe—variations that reflect the preferences of individuals or groups, changes in usage over the years, and other factors.

A note on style: THROUGH INDIAN EYES draws extensively on the oral histories and storytelling traditions that have enriched native American life from the beginning. The words of Indian people appear throughout the book; the diversity of their voices is itself part of the story. To accommodate as many as possible, some quotations have been excerpted or abridged without the insertion of an ellipsis each time words are omitted. Nowhere, however, has the editing been allowed to alter the tone or meaning of the original.

There is far more to this story than any one book can tell, but it is important to begin. As this book begins, the editors turn to a contemporary author to set the scene:

I wish for the reader to imagine a Seneca storyteller. He is a hard-working man with signs of advancing age on his face. . . . It is eveningtime. . . . He waits for us, and we come up to him and say, "Grampa, tell us ghost stories." He would blow out a big puff of smoke, and he would begin: "Now this happened one time. . . ."

—Duwayne Leslie Bowen, Seneca

There is a commonly held
belief that thousands of years ago,
as the world today counts time,
Mongolian nomads crossed a land bridge
to enter the western hemisphere, and
became the people now known
as the American Indians.
The truth, of course, is that
the Raven found our forefathers in a
clamshell on the beach at Naikun.
At his bidding, they entered a world
peopled by birds, beasts, and
creatures of great power. . . . At least,
that's a little bit of the truth.
— Bill Reid, Haida

1

IN THE DAYS OF THE ANCESTORS

THE VOICES OF MEMORY

In the beginning, according to a story told by the Tewa Pueblo, the People lived underground in blackness. They did not know that their world was dark because they had never seen the sunlight or the blue sky world. After a long time, the People began to get restless and said to one another, "Is this all the world there is? Will there never be another world?" Then Mole came to visit them, digging his way along through the darkness with his little paws and sharp-pointed nails. The old men of the People asked Mole, "Is there more of a world than this, friend?" Mole replied, "Follow along behind me."

Then the People formed themselves into a line behind Mole and he began to dig his way upward. As Mole clawed away in the earth, the People took the clay from his paw-hands and passed it back along their line to get it out of the way. That is why the tunnel that Mole dug upward was closed behind them and why they could never find their way back to their old dark world. So ended the story.

A brighter beginning occurred one sunlit spring day somewhere along the coast of what we know as Alaska. The sound of two stones rang out through the ancient stillness, two stones striking together hard enough to break. It was an alien sound to any animals that heard it—yaks, mammoths, short-faced bears perhaps—because two stones rarely collide in nature. Thousands of stones, yes, when surf pounds a rocky beach or a mountain crumbles in a landslide. But not just two.

The sound was an audible omen, a tattoo that drummed in the arrival of a new species on this side of the planet, creatures that would bring change across the face of two continents. The stones striking each other, rhythmically, purposefully, could only have been held by a dexterous alien, an invader with a curious brain and prehensile hands. Slower than most beasts, weaker and smaller than many, he had an advantage in knowing how to make weapons to hunt the faster, fiercer animals that were his quarry. Here was something new under the Arctic sun.

Clockwise from right: Prehistoric panther images on the walls of a Pecos River canyon shelter are likely contemporaries of a whale pictograph found in Ozette, Washington. The bear or opossum on this shell sandal ornament from the Great Lakes region was etched between 1500 and 500 B.C.

◄ Preceding page: From ancient Cahokia, a ceramic figure celebrates the renewal of life in the bond of a mother and child.

The 500-year-old shell artifact below, from Ozette, Washington, illustrates a Makah creation story in which moisture from a weeping mother's nose fell onto a mussel shell and became an infant.

How can it be known for sure that skillful man came to this hemisphere fully human—that this continent is one of immigrants? Because all the remains of ancients ever found here have been *Homo sapiens*. In the Americas no trace has ever been found of *Homo sapiens'* forebears or cousins, the species and subspecies nearly like modern man, if generally older. These precursors emerged elsewhere more than a million years ago; their fossil bones are found scattered in Africa and in various sites across Europe and Asia—indicating that their restless descendants dispersed far and wide from their African origins.

Like "the People" who followed Mole, the earliest immigrants labored blindly to reach the New World. It happened at least 12,000 years ago, probably three times as far back as that, and possibly much earlier. Whenever they came, the sound they made cracking two stones together was the noise of human technology, as surely as the roar of an engine is today. Paleolithic tools—rocks shaped and sharpened to stab, slice, scrape, or stun—constituted the single most important innovation that ancient people brought here. With such tools, and the imagination behind them, these first immigrants launched the first American revolution.

Huge mammals had evolved on this continent: elephantine mastodons, hairy mammoths, saber-toothed tigers, bears and wolves of enormous size and ferocity, 20-foot-tall ground sloths, and the lumbering Bison antiquus, larger cousin of the species that survives—barely—today. It is probably more than coincidental that those enormous animals died out during the period when man was roaming the continent freely. While a warming climate and biological forces were already pushing the animals toward extinction, human hunters may have literally run some species over the edge. Armed with stone weapons, small bands of small men brought down individual mastodons and other beasts 10 times their size. Made powerful by cleverness, men stampeded to their deaths herds of bison numbering many times more animals than hunters.

The ancients all had greater powers and cunning than either animals or people. Besides the ancients, real people lived on the earth at that time. Old One made the people out of the last balls of mud he took from the earth. They were so ignorant that they were the most helpless of all the creatures Old One had made.

The difficulty with the early world was that most of the ancients were selfish, and they were also very stupid in some ways. They did not know which creatures were deer and which were people, and sometimes they ate people by mistake.

At last Old One said, "There will soon be no people if I let things go on like this." So he sent Coyote to teach the Indians how to do things. And Coyote began to travel on the earth, teaching the Indians, making life easier and better for them, and performing many wonderful deeds.

— *Salish creation story*

Whatever early man's role in the North American extinctions, the first invaders were the vanguard of a species that uniquely could adapt to any environment and change the very shape of the land. Here was the primate whose brain enabled its body to compensate for physical limitations, and whose mind weighed matters beyond physical and reproductive needs. Humans could kindle fire and preserve food and in time would domesticate other animals and nurture native plants into crops. Here was a creator of cultures, each one a constellation of language, religion, tools, skills, and knowledge that one generation passed on to the next. This formidable creature would invent things for its own pleasure, comfort, and posterity.

Honoring the Powers of the Sky

Created in every region of the continent — carved, chipped, or painted on stone, wood, animal hides, and other objects — images of suns and stars, comets and spirit beings paid tribute to the awesome powers many early cultures associated with celestial bodies and their movements across the heavens.

Carved by a Great Lakes warrior, the thunderbird, moon, and star represent powerful spirit helpers.

A symbol of vital power, this sun pendant was worn by Caddoan chiefs at Temple Mound in Oklahoma.

This rock painting in Chaco Canyon may record the appearance of a supernova near the crescent moon in A.D. 1054.

Chumash priests may have made this cave painting of a comet, a sign of disharmony in the upper world, to ward off the evil omen.

A stylized constellation of stars appears on an early Arctic reindeer-skin coat.

The winter solstice is heralded one sunrise each year by a shaft of light crossing this Arizona petroglyph.

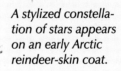

Many sunlike symbols are carved on a bluff top overlooking the Pecos River, an ancient ceremonial site.

This sun has feathers because a Sioux artist thought of it as a bird that flew across the sky.

A Hopi emblem incorporates the symbols of a star, a crescent moon, lightning, and clouds with rain.

This pair of "star beings" was artfully envisioned in a petroglyph left by the Anasazi of New Mexico some 800 years ago.

Morning Star, the son of Sun and Moon, helped to bring the sacred Sun Dance to the Great Plains.

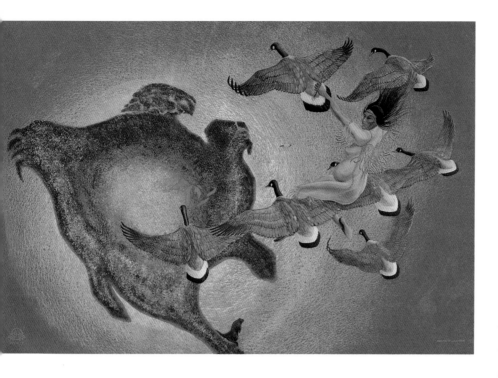

The Iroquois trace the beginning of human life to a time when Sky-woman fell to an island created by a giant turtle, which grew in shape and size to become North America. There she gave birth to a daughter, whose children propagated the human race. This painting, "Sky-woman Descending Great Turtle Island," is by Onondaga artist Arnold Jacobs.

Furthermore, these immigrants and their descendants accomplished feats of civilization comparable to those appearing elsewhere on the planet. The Maya of Mexico developed a calendar more accurate than any used in Europe. The Olmec and Aztec constructed many more pyramids than the Egyptians. The Anasazi of the Southwest built apartmentlike dwellings of a size and complexity not matched until the coal-powered urbanization of the 19th century. The Great Lakes area was the center of what may have been the first organized metalworking in the world, between 4000 and 5000 B.C.

Civilization had come to stay. Speaking 2,000 separate languages and dialects and practicing a wider array of lifeways than those found in Europe, these earliest Americans created trading networks that spanned thousands of miles. Collectively, they developed the indigenous plants they found into agricultural crops that account for much of the food grown around the world today.

Physical traces of early peoples are few and far between. Yet studies in many disciplines of our own time—archeology, biology, genetics, linguistics, and physics among them—offer compelling evidence that Native Americans descended from people of various groups who emigrated out of Asia, bringing different skills, beliefs, and traditions with them. Once here, they radiated farther and farther across the Americas, and in the process they became more and more distinct from each other in their cultures and ways of life. Just when they came and by what means are questions yet to be answered conclusively.

Retracing the Journey

For decades the opinion of most archeologists was that about 12,000 years ago bands of the first Americans walked across a land bridge from Siberia to Alaska—in reality, a 1,000-mile-wide swath of wilderness—that now lies beneath the shallow Bering Sea. This land expanse, called Beringia, was exposed when Ice Age glaciers impounded huge quantities of the world's water: sea level fell to at least 300 feet lower than it is today. When the last ice age ended, the glaciers began to melt. Sea level rose to flood Beringia and give the world's continents approximately their present shape about 8000 B.C.

The first immigrants survived by hunting the ancient mammoths, mastodons, and other huge animals so long as the animals remained. They armed themselves with arsenals of stone weapons of a type archeologists call Clovis (for the New Mexico site where this kind of implement was first found), relatively large stone knives, arrow points, and spearheads shaped on both sides by skillful chipping.

Clovis points have been found among the bones of prehistoric animals and identified as the instruments of their death and butchering. Durable and well made, they were excellent weapons for hunting big mammals that had thick, tough hides. Between about 9500 and 8500 B.C., Clovis points spread throughout the continent; they have been uncovered in virtually every section of North America, from Nova Scotia to Mexico.

What this means, however, is far from clear. Evidence of people arriving before the Clovis period has turned up in bewilderingly distant places, from the Alleghenies to California to the Andes of South America. One site,

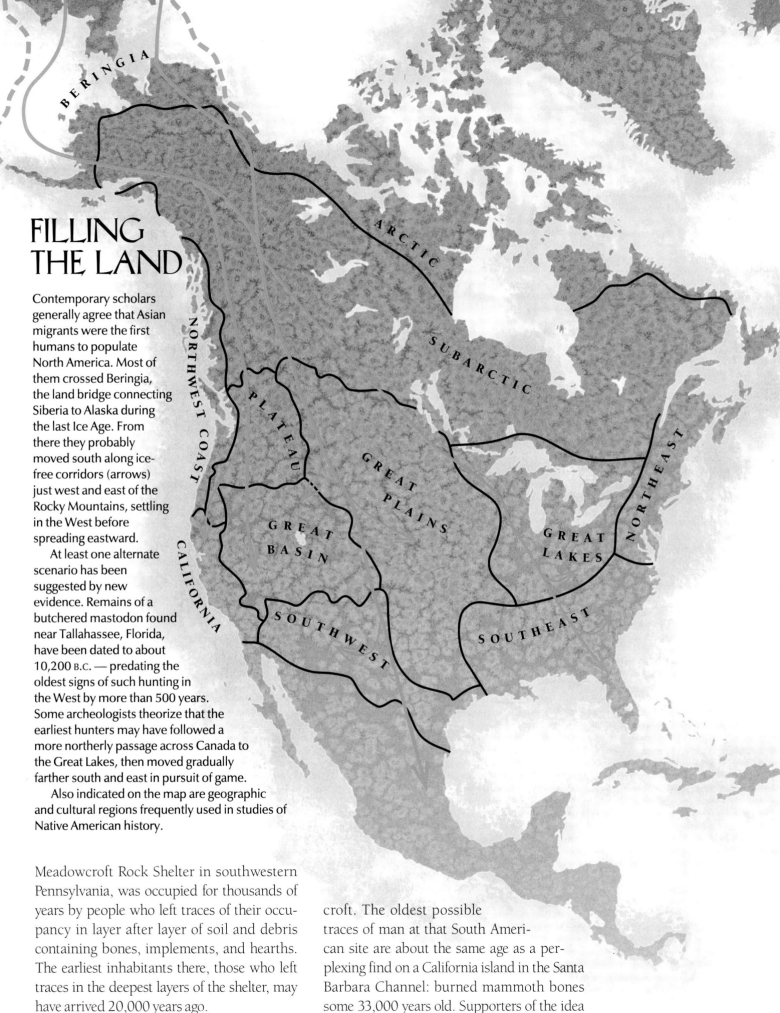

FILLING THE LAND

Contemporary scholars generally agree that Asian migrants were the first humans to populate North America. Most of them crossed Beringia, the land bridge connecting Siberia to Alaska during the last Ice Age. From there they probably moved south along ice-free corridors (arrows) just west and east of the Rocky Mountains, settling in the West before spreading eastward.

At least one alternate scenario has been suggested by new evidence. Remains of a butchered mastodon found near Tallahassee, Florida, have been dated to about 10,200 B.C. — predating the oldest signs of such hunting in the West by more than 500 years. Some archeologists theorize that the earliest hunters may have followed a more northerly passage across Canada to the Great Lakes, then moved gradually farther south and east in pursuit of game.

Also indicated on the map are geographic and cultural regions frequently used in studies of Native American history.

Meadowcroft Rock Shelter in southwestern Pennsylvania, was occupied for thousands of years by people who left traces of their occupancy in layer after layer of soil and debris containing bones, implements, and hearths. The earliest inhabitants there, those who left traces in the deepest layers of the shelter, may have arrived 20,000 years ago.

Chile's Monte Verde appears even older— perhaps 13,000 years older than Meadowcroft. The oldest possible traces of man at that South American site are about the same age as a perplexing find on a California island in the Santa Barbara Channel: burned mammoth bones some 33,000 years old. Supporters of the idea that migrants arrived long before 9500 B.C., when the Clovis period began, argue that

these mammoth bones were charred on a hunter's hearth. Proponents of the more orthodox view, that the "Clovis people" were the first here, say the mammoth could have died in an ordinary forest fire started by lightning.

To complicate the issue further, who is to say everyone came by land? Why not by sea? In the 19th century a simple sailing boat landed on the California coast with survivors after being blown off course—from Japan. Doubtless it was not the first time; maritime cultures have thrived on China's mainland for at least 40,000 years, and people might well have reached this hemisphere that long ago. Northeast Asians could have sailed to the Americas by a shorter and faster route than mainland Beringia offered. When the sea level was lower, they would have crossed northern Japan to reach Kamchatka

This Clovis tool kit has fluted points (second and third from right) and stone tools with single and double edges (far left and right). The bone shaft wrench (center) may have straightened spear shafts, while the foreshaft to its left may have attached Clovis points to shafts.

and the Aleutian Islands. From there these ancient mariners could have plied the coast as long as fish and game held out. Such a theory may be impossible to test, however, since rising sea levels would long since have erased any traces of coastal settlements.

Speculations of this kind lead to a larger question: what caused the earliest immigrants to migrate in the first place? The answer is twofold—some were pushed into it; some were pulled. The "push" is easy enough to understand. When food becomes scarce, whether because of a drought or overpopulation of an area, the scarcity forces some to leave. Likewise, people move when confronted with hostile neighbors, plagues of locusts, or any number of other difficulties .

The "pull" that inspires emigration is not so clear-cut. People who live by hunting, fishing,

and gathering cannot cluster in large groups for very long or stay in one place indefinitely, lest they exhaust the supply of game animals and edible plants. Such people habitually move on, often in repetitive patterns, because they know the larger region and its resources either by firsthand experience or through inherited lore. While they value a location rich in game, for instance, they may not linger there for fear that overhunting will diminish the herds or drive them away.

As they return to a series of such remembered places, nomads may travel in a rough circle over a period of many years. So it was that the tribes or clans of Asians who drifted into Beringia probably lingered in the thousand-mile-wide region for generations, even centuries, before moving on in any direction ahead of the slowly rising sea. They were in no hurry to reach a chosen destination. They could not have known where they were going. They may not even have known they were going anywhere.

In any event, migration certainly happened more than once. It may have been continuous over long spans of time, though it seems to have stopped when the Ice Age ended and rising seas flooded Beringia. Migrant bands almost certainly found their way east of the Canadian Rockies through ice-free corridors. From there they explored the Great Plains, the Mississippi Valley, the Eastern Woodlands, and the Canadian Maritimes. Others worked their way southward into Mexico and beyond or colonized the islands of the Caribbean.

By whatever means and routes, they came. The details of countless epics may remain obscure; what matters is that they spread across the land and got on with the business of survival. Continually adapting and improvising, people in each region would invent ways of life as varied as their newfound homes and the paths that brought them there.

◀ Overland migrations from Asia ended when rising sea levels flooded Beringia, leaving a landscape of ice, ocean, and jagged peaks.

ANCIENT MILESTONES

2,000,000 – 10,000 B.C. Pleistocene Epoch. The land bridge between Alaska and Siberia was exposed for two prolonged periods. Occasional openings of ice-free corridors gave Asian migrants passage to the continental heartland. The end of the Pleistocene, or Ice Age, coincided with the submergence of the Bering land bridge and the extinction of more than 60 species of large mammals, including the mammoth and the saber-toothed cat.

11,000 – 6000 B.C. Paleo-Indian Period. North American peoples hunted large mammals, using Clovis and other stone weapons during this epoch, which is also known as the Stone Age in Europe.

8000 – 1000 B.C. Archaic Period. This was a preagricultural era characterized by hunting and gathering and the development of a wide variety of tools. People hunted antelopes, rabbits, and other smaller game, fished the rivers and oceans, and foraged for vegetables and grain. About 5000 B.C. they became metalworkers with the development of the Old Copper Culture of the Great Lakes, which produced chisels, spear points, axes, and knives from copper. Around 4000 B.C. the early forebears of the Eskimo, or Inuit, culture appeared in the North. In 1500 B.C. Poverty Point emerged as a major trade center in the Lower Mississippi Valley.

1000 B.C. – A.D. 1000 Formative Period, also known in the East as the Woodland Period. Various societies developed pottery, stable village life, trade, and the beginnings of agriculture. By 200 B.C. the Hopewell culture produced large earthworks, a stratified society, and agriculture from the Ohio and Illinois river valleys across much of the Midwest and East. In A.D. 900 the Mississippian culture stretched from the Mississippi River to the Atlantic Coast and included the most complex societies in North America. Sometimes called the Moundbuilders for the elaborate earthwork temples they created, the Mississippians derived their sustenance from raising large crops of corn. In the West the Anasazi community of Pueblo Bonito was built by A.D. 900 in Chaco Canyon, New Mexico.

A.D. 1000 –1500 The first known contact with Europeans occurred about A.D. 1000 between Vikings and Inuit people on Newfoundland. The Iroquois Confederacy, probably formed in the 1400's, emerged as the most sophisticated political alliance in North America. Columbus landed in the West Indies in 1492. The Thule Eskimo culture was established across the Arctic, from the Bering Sea islands to Greenland, by 1500.

The Far North

Men say that the world was made by Raven. He is a man with a raven's beak. When the ground came up from the water it was drawn up by Raven. He speared down into it, brought up the land and fixed it into place.

The first land was a plot of ground hardly bigger than a house. There was a family in a house there: a man, his wife, and their little son. This boy was Raven. One day he saw a sort of bladder hanging over his parents' bed. He begged his father for it again and again, but his father always said no, until finally he gave in. While playing, Raven broke the bladder, and light appeared. "We had better have night too," said the father, "not just daylight all the time." So he grabbed the bladder before the little boy could damage it further. And that is how day and night began.

— *Inuit creation story*

The creation of day and night in the Far North did not carry with it a guarantee that they would follow each other in the same balanced, moderate intervals as they did elsewhere. The Arctic was and is a realm of excesses—in its extraordinary lengths of darkness and light, its depths of cold, and the lack of variety in its plant life. Excessive also was its wealth and variety of animals. The northern rim of the continent featured the richest possible array of sea mammals—seals, whales, walrus—to say nothing of fish and shellfish of many kinds. The tundra marshes attracted enormous numbers of breeding birds and waterfowl each spring and summer; the coast had myriad seabirds; the interior, ptarmigan. In addition, there were caribou and musk ox, polar bears and a profusion of smaller mammals, down to micelike voles—in short, a vast storehouse of sustenance for anyone with the skills, courage, and perseverance to exploit it.

Learning to survive in the exceedingly harsh conditions of the Arctic, the ancestors of today's Northern peoples seem to have passed on to their posterity a surprising but unmistakable social trait: they shunned hierarchies. Great chiefdoms and stratified societies arose in gentler regions where, perhaps, nature was more forgiving of a mistake in judgment or hunting tactics. In the Far North, where the environment presented dangers on a daily basis, egalitarian societies seem to have had the edge. Where there was less margin for error, each person remained responsible for his or her own actions.

If most immigration proceeded across Beringia, then most immigrants passed through the Arctic on their meandering way to temperate latitudes. The remains of ancient residence that have been found in the Arctic generally date a few thousand years after the Clovis period, as if all the early venturers continued south, leaving vacant space for later immigrants who came this way. For these and other reasons, it seems likely that the forebears of modern Inuit and Aleut peoples were in the last "wave" of migrants from Siberia.

Some of these newcomers showed amazing stability. One community numbering perhaps 75 at any given time abided on the Aleutian island of Anangula for at least 500 years during the seventh millennium B.C. That is longer than the Roman Empire would last (and longer so far than any settlement of European descendants in what they were taught to call the New World). The Anangulans might have stayed even longer had they not been driven away when volcanic ash blanketed their domain in 6250 B.C. They lived in small semi-subterranean houses built of driftwood frames covered with living sod. Evidently there was a strict division of labor: the women performed domestic work such as sewing animal-skin clothing, while the men spent daylight hours on the roofs making stone tools and weapons

As if swimming in a quiet pond, a polar bear seems to poke its head above the pool of sea-mammal oil used in this stone lamp from Kodiak Island, Alaska; it was made between 500 B.C. and A.D. 500.

as they watched for marine mammals and other game. Their descendants were the Aleut, who settled on the Aleutian Islands and parts of the Alaskan mainland; closely related by language and facing similar challenges were the Inuit, known to whites as Eskimos.

The distinctive culture that gradually developed in this region was fed by two main tributaries, both of which emerged around 4000 B.C.—the Norton tradition, spreading out from Norton Sound along Alaska's perimeter, and the Dorset tradition (named after Cape Dorset, one of the culture's major sites), reaching eastward from the Mackenzie River. The Norton people used stone lamps to burn oil for heat and light. They contrived the first toggle harpoons, which they hurled at seals and other marine mammals from the light, maneuverable kayaks they built to ply the frigid coastal waters.

Carved perhaps 2,000 years ago, this ivory harpoon tailpiece typified an Inuit tradition: fashioning tools that were also works of art.

The Thule people of Skraeling Island built sunken whale-rib-and-sod houses when the weather grew too bitter for tents. Polar bear skins, stretched out to dry, were used for clothing; the bowhead whale being butchered would feed several families through the winter.

At about the same time, as the Canadian glaciers retreated, Dorset people moved into the virgin territory of the new coasts and subsequently moved eastward all the way to the Atlantic and Greenland. They lived in all manner of dwellings—pit houses, sod houses, and skin tents stretched tight over animal-bone frames. They were apparently conservative in their hunting, however, taking only caribou and seals.

This specialized hunting may have been detrimental, because around A.D. 1000 the Dorset people gave way to the Thule culture, which lasted 700 years. Starting on Siberian and Bering Sea islands, Thule hunters built seagoing boats and broadened their hunting repertoire to take whales, big seals, and walrus —and became so successful that their way of life spread clear across the Arctic to Thule, Greenland (from which the culture later derived its name). In due course, the Thule peo-

Emblem of the vast Subarctic, the migratory caribou were an indispensable source of food and hides for peoples scattered across the Far North.

Below, wooden snow goggles of the Thule culture (A.D. 1000 – 1700) prevented snow blindness during hunting. Below right, a handle of horn or wood fitted with a sharpened slate blade produced the versatile ulu, used for cutting and scraping.

ple, with shared customs and essentially the same language, inhabited coastlines spanning 6,000 miles. Their descendants would continue to use a common language from Siberia to Greenland well into modern times.

Though a demanding Arctic environment would seem to have left no place for artistic expression, for centuries the Aleut's and Inuit's ancestors brought extraordinary care and skill to virtually everything they made, achieving high artistry in their weapons, implements, and accessories. A keen sense of beauty, even in everyday objects, was everywhere apparent. Wooden goggles that enabled a hunter to see in the blazing sun of an ice field took on a design that transcended their utility. So, too, a scratcher made of a seal's claw and used to coax live seals out of hiding had to be pleasing in form. Likewise ivory toggles that linked loops of leather thongs (knots were not used because they could not be untied when frozen). Most objects were decorated, and many took forms that are recognizable a hundred generations later—buttons shaped like animals, for instance.

Typically, every adornment had an animal motif in order to please the animal's spirit, or *inua*. The inuas were known to dislike ugliness, and the spirit of a bird or seal that was slain by an ill-crafted weapon would carry that message to its kind in the spirit world. If, however, an animal was killed with a fine weapon, the beast's spirit would return in the body of a similar animal and repopulate the earth. In the dangerous North, beauty may have been a form of insurance against weapons that might fail; thus the higher the degree of esthetics, the more food at hand.

The Subarctic Wilds

Inland from the Northern coast, the landscape rolls out into the vast Subarctic, a transition zone embracing some 2 million square miles of mountains, lakes, marshes, forests, and tundra. This immense realm gradually came to be inhabited by members of two very different linguistic families: Athabascan speakers to the west of Hudson Bay and Algonquian speakers to the east. The Athabascans, descendants of an ethnically distinct people called the Na-Dene, appear to have established themselves in the area relatively late—though still before the last wave of migrants from Asia spread across the Arctic. They may have returned northward after reaching more southern regions on the Canadian plains.

As if anticipating the successful Thule strategy, the Athabascans hunted whatever came their way—in particular, the caribou. In this harsh region animal populations fluctuate widely from year to year, and in order to survive, the people of the Subarctic became adept at hunting all of them in their seasons.

Over time the ancestral Na-Dene continued to disperse. Some moved into the Pacific Northwest, giving rise to such peoples as the Haida, Tlingit, and Hupa. Other Na-Dene went farther south late in the prehistoric period: to this day the Athabascan language family is represented in the Southwest by the Navajo and Apache.

The West

The People went through four worlds before they walked up a reed from the bottom of the Lake of Changing Waters into the present world. First Man and First Woman led the others, and with them came their two first children, the Changing Twins.

One took some clay from the stream bed in his hand and it shaped itself into a food bowl. The other Twin found reeds growing and with them he shaped a water basket. Then they picked up stones from the ground, and the pieces became axes and hammers, knives and spear points in their hands. Last of all the Twins shaped digging sticks from branches of mountain mahogany, and hoes from deer shoulder blades.

They found the Kisani, a different people growing gardens in the valleys, and the People traded their tools and baskets and bowls and weapons for seeds to plant in their own places along the rivers. They learned how to build dams and spread the water on the dry ground where it was needed.

— Navajo creation story

To survive in a desert world, people must ration water, as the ancestors of the Paiute did while inhabiting an inhospitable realm and pursuing a life that hardly changed in the course of a few thousand years before Europeans came. To thrive in the desert, people must manage water on a large scale through engineering. To be an engineer is to be a

builder—as the Hohokam surely were 2,000 years ago when they built a system of canals that the city of Phoenix mimicked when it built its modern water works. To be builders, people must erect things that outlast them, as the Anasazi surely did in the prehistoric cities at Mesa Verde and Chaco Canyon. To build a city is to be a governor, a manager, a merchant, a farmer; it means surrendering the liberties of hunting and gathering as a way of life in exchange for the luxuries of settlement.

Thus the arid conditions of the Southwest, rather than discouraging the growth of large, settled communities, seemed to spur development. Having mastered the problem of water supply for drinking and irrigation, the people of the Southwest stood on the brink of a thriving agriculture—and urban living. Farming in this part of the Americas, at least on a scale that allowed permanent settlement, evidently appeared first in Mexico around 3,500 years ago. Yet the domestication of crops began long before and must have occurred widely in small, slow increments over the centuries.

Between mastodon kills, for instance, Clovis hunters took small animals when they could (as the Arctic hunters of walrus and polar bear stalked field mice), and doubtless they gathered fruits, roots, and legumes in season as well. During the preagricultural period in the Southwest, bands of nomads remembered where they had found piñon nuts and returned regularly to those places. As they discovered edible wild plants, they must have encouraged their growth or dispersal, even inadvertently, as squirrels encourage oak forests when they bury acorns.

Among the early plants to be nurtured systematically were squash, beans, and avocados. Even prickly pears were planted, evidently in hedges for protection and as a source of seasonal fruit. Corn came later with the domestication of a wild grass called teosinte, which developed into maize in its many varieties, each suited to a different habitat. The implications of these changes were enormous. The cultivation of crops provided larger yields than foraging, and larger food supplies sup-

Dancing figures from a 1,000-year-old pot attest to the artful touch that the Hohokam brought to the making of pottery.

ported higher population densities, which led to social specialization and stratification—which in turn encouraged dependency on the higher food production provided by people who became farmers.

Whereas the nomadic life meant traveling light, settlement permitted the acquisition of treasured permanent possessions—witness the beautiful Mimbres pottery of the Mogollon culture. The people now called Mogollon grew corn and other crops casually in the game-rich highlands of Arizona and New Mexico 3,000 years ago. They lived in shallow pit houses clustered together, the roof of each one pitched around a single post.

Over time the dwellings here became more stylized: D-shaped in plan, then featuring more rooms in apartment-style complexes. So, too, Mogollon pottery evolved from plain brown and red earthenware to painted vessels—red designs on white ground, black on white, and polychrome. Whether the stylized figures of animals and people had spiritual meanings cannot be known; in any case they marked a high level in artistic creation that peaked in the second century A.D. and disappeared a millennium later.

A wonder of the age, the irrigation system engineered by the Hohokam was the most sophisticated in the Western Hemisphere.

The Hohokam developed the art of etching around the 10th century. Fermented cactus juice was applied to this cockleshell (acquired in trade from the California coast) to produce the design of a horned toad in relief.

Making the Desert Bloom

During the same general period, the Hohokam people lived handsomely in the semiarid Sonoran Desert to the west, masterfully adapting to their parched environs. Where water was lacking, they transported it through a system of canals that ultimately stretched hundreds of miles. These aqueducts were built remarkably well: many remain, and they testify to their builders' understanding of such matters as the mechanics of evaporation. (For example, the Hohokam enlarged the carrying capacity of a canal by digging it deeper rather than taking the easier solution of making it wider, which would have allowed more water to evaporate.) Like the neighboring Mogollon, with whom they traded, the Hohokam made pottery and decorated it with painted designs. They also etched seashells with acidic liquids—centuries before Europeans developed similar etching techniques.

Overlapping both of these cultures to the north were the Anasazi, who left impressive and mystifying monuments in the cliff dwellings of Mesa Verde and the astonishing pueblo cities of Chaco Canyon in present-day New Mexico. Within an area of 32 square

miles are nine old Anasazi towns, each containing hundreds of rooms capable of housing thousands of people. These communal dwellings were "solar powered" in that their dressed stone walls were built to take maximum advantage of the sun's heat in winter and to limit exposure in summer.

Chaco was busy; it commanded trade in marine shells from the Gulf of California, in turkeys and parrots from Mexico, and in ores, minerals, and metals from throughout the Rocky Mountains. In a manner of speaking, Chaco was a capital of capitalism, for it appears to have been the center of a turquoise-based economy in which that blue gemstone was traded for food and other necessities. It was also a center of learning, certainly in astronomy as well as architecture.

But it remains an enigma. Why was it abandoned in the 15th century? Why have

The Anasazi were renowned basket makers. The one above, made of sturdy yucca fibers and decorated with plant and mineral pigments, still had 48 ears of corn stored in it when it was discovered in a cave in Arizona.

few human remains been found there? Why did Chaco have the capacity to house a population several times larger than what the land surrounding it could possibly support? Why did its people expend such extraordinary energies making their roads straight?

One thing that now seems clear is the reason for Chaco's abandonment, which occurred around 1450, some two centuries after the eclipse of the Hohokam and Mogollon cultures. Chaco spun off a network of outlying farm communities and hamlets, evidently on the theory that the region's scattered rainfall must water one arable area if it misses another. But even the experience accumulated over several centuries could not prepare the Anasazi for decades of drought. The relentless dry spell forced the population away from Chaco to find water elsewhere—perhaps in the San Juan Basin and the Rio Grande valley, home of today's Pueblo peoples.

LIVELY RECORDS, VANISHED LIVES

Ancient cultures do not often leave behind pictorial records of their pastimes, work days, family life, or sense of humor, but the Mogollon people did just that. Inhabitants of the Mogollon Mountains of central New Mexico and Arizona, they were the first to make pottery in the Southwest, beginning perhaps as early as 300 B.C.

By A.D. 700 they were embellishing their pots with painted designs. Both decoration and craftsmanship reached a high point in the work of one Mogollon group, the Mimbres people, between 900 and 1200. Their subjects ranged from insects and animals to people engaged in all sorts of activities, from sexual to sacred. When someone died, a bowl with a hole punched in the bottom was placed over his or her face to let the spirit out.

The examples above date from between A.D. 950 and 1150. On the left, a husband and wife lie in bed under a blanket. Next is a scene of four women and a baby that is thought to depict a naming ceremony. In the center, the two men sitting on a crane's neck are legendary characters who helped the People emerge from the underworld. On the fourth pot, three men wearing horned helmets are playing a ball game, and on the last, a male weaver is posed next to his loom and a water vessel.

No one knows the exact fate of the Mogollon. They were probably absorbed into the larger Anasazi culture during the droughts and mass migrations of the 13th and 14th centuries and so were part of the process that helped produce today's constellation of Pueblo societies.

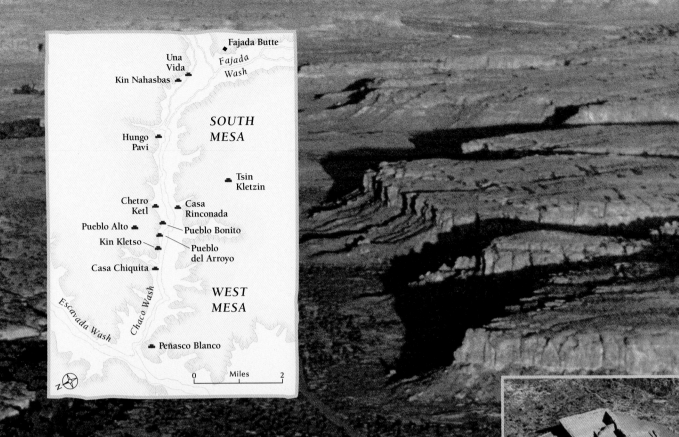

THE WORLD OF CHACO CANYON

Nestled in the San Juan Basin, Chaco Canyon — seen here in an aerial photograph — was the center of a far-flung cultural area, its parts connected by a starburst of roads that stretched as far as 400 miles in unerringly straight lines. Sometimes several yards wide, these roads ignored topography, running in carved steps straight up and down canyon walls. Since the Anasazi had neither vehicles nor beasts of burden, the design of these roads must have had symbolic importance; they manifested community and communication at least as much as they carried freight. (Some material did come by the roads, to be sure; the trees that provided logs for building the great houses grew no closer than 40 miles away.)

One site of particular note is Casa Rinconada (above right). This circular building, 60 feet in diameter, was designed and built perfectly round: each axis is aligned in a cardinal direction, and the midpoints of all

its diameters fall within four inches of each other. Casa Rinconada is a *kiva* — a place for sacred ceremonies that physically reflects its occupants' view of the world. In the center of the floor is a *sipapu* — a hole symbolizing the entry into this world that the first ancestors used when leaving a lower one. Further, its walls have niches and a window that, at dawn on the summer solstice, admits a beam of sunlight to strike a niche across the room.

As shown on the map above, various towns populated Chaco Canyon. Predominant among them was Pueblo Bonito, whose D-shaped ruins can be seen in the left foreground of the photograph. In an artist's depiction (above left), Pueblo Bonito is seen on one of its festival days, which were held regularly in the summer months to bring rain for the crops. A few men can be seen ascending in costume from a kiva, while other celebrants file down the road from Chetro Ketl and into the plaza.

This ancient figure of a woman from Sucia Island, one of the San Juan Islands south of Vancouver, was carved from elk antler. Her elongated forehead reflects the practice among early peoples of the Northwest Coast of shaping infants' skulls to beautify them.

A 2,000-year-old duck decoy (right) found in Nevada was woven from reeds and probably used by Paiute hunters to lure ducks to Humbolt Lake, a remnant of a once vast inland sea.

And just when these longtime inhabitants of the Southwest were adjusting to new conditions, new immigrants were infiltrating their homeland from far to the north. Seminomadic Athabascan-speaking groups, later known as the Apache and Navajo, arrived during the 15th and 16th centuries—in time to confront bearded newcomers from even farther away.

Survival and Surplus

Elsewhere in the West, some native peoples developed ways of life that would last thousands of years virtually unchanged and even survive the first ravages of contact with the Europeans. Early inhabitants of the Northwest Coast, for example, developed a culture based on the natural bounty of warm ocean currents and maritime rain forests. This was one of the most naturally abundant regions on earth, and the ease of living there left the people time to devote to material culture—wood carving, totem poles, large wooden houses, and seaworthy log canoes. They developed an economy of plenty and a society built on surplus.

When the ancestors of the Kwakiutl people of the Northwest Coast settled down for winter, they organized feasts known as potlatches, parties designed to display the wealth taken from the waters and forests. A chief would show fabulous hospitality to a rival chief from a neighboring clan—and in so doing threaten the other's bankruptcy, since the guest was honor bound to repay the favor. Thus the ancestral Kwakiutl built a culture in which clans and families were tied together in webs of mutual indebtedness that lasted generation after generation—as did the communities of substantial log houses that they built.

When the Chinook people of the Columbia River Basin caught the first salmon of the year as it swam up its natal river to spawn, they treated it with ritual respect, as their forefathers had learned to do: They placed the honored fish on an altar facing up-

stream, prayed, and roasted it. Each person in the community tasted its flesh, and then its intact skeleton was carefully returned to the river, whence it would swim to the marine world of the salmon people and report that it had been properly treated. Well into historic times, it appears that an ancestral claim in the annual salmon run was a perpetual legacy. Tribes that had moved away from the riverside continued to have absolute fishing rights when the salmon returned—as if their treating the salmon with respect had earned them the respect of other peoples as well.

Life was a very different experience for ancestors of the Paiute in the Great Basin, one of the least hospitable places on earth, an arid expanse bounded by the Rocky Mountains on the east and the Sierra Nevada on the west. These people were on the move more or less constantly, traveling in small bands, carrying most of their worldly goods with them as season by season they ranged across the landscape in search of edible plants and game.

Periodically some of these mobile bands joined forces to hunt and socialize. Each family owned a net made of twisted fiber, and several of these could be tied together into a single barrier that might be several hundred yards long. Then the people beat the desert bushes and drove rabbits into the net, hundreds and sometimes thousands of them. The bag would then be divided among the families, and doubtless a celebration ensued. When the hunt and festivities were done, the family bands parted again to go their separate ways.

Two other regions west of the Mississippi are worth noting, one for its vast size, the other for its complexity. The Great Plains, comprising an area of almost a million square miles, stretch from near the Mississippi to the east slope of the Rocky Mountains and from Texas well into Saskatchewan. For thousands of years people thrived here: first with spears, then atlatls, and later bows and arrows, they hunted the big Pleistocene beasts and then the lesser ones—bear, sheep, deer, antelope, bobcat, coyote, and others. But foremost among their prey was the bison. This herding animal was hunted throughout ancient times using methods that were models of cooperative effort. Many kill sites have been excavated that show where hunters stampeded herds of bison in a certain direction and drove them off cliffs or into dry gullies where they were trapped and killed. With dogs pulling the sledges on poles called travois, early Plains peoples moved often in summer, when traveling and hunting were easiest, then tended to stay put for the winter, waiting out the cold weather.

The societies of California are more difficult to summarize because then, as now, the land was a patchwork comprising seacoast, lush forest, desert, mountain, and fertile valley. Culturally it became as complex as it was geographically, with perhaps one-third of a million people living in hundreds of distinct communities when Europeans first arrived.

Pottery was of only minor importance here; instead, early Californians brought the craft of basketmaking to peaks of artistry and utility. Many nations produced exquisite baskets, decorating them with woven designs, feathers, and beads made of abalone shell and other color-rich materials. The most gifted basket makers used their wares instead of pots, plaiting them so finely that they were watertight and could be used for storing liquids—even for cooking with heated stones.

A triumph too often overlooked was the use of acorns as a dietary staple. Acorns contain lethal quantities of tannin, yet native Californians had discovered that when acorns are soaked, ground into flour, mixed with water, and baked, they make a highly nutritious food. Just as the processing of wheat and rice marked a breakthrough in the distant worlds of Europe, Africa, and Asia, the processing of acorns to remove active poisons represented an epochal milestone here.

This tightly lidded Chumash basket exemplifies the quality of California basketry, long considered among the best ever produced in North America.

Snowshoes gave Plains Cree buffalo hunters a vital advantage over their prey, whose mobility was hampered by early spring snow.

The Eastern Woodlands

Too vast and rich in resources for one culture to claim, the eastern third of North America was unsurpassed in attracting a variety of prehistoric settlers. Numerous monuments—"mounds" of many sizes, shapes, and ages—arose here and there from Labrador to Louisiana to the Great Lakes. A political confederation forged in the Northeast brought amity among nations that had battled each other for generations. Easterners also created new sorts of useful and decorative media, from the continent's first pottery (in Georgia about 4500 B.C.) to what were among the world's first copper implements (in the Great Lakes region at about the same time). Finally, peoples of this region independently invented the rudiments of agriculture as they discovered and developed small-plot farming in far-flung localities.

Archeologists now believe that riverside settlements and backwaters sustained small clans generation after generation throughout the East. By roaming a single area and coming to know which of its plants were edible, early Woodland peoples learned to manage and plant a variety of crops that differed from place to place across the midsection of eastern America, extending from the Atlantic Coast to the Great Plains.

Such crop-tending appears to have been women's work, and it went on without pause during the long intervals when the men were off hunting or fighting. This might explain why many Eastern peoples traced their lineage through female lines, since children naturally formed their primary affiliation with the

Abundance is evident in this 16th-century Algonquian village situated on a riverbank in North Carolina, where garden plots yield corn, sunflowers, beans, pumpkins, melons, and tobacco. The river teems with black drum and Atlantic croaker, shellfish is plentiful on the shore, and the forest is a rich source of game. Algonquian peoples lived in longhouses with coverings that could be kept down or rolled up in sections according to the weather.

parent who was seen as the more reliable provider. Women were indeed a stabilizing force, guaranteeing the community a supply of food from the plants they nurtured.

When Kloskurbeh, the All-Maker, lived on earth, there were no people yet. But one day a youth appeared, born from the foam of the waves, and became his chief helper. After these two beings had created all manner of things, there came to them a beautiful girl. She was born of the wonderful earth plant, and of the dew, and of warmth.

First Mother (as she was called) married the chief helper of Kloskurbeh. When their children multiplied until there was not enough game to feed them all, First Mother made her husband kill her. Then he and his children dragged her body back and forth across a barren plot of land, as she had ordered, and buried her bones in the center of the field. Seven months later they returned and found the field green with ripe corn and, in the center, fragrant tobacco.

— Penobscot creation story

Probably the women experimented with many kinds of plants. Those that produced rich returns were the hardy, seed-producing plants of the floodplains: sunflower, marsh elder, goosefoot, squashlike gourds, knotweed, little barley, and maygrass. As these plants proved their worth, the basis of sustained agriculture was born—sporadically, almost imperceptibly. It has been estimated that for upwards of 4,000 years the scattered peoples of the East learned by trial and error how to sow crop plants, take their produce of seeds, store them, and be sustained by them throughout the following winter.

The Northeast coastal regions were occupied for many ages by tribes of people who spoke Algonquian languages—the Narragansett, Delaware, and others. Descended from earlier immigrants to the region, the Algonquians had found ingenious ways to use its resources. One archeological site in Massachu-

SACRED MEDICINE WATER

The favor of the Great Spirit rested on the abundant forest, flowers, songbirds, and small animals of these quiet hills. Then a fierce dragon devastated the land, bringing disease and hunger on the people. The Indian Nations pleaded with the Great Spirit to subdue the dragon, and the might of all the heavenly forces contrived to bury it deep under the mountain, where it shakes the earth even today. Once the Great Spirit had reclaimed his beautiful resting spot, he caused pure water to gush from the earth, and asked that his favorite place be held neutral ground, so all can share in the healing waters.   — Caddo legend

Since that distant, unknown time thousands of years ago when the first Indians discovered the steaming waters of Arkansas's hot springs, its fame has spread far and wide. Evidence from stone artifacts shows that ancient peoples lived in the region, quarried stone from along the mountain ridges, and looked to the thermal waters and healing mud baths to restore health to the infirm. In historic times tribes as distant and various as the Crow, Blackfeet, Comanche, Quapaw, Sioux, Osage, and Choctaw gathered together to hunt, trade, and take the healing waters. Even when their peoples were at war, individuals of opposing tribes could come together here in safety and peace. In addition, a Caddo creation story tells of the birth of their ancestors from these invigorating waters.

The creative energies of nature are clearly at work here. As rain falls on the mountains and sinks down into the warm rock, minerals dissolve while the underground heat sterilizes and filters out impurities in the liquid. The water seeps slowly through the porous sandstone on the lower west side of Hot Springs Mountain until it flows out through cracks in the rock at a rate of about 850,000 gallons a day — the end of an eventful 4,000-year journey through the mountain. Thus the Great Spirit provides voluminous streams of sacred medicine water to all his tribes.

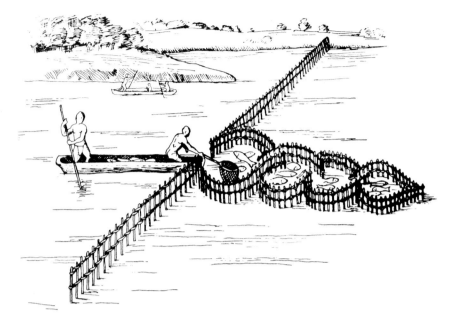

The major Northeastern nations might have destroyed each other in due course, but around the 15th century A.D.—dates and details differ in tribal traditions—a peacemaker came among them, and rival Iroquois tribes formed a political confederation. Leaders thereafter met regularly in a ceremonial long-house, where they negotiated their differences and agreed upon policies for the near future. So effective was this union that when Europeans came in numbers to North America, they encountered a league of nations that was a viable political force, one they would have to reckon with for generations.

The Hopewell Phenomenon

While agricultural and political innovations helped early peoples flourish in forests, on floodplains, and along rivers, the accomplishments that would give their societies lasting stature were more concrete—the celebrated earthworks known as mounds. Some of the most intriguing are clustered along the Mississippi River in northeastern Louisiana. This site, named Poverty Point, was best known for its huge "bird mound," which rose to a height of 70 feet above the surrounding terrain and had a span of 640 feet. A flourishing center of trade around 1500 B.C., Poverty Point proved to be well ahead of its time, anticipating the widespread building of mounds by at least 500 years.

The systematic building of mounds across much of the Northeast, called the Hopewell phenomenon (after the owner of one of the principal sites in the Ohio Valley), originated with an early Woodland people known as the Adena, who first appeared in the Ohio Valley in about 1000 B.C. Around 200 B.C. the Adena culture began to be eclipsed by that of the Hopewell, which flourished for at least seven centuries thereafter, until A.D. 500.

Not confined to any single native people or language group, the Hopewell tradition embraced a way of living. Inhabiting fairly permanent villages ranging from Ontario down to Arkansas and Florida, Hopewell people traded staples and exotic luxury items that in-

setts revealed food remains that included beaver, dog, fox, bear, mink, seal, deer, heron, duck, hawk, eagle, turtle, stingray, sturgeon, bass, scallop, clam, and snail. In short, these people left no potential food source untapped—sea, lake, forest, or air. They gathered wild plants and cultivated domestic ones, including squash and later a hardy kind of corn adapted to the shorter growing season. Their villages were more or less permanent and had domed houses framed with saplings and covered with bark and animal skins.

Occupying the inland forests that skirted Lakes Ontario and Erie were people of a different heritage, the Iroquois nations of present-day Canada and New York State. At least five related populations—ancestors of the Mohawk, Oneida, Onondaga, Cayuga, and Seneca—lived in large fortified villages. They moved from time to time, and they used fire to clear land for crops and to keep the forests open, a practice that encouraged the growth of brushy browse for deer and other animals.

These peoples also shared a tradition of warfare that centered on taking prisoners and either adopting them into the captor's society or, more often, sacrificing them. Evidence that enemies raided each other's towns regularly appears in distinctive pottery styles found at different sites—the work of captive women who continued to make their highly personalized pottery after being forcibly resettled.

In the sketch above, Indians in Virginia are seen trapping fish in reed weirs, where they could then be speared with lances. A slate bannerstone (below) found in Indiana and dating from 2000 – 1000 B.C. was meant to be attached to a spear thrower; it increased the hunter's thrust and balance, enabling him to throw the weapon farther and with greater accuracy.

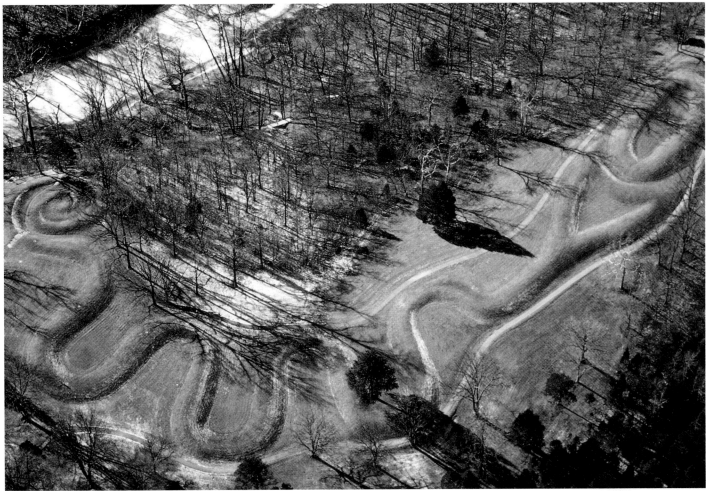

cluded copper from the Great Lakes, mica from Appalachia, seashells from the Atlantic and Gulf coasts, and glasslike obsidian from the Rocky Mountains. Although different groups developed their own styles of material goods, all the Hopewell peoples shared a fascination with earthworks—the most spectacular of which were animal effigies such as the 1,200-foot-long Great Serpent Mound, erected by their Adena predecessors along a river bluff near Chillicothe, Ohio. In other locations earthworks were built in geometric shapes to surround and protect religious ceremonial centers or to provide a stage for the ceremonies themselves.

Hopewell societies devoted extraordinary energy and resources to the burial of their dead, whose lavish tombs they furnished with a large array of items. Their artisans were among the most accomplished in North America, as reflected in the craftsmanship of objects recovered from their burial mounds. They created sophisticated pottery and ceramic figures, fashioned exquisitely wrought objects of bone and wood, and crafted the finest tools and ornaments of their time out of copper, silver, and gold.

Along the great rivers serving the continent's heartland, the Hopewell family of cultures was followed by another constellation of societies known collectively as the Mississippians. This way of life arose by the middle of the first millennium A.D. and proved remarkably durable, continuing to thrive in several areas up to the time of the first European incursions 1,000 years later.

Mississippian Monuments

Mississippian cultures could depend more heavily than did their predecessors on systematic agriculture, since corn had gradually become a staple—perhaps after being imported from Mexico, but in any case after the development of hardier varieties from early Southwestern strains. These nations also displayed the increased social organization needed to erect even larger earthworks, such as those at Moundville, Alabama—one of which required 4 million cubic feet of earth. This was a temple mound, the centerpiece of a cluster of

The Great Serpent Mound in Ohio (top), like other elaborate burial mounds, contained rich caches of Hopewellian artifacts, such as this ceramic figure of a mother and child, unearthed in Illinois.

EARTHEN MASTERWORKS OF POVERTY POINT

When Solomon succeeded David as king of Israel around 1000 B.C., this site — half a world away, in what is now northeastern Louisiana — was a crossroads of commerce for the whole Lower Mississippi Valley. Located at a junction of major rivers, it tied together a waterborne network that brought goods from as far away as the the Appalachian Mountains and the Great Lakes.

The curious name Poverty Point was given to the site in the 19th century because it was considered a poor spot for a plantation. But during its heyday around 1500 B.C., this was the largest, most prosperous locality in North America — and it celebrated the fact with a complex of earthworks so sprawling that their very existence was revealed only several decades ago by aerial photography.

Since then, archeologists have pieced together an astonishing picture: a semicircle of six concentric ridges 4 to 6 feet tall, each between 50 and 150 feet wide and spaced 50 to 150 feet apart, stretching almost three-quarters of a mile from one end of the outer arc to the other. The dramatic bird-shaped mound at the back of the semicircle — measuring 640 feet by 710 feet — was probably used for religious ceremonies. The conical

mound across the roadway and the oval mound in the plaza are among other examples of the earliest earthworks created anywhere on the continent.

The site could accommodate thousands of people at once, though whether they resided there for seasons or years at a stretch cannot be said. It may have been a gathering place for special ceremonies such as solstice observances or for trade fairs. However long they stayed, the majority lived in houses of cane thatch and daub built on the semicircular ridges; others probably lived on the land behind the complex and in dwellings scattered along the bluff outside the 37-acre central plaza. There is no evidence of major agricultural crops at Poverty Point, although the people could have survived by hunting, fishing, and gathering, since wild plants and animals were abundant all year long. But there is ample evidence of social cohesion in the thousands of artifacts left behind. And proof of political organization is manifest in the very fact that these people, using Stone Age digging tools and woven baskets, created earthworks that contained nearly 1 million cubic yards of dirt and required perhaps 5 million man-hours of sustained, coordinated effort.

Obsidian cutting tools from Arctic and Sub-arctic sites were traded far to the south.

The Grand Portage, a river-and-land network linking the Great Lakes with central and northern Canada, was the scene of ongoing trade in copper utensils and ornaments.

Blankets, canoes, whale oil, and shells from the Northwest Coast moved inland in exchange for pelts and obsidian from the Plateau.

Mandan villages on the Missouri River were magnets for commerce in buffalo robes, deer hides, dried foods, flint, and craft items.

Wampum beads from Long Island Sound traveled north to Nova Scotia, gaining value along the way.

Ornamental shell beads from coastal California were traded for cotton blankets, pottery, and stone axes from the Southwest.

Woven garments from the Southeastern interior were taken downriver to trade for saltwater fish and other coastal items.

Cahokia

Chaco Canyon

Bird feathers and turtle eggs from Florida were prized items in Cuba and the Bahamas.

Poverty Point

ANCIENT TRADERS

North America's original trail blazers, the earliest entrepreneurs began by traveling along familiar trails to trade with their nearest neighbors. In time, though, virtually all tribal groups became aware of a world beyond their immediate territories and a much greater variety of goods available for barter. Of special interst were materials and products unavailable locally — obsidian blades and drills, copper for both decorative and practical objects, and other valuable minerals from salt and silica to turquoise and meteoric iron.

Caddoan merchants delivered valuable bow-wood to customers in the Southwest.

Eventually a loose trade network spanned the entire continent, with routes typically following rivers and moving across or around bodies of water: the Mississippi, Ohio, Missouri and other rivers were all major arteries. This web of trails allowed copper implements forged in the upper Great Lakes region, for example, to be exchanged for ornamental shells from the Gulf of Mexico at the trading junction of Cahokia in Illinois. At different times, Poverty Point in Louisiana, Chaco Canyon in Arizona, and other strategic centers grew prosperous as crossroads for commerce that appeared from the Atlantic to the Pacific and from the Far North to Mesoamerica centuries before any Europeans set foot on the continent.

▲ Obsidian

◆ Copper

■ Other Minerals

earthen platforms that supported the homes of the local aristocracy and symbolically raised them closer to the sky. The common folk had their less exalted homes in outlying communities along the Black Warrior River.

Life was good for the Mississippians. At Moundville they cultivated an array of grasses, including corn, as well as legumes and gourds. They fished the river and hunted the game-rich woods—which, much like the peoples of the Northeast, they kept in a condition Europeans later described as parklike by burning back the underbrush.

Other ceremonial centers arose in Georgia, in Oklahoma, and most impressively in Cahokia, Illinois. Here, across the Mississippi from present-day St. Louis, a central mound covering some 15 acres towered over a city that in A.D. 1200 had perhaps 40,000 residents. These extended communities, stable and prosperous, represented a new form of social and political organization. They were chiefdoms, governed by an elite hereditary sect, class, or clan—which in turn was usually ruled by a single individual.

So it is that the development of a highly complex social structure should be added to the wealth of cultural assets indigenous to this hemisphere. Among these assets are any number of masterpieces—monumental architecture, practical artistry in ceramics and basketmaking, applied physics and astronomy, dramatic advances in agriculture, dynamic politics, devout spirituality, and an accumulated wealth of myth, legend, and oral literature. It is especially intriguing to consider that all these things and more had been woven into the fabric of American life long before ambitious mariners from Europe accidentally learned of the existence of this vast, ancient land.

> Will you ever begin to understand the meaning of the very soil beneath your feet? From a grain of sand to a great mountain, all is sacred. Yesterday and tomorrow exist eternally upon this continent. We natives are guardians of this sacred place.
> — *Peter Blue Cloud, Mohawk*

A howling coyote perched on a platform concealing a pipe stem is typical of the animal effigy pipes found in Hopewell tombs; the one above was carved in Ohio before A.D. 100. Below, the lofty position of this reconstructed dwelling at Moundville proclaims the eminent status of its former occupant.

When the first white man
came over the wide waters, he was
but a little man . . . very little.
His legs were cramped by sitting long
in his big boat, and he begged for
a little land. But when the white man
had warmed himself at the
Indian's fire, and had filled himself
with the Indian's hominy,
he became very large. . . .
— Speckled Snake,
Creek

2

NEW FACES IN AN OLD WORLD

THE SOUTHEAST

The old people told it best, the ancient tale of land and water, darkness and light. This was how children in towns and villages across the Southeast learned who they were, where their ancestors had come from, how the world itself had come to be. There were different versions—probably as many as there were old people—but the heart of the story was the same. Around the home fires of a Cherokee town, it might have gone this way:

Long ago, before there were any people, the earth was a great island floating in a sea of water, suspended by four cords hanging down from the sky vault, which was made of solid rock. It was dark and the animals could not see, so they got the sun and set it in a track to go across the island every day from east to west, just overhead.

The Creator told the animals and plants to stay awake for seven nights. But only a few of the animals were able to, including owls and panthers, and they were rewarded with the power to go about in the dark. Among the plants, only the cedars, pines, spruces, and laurels stayed awake, so they were allowed to remain green year-round and to provide the best medicines. The Creator chided the other trees: "Because you have not endured to the end, you shall lose your hair every winter."

People appeared last, after the animals, the sun, and the plants, but they multiplied so quickly that they threatened to overrun the world. So it was decided that each woman would have only one child a year, and it has been that way ever since.

The old storytellers described other wondrous things from long ago: the turkey buzzard's flapping wings that scooped out all the hills and valleys, and the water spider who brought fire from a hollow sycamore tree on a distant island. They also spoke of great troubles yet to come. The world would grow old and worn out, they said. The people would die, the four cords would break, and the earth would sink into the ocean. Future generations had reason to remember these prophetic stories. The earth did not sink into the sea, perhaps, but it was from the sea that the strangers came—strangers who would overturn the world as they had known it.

◄ Preceding page: Tomo Chachi, member of a Creek trade delegation to London, sat for this portrait with his nephew during the 1754 visit.

The Blue Ridge Mountains were part of the sprawling domain of the Cherokee, a bountiful land that would meet all their needs, it was said, so long as they took care to preserve the intricate harmony of the Creator's work.

Gifts of the Earth

That world was one of natural abundance. From Chesapeake Bay south to the Gulf of Mexico and west to the Mississippi Valley, the Southeast comprised a generous mix of mountains, tidal lowlands, rolling uplands, and expanses of forest everywhere. In the Florida flatlands Timucua and Calusa children grew up gathering wild grapes, persimmons, and the fruit of the prickly pear. Farther north, in the hill country of Alabama and Mississippi, the Chickasaw, Creek, and Choctaw collected acorns, chestnuts, wild strawberries, and blackberries from the forests and fields. And throughout the region a moist, warm climate and long summer season allowed most communities to plant two corn crops each year. The Tuscarora and Pamlico

grew corn in the sandy loam of the Carolina coastal plain, while the Powhatan and their neighbors farmed alluvial soil along the rivers that fed Chesapeake Bay.

The Southeast was also a land of many rivers. In the Mississippi Valley, the Natchez people took bream, catfish, and eels from the great river and the streams that fed it. Along the Atlantic coastal plain each spring, fishermen built weirs to trap oceangoing fish that came up the rivers to spawn. People of the tidewater regions were especially fond of Atlantic sturgeon, giant bottom-dwelling fish that appeared in March and often remained in the rivers until early fall.

Everywhere the routines and rhythms of life followed the wheel of the seasons. For the Cherokee, *gogi*—the warm season between April and October—was the time to travel, to make war, to plant and harvest. The cold *gola*, from October to April, was the time to collect

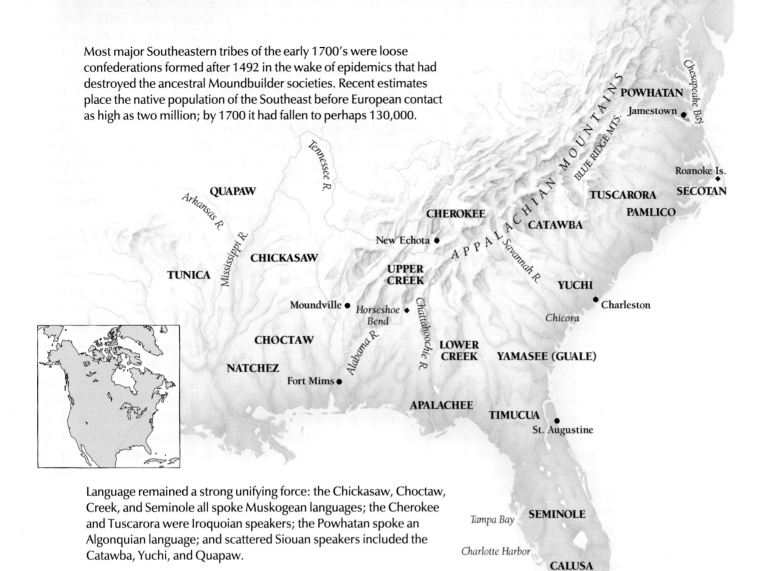

Most major Southeastern tribes of the early 1700's were loose confederations formed after 1492 in the wake of epidemics that had destroyed the ancestral Moundbuilder societies. Recent estimates place the native population of the Southeast before European contact as high as two million; by 1700 it had fallen to perhaps 130,000.

Language remained a strong unifying force: the Chickasaw, Choctaw, Creek, and Seminole all spoke Muskogean languages; the Cherokee and Tuscarora were Iroquoian speakers; the Powhatan spoke an Algonquian language; and scattered Siouan speakers included the Catawba, Yuchi, and Quapaw.

nuts, to hunt for deer, black bears, wild turkeys and other game, and to gather inside to tend the fires and retell the stories. Plants and animals, too, knew their seasons. March was herring month; in late April the turkey-cocks were on the prowl; June was the lush strawberry season; late autumn, when white-tail bucks were competing for mates, was also the season when they abandoned some of their usual caution and so made themselves easier targets for hunters.

Herds of more than 200 browsing whitetails were a common sight in the rich bottomland forests and yielded a good supply of both venison and hides, which could be scraped clean of hair and tanned into velvety, buff-colored leather for moccasins and clothing. Black bears were dangerous quarry but worth the risk: a single kill rewarded the hunter with abundant meat and fat for cooking, a warm blanket for winter, and

the esteem of family and neighbors. True success, however, involved more than an individual's skill and courage in the forest.

In the old days, the storytellers said, all the animals and plants had lived together in peace with the people. But as time went on, men invented knives and bows, blowguns, spears, and hooks and began to slaughter the animals for their flesh and skins. So the animals held councils to discuss these grave threats. The deer decided they would send rheumatism to any hunter who killed one of them without at least asking their pardon. To enforce this policy, they agreed that Little Deer—who was swift as the wind and could not be seen—would race to the spot the moment a deer was shot and ask the animal's spirit if it had heard the hunter's prayer for forgiveness. If so, all was well. But if not, Little Deer would follow the hunter back to his village and cripple him with rheumatism. So it was that young men were taught prayers asking the Creator that

Deer, I am sorry to hurt you, but the people are hungry.

— *Choctaw hunter's prayer*

A plant more precious than gold: For at least 500 years before Columbus, the great Mississippian societies of the Southeast were organized around the cultivation of corn, a food then unknown to Europeans.

the spirit of a slain deer return in the body of a fawn. Likewise, many new hunters were forbidden to eat the first bear, deer, or turkey they killed: this was a momentous occasion, meant to renew the sacred bond between human and animal for another generation—not merely to indulge the appetite of a single day.

Tradition also dictated the protocol to be followed in dealings between humans and plants. The Cherokee and others believed, for instance, that ginseng, an aromatic medicinal herb that grew wild in the mountains, was a conscious being and that it could make itself invisible to anyone unworthy of gathering it. The women who went out searching for ginseng were thus instructed to show their respect by leaving the first three plants they found untouched and, before digging up the fourth, to say a prayer and place a small bead on the ground as compensation to the plant's spirit.

Native farmers took similar care to balance their needs against those of the land itself. At the start of the warm season, most farmers

planted bean and corn seeds together in the hills, while squash and pumpkins were usually sown in rows on level ground. As the crops sprouted, the beans helped replace nutrients the corn took from the soil. Within a few weeks the plants formed a tangle of leaves and stalks that was usually thick enough to prevent weed growth and keep erosion to a minimum. After the harvest, farmers set fires to clear away the dead plants and make way for a new crop, leaving nitrogen-rich ashes to help renew the soil. Through such methods it was possible to get 15 years or more of continuous yields from a planting ground before its fertility was used up and new land had to be cleared.

In the Southeast, as elsewhere, ground fires were also used to clear the undergrowth in oak and hickory forests. The fires rarely burned hot enough to ignite the larger trees, but they did consume the tangle of woody plants and saplings that grew on the forest floor, fertilizing the soil and creating woodlands that were open and parklike. After the burn a new growth of vegetation attracted deer, which fed on the sprouts of grass and new bushes; thus the fires helped sustain the animals on which people depended.

Nature, of course, was not always predictable. Droughts, floods, early frosts, and fierce winters caused occasional crop failures, and many native settlements kept communal storehouses of corn to ward off starvation during lean seasons. Nevertheless, in late winter and early spring, when grain supplies dwindled and game was scarce, villages sometimes had to go for days without food, and there was nothing to do but endure. Even in good times children were encouraged to skip meals and to share food with the sick or elderly—important lessons that prepared them to face times of shortage or other hardships without complaint.

The art of camouflage required more than a deerskin. Only years of experience taught these Timucua hunters the patience and stealth needed to approach their prey undetected.

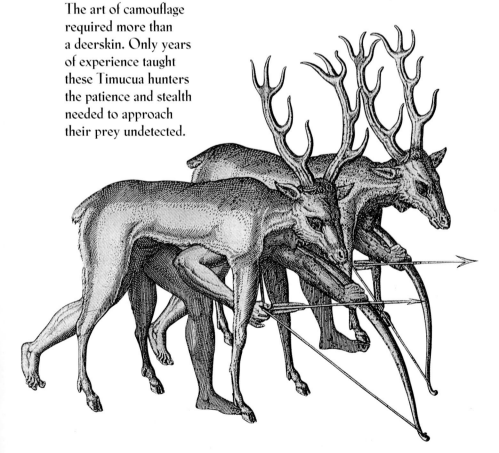

THE GREEN CORN CEREMONY

In almost all Southeastern communities, the most important rite each year was the Green Corn Ceremony (or Busk, from the Muskogean word *baskita,* meaning "to fast"), which celebrated the ripening of the corn in late summer. The rituals varied , but preparations generally involved the cleaning out of houses and public buildings, a period of fasting followed by a feast in the town square, then the extinguishing of every household fire and the solemn kindling by the high priest of a new fire, from which the home fires were in turn relit. Finally, the priest led the town elders in a ceremonial dance around the sacred flame. Past transgressions were forgiven; the community was reaffirmed and made pure. The new year had begun.

The layout of a Southeastern square ground — the sacred fire at the center, with logs aligned in the four cardinal directions, and four shedlike "clan beds" in which seating was assigned by age and status — mirrored the tribe's concept of the universe and its own social order. Those ideas are echoed in an early shell amulet and a diagram of a Yuchi Green Corn Dance (right, above), which symbolically trace the annual circuit of the sun and the stages of life from youth to adulthood, old age, and death.

In "Creek Baskita Green Corn Dance" (above), by Creek artist Fred Beaver, the new fire has just been kindled on the square ground; beyond it stands the circular council house, where the flame is kept alive and ceremonies are held in winter.

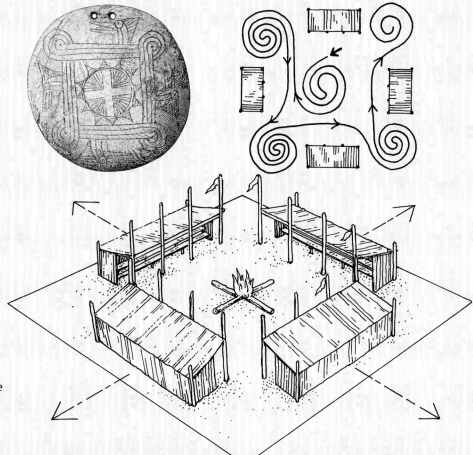

Emblems of Power Engraved on Shell

In temple mounds and burial sites from Virginia to Arkansas and beyond, early inhabitants of the Southeast left a treasure trove of ceremonial objects: bowls, beads, daggers, drinking cups, ornamental neck plaques called gorgets, and much else. Some were ceramic, some stone, and huge quantities were made of seashells brought from the Gulf Coast by traders. Most, like those illustrated here, date from between A.D. 1000 and 1600 and were incised with evocative designs meant to bestow grace, courage, and spiritual power.

A hand-and-eye motif frequently symbolized the power of ancestors. This one was incised on red Alabama slate.

This stylized skull design from Moundville, Alabama, may have been rendered in honor of a departed ancestor.

This bird-head effigy has a raven's keen eye — indicated by the three-pronged eye design — meant to convey the speed and aggressiveness of a bird of prey.

A face mask with "weeping" eyes probably invoked the might of an ancestral warrior; the lightning-bolt zig-zag of its tears recalls the mythic Thunderbird.

A pair of plump woodland turkeys — perhaps the wearer's cult animal — decorates a carved shell gorget from Georgia.

A shell gorget from Mississippi displays an elaborately costumed figure, mysterious and powerful. Words flow from his mouth as an S-shaped scroll.

Four winged cat-serpents symbolizing cosmic unity adorn a conch-shell drinking cup from Spiro, Oklahoma. The cross within a circle was a common device indicating the sun.

A Season for War

Each tribe, clan, and village fiercely defended itself and its territory against hostile neighbors. Any injury done to a kinsman by an outsider had to be avenged by the injured person's family—though not necessarily right away. Justice, too, was governed by the cycles of nature, and summer was the time for war.

Long before boys were old enough to join the war parties, they wrestled, ran foot races, and played increasingly rugged ball games to build their strength and hone their competitive skills. They slept on panther or bobcat skins, hoping to absorb some of the courage and cunning of those animals. When they became men, combat would be a means of proving their bravery and their value to the community. In the warm season danger was always in the air. Enemies attacked without warning, swooping down on unprepared villages or travelers. If a warrior's courage failed at such a moment, death could come quickly —to him and to others of his town.

Most fighting among Southeastern tribes grew out of blood feuds with neighboring groups. Kinsmen killed or captured in previous summers had to be avenged, hunting grounds protected, insults from other groups answered. When village elders determined that a raid was in order, the volunteers—no one was ordered to go—fasted and drank strong herbal potions to fortify their spirits.

A raiding party typically numbered between 20 and 40 men. Armed with war clubs, spears, and bows and arrows, their bodies painted black and red, they were cheered out of the village by the cries and howls of those who stayed behind. Advancing silently in single file through the foe's territory, counting on surprise to give them the advantage, the warriors split into small groups to surround the targeted village or camp.

At a signal—it might be an imitation bird call or animal cry—the men first launched a barrage of arrows, then fell on their enemies

A ceremonial dance (right) performed on the eve of battle by Yuchi warriors — originally from Tennessee, they later settled in Georgia — was recorded in the 18th century by German artist Philipp Georg Friedrich von Reck.

with clubs and lances. Battles were fierce and usually short. Victors took the scalps of those they killed; live prisoners were taken back to the home village, heralded by a chorus of victory shouts from the warriors that grew louder as they neared their destination.

There were no clear-cut rules governing the treatment of captives. Some were tortured and then put to death—especially those with reputations as great warriors, who were expected to show their courage by singing war songs until they lost consciousness. Others were enslaved and forced to work for their captors. Occasionally a fortunate prisoner was shown kindness and taken into a family, perhaps to replace a fallen son or kidnapped daughter.

Ways of Healing

The life of America's native peoples, although bountiful in many ways, was hardly the carefree, idyllic existence portrayed by some European chroniclers. In addition to sporadic food shortages and seasonal warfare, people had to

The spirit of the falcon is invoked by a dancer on this embossed copper plate from a burial ground in Georgia. Impersonating a bird-warrior deity, the dancer holds a war club in his right hand and a severed head in his left. On his forehead he wears a copper plate — much as this plate itself might have been worn.

deal with their share of illness and injury. Particularly where populations were dense, as in the Virginia piedmont or Chesapeake Bay area, outbreaks of diarrhea, yaws, tuberculosis, and other ailments could attack whole communities.

Tribal healers knew that one way to fend off disease was to rid the body of impurities. A sick person (or someone wishing to stay well) might visit a sweat lodge, a small hut covered with bark or animal skins. Inside were red-hot stones or perhaps a pot of steaming water. Leaving their clothes at the door, the people crowded together in the steamy interior and sang or chanted until they were covered with perspiration. They then ran outside and plunged into a nearby stream to wash away any foul matter that had been brought out of their bodies by the sweat. For ailments such as arthritis and rheumatism, the sweat lodge treatment may have been as effective as anything developed since.

Pigments and medicines derived from plants were ground on flat stone discs, often intricately incised (left) with symbolic imagery — hands with eyes, entwined death heads, and other ancient motifs. The yaupon plant (below) produced the Southeast's most widely used ceremonial medicine, the stimulating brew called the black drink.

Plants were the humans' chief allies in the fight against illness and injury. To neutralize the venom of snakes or poisonous insects, medicine men relied on a number of snakeroots, the most potent of which were herbs belonging to the chicory family. These produced a milky liquid that could be taken internally while a poultice of their medicinal leaves was placed directly on the bite. Medicine men applied dressings made from dogwood, sassafras, or poplar bark to wounds, rashes, and inflammations. They ground up bark of the wild cherry tree to make cough syrup and

Frenchmen look on as Timucua council members consume the black drink to induce vomiting as a means of self-purification. The purgative was usually swallowed in large quantities from conch shells or pottery vessels. The ceramic bowl below, designed to resemble a conch shell, bears a spiral pattern suggestive of the world's four sacred directions.

knew that oak bark (which contains tannin, an antiseptic) made an effective solution for washing out wounds. Salicylic acid, the main ingredient of aspirin, was extracted from the bark, leaves, and roots of various willow trees and prepared in compounds to treat an assortment of aches and pains.

The Black Drink

A favorite beverage all over the Southeast was a dark, potent, somewhat bitter tea many believed to be a gift from the Great Spirit. Many Indians knew it as the white drink, so called for the froth that formed during its preparation. But English traders dubbed it the "black drink" for its color when brewed to full strength, and the term endured. Brewed from the leaves of a variety of holly called yaupon, or cassina, it was widely consumed in the morning, much like coffee, for its stimulating effect. On important occasions a stronger version of the black drink was taken ritually as an emetic to cleanse body and mind; it was thought to provide the user with energy, stamina, and clear thinking. Warriors of many tribes drank it while otherwise fasting, before going out on raids. In Virginia and the Carolinas, the black drink was part of the ceremony marking a boy's passage to manhood.

Dreams, too, were powerful agents in maintaining physical and spiritual health. During a dream the spirit temporarily left the body and experienced things that no conscious person could know. Because dreams gave access to the spirit world, they could also serve as warnings of impending peril. To the Choctaw, for instance, a dream in which a bear was encountered meant that either the individual or the community would soon meet trouble. A dream might also reveal hidden yearnings in a sick person that had to be satisfied before the patient could recover. No such message could prudently be ignored, and most towns had a shaman to whom any vivid dream had to be reported. The holy man explained its meaning and advised the dreamer and the community on how to deal with it.

DISCOVERING COLUMBUS

On a fateful October morning in 1492, Christopher Columbus stepped ashore on the tiny Bahamian islet of San Salvador and claimed the land for Spain. To the resident Arawak Indians, his arrival must have seemed like a visitation from outer space. Not in their wildest dreams would they have envisioned beings such as these, with their heavy Spanish tunics, glittering armaments, pale skin, and strange facial hair. They welcomed the newcomers as if they were heavenly spirits, offering food and drink and catering to their every wish.

Columbus was enchanted. Sailing on to Cuba and Hispaniola, he encountered the Taino, an Arawak-speaking people who grew corn and smoked tobacco and lived in cities with up to 3,000 inhabitants. "There is no better race or better land," the navigator wrote. "They have the softest and gentlest voices in the world, and they are always smiling. . . . The king maintains a marvelous state, of a style so orderly that it is a pleasure to see it." Columbus also took note of the gold necklaces and nose rings worn by Taino nobility.

On his second voyage, in 1493, Columbus arrived with 17 ships and 1,000 men and set up a colony in Hispaniola. Disappointed in his hopes of striking gold — in the Caribbean it came mostly from Mexico — he decided instead to get rich through agriculture. The Taino would provide the labor.

The agonized face on this Taino stone carving, made in Puerto Rico between A.D. 1200 and 1500, conveys a mournful premonition of the tribe's future.

All warmth of feeling between Taino and Spaniard soon evaporated. Before Columbus, the region's only human menace had been from raids by predatory Caribs living in the lower islands; perhaps the Taino hoped the strangers would give them protection. Instead, the Spanish enslaved them, forcing them to toil on colonial plantations and sending them in chains to work the newly discovered silver mines in Mexico.

The newcomers also brought the scourge of European disease. A single outbreak of smallpox on Hispaniola in 1518–19 killed more than one-third of the million or so Taino who lived there. Later epidemics took an even heavier toll. By 1570 the Taino were virtually extinct, their only legacy a few stone carvings and ceramic pots, plus a handful of surviving words — among them canoe, hammock, and tobacco.

A Calusa man painted on a valve shell (above) wears a headdress and displays symbols on his hands that suggest a ceremonial event. The shell was found on Key Marco, near the southern limits of a watery realm that included today's Florida Everglades (opposite).

The Calusa and the Stranger

In years to come, tribal stories in the Southeast would include tales of people whose dreams or visions had foretold the European invasion. Certainly, almost from the time of Columbus's landfall in the Caribbean, unsettling reports began to circulate on the mainland. The Calusa, who lived in the fertile mangrove swamps, savannas, and marshlands of southwestern Florida, would have been among the first to hear news of strangers from across the water. Numbering perhaps 10,000, the Calusa were a maritime people who derived such a copious harvest of fish from the rivers and sea that they never learned to cultivate corn—and never needed to. The center of their society was a large town called Calos, probably located on Mound Key in Estero Bay, from which a primary chief governed some 50 smaller settlements scattered from Lake Okeechobee south to the Florida Keys.

Inveterate travelers, the Calusa built networks of canals to connect their villages and navigated them in dugout canoes. Fishermen worked the offshore waters and made voyages that put them in contact with people from the Bahamas and other Caribbean islands. It was probably on such fishing expeditions that the Calusa first heard tales of the Spanish explorers, men from another world who traveled not in canoes but on what some described as giant floating islands covered with clouds.

They probably saw the strange vessels off their coast as early as 1499. But the first face-to-face encounter did not occur until the spring of 1513, when Juan Ponce de León landed on the eastern coast of the peninsula the Spaniards called La Florida, the "Flowery Land." By this time word had spread that the light-skinned, bearded people were not to be trusted. Despite their gifts of wonderfully useful tools and intriguing trinkets, despite their warm avowals of friendship, they really wanted only two things: gold for their treasure

ships and slaves to work their island plantations. The Calusa chiefs, rightly suspicious, reacted as they would have to any hostile intruder—with a surprise attack.

While Ponce de León's fleet lay anchored near what is now Charlotte Harbor, some 20 canoes filled with warriors came to meet him. Communicating with hand signals and in pidgin Spanish picked up from Caribbean natives, the Calusa informed Ponce de León that they were indeed interested in trading. But as the strangers prepared to show their wares, the warriors struck with spears, darts, and arrows. After a brief skirmish the Calusa withdrew. The Spanish, seeking peace, sent an envoy to meet with the primary chief at Calos. The chief—"Carlos" to the Europeans—agreed, but he did not come alone. This time Carlos brought 80 war canoes, and the ensuing battle lasted from late morning until dark.

Shortly afterward, the Spaniard left Florida with no gold and no slaves. Eight years later he

returned, hoping to set up a colony; again the defenders got the better of it. During one of the skirmishes, a Calusa arrow found Ponce de León, inflicting a wound from which he later died. Duly impressed by this further display of the "primitive" inhabitants' fighting skills, the Europeans temporarily abandoned their plans for colonizing La Florida.

Harvesting a good life from the rich waters off the Florida Keys, a Calusa fisherman unloads the day's catch from his dugout canoe, hollowed from a cypress tree. His net, spear, cord, hooks, and other tools are fashioned from shells, plant fibers, and wood. The woman sorts shellfish; some of the shells will be crafted into jewelry, bowls, and other valuables bound for far-reaching trade routes and distant customers.

Awe and Terror in Our Hearts: De Soto's Rampage

A half century after Columbus, most people of the Southeast had still not seen a white face. But around the council fires, stories and rumors continued to spread. There was talk of the white man's deadly sticks, which spewed fire and filled the air with thunder, and of the huge four-legged animals that men sat on and that ran as fast as a deer and obeyed their masters' commands.

Beginning in 1539, the talk became all too real for some of the communities of the interior. In that year a Spanish explorer called Hernando de Soto began a journey across the Southeast, and one thing soon became clear:

FRANCISCO DE CHICORA

While the Calusa were defending their Florida beaches against Ponce de León, inhabitants of the Carolina coast had a brush with other marauding Spaniards. In the summer of 1521, Lucas Vásquez de Ayllón, a major landholder on the island of Hispaniola, sent agents up the Atlantic seaboard looking for slaves to work his sugar plantations. They landed along the South Santee River, in an area the Spanish called Chicora. Here the people knew nothing yet of Spanish motives. Eager to view the wonderful floating islands on which the foreigners had arrived, a group of natives trustingly boarded one of the ships — and the captain promptly set sail for Hispaniola with about 60 kidnapped slaves.

Many died of sickness on the way. But one became a useful ally of the Spanish: Francisco de Chicora, as his captors dubbed him, learned their language and journeyed with Ayllón to Spain, where his glowing descriptions helped convince the authorities to found a colony in Chicora. Francisco sailed back to his home waters with the Spanish expedition; then, almost as soon as the ships dropped anchor in 1526, he escaped and obviously wasted no time warning his people. When Ayllón began to explore, there were no inhabitants to be found. The chagrined Spaniard tried again farther south, in Georgia, but disease and near starvation drove his followers from the coast after only six weeks — and spared the people of Chicora and their neighbors the worst effects of the European invasion.

These hairy-faced men were more dangerous than anyone could have imagined. De Soto was an explorer—a *conquistador,* as the Spanish said—who had earned a reputation for courage and ruthlessness while fighting the Inca in Peru (and had also reaped a fortune in plundered gold). But De Soto's ambitions still burned, and so, using his wealth to outfit a new venture, he set off to explore and conquer the vast region north of the Florida peninsula.

When he landed at Tampa Bay on the west coast, De Soto led an entourage that must have made people disbelieve their eyes. For transport he had some 220 horses; for food and soap he brought 300 hogs—which were also useful for sniffing out hidden Indians; for fighting there were 600 men with powerful weapons and armor; finally, 100 African and Mexican slaves carried the army's provisions.

> Think, then, what must be the effect of the sight of you and your people, whom we have at no time seen, astride the fierce brutes, your horses, entering with such speed and fury into my country . . . things altogether new, as to strike awe and terror into our hearts.
> — *Chief of Ichisi, 1540*

During the first weeks, in the lands of the Timucua people, the Europeans found numerous villages surrounded by large fields of corn. De Soto's men noted storehouses full of harvested corn and high palisades built to protect the towns. They remarked on the appearance of those they encountered, especially the tall, muscular chiefs, elaborately tattooed and dressed in feathered robes.

But De Soto himself showed little interest in the people or their culture. He moved through the towns like a restless predator, taking food to sustain his army, kidnapping men to carry his supplies and women to entertain his soldiers. When the natives fought back, his men burned fields, tore apart houses, and plundered burial sites; anyone who angered the Spaniard might be thrown to the terrifying attack dogs that were also part of his retinue.

THE TRACK OF AN INVADER

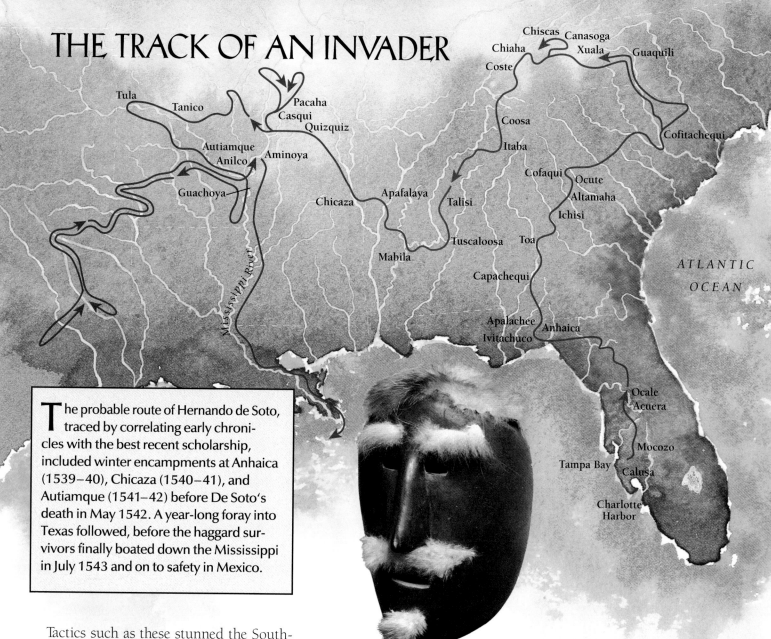

Chiscas
Canasoga
Chiaha
Xuala
Coste
Guaquili
Tula
Tanico
Pacaha
Casqui
Quizquiz
Autiamque
Coosa
Anilco
Aminoya
Itaba
Cofitachequi
Guachoya
Cofaqui
Ocute
Chicaza
Apafalaya
Talisi
Altamaha
Ichisi
Tuscaloosa
Toa
Mabila
Capachequi
ATLANTIC
OCEAN
Apalachee
Anhaica
Ivitachuco
Mississippi River
Ocale
Acuera
Mocozo
Tampa Bay
Calusa
Charlotte
Harbor

The probable route of Hernando de Soto, traced by correlating early chronicles with the best recent scholarship, included winter encampments at Anhaica (1539–40), Chicaza (1540–41), and Autiamque (1541–42) before De Soto's death in May 1542. A year-long foray into Texas followed, before the haggard survivors finally boated down the Mississippi in July 1543 and on to safety in Mexico.

Tactics such as these stunned the Southeasterners. War, pain, and death were nothing new to the Timucua or other native peoples. But when they fought, they rarely intended total destruction. Nor did they routinely pillage and plunder for no apparent reason. To them the European way of making war was brutal, excessive, mindless—in a word, barbaric.

The Lady of Cofitachequi

After spending the winter in Apalachee country, De Soto pressed north through Georgia into the Carolinas. He had heard of a rich and prosperous kingdom called Cofitachequi, and in the spring of 1540 he found it along the Wateree River in what is now South Carolina. As the Spaniards drew near, six emissaries came out to meet De Soto, sharply asking, "Do you seek peace or war?" When De Soto said, "Peace," the spokesmen left and shortly returned with their ruler, identified in Spanish chronicles as the Lady of Cofitachequi.

She rode on a litter of white linen and was clearly a figure of great authority (one of De Soto's men lyrically compared her to Cleopatra). Seeing that the strangers took a keen interest in her freshwater pearls, she directed them to a large temple in the nearby town of Talomeco, in which her people housed their dead. Finding more pearls and a sizable cache of weapons there, the Spaniards sacked the temple and its graves, carrying off anything that looked valuable. De Soto then seized the Lady and made her lead his troops northwest toward the Blue Ridge Mountains, where they still hoped to find gold. Not long afterward, according to Spanish chronicles, the Lady vanished into the forest (along with her private collection of pearls, which De Soto had planned to seize) and in all likelihood made a safe return to what remained of her domain.

Boorish and bushy-haired, this Cherokee booger mask is used during a riotous ceremonial dance that may have originated as a reenactment of De Soto's invasion. Dancers wearing the masks ("booger" refers loosely to any ghost or monster) burst loudly into the room and launch a manic display of lewd, aggressive behavior that leaves no doubt about the Cherokee's opinion of the celebrated conquistador.

A LANDMARK FOR CASQUI

As Spain's conquistadors ventured forth in search of gold and glory, they had a further mission: to win converts to Christianity. Among the horsemen and foot soldiers who accompanied Hernando de Soto were 12 Catholic priests, and one place that seemed receptive to their message was Casqui, a town of about 2,000 people on the St. Francis River in present-day Arkansas.

Chronic warfare with neighboring tribes had drained Casqui's resources; drought was shriveling the corn crop. These troubles may have given the priests' gospel of salvation special appeal. In any event, in June 1541 the people of Casqui raised a 50-foot-high cross beside the house of the chief, atop a massive earth mound overlooking the rest of town.

Everyone gathered to watch. The chief — also named Casqui — sat beside De Soto, draped in a splendid feather cloak and crowned with a copper headband holding woodpecker plumes. The diminutive town shaman hovered nearby, turtle-shell rattle in hand. Two of Casqui's wives sat in front of him on grass mats. Soldiers of two continents stood guard: the Spanish in quilted cotton armor — somewhat frayed after two years on the march — and the men of Casqui with ear plugs and bracelets, their heads shaved and painted, their bodies tattooed. The cross, made of two enormous cypress trunks, was heaved upright. The priests celebrated Mass.

Whether Casqui's people defeated their enemies, whether rain revived the corn crop — these facts are unknown. The town is gone, its Quapaw descendants long since dispersed, and the Spaniards soon moved on through the forest to their own uncertain destiny.

This carved eagle effigy stood watch over the dead in a charnel house in Florida; it dates from A.D. 500–1000.

Cofitachequi had earlier been ravaged by disease, probably smallpox. The epidemic may have begun with a Spanish landing on the Atlantic coast and spread from there to the interior. The sickness was unlike anything the people had seen before, racing unchecked through whole villages, leaving behind heaps of scarred corpses and the mournful wails of a few grieving survivors. By the time De Soto arrived, the bustling capital of Talomeco had been abandoned to the dead.

The Spaniards crossed the Blue Ridge Mountains in May of 1540, encountering little hostility but also finding few stockpiles of corn to steal. The area was controlled by people whose descendants would be known as the Cherokee; they spoke an Iroquoian language and were related to other Iroquoian tribes in the Northeast. (One township visited by De Soto was called Chalaque, similar to a Muskogean word meaning "people of a different speech.")

Pushing west and south during the summer, De Soto spent more than a month in the powerful Muskogean chiefdom of Coosa, which in later times would become the powerful Upper Creek Confederacy. Then, in October 1540, the Spaniards reached the territory of the great Choctaw chief Tuscaloosa.

The chief, seated on cushions in a raised pavilion in the town plaza, received the strangers with regal pomp. About his shoulders hung a floor-length feather cape; behind him stood an attendant holding a fan-shaped parasol. De Soto demanded 400 bearers, which Tuscaloosa graciously provided, and also 100 women. These, the Choctaw said, would be waiting at the next town, Mabila.

So the Spanish set off. At Mabila they entered a massive stockade with 15-foot-high mud-plastered walls and tall defensive watchtowers. Suddenly Choctaw warriors poured into the central plaza and fell upon the intruders. De Soto had been ambushed. After hours of ferocious combat, thousands of Tuscaloosa's men had fallen to the Spaniards' guns and swords; tribal legend tells that the survivors hanged themselves rather than surrender.

The conflict was also devastating to the Spaniards. The Choctaw cut down many of their horses, destroyed most of their supplies, killed perhaps 40 Spanish soldiers, and wounded almost all the others. It was a hungry and haggard force, then, that De Soto led west to Chicaza on the Mississippi-Alabama border. There, subjected to numerous hit-and-run attacks by the local people—the Chickasaw—he sought to rest his troops and restock his supplies before moving on to the Mississippi River in 1541.

The silent remains of Moundville (below) in Alabama bear witness to the scale of ceremonial life in the ancient Southeast. The carved sandstone figure from about the 14th century (inset), portraying the man with whom it was buried, is a type that De Soto's men would have found in the temple at Talomeco. A bauxite frog-effigy pipe (below left) linked the sacred act of smoking with an animal spirit that moved freely between this life and the watery underworld of the next.

*I have long since learned who you Castilians are. . . .
To me you are professional vagabonds who wander from place to place, gaining your livelihood by robbing, sacking, and murdering people who have given you no offense.*
— Florida chief, 1539

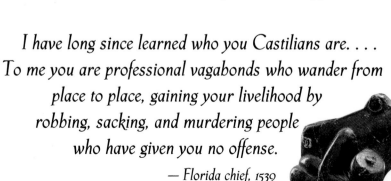

The Moundbuilders

As De Soto bullied and looted his way across the Southeast, he passed through a succession of towns whose names have all but vanished from memory. Their most striking features were great earthworks and ceremonial mounds, some small enough for a man to jump over, others enormous structures with flattened tops standing more than 50 feet tall, complete with walkways and staircases.

De Soto did not know it, but his men were the last Europeans to see the great chiefdoms of the ancient Moundbuilder societies. By the time French and English explorers returned to the area in the 1700's, it was a scene of desolation, scoured by wave after wave of European disease. Sacred mounds had long since fallen into disrepair; clearings once used for villages were covered with a thick growth of forest.

Nevertheless, the Moundbuilders' legacy endured in tribal traditions. To this day the Choctaw speak of a great mound, Nanih Wiya, from which the Great Spirit created the first of their people, who then crawled through a cave into the light of day. The Creek tell of a battle long ago when their warriors hid in an earthen mound to surprise and defeat a Cherokee war party. When Oklahoma Muskogee and Seminole gather for the Green Corn Ceremony, singers and dancers perform on small square mounds reminiscent of their ancient predecessors'.

For another year De Soto and his men wandered across Arkansas, stopping at Casqui, Pacaha, and other impressively fortified towns but still failing to locate the gold-laden cities that had been their objective from the start. In the spring of 1542, they returned to the Mississippi. There De Soto and others succumbed to an illness that began with low fever and ended in death—an ironic fate for an expedition that had left so much disease and death in its own wake.

Finally, in the summer of 1543, some 320 Spanish survivors and 100 native slaves built seven boats and made their way downriver, harassed by tribes along the route, bound for the safety of Mexico. As they reached the Gulf, one Spaniard remembered that a lone Indian stood in his canoe and called after them:

*If we possessed such large canoes,
we would follow you
to your land and conquer it,
for we too are men.*

Incised on a shell gorget dating from about the 14th century, a horned serpent (agent of the underworld) is locked eternally in battle with a falcon (champion of the upperworld). Caught in between is the earth itself, whose human caretakers must keep these two forces in balance to ensure the well-being of all.

The thatch-roofed great house of the Seloy chief, placed at the Spaniards' disposal in 1565, was soon fortified for long-term defense with a moat and log palisade. A newly found site in St. Augustine marks the likely location of this "Spanish Plymouth Rock," Europe's first permanent outpost on North American soil.

The Next Wave

Undeterred by De Soto's failure, Europeans continued to probe and punch at the Southeast with what, for them, were disappointing results. Spain tried unsuccessfully to found a colony at Pensacola between 1559 and 1561. About the same time the French established two outposts on the Atlantic coast. One of them, Fort Caroline near present-day Jacksonville, became the target of Pedro Menéndez de Avilés, who landed in 1565 with 1,500 men and promptly reduced it to ashes. His next step was to subjugate the Seloy tribe that controlled the area—Timucuan people who, like so many others, at first extended a friendly welcome. Within months their welcome was repaid with brute force, and Spain had accomplished its goal of establishing a permanent settlement in North America, one that it named St. Augustine.

A half century of costly expeditions had netted the conquistadors no gold and precious little glory, but there was another kind of prize to be sought. In 1566, Spanish missionaries began fanning out from tiny mission outposts along the southern Atlantic coast, trying to "civilize" the Indians and convert them to Christianity (though how fully they succeeded remains unclear). To early converts Jesus may well have been a new spirit-helper from whom they could seek relief from drought and flood—or from the new diseases ravaging the countryside.

North of Florida native communities had only occasional contact with Europeans until late in the 16th century, when the foreigners began to come again. English explorers landed at Roanoke Island in 1584, but two ill-advised attempts at settlement there are notable only for the mysterious disappearance of what would be remembered in American lore as the Lost Colony. Almost two decades passed before the next band of colonizers arrived, and this time they stuck. In 1607 a band of English landed a bit farther up the Atlantic coast and settled near a river that flowed into a large body of water the natives called Chesapeake, the "Great Salt Bay." The settlement, named Jamestown by the newcomers, became the first permanent English foothold in America (or as they and other Europeans were calling it, the New World). By chance, the site they chose was not far from the home of one of the most powerful men on the continent.

In many ways the native people of Virginia were similar to other societies up and down the eastern seaboard—in their view of the world, their ceremonial calendar, the ways they made a living. But in their political organization they were unusual. Along Chesapeake Bay and the rivers that fed it, some 15,000 people lived under a single ruler; his name was Wahunsonacock, but the English knew him as Powhatan, "the great king" of Virginia's Indians.

Powhatan had probably first come to prominence as a warrior and local chieftain late in the 1500's. Waging war against a succession of other local chiefdoms, he had gradually subdued about 30 of them and forged what amounted to a small empire. The various groups kept their tribal names but also referred to themselves as residents of Tsenacomoco, the name of Powhatan's chiefdom. As a paramount chief, Powhatan received appropriate tribute from his

subject towns and villages—shell beads, deerskins, and other valuables—and enjoyed such privileges as a private hunting preserve and cornfields planted especially for his use. When he decided to wage war, he selected a war captain who solicited fighters from the various districts and villages. In return Powhatan offered a strong trading alliance and protection from invaders, native and European alike. And as the English discovered, he was indeed a force to be reckoned with.

Not long before the Jamestown settlers arrived, Powhatan had heard an ominous prophecy. A shaman warned

An elder of one of the Powhatan towns wears a fringed deerskin mantle, an indication of his prominence in the community; the engraving was based on a painting by John White.

The famous deerskin robe known as Powhatan's Mantle (far right) artfully suggests the chief's view of his world — with a human standing at the center of the shell-bead design, flanked by two animals symbolic of wealth and power, and 34 circles that likely represent the towns of his domain. Similar imagery appears on a Catawba map (right) from about 1721: circles showing the Catawba and other tribes are connected by paths that suggest political and trading ties — with other tribes and with colonists in Virginia (rectangle, upper right) and Charleston (grid at bottom, with a ship anchored in the harbor).

THE SACRED WEED

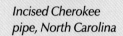

Almost no public ceremony could take place without it. Every tribal council, each call to arms or move toward peace was prefaced by smoking it. Cherokee medicine men squeezed its juice on bee stings and snakebites and boiled its leaves into tea as a cure for

Incised Cherokee pipe, North Carolina

fever. The Creek crumbled it into the postholes of new houses, believing it would drive away ghosts. Such were the virtues of tobacco, a substance of countless uses — and deep mystical importance.

For longer than anyone can remember, native peoples throughout North America have consumed tobacco in one form or another; it was grown even in regions too cold for the cultivation of corn. More than 1,000 years before De Soto, Indians of the Mississippi Valley were smoking a pungent local variety in handsomely carved soapstone pipes — prototypes of the pipes shown here. Because of its harshness, smokers often cut the native plant with sumac leaves. Tribes of California and the Northwest chewed it with mollusk-shell lime to release the nicotine. Among the Creek, an infusion of tobacco increased the potency of the black drink.

Indians used tobacco to clear the mind, calm the soul, stave off hunger, and for sheer enjoyment. Its principal virtues, however, were spiritual. Just as the flame of a council fire was thought to be a piece of the sun transported to the earth, so the smoke from burning tobacco was seen as a prayer rising up to the Great Spirit. Before the high priest lit the New Year's fire in the Green Corn Ceremony, leaves of tobacco were placed in the fire pit. Tribal members smoked tobacco to ward off evil, cast out witches, heal the sick, bring rain, and ensure fair weather before a journey. So potent were its effects, in fact, that when someone rose in council with a pipe in his hand, his listeners knew he would speak only the truth. And whenever two foes sat down to parley, the smoke of the peace pipe would cleanse their hearts and ensure that their accord would last forever.

Stone effigy pipe, Kentucky

him—as it was later transcribed—that "from the Chesapeake Bay a nation should arise, which should dissolve and give end" to Powhatan's empire. No leader could lightly ignore a shaman's admonition, and Powhatan took bold action. He ordered his forces to go to war against the Chesapeake, a tribe that lived west of the bay, and his warriors did their work well: by May of 1607 the Chesapeake were virtually exterminated.

But Powhatan had picked the wrong enemy. It was the small band of 104 English men and boys who settled at Jamestown the same year that he should have feared. Like native leaders elsewhere along the eastern seaboard, he at first made every effort to accommodate the newcomers, who probably would not have survived the first hard winter without his gifts of food. Perhaps Powhatan anticipated that English swords and guns might help him extend his domination of other Indian communities. In any case, he negotiated an uneasy alliance that seemed to be cemented in 1614 when his daughter, Pocahontas, married the English colonist John Rolfe.

> Why should you take by force that from us which you can have by love? Why should you destroy us, who have provided you with food? What can you get by war?
>
> I am not so simple, as not to know it is better to eat good meat, lie well, and sleep quietly with my women and children; to laugh and be merry with the English; and, being their friend, to have copper, hatchets, and whatever else I want, than to fly from all, to lie cold in the woods, and to be so hunted, that I cannot rest, eat, or sleep.
>
> — *Wahunsonacock (Powhatan), 1609*

But whatever slim prospect there might have been for real peace ended when the Europeans discovered the delights of tobacco. Like all Southeastern peoples, the Powhatan (Europeans often referred to a tribe by its chief's name) considered tobacco sacred. Its smoke helped shamans communicate with

"The Baptism of Pocahontas," a 19th-century painting by John Gadsby Chapman, typifies a popular notion of Indians "civilized" by European culture. In fact, through the one son she bore before her death at 22, Pocahontas initiated a line of descendants that would include such eminent Virginia families as the Jeffersons, Lees, and Masons.

important spirits, and tobacco pipes were indispensable at trade and peace negotiations. But the white strangers saw things differently. What the Indians revered as a sacrament, the whites regarded as an opportunity.

Touting it as a healthful and stimulating herb, merchants began selling American tobacco at exorbitant prices to the English upper classes. Then in 1612 John Rolfe managed to cross the harsh-tasting variety grown by the Powhatan with a milder strain from the West Indies. The new hybrid flourished in Chesapeake soil, and within five years Virginia tobacco became an addictive luxury that almost any Englishman could afford. Suddenly the settlers had hit upon a sure way to make their colony pay. As Jamestown founder John Smith noted, people were cultivating the plants in "the market-place, and streets, and all other spare spaces" around their village.

For the Powhatan, growing tobacco for profit added insult to injury. Not only were the whites defiling a sacred plant, but as the number of colonists grew, the tobacco fields encroached more and more on Powhatan farming and hunting grounds. Inevitably, the course was set for a collision between two very different views of the world.

Like most native societies in America, the Powhatan did not believe in individual ownership of land. Tribes or smaller bands traditionally occupied certain territories and were fiercely attached to them. But land itself could no more belong to any one person than did sunlight or air.

The invaders lived by different rules, of course. Coming from a nation where boundaries were explicit and land ownership served as a measure of status, they assumed it was the same everywhere. Most land in England belonged to the very few, and prison awaited any who trespassed. Here, on the lush shores of the Chesapeake, there were no fences or game wardens, and since the natives did not clear the land and divide it into neat fields, the English concluded that they were not making the best use of it. As one observer said, the Powhatan had "no particular property in any part or parcell of the country, but only a general residencie there, as wild

Hailed for its ability to purge "superfluous fleame" and "gross humors," among other things, the Virginia tobacco (below) developed by John Rolfe was a big hit in England. It spawned a bumper crop of rival brands, packaged with exotically eye-catching labels.

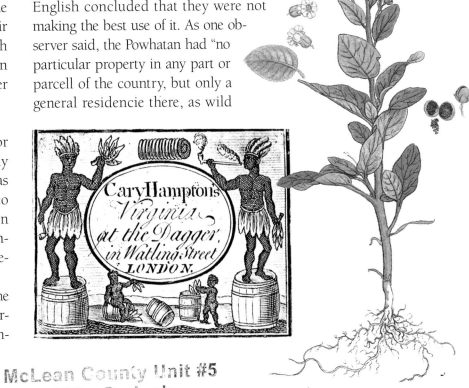

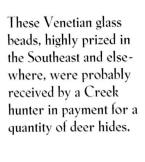

These Venetian glass beads, highly prized in the Southeast and elsewhere, were probably received by a Creek hunter in payment for a quantity of deer hides.

beasts have in the forest." Besides, like De Soto before them, the English had more powerful weapons than the natives; why should they not lay claim to whatever land they wanted?

But the Powhatan were not about to give away their birthright. Even as their chief pursued friendship, others plotted to rid their territory of the invaders. Powhatan's half brother, Opechancanough, led the dissidents, and after Powhatan died in 1618 their pent-up rage finally boiled over. On Good Friday of 1622, Opechancanough and his followers staged a surprise raid on the English plantations and the tobacco ships anchored in the rivers. Before it was over, the Powhatan warriors had burned several villages and killed a quarter of the English men, women, and children in Virginia.

The raid did not succeed in driving out the strangers, but it ended all pretense of amity between the two sides. To the English, the Indians' "true" nature had at last been revealed, and they could turn all their resources against the savages without nagging qualms about dispossessing a peaceful people. To the Powhatan, a surprise attack was the only realistic means of resisting better-armed invaders.

On and off during the next two decades, English and Powhatan forces clashed inconclusively. Then, in 1644, Opechancanough launched another all-out assault on the white settlements—but now there were three times as many settlers as in 1622. The English survived and struck back, capturing Opechancanough, by then almost 100 years old, and

defeating his warriors. Reviled by the English as "the bloody monster," Opechancanough was imprisoned in Jamestown, then shot. From that day forward the Powhatan were, in effect, subjects of the English Crown. The shaman's prophecy of a nation rising from the East, it seemed, had been fulfilled.

Victory over the Powhatan made the Europeans bold. English explorers and traders began pushing inland to the lands of the Tuscarora, Catawba, and Cherokee. In 1670 another group of English colonists founded Charles Town (later Charleston) on the Carolina coast. From there traders made their way west to contact the Creek, Choctaw, and Chickasaw. The Creek—so named by the English because of the countless watercourses that crisscrossed their territory—were actually a sprawling confederacy of Muskogean-speaking groups that occupied most of Alabama and Georgia. During the period of trade with the English, they numbered perhaps 30,000 people, living in some 50 towns situated mainly along the Coosa and Tallapoosa rivers (tributaries of the Alabama River) and the Flint and Chattahoochee rivers.

A Web of Commerce

Charleston was to become the hub of trade between whites and Indians throughout the Southeast; within a few decades its wharves were lined with ships that brought in manufactured goods from Europe and took back to London's merchants the wealth of America's natural bounty. The white traders who trekked through the Southeastern interior in the late 17th century were no longer looking for gold or precious jewels but for more prosaic treasure—in particular, the hides of whitetail deer. For centuries women in villages from the Virginia piedmont to the Gulf Coast had tanned deer hides into beautiful soft, chamois-like leather. White traders soon learned that these deerskins, particularly the heavy buckskins, brought good prices in Europe, where they were made into luxurious bookbindings, elegant gloves, and other merchandise of high value.

Commerce was something the Southeastern peoples understood and relished. Since the earliest times tribes of all regions had traded with one another: coastal societies supplied the interior with shells, fish, salt, and yaupon leaves for brewing the black drink. In exchange, communities of the piedmont and the mountains offered flint for arrowheads, turkey feathers, animal skins, and various roots useful in making paints and dyes. For these veteran traders the Europeans were simply new people with different products.

And most native communities were eager to acquire those products. Europeans had metal pots that did not crack in cooking fires; they had knives, hatchets, and hoes to ease the labor of clearing fields and skinning animals; they had colored cloth for new clothing. And they had guns. Muzzle-loading firearms of the 17th century were scarcely an improvement on bows when it came to killing deer—they

Ginseng, new to Europeans but long valued here for its curative powers, was an unexpected and lucrative trade item.

Swapping metal tools for farm produce at the turn of the 19th century, Indian agent Benjamin Hawkins (the first such official in the Southeast) encourages a Creek family to embrace the ways of white farming.

were slow to reload, not especially accurate, and often failed in wet weather. But in times of war, guns terrorized enemies with their thunderous noise, smoke, and fire. To most Southeastern peoples, exchanging ordinary deerskins for these potent weapons and other prized items was almost too good a deal.

At first, trading between Europeans and Indians followed customs that had governed the exchange of tribal goods for centuries. Etiquette varied from place to place, but anyone who traveled much knew the general rules. When village leaders, or headmen, sighted an approaching white trader followed by his train of pack horses or by a crew of Indian "burdeners," they first sent warriors out to greet him and make sure he came in peace; then he was invited into a house for food.

If at any point the headmen detected hostility or bad faith—raised voices, staring, rapid gestures were all considered bad form—com-

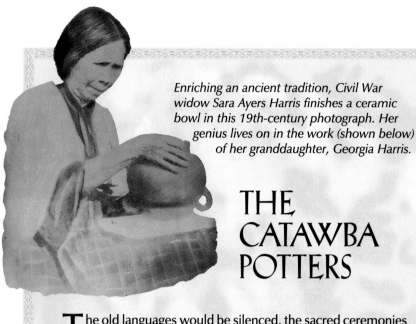

Enriching an ancient tradition, Civil War widow Sara Ayers Harris finishes a ceramic bowl in this 19th-century photograph. Her genius lives on in the work (shown below) of her granddaughter, Georgia Harris.

THE CATAWBA POTTERS

The old languages would be silenced, the sacred ceremonies abandoned, the people scattered — and too often the ancient skills of survival would disappear as well. But for the Catawba, a once-powerful nation in the Carolina piedmont, a tradition of pottery-making has been a lifeline to their past. Long before Columbus, Catawba women were fashioning sturdy cookware and handsome ceremonial vessels; when the English settled Charleston, the women bartered pots for metal tools, clothing, and other necessities. In the 1860's the Catawba were confined to a tiny reservation in South Carolina — which by chance contained the deposits of distinctive reddish clay they had used for years. Pottery became a key to their very survival.

Now as then, Catawba potters eschew kiln firing, modern glazes, and potter's wheels. Using techniques handed down from mother to daughter for generations, they build their vessels from clay coils, polish them with quartzite pebbles, decorate them with ancient designs, and fire them on the hot coals of an open fire. The resulting hard finish produces a metallic ring when tapped — the echo of a well-tended tradition, still audible among the red-clay hills of South Carolina.

merce ceased and the visitor might be sent on his way. But if he behaved properly and ate heartily, his hosts would offer him lodging and perhaps female company for the night. If a village became especially fond of a newcomer, he might be adopted into the community; by the early 1700's it was common for white traders to take Indian wives and live with them for as long as they stayed in the villages.

The headmen of the towns expected gifts from their visitors, whether native or European. Before doing any business, a white trader offered his hosts such tokens of friendship as earrings, belt buckles, mirrors, or jewelry. To the headman he might give a "ten-striped shirt"—a garment of European cut that was highly prized and enhanced a man's standing in his town. During these preliminaries the visitor and his hosts smoked tobacco and engaged in "strong talk" (that is, hard bargaining) about the quality and prices of their goods; only then did the actual trading begin.

The trader's wares included coarse cloth, which was a basic article of trade, plus glass beads, blankets, hatchets, brass kettles, adzes for hollowing out tree trunks—the inventory was extensive. It was also habit-forming: as native communities became more dependent on European goods, their needs came to include such items as needles, thread, perhaps even laced coats and hats for the chiefs, as well as guns and ammunition. In return the trader took as many deerskins as the village's hunters and tanners had been able to amass since his last visit. The hides were packed up on horses or shouldered by the burdeners, each of whom carried a bundle of 30 skins, and the trader's entourage made its way back to the wharves of Charleston.

As prosperous Europeans ordered more and more deerskin gloves and book covers, Southeastern Indians were pressed by traders to kill more and more deer. In the 1750's more than 150,000 deerskins a year were being shipped across the Atlantic from Charleston alone, with additional routes operating out of Savannah and other ports.

Remarkably, the deerskin trade did not lead to extinction of the whitetails; deer reproduce quickly, and sporadic lulls in the hunting gave the herds a chance to replenish their ranks. But their numbers did decline over the long run and steadily enough so that virtually all Southeastern tribes faced periodic shortages of venison and skins.

Slave Traders and the Tuscarora

For the most part, however, commerce worked to the short-term advantage of both Indians and whites. It was what came next that did the real damage. By the early 1700's the peoples of the deep Southeast discovered what the Powhatan had learned nearly a century earlier: prolonged contact with whites eventually brought terrible disruption.

Among the first to suffer were the Tuscarora, an Iroquoian tribe living in the piedmont region of what is now North Carolina. For years they had bartered deerskins for hatchets, cloth, and other goods. But not all traders dealt honestly, and time after time the Tuscarora found themselves defrauded. Raids by hostile Indian neighbors—encouraged by Charleston slave traders who dealt in Indian captives—were depleting their numbers. Then, during the first decade of the 18th century, the Tuscarora watched with mounting apprehension as white settlers from Charleston and elsewhere began pouring into their traditional hunting territory. Reluctant at first to fight, they turned for help to the Quaker government of Pennsylvania, which had a reputation for fair dealing. The Tuscarora leaders presented eight separate petitions, each accompanied by a wampum belt, ranging from a request for hunting rights to a plea for asylum. But the Quakers, with problems of their own, turned them down one after another.

Rebuffed by the whites, the Tuscarora took up arms. Aided by warriors from nearby tribes—Coree, Pamlico, and others—they attacked the Carolina settlements with devastating effect. The Carolinians struck back even harder, marching into Tuscarora country in 1712 with a powerful force of colonial militia and more than 1,000 Indian allies. Within a year the Tuscarora had been routed, and some 700 men, women, and children were captured and sold into slavery in Charleston. The tribe's survivors made their way north during the next decade to find refuge among their Iroquois kin, later winning formal adoption as the Sixth Nation of the Iroquois Confederacy.

The experience of the Tuscarora was hardly unique, for the rise of the slave trade in the late 1600's had injected an explosively volatile fuel into the commerce between Indians and whites. Slaves were now vital to the colonial American economy; English, French, and

Held captive by the Tuscarora, land developer Christopher von Graffenried and two companions await trial; his seizure of Indian territory had sparked the Tuscarora War. The tribal council freed Graffenried — who lived to pen this sketch — but executed land surveyor John Lawson, seated beside him. The fate of the third captive, a black servant, is unknown.

At a Choctaw village in northern Mississippi, Old World influences mingle with traditional folkways — from the European-style clothes to the log-cabin construction of the house to the chickens and the sheaf of wheat in the foreground. The painting is by 19th-century artist François Bernard.

Spanish merchants all carried on an extensive trade in Indian as well as African slaves. West Indian natives worked beside Africans in the Caribbean sugar plantations. In Virginia captive Powhatans were put to work in the colonists' tobacco fields. Soon both Africans and Indians would be needed for the sprawling cotton plantations of the South.

Slavery of a sort had long been common among Southeastern tribes, to be sure. But the numbers were small. Most slaves were war captives who had been spared from death, and some were eventually accepted into the tribe by adoption or marriage. To the Europeans, however, slaves were a bulk commodity. Those bought and sold on the auction blocks of Charleston were shipped off in miserable bunches to New England or the West Indies. To satisfy the demand, white traders encouraged Southeastern Indians to wage war against each other for prisoners who could be exchanged for trade goods.

Setting tribe against tribe not only produced slaves for the market but also reduced the threat that Indians would unite in large numbers against the whites. By 1700 most of the Choctaw had joined forces with the French against the British and their allies, the Chickasaw and the Natchez, for colonial territories and trading rights. In 1702 a French official charged that in the previous decade Chickasaw warriors had taken 500 Choctaw prisoners at the urging of the English and killed three times as many more.

The slavers also found easy pickings in northern Florida, where thousands of Apalachees and Timucuas had been converted to Christianity and turned into farmers by Spanish missionaries. English raiding parties from the Carolinas swooped down on the mission towns, rounded up the sedentary Indians, and marched them back to the slave markets. By 1710 as many as 12,000 had been auctioned off and shipped out of Charleston.

Rotten Grain and Strong Spirits

Before the European invasion, the Southeastern peoples had used no fermented drinks of any sort, and when they were introduced to hard liquor, the impact was devastating. Warriors who valued courage imagined that whiskey made them fearless. Shamans believed that rum helped them achieve a dreamlike state in which they were better able to communicate with the spirit world.

The truth was appallingly different. Lacking any tradition of moderate social drinking in the European sense—and perhaps genetically more vulnerable to alcohol's toxic and addictive effects—untold numbers of Indian men fell victim to the bottle. Entire communities were thrown into turmoil. Rum and whiskey became one of the white traders' most effective bartering devices for gaining an edge over their native counterparts—who in some cases were willing to trade a whole season's supply of hides for a jug or two.

Native leaders were not blind to such problems, and by the 1750's many were speaking out against the alcohol trade. One of the most eloquent was a Catawba chief known as King Haglar, who lived near the border of North and South Carolina. In 1757 he chastised traders who would "rot your grain in tubs, out of which you take and make strong spirits," and vainly urged colonial officials to stem the flow of Caribbean rum and English whiskey into his people's villages.

> You sell it to our young men, and give it to them, many times . . . it rots their guts and causes our men to get very sick, and many of our people have lately died by the effects, and I heartily wish you would do something to prevent your people from daring to sell or give them any of that strong drink.
>
> — *King Haglar, Catawba*

Unscrupulous white traders had still another potent weapon in their dealings with the Indians—easy credit. They offered valuable European goods in exchange for hides to be delivered later; the details of the transaction, typically including outrageous prices and exorbitant interest, were duly recorded on paper before witnesses.

Like many other European practices, buying on credit was an alien idea in native societies. To get something for nothing seemed too good to be true—and in the long run, of course, it was. Credit turned quickly to debt, and eventually, no matter how hard they hunted, many Indians had little hope of ever clearing their ledgers. It is said that early in the 18th century the Yamasee tribe of South Carolina ended up owing their Carolina creditors some 100,000 deerskins—a debt that would have taken four years of hunting to repay.

A Lengthening Shadow

While the natives haggled with traders and struggled to cope with the effects of rum and debt, other old and invisible enemies began to revisit their villages. Spread by the widening net of commerce, European diseases again ravaged the Southeast, which suffered at least five major epidemics of smallpox and four of measles (often compounded by deadly outbreaks of influenza) between the 1690's and 1770's. Once introduced into an Indian village, smallpox usually killed between 50 and 90 percent of the inhabitants. Moreover, all the people usually fell ill at the same time, leaving no one healthy enough to hunt, tend crops, or nurse the afflicted. And both smallpox and measles typically struck in late winter or early spring, when stored food was scarce and new fields had not been planted yet—raising a threat of malnutrition that left survivors all the more vulnerable to future epidemics.

As with other things that arrived with the Europeans, these afflictions were interpreted by native people from the standpoint of their own traditions. Animals, for instance, were considered the source of most common illnesses, but these diseases were unlike anything ever seen before and so were presumed to have some other cause. Cherokee elders, wondering if a smallpox epidemic in 1738 might be retribution for sins committed

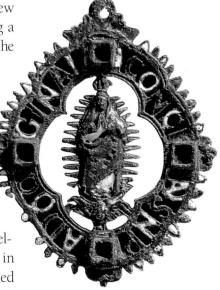

A 16th-century medallion of the Virgin Mary, buried in a convert's grave on St. Catharines Island, Georgia, reflects the early inroads made by Spanish missionaries in the region.

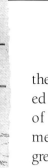

the Cherokee, recorded a powerful account of the physical and mental anguish of a great warrior who had been stricken in 1738: "When he saw himself disfigured by the small pox, he chose to die, that he might end his shame. When his relatives knew his desperate design, they watched him, and took away every sharp instrument. He fretted and said the worst things their language could express, and showed all the symptoms of a desperate person forced to live and see his ignominy; he then darted himself against the wall, with all his remaining vigor. . . . His strength being expended by the force of his friends' opposition, he fell sullenly on the bed, as if he was overcome, and wanted to repose himself. His relatives left him to his rest—but as soon as they went away, he raised himself, and finding nothing but a thick and round hoe-helve, he took the fatal instrument, and having fixed one end of it in the ground, he repeatedly threw himself on it, till he forced it down his throat, when he immediately expired. He was buried in silence, without the least mourning."

The Fall of the Natchez

For many Southeastern tribes, the invasion from Europe meant warfare and disease; for some it meant the end of a way of life. For the Natchez it meant the end of everything. With a population of about 5,000, the Natchez controlled a large territory along the southern Mississippi River, near the city that would later bear their name. Their society was more highly organized and formally religious than most others in the region, hearkening back to the great Mississippian cultures that had dominated the area before contact with the Spanish.

The ruler of the Natchez, called the Great Sun, was revered by his people as a living god. They believed that he was descended directly from the supreme deity, whom the Natchez identified with the sun. He lived in a huge house on a tall, flat-topped mound and dur-

The funeral rites of Tattooed Serpent, a Natchez prince (shown here in a 1725 eyewitness drawing by French explorer Le Page du Pratz), included the ritual strangulation of the dead man's principal wives and retainers so that they could accompany him to the next world. Du Pratz also drew the supreme Natchez ruler (inset), called the Great Sun, being carried in a litter.

by some of the young people, had their shamans lead rituals of contrition to appease the offended spirit. But such measures often failed, and when they did, some townspeople began to question the power of their shamans.

Traditional cures also had little effect on the new sicknesses. Poultices of herbs or bark were useless against the virulent red rash of measles and the noxious pustules of smallpox. The sweat lodge, too, proved no place for the victims of communicable disease. Crowded together in the tiny enclosures, the sick often infected the healthy, and the cold bath that usually followed the sweat only invited pneumonia or other respiratory problems.

Of all the European diseases, smallpox was the most devastating, but not just for the physical suffering and high death toll it inflicted. Survivors were left with severe, permanent pock marks—which inflicted even crueler psychological scars among a people who took great pride in their personal appearance. James Adair, a white trader among

ing harvest festivals was carried on an elaborate litter by relay teams of eight warriors each, as befitted a great king. When a Great Sun died, many of his closest kin and attendants committed suicide in order that they might follow him into the next world.

The Frenchmen (who not long before had given fealty to an exalted monarch, Louis XIV, who was himself known as the Sun King) showed no sign of understanding the Natchez's reverence for their ruler or their land. In 1729 French officials abruptly called on the Natchez to abandon their principal village so that the French governor could build a home on the site. But to the Natchez the land on which the village stood was the sacred domain of the Great Sun—no white man, however powerful, could be allowed to live there.

In the fall of 1729, therefore, Natchez warriors attacked the French settlements without warning, killing 200 of the intruders and win-

ning a great victory. But it was not enough. Two years later the French struck back with a large army that included a contingent of Choctaws and other native fighters who regarded the Natchez as their enemies.

For the Natchez it was a cataclysm: More than 1,000 men, women, and children died defending the Great Sun—and French slave traders took almost 500 others to sell to merchants in the Caribbean. Natchez prisoners deemed unfit for slavery were tortured or burned. Those who survived fled the region and sought refuge in Cherokee and other native communities. With a persistence shown again and again by displaced tribal groups, the refugees managed to preserve aspects of their culture in new surroundings—even continuing to use the Natchez language for several generations. But the ancient and majestic Natchez kingdom itself, at the whim of an alien empire, had in the span of a few years been extinguished forever.

The French alliance against the Natchez included Illinois warriors brought down to Mississippi. Here, four Illinois men (at left, one crouched) arrive with relatives and belongings, including a mother and child and a female captive. Standing at right are a black slave and a local Attacapa warrior.

A People Untamed: The Seminole

The fate of several tribes in the Florida region, if not as cataclysmic as that of the Natchez, was just as bleak. Many of those who had endured De Soto's marauding —the Calusa, Timucua, Apalachee, and others—were dealt blow after blow in the following years by disease and the slave trade. The toll was staggering: by the 18th century much of the land they had occupied was empty.

During the early 1700's various bands of Muskogean-speaking people—many of them Creeks displaced by wars with white settlers in Georgia and Alabama—filtered south to take refuge in the deserted Florida territory. The refugees adapted to living in the tropical flatlands there, and gradually the separate bands coalesced into a new, larger tribal grouping—in effect repeating the process that

had produced most of the major tribes and confederations of the Southeast. By about 1775 traditional Creek communities were using the term *seminole*—"runaways" or "untamed people"—for this new coalition.

Some Seminole groups retained their own language or dialect, and most continued to follow their own customs under local village leaders. Each town grew its own communal corn crop, in which every individual shared, with a portion set aside for the *mico,* or local chief. Europeans who inquired about this practice learned to their surprise that the corn did not serve as tribute but rather as a sort of public treasury, which any needy citizen could dip into when times were bad. The communal cache might also be shared with neighboring villages whose crops had failed.

As farmers, the Seminole, like other Southeastern peoples, annually celebrated the new year with the Green Corn Ceremony. They were also hunters and fishers, as their prede-

"Two Cranes in Nests," by Seminole artist Paul Billie, evokes the lush, secret Everglades landscape the Seminole made their home.

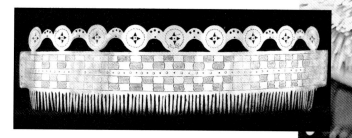

cessors in the region had been. But it became harder and harder to pursue those activities in traditional ways. Extensive deerskin trade with Europeans periodically depleted the deer herds, which limited the annual winter supply of venison. Dams built by colonists along the coast restricted the spawning runs of saltwater fish. By the late 18th century, the Seminole were turning more and more to the whites' farming methods and to the domestication of cattle, pigs, and other alien livestock.

It was not an easy adjustment. Many were loath to eat pork: somehow pigs reminded them of opossums, ugly beasts long deemed unfit for human consumption. There was also a reluctance to raise cattle—the "white man's deer," unworthy of a hunter's skill.

> You say: Why do not the Indians till the ground and live as we do? May we not ask, why the white people do not hunt and live as we do?
>
> The great God of Nature has given each their lands . . . he has stocked yours with cows, ours with buffalo; yours with hog, ours with bear; yours with sheep, ours with deer. He has indeed given you an advantage, in that your cattle are tame and domestic while ours are wild and demand not only a larger space for range, but art to hunt and kill them.
>
> — *Corn Tassel,*
> *Cherokee, 1785*

In time, declining populations of deer and other game forced most tribes to come to terms with the demands of livestock raising. The results were mixed, to be sure. In many places tribal cattle were allowed to roam semi-wild in the woods, where it was difficult to round them up. Also, domesticated cattle became reservoirs of microorganisms that contributed to periodic outbreaks of sickness in native communities.

An elegant Seminole trio of mother, daughter, and child was photographed at Cypress Swamp in 1910, wearing patchwork tribal dresses and African-style shell necklaces. Seminole artisans also fashioned the delicate silver comb (top) and silver buckle (above).

Among the Seminole another traditional pattern was undergoing a remarkable change. During the 17th and 18th centuries, many Southeastern Indians had looked with a certain disdain upon the region's African blacks. Plantation owners often hired Indians to catch slaves who had fled to the frontier forests, offering trade goods and other prizes as bounties. But in Seminole country, which from the start had been a sanctuary for runaways and the dispossessed, the climate was different.

The Seminole, themselves victims of the white man, shared their refuge with escaped African slaves, who supplied the villages with part of their crops in return for the right to work the land. Shared hardships, a common enemy, and intermarriage brought the two cultures together. By the early 19th century, former slaves (called Seminole Negroes or Indian Negroes by white Southerners) frequently served as interpreters when Seminole leaders parleyed with whites, and when negotiations broke down, as they often did, the Africans and Indians fought side by side to defend their common interests.

While Andrew Jackson (above) rode to triumph in the Creek War, most Indian leaders met disaster. William McIntosh (left), a White Stick Creek commander who fought beside Jackson, was later assassinated for betraying his tribe. Red Stick war chief Menewa (right) took eight enemy bullets at Horseshoe Bend, then recovered — only to lose all his lands and possessions to the whites.

Sharp Knife and the Red Sticks

Last night I saw the sun set for the last time, and its light shine upon the tree-tops and the land and the water that I am never to look upon again.

— Menewa, Creek, 1836

The largely peaceful existence of the Seminole was shattered in 1817 when Gen. Andrew Jackson led 1,700 American troops into Spanish-held Florida, ostensibly in search of escaped slaves. His campaign, the first of many brutal U.S. sorties into the region, savaged both blacks and Seminoles, and it ended with the United States taking possession of Florida. It also confirmed Jackson's reputation as a no-holds-barred Indian fighter.

A few years earlier Jackson had stormed into national view with a series of resounding victories against a coalition of Creek tribesmen in Alabama and Georgia. War had broken out in 1812 between the United States and Britain, and a number of Indian leaders across the eastern part of North America had seized the opportunity to assert their own national independence. Tribesmen from the Indian lands of the Ohio Valley, commanded by the great Shawnee warrior Tecumseh, marched with the British against American troops in the Great Lakes region. In the Southeast a faction of Red Stick Creeks—so called for the color of their war clubs—began attacking American frontier settlements there.

The Creek War flared up in sharp, sudden assaults that ranged from the Ohio River south to the Gulf of Mexico. In one attack, in August 1813, a force of 1,000 Red Sticks swooped down upon the U.S. stronghold of Fort Mims, Alabama, setting the compound ablaze and killing some 400 white defenders. The victims also included a number of White Sticks, members of a more peaceable and Europeanized Creek faction that had hoped to remain neutral during the conflict.

The Fort Mims Massacre (as whites liked to call it) inflamed American opinion. In response the government called in Jackson to smash the Red Stick coalition. Moving quickly, he assembled 3,500 Tennessee militiamen and a force of Cherokee, Choctaw, and White Stick Creek allies. By November Jackson was ready to march.

Jackson's antagonist was a remarkable Creek patriot of mixed blood who is sometimes referred to as William Weatherford in history books. At an early age, so the story goes, Weatherford had been given a choice: to grow up white, like his Scottish father, or to remain with his Creek mother. He had picked the latter and proudly assumed his tribal name: Lumhe Chati, or Red Eagle. Inspired by the dream of Creek independence, he now led the Red Sticks into battle.

Jackson thrust deep into Creek country—Sharp Knife, the Indians called him—determined to eradicate the Red Stick challenge. For nearly four months he stalked them, winning a few skirmishes but never finding the pitched battle he sought. Finally, in March 1814, he cornered the main force of warriors at Horseshoe Bend on the Tallapoosa River in Alabama. The bloodshed began in early morning, and it lasted all day. By dusk some 750 of the 900 Red Stick defenders lay dead or dying.

Red Eagle was not among them. By chance, the Creek war leader had been traveling elsewhere and missed the battle entirely. But he knew defeat when he saw it. Several days later he strode into Jackson's compound, stony-faced, and surrendered. These were his words:

I am in your power. Do with me what you please. I have done the white people all the harm I could; I have fought them, and fought them bravely: if I had an army, I would yet fight . . . but I have none; my people are all gone. I can now do no more than weep over the misfortunes of my nation.

Jackson was seldom known to show leniency toward a captured or defeated Indian. But perhaps because of Red Eagle's eloquence, the American general was moved to pardon him. Red Eagle retired to a plantation in Tennessee where, until his death in 1822, he worked for peace between his people and the whites. Jackson, meanwhile, soon reverted to form. That summer he called the chiefs together to dictate the terms of peace. The resulting Treaty of Horseshoe Bend forced all Creek factions, including those who had fought beside him, to hand over some 23 million acres of tribal land—about 60 percent of Alabama and 20 percent of Georgia.

Shrinking Worlds

By this time more than 300 years had passed since the first Europeans stepped into the Southeast. Formerly vast Indian territories had been reduced to tribal enclaves surrounded by white settlement—the cumulative result of armed conflicts, one-sided peace treaties like Horseshoe Bend, and outright land grabs. The Seminole were limited to a tract in central Florida, while the Cherokee clung to the hill country of northwestern Georgia and southeastern Tennessee. In Mississippi, where few lands had been opened to white settlement, the Chickasaw still held the northern third of the state. The Choctaw retained the middle third, with holdings extending into eastern Alabama.

Yet even those who held fast to tribal identities were much changed from the ancestors who had greeted the early white explorers. Many native people now wore European-style clothing. Some—especially the more assimilated "mixed-bloods"—practiced Christianity, owned black slaves, and built and lived in houses like those of white Southerners. Some Indian communities had mills for grinding grain, and Indian women wove cloth on European looms. The Cherokee had their own written language, thanks to the genius of Se-

We never had a thought of exchanging our land for any other . . . fearing the consequences may be similar to trans-planting an old tree, which would wither and die away.

— Levi Colbert,
Chickasaw, 1826

quoyah, and their own newspaper, *The Cherokee Phoenix,* with a readership reaching well beyond the tribal homelands.

⤙

The Great Spirit is displeased with you for accepting the ways of the white people. You can see for yourselves — your hunting is gone and you are planting the corn of the white men. . . .You yourselves can see that the white people are entirely different beings from us; we are made from red clay.
— *Tsali, Cherokee shaman*

⤙

The change was never easy. Each step in the direction of European methods and manners was taken at the cost of profound, often wrenching self-scrutiny. Tribal leaders split into bitterly antagonistic factions, with the "progressives" (usually of mixed-blood parentage) favoring assimilation and the full-blood "traditionalists" denouncing it as a betrayal of all that was sacred. But change, like it or not, was unstoppable: little by little the progressives were winning.

The Cherokee Nation

No group succeeded more dramatically in modernizing itself than the Cherokee. Taking new European ideas of republican government and blending them with their own tradition of tribal councils, progressive Cherokee leaders attempted to construct a model society. They built a capital, New Echota, in Georgia (their original capital in Tennessee having been lost by treaty), established a 32-member legislature, wrote a constitution, and framed a judicial system. Propelled by the popularity of *The Cherokee Phoenix,* the literacy rate among their people was higher than that in surrounding American communities.

But to the growing white majority on the western frontier, the presence of any Indians at all, "civilized" or not, was unacceptable.

Every perceived failing was dredged up to discredit the Cherokee—including the fact that they had sided with the British during the American Revolution. (No matter that more recently, in the War of 1812, Cherokee warriors had allied with Jackson to defeat the Red Sticks.) Meanwhile, white planters and land speculators continued to pour in. Hungry for new acreage on which to raise cotton and expand the slave system, they relentlessly pressed the federal government to remove the Cherokee, along with the other Southeastern tribes, and open their territories to settlement.

In 1828 gold was discovered on the edge of Cherokee territory, and the cries for removal reached a crescendo. Then later that year the expansionists gained the ally they needed: Andrew Jackson was elected president.

Cherokee villages dot the Tennessee River valley in this 1762 map drawn by Lt. Henry Timberlake, a British officer who hoped to secure their friendship. A year earlier Cherokee chief Oconostata had signed a peace treaty (inset) with the French.

Where now are our grandfathers, the Delawares? We had hoped the white man would not be willing to travel beyond the mountains; now that hope is gone. They have passed the mountans, and have settled on Cherokee lands. . . .The remnant of the Ani-Yunwiya, the Real People, once so proud and formidable, will be obliged to seek refuge in some distant wilderness.

— *Dragging Canoe,*
Cherokee, 1768

The idea of removal was not a new one. Years earlier Thomas Jefferson, among others, had advocated moving all Indians west of the Mississippi River until they became accustomed to white ways. Jackson's reasons were of a different sort: he objected to the existence of sovereign Indian nations within the bound-

aries of the United States. He feared they might make their own alliances with Spain or England, which still posed a real threat to America's national ambitions.

Jackson's security policies meshed perfectly with the land hunger of white settlers and their political allies. After a furious debate, Congress passed the Indian Removal Act of 1830 by one vote. The bill allowed the president to give the Five Civilized Tribes land in Indian Territory, later named Oklahoma, in exchange for the Southeastern lands they now occupied. That was the carrot. The stick was a provision that the new law could be enforced, if necessary, with military action.

The Removal Act caused a storm of national controversy. The Indians had many champions among white Americans — traders, missionaries, even planters and politicians

MAKING THE LEAVES TALK

He was an illiterate Arkansas Cherokee who spoke no English and knew nothing of writing except that it existed and that the "talking leaves" gave whites who could read them many advantages. In English he was called George Guess or Guest; his Cherokee name was Sequoyah. His leg, withered since birth, consigned him to a reflective life. He became a fine silversmith and had a gift for drawing.

About 1809, after an argument with friends on the nature of writing, Sequoyah began from curiosity to devise signs for words. It became an obsession. He neglected his farm and his family; he ignored those who laughed at him; he kept going when his wife and neighbors threw his early work into the fire. In 12 years he trod much of the ground covered by entire civilizations over centuries. At length he discovered that by breaking words into syllables, every sound in the Cherokee language could be represented by 86 characters. These were initially of his own design; later he took letters from the Roman and Greek alphabets to allow easy use by a printing press.

The result was the first full writing system ever devised by a native North American. It proved easy to learn; most Cherokees mastered it in days, and it was soon adapted for use in other native languages. At one stroke he had broken the monopoly of letters enjoyed by whites and a select few Indians. In 1826 one of the latter, a brilliant young Cherokee named Elias Boudinot, began raising funds for a press with Sequoyan type. He got it, and in 1828 Boudinot began publishing his groundbreaking weekly, *The Cherokee Phoenix,* filling it with incisive articles and editorials — many of which were reprinted by sympathetic papers across the country. For the first time, a native voice reached a wide audience through the printed page.

Prophet of Cherokee literacy, Sequoyah (above) displays his new syllabic alphabet. Love of the printed word proved to be the best hope for his peoples' future (left).

who applauded their efforts to assimilate. But the pressures for removal had been building for decades, focused especially on individual state governments. They came to a head in a landmark legal confrontation between the Cherokee Nation and the state of Georgia.

"Now Let Him Enforce It"

In 1828, two years before the Removal Act, the Georgia legislature passed a bill denying Indians the right to testify against whites in court. The Cherokee, realizing that this measure would deny them all legal protection and allow whites to seize Indian lands at will, brought suit. The case moved up through the judiciary until it reached the Supreme Court. By then the Removal Act of 1830 had been signed, so the Cherokee asked the court for a ruling on its legality as well.

In their battles against removal, the Cherokee were led by their principal chief, John Ross, the de facto head of government at New Echota. Born in 1790, Ross was the son of a Cherokee-Scotch mother and, like Red Eagle before him, a Scottish father. Educated in white schools, he had fought on Jackson's side at Horseshoe Bend. But Ross was adamant in opposing Jackson's removal plans: the Cherokee were a sovereign nation, he argued, whose territory the federal and state governments must respect. Ross gained the support of several prominent white politicians, including Senator Henry Clay of Kentucky and the great Massachusetts orator Daniel Webster. Yet he never succeeded in winning over all of his own people.

One of those who disagreed was a Cherokee Council speaker called The Ridge (known also as Major Ridge), who, like Ross, had served with Jackson at Horseshoe Bend. Ridge believed it was in the tribe's interest to negotiate with Washington, make the best deal possible, and move west. Ridge had another motive as well—he wanted to replace Ross as principal chief. In this he had the support of

Rival Cherokee leaders meet in 1835 to debate the Treaty of New Echota: Should they exchange their ancestral lands for $5 million and a new home in Oklahoma? The treaty's main supporter, John Ridge (owner of the plantation house in the background), has the podium. Beside him sit two allies: news-

his son, John; his brilliant young cousin, Elias Boudinot, editor of *The Cherokee Phoenix;* and Boudinot's brother, Stand Watie. The "Ridge Faction," as it was known, inspired little enthusiasm from the rest of the tribe; only a few hundred favored accommodation. Nevertheless, the internal division gave single-minded white expansionists a valuable opening to exploit.

When the Supreme Court handed down its verdict, the result at first seemed ambiguous. In *Cherokee Nation* v. *Georgia* (1831), Chief Justice John Marshall ruled that Indian tribes were "domestic dependent nations"—wards of the federal government, in effect, with no right to file suit. Then, in a second case (*Worcester* v. *Georgia*), the court held for the Cherokee, declaring them to be "a distinct community, occupying its territory," which the people of Georgia had no right to enter without Cherokee consent.

It was a strong statement, issued by the highest tribunal in the land. But President Jackson simply sneered at it. "John Marshall has made his decision," the president said. "Now let him enforce it."

Government negotiators soon began talks with the Ridge Faction and its supporters. In 1835, at the Cherokee capital of New Echota, Ridge and a group of several hundred supporters agreed to trade the remaining Cherokee lands for territory west of the Mississippi. Remembering a Cherokee law of 1829 that decreed death to anyone selling land without the consent of all Cherokee people, Ridge grimly remarked, "With this treaty, I sign my death warrant." (He was right. Four years later Ridge, his son, and Elias Boudinot were put to death for their actions.) But the Treaty of New Echota—which was never approved by the Cherokee Nation nor by John Ross nor by anyone seriously considered a leader—was ratified by the U.S. Senate and became the legal basis for exiling the Cherokee people.

paper editor Elias Boudinot, cradling his chin in his hand, and Major Ridge, founder of the Treaty Party. Determined at all costs to kill the treaty, Principal Chief John Ross (seated at far left) confers with another treaty opponent. The painting is by Cherokee artist Robert Annesley.

The Removal Begins

Coerced by illegal treaties and bullied by federal troops, the last of the Southeastern Indians were finally forced off what was left of their land. The Choctaw were first to leave, moving from Mississippi to eastern Oklahoma in large groups between 1830 and 1846. Some went by boat up the Arkansas River; others trekked overland. For all, it was a long and sorrowful trip. The boats were crowded and unsanitary; the land convoys poorly supplied and ill equipped for cold weather. During the bitter winter of 1831–32,

IN HISTORY'S PATH: THE BOUDINOTS

Under different circumstances their story might have been one in which love conquered all and conflict dissolved into a happy ending. The two young protagonists could hardly have been more appealing: Harriet Ruggles Gold, "one of the fairest, most cultured young ladies" of Cornwall, Connecticut, and the dashing Elias Boudinot, brilliant, handsome — and Cherokee, a student at the Foreign Mission School in Cornwall. The two had met and fallen in love, and Harriet — to the dismay of her Protestant parents — announced her intention to marry Elias. When this became public knowledge, reaction was swift. The girls' choir at the Golds' church wore black armbands on their white robes. The family received hate-filled letters from neighbors. Officials of the mission school circulated a notice condemning "this evil." The night before the ceremony, in March 1826, Harriet, her mother, and Elias were burned in effigy on the village green as a mob howled its approval.

The marriage was performed privately in the Golds' home, and the couple left immediately for New Echota. There Harriet lived with her husband, founding editor of *The Cherokee Phoenix,* in a two-story clapboard house that seemed like a bit of New England transplanted. Harriet bore Elias three sons and three daughters, maintained open house for an extended new family of Cherokee nieces, nephews, and cousins, served tea shipped in from Boston, and gave piano lessons on the side. Even as the shadow of Removal grew darker, she voiced no regrets at her decision: "The place of my birth is dear to me," she wrote, "but I love this people and with them I wish to live and die."

But Elias would have to make the journey west alone. As the entire Cherokee world seemed to be collapsing, Harriet's health failed; soon after delivering a stillborn child, she died at New Echota in 1836.

one party of Choctaws walked for 24 hours barefoot through the snow and ice. An army officer supervising the operation sadly noted, "Our poor emigrants, many of them quite naked, and without much shelter, must suffer, it is impossible to do otherwise."

> We are exceedingly tired. We have just heard of the ratification of the Choctaw Treaty. Our doom is sealed. There is no other course for us but to turn our faces to our new homes toward the setting sun.
> — *David Folsom, Choctaw, 1830*

Cholera and other diseases swept through the boats and the caravans. By the end of 1832, approximately 20 percent of the 3,000 Choctaws who had left Mississippi were dead. Better planning and more provisions made the process less hazardous to life and limb in later years, but nothing could heal the suffering of those leaving the soil of their ancestors. It was a journey, wrote one mournful Choctaw, "calculated to embitter the human heart."

The Chickasaw began their migration from northern Alabama and Mississippi in 1837, after buying land in Oklahoma from the Choctaw. Most went by boat, and because conditions on board were generally healthful, the Chickasaw were spared many of the physical hardships endured by other tribes. But as soon as they arrived, they were challenged by Plains Indians who claimed the newcomers had stolen land from local tribes. It would be years before they knew peace.

Removal of the Creek began in 1836, but it did not go smoothly. Eneah Emathala, a Creek leader in his eighties who had fought with the Red Sticks, refused to move. He and about 1,000 followers somehow acquired guns and took refuge in the Alabama back country. The army sent Gen. Winfield Scott to ferret them out. Scott finally caught up with Emathala and arrested him. Designated as "hostile" because of their resistance to removal, Emathala and the thousand men, women, and children with him were shackled hand and foot and

Seminole war chief Osceola led his people in a three-year war of resistance until his death in prison in 1858; this portrait by George Catlin was made during Osceola's last weeks. The war raged on without him, the rebels' hit-and-run tactics inflicting heavy losses. Above, the night is illuminated by a Seminole village set ablaze by U.S. troops.

They could not capture me except under a white flag. They cannot hold me except with a chain.

— Osceola, Seminole, 1838

marched 75 miles across Alabama to Montgomery. Its job not finished, the federal government then forcibly removed some 14,000 more Creeks, a process finally completed in December 1837. More than a thousand died before reaching the Western territory.

Next to leave were the Seminole, and they did not all go gently. After Andrew Jackson's earlier foray into Florida, the region had enjoyed a period of relative calm. Then in 1831 a drought struck Seminole crops in central Florida, and by the spring of 1832 many were going hungry. U.S. agents swiftly moved in with offers of food and clothing to any Seminole who would emigrate west; land was available in Indian Territory alongside the Creek. Dispirited by the drought, a small group of chiefs reluctantly signed two treaties agreeing to removal of the Seminole by 1835. But one refused to budge. His tribal name, which meant "black drink crier," was Osceola.

When the army came after him, Osceola took his warriors into the Florida swamps. There they abandoned guns in favor of bows and arrows so that they could hunt without being detected. Seminole fighters attacked government forces when they least expected it, harassing and frustrating the troops with resourceful guerrilla tactics. At one point the army even tried using specially trained Cuban bloodhounds to roust the Indians from their hiding places, but without success.

You have guns, and so have we. You have powder and lead, and so have we. You have men and so have we. Your men will fight and so will ours, till the last drop of the Seminole's blood has moistened the dust of his hunting ground.
— *Osceola, Seminole, 1836*

In the fall of 1837, Gen. Thomas S. Jesup asked Osceola to meet him under a flag of truce. When the Seminole came to talk, Jesup arrested him and threw him into a federal prison in South Carolina. Osceola died three months later. This act of treachery only deepened Seminole resolve, and the conflict dragged on for seven years, until at last in 1842 a series of treaties officially ended it.

About 4,000 Seminole survivors were duly moved west to Indian Territory, where U.S. authorities, citing their Creek heritage, settled them in Creek lands—among people some Seminoles regarded as enemies. Before long, Creek slaveholders in Oklahoma charged that the Seminoles were luring Africans from Creek farms with promises of freedom. When news of this was received back East, some of the Seminoles still in Florida refused to move. Like Osceola's warriors, they retreated into the Everglades and the Big Cypress Swamp and eluded the federal troops that came for them. Several thousand of their descendants live in Florida to this day, unmoved and immovable.

ECHOHAWK

The punishing trek to Oklahoma — here commemorated in a 1957 oil by the Pawnee artist Brummett Echohawk — took an immeasurable toll on the thousands of deportees. Recalled one Creek survivor, "We were drove off like wolves . . . and our people's feet were bleeding with long marches."

"The Trail Where They Cried"

It was the Cherokee who suffered most. To force compliance with the illegal Treaty of New Echota, the U.S. government sent more than 7,000 troops into Cherokee country; state militias swelled the army of occupation to more than 9,000 men. The soldiers built stockades in key locations and in late May of 1838 began to fill them with ordinary people pulled from their homes.

Years later an eyewitness remembered the scene: "Families at dinner were startled by the sudden gleam of bayonets in the doorway and rose up to be driven with blows and oaths along the trail that led to the stockade." Individuals were seized "in their fields or going along the road, women were taken from their spinning wheels and children from their play."

As soon as soldiers removed the Indians, local whites rushed in, ransacking their abandoned homes and stealing anything of value. Even the dead were not safe. Searching for Cherokee gold that was rumored to have been hidden, white mobs feverishly ripped apart burial grounds and opened old coffins, tossing aside the sacred remains of Cherokee ancestors. Within a single month more than 8,000 Cherokees had been rounded up and herded into the stockades. Only one small group managed to escape the soldiers; they took refuge deep in the North Carolina mountains, where their descendants remain today.

I have a little boy. . . . If he is not dead, tell him the last words of his father were that he must never go beyond the Father of Waters, but die in the land of his birth. It is sweet to die in one's native land and be buried by the margins of one's native stream.

— *Tsali, Cherokee shaman awaiting execution, 1838*

For most of the tribe, the worst was still ahead. Drought again struck the Southeast, drying up wells and streams and destroying crops. Cholera and dysentery broke out in the stockades. Watching their people die, Cherokee leaders negotiated an agreement that allowed them to control their own removal. But nothing could stop the impending tragedy. As the long caravans began to move toward Oklahoma, the emigrants were already running short of food and supplies.

Tuberculosis, pellagra, pneumonia, and other diseases stalked the wagon trains. Of the 16,000 men, women, and children forced to relocate, more than 4,000 died either in the stockades or on the way west. The tragedy of the removal still lingers in the memory of the Cherokee. They call it *oosti ganuhnuh dunaclohiluh,* "the trail where they cried."

By 1850 the Five Civilized Tribes had been relocated on the distant soil of Oklahoma. But their ordeal was hardly over. On June 22, 1839, Major Ridge, his son John, and Elias Boudinot were stabbed to death by unknown assailants, their punishment for signing the infamous 1835 treaty. Amnesty was subsequently granted to others who signed—and to the unidentified executioners.

Externally, much of the region was inhabited by bands of Plains Indians, fast-moving hunter-warriors to whom the Southeastern tribes were as alien and unwelcome as white farmers. Even so, in some ways the new land seemed remarkably like home—especially the wooded, hilly eastern portion.

The Creek moved in along the Arkansas and Canadian rivers, cleared the land, and planted crops. The Cherokee laid out a new capital, Tahlequah, and revived their constitution. John Ross won reelection as principal chief. A public school system was in operation by 1841. *The Cherokee Advocate,* first newspaper in Indian Territory, appeared in 1844 and was soon joined by publications from other tribes. The Choctaw and Chickasaw nations drew up constitutions of their own, modeled on U.S. political procedures. More schools were established, and missionary societies were invited to open churches. (The Choctaw also set aside their own concerns long enough to raise $710 in 1847 for victims of the potato famine in Ireland.) The Seminole at length were recognized as a tribe and in 1856 given territory separate from the Creek's.

Thus, step by step, the Five Tribes began to recover. By the time of the Civil War, in fact, despite hardship, bigotry, and official persecution, many had reached a level of prosperity well above that of most frontier whites.

Yet even then their struggle was not done.

First elected principal chief of the Cherokee Nation in 1828, John Ross would remain in that post for nearly 40 years, leading his people through the trauma of forced relocation and the long process of rebuilding their society until his death in 1866.

Nearly a century after Removal, the Green Corn Dance was still being performed not only by tribes in Oklahoma but also by the Eastern Band Cherokee of North Carolina (below), whose ancestors had eluded white troops and found sanctuary deep in the Appalachians.

We have lived upon this land from days beyond history's records, far past any living memory, deep into the time of legend. The story of my people and the story of this place are one single story. We are always joined together.
— *Pueblo elder*

3

SPIRITS OF A SACRED LANDSCAPE

THE SOUTHWEST

Trouble had come to one of the Hopi villages in Arizona. The people were refusing to dip their sheep in disinfectant, as regulations demanded. Even worse, since this was during World War II, they were refusing to register for military service. A government official drove up the mesa road to the village to ask why these things were. Perhaps there was a misunderstanding.

The Hopi spokesman arrived from the fields in work clothes, and as the afternoon wore on, he talked to the official of the things that troubled the villagers. His words had a terrible urgency.

"When the Hopi people came from the underworld," he said, "they found people living in this land before them. Our Hopi people went to them and said, 'We would like to live here with you.' They replied, 'All right. You can stay here. We have certain rules here, ways of living, and you will have to follow these rules. Then there will be no trouble.' That's how it was. The Hopis did as they were told and they never had trouble.

"After a while the white men came. They did not ask if they could live with us. They just moved in. They did not ask what our rules were; instead, they wrote rules for us to follow. 'Now you just obey these, and you won't get into trouble,' they said. How do you explain that?" The speaker did not wait for a response.

"Why do you put us in jail?" he asked. "You bring us laws and rules which are not even our own, and then you send us to jail for not obeying them. How do you explain that?"

Still he went on. "Now we have a drought. It has been bad for years and seems to get worse. The rains come less often. The grass is dying everywhere. You tell us we will have to give up our sheep. They are the only food we have. Is this sensible?

"The sheep did not stop the rains. It is you who have caused that. You have put so many of these regulations on us that we are not able to concentrate on the things a Hopi must do, the ceremonies he must keep and the thoughts he must have. That is why it never rains and why the grasses are scarce. That is what I say."

The government official could think of no good reply. He had bumped hard against a re-

Soaring majestically above the timberline, the 12,633-foot-high San Francisco Peaks (above), near Flagstaff, Arizona, are held sacred by the Hopi, the Apache, and the Navajo alike. In the painting below, by Hopi artist Milland Lomakema, powerful spirits called kachinas — who make the peaks their home — perform rainmaking ceremonies that will help ensure a successful corn crop.

ality as old as the first moment of contact between Native Americans and Europeans centuries earlier. Even as they began to share this starkly beautiful landscape, the two peoples continued to live in two separate worlds—one governed by calendars and account books and bureaucratic need, the other by a tradition as old and powerful in the eyes of its followers as the mountains themselves.

In the view of the Hopi and of other Pueblo groups in the Southwest, a single, powerful force pervaded the universe. Every mountain had a soul, every tree, every rock, every living creature, and through them all flowed the Great Spirit, holding nature and mankind in perfect balance. In such a world, religious belief and daily life became one and the same. Every action had a spiritual consequence: think the right thoughts, perform the proper ceremonies, and the balance would prevail; neglect them, and nature would be offended. In such a world, right thinking and proper conduct encompassed many things—but not dipping sheep in disinfectant.

◄ Preceding page: A Santa Clara Pueblo leader of the late 19th century; in the background is Enchanted Mesa, near Acoma Pueblo, New Mexico.

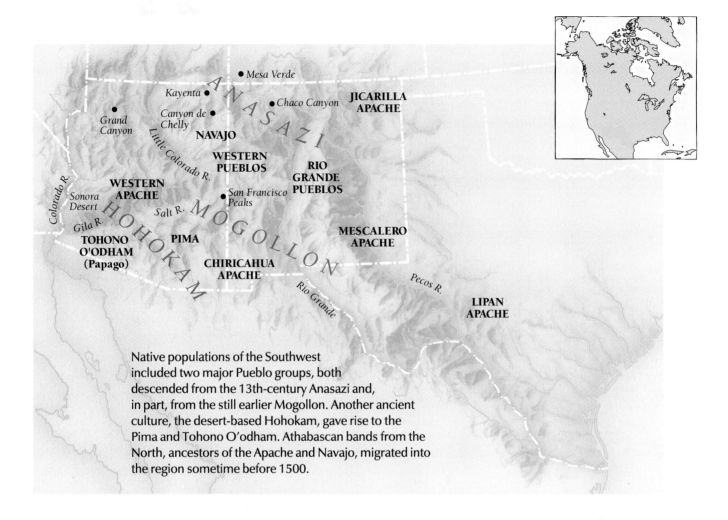

Native populations of the Southwest included two major Pueblo groups, both descended from the 13th-century Anasazi and, in part, from the still earlier Mogollon. Another ancient culture, the desert-based Hohokam, gave rise to the Pima and Tohono O'odham. Athabascan bands from the North, ancestors of the Apache and Navajo, migrated into the region sometime before 1500.

What we are told as children is that people when they walk on the land leave their breath wherever they go. So wherever we walk, that particular spot on the earth never forgets us, and when we go back to these places, we know that the people who have lived there are in some way still there, and that we can actually partake of their breath and of their spirit.

— Rina Swentzell, Santa Clara Pueblo

The traditions of the Pueblo peoples had arisen during centuries of habitation in one of the world's most majestic landscapes. From high on a desert cliff in central Arizona, the eye sweeps out across a panorama of sage land and alkali flats, of red-rock canyons and juniper-studded hillsides. Farther off, in the violet distances, snow-capped peaks rise thousands of feet above sea level. The land is harshly unforgiving. Nighttime temperatures can drop below freezing in the clear desert air;

the afternoon sun beats down mercilessly. Rainfall is sparse—less than 10 inches a year in most of the region. It is also erratic. Scattered midsummer thunderstorms roar in from the west, drenching some areas while leaving others dry. More rain and snow falls in the mountains, where dark forests of Douglas fir and ponderosa pine cloak the slopes below the tree line. Game abounds: deer, bear, elk, and wild turkey in the high country; rabbit, antelope, and wild pig in the desert scrub.

Within this varied world the ancestors of today's Pueblo peoples made their homes. The Hopi's earliest forebears may have wandered in from the Mojave Desert to the west, then merged with other groups filtering down from the north. The Zuni of western New Mexico are thought to be descended from the ancient Mogollon, who dwelt in the mountains to the south. In the Pueblo villages along the upper Rio Grande, the number of different local languages suggests a variety of ancestral stocks. Most people speak various dialects of Tanoan,

The landscape is our church, a cathedral. It is like a sacred building to us.

— Zuni saying

a language group associated with the Great Plains. Others, along with the residents of Acoma to the west, converse in Keresan, a language unique to the Southwest. Yet for all their diversity of speech and lineage, the Pueblo communities share a single, unifying heritage.

Venerable Forebears

Their main cultural ancestors are the Anasazi, a succession of builders and farmers who emerged into prominence around A.D. 900 and

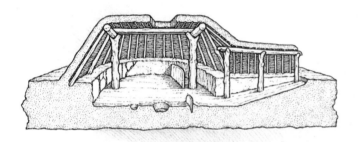

Some 2,000 years ago the pit house — in its many variations — was a common type of dwelling in the Southwest. The example at top includes a tunnel entrance and an interior wall that doubles as seating. After about A.D. 850 some people built rectangular aboveground housing (as above) out of stone, mud plaster, and timber bracing. When joined by common walls, these houses evolved into apartmentlike pueblos (below), while the pit house was retained as an underground kiva.

spread their influence throughout the Southwest. No one knows what language the Anasazi spoke or even what they called themselves. Their modern name is a Navajo word meaning "enemy ancestors." But evidence of their presence is everywhere: in the monumental cliff-side apartment dwellings at Mesa Verde, Colorado; at Kayenta and Canyon de Chelly in Arizona; at the sprawling urban complex of New Mexico's Chaco Canyon, and at many other sites.

The Anasazi heartland was a lofty, semiarid plateau in the Four Corners region, at the junction of present-day Utah, Colorado, New Mexico, and Arizona. Here, after centuries of nomadic hunting and foraging, they settled in and began to raise corn, make pottery, and acquire the amenities of permanent habitation. Like many Southwestern groups, they lived partly underground at first, in circular or oval-shaped pit houses. Cool in summer, warmed in winter by a central hearth, these dwellings gave rugged but adequate shelter in the harsh up-country climate. Then gradually a transformation occurred.

To store their annual harvests, the Anasazi began building aboveground granaries—first of mud-covered latticework and then of stone and mud mortar. So sturdy and comfortable did these structures prove to be that the Anasazi started living in them. This move to

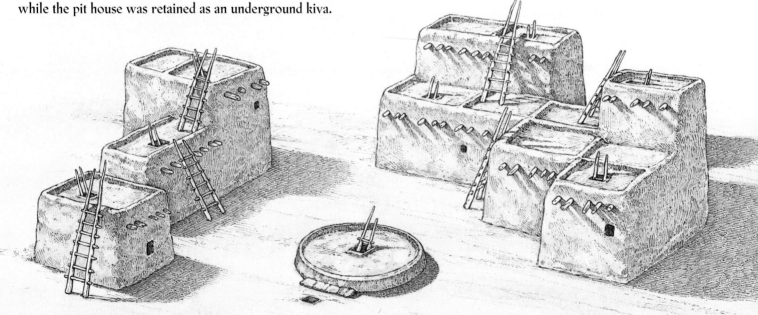

Petroglyphs overlooking the Rio Grande in northern New Mexico include stylized ritual figures and a naturalistic horse — an animal unknown here until the 16th century.

the surface marked the beginning of a cultural ascent that would lead from Anasazi to Pueblo. As their communities grew in size and number, the Anasazi builders achieved an astonishing degree of architectural mastery. Mesa Verde's fortresslike Cliff Palace, tucked under the sandstone rimrock, contained some 220 adjoining rooms of carefully dressed stone, with squared-off windows and clay-plastered walls. The 600 rooms of Pueblo Bonito, a five-story crescent-shaped structure erected in Chaco Canyon between A.D. 1050 and 1100, housed perhaps 1,000 people.

Many Anasazi communities were situated with a clear eye toward defense. The cliff-side structures of Mesa Verde could be reached only by an arduous climb using footholds carved into the rock. The buildings were constructed in tiers, so that the roof of an apartment formed the front porch of the one above it. In most settlements the ground-floor apartments lacked doors, and access was down a ladder through a hole in the roof. Even so, all dwellings looked out onto a central plaza, which served as the focus of daily life. This architectural plan would later prompt Spanish conquistadors to dub the settlements pueblos, or "villages," and the people themselves Pueblo.

Like all aspects of Anasazi life, these dwellings had spiritual meaning. The stone and mud of their massive walls recalled the

Prayers, Myths, and Messages Encoded in Stone

On boulders and canyon walls, the native peoples of the Southwest left a heritage coded in petroglyphs — pictures pecked into the rock with stone chisels. Each image may contain several meanings, and together they tell of ancient lore, of appeals for rain or hunting prowess, and of the quest for spiritual power. These examples date from A.D. 650 to 1700 and were found in New Mexico, Utah, and Arizona.

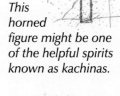

A humpbacked deity with a flute calls for rain; a duck carries the message; a third figure holds the disc of the sun.

A bird soars upward toward a rainbow and a bank of clouds.

This horned figure might be one of the helpful spirits known as kachinas.

Two mythic sisters, the mothers of us all, may have left these footprints.

Spirals could stand for journeys, water, or perhaps wind. But a star was always a star.

Mountain sheep and other game frequently appear in petroglyphs.

Several kinds of deer roamed the Southwest, but few were so elaborately antlered as this one.

This creature may have been a local variety of turtle, which had the power to bring rain.

Bears are associated with both war and healing. Three stars emblazen this six-foot-long specimen.

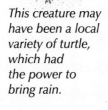

A giant hunter with a body-sized shield looms above a small human and a tiny deer.

The horned serpent controlled earthquakes and floods. The cross on this one's tail may symbolize Venus, the morning star.

READING THE SKY

The tower at Hovenweep, an Anasazi ruin in Utah, was designed for solar observation. Openings in the masonry (diagram, right) align with key sunset positions.

Summer
solstice
sunset

Equinox
sunset

Winter
solstice
sunset

To plan their farming and ceremonial cycles, the Anasazi watched the skies, noting the positions of the sun, moon, and stars. Each month began with the crescent moon, and the days to the next new moon were recorded by cutting notches into sticks. Carved symbols on these calendar sticks indicated the dates of rituals, which often depended on a close calculation of both solar and lunar events. Even today the Zuni of New Mexico use a similar system, observing the sun's progress and the phases of the moon to determine the date of their late-autumn Shalako festival.

←—NE   SW—→

Earliest date
for planting
corn

Winter
solstice
(December 21)

Summer
solstice
(June 21)

The primary focus was the life-giving sun. Each morning at dawn the village high priest would make careful note of the place on the horizon where the sun's first rays appeared. Since this point shifts during the season, moving north as the days grow longer, the priest's observations served as a kind of landscape calendar (left), allowing him to calculate the time for planting crops or for staging certain festivals.

Some solar events, such as solstices and equinoxes, were so important that the Anasazi sky watchers took readings at both dawn and sunset. They also built special structures for solar observation. When the sun was perfectly centered on a particular opening (above), they knew that the anticipated date had arrived.

Certain sun rituals were common to all Anasazi groups. They greeted the morning sun by facing east and offering a pinch of cornmeal. Mothers held newborn babies up to the dawn to receive the sun's blessing. As with all things, the Anasazi knew their bond with the sun was based on mutual obligation: show it proper respect, and it would reward you with the gift of fine weather.

earth from which the tribe had first emerged in the days of creation. The arrangement of dwellings around a central plaza echoed the builders' image of the universe: a huge clay pot, covered by the dome of a wicker basket. This living symbolism, along with the architecture itself, became a vital part of the Pueblo peoples' shared heritage.

> The Pueblo have no word that translates as "religion." The knowledge of a spiritual life is part of the person 24 hours a day, every day of the year. Religious belief permeates every aspect of life; it determines man's relation with the natural world and with his fellow man. The secret of the Pueblo's success was simple. They came face to face with nature but did not exploit it.
> — *Joe S. Sando, Jemez Pueblo*

Also incorporated into Pueblo tradition were legendary accounts of the world's beginnings that closely mirrored the Anasazi's own tribal genesis. Somewhere to the north, so the story was told, the first humans climbed into the sunlight through a hole in the earth from a sacred underground place called Sipapu. Guided by the Great Spirit, they wandered for many years, seeking food, fleeing drought or tornadoes or wicked shamans, always searching for a land of harmony and plenty.

At last they found it. The Great Spirit taught them to plant and harvest crops—especially corn, the staff of Pueblo life—and to build their fortresslike communities. Then, after appointing a pair of twin warrior gods (Maseway and Sheoyeway, in the Hopi account) to guard over them, he returned to his home beyond the clouds.

Variations of this story, elaborated with songs and dances added over the generations, are told and retold by today's Pueblos. Each community has added its own unique details. The Tewa, who settled in the Rio Grande basin, made their first home under the surface of a sacred lake. The earliest forebears of the Zuni came into a world with

webbed feet, long ears, hairless tails, and moss-covered bodies and acquired human form after bathing in the waters of a sacred spring. In every case the birth of humankind was a saga of upward emergence—from darkness into sunlight, from ignorance to wisdom.

The myth of creation was enshrined in each village plaza in an underground ceremonial chamber that had evolved from the traditional pit house; the Hopi called it a *kiva*. A small village might have only one kiva, larger settlements as many as 20 or more, with a

Both the Anasazi and their descendants used digging sticks to plant crops. Made of a hardwood like scrub oak or mountain mahogany, the sticks sometimes had a foot brace for easier penetration into hard, sun-baked soil.

Zuni farmers conserved moisture and guarded against erosion by molding their fields into waffle patterns like the ones shown here.

Working together in a family corn patch, the farmers on this 1,000-year-old Mimbres food bowl use digging sticks to cultivate the soil. The animal at top may be a mountain lion, symbol of spiritual power.

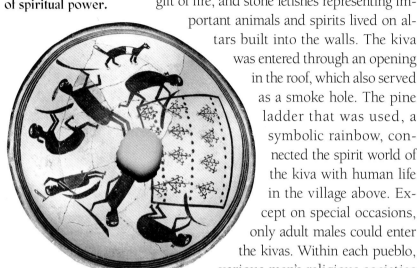

You can look back at the old Mimbres pottery, at petroglyphs and rock art . . . there is that presence there . . . people are aware of where they came from and they are leaving images for other people to see.
—Gail Bird, Laguna Pueblo

principal grand kiva that could reach up to 70 feet in diameter. Every feature of these subterranean sanctuaries carried meaning. A small "sipapu hole," dug into the earthen floor, represented the world navel from which life first sprang and through which each human spirit would one day return. A fire altar recalled the gift of fire, and stone fetishes representing important animals and spirits lived on altars built into the walls. The kiva was entered through an opening in the roof, which also served as a smoke hole. The pine ladder that was used, a symbolic rainbow, connected the spirit world of the kiva with human life in the village above. Except on special occasions, only adult males could enter the kivas. Within each pueblo, various men's religious societies took responsibility for communicating with the spirit world, and the kivas served as their lodge houses. Here initiates met to plan and perform the ceremonies that brought the summer rains, caused the corn to sprout, and ensured success in battle and the hunt.

Prayers to the Sun

Standing at the center of the pueblo's spiritual life was an official known in some areas as the *cacique*, who served as both high priest and political chief. Claiming spiritual descent from the sun itself—the Zuni called him Sun Speaker; the Hopi, Sun Watcher—the cacique held council with the town's leading men to resolve disputes, hand down justice, and decide all matters important to village welfare. He was also charged with maintaining harmony between his people and the spiritual forces that controlled the universe.

Each morning he would greet the rising sun with a welcoming prayer. Also, by close observation of celestial events, he drew up the village calendar, marking out the times for planting and harvest festivals, for rain dances and puberty rites, and for the many other sa-

cred events that gave shape to the Anasazi year. Periodically he would enter the main kiva to ritually re-create the time of emergence, thereby restoring his people to a state of primordial grace

Way back in the distant past, the ancestors of humans were living down below in a world under the earth. They weren't humans yet, they lived in darkness, behaving like bugs.

Now, there was a Great Spirit watching over everything; some people say he was the sun. He saw how things were down under the earth, so he sent his messenger, Spider Old Woman, to talk to them. She said, "You creatures, the Sun Spirit doesn't want you living like this. He is going to transform you into something better, and I will lead you to another world."

When they came out on the surface of the earth, that's when they became humans. In the journeys that followed, they were looking for a place of harmony where they could follow good teachings and a good way of life.

— Albert Yava, Tewa/Hopi

In the Keres culture of Acoma Pueblo, the cacique bore the title of Inside Chief, signifying his power within the village. Beyond the pueblo walls, power passed to one or more war leaders, or Outside Chiefs, who were responsible for constructing defenses and keeping watch against invaders. The war leaders guarded the pueblo's essential resources, from woodlands to water supplies, from turquoise mines to salt beds and hunting grounds.

Virtually every adult male belonged to a warrior society, having gained membership through arduous physical and spiritual preparation. Young initiates learned to chip a flint arrowhead, carve a hardwood bow, and use the combination with deadly accuracy. Equally important were the chants and dances, performed in the society's kiva, that gave them the predatory powers of such animals as the puma, eagle, badger, and bear.

SACRED KERNELS OF LIFE

Kachina dancers representing powerful rain spirits gather by lantern light at the entrance to a kiva in "Night Dance" by Hopi artist Neil R. David, Sr. Some hold rattles; others carry ears of corn, symbolic of the crop the villagers hope to raise during the year ahead. The Hopi celebrate the Night Dances in February, well before the first planting.

All the achievements of Pueblo civilization rested upon a single piece of knowledge: the ability to grow corn. The first usable kernels, arriving from Mexico around 1000 B.C., gave rise to an agricultural way of life that allowed towns to be built and arts to flourish. Pueblo farmers harvested at least 19 varieties, including blue corn, white corn, yellow corn, and black corn. Corn was both dietary staple and religious sacrament, revered in ancient story and celebrated in numerous festivals. To the Keres people, life began with a Corn Mother, who planted the seeds of all the earth's flora and fauna. Other groups pay homage to Corn Maidens, who personify corn in its various types and colors. To this day Pueblo children are given a perfect ear of corn — their own symbolic Corn Mother — when they are born. They keep it for life, its dried kernels a continual reminder of this most basic aspect of their Pueblo heritage.

A trio of Corn Maidens, depicted above by Hopi painter Milland Lomakema, recalls the tradition of mythic females who supplied the Pueblo world with its most basic food stock. At right, in a painting by L. Honewytewa, sacred Hopi clowns dine on piki, a rolled waferlike bread made from blue corn flour and served here by Corn Maiden dancers.

Nestled beneath a giant sandstone arch in Arizona's Tsegi Canyon, the Betatakin cliff dwelling was built in 1267 to house an entire community in more than 100 rooms. Facing south, it took warmth from the winter sun, while the rock overhang gave shade in the hundred-degree heat of midsummer. Despite its ideal setting, Betatakin was abandoned by 1300 during the massive population shifts of the Great Migration. At right, Anasazi men meet in a kiva below another cliff pueblo.

Three other male ritual societies—rain, medicine, and hunt—also maintained kivas where youths lived while learning the organization's secrets. Because rain was sparse and crucial, the rain chief was very powerful. He could summon the Horned Water Serpent, whose slithery, lightning-fast habits linked the masculine, rain-bearing sky with the feminine, fertile earth. Both had to work in harmony for the community to prosper.

> We perform the Snake Dance for rain to fall to water the earth, that planted things may ripen and grow large; that the male element of the Above, the Yei, may impregnate the female earth virgin, Naasun.
> — *Hopi man, 16th century*

In addition to their ceremonial duties, and along with their roles as hunters of game and

defenders of the peace, men spent much of their time farming. In carefully tended plots outside the pueblo walls, they grew beans, squash, gourds, and in later years cotton and tobacco. The main crop was corn, the staple of Pueblo existence. But although men worked the fields, it was a woman who first taught them how. The story is still told by the people of Acoma Pueblo in present-day New Mexico.

Thought Woman

The earth was formed, the Acomans say, when the Great Father Uchtsiti, Lord of the Sun, hurled a clot of his own blood into the heavens. In the soil of this new world, he set germinating the souls of two sisters, the Corn Mothers, who were raised to maturity by a spirit called Thought Woman. When the time was ripe, Thought Woman gave the two sisters baskets filled with seeds and showed them the way to the earth's surface. Corn was the first thing they planted. They learned to cultivate and harvest it, to grind and cook it, and to make daily offerings of cornmeal and pollen to their father, Uchtsiti. These lessons the Acomans would practice each day of their lives.

Women thus held positions of unusual power in the Pueblo world. The cornfields belonged to them, as did the houses in each town. Usually a household was managed by a grandmother, whose husband, in-laws, daughters and sons-in-law, grandchildren, and others lived under her sway. She controlled the food bins, the seed supplies, the clan fetishes, and all the implements of domestic life. When a man married, he went to live in his wife's household, although he returned to his mother's home for important occasions.

Much of a woman's day went into food preparation. The grinding of corn into meal, by rubbing the kernels with a handheld stone mano against a stone metate, was an endless, ongoing process. A pot of stew simmered day and night, replenished by handfuls of meal, beans, or squash, plus any available game, from rodents to buffalo. Women also went foraging for pine nuts, ju-

THE FINE ART OF TRADE

A ceremonial wooden body ornament of the 11th or 12th century mimics the look of macaw feathers; below, turquoise adorns a bone hairpin.

The woven yucca-fiber bracelet below still bears its turquoise mosaic outer shell. The rich, delicate cotton lace poncho in the background was woven at an Arizona pueblo around 1350.

Unglazed black-on-white Kayenta pottery featured elegant geometric designs painted with a pigment extracted from wild aster plants. These jars, which stand between 14 and 17 inches tall, were made between 1100 and 1280.

The far-reaching influence of Anasazi culture was spurred, in part, by the superb talents of Anasazi craftsmen. Along with a rising population and the movement to larger settlements around A.D. 1100, the Anasazi reached new levels of mastery in the arts of weaving, ceramics, basketry, and mosaic work. Fueling this creative ascent was an outpouring of wealth from the turquoise mines near Chaco Canyon. Anasazi merchants exported the precious blue stone throughout the Southwest region and beyond.

Anasazi trade routes stretched to the Great Plains, the California coast, and deep into Mexico. Objects, ideas, raw materials, and artistic styles flowed freely in all directions. The black-on-white pottery designs developed in the Kayenta region, for instance, were widely copied. And among the valuables the Anasazi brought back from Mexico, in return for their turquoise, were macaw feathers and copper bells.

niper berries, chokeberries, cactus fruit, sage, wild oregano, and other herbs. They tanned hides and made clothes from cotton cloth woven by men in the kivas. Their pottery and basketwork reached a high level of artistry.

> Our art is not a separate entity. It is a universal gesture of prayer.... And it harmonizes with the expression of life.... Art is always there. There is always something done, something woven, something painted, something sculpted.
>
> — *José Rey Toledo, Jemez Pueblo*

Such was the heritage bequeathed to the Pueblo people by their Anasazi ancestors. Their influence spread across the Southwest during a 350-year period of vigorous expansion that began around A.D. 900 and saw the construction of the great pueblo sites of Chaco Canyon, Mesa Verde, and scores of other locations. Altogether, Anasazi settlements may have held as many as 50,000 people.

The Anasazi ushered in a golden age of commerce, with a trading system that reached deep into Mexico and as far west as the Pacific Ocean. The main export was turquoise, which traders exchanged for seashells from the California coast and for obsidian, copper bells, and brightly colored macaw feathers from the jungles of Central America. Equally prized were the macaws themselves, which were petted and pampered, fed on roasted agave fruit, and used in important ceremonies.

End of an Era

As quickly as it had blossomed, the Anasazi exuberance began to wane. By 1150 new construction ceased in Chaco Canyon, and the region was eventually abandoned. Populations to the north, in such places as Hovenweep and Mesa Verde, enjoyed a final flowering; then they, too, vanished. Perhaps overfarming had depleted the soil, or the cutting of timber to build roofs had destroyed fragile watersheds. Raids by enemy tribes may have driven some settlers away in search of more defendable terrain. But the main reason almost certainly was

a shift in the weather. Severe cycles of drought hit the region beginning in the mid-1100's and culminated in a devastating 23-year dry spell between 1276 and 1299. Without rainfall the land burned dry, rivers and streams vanished, and the corn crop died even as it sprouted.

Drought was the explanation of Acoma storytellers, who say that one night the Horned Water Serpent, spirit of rain and fertility, abruptly left his people. No amount of prayer, no charms or dances of the rain priests, would bring him back. Unable to survive without their snake god, the people followed his trail until it reached a river. There they established a new home.

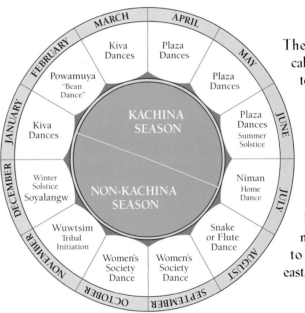

The Hopi ceremonial calendar — still in use today — divides the year in half, based on the visits of the kachinas. These ancestral spirits arrive with the first new moon after the winter solstice, then leave in high summer for their homes to the north, south, east, and west.

> There are stories and stories.... There are the songs, also, that are taught. Some are whimsical. Some are very intense. Some are documentary.... Everything I have known is through teachings, by word of mouth, either by song or by legends.
>
> — *Terrance Honvantewa, Hopi*

Another version survives in the stories of the Zuni. They tell how Cloud Swallower, a mighty giant, devoured the thunderheads that brought the summer rains. For good measure he gulped down a few humans as well. The Warrior Twins and Grandmother Spider, a

Purveyors of ritual mayhem, sacred Pueblo clowns included long-eared, striped Tewa koshares (top), known for gluttony and bawdiness, and long-skirted Hopi mudheads, or koyemshi. Both are shown as carved wooden effigies.

powerfully protective goddess, managed to drive him away, and the rains returned. But the event so frightened the people that they decided to move on.

The Great Migration

However it happened, during a 150-year period known as the Great Migration, the Anasazi abandoned their larger pueblos and wandered from place to place. By 1300 virtually all the settlements in the San Juan and Chaco river drainage basins were left empty. The inhabitants of Kayenta drifted south, perhaps mingling with other groups on Arizona's Black Mesa to become the people known in historic times as the Hopi. A construction boom occurred at Zuni, in the land of the ancient Mogollon people, where Anasazi migrants by the thousands built houses for themselves. Some refugees from the Chaco and Mesa Verde areas established homes at Acoma and Laguna, while others pushed farther east across the mountains to populate the fertile valley of the Rio Grande.

There's a story in Acoma history that talks about a place like Chaco Canyon, a place where Acoma people migrated from.

I remember my grandparents going to Chaco Canyon, and late at night as they were praying, my grandmother later told me she thought she heard someone, somebody, singing.

— *Conroy Chino, Acoma Pueblo*

The upheavals of migration brought further changes in culture and tradition, as the ancestral beliefs of the Anasazi intermingled with the ideas and practices of their new neighbors. Differences in social structure also began to appear. Among the Rio Grande Tewa, for example, governance of the village alternated by season between two roughly equal segments of the population. Membership was hereditary, and everyone joined his or her father's group (sometimes called a moiety) to become

either a Summer Person or a Winter Person.

Among all Pueblo people, religion continued to play a vital role in daily life. At the heart of religious life, particularly among western groups like the Hopi and Zuni, were the infinitely helpful kachinas—also sometimes called *katsinas*. In a world infused by supernatural forces, each visible object had a spiritual counterpart, a divine essence as real as the thing itself.

A *katsina* can be an ancestor spirit, or it can be the spirit of an animal or a plant or anything that is beneficial to the Hopi. . . . We even have a dog *katsina*: dogs help the Hopi hunt. And then a *katsina* can be just an abstract thing. You don't know the meaning behind it — all you know is that it will perform for you, it brings rain, it carries messages back to whoever is making rain.

— *Michael Lomatuway'ma, Hopi*

Six months of every year, the kachinas resided in the mountains to the west, where they could be seen as cloud banks gathering above the peaks. Then shortly after the winter solstice, they would return to the pueblo. Summoned in secret kiva ceremonies, the kachinas arrived through the sipapu hole in the floor to act as intermediaries between the spirit realm and the world of humans.

During their stay the kachinas became the center of the pueblo's ceremonial life. On important occasions the men of the kachina society, gloriously masked and costumed, would emerge from the kivas and pour into the village square to dance and chant. As each dancer performed, he would receive the spirit of the kachina he represented and so acquire the power to send prayers to the deities.

One of the kachinas' tasks was to maintain discipline among the pueblo's children and to instruct them in religious matters. Each boy and girl at an early age received a wooden kachina doll, called a *tithu* in Hopi, carved from cottonwood root by the

LEGACY OF THE KACHINAS

Even today, powerful sacred beings arrive at the Pueblo villages when summoned. Men representing the kachinas, or cloud spirits, emerge masked and costumed to participate in line dances and other rites that can last for days. Once invoked, the kachinas may bring rain and prosperity. In addition, impudent clown figures called koshares add leaven to the occasion — at the same time illustrating the folly of moral indiscretion. Feasts are prepared and shared among villagers, while the kachinas give away dolls made in their likenesses to teach children the ways of the spirit world.

Bursting in on the scene like a human rockslide, gleeful koshares upset the decorum of a Hopi ceremony with their special brand of chaos in "The Delight Makers," by the artist Fred Kabotie.

A kachina doll representing the chief female spirit of the Bean Dance ceremony (above) bears a tray of corn sprouts. At left, she leads other kachina figures into the sunset on the ceremony's final evening.

Kachinas, clowns, and villagers celebrate together during a Zuni Shalako festival in "Dancing Spirits," painted in 1947 by Pueblo artist José Rey Toledo.

men of the kiva and given out during the dances. When children were good, the kachinas would leave them presents. But should they misbehave, a kachina would appear, brandishing a yucca whip or cottonwood switch, and treat them to the fright of their young lives.

~

Some observers have said that the Pueblo "dance all the year round." This may be true, and was more the case in the past, since their ceremonial calendar covers the whole year. Through dance and song one can realize a sense of rebirth and rejuvenation.

— *Joe S. Sando, Jemez Pueblo*

~

During the February Bean Dance festival, boys eight or nine years of age were assembled in the kiva, where the Kachina Chief recited the creation story. Suddenly, with a terrifying cry, other kachinas entered, carrying whips. Each boy received four memorable lashes, after which gifts of sacred feathers and cornmeal were presented. Then, after further ceremony and a sumptuous feast, the kachinas peeled

off their masks—showing themselves to be men of the village. Then began the serious business of instructing the children in the moral and spiritual truths of Pueblo life.

Life in the villages settled into the traditional rhythm of planting and harvesting, hunting and worshiping. The scale was smaller than in the Anasazi past. Never again would the Pueblo people erect huge 600-room edifices like the ones at Chaco Canyon. The far-flung network of Anasazi trade routes contracted and disappeared, and individual villages became increasingly self-sufficient.

~

The most important of the traditions is to recognize the value of what is the Hopi way of life. It is not only ceremonies . . . you grow up into these traditions. It is a whole social structure that is involved.

— *Terrance Honvantewa, Hopi*

~

Once established in their new homes, the Pueblo people prospered and multiplied. By about the year 1500, they had grown to a population approaching 250,000, living a settled, self-contained existence in 134 or more villages reaching from the fertile Rio Grande Valley in New Mexico to the more isolated Hopi mesas of Arizona.

Menacing Strangers

Even so, the Pueblo world remained in precarious balance. An ominous signal of future discord occurred as bands of nomadic strangers moved in from the wilderness. The newcomers dressed in animal skins, used dogs as pack animals, and pitched tentlike dwellings made of brush or hide. None of the Pueblo villagers could understand what they said, for they spoke an Athabascan language that had originated in their former homeland: the vast subarctic taiga of northwestern Canada.

No one knows when the Athabascans first ventured into the Southwest or just how they got there. The process may have taken centuries, with small bands trekking down through the Rocky Mountains and onto the Great Plains. But by the early 16th century, they had arrived and were setting up camp on the outskirts of the pueblos.

In their packs they carried the wealth of the Plains: buffalo hides, tallow and meat, bones that could be worked into needles and scrapers, and salt from the desert. In exchange they sought the riches of the Pueblos—pottery, cotton, blankets, turquoise, corn, and other goods. But if most of the time they were content to barter, upon occasion they simply saw what they wanted and took it. They became known among the villages by another name: the Apache.

Despite occasional friction, the Apache and Pueblos managed to maintain generally peaceful relations. Not so with the next wave of newcomers: midway through the 1500's, the first Europeans came marching across the sagebrush in a haze of desert dust.

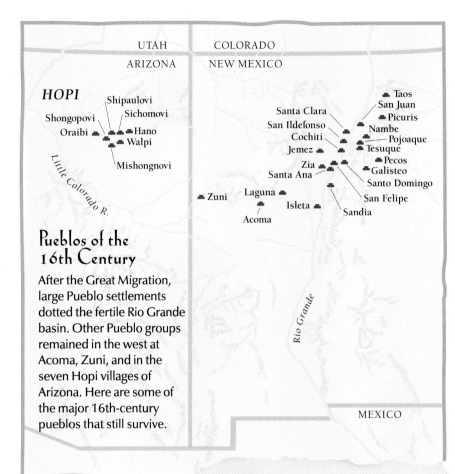

Pueblos of the 16th Century

After the Great Migration, large Pueblo settlements dotted the fertile Rio Grande basin. Other Pueblo groups remained in the west at Acoma, Zuni, and in the seven Hopi villages of Arizona. Here are some of the major 16th-century pueblos that still survive.

The multitiered adobe building style of Taos Pueblo, as captured in this 1870's photograph, remained remarkably faithful to a description of Taos — "the houses are very close together and have five or six stories" — given by Spanish explorer Hernando de Alvarado after a visit in 1540.

First Encounters

It is not always easy to separate legend from truth in the early chronicles of Spanish colonial history. Tall tales grew up right from the start, in 1536, when four sun-dazed travelers showed up in Mexico City, capital of the newly proclaimed province of New Spain.

The four men, sole survivors of a Spanish shipwreck, had spent eight years wandering through the prairies and deserts of present-day Texas and New Mexico. One was the conquistador Cabeza de Vaca; another, his Moorish slave Esteban. And although they arrived half dead, they were filled to bursting with wondrous stories. They told of grassy plains teeming with *cibolos*—as they called the buffalo—of industrious farmers and well-built villages, and of cities resplendent with multistoried houses and accumulated riches.

In Mexico City this was sensational news. According to an old Spanish legend, somewhere in the far reaches of the New World there existed seven ancient cities of fabulous wealth. Now, with the reports of Cabeza de Vaca, the viceroy of New Spain authorized an expedition to find the Seven Cities of Cíbola. Headed by a missionary named Fray Marcos de Niza and with Esteban as guide, the party set out in 1539. Esteban was sent ahead to reconnoiter: if he found nothing of note, he was to send back a cross the length of his hand; a larger cross would mean an important discovery. Four days later, the story goes, Fray Marcos received a cross as tall as a man.

Esteban had reached the Zuni town of Hawikuh in western New Mexico. It was May, and Hawikuh's residents were preparing for their main spring festival, the plaza dances heralding the annual arrival of the kachinas from their winter abodes. But this year lookouts spotted something that looked like no kachina they had ever seen—a figure with dark skin and gaudy attire coming toward them across the desert.

Esteban, the Moroccan slave who helped lead the first Spanish expedition, lives on in the form of Tsa'kwayna, a kachina doll.

Visitors to a town customarily sent a gift before arriving, and a member of Esteban's entourage duly approached with his offering— only this time the Moor had blundered.

> Esteban learned a few tricks of the trade of being a medicine man. So he sent this gourd that was supposedly his medicine gourd, which had two feathers, one white, one red, and a couple of copper bells. At that point the Zuni chiefs flung the gourd to the ground and said, "This is not from our people, this person must be a spy."
> — *Ed Ladd, Zuni*

Esteban was undeterred, however, and strode up to issue demands for turquoise and women, boasting of powerful friends not far behind. But bravado and bluster did not impress the Zuni chiefs. They ordered him seized, conferred briefly, then announced their decision. The intruder was put to death.

When Fray Marcos learned of Esteban's fate, he prudently changed his plans to visit Hawikuh and instead ascended a hill nearby. Looking down, he saw what he wanted to see: not a muddy village, but a magnificent town with gleaming terraces, houses with jeweled doors, and streets lined with silversmiths' shops. Claiming the region for Spain, he made haste for Mexico City to deliver his breathless report to the viceroy.

The result of Fray Marcos's fantasy was a much larger incursion, led this time by a soldier. Francisco Vásquez de Coronado commanded an impressive force: 230 soldiers on horseback and 62 on foot, nearly 1,000 Indian allies from the south, 600 pack animals, and 1,000 horses. It was an awesome spectacle: never had anyone in the Southwest seen such warriors. Some carried deadly sticks that shot fire and barked like thunder, and it was rumored that the horses, with their massive heads and huge teeth, liked to eat people.

Coronado soon discovered that Fray Marcos had not merely exaggerated—he had lied in every detail. There were no terraced mansions and not one ounce of gold. What Coro-

nado found instead was trouble. The people of Hawikuh, seeking to protect themselves from the horses, sprinkled a barrier of sacred corn-meal in their path. But the horses kept coming. Terrified, the villagers unleashed a barrage of arrows. The Spaniards responded with a cavalry charge and a salvo of gunfire that sent the defenders reeling and gave the soldiers time to loot their food supplies.

News of the attack swept from town to town. Who were these beings, with their fear-some animals and fire sticks? Could they be the white gods spoken of in the old stories, mighty kachinas who had said they would come again from the south? The strangers were brutal and greedy—that much was certain—and the local people could not wait for them to leave.

Zuni villagers look with silent disbelief upon the gaudy figure of Esteban, the first non-Indian they had ever seen. To impress the local population, Esteban bedecked himself in feathers and bells, kept a pair of greyhounds, and traveled with an entourage of Mexican retainers and beautiful women.

Coronado sent out search parties to look for gold, but all in vain. Moving east, he reached a cluster of pueblos at Tiguex, on the Rio Grande, and settled in for the winter. Further depredations, including the wholesale theft of corn and the rape of Pueblo women, made it clear that these intruders were no gods. As the Spaniards tightened their hold, several pueblos rose in revolt. Coronado replied with a savagery calculated to discourage any further thoughts of resistance. One hundred Pueblo warriors were burned at the stake, and hundreds more were hunted down as they fled north into the mountains.

The following spring Coronado set out again on his quest for gold. The cities he was looking for, the natives told him, lay in the plains to the east, in the land of Quivira; there

ANCIENT NATIVE TRADE ROUTES

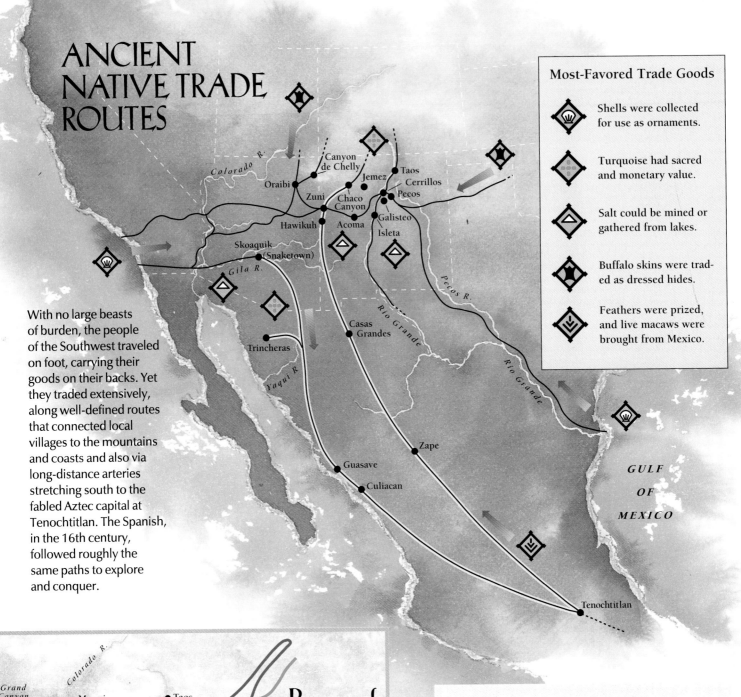

Most-Favored Trade Goods

Shells were collected for use as ornaments.

Turquoise had sacred and monetary value.

Salt could be mined or gathered from lakes.

Buffalo skins were traded as dressed hides.

Feathers were prized, and live macaws were brought from Mexico.

With no large beasts of burden, the people of the Southwest traveled on foot, carrying their goods on their backs. Yet they traded extensively, along well-defined routes that connected local villages to the mountains and coasts and also via long-distance arteries stretching south to the fabled Aztec capital at Tenochtitlan. The Spanish, in the 16th century, followed roughly the same paths to explore and conquer.

Routes of the Spanish Explorers

— de Vaca 1528-36
— Coronado 1540-42
— Oñate 1598-99

Tracking the Salt Mother

Salt was a widely traded commodity, valued for its use in healing rituals, burial rites, love potions, and as a flavoring and preservative. The Pueblos revered it as the Salt Mother, an elderly matriarch who gave herself freely to anyone who sought her. They made pilgrimages to places she was known to inhabit.

The people of Acoma — so the elders recounted — once followed the Salt Mother's trail far into the wilderness, trekking past dry gulches and sage-purpled hills for days on end. Finally they reached a large salt lake. "This is my home," the Salt Mother declared. After that, all who traveled there read their fortune in the water, and if ailing in body they were made well again.

he would find all the gold, silver, silks, and precious stones his heart desired. In fact, Quivira turned out to be a dusty settlement of grass huts occupied by the Wichita Indians.

Bitterly disappointed, Coronado marched his treasure-seekers back to Tiguex for a second winter's retreat. When the conquistadors returned to Mexico in the spring of 1542, their reports of a harsh desert, cold winters, mud towns, impoverished Indians, and the continual threat of revolts finally put to rest the dream of Cíbola. And with no golden cities to quicken the Spaniards' pulse, the Pueblos were left undisturbed for the next 40 years.

The Second Wave

But the imperial impulse of the Spanish crown was strong—as was the missionary zeal of the Catholic Church. Groups of brown-robed friars and freebooting conquistadors ventured into Pueblo country over the years in search of fortune and converts. All ended in failure. Then in 1595 the king of Spain decided to make New Mexico a colony, and he issued a license to Don Juan de Oñate, scion of a wealthy Spanish mining family.

Oñate set out from Mexico with 400 soldiers, settlers, servants, Franciscan priests, and a clear mission: "the service of the Lord Our God, the spreading of His holy Catholic faith, and pacification of the natives."

When the Spanish arrived in New Mexico, they established their first capital in San Juan Pueblo. It was clear that this group of invaders was different from Coronado's expedition. They brought their families, mission supplies, wheat seed, fruit trees, and thousands of horses, cattle, sheep, pigs, and chickens. The Spanish were here to stay.

— *Conroy Chino, Acoma Pueblo*

The Pueblo people looked upon the intruders with a mixture of fascination and dismay. Some fled into the hills. Others greeted the Spaniards as they would any other powerful visitors, offering gifts of water and corn. Confronted with the white men's determination to save their souls, they invited the missionaries into their villages, intending to adopt the new teachings only if they liked what they heard. That was good enough for the Spanish. Friars scattered throughout the pueblos, setting up crosses and staging morality plays on the life of Christ. To the Indians the crosses resembled giant prayer sticks; Christ seemed like nothing so much as a powerful new kachina.

Oñate moved up the Rio Grande, demanding allegiance as he went. At one pueblo he evacuated the villagers, renamed the site San Gabriel, and established the region's first Spanish capital. Within two months he had built a church, largely with Indian labor. Then, like Coronado before him, Oñate went looking for gold. When he needed supplies, he took from the villages. "The Spaniards seize their blankets by force," wrote one of his captains, "leaving the poor Indian women stark naked, holding their babies to their breasts."

The first rebellion against Oñate's brutality, at Acoma in 1599, left the colonists severely shaken. Similar outbreaks at two other pueblos forced an uneasy peace. Finally, word of Oñate's ruthlessness filtered back to Mexico, and he was removed from office. His succes-

A Navajo rock painting of Spaniards on horseback recalls the impact of the conquistadors and all they introduced — horses, religion, and a myriad of other changes, vast almost beyond measure.

THREE DAYS AT ACOMA

When the column of Spanish troops came into view on a cold winter afternoon — January 21, 1599, by European reckoning — the fighting men of Acoma fanned out from their village to guard the edge of the mesa. As the Spaniards drew closer, the defenders unleashed a barrage of insults, rocks, and arrows from more than 300 feet above. Just seven weeks earlier, a party of Spanish soldiers seeking food had been treated in a friendly manner until their demands turned aggressive — and provoked a furious reaction. When it was over, almost all the intruders were dead, including their commander, Juan de Zaldivar, nephew of the military governor of New Mexico, Juan de Oñate.

Resolved to make an example of Acoma, Oñate dispatched 70 of his best men under the command of Vicente de Zaldivar, Juan's brother. These were the troops approaching the seemingly impregnable "Sky City" that January afternoon, and with them arrived a harsh new reality. Over the next three days the Spaniards fought their way to the top of the mesa, where they rolled out a fearsome new weapon — a cannon that spewed thunderous blasts of small stones, tearing flesh and shattering bones. The battle became a massacre. As many as 800 Acomans soon lay dead in the rubble of their ruined city. Some 500 survivors were herded into dismal captivity: all males over the age of 12 were condemned to 20 years' servitude; those over 25 were also sentenced to have one foot cut off. In time some of the Acomans managed to escape and made their way home, there to begin the long process of rebuilding. The Sky City has been continuously inhabited since then, and never again has it fallen to an invader.

In their campaign to win converts, missionary friars set up schools to teach reading and singing, along with the rudiments of Christian doctrine. The catechism above, made by Franciscans in Mexico around 1540, used easily understood pictographs to carry the message.

sor arrived in 1610 and founded a new capital at Santa Fe. The move symbolized a new reality: the riches of conquest would arise from the land and from the sweat of the conquered.

Oppression and Revolt

Under the new regime an ancient way of life was utterly transformed. People who had farmed their communal village holdings for centuries suddenly found the fields staked off and parceled out to Spanish colonists. For societies that saw the earth as sacred and had no notion of land as private property, this made no sense. The *encomiendas,* as the land grants were called, seemed to defy the basic harmony between man and nature. Furthermore, the Spanish instituted a system of *repartimiento,* which allowed each landowner to exact annual taxes of corn and cloth from the native residents on "his" property. Even worse, the same

people could be drafted to labor in the landowner's fields or orchards, to drive his cattle, or to build his barns and dwellings.

The encomienda system proved highly productive. Goods made in the pueblos were sold in Mexico, with profits going to the landowners and to colonial authorities. But Spanish prosperity was bought at the price of Pueblo freedom. Barred from leaving their assigned encomiendas, denied access to both guns and horses, the people became serfs in the land of their ancestors.

> All of a sudden here come these invaders who begin to tell you, well, things are going to change here now and you can't leave your pueblo, you can't travel as far as you want any more, because we don't want you leaving your area.
>
> — *Glenabah Martinez,*
> *Taos Pueblo/Navajo*

The church also imposed a heavy burden, demanding regular tithes of food and labor. In return, it strove to save Pueblo souls. Franciscans built impressive churches in the largest pueblos, such as Pecos and Acoma, and chapels in the smaller ones. The friars often commanded as much respect as any town cacique. Some were trained doctors, able to cure everyday ailments. They were also aided by surface similarities between Christian and Pueblo beliefs. Christmas, for instance, coincided with rites marking the winter solstice. The Virgin Mary and various saints were likened to kachinas in their roles as intermediaries with the spirit world. Portraits of the Virgin sometimes depicted her surrounded by corn ears, flowers, butterflies, and other traditional symbols of fertility.

At first the Pueblos seemed eager disciples. Entire towns would gather for communal baptism, joining the "wet heads" in the new religion. By 1626 the missionaries claimed as many as 30,000 converts. Yet even while they called themselves Christians, many Pueblo people continued to follow the old ways, meeting in secret to perform their own rituals. If caught, they risked terrible punishment. The Spanish, in an effort to stamp out "devil worship," forbade kachina dances, filled kivas with sand, and burned every mask, prayer stick, and effigy they could lay their hands on.

Priests used to see the curing ceremonies, the medicine men. They were allowed to see a lot of this, in the beginning. But . . . they were proselytizing Christianity, and at the same time turning the people against their own way. They burned up the chambers and they punished the shamans. They killed them. . . . That is when the ceremonies went underground.

— *Joe Herrera, Cochiti Pueblo*

Such cruelties spawned bitter resentments: surely priests of the Great Spirit should not behave this way. At the same time, continual feuding between church and civil government eroded the authority of both. Governors

Enforcing Spanish rule, the civil authorities used any means that worked, including torture. In this 1598 engraving, soldiers hold a captive's feet to the fire while burning his belly with hot wax. Most missionaries abhorred such practices — except to root out "devil worship" within the pueblos.

A MISSION TO BUILD

Wherever the Spanish came to colonize, the Catholic Church was never far behind. Disciplined squads of brown-robed Franciscan friars moved into the Southwest in the wake of Oñate's conquest. They were armed with prayer books, crucifixes, axes, saws, chisels, and shovels, for their first priority was to build a mission. By 1630 the Franciscans had erected several dozen large mission compounds and no less than 90 village churches and chapels.

Funding for construction came from the Spanish king, who donated supplies and equipment. Labor was free of charge, provided by the Pueblo subjects themselves — sometimes willingly, occasionally at swordpoint. For building a mission entailed thousands of man-hours of back-breaking toil. A full-sized compound normally included workrooms and craft shops, granaries and farm buildings, a school, and a residence for at least one priest. The centerpiece was the church itself, a massive, adobe-plastered structure with a long, narrow nave and one or more bell towers.

Beams the size of tree trunks supported the roof. These massive timbers often had to be cut and hauled from forest stands located miles from the mission site. The spruce beams for the church at Shungopovi, a Hopi village on Arizona's Black Mesa, came from the San Francisco Peaks, more than 60 miles to the southwest— down a mountainside, across the Little Colorado River, up and down canyon walls, and finally up the mesa itself. Each log took more than 20 men to lift.

As in traditional Pueblo architecture, women and children built the walls. In some areas they followed the centuries-old practice of setting stone slabs in mud mortar, but along the Rio Grande they adopted a Spanish innovation — adobe brick, made by mixing mud with straw and molding it in wooden forms.

Along with mission-building techniques — and, of course, instruction in Christianity — the Franciscans introduced a number of useful new dimensions to Pueblo life. Mission workshops taught carpentry, leatherwork, and blacksmithing. Pueblo farmers learned to plant wheat fields and peach orchards. And from tending mission livestock, Pueblo herdsmen developed a vocation for cattle and sheep raising that would sustain their descendants for centuries to come.

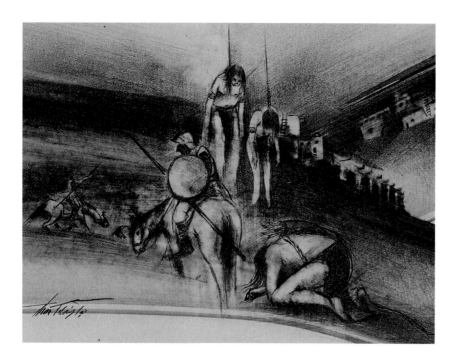

A grim assault on Pueblo religious pride occurred in 1675, when Spanish authorities hung three Tewa medicine doctors for practicing "sorcery." The execution, depicted here by Tommy Montoya of San Juan Pueblo, helped fuel the resentment that triggered the Pueblo Revolt of 1680.

charged friars with mistreating the Indians; friars cited governors for womanizing, corruption, and other immorality. Each side accused the other of profiteering at Pueblo expense.

A series of natural disasters further undermined Spanish rule. Diseases like smallpox and measles, imported by the foreigners, took a dreadful toll among the Pueblos, whose lack of natural immunity left them defenseless. Calamitous droughts also hit the region in 1640 and again in the late 1660's.

⌖

> It was a time when the world was out of balance; it was a time of death. The rain ceased to fall; the corn withered. Thousands of Pueblo people died in a great famine.
>
> — *Conroy Chino, Acoma Pueblo*

⌖

And in Pueblo eyes the cause was clear. Frictions with the Spanish had produced isolated acts of violence over the years, and by the mid-1670's hatreds had reached a flash point. The spark that set them blazing was a witchcraft trial at Santa Fe in 1675. Some native Tewa priests were accused of casting spells on local missionaries, causing them to sicken and die. Hauled into court, the Tewas were summarily convicted and sentenced—4 to death by hanging, 43 others to long terms of slavery

or prison or else to the shame of public flogging. Among those whipped was a man called Popay from San Juan Pueblo. His name would be long remembered.

The harshness of the sentences sparked an immediate uproar. A delegation of Tewa leaders marched on Santa Fe to demand the prisoners' release. A new governor sat in power at Santa Fe, and alarmed by the belligerence of the protesters, he thought it best to give in. This was a mistake. Popay (spelled Popé in Spanish), once freed from arrest, began meeting secretly with other Pueblo leaders to plot revenge. Their purpose: armed rebellion against colonial rule.

The People Rise Up

By 1680 the conspirators were ready. They outnumbered their oppressors by a wide margin, with some 17,000 Pueblos, including 6,000 armed fighters, against 2,800 colonists. Even so, surprise was essential. To synchronize the uprising, Popay and his fellow leaders used a simple but ingenious plan. Young couriers trained to run long distances were sent from pueblo to pueblo delivering knotted cords; one knot was to be untied each morning, and when the last knot was reached, the uprising would begin.

Somehow details of the plot leaked out, and the Spanish governor moved to arrest the ringleaders. He was too late. Violence had already erupted at Tesuque Pueblo, near Santa Fe, and it soon spread across the region. From Taos to Santa Clara, from Pecos and Galisteo to San Cristobal and San Marco, rebellion raged. Missionaries who elected to stay in the pueblos and landowners and their families in outlying areas were all slaughtered.

In Santa Fe itself, about 1,000 frightened colonists gathered behind the city walls, protected by only 50 soldiers. The insurgents surrounded the city, cutting off its water supply. Equipped with captured guns and horses, they gained strength daily. On August 16 the Pueblos, some 2,500 strong, attacked. For two days the fighting continued through the capital, hand to hand, street by street. The Spanish

REMEMBERING THE PUEBLO REBELLION

T hree hundred years after the Pueblo Revolt, in the summer of 1980, all the native villages of the Southwest joined in a great celebration. There were plaza dances and parades, sumptuous feasts and scholarly seminars, and a reenactment of the 400-mile relay in which Pueblo runners carried the signal to start fighting — all commemorating the only successful rebellion in American history against white domination. These tercentennial paintings by San Juan Pueblo artist Tommy Montoya depict key events. Clockwise from top right: the heroic Popay confers with other rebel captains; Tesuque runners spread the word; Pueblo soldiers battle Spanish horsemen in Santa Fe; Spanish refugees begin their exodus.

At the Hopi pueblo of Shongopovi, insurgent villagers exacted terrible revenge — as this 1976 painting by Fred Kabotie attests. After years of harsh treatment by a resident friar who whipped converts and seduced Pueblo women, they strung the priest up to burn and dismantled the church he had forced them to build.

In a harmonious blending of Christian faith and Pueblo belief, wall paintings in traditional style represent the tombs of parishioners at this Catholic church in Laguna Pueblo.

briefly turned back the attackers, but in the end they lost heart. On August 21, after generations as lords of Pueblo country, they quit the capital and headed south for Mexico.

The Pueblos simply let them go; exodus, not slaughter, was their goal. The victors threw themselves into the task of ritual purification, symbolically washing away all traces of Christianity. They held ceremonies to thank the war spirits. They discarded their baptismal names. Churches and mission buildings were put to the torch. The Spanish language was banned.

Yet life after the rebellion was not as harmonious as might have been expected. People missed the farming tools and household goods brought by the colonizers. And with Spanish garrisons no longer close by, nomadic raiders swept down at will to seize food, livestock, and women from the Pueblo settlements. Even Popay himself was said to have taken on imperial airs, riding around in the governor's carriage and stamping out dissent with Spanish-style harshness. As disputes multiplied and pueblo turned against pueblo, the region's defenses fell into neglect.

At length, in the summer of 1692, just 12 years after the revolt, the Spanish returned. A small force under Diego de Vargas quickly brought 23 pueblos back under colonial control—all, he boasted, "without wasting a single ounce of powder." In fact, some areas held out stubbornly. Revolt erupted along the Rio Grande in 1696 and continued until its leader, Lucas Naranjo, was cut down in battle. In

1700 Hopi warriors attacked the only mission in their territory (after the friars refused to leave voluntarily) with such resounding fury that no further attempts were made to convert or conquer the Hopi. But elsewhere Spanish colonial rule was effectively restored.

A New Cooperation

The new regime seemed to have learned some lessons. The encomienda system was abandoned: no longer would the Pueblo people live as serfs on colonial estates, and those drafted for repartimiento labor were at least entitled to wages for their work. The civil authorities seemed to have realized the practical value of treating native customs with respect. Each pueblo kept its own spiritual and ceremonial leaders in addition to electing a *gobernadorcillo* ("little governor") to represent it before the colonial administration. New gobernadorcillos would pay a formal visit to Santa Fe to receive their badge of office: a black cane with ribbons and silver bands.

A new kind of toleration also evolved in religious matters. Missionaries still built churches, baptized converts, and condemned most native beliefs. But when kiva members met in secret to perform traditional rites, the friars discreetly looked the other way. (On hearing complaints that the Indians were decorating themselves with forbidden war paint, one cleric observed that Christian colonists also painted their faces—before going to Sunday Mass.)

As trust developed between newcomers and natives, the Spanish lifted their prohibition against the Pueblos carrying firearms. In times of unrest the villagers organized militias and fought alongside the colonists to repel attackers. The Pueblo men were exemplary soldiers, according to Spanish reports, superior in courage and skill to the poorly disciplined Spanish residents. And that courage was essential, for the region came under ever fiercer assault from all directions—from the Ute to the north and west, from the Comanche to the east, and most of all from the Apache.

THE SUN, THE HORSE, AND THE SETTLING OF THE SOUTHWEST

Way back in time, say the Hopi storytellers, all the tribes and races of mankind emerged from a single hole in the earth. A mockingbird sitting on the surface gave them their names and languages. To one person he would say, "You shall be a Hopi, and that language you shall speak." To another, "You shall be a Navajo, and you shall speak that language." And so it went for everyone, including the White Men.

A darkness still covered the face of the land, back in those early ages. Then one day the people came together and decided to change things. They fashioned the silver ball of the moon and the fiery globe of the sun and threw both into the sky. The world was transformed. With the sun's warmth and light, food became more plentiful, and work easier. Nor was it necessary for everyone to huddle together for mutual protection and support. So the chiefs of all the races met together and decided to break up.

"We will go eastward to find out where the sun rises," they declared, "but let us travel by different routes and see who gets there first." When the first party arrived at the place where the sun rises, the chiefs agreed, a shower of stars would fall from the sky. At that moment everyone would stop where they were and settle down.

The journey began. Everyone set out on foot, carrying their children and all their belongings on their backs. The Hopi took a northern route, the various Pueblo peoples of New Mexico traveled a more southerly one, and the White People trekked along still farther to the south. But the Whites, always impatient, quickly grew tired and footsore. So one of the white women rubbed flakes of skin from her body and molded them into horses.

Mounted on these marvelous new creatures, the Whites could go faster, and they reached the place where the sun rises before anyone else. Immediately a fountain of stars cascaded from the sky. "Look," cried the others, "someone has arrived." So everyone stopped and settled down. And that is why the sun shines, why the world has horses, and why people live where they do.

An Apache war party
thunders into action
in this 1952 painting by
Apache artist Allan
Houser. After the
Spanish conquest some
bands were quick to
adopt the horse for
warfare, while others
continued to fight
on foot.

People of the Mountain Spirits

The Zuni called them *ápachu,* "the enemy," for the havoc they caused. Moving
against the Pueblo villages in small,
highly mobile groups, they would sweep in
without warning to carry off food, weapons,
children, and anything else they could find. To
the Spanish they were a constant threat. Attacks by Apachean nomads on the first colonial capital at San Juan Pueblo (temporarily
renamed San Gabriel by the Spanish) had
prompted the government to move its headquarters to Santa Fe. From then on, warfare
flared almost continuously between the
Spaniards and one Apache band or another.
Their prowess in battle became the stuff of legend. An Apache warrior, it was said, could run
50 miles without stopping and travel more
swiftly than a troop of mounted soldiers.

At first they had hardly seemed menacing.
Coronado, who had come upon a band of
Plains Apache while searching for the mythical Quivira, had found them to be "gentle people, faithful in their friendships." With the

Pueblos, too, the Apache had at first remained
mostly at peace, showing up at the villages to
trade as often as to raid. But the arrival of the
Spaniards changed everything. One source of
friction was the activity of Spanish slave
traders, who hunted down captives to serve as
labor in the silver mines of Chihuahua in
northern Mexico. The Apache, in turn, raided
Spanish settlements to seize cattle, horses,
firearms, and captives of their own.

Each generation the violence grew worse.
During the drought of 1640, Apache war parties rampaged through the Rio Grande area
and burned some 30,000 bushels of corn. In
1673 an Apache force hit the Zuni town of
Hawikuh, where the Spanish operated a mission; they killed the Spanish friar and 200
Zuni residents, took 1,000 captives, and
burned the village. Apache raids into Sonora
in the 1680's threatened to drive out Spanish
settlement there. During one especially bad
period in the mid-1700's, as many as 4,000
colonists lost their lives to Apache assaults.
And so on into the late 1800's, when one U.S.
Army general who had fought them meant it
as a grudging compliment when he described
the Apache as "tigers of the human species."

The Apache saw themselves differently. Living as nomads in the rocky deserts and tablelands of the Southwest, they faced a constant struggle to survive. When they raided a village, they did so from pure necessity, to provide corn for their families when game was scarce. Most of the time they went their own way, moving from camp to camp in pursuit of deer and buffalo, collecting roots and berries, sometimes planting seeds that they later returned to harvest. Proudly independent, they called themselves *Nidé*, an Athabascan word meaning "the people," and like other native societies they considered themselves to be a very special breed.

You always work as a group, not somebody just singled out. There is no such thing as that with the Apache. We say, "I walk with you," not "I walk before you" or "I walk behind you".... You are not a leader, you are a part.

— *Philip Cassadore, Apache*

During their wanderings the Apache lived in extended family groups of perhaps several dozen members, all loosely related through the female line. Generally speaking, each group operated independently under a respected family leader — hunting and marauding on its own, settling its own disputes, answering to no higher human authority.

The main exception to this occurred during wartime, when neighboring groups banded together to fight a common enemy. Unlike ordinary raiding, where the main object was to acquire food and possessions, war meant lethal business: an act of vengeance for the deaths of band members in earlier raids or battles. Leaders of the local family groups would meet in council to elect a war chief, who led the campaign. But if any one group preferred to follow its own war chief, it was free to do so.

While they acknowledged no central government, Apache bands that roamed the same area admitted to a loose cultural kinship. Thus, the Jicarilla of northeastern New Mexico hunted buffalo in the plains, planted corn in the mountains, and thought of themselves as one people. By contrast, the Mescalero to the south were hunter-gatherers who developed an appetite for the roasted heads of wild mescal plants. The Chiricahua, fiercest of all tribal groups, raided along the Mexican border, while the more peaceable Western Apache of Arizona spent part of each year farming. Two other tribal divisions, the Lipan and Kiowa-Apache, lived as plainsmen in western Kansas and Texas. Despite these differences, all Apache groups spoke variations of the same Athabascan language. And all subscribed to certain common customs and beliefs.

Tradition and Family

A strict code of conduct governed Apache life, based on strong family loyalties. The most important bond led from an Apache mother to her children and on to her grandchildren. A

Clashing petroglyphic warriors from a Utah cliff dwelling (below) may represent Pueblo villagers fending off Apache raiders. The painted insignia on the leather Apache shield at bottom — other images included birds, animals, and lightning bolts — was meant to give its owner strength in battle.

They had war dances at night before battle . . . keeping time with the drum, ducking down and moving with their shield . . . and people would say you could hardly see them because they did it so fast.

— *Allan Houser, Apache*

wedded couple usually took up residence near the dwelling of the wife's mother, and their children would be born into the wife's clan. The husband always treated his mother-in-law with extreme respect, often supplying her with game. At the same time he was expected to preserve his ties with his own mother's household. When his sisters married and had children, it was often his responsibility to teach his nephews to hunt game and to wield the weapons of battle. Should a husband shirk his family duties or treat his bride cruelly, he could be expelled from the settlement, ending the marriage.

Beyond this common code of propriety and family obligations, the Apache shared a rich oral history of myths and legends and a legacy of intense religious devotion that touched virtually every aspect of their lives.

We had no churches, no religious organizations, no sabbath day, no holidays, and yet we worshiped. Sometimes the whole tribe would assemble to sing or pray; sometimes in a small number, perhaps only two or three. Sometimes we prayed in silence, sometimes each one prayed aloud.

— Geronimo, Apache war chief

Every Apache paid homage to a trio of ancestral beings who together helped create the present world. First to arrive on earth were White Painted Woman and a man (her brother in some versions, her son in others), Killer of Enemies. It was his job to hunt game, but every time he shot a deer, the terrifying Owl Man Giant would swoop down and gobble it up. The two grew hungrier until one day a friendly spirit, Life Giver, arrived in the form of a thunderstorm. Nine months later White Painted Woman—also known as Changing Woman—delivered a baby, Child Born of Water, who grew to heroic manhood and in a pitched battle slew Owl Man Giant.

Beginning with the bond between mother and child, close ties of love and duty united Apache family groups; like all babies under six months old, this one is swaddled and secured to a cradle board. Women built the family wickiups — temporary shelters of brush and grass matting laid over a frame of willow boughs.

Reenactments of this legend formed the basis of many Apache ceremonial rites. Warriors on the eve of battle danced the roles of Killer of Enemies and Child Born of Water. Even today young girls entering puberty don the costume and assume the identity of White Painted Woman in a ceremony intended to ensure fertility and promote spiritual well-being.

Behind all myths and ceremonies lay the core belief in a cosmic force that permeated all things, from the merest grain of sand to the loftiest dreams of the human heart. Sometimes the power operated as a life force, imparting health and vigor.

> Lightning is good. When lightning strikes a tree, people say that tree has been blessed and go to gather that wood for special purposes.
>
> — *Delmar Boni, Apache*

On other occasions it could produce the opposite effect, causing misfortune and even death. To avoid such outcomes, Apache priests took meticulous care in performing each rite: the slightest mistake or omission might prove disastrous for everyone.

The most direct link to the cosmic power was through a shaman, often an elderly man or woman who had been visited by a divine vision. Performing special rites, shamans could enlist the life force to ward off harm, find water in a drought, ensure success in battle, see into the future, or expose an enemy. Should an Apache fall ill, a shaman would be called in to exorcise the ailment—caused, perhaps, by an affronted spirit or some other evil agent. The mere sight of an owl, snake, coyote, or other spiritually contaminating creature required ritual purification.

With their intimate connection to the spirit world, shamans could generate untold harm if they employed their talents maliciously. The misuse of such power was held to be a form of witchcraft, deeply disruptive to the public welfare. A shaman-turned-sorcerer, the Apache believed, might strike down his victims with a mumbled phrase or even a single dark glance. Since they worked their witchcraft in secret, witches were difficult to ferret out. Any individual who dressed oddly or spoke strange words became suspect. So did anyone caught in the crime of

In a sacred coming-of-age rite, an Apache medicine man chants prayers and blessings for two adolescent girls on the verge of womanhood. Each is dressed in the fringed rawhide tunic of White Painted Woman and is attended by an older female sponsor. The ceremony, shown here in a 1938 painting by Allan Houser, lasts four days and nights and ends in a joyous feast. Afterward, both girls will be ready for marriage.

incest. Once a witch was exposed, he or she faced a slow and painful death, often being suspended by the wrists over a fire.

So long as the world's unseen powers remained in balance, however, even death itself was not something to be feared.

> The Apache seem to be very strong when somebody dies, very strong about death. There is a reason for that.
> When somebody dies, when you hear thunder way over there — so that you just hardly hear it — that means that the white cloud is taking him to another world. They travel for many days, and then sometimes on the fourth day it rains. When that rain drops on you, they are touching you.
>
> — *Philip Cassadore, Apache*

As the Apache tribal groups moved about in their home territories, they incorporated beliefs and living habits from other Indians in the area. While most Apaches dwelt in dome-shaped wickiups, those in the Great Plains favored the buffalo-hide tepees common to that region. The groups that farmed, such as the Western Apache, learned the techniques of agriculture from the Pueblos. And one religious ceremony of the Jicarilla was an intricate blend of borrowed elements: an ancient Athabascan campfire ritual,

Hand-painted rawhide playing cards reflect the traditional Apache love of gambling, a pastime that took on new dimensions after contact with the Spanish. An Apache craftsman made these as part of a 40-card monte deck, which called for four suits: cups, swords, clubs, and coins.

a dance from the Great Basin in which men and women performed together, the use of Navajo sand paintings, and a Pueblo-style dance with masked performers.

Eventually most Apache groups adopted a variation of the Pueblo kachinas—a population of benevolent beings they called *gaan*, the mountain spirits. Intermediaries between humans and the higher powers, the *gaan* protected people and could be summoned from their homes inside the sacred mountains when needed. On such occasions, usually rituals to cure the sick or mark the onset of a girl's puberty, the mountain spirits were represented by specially trained and costumed dancers.

> There is a circle of people, so many hundreds of people there, watching and being a part of it. Young and old alike are out there dancing towards the center, where the dancers are. . . . When you are there in that circle you can't help but feel the energy go around and around and around. . . . You can just feel it.
>
> — *Delmar Boni, Apache*

After the arrival of the Spaniards, Apache life changed even more profoundly. At trading posts in northern Mexico, Apache bands from the Plains would swap buffalo hides for grain, clothing, and trinkets. Raids on colonial settlements yielded guns and livestock. The Apache acquired a taste for beef. Horses, too, were thought to make particularly fine eating until the Apache learned their far greater value as war steeds and pack animals.

A measure of tranquillity took hold in the late 18th century as a succession of Spanish governors tried to improve relations. The colonists forged a peace alliance with the Jicarilla Apache and Navajo and with the nomadic Ute and Comanche. But other Apaches remained at war.

The Chiricahua of southern New Mexico and Arizona became particularly fierce combatants. One of their leaders was a lapsed Catholic

convert named Juan José, who in 1835 learned that his father had been murdered by Mexicans. Taking justice into his own hands, Juan José began launching raids on Mexican settlements. He would then sell the loot to a white trader from the United States, James Johnson. But the trader was no true friend of the Indian. In return for a handsome reward from the Mexican government, Johnson paid a visit to the Chiricahua camp, carrying a small howitzer concealed under a pile of gifts. After an exchange of pleasantries, he opened fire and shot Juan José dead.

Similar acts of vengeance and betrayal continued to escalate the conflict. In one notorious incident of 1850, at the Mexican town of Ramos, local citizens plied some visiting Chiricahua traders with strong drink and sent them reeling back to camp—then followed that night to slaughter them in their sleep. And so the strife continued. So troublesome did raids into Mexico by Chiricahua and other bands become that one 19th-century governor of Sonora put a price on the scalp of every Apache man, woman, and child.

A New Lifeway: The Navajo

One Athabascan group, known to outsiders as the Navajo (and to themselves as *Diné*), became increasingly distinct from their ancient Apache kinsmen. Settling in scattered groups throughout northern New Mexico in a land they came to call *Dinetah*—"home of the people"—they adapted so thoroughly to this new environment that they virtually reinvented themselves.

The Navajo, like other nomadic tribes, had arrived in the Southwest with a rich spiritual tradition but few material possessions. They dressed in skins, wove reed baskets, hunted and foraged for food. To them the Pueblo villages, with their well-stocked granaries and abundant stores of pottery and blankets, must have seemed like centers of fabulous wealth. Their hunger whetted for the amenities of Pueblo life, the Navajo began by raiding. Gradually, though, as they settled in, they turned from plunder to emulation.

On the first day of creation, First Man and First Woman produced North Mountain, sacred to the Navajo. They fastened down the peak with a rainbow and populated it with plants and animals. Since north is associated symbolically with the color black, on the very tip they placed an obsidian bowl with two blackbird eggs, as shown here by Navajo painter Harrison Begay.

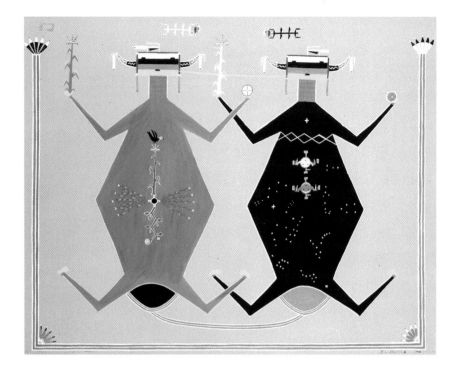

For a powerful Navajo sand painting, the artist has used crushed colored stone and charcoal to depict Father Sky on the left, adorned with symbols for the sun, moon, and Milky Way, and Mother Earth, with four plants growing from a spring. This painting was made for a Shootingway rite, sometimes used to treat accidental injury.

No other Athabascan group took so readily to farming. Picking up the basics from their Pueblo neighbors, they were soon harvesting family plots of beans, squash, tobacco, and corn; their very name derives from the Tewa *nava hu,* meaning "place of large planted fields." Their clothing changed as well. Discarding their buckskin tunics, they began wearing cotton shirts and richly dyed cotton blankets in the Pueblo fashion.

Pueblo influence increased during the Spanish wars of the late 1600's, as thousands of displaced villagers from the Rio Grande battlegrounds fled west into Navajo country. The Navajo gave the refugees protection, and soon the two groups began to intermarry. The Navajo learned the refinements of weaving, sandal making, and ceramics, and they acquired the technique of diverting streams to irrigate their cornfields. Overtones of Pueblo rituals and beliefs crept into Navajo religion. Celebrations began to center on the agricultural cycle of planting and harvest, and kachina-like masked figures called *yeibichai* would dance the appropriate rites. Navajo priests developed the Pueblo-inspired technique of ritual sand painting into a high art. Corn pollen became an essential sacrament, used to promote fertility and prosperity.

The Colorado River, you bless it. Every time you go across it, you say a few prayers. To go across it, you get your corn pollen — we carry it around all the time, corn pollen — so we take it out and bless the water. If we don't have water, we can't get anywhere.

— *Navajo medicine man*

The Navajo also took freely from the Spaniards. Metal tools and firearms, the cultivation of fruit trees and other European crops, all became part of Navajo tradition. So did livestock—not just horses and cattle but, most important of all, sheep. The Navajo became the great master shepherds of the Southwest. Family flocks sometimes numbered in the hundreds, and every child, as part of his or her education, would be given a lamb to raise. Wool from the flocks, carded and dyed, was woven into blankets of remarkable beauty. Even today, Navajo blanket weaving still counts among the highest expressions of Native American artistry in the Southwest.

Yet even as they borrowed from others, the Navajo retained key elements of their Apachean heritage. Resisting all overtures by Spanish missionaries to learn Castilian and convert to Christianity, they continued to speak an exceptionally pure form of Athabascan. Even as they intermingled with the Pueblos, they continued to live in hogans—mud-plastered, log-framed structures that resembled permanent wickiups. Like their Apache cousins, they cherished independence while at the same time observing a complex code of family obligations. Women played an equally powerful role as owners of property and as family matriarchs. Newlyweds set up housekeeping near the bride's relatives, even as the groom maintained close ties to his own parents. To avoid family conflicts, Navajo men treated their sisters-in-law with distant courtesy; if their mother-in-law so much as entered the same area, they had to leave without speaking a word.

The Navajo strove to avoid external conflict as well. A people who in earlier times had made their way by marauding, they now went to extreme lengths to prevent confrontation. A traditional tale describes how the first ancestral humans wandered through successive worlds of chaos and confusion, then eventually arrived in a land of perfect harmony.

Exile and Ascent

The original world lay deep within the present earth. Lit by neither sun nor moon, it contained dimly colored clouds that moved around the horizon to mark the hours. At first life was peaceful; then the evils of lust and envy took hold, and violence broke out. So the ancestral Navajo fled into exile, grappling upward through a hole in the sky to another world directly above. Here, where the light was blue, harmony at first prevailed. Then again the same story: bitter quarreling, followed by escape and a climb to yet another world, and then another.

Finally, First Man and First Woman, the direct ancestors of humankind, emerged on the present earth. Water covered the earth's surface, but sacred winds gusted in to blow it away. With the aid of a sacred medicine bundle, and guided by beings known as *diyin diné*, the holy people, First Man then filled the world with all its natural bounty and wonder. He laid out each object in the bundle and by chanting transformed it into an animal, a plant, a mountain peak, an hour of the day.

> All the mountains have their prayers and chants . . . as have the stars and markings in the sky and on the earth. It is their custom to keep the sky and the earth and the day and the night beautiful. The belief is that if this is done, living among the people of the earth will be good.
> — *Sandoval, Navajo*

Everything in the new universe resided in perfect balance, controlled by a kind of spiritual symmetry: four directions, four winds, four seasons, and the four basic colors of

SPIDER WOMAN'S LEGACY

Like so much else in Navajo tradition, the supreme artistry of tribal weavers had divine origins. Legend recalls the many deeds of Spider Man, who taught the Navajo how to make the loom, and even more importantly of Spider Woman, who taught them how to use it.

In one tale a Navajo girl was walking through the barrens when she saw smoke rising from a tiny hole in the ground. Looking inside, she spied an ugly old crone — Spider Woman. "Come down and sit here beside me and watch what I do," said the old woman. She was passing a wooden stick in and out between strands of thread. "What is it that you do, Grandmother?" asked the girl. "It is a blanket that I weave," the ancient woman replied.

Over the next three days, the Navajo girl watched Spider Woman weave three different blankets of wonderful design. She then went home and showed her people all she had learned. Later she visited Spider Woman again and told her how everyone was now busy weaving. "That is good," the old woman replied. But she also gave the girl this warning: "Whenever you make a blanket, you must leave a hole in the middle. For if you do not, your weaving thoughts will be trapped within the cotton — not only will it bring you bad luck, but it will drive you mad." Since then, Navajo women have always left a spider hole in the middle of their blankets.

Weaving, spinning, and sheep raising are among the arts and occupations portrayed in this detail from a monumental 1940's mural painted by Gerald Nailor for the Navajo Tribal Council.

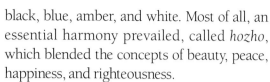

DESERT PEOPLE DEFEND THEIR PEACE

For many generations the Pima and Tohono O'odham had scratched a living from the harsh Sonoran Desert of southern Arizona, dwelling in harmony with the land and their neighbors. Both groups were descendants of the ancient Hohokam. The Pima, known as the River People, lived in villages like their forebears and irrigated their corn and cotton with water from the Gila and Salt rivers. Their cousins the Tohono O'odham (formerly called the Papago, from a Pima term meaning "bean people") hunted and foraged in the drier hills along the Mexican border.

Although generally peaceful, they could be formidable opponents. Forced to defend themselves against Apache raiders, they battled with heavy clubs and shot arrows tipped with rattlesnake toxin. Yet the Pimans saw war as evil, and if a Pima warrior killed a man, he cleansed himself by fasting in seclusion for 16 days while a shaman performed special rites to decontaminate his weapons.

With the arrival of the Spanish, the Pimans forged an alliance with the newcomers against their Apache foes. The raids began to subside. When the first Spanish missionary, Jesuit Father Eusebio Kino, came to live with them in 1687, they took up wheat farming, along with cattle and horse ranching. But if the Pimans hated the Apache, neither would they sit content under white domination. They staged major revolts against the Spanish in 1695 and 1751. And until 1856, when Mexico lost control of the region, foreign governors were never quite sure if the Pimans were their friends or foes.

Pima men grew cotton and wove it into fabrics like the turban cloth worn by 19th-century chief Antonio Azul (above). At left is a Tohono O'odham calendar stick, which served as a kind of tribal diary; lines, dots, circles, and crosses all represented significant events. Most calendar sticks were considered so personal that they were destroyed when the owner died.

black, blue, amber, and white. Most of all, an essential harmony prevailed, called *hozho*, which blended the concepts of beauty, peace, happiness, and righteousness.

As every Navajo still knows, *hozho* must be maintained. The principal method was to follow closely the strict codes of behavior and custom laid out by the Holy People, in which any careless or unseemly act might upset the delicate balance of the universe. An unintended lapse of good manners, a clumsy movement while hunting, even a badly made basket might throw the world into turmoil.

This covers it all, the Earth and the Most
High Power whose ways are beautiful.
   All is beautiful before me,
   All is beautiful behind me,
   All is beautiful above me,
   All is beautiful around me.
                — Navajo song

To ensure the preservation of *hozho*, the Navajo accompanied virtually any important activity with a song or chant. There were hundreds of songs, all in some way drawing on tribal myth and legend. Sometimes they would be chanted as people went about everyday tasks—herding sheep or grinding corn on a metate. On other occasions, lengthy rituals were held for specific purposes—to cure the sick, ward off evil, bring good luck, commemorate a birth or a housewarming, or simply to maintain tribal harmony. Perhaps the most important was, and is, the Blessingway.

Of all these various kinds of holy ones
that have been made, you the first one will
be their thought, you will be called *Sa'ah
Naghai*, Long Life . . . and you who are the
second one, you will be their speech, and
will be called *Bik'eh Hozho*, Happiness.

   All will be long life by means of you
two, and all will be happiness by means
of you two.

                *— from creation story told
                in the Blessingway*

Even today in Navajo country, the sacred rites endure. Navajo men who joined the U.S. Army during World War II took part in a Blessingway ceremony much like those sung in ancient times to ensure the protection of warriors going into battle. Many who returned from combat were purified in an Enemyway ritual designed to protect them from the spirits of slain enemies.

I guess these old people, our great ancestor people, they said that one day you will forget all your religion and your culture and all that. . . . If we forget all about our culture and religion, we have nowhere to go, we don't know how to pray, we don't know how to use our corn pollen, corn meal, anything that we pray with, we forget all about that.

Before that happens, we'd better do something.

— Jimmy Toddy, Navajo

And the Navajo are not alone. In communities throughout the Southwest—among the Apache, Pima, Tohono O'odham, and others, on the mesas of the Hopi, in the pueblos at Zuni and Acoma and along the Rio Grande— sons and daughters of the tribal groups remember the old ways. Each time they perform a sacred ceremony, they breathe new life into the traditions, summoning up spirits that have dwelt in this stark, spectacular landscape since the earliest days of human habitation.

The Blessingway ceremony might last anywhere from two days to four. Chanters versed in tribal lore would reenact an episode from the creation story or other pertinent myth, all the while manipulating holy talismans and praying over a medicine bundle containing earth from each of the four sacred mountains. A priest might fashion a dry painting of colored sand, corn pollen and crushed flowers. Variations of the Blessingway rite would be held to celebrate a marriage, to protect a mother in childbirth, to guide a pubescent girl into womanhood, or to ensure success in any great enterprise.

Sturdy Navajo dancers transport a fellow tribesman in "Mud Dance," a painting by Beatian Yazz; the dance is part of an Enemyway rite used to cure illness and protect against enemy ghosts. By such rituals the Navajo help preserve harmony in their homeland, which includes this dramatic stretch of Monument Valley in Arizona.

*Your forefathers crossed the great
water and landed on this island.
Their numbers were small.
We took pity on them, and they
sat down among us. We gave them
corn and meat. They gave us
poison in return.*
— *Sagoyewatha (Red Jacket),
Seneca*

4

FROM THE DAWNLAND TO HANDSOME LAKE

THE NORTHEAST

Many centuries ago, it is said, a young Micmac woman living on the coast of Nova Scotia dreamed one night of an island that floated in from the sea. Dreams were powerful revelations to native people of the Northeast, as they were elsewhere, offering guidance and predicting future events. The next morning the Micmac village awoke to find that something like an island had drifted close to shore. "There were trees on it," a villager later recalled, "and branches to the trees, on which a number of bears were crawling about." The Micmac hunters grabbed their bows and arrows and rushed to the shore. To their surprise, the island turned out to be a French sailing ship, and the bears were crewmen climbing its masts and rigging.

All along the Northeast coast, as European seafarers began arriving in the early 1500's, people greeted the newcomers with a mixture of curiosity, astonishment, and wild misunderstanding. The Montagnais, who inhabited the north shore of the St. Lawrence River, also mistook the first ship they saw for a floating island. Paddling out in their birchbark canoes, they discovered that the island was inhabited by a new kind of human who wore chest armor and who lived on dry sea biscuits and red wine. Europeans, the Montagnais concluded, belonged to a tribe that dressed in iron, ate bones, and drank blood. Other native peoples living on the coast of New England thought the first sailing ships they saw were huge sea birds. And Delaware and Mahican men near what is today Manhattan Island remembered seeing "a house of various colors . . . crowded with living creatures" who turned out to be Dutch sailors. They welcomed the foreigners ashore; the sailors gave them alcohol, and they got drunk for the first time.

The newcomers' large ships, along with their metal tools and firearms, deeply impressed the Indians. Then hard on the heels of the first fishermen and explorers there came wave upon wave of other Europeans—fur traders, colonists, soldiers, land speculators, Christian missionaries—and the natives began to have second thoughts. As the number

◄ Preceding page: Mohawk chieftain Tiyineenhoharo—He Who Tells the Stories —displays a wampum belt signifying friendship between his people and the British; he is dressed for a visit to the British court, made during a trip to England in 1710.

Carved into the wood of a living tree, an Iroquois mask depicts the Great Defender, a legendary giant who smashed his nose during an encounter with the Creator. This mask was carved by Iroquois artist Jake Thomas of the Six Nations Reserve in Ontario for museum display, not for ceremonial use.

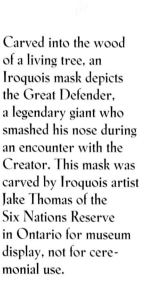

of contacts increased, so did the misunderstandings. It soon became clear that these strange and bearded foreigners, emerging out of dreams and floating islands, would be powerfully disruptive to the native way of life.

The Indian peoples who dwelt in the broad expanse of shoreline and woodlands reaching south from present-day Quebec to Chesapeake Bay thought of their homeland as the center of the world. It had been the land of their ancestors longer than anyone could remember. Iroquoian peoples recounted how the world had grown into being from a blob of mud on the back of a giant turtle. The Abenaki in Vermont learned from childhood that the Creator, Tabaldac, had set aside the rivers and mountains of their homeland for their eternal use. Each landmark had a story: An enormous boulder in Lake Champlain, for instance, contained the spirit of the giant Odzihozo, who in his birth pangs had gouged out the basin that held the lake's waters. These stories, told by firelight during long winter evenings, reminded people of why things were the way they were, and of their own place in the world around them.

There was a time when our forefathers owned this great island. The Great Spirit had made it for the use of Indians. He had created the buffalo, the deer and other animals for food. He had made the bear and the beaver. Their skins served us for clothing. He had scattered them over the country, and taught us how to take them. He had caused the earth to produce corn for bread.

— *Red Jacket, Seneca*

Life followed a natural rhythm of hunting and fishing, agriculture, and food gathering. As the men tracked deer, moose, and other game, the women combed the woodlands for wild fruit, berries, nuts, and other plants. There were onions and fiddlehead ferns, strawberries and raspberries, beach plums and beech nuts, lily roots and grapes, cran-

berries, elderberries, and more. In early spring, when the maple sap started running, the women would boil it down to make sugar.

Except in the northernmost areas, a majority of tribes also grew corn. Men cleared the fields by girdling the trees, setting fires at their bases, and then felling the charred trunks with stone axes. Vast acreages were transformed this way; European explorers of the New England coast described open plains as much as 70 miles in length, entirely free from trees, and extensive plantations around Massachusetts Bay and elsewhere. After the timber and underbrush were burned, the women took over. They broke the ground with bone or wood hoes and planted kernels of hardy flint, flour, or pop corn in small mounds formed by hand. Like growers in the Southeast, they often planted beans in the same hillocks; the bean plants climbed the cornstalks, while the roots added nitrogen to the soil. When the crops ripened, women brought in the harvest.

Seasons in the Dawnland

Native communities tended to move about seasonally. In the northeastern part of New England, known traditionally as the Dawnland, Abenaki groups congregated in farm villages for planting and harvesting but migrated to waterfalls and other choice sites when

Two views of contact: Henry Hudson (top) lands in 1609 at an Indian encampment on the river later named for him in an idealized scene by 19th-century painter Albert Bierstadt. Six decades after Hudson's voyage, a Cayuga craftsman carved this ornamental comb showing European traders riding into upstate New York.

salmon, shad, and alewife headed upstream to spawn in the spring. At such times the Abenaki encampments hummed with activity. Families exchanged visits, and the shouts of children playing filled the air. Then late in the year, as autumn turned to winter, family bands dispersed into distant hunting territories, and the villages fell silent.

Each season brought its round of traditional ceremonies. The Abenaki held celebrations to mark the time of spring planting, the ripening of the blueberries, the bringing in of the corn. Iroquois peoples took part in a nine-day Midwinter Ceremony at the start of the year, then followed it with other events that included a Maple Sugaring Feast, a Strawberry Festival in June, a Green Corn Dance in late summer, and a Feast of Thanksgiving in autumn. The ceremonies were both social gatherings and vitally important religious events. Should people neglect these sacred rites of dance and prayer or forget to show gratitude for nature's bounty, it was thought that the world itself might fall into chaos.

The activity of the hunt—the basis of life for peoples like the Micmac and Abenaki, who dwelt in the more northerly areas—also required powerful rituals to ensure success. Hunters knew the habits and habitats of the animal world intimately, and they felt an almost personal bond with the animals they tracked. Before setting out, each hunter sought to discover his quarry in a dream—a sign that the creature would willingly surrender itself to his spear or arrow. Prayers would be offered and tobacco burned. After making the kill, a hunter treated the carcass with respect, ceremoniously burying the bones lest the animal's spirit take offense and depart forever from the hunting grounds.

Farther south, from central New England on down toward Chesapeake Bay, the growing season was longer and agriculture more secure. Groups like the Patuxet of Massachusetts, the Narragansett of Rhode Island, and the Delaware, or Lenni Lenape, of New Jersey and Pennsylvania hunted primarily in winter and spent the summers farming—the men

clearing land, the women planting and cultivating. The country was rich and varied, with plentiful game, fertile soil for crops, fish-filled rivers, and a profusion of clam and oyster beds along the coast. Populations were more heavily concentrated here than in the north, with villages that were usually larger and more permanent. Oval-shaped wigwams, constructed of saplings covered with sheets of birch bark, provided shelter. In southern New England, hereditary chiefs called sachems, who were usually male members of elite families, took responsibility for looking after the community and its lands.

Most of the region's peoples spoke some dialect of Algonquian, the most widespread linguistic family in North America. Between Lake Huron and the Hudson River, however, the in-

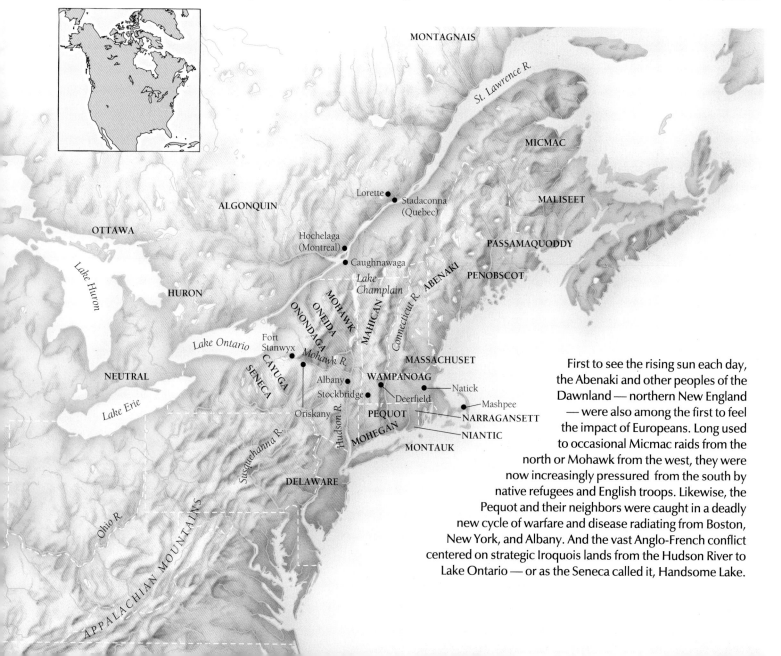

First to see the rising sun each day, the Abenaki and other peoples of the Dawnland — northern New England — were also among the first to feel the impact of Europeans. Long used to occasional Micmac raids from the north or Mohawk from the west, they were now increasingly pressured from the south by native refugees and English troops. Likewise, the Pequot and their neighbors were caught in a deadly new cycle of warfare and disease radiating from Boston, New York, and Albany. And the vast Anglo-French conflict centered on strategic Iroquois lands from the Hudson River to Lake Ontario — or as the Seneca called it, Handsome Lake.

habitants spoke Iroquoian, a language group as different from Algonquian as English is from Chinese. The Huron, Erie, Tobacco, Petun, and other residents of the upper St. Lawrence Valley were all Iroquoians, as were scattered groups to the south, among them the Tuscarora of North Carolina. But the most famous were five tribes that dwelt in what is now upper New York State: the Seneca, Cayuga, Onondaga, Oneida, and Mohawk. Outsiders referred to them as the Five Nations—or, because of their ferocity, as the *iriakoiw*, an Algonquian word that meant "rattlesnakes." To themselves they were the Haudenosaunee—the People of the Longhouse—and they constituted the single most powerful confederation of native North Americans in recorded history.

The Great League of Peace

L
ong before, in a dark time of troubles, the Iroquois had fought among themselves in a destructive cycle of killing and retribution. A dispute might break out between two villages over hunting rights, for example; angry words would lead to blows; and in the end one of the villages would be mourning the loss of a young warrior. The dead man's relatives, seeking compensation, would launch a raid on the offending village. The object was to take captives, but as often as not, more blood would be spilled and the deadly cycle would spin out of control.

No one wanted to become an Iroquois captive. Led back to the enemy village, the prisoner would be beaten, sometimes bitten, and forced to run naked through a gauntlet of alternately angry and festive villagers. If he stood up bravely to this abuse, he might be adopted into a family who had lost a son in battle. Otherwise, his fate was sealed. His captors would tear his hair, pull out his fingernails, burn his flesh with hot coals, break his bones. At the end he would be put to death. Sometimes the villagers would eat bits of his flesh in a sacrificial rite designed to appropriate the victim's wisdom and strength.

Bringing an end to these blood feuds was a matter of self-preservation. At the dawn of time, the Master of Life had commanded all people to live in love and harmony. Clearly the message had been forgotten, so the Master decided to repeat it. According to most versions of the story, his spokesman was a Huron holy man, Degana-

Algonquian hunters—perhaps Ottawa or Montagnais—chase a moose from its marshy feeding grounds into the deep waters of a Northern lake. Their canoe is birch bark waterproofed with spruce gum.

Commanding the attention of anyone who beheld it, an Iroquois mask made of braided corn husks (left) was worn by a dancer of the Husk Face Society. A religious group with shamanistic powers, the society performed at midwinter festivals and various healing rituals.

widah—the Peacemaker—who set out across Lake Ontario in a stone canoe. Landing on the southern shore, the holy man came upon Hiawatha, a clan leader of Mohawk descent who had lost all his daughters to tribal strife. Deganawidah offered words of condolence that lifted Hiawatha's grief and dried his tears; the same consoling words would later be repeated at Iroquois council meetings to promote good feelings and open minds. Then the prophet described a great Tree of Peace under whose branches the tribes would meet to resolve their differences. He enunciated principles of justice and equality; bloodshed would yield to a new sense of brotherhood among the people.

Deganawidah was a man of powerful vision; Hiawatha possessed the gifts of oratory and persuasion. Together the two men traveled the length and breadth of Iroquois country, forging alliances, teaching the Great Law of Justice, and spreading the gospel of the Tree of Peace. Finally, so legend tells it, only an Onondaga chief named Atotarho resisted. Atotarho was a fearsome wizard—his body crooked, his mind twisted, his hair a mass of tangled snakes—but eventually even he was persuaded to embrace the accord.

The Five Nations that entered the league retained full control over their own affairs. But matters of mutual importance—peace and war, for example—were debated by a Grand Council, which met periodically on a hilltop at Onondaga. The first meeting took place, according to tribal lore, under a giant evergreen tree where an eagle perched, its eyes scanning the horizon for signs of approaching trouble. Fifty chiefs attended, selected from

Right: Enlisting the final league member, founders Hiawatha (with spear) and Deganawidah confront the serpent-wizard Atotarho. The scene is from an 1853 book of drawings by West Point officer Seth Eastman.

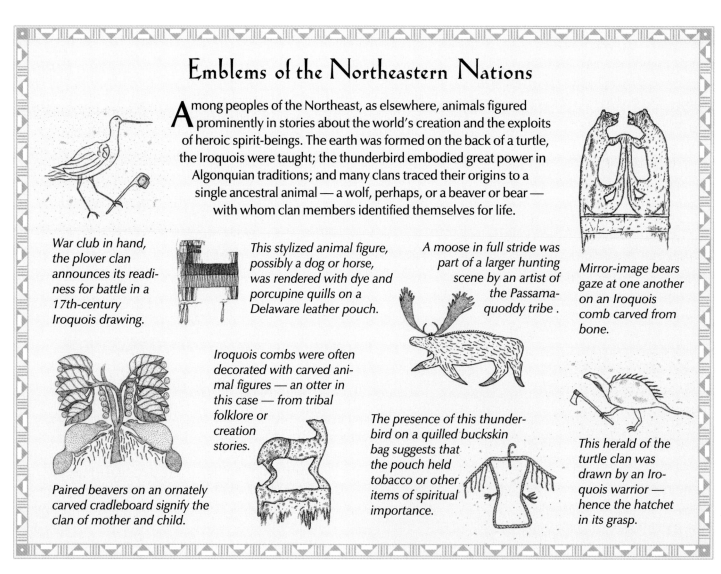

Emblems of the Northeastern Nations

Among peoples of the Northeast, as elsewhere, animals figured prominently in stories about the world's creation and the exploits of heroic spirit-beings. The earth was formed on the back of a turtle, the Iroquois were taught; the thunderbird embodied great power in Algonquian traditions; and many clans traced their origins to a single ancestral animal — a wolf, perhaps, or a beaver or bear — with whom clan members identified themselves for life.

War club in hand, the plover clan announces its readiness for battle in a 17th-century Iroquois drawing.

This stylized animal figure, possibly a dog or horse, was rendered with dye and porcupine quills on a Delaware leather pouch.

A moose in full stride was part of a larger hunting scene by an artist of the Passamaquoddy tribe .

Mirror-image bears gaze at one another on an Iroquois comb carved from bone.

Iroquois combs were often decorated with carved animal figures — an otter in this case — from tribal folklore or creation stories.

Paired beavers on an ornately carved cradleboard signify the clan of mother and child.

The presence of this thunderbird on a quilled buckskin bag suggests that the pouch held tobacco or other items of spiritual importance.

This herald of the turtle clan was drawn by an Iroquois warrior — hence the hatchet in its grasp.

each tribe by its leading older women, the clan mothers (in later years only 49 clan representatives would take part because no one was deemed worthy of filling the seat originally occupied by Hiawatha). Each tribe had one vote, and decisions were always unanimous, reached by consensus usually after lengthy discussion. No one was obliged to accept a conclusion he did not agree with.

⁂

A council fire for all the nations shall be kindled. It shall be lighted for the Cherokee and for the Wyandot. We will kindle it also for the seven nations living toward the sunrise, and for the nations that dwell toward the sunset. All shall receive the Great Law and labor together for the welfare of man.

— Attributed to Deganawidah

⁂

Much the same system prevailed within the tribes themselves, down to the village level. The basic unit in Iroquois life was the "fireside," consisting of a mother and all her children. Related families lived together in sturdy wooden longhouses, some of which reached 400 feet in length. A dozen or more family groups might share a single longhouse, resid-

Below, the sheltering Onondaga pine tree stands at the center of the Five Nations in the famed Hiawatha Belt. Honored regalia of the Iroquois League included a notched maplewood staff (right) with pegs and pictographs representing the ancestral titles of the league's 50 chiefs. Allocated by tribe and clan, the titles were read during the Roll Call of the Chiefs that took place at major ceremonial meetings. Reflecting their status as keeper of the league's wampum records, the Onondaga had 14 chieftainships, more than any other tribe; their pictographic names are shown (far right) with the clans that held them.

ONONDAGA

Thadodaho
] Beaver
Snipe
Hawk
Turtle
] Wolf
] Deer
] Eel
] Turtle

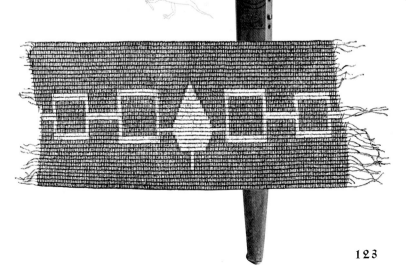

Ancestral clan animals of the Iroquois League gather in the spiritual radiance of the great Tree of Peace, as envisioned here by Onondaga artist Arnold Jacobs; the league's eagle sentinel hovers overhead, ever alert against outside danger.

ing in compartments on either side of a central aisle and sharing a central hearth with the family opposite them. Each longhouse bore above its door the symbol of the clan to which its inhabitants belonged. There were ten clans in all, each named for the animal considered to be the clan members' original ancestor.

Ultimate power, both within the longhouse and beyond it, rested with the leading older women. Clan membership passed through the female line: A woman who was a member of the Turtle clan had children who were Turtle clan. A husband generally moved into the longhouse of his wife's clan, where the senior clan mother held sway. Women named the male delegates to clan and tribal councils and also the tribal representatives to the league's Grand Council at Onondaga.

The Iroquois conceived of their league as a great longhouse stretching from the Mohawk Valley almost to the Pennsylvania border in the west. In it the five tribes gathered around five fires. The Mohawk guarded the eastern side; to their west were the Oneida, then the Onondaga, who tended the central hearth; following them were the Cayuga and then the powerful Seneca, keepers of the western door. The Iroquois Trail, spanning the length of what is now upstate New York, provided moccasined runners with easy access to any part of the longhouse.

A LEGEND OF THE LITTLE PEOPLE

Long ago, when the world was young, the storytellers say, an Iroquois youth went hunting with his bow and arrow. All at once he heard voices drifting up from the bottom of a dark ravine. Peering down, he saw two tiny men no taller than his shinbone. He offered them a squirrel he had shot; they, in turn, invited him to dinner.

So began the special friendship between the Iroquois and the Little People, a powerful race that lives deep in the forest and helps control the forces of nature. Some are so strong they can hurl rocks and uproot trees. Others have the job of waking up the plants each spring. Still others guard the gates of the underworld, protecting mankind from chaos and disease.

Back at their village, the Little People fed the young hunter corn soup from a bowl that never emptied, and they gave him a round white stone as a hunting charm. Then they summoned their kinsmen to a great feast. Soon the whole tribe had gathered to burn tobacco and perform the sacred rite of the Dark Dance (shown in this 1948 watercolor by Cheyenne artist Dick West). The youth looked on in wonder, learning to mimic their chants and gestures, which he later taught to his own people. When it came time to leave, his hosts made a promise: In exchange for gifts of tobacco (which they prized) the Little People would come to feast with the Iroquois, gracing the Iroquois rituals with their invisible presence whenever the drums of the Dark Dance began to sound.

Now we will speak again about him, Our Creator. He decided, "Above the world I have created . . . I will continue to look intently and to listen intently to the earth, when people direct their voices at me."

Let there be gratitude day and night for the happiness he has given us. He loves us, he who in the sky dwells. He gave us the means to set right that which divides us.

— *From Iroquois Thanksgiving ritual*

Like a domestic longhouse, the league could be extended to shelter other peoples. In 1722, Tuscarora refugees from war with the English migrated north from the Carolinas and were soon accepted as a Sixth Nation. During the course of the 18th century other refugees filtered into Iroquois country, and several new communities of displaced peoples grew up under the protective Tree of Peace.

Not all Iroquoian nations joined the league, to be sure, nor did warfare cease. Simmering hatreds continued to divide league members from their cousins, the Huron. Seneca raiders ventured as far south as Virginia to test their mettle against the Cherokee, another Iroquoian group. "We have no people to war against nor yet no meal to eat but the Cherokee," one Seneca man explained. But Deganawidah's vision put an end to the fratricidal feuding, and the combined strength and political sophistication of the league gave the Iroquois a dominance that would continue to shape the region's history for years to come.

Welcoming the Strangers

The dream of peace soon turned into a nightmare, however, as European explorers, European microbes, and European guns and sharpened steel blades began to penetrate North America. Sailors and soldiers, traders and fur trappers, missionaries and colonists arrived from France, England,

Watcher was chief; he looked toward the sea. At this time, from north and south, the whites came. . . .Who are they?

— *Walum Olum, Delaware epic*

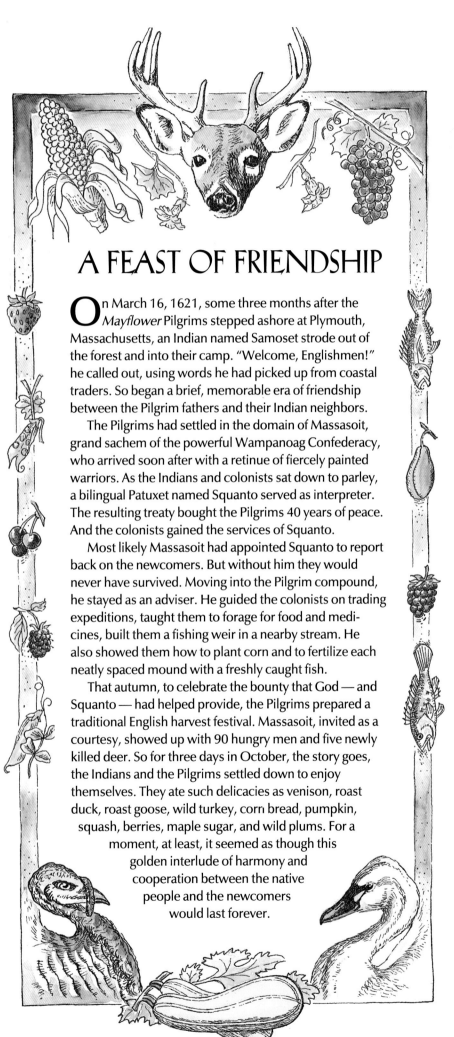

A FEAST OF FRIENDSHIP

On March 16, 1621, some three months after the *Mayflower* Pilgrims stepped ashore at Plymouth, Massachusetts, an Indian named Samoset strode out of the forest and into their camp. "Welcome, Englishmen!" he called out, using words he had picked up from coastal traders. So began a brief, memorable era of friendship between the Pilgrim fathers and their Indian neighbors.

The Pilgrims had settled in the domain of Massasoit, grand sachem of the powerful Wampanoag Confederacy, who arrived soon after with a retinue of fiercely painted warriors. As the Indians and colonists sat down to parley, a bilingual Patuxet named Squanto served as interpreter. The resulting treaty bought the Pilgrims 40 years of peace. And the colonists gained the services of Squanto.

Most likely Massasoit had appointed Squanto to report back on the newcomers. But without him they would never have survived. Moving into the Pilgrim compound, he stayed as an adviser. He guided the colonists on trading expeditions, taught them to forage for food and medicines, built them a fishing weir in a nearby stream. He also showed them how to plant corn and to fertilize each neatly spaced mound with a freshly caught fish.

That autumn, to celebrate the bounty that God — and Squanto — had helped provide, the Pilgrims prepared a traditional English harvest festival. Massasoit, invited as a courtesy, showed up with 90 hungry men and five newly killed deer. So for three days in October, the story goes, the Indians and the Pilgrims settled down to enjoy themselves. They ate such delicacies as venison, roast duck, roast goose, wild turkey, corn bread, pumpkin, squash, berries, maple sugar, and wild plums. For a moment, at least, it seemed as though this golden interlude of harmony and cooperation between the native people and the newcomers would last forever.

At the future site of Montreal, Iroquoian-speaking Hochelaga Indians greet French explorer Jacques Cartier. This schematic drawing, made soon after Cartier's 1535 visit, shows blocks of longhouses within a surrounding palisade.

Sweden, and the Netherlands. The influx transformed the Northeastern forests into a cauldron of competition that pitted Indians against Europeans, Indians against Indians, and rival European empires against each other. Even worse, the most devastating part of the invasion was invisible.

Among the first Europeans to explore beyond the seacoast was the French navigator Jacques Cartier, who sailed up the St. Lawrence River in 1535. Cartier landed at the Iroquoian-speaking town of Stadaconna, the site of present-day Quebec City, then proceeded upstream past rich orchards, shimmering cornfields, and thriving Indian villages. In early October he dropped anchor at Hochelaga, a town of some 3,600 people living in 50 elm-bark longhouses protected by an 18-foot-high stockade.

Extending a greeting customary for powerful visitors—and no doubt eager to trade—more than a thousand people turned out to welcome the explorer and his crew, showering them with gifts of fish and corn bread. The residents took Cartier to the top of a steep hill that towered over their village and pointed out distant peaks and mountain ranges that must have been ablaze with fall colors.

"Their Wisdom Is Buried With Them"

Soon after Cartier departed for home, an alien virus—brought either by him or by other visitors from the disease-ridden ports of Europe—swept through the St. Lawrence Valley. The local inhabitants, lacking immunity, began losing friends, relatives, and loved ones to horrible deaths. As the contagion spread, it wiped out entire communities. Bustling villages were silenced; abandoned cornfields reverted to wilderness. Neither the rites of the shamans nor the skills of native herbalists could quell the wrath of this devastation.

> They will forget their old laws; they will barter their country for baubles. Then will disease eat the life from their blood.
> — Hanisse'ono, the Evil One, from Iroquois legend

The same grim tale repeated itself throughout the Northeast. Smallpox, bubonic plague, measles, and influenza became regular and deadly visitors. Between 1616 and 1619 an unidentified epidemic ravaged the coast of New England. "They died in heapes, as they lay in their houses," wrote a sympathetic Englishman, Thomas Morton, describing the fate of the Massachuset tribe. "For in a place where many inhabited, there hath been but one left alive to tell what became of the rest, the living being (as it seems) not able to bury the dead." Squanto—the intrepid Wampanoag who would be remembered fondly in the history books of later generations for befriending the *Mayflower* Pilgrims—had been kidnapped in 1614 by the English and taken to Europe. He made his way home aboard another English ship in 1619, only to find his village abandoned: Everyone had died or else fled the terrifying pestilence.

Smallpox hit the Northeast in 1633–34, causing 95 percent mortality among some native communities on the Connecticut River. Illness swept across Martha's Vineyard in 1645; the next year a sachem named Tawanquatuck lamented that the elders who had taught and guided the people were now dead, "and their wisdom is buried with them."

A decade later, Indians living on the Hudson River told a Dutch settler that they had been 10 times more numerous before the Europeans arrived and brought their diseases with them. Recurring outbreaks continued to depopulate villages, disrupt economic activities, and fracture social ties. Many of the heartbroken survivors blamed the newcomers; most Europeans, for their part, regarded the catastrophe fatalistically as "God's work."

"The last of the pure-blood Huron," as he described himself, Montreal artist Zacharie Vincent made this 1845 self-portrait with his son Cyprien. By that time, the mighty Huron nation had long since been scattered and virtually exterminated by warfare and disease.

Two Centuries of Conflict

Escalating warfare speeded the already rapid decline of Indian populations as the European invasion introduced new reasons for going to war and deadly new ways of waging it. Guns and metal weapons altered the face of battle beyond recognition. In the past, most intertribal warfare had been relatively modest in scale, with opponents meeting to settle local disputes or to boost tribal prestige. Warriors often went into battle wearing armor made of wooden slats, and stood in ranks to engage the enemy in ritualistic combat with stone-tipped arrows and wooden clubs. That quickly changed. The fighters gave up their bows for muskets, and their war clubs for steel-headed tomahawks. Shedding their wooden armor, they ventured forth in mobile

Geared up for ritualized combat against a rival tribe, a 16th-century Huron warrior wears body armor made from sticks laced together with sinew.

Equipped for killing, not ceremony, an Iroquois warrior of the 18th century brandishes a traditional war club but also carries a steel tomahawk made in Europe and, over his shoulder, a musket bedecked with the scalp of an enemy. (The snowshoes worn in summer are a fanciful artist's touch.)

bands to stage surprise raids on enemy villages, hijack trading parties, and generally spread terror and mayhem. Armed with the new metal weapons, Montagnais and Algonquin warriors north of the St. Lawrence fought with Mohawks and other Iroquois to the south, turning the once populous and prosperous region into a no-man's-land.

Adding to the new intensity of combat was the foreigners' desire for a wonderfully sleek and profitable animal: the beaver. Shortly after Cartier's voyage, French hat manufacturers discovered that the fur of this North American creature made handsome, almost indestructible felt. The price of beaver pelts shot upward in European markets. When buyers arrived in America with glass beads, copper kettles, steel tomahawks, muskets, and other manufactured items, Indian hunters vied with each other for exclusive trade rights. Bloodshed became inevitable.

One early confrontation took place when the explorer Samuel de Champlain, in search of beaver, ventured into Iroquois territory with a party of Indian allies. Champlain had made earlier trips to the Northeast, following Cartier's route up the St. Lawrence toward the Great Lakes. Along the way he had made friends with the Algonquin, the Huron, and the Montagnais, forging trade pacts and exchanging furs and wampum. In the spring of 1609, accompanied by some of his new allies, Champlain headed south through upstate New York and "discovered" the lake that bears his name. At the lake's far end they came upon a group of Mohawk warriors, traditional enemies of the Huron. French musket fire sent the Mohawks fleeing.

This brief skirmish helped draw lines of combat that prevailed for the next two centuries. In battles that followed, the Huron and northern Algonquian tribes generally sided with the French. Against them were the Five Nations of the Iroquois League. Searching for trading partners, the Iroquois turned first to the Dutch along the Hudson River and then to the English. At the same time, threatened by an encircling French alliance of traditional rivals—all determined to exclude them from the beaver trade—they went on the offensive.

Iroquois war parties fanned out across New England, up the St. Lawrence, and west into the Ohio Valley. Sometimes they raided hunting grounds. More often they pillaged rival tribes of furs already harvested or trade goods being taken home from market. So began the devastating cycle of intertribal carnage known to historians as the Beaver Wars.

The Fate of the Huron

Mohawk and Mahican warriors clashed in a bloody four-year dispute that by 1628 destroyed the latter's trade monopoly with the Dutch at Albany. The next target was the powerful Huron Confederacy, which dominated the beaver trade in New France. In 1649 a force of 1,000 Iroquois warriors, mostly Seneca, hit a pair of Christianized Huron towns on Lake Huron's Georgian Bay, setting fire to the longhouses and "baptizing" the two resident Jesuit priests in boiling water. From there they surged inland through Huron country, burning and slaying and rounding up captives. They ravaged the Neutrals, the Nipissing, and the Tobacco Huron. Moving west through the Great Lakes and south into Ohio, they hit the Ottawa, the Erie, the Miami, and the Illinois. Over the next half century, the People of the Longhouse would extend their power as far west as Lake Michigan and south into the Carolinas. The Huron, meanwhile, were destroyed as a nation. Some survivors fled west; others were absorbed into the Iroquois Confederacy.

While warfare raged between the tribes, Indian peoples also faced increasing aggression from European colonists who wanted their lands. In 1637 a Puritan army surrounded the

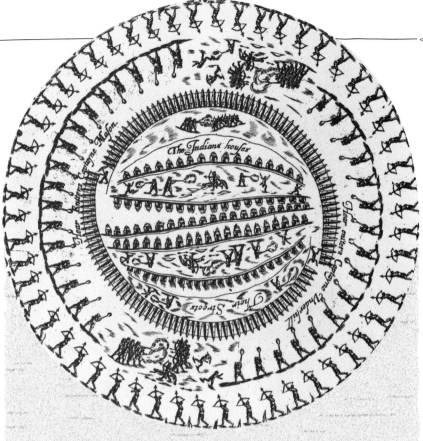

A Penobscot powder horn, used to funnel gunpowder into a musket's firing pan, is adorned with carvings of traditional Indian design.

THE PEQUOT HOLOCAUST

It began with a set of isolated clashes along the Connecticut frontier. Colonists from Massachusetts Bay began pushing into territory claimed by the Pequot; disputes broke out, some leading to fatalities. Soldiers from Boston burned several Pequot villages, and tribesmen responded by raiding colonial settlements. So in the spring of 1637, a well-armed force of 250 colonial soldiers moved into Pequot country to take reprisals. Along the way they picked up perhaps 1,000 warriors from the Narragansett and Mohegan, traditional foes of the Pequot.

The combined armies headed for the main village of the Pequot grand sachem, Sassacus, on Connecticut's Mystic River. At dawn on May 25, they attacked. The first assault, against the village gates, was turned back by archers firing down from the stockade. Then the attackers managed to set fire to the Pequot wigwams, and the tide of battle shifted — as shown in the woodcut above by James Underhill, one of the militia captains. Villagers who fled the fire were cut down as they emerged. Those who stayed, mostly women and children, burned to death. "It was a fearful sight," a colonist recalled, "to see them thus frying in the fyer, and the streams of blood quenching the same." More than 600 Pequot people died.

Survivors were hunted down and killed, or else sold into slavery. Even using the tribal name was banned. Chief Sassacus sought refuge with the Mohawk — but they, anxious to maintain good relations with the colonists, beheaded him and sent the scalp to Hartford. By the end of 1638, the Pequot had been largely wiped out (though in a later era their descendants would dramatically revive the tribe's fortunes) and a dark precedent set for colonial expansion.

"But little remains of my ancestors' domain," declared the Wampanoag war chief Metacom, "and I am resolved not to see the day when I have no country."

main village of the Pequot on the Mystic River in Connecticut and put it to the torch; hundreds of men, women, and children perished. In 1642 a Narragansett sachem called for united resistance before it was too late:

> Brothers, we must be one as the English are, or we shall all be destroyed. You know our fathers had plenty of deer and skins and our plains were full of game and turkeys, and our coves and rivers were full of fish.
>
> But, brothers, since these Englishmen have seized our country, they have cut down the grass with scythes, and the trees with axes. Their cows and horses eat up the grass, and their hogs spoil our bed of clams; and finally we shall starve to death; therefore, I ask you, resolve to act like men.
>
> — *Miantonomi, Narragansett*

But it was already too late: Miantonomi died at Mohegan hands by English instigation the next year. On the lower Hudson River and Long Island, as many as 1,000 Wappinger and Delaware Indians died at Dutch hands in Governor Kieft's War between 1643 and 1645. Susquehannock Indians in the late 1600's found themselves caught between Iroquois enemies to their north and west and colonists from Virginia and Maryland to the east.

After years of uneasy coexistence in southern New England, tensions exploded again in 1675 when Metacom, the Wampanoag leader known to the English as King Philip, launched a war of resistance against the settlers. Metacom was the son and heir of Massasoit, the grand sachem who had befriended the tiny band of *Mayflower* Pilgrims. Few in number, the colonists had been no threat to anyone. But by now the colonial population of New England had grown to perhaps 40,000, while Indian strength had dwindled. Determined to restore the balance, Metacom rallied the region's tribes. War parties of Wampanoag, Nipmuc, and Narragansett attacked more than 50 English settlements, destroying 12 and sending out shock waves of terror and dismay.

After a year of combat the alliance succumbed to disease, internal division, Mohawk counterattacks, and the weight of English fire-

Campaigning against the Iroquois, the French and their Indian allies destroyed villages and burned prisoners. Here, an Onondaga warrior (at rear, against a tree) stoically awaits his fate, while the governor general of New France, Count Louis de Frontenac (seated, at right), looks majestically on.

power. Metacom was hunted down and killed, and his severed head put on display above the blockhouse at Plymouth; his wife and children were sold into slavery. Many survivors of the war fled north, seeking refuge in Abenaki communities or with the French in Canada.

A Duel of Distant Giants

Increasingly, the peoples of the Northeast became reluctant antagonists in a worldwide battle being waged among European superpowers. After the English expelled the Dutch from New York in 1664, France and England squared off in the contest to dominate eastern North America. Beginning in 1689, a period of intermittent bloodshed known as the French and Indian Wars embroiled the region for nearly three-quarters of a century. Indians marched into battle on both sides. As alliances shifted from group to group, Indian runners

sped down forest trails, carrying wampum belts summoning the tribes to meet with representatives of one or another of the contending monarchs.

The recruitment of native allies by the European rivals took full advantage of old tribal antagonisms and so reduced whatever chance there might have been for a united front against the foreigners. But their foreignness was never forgotten. One Iroquois leader pointedly reminded the governor of Canada in 1694 that his own people were the original human beings and that the Europeans—Axe-Makers, he called them—were latecomers.

> You think that the Axe-Makers are the eldest in the country and the greatest in possession. We Human Beings are the first, and we are the eldest and the greatest. These parts and countries were inhabited and trod upon by the Human Beings before there were any Axe-Makers.
>
> — *Sadekanaktie, Onondaga*

Nevertheless, individual tribes had to protect themselves. In Canada and northern New England, the Montagnais, Abenaki, and other Algonquian peoples continued to side with the French. Mainly interested in Indian furs, the French seemed less threatening than the English settlers to the south, with their insatiable hunger for Indian lands. Many Indian refugees from earlier conflicts had regrouped around French mission villages on the St. Lawrence. From there they continued the battle, sallying forth with their new French allies to raid English settlements in territory that had once been their own.

Although allied with foreigners, most Northeastern tribes fought on their own terms and for their own interests. In the 1720's, while France and England kept an uneasy truce, Chief Grey Lock of the Abenaki made lightning raids on the Massachusetts frontier, battling the colonial militia to a standstill. In 1752, as English settlers edged north up the Connecticut Valley, an Abenaki speaker warned them not to steal another inch of

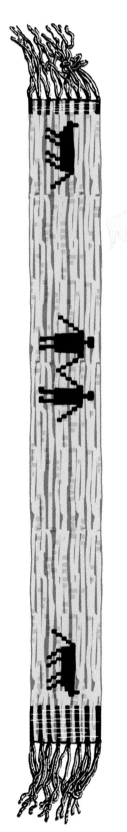

Proclaiming their neutrality, the Iroquois in 1701 made peace with everyone—as attested by the Wolf Clan Belt, believed to represent a Mohawk pact signed with the French.

Despite the Iroquois revival, generations of armed conflict had a devastating impact on the Indian way of life. Young men left their families and villages to serve as scouts and forest soldiers for European armies; Indian raiding parties ranged far and wide; colonial armies tramped into Indian country to burn towns and crops. Wars disrupted normal cycles of hunting, gathering, planting, and harvesting. Rituals and ceremonies that ensured the health of the community, the success of the hunt, the fertility of the crops, and even the protection of warriors—all suffered neglect and disruption. As men fell in battle, populations plummeted; birth rates dropped, and famine stalked in the ashes of burning food supplies. Diseases returned, finding easy targets in hungry children.

One way for a tribe to rebuild its population was to take large numbers of captives and adopt them. This was an accepted, time-honored practice: By the late 1600's some Iroquois towns contained as many adoptees as native-born inhabitants. Nor was it uncommon for some of the new faces to be white.

The Deerfield Captivity

In the winter of 1703–04, a raiding party of French, Abenaki, and Mohawk fighters from the Catholic mission village of Caughnawaga, near Montreal, made a grueling snowshoe trek across the Green Mountains of Vermont and south into Massachusetts. Their target: the English settlement of Deerfield. They caught the sleeping town unawares one February dawn and burned most of it to the ground. More than 100 Deerfield residents became captives, including the town's minister, the Reverend John Williams. Hurrying up the frozen Connecticut River to escape pursuing militia, the raiders tomahawked anyone unable to keep up—including Williams's wife—though they treated the children far more leniently. The captors carried Williams's seven-year-old daughter, Eunice, on their shoulders and looked after her with what even her father later described as "a great deal of tenderness." When the prisoners reached their

French and Indian raiders from Montreal prepare for their dawn assault on the English colony at Deerfield in February 1804. They are leaving a cache of food and equipment, which they will pick up on their return across the mountains to Canada.

Abenaki land and emphasized that he was speaking for himself, not the French. "We are entirely free," he declared at a council in Montreal in the presence of both his English enemies and his French allies. And he made it clear they intended to stay free.

For members of the Iroquois Confederacy, the colonial wars at first exacted a heavy toll as French troops invaded their country time and again. "All those who had sense are dead," lamented one Mohawk man as early as 1691. By 1698, according to some estimates, Iroquois fighting forces were down to perhaps 1,200 warriors, having lost half their strength in less than a decade.

Iroquois chiefs convened at Onondaga to try to halt the downward spiral. Recasting the league's earlier policy, they made peace with their Indian enemies. They then traveled to Albany and Montreal, entering into additional peace treaties with the English and French. Henceforth, the Iroquois would remain neutral in the wars of their European neighbors. It was a wise decision. Using their strategic location to play the colonial rivals against each other, the People of the Longhouse once again held the balance of power in the Northeast.

destination after 25 cold, arduous days, Eunice was adopted by a Caughnawaga family.

Life in the motherly embrace of a native village was in some ways much more pleasant than a typical upbringing in Puritan Massachusetts. She would be taught by example rather than punishment—by love, not the birch rod. So when Eunice's father, who had been ransomed, tried to get her back, she said no. Eunice converted to Catholicism; at age 16 she married a Caughnawaga man; and except for a few brief visits to New England, she spent the rest of her 80 years as a tribal woman.

Challenge of an Alien Faith

Northeastern Indian people were also caught up in a war for their souls. No sooner had the first traders and colonists stepped ashore than a small army of priests and clergymen moved in after them to spread the gospel of Christ. The Black Robes (as French Jesuits came to be known) left their headquarters at Quebec to trek and paddle far into the Canadian woodlands, staying in local wigwams, learning the languages, and rounding up significant numbers of converts. Often they traveled alone. With their black robes and Bibles and their strange indifference to women, the Jesuits were clearly men of special power. Whether they would use their powers for good or evil, no one could tell.

One of the Jesuit missionaries in the Northeast, Paul Le Jeune, spent the winter of 1633–34 with a band of Montagnais hunters. Beset by illness much of the time, the Black Robe drew strength from his friendship with the chieftain Mestigoit. "Seeing that I was very weak and cast down," Le Jeune wrote of a day at a lakeside camp, "he consoled me, saying, 'Do not be sad; if you are sad, you will become still worse; if your sickness increases you will die. See what a beautiful country this is; if you love it and take pleasure in it you will become cheerful, and if you are cheerful you will recover.'"

Farther south in New England, the missionary impulse took longer to catch hold. The *Mayflower* colonists at Plymouth had enough to do trying to survive, without going out of their way to make converts. Puritan authorities in Boston were busy absorbing thousands of English settlers flowing into the new Massachusetts Bay Colony. But an injunction to convert the Indians was written into the colony's charter, and in the mid-1640's the Reverend John Eliot took up the challenge.

Eliot learned the local Algonquian dialect and began preaching. He persuaded converts to settle in "praying towns" like Natick and Punkapoag, where they could work, study, go to church, and learn to behave like the English. Eliot's followers lived in houses of English design and wore English-style clothing; men were told to cut their tribal topknots, and everyone had to wash off the bear grease that protected them from mosquitoes. In return, Eliot provided spades, axes, looms, and other tools, along with instruction in the Protestant faith. Indians who broke Eliot's rules ran the risk of being fined or whipped.

Despite the Puritan rigors, Eliot's towns attracted a considerable number of Christianized natives. Some went on to the newly founded Harvard College, becoming teachers and ministers in order to spread the faith in the woodlands. The results were mixed: "We are well as we are," one of Eliot's missionaries was politely told, "and desire not to be troubled with these new wise sayings." Even so, the movement grew to include a total of 14 towns and as many as 4,000 "praying Indians" at its height. Other evangelists of various denominations won victories elsewhere in the Northeast—but for every Indian who accepted Christianity, others found the new faith profoundly disturbing.

> It is a strange thing, that since prayer has come into our cabins, our former customs are no longer of any service; and yet we shall all die because we give them up.
> — *Algonquin sachem*

The new religion struck at the very foundations of Indian life, in fact. For as long as anyone could remember, the Indians had maintained harmony with the spirit world by means of time-honored rituals and ceremonies. Passing a prominent rock in the forest, for example, a traveler would make an

The serenity of Lake Placid, in the Adirondack Mountains of upstate New York, made it an ideal site for an Iroquois youth on a vision quest.

John Eliot spread the word of God to the natives of Massachusetts, aided by a New Testament he had translated into Algonquian. It was the first Bible printed in America.

I have seen the time when my dreams were true; when I had seen moose or beaver in sleep, I would take some. Now, our dreams and our prophecies are no longer true — prayer has spoiled everything for us.

— *Algonquin hunter*

Adding to the spiritual turmoil, rival Christian sects waged a heated competition for Indian converts, particularly in the border areas between colonies. French Catholics and English Protestants both attempted to proselytize in Iroquois territory—to the growing dismay of the intended proselytes. "You both tell us to be Christians," the Onondaga headman Dekanissore lashed out at officials of New York and Canada in 1701; "you both make us mad; we know not what side to choose." At length the pragmatic Dekanissore advised his people to pray with the side that offered them the best deals in trade.

But even as the world of their ancestors fell apart around them, some people found solace in the words of Christ. The Wampanoag on

Since you are here as strangers, you should rather confine yourselves to the customs of our country than impose yours upon us.

— *Wicomesse leader, 1633*

offering of food or tobacco to propitiate the rock's spirit. Such acts of homage were frequent, for the Northeast was alive with deities. Virtually everything—plants, animals, physical objects, even abstractions such as colors and seasons of the year—had spiritual counterparts that needed to be treated with respect. The Algonquians referred to these spirits as *manitous* and believed they wielded a powerful influence over human events. Manitous visited tribal shamans in prophetic dreams and visions, and they were invoked in ceremonies to cure disease.

To the European priests and pastors, such beliefs were little better than devil worship. In their place, the missionaries offered disquieting concepts like sin, guilt, and damnation—all alien notions to a people who, as one colonist put it, had known neither "of a Hell to scare them, nor a Conscience to terrifie them." No longer would the soul of a deceased Algonquian or Iroquois go to live with its departed kinsmen at a village in the western sky. From now on, the soul after death would descend directly to the torments of purgatory.

Martha's Vineyard became devout Protestants, supplying their own pastors and lay preachers to the local church. In a period of terrible hardship, their message brought comfort. "Be not overmuch grieved," a 16-year-old Wampanoag girl told her family as she lay stricken during a 1710 epidemic, "for I have hopes in the mercy of God, through Jesus Christ my only Saviour, that I shall when I die leave all my pain and affliction behind me, and enter into everlasting rest and happiness."

The wondrous feats of Gluscap—demigod, sage, trickster—still echo in Algonquian lore. Above, Gluscap sets his dogs on a pair of forest witches (left), and waves goodbye to a friendly whale who, in exchange for a gift of pipe tobacco, has given him a ride.

A candidate for saint-hood, Kateri Tekakwitha was a Mohawk woman who in 1677 became the first Indian nun. So great was her piety, it is said, that when she died a miracle occurred: Smallpox scars that had disfigured her face since childhood abruptly disappeared.

A mass religious revival known as the Great Awakening swept the English colonies in the 1730's and 1740's, and it pulled in many thousands of Indian converts. One was Samson Occum, a young Mohegan from Connecticut. Adopted into the household of the Reverend Eleazar Wheelock, he mastered English, Latin, Greek, and Hebrew and became a minister himself. After preaching to the Montauk on Long Island, he journeyed to England to help raise funds for Wheelock's Indian School, the future Dartmouth College. Strong in his faith, Occum turned a withering eye upon the occasional failings of more ordinary, everyday Christians. Here is his account of a visit to the outskirts of New York City one Sunday in June 1761: "Drunkards were reeling and staggering in the streets, often tumbling off their horses; there were others at work in their farms, and if ever any people under Heaven spoke Hell's language, these people did, for their mouths were full of cursings." Occum concluded that New Yorkers were "worse than the savage heathens of the wilderness."

Occum remained steadfast in his convictions—despite his dismay at New York City boorishness. But many Indian people judged Christianity by the example set by its practitioners, and they were rarely impressed. Better stick to the ways of their ancestors, they felt, than submit to a culture with so many undesirable side effects.

Given the powerful emotions Christianity sparked, converts often faced terrible sacrifices. Communities divided between Christians and traditionalists—or between adherents of different Christian denominations. Mohawks who espoused Catholicism moved away to form new enclaves at French mission villages like Caughnawaga and St. Regis on the St. Lawrence River. Most of their relatives who stayed at Fort Hunter and Canajoharie, on the Mohawk River, became Protestant. Oneidas in 1772 complained that "we are despised by our brethren, on account of our Christian profession." Some people tried to resolve the conflicts between native tradition and Christian belief by following both at once—going to Mass on Sunday, and honoring the Great Manitou on Monday. There was

Sky Woman, the goddess of Iroquois creation, plunges from heaven through a hole left by an uprooted tree. A flock of geese breaks her fall, and a giant turtle, on which the earth will form, rises to catch her. The painting, "Our Earth, Our Mother," is by Seneca artist Ernest Smith.

peans arrived with their glass beads and woolen blankets, their copper kettles, iron axes, and steel knives, the Indians wasted no time gathering the newcomers into their existing trade networks. Before long, everyone was scrambling to get metal tools and utensils of European or colonial manufacture. Even objects that at first made no sense were eagerly accepted: When the Dutch offered stockings, Delaware Indians used them as tobacco pouches. Best of all, these many wonders seemed to cost almost nothing. "The English have no sense," scoffed one Montagnais trader in the 1630's. "They give us twenty knives like this for one beaver skin."

room for more than one divinity in Iroquoian religion, after all, and a convert could read the Bible and still believe in the magic of dreams. Still, the Christian path to salvation often proved a hard road in Indian country.

A Mohawk schoolmaster drills his class in the basics of reading and writing in this drawing from a 1786 English-language primer.

Copper Kettles and Hidden Costs

Even as Northeastern Indians wrestled with alien ideas, they became devoted admirers of European technology. The region's tribes had always engaged in commerce, exchanging gifts of wampum, animal pelts, tobacco, shells, reed mats, pottery, pigments, and other items. In the process, they forged lasting ties of friendship and alliance. So when the Euro-

But the inflow of European trade goods proved to be another cultural time bomb. As the people grew accustomed to metal tools, they lost the arts of chipping flint into arrowheads and shaping pieces of bone into knives and scrapers. As a result, foreign-made articles that began as luxuries were soon necessities. Without metal farm tools, Indian villagers could not raise enough food to sustain themselves. They were growing dependent on the white traders for their very survival.

The principal item the traders wanted in return was fur, especially beaver pelts. And the fur trade carried its own hidden costs. As Indian hunters strove to meet the demand for

CANASATEGO ON HIGHER EDUCATION

While most colonial administrators did their honest best to educate and "civilize" their Indian neighbors — hoping perhaps to tame their highly independent ways — the Indians themselves remained doubtful. In 1744, when the Virginia legislature offered free tuition at the College of William and Mary to six Iroquois youths, the Iroquois politely declined. Explaining their reasons, the great Onondaga spokesman Canasatego told why a college education made no sense at all:

"We have had some experience of it. Several of our young people were formerly brought up in the colleges of the Northern provinces; they were instructed in all your sciences; but, when they came back to us, they were bad runners, ignorant of every means of living in the woods, unable to bear either cold or hunger, knew neither how to build a cabin, take a deer, nor kill an enemy, spoke our language imperfectly, were therefore neither fit for hunters, warriors, nor counselors; they were totally good for nothing.

"We are however not the less obliged for your kind offer, though we decline accepting it; and to show our grateful sense of it, if the gentlemen of Virginia shall send us a dozen of their sons, we will take great care of their education, and instruct them in all we know, and make men of them."

pelts, many neglected the time-consuming ancient rituals that had once bound them spiritually to the animals they hunted. At the same time, the ever-increasing volume of trapping and shooting depleted the region's animal populations. Deer and bears became scarce. Ponds and streams that once thronged with beavers now stood empty and still.

We lived before they came among us,
and as well, or better. We had then room
enough, and plenty of deer, which was
easily caught; and tho' we had not knives,
hatchets, or guns, such as we have now,
yet we had knives of stone, and bows and
arrows, and those served our uses
as well then as the English ones do now.
— *Canasatego, Onondaga*

Alcohol helped accelerate the Indians' decline. To lubricate the wheels of commerce, many colonial traders plied their Indian customers with rum and whiskey. This led in turn to even greater dependency on the traders. "When our people come from hunting to the town or plantations and . . . want powder, and shot and clothing, they first give us a large cup of rum," a Mahican delegation complained to the governor of New York in 1722. "After we get the taste of it we crave for more so that in the end all the beaver and peltry we have hunted goes for drink, and we are left destitute either of clothing or ammunition."

This ornamental bird (top) was shaped by a Pennacook craftsman from part of a copper pot obtained by trade. An Iroquois-made silver brooch (above) includes a surprising European touch: the familiar compass-and-arc emblem of the Freemasons.

A birch-bark work basket embroidered with caribou hair exemplifies the distinctive artistry of Huron converts who settled near the Jesuit mission at Lorette in Quebec.

Alcohol brought chaos to Indian villages as people killed each other in drunken brawls; men who exchanged pelts for bottles often neglected their hunting and their families. In effect, alcohol addiction joined the list of new killer diseases. "You may find graves upon graves along the lake, all of which misfortunes are occasioned by selling rum to our brothers," one Iroquois reflected sadly in 1730. "These wicked whiskey sellers will be our ruin," declared another.

"Pen and Ink Work"

With their thirst for European goods and liquor, many Northeastern natives fell deep into debt. Searching for ways to pay their creditors, they turned to the one asset they held in seemingly endless supply: land. The dense woodlands that blanketed the region were sparsely populated and appeared extensive enough to contain everyone. No deeds of ownership marked the boundaries of tribal territories, which had been established over centuries by custom and usage: Here the Narragansett dug for clams; here the Cayuga farmed and foraged. And so if the newcomers wanted to bargain for the use of a tribe's ancestral hunting grounds, there seemed to be no harm in letting them do so.

The settlers had different ideas, of course. Once they took possession, they set about transforming the land to match their vision of civilized life: a world of farms, fields and fences, roads and bridges, prosperous mills and bustling towns.

Confronted with the newcomers' bewildering land hunger, Indian leaders tried to strike the best deals they could. They attempted to master the complexities of colonial deeds and to slow down the rate at which their homelands were being overrun. But the process was unstoppable. Land speculators, in the business of acquiring woodland property for future development, made offers to individual villages and families that seemed too tempting to refuse. Sometimes, because of shady dealing and the clever phrasing of property deeds—what the Onondaga leader Canasa-

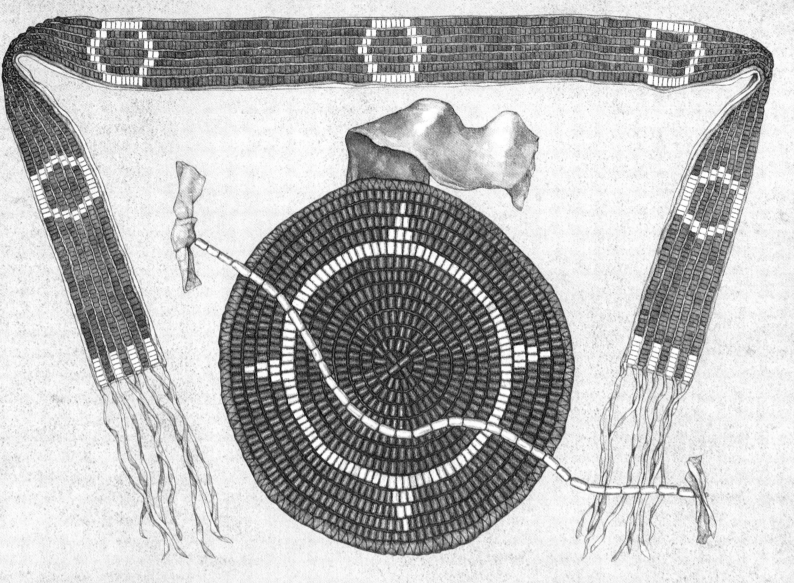

THE WAYS OF WAMPUM

An array of Iroquois wampum shows (from the top) the Champlain Belt, with each circle representing an attack by the French; an unusual wampum disc; a condolence string used at Iroquois council meetings to honor departed chieftains; and a string of invitation wampum (far right) for summoning village leaders to tribal meetings. Sorted and strung together (bottom right), beads might travel long distances before finally being woven into objects such as those illustrated here.

For a people with no written alphabet, wampum carried an almost mystical weight of meaning. Bits of polished shell or glass roped together into strands, belts, or other shapes, wampum (the term comes from an Algonquian phrase meaning "string of white beads") served as ornament, archive, trade item, and medium of communication. No diplomacy could take place without it. Runners relayed messages using wampum: red beads meant war; white, peace.

Iroquois orators opened councils by offering wampum strings to quiet anger, wipe away tears, and open the hearts of listeners. Each speaker in turn punctuated his remarks by handing wampum belts across the council fire; if a listener threw a belt aside, it meant that he doubted the speaker's words — or rejected his proposal. When the talks were over, the wampum became a part of the tribal record and a guarantee of promises made.

European colonists learned the etiquette of wampum diplomacy and some other uses of wampum as well: paying a debt, for instance, giving a gift, offering tribute, or atoning for one's misdeeds. A gift of wampum might accompany a proposal of marriage. In the cash-poor colonies, it became a widely accepted form of hard currency. But for the people who created it, wampum was always something more — an object imbued with honor, tradition, and spiritual resonance.

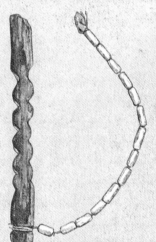

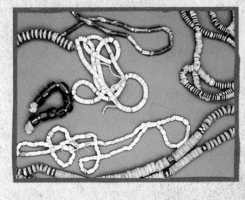

At a reconstructed Delaware village in Waterloo, New Jersey, part of the original Lenape homeland, corn porridge simmers on a stone hearth. Wooden stirring paddles hang from the fire bar, along with drying corn cobs, and two wooden fire drills rest in the left foreground. The bark-covered longhouse at the rear would have sheltered perhaps a dozen people.

tego scornfully called "pen and ink work"—the land slipped from the Indians without their full consent or even their knowledge. So by fair means and foul, the tribal territories were steadily whittled away. "Our hearts grieve us when we consider what small parcel of lands is remaining to us," Mohawk headmen complained to Albany in 1730.

> We know our lands are now become more valuable. The white people think we do not know their value; but we are sensible that the land is everlasting, and the few goods we receive for it are soon worn out and gone.
>
> — *Canasatego, Onondaga*

No group signed away land more often than the Lenape—or Delaware, as they increasingly came to be known—who first encountered Europeans when living in what is

today New Jersey. Between 1630 and 1767 the Delaware inked their personal marks on nearly 800 different land deeds. On the surface many of these documents were reasonable and fair. William Penn, the first governor of Pennsylvania, set an example of honest dealing when he drew up a celebrated peace treaty with the Delaware leader Tammany in 1682, ushering in a half-century of trust between his Quaker colony and the local tribes.

Unfortunately, the legacy of William Penn did not long outlive him. In 1737 his son, Thomas Penn, convinced some Delaware chiefs to sign a deed that granted the colony as much land as a man could walk across in a day and a half. The Pennsylvanians cleared a path through the forest, but instead of one man walking, they produced a team of three runners. At noon of the second day, the last runner reached the end of his endurance—a full 65 miles from the starting point.

A portrait of Tishcohan, one of the Delaware leaders defrauded by the 1737 Walking Treaty.

The Delaware protested in vain. Time and again they sold lands and moved away, but the settlers kept coming, pushing them farther and farther west. By 1751 they had been forced beyond the Alleghenies. They migrated to Ohio, then across the Mississippi and out onto the Great Plains, until at last the majority of their descendants would settle in the far, dusty reaches of Kansas and Oklahoma.

Rebellions and a Revolution

By 1763 the British had won the last of their wars with the French, who surrendered all their disputed land claims. But peace between the colonial powers brought no rest for native communities. No sooner had the French departed than some of their Indian allies, fearing harsh treatment by the British, banded together in a new round of resistance in the Ohio Valley and Great Lakes regions.

As a peace offering, the British government officially forbade settlement beyond the crest of the Appalachian Mountains. All lands west of this barrier would belong to the tribes, and they could be relinquished only by treaty between tribal leaders and the government. But almost immediately land developers and would-be settlers were contriving to break the decree's provisions. With the French wars over —and no troops on hand to enforce the new policy—white colonists poured across the mountains in ever greater numbers.

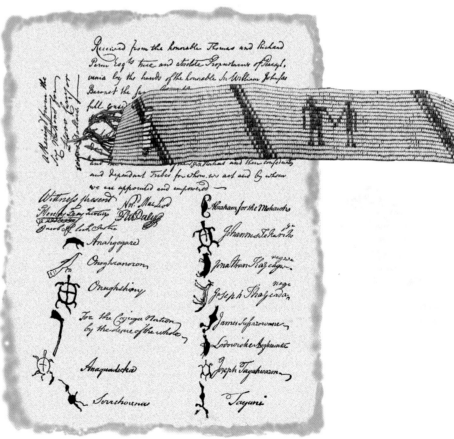

William Penn's original 1682 Peace Treaty was commemorated in separate ways by the 19th-century painter Edward Hicks (top) and in the Great Treaty Wampum Belt (above), which pledges eternal friendship between the Quakers and the Delaware. In the background is a 1769 Quaker land deed signed by clan representatives of both the Delaware and the Iroquois.

A VERDICT FOR MARY JEMISON

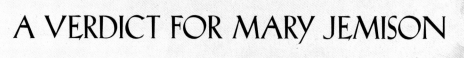

On a summer's day in 1764, the chiefs and elders of Little Beard's Town, a Seneca village on the Genesee River in New York, met to decide an issue of vital importance. More than a year had passed since the end of the last French and Indian War, and the British colonial government was now offering a bounty for the return of all settlers taken hostage during the conflict. Most were overjoyed. But at least one, 21-year-old Mary Jemison, wanted to stay where she was. Ever since her capture six years earlier, during a raid on her parents' wilderness farmstead, Mary had lived as a Seneca. Her captors treated her with kindness and affection and had adopted her into the tribe; she had taken a native husband and had given birth to a Seneca son. Since her parents had been killed in the raid, this was now her family.

And so the chiefs of her village met around the council fire, in front of the main longhouse, to hear the senior clan mother plead Mary's cause. (By tribal custom, Mary did not attend.) Beyond their fondness for their adopted sister, the council's decision had larger implications. According to Iroquois belief, each individual possesses an inner spiritual power, which contributes to the overall strength of the tribe. To ransom Mary back to the white men would be to barter this power for money. Such a thing seemed unthinkable, and Mary was told she could stay as long as she wished.

But money itself is a powerful force, and a few days later a high-ranking Seneca chieftain arrived at the village to take Mary away. The villagers were outraged. One Seneca brother showed his defiance by offering to kill Mary rather than give her up. Faced with this option, she fled into the woods with her infant son until the chieftain departed and passions cooled. Then she returned, to the joy of her adopted tribespeople. She remained among them, raising five Seneca children and numerous grandchildren, until her death in 1833 at age 91.

Colonial administrators tried to bring the tide of settlement under control, and some succeeded better than others. One of the most able—and controversial—was Sir William Johnson, England's superintendent of Indian affairs in the Northeast. Johnson had moved into Iroquois country and made a fortune in land development and fur trading while at the same time earning the lifelong trust of the Iroquois nations. During the recent wars, he had led a combined force of Mohawks and colonists into battle against the French. His Mohawk wife, Mary Brant, gave him eight mixed-blood children. The Mohawk people, in turn, took Johnson into the tribe under the name Brother Warraghiyagey (He Who Does Much Business) and moved their council fire to the grounds of his estate.

It was Johnson who negotiated the end of Chief Pontiac's rebellion after luring the Seneca back to the British side. Then, resolving to settle once and for all the boundary between white settlement and Indian hunting grounds, he called a summit council of tribal and colo-

Crown agent William Johnson won Iroquois loyalty by his adroit frontier diplomacy. An Iroquois council meets at his baronial estate on the Mohawk River (below), where he kept open house for all Indian visitors. The silver medal at right celebrates Johnson's friendship with the western Iroquois.

nial delegates. Some 3,000 Indians showed up in 1768 to attend the meeting at Fort Stanwix on the upper Mohawk River. The outcome was a cash payment to the Iroquois and the promise of a perpetual homeland north of the Mohawk River, in return for which they gave up large stretches of territory to the south and west. But much of this region was also claimed by the Shawnee, Cherokee, and others—whose expressions of outrage and open contempt brought Iroquois prestige to its lowest ebb in many years. (The only real victor was Johnson himself, who lived up to his tribal name by coming away with 100,000 acres of Mohawk Valley land.)

The close ties between the Iroquois and Johnson would have further consequences during the next great conflict, the War for Independence. As a British official, Johnson used every opportunity to enlist the goodwill of the Six Nations on behalf of their "Father, the Great King." When the aging Johnson

died shortly before the outbreak of hostilities, the Iroquois Confederacy found itself near stage center in the drama about to unfold.

The Battle of Lexington and Concord in April 1775 sent British and American agents hurrying into Indian country to recruit warriors for their respective sides. In Massachusetts, men from the Indian towns of Stockbridge and Mashpee promptly joined their American neighbors; they served in George Washington's Continental Army and suffered heavy casualties. The Penobscot likewise aided the Patriot cause in Maine.

But most Indian people tried to remain neutral. Caughnawaga and Abenaki on the St. Lawrence kept both sides at arm's length, knowing they had little to gain and much to lose if they got involved. The Iroquois also attempted to remain on the sidelines—at first.

> We cannot intermeddle in this dispute between two brothers. The quarrel seems unnatural. If the great king of England apply to us for aid, we shall deny him; if the Colonies apply, we shall refuse.
>
> — *Oneida delegation to governor of Connecticut, 1775*

Slowly, however, the Iroquois were pulled into the conflict, and the resulting split in loyalty crippled the league as an effective force. The Oneida and Tuscarora generally supported the Americans; the Mohawk, Cayuga, Onondaga, and Seneca sided with England. The man most responsible for the latter was Thayendanegea, a Mohawk chief better known by his English name: Joseph Brant.

The late William Johnson's brother-in-law, Brant had fought under Johnson against the French as a teenager and later served as Johnson's interpreter. Along the way he picked up a first-rate mission-school education, became close with his Johnson in-laws, and translated the Christian Gospels into Mohawk. He also became an eloquent speaker at Mohawk councils. Not surprisingly, when the British started courting the Iroquois, they turned to Brant.

Invited to visit London in early 1776, Brant was feted and lionized. King George III granted him an audience, and the Prince of Wales took him out for a night on the town. So great was Brant's celebrity that London street gangs began shaving their hair into spiky Mohawk topknots. But before he agreed to anything, Brant wanted concessions in exchange.

> The Mohawks have on all occasions shown their zeal and loyalty to the Great King; yet they have been very badly treated by his people. Indeed it is very hard, when we have let the King's subjects have so much of our lands for so little value. We are tired out in making complaints and getting no redress.
>
> — *Thayendanegea (Joseph Brant) Mohawk, 1776*

Apparently the royal reply satisfied him, for on returning to Iroquois country, Brant began raising troops to fight the Americans. Amassing a force of Mohawk and other Iroquois warriors, he joined the British in an assault through western New York in the summer of 1777. The combined force of Redcoats and In-

The first to fall in the Boston Massacre of 1770—shown below in a Paul Revere engraving—was an escaped slave named Crispus Attucks, whose father was African and whose mother was a member of the Massachuset tribe.

Brant remained in the field, leading his Mohawks in raids on frontier settlements in New York and Pennsylvania, sometimes with British troops or with colonial militiamen who had remained loyal to the Crown. Reports of atrocities began to circulate. A combined force of Iroquois and Tory militia struck the prosperous farmlands of northeastern Pennsylvania, burning houses, driving off livestock, and killing 227 armed defenders, along with many women and children.

After one attack on an American fort in 1777, Brant found that a child had been carried away by some of his men. The child was returned unharmed to the commandant the next morning, along with a note that made pointed reference to white militiamen sometimes allied with Brant's Mohawk warriors.

Sir: I send you by one of our runners the child which we will deliver, that you may know what ever others do, I do not make war on women and children. I am sorry to say that I have those engaged with me in the service who are more savage than the savages themselves.

— *Joseph Brant, Mohawk*

The Americans struck back with avenging fury, invading Iroquois towns in the Susquehanna Valley in 1778 and again the following spring. "They put to death all the women and children," lamented an Onondaga chief, "excepting some of the young women, whom they carried away for the use of their soldiers and were afterwards put to death in a more shameful manner." (Nowhere was there a starker contrast in the conduct of whites and natives. "Bad as these savages are," wrote Gen. James Clinton, no friend of the Iroquois, "they never violate the chastity of any woman.")

George Washington, determined to extinguish the Indian threat once and for all, then ordered a massive sweep of Iroquois country, specifying that it should "not merely be overrun, but destroyed." In August 1779, Gen. John Sullivan marched north from Pennsylvania with 2,500 men. Many later described the

dians struck Fort Stanwix, was turned back, then moved on to intercept a relief force of Patriot militiamen at the Battle of Oriskany.

Streams Red With Iroquois Blood

A contingent of Senecas also fought for the British at Oriskany; ranged against them on the American side were companies of Oneida and Tuscarora warriors. Earlier that year, in the wake of a smallpox epidemic that killed three Onondaga chiefs, the council fire of the Iroquois League had been ritually extinguished. Now, in the smoke of battle, the great Longhouse Confederacy was truly ended. Brother fought against brother in bitter hand-to-hand conflict, leaving the ground heaped with bodies and tinting the streams red with blood, in an engagement long remembered with horror by those who survived it.

Mohawk war chief Joseph Brant helped split the Iroquois Confederacy by siding with Great Britain in the American Revolution. After the British surrender he moved to Canada, where a local artist painted this portrait. The tomahawk is a gift from a British friend, the duke of Northumberland.

richness of the land, with its neat frame houses and broad, verdant cornfields. But their mission was to scorch the earth, and that they did—burning towns, pillaging longhouses, uprooting crops, chopping down orchards, slaughtering cattle, and destroying grain supplies. Some units stopped to plunder graves for burial goods; others skinned the bodies of dead Iroquois to make leggings.

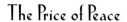

> There was nothing but bare soil and timber, not a mouthful of any kind of sustenance, not even enough to keep a child one day from perishing from hunger.
> — *Seneca survivor of Sullivan's campaign*

Most residents, forewarned by lookouts, fled into the woods and so sustained few casualties. But their homeland lay devastated. Many fled to the British fort at Niagara, where they huddled in squalid refugee camps through one of the coldest winters on record. Some starved; some froze to death. Ever after, the Iroquois remembered George Washington as Caunotaucarius—Town Destroyer.

In 1783, Great Britain and the United States signed a peace accord in Paris. Along with independence, the new nation won title to all territory south of Canada that had been claimed by the British. To the mind of the victors, this included lands rightfully belonging to the Indians. And so for the region's original inhabitants, the Treaty of Paris was an act of terrible betrayal. Virtually all prior government agreements were rendered void. The Royal Proclamation of 1763, already broken a hundred times over by land-hungry frontier farmers, became so much scrap paper. With the departure of the British, Indian warriors who had supported them were left stranded. Even those allied with the Patriots, who had fought and bled in the cause of liberty, received little thanks.

The Price of Peace

In New England unpaid Revolutionary War soldiers were given Indian lands instead of currency. Massachusetts settlers pushed steadily into the hunting territories of the Penobscot and Passamaquoddy, their former allies. The two tribes appealed to the new U.S. Congress, demanding the freedom and justice "which we have been fighting for as other Americans." Eventually Congress passed the Indian Trade and Non-Intercourse Act, declaring illegal any sales of Indian land that Congress itself had not specifically approved, but the measure had little effect. Massachusetts continued to pressure the Penobscot into giving up their territory.

The self-governing Indian town of Mashpee, on Cape Cod, had lost so many of its young men to Tory bullets that Mashpee women were obliged to look for husbands among Anglo-Americans, African-Americans, and some stray Hessians—German mercenaries sent over by the British—who had been captured by the Americans and then released. Yet the town's great sacrifice earned it nothing. The Massachusetts Department of Indian Affairs dissolved the local Indian council and placed Mashpee under state-appointed

American troops under Gen. John Sullivan sweep into Seneca country in 1779, following orders by George Washington to "lay waste all the settlments." Sullivan's men ravaged 40 villages, burned 500 houses, and destroyed 160,000 bushels of corn. This scene of the campaign — an infamous chapter in Iroquois memory — was painted by Ernest Smith, whose Seneca ancestors were among the dispossessed.

guardians. Indians from Stockbridge returned from battle to find that their neighbors had seized control of both their town government and their real estate. The Stockbridge Indians left home and moved west, taking up residence near the Oneida in upstate New York.

The Revolution left the Iroquois Confederacy in ruins. An embittered Joseph Brant, preferring to live in exile rather than remain at home among the Americans, led his Mohawks and some other Iroquois allies to the Grand River in Ontario. On a small stretch of land set aside for them by the British government—and where their descendants still inhabit the Six Nations Reserve—they built new homes and churches and rekindled their sadly diminished council fire.

> Every man of us thought that, by fighting for the King, we should ensure for ourselves and children a good inheritance.
>
> — *Joseph Brant, Mohawk*

The government of the Iroquois was now permanently divided between Brant's followers in Canada and groups remaining in New York. To mark the split, tribal leaders physically cut the great founding wampum belt of the confederacy into two separate parts. The New York chiefs then began negotiating their own peace agreements with the Americans.

They met at Fort Stanwix in 1784, and under the circumstances they probably did the best they could. The Americans, as victors, held most of the high cards. Maintaining that Washington's troops had "conquered" the Iroquois, the American treaty commissioners demanded huge land concessions as the price of peace. The terms were an exercise in humiliation. All Iroquois-held territory in Pennsylvania and Ohio and much of the western New York heartland—the same areas that soldiers in the Sullivan expedition had praised for their rich, productive soil—had to be signed away. The domains of the Seneca, the Cayuga, and the Onondaga shrank to a tiny portion. Even the Oneida and Tuscarora, who as wartime allies had expected to remain whole, lost out. Later agreements with private land companies and the state of New York cost the Oneida so much acreage that most of them pulled up stakes and moved to either Wisconsin or Ontario.

Virtually all Northeastern Indians who opted to remain in the United States found themselves living an increasingly marginal existence. With their homelands gone and the fur trade long since exhausted, many people took jobs as day laborers working for meager

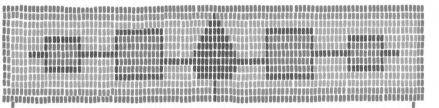

A MODEL FOR UNION?

When delegates of the newly independent American Colonies met in Philadelphia in 1787 to write a Constitution, they took inspiration from many sources: the ancient Greek democracies, British parliamentary tradition, the writings of John Locke and Jean-Jacques Rousseau—and the practical example of the Iroquois League.

"We are a powerful confederacy," the Onondaga leader Canasatego had advised colonial officials back in 1744, "and by your observing the same methods our wise forefathers have taken, you will acquire fresh strength and power." The words prompted a bright young journalist named Benjamin Franklin to make a study of the Iroquois system. Franklin discovered a fine working example of representative democracy, with an unwritten constitution that spelled out checks and balances, rules of procedure, limits of power, and a stress on individual liberty. Deeply impressed, Franklin drew up a scheme, called the Albany Plan, for joining the Thirteen Colonies into a similar confederation.

Franklin's proposal languished for several decades. Then, at Philadelphia, the delegates turned to its provisions; much of the final Constitution thus came to reflect Iroquois ideals. So, too, did an important piece of national symbolism: the American eagle. Like the majestic bird that guards the Iroquois Tree of Peace, the American eagle stands for unity and power. There is one further echo. The Iroquois eagle holds six arrows, one for each of the Six Nations; the United States eagle grasps 13 arrows, a reminder of its 13 original member states.

wages. Some coastal groups went to sea as sailors. Others eked out a living peddling baskets and other tribal handicrafts. Abenaki in northern New England tried against all odds to maintain their ancient way of life—hunting, gathering, roaming the fringes of what had once been extensive homelands. Other Indians dwelt anonymously in the towns and cities of the new nation. Families broke up. Alcoholism increased dramatically.

The fall from grace was particularly steep for the Seneca, once the most numerous and powerful of the Iroquois nations. Now isolated in small pockets of their ancestral hunting grounds, surrounded by hostile new neighbors, they seemed destined for total extinction. Yet the Seneca held on. And through sheer grit and intelligence—and the spiritual force of some exceptional leaders—they slowly began to recover.

He Keeps Them Awake

One of the greatest of those leaders was Red Jacket. Like many Senecas, he had fought on the Tory side during the Revolution (thus acquiring the red British army officer's coat that inspired his English name). But his true weapons were words. In speech after speech, at tribal councils and at treaty conferences with the American government, Red Jacket gave voice to the independent spirit of Iroquois tradition and decried attempts by federal officials to treat them as a subjugated

Red Jacket defends himself against charges of witchcraft made in 1801; he points at one accuser, the war chief Cornplanter, seated at right with a red blanket. His main accuser, the prophet Handsome Lake, stands at far left, arms folded. Red Jacket wears a peace medal (inset) given to him by George Washington.

people. His tribal name was Sagoyewatha—He Keeps Them Awake—and he spoke with a riveting blend of passion, poetry, common sense, and bitter irony.

To Red Jacket any concession to American interests was an act of treason. Decrying the huge losses of tribal territory at the hated Stanwix peace settlement, he later helped roll back some of its worst provisions and managed to regain a measure of local sovereignty for the Seneca. A strict traditionalist, he scorned all attempts to convert the Iroquois to white men's ways—especially their religion.

You have now become a great people,
and we have scarcely a place left to spread
our blankets. You have got our country now,
but you are not satisfied. You want to force
your religion upon us.

We are told that you have been preaching to the white people in this place. These people are our neighbors. We will wait a little while, and see what effect your preaching has upon them. If we find it does them good, makes them honest and less disposed to cheat Indians, we will then consider again what you have said.

*—Red Jacket, Seneca,
to Protestant missionaries*

The principal rival to Red Jacket's hard-line approach was the Seneca leader Cornplanter. A bold and talented warrior who had fought

Some of our chiefs make the
claim that the land belongs to us.
It is not what the Great Spirit told
me. He told me that the land belongs
to Him, that no people own the land,
and that I was not to forget to tell
this to the white people.

—Kannekuk, Kickapoo prophet

Then one June day in 1799, during the Strawberry Festival, Handsome Lake attempted to rouse himself from his stupor. He let out a mighty cry, collapsed, and lay still as death. Mourners were summoned, and relatives began preparing his body for burial. But astonishingly, the dead man's breath returned. His eyes fluttered open. "Never have I seen such wondrous visions!" he exclaimed, and he went on to tell how three magnificent angels in ancient Iroquois regalia had taken him on a profound spirit journey so that he would hear the will of the Creator. And the message was loud and clear. First, the Iroquois must renounce liquor. They should then dedicate themselves to a process of complete spiritual renewal.

Handsome Lake awoke a changed man. For the next 15 years, until his death in 1815, he traveled the reservations preaching the new religion. His gospel, the *Gaiwiiyo*, blended ancient customs and traditions with certain key aspects of Christianity —particularly the beliefs of the Quakers in temperance, frugality, and nonviolence. It emphasized the age-old values of family and clan and the importance of seasonal rituals such as the Green Corn Ceremony and the Midwinter Ceremony. Its symbol became the Iroquois longhouse.

Yet it also embraced the benefits of European-style education and of new, more productive agricultural practices.

These teachings generated passionate feelings, to be sure, both for and against. Farming had always been considered women's work, and it took some powerful convincing to persuade a former Seneca warrior to step behind a plow. Furthermore, spiritual renewal was taken to mean that the tribes must be cleansed of sorcery and black magic—terms that were thrown around loosely at the time—with the result that several unfortunate people were accused, hunted down, and put to death.

But within a few years Handsome Lake had acquired a large, deeply committed following. Thomas Jefferson gave the new faith his blessing and encouragement, seeing it as a step on the path to assimilated living—a view shared by the Seneca's Quaker neighbors. By preserving what was best in Iroquois tradition and incorporating useful innovations from the white man's world, the Longhouse Religion (as it came to be called) seemed to promise both social reform and cultural rejuvenation.

Whiskey is a great and monstrous evil and has reared a high mound of bones. So now all must say, "I will use it nevermore."

The married should live together and children should grow from them. Man and wife should rear their children well, love them, and keep them in health.

Love one another and do not strive for another's undoing. Even as you desire good treatment, so render it.

— *Handsome Lake, Seneca*

Gradually the promise was fulfilled. In the generations that followed, increasing numbers of disciples spread the message of Handsome Lake, and converts flocked to longhouses throughout the remaining Iroquois lands. And ultimately it became apparent that the Six Nations, like many other native nations, would survive despite everything—that they would persist, adapt, and in time perhaps recover some measure of what was once theirs.

Our religion is not one of paint and feathers; it is a thing of the heart.
— *Follower of Handsome Lake*

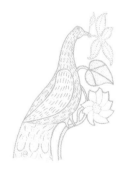

Some of our chiefs make the claim that the land belongs to us. It is not what the Great Spirit told me. He told me that the land belongs to Him, that no people own the land, and that I was not to forget to tell this to the white people.

—Kannekuk, Kickapoo prophet

wages. Some coastal groups went to sea as sailors. Others eked out a living peddling baskets and other tribal handicrafts. Abenaki in northern New England tried against all odds to maintain their ancient way of life—hunting, gathering, roaming the fringes of what had once been extensive homelands. Other Indians dwelt anonymously in the towns and cities of the new nation. Families broke up. Alcoholism increased dramatically.

The fall from grace was particularly steep for the Seneca, once the most numerous and powerful of the Iroquois nations. Now isolated in small pockets of their ancestral hunting grounds, surrounded by hostile new neighbors, they seemed destined for total extinction. Yet the Seneca held on. And through sheer grit and intelligence—and the spiritual force of some exceptional leaders—they slowly began to recover.

He Keeps Them Awake

One of the greatest of those leaders was Red Jacket. Like many Senecas, he had fought on the Tory side during the Revolution (thus acquiring the red British army officer's coat that inspired his English name). But his true weapons were words. In speech after speech, at tribal councils and at treaty conferences with the American government, Red Jacket gave voice to the independent spirit of Iroquois tradition and decried attempts by federal officials to treat them as a subjugated

Red Jacket defends himself against charges of witchcraft made in 1801; he points at one accuser, the war chief Cornplanter, seated at right with a red blanket. His main accuser, the prophet Handsome Lake, stands at far left, arms folded. Red Jacket wears a peace medal (inset) given to him by George Washington.

people. His tribal name was Sagoyewatha—He Keeps Them Awake—and he spoke with a riveting blend of passion, poetry, common sense, and bitter irony.

To Red Jacket any concession to American interests was an act of treason. Decrying the huge losses of tribal territory at the hated Stanwix peace settlement, he later helped roll back some of its worst provisions and managed to regain a measure of local sovereignty for the Seneca. A strict traditionalist, he scorned all attempts to convert the Iroquois to white men's ways—especially their religion.

> You have now become a great people, and we have scarcely a place left to spread our blankets. You have got our country now, but you are not satisfied. You want to force your religion upon us.
>
> We are told that you have been preaching to the white people in this place. These people are our neighbors. We will wait a little while, and see what effect your preaching has upon them. If we find it does them good, makes them honest and less disposed to cheat Indians, we will then consider again what you have said.
>
> —*Red Jacket, Seneca,*
> *to Protestant missionaries*

The principal rival to Red Jacket's hard-line approach was the Seneca leader Cornplanter. A bold and talented warrior who had fought

149

beside Brant at Oriskany and elsewhere, Cornplanter turned to diplomacy at the war's end. Compromise, he felt, would win more favor from the American victors than a continued show of opposition. He spoke for the Seneca nation at Fort Stanwix and in a succession of later treaty negotiations, although he could do little to prevent the erosion of Seneca territory. "If we do not sell them the land, the whites will take it away," he reasoned. And he did manage to cultivate amiable relations with the new government. Even the infamous Town Destroyer became a friend.

> When your army entered the country of the Six Nations, we called you Caunotaucarius, the Town Destroyer; and to this day when that name is heard, our women look behind them and turn pale, and our children cling to the knees of their mothers.
>
> Our councilors and warriors are men and cannot be afraid; but their hearts are grieved with the fears of their women and children, and desire that it may be buried so deep as to be heard no more.
>
> When you gave us peace, we called you father, because you promised to secure us in possession of our lands. Do this, and so long as the lands shall remain, the beloved name will remain in the heart of every Seneca.
>
> — *Cornplanter, Seneca, to George Washington, 1790*

When fighting subsequently broke out between American settlers and native tribes in Ohio, Cornplanter helped negotiate a peace accord. In payment he was given a 1,300-acre tract of Pennsylvania farmland. Inviting his followers to join him, he founded what in effect was a private Seneca reservation. Here, at his urging, residents practiced the latest American farming techniques, lived in American-style houses, and generally tried to fit into the new culture surrounding them. One of the residents on this estate was a half-brother of Cornplanter (and also, as it happened, an uncle of Red Jacket), who, like his two famous relatives, had fought for the British.

The Iroquois prophet Handsome Lake, depicted here in an Ernest Smith painting, preaches his code of temperance and self-esteem at the Seneca longhouse in Tonawanda, New York. His teachings became the foundation of the Longhouse Religion.

The Vision of Handsome Lake

This half-brother had once held a voice in tribal councils; as a sachem of the Turtle clan, he had received the title Ganeodiyo, or Handsome Lake (the Seneca name for Lake Ontario). But in the grim dissolution of the post–Revolution era, Ganeodiyo succumbed to alcohol and despair. For four years he lay bedridden in his cabin, cared for by a daughter. The end seemed only a matter of time.

The Seneca war chief Cornplanter, who terrorized frontier farmsteads during the Revolution—then turned to farming himself—smokes the pipe of peace in this late-18th-century portrait.

5

WAVES OF CHANGE IN THE UPPER COUNTRY

THE GREAT LAKES AND OHIO VALLEY

n an island in Chequamegon Bay near the western end of Lake Superior, the old Ojibwa people told the story of the Man with a Hat—the first being from across the salt sea they had ever encountered. It happened, as many things happen, because of a dream. One of the Ojibwa holy men saw a vision of "white spirits," their heads covered, approaching from the direction of the rising sun with smiling faces and outstretched hands. So to seek them out, the old man worked all winter building a birchbark canoe, curing meat for travel, and preparing furs to have ready for an exchange of gifts.

In the spring he and his wife set out for the East, retracing the course their westbound ancestors were said to have used centuries earlier to reach Lake Superior. The two paddled along the lake's south shore to its outlet, the present St. Mary's River, probably stopping at Bawating, the principal village at the rapids. Heading on, they reached Lake Huron, then turned up the French River to Lake Nipissing.

From there the old couple labored through 36 portages around dangerous rapids, unloading the boat and carrying it overland, before they reached the Ottawa River and rode it down to the St. Lawrence. Moving northeast through friendly Algonquin country, then through dangerous Iroquois territory, they reached the broadening of the river where the St. Lawrence Seaway begins—and soon saw a cabin with smoke coming out of the top. There they found the Man with a Hat, a bearded human wearing a head covering—a "white spirit," they later said. He came forward, shook their hands, and gave them food and wondrous gifts: a metal ax and knife, a piece of beautiful red cloth, and brightly colored beads that could be strung on a length of sinew.

The old man and his wife made the slow upstream journey back to their island in Chequamegon Bay. (The people there later calculated that, by the European calendar, this encounter took place about 1612.) Before the village they opened their medicine bundle with its exotic contents and told of the Man with a Hat. The next spring neighbors made the same trip and returned with more valuable

◀ Preceding page: Wah-com-mo (Fast Walker), a Fox war leader, wears a grizzly bear claw necklace and holds an eagle feather fan and a tomahawk-pipe, all traditional emblems of rank. Background: the shoreline of Lake Superior.

objects from the "white spirits," including the first gun and a bottle of whiskey. They tested the liquor on an old woman, in case it was poison; when she recovered from her stupor, she asked for more. The men promptly drank the rest, calling it "mother's milk" and agreeing that it was worth a trip of many miles.

Young Frenchmen, runaways from settlements on the lower St. Lawrence River, soon learned the river route to the environs of the upper lake—what they called the *pays d'en haut*, the Upper Country. Pausing at Bawating,

"the place at the falls," they dubbed it Sault Ste. Marie. The village became a focal point of trading systems that extended through the entire Great Lakes and Ohio River valley regions and beyond.

Besides its central location, another factor made Bawating a gathering point. St. Mary's River had an abundant year-round supply of whitefish, enough to feed the 3,000 or more people who converged for summer trading, ball games, gambling, sports events, seasonal festivals, and religious ceremonies.

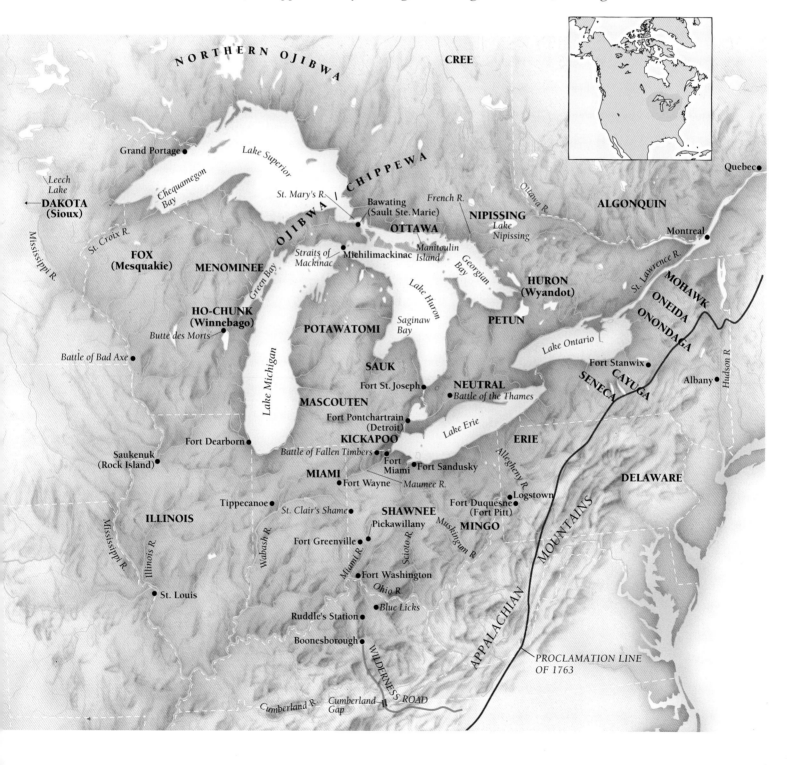

Right: A Northern Ojibwa family, painted by Swiss artist Peter Rindisbacher, lives in a traditional Indian village but owns various items — including brass nose pendants, bracelets, and beaded chokers — acquired through trade with Europeans. Below right: This richly ornamented cradleboard was used by an Ojibwa mother to carry her baby, which was wrapped securely to the board and protected from falls by the decorated hoop at the top.

◄ Almost from the first appearance of European fur traders and colonists, native societies around the Great Lakes and Ohio River valley were caught up in a relentless cycle of violence, dispersal, and relocation. Most of the tribal territories shown at left were those occupied in the early 1600's; events of the next 200 years would leave a drastically altered landscape. Also shown are settlements of the French, English, and Americans and locations of important events.

Radiating outward from the hub at Bawating and from the equally strategic Straits of Mackinac to the south, a great arc of more than 20 tribes stretched south to the Ohio Valley and west to the Mississippi. They had lived there for centuries, shifted sometimes by population pressures or the gains and losses of land in war.

In the north those later called Ojibwa or Chippewa (Anishinabe, "original people," to themselves; Ojibwa and Chippewa were variants of a Dakota name for them) overarched the entire Great Lakes region, with a population of as many as 100,000 people. In ancient lore, the Ojibwa shared with the Ottawa and the Potawatomi a tradition of having migrated from the St. Lawrence Valley. At the Straits of Mackinac they split: the Ojibwa settled first at Bawating, and the Ottawa on Manitoulin Island, while the Potawatomi ventured south to the Lower Peninsula of Michigan. The three groups, who speak similar Algonquian languages, still refer to their tribal alliance as the Three Fires, and to the Potawatomi as the Keepers of the Fire.

On the eastern flank of the Great Lakes region were the Wyandot, an alliance of Iroquoian-speaking communities. Because of the spiky coiffure of their warriors, the French called them Huron, "bristly head." They lived in a cluster of densely settled longhouse villages on good agricultural land southeast of Lake Huron's Georgian Bay. Here they raised large crops of corn and tobacco, which they traded along with fishnets and pottery to tribes in the interior. Two allies ferried these goods on their way: the Nipissing, who dealt with the Cree to the north, and the Ottawa, who operated west to Lake Superior and Lake Michigan. In return came cured meat, dried fish, copper, and high-quality furs.

When the French arrived they found skillful allies in the Huron, who became middlemen in the hugely profitable fur trade and acquired iron, cloth, and other European valuables. But there was a hidden price. In 1620 the Huron numbered perhaps 20,000 people; by 1640 they had lost about half their population to measles, smallpox, and other alien diseases.

Farther west, the mosaic of tribal groupings became even more complex. Green Bay was the ancient homeland of the Winnebago (today called Ho-Chunk), the only Siouan-speaking group in the Great Lakes region. To their north lay the country of the Menominee, the Wild Rice People; to the west of them lived the Mesquakie, or Red Earth People, better known by the name French traders gave them — the Fox.

The Fox were ancient enemies of the Ojibwa and also of the Dakota (or Sioux) to their

west in Minnesota. The Ojibwa, in turn, were enemies of both the Fox and the Dakota. Seasonal warfare was constant in this area.

South of Lake Michigan were the Illinois people, who lived in a dozen separate villages on both sides of the Mississippi River. In this region of fertile prairie, the Illinois were a gardening and buffalo-hunting people (bison remained common here into the 18th century). But the inevitable effects of disease and warfare reduced the tribe to five towns clustered on the Illinois and Mississippi rivers. To compensate, they periodically raided west of the Mississippi and brought back slaves captured from Pawnee and other Plains villages.

The home territory of the Miami centered at what is now Fort Wayne, Indiana, a strategic location at a portage point to the Wabash River. The Miami maintained generally unfriendly relations with their western neighbors, the Illinois. Farther east, in Ohio, the dominant people were the Shawnee (from an Algon-quian term meaning "southerners"). The palisaded towns of the Shawnee lined the region's waterways, and their cornfields spread for miles across the rich bottomland.

Land, Family, and Tradition

Despite myriad differences in local customs, the peoples of the entire region—from the Ojibwa in the north to the Shawnee in the south—were part of the same larger social order. Except where the growing season was too short, they all raised the storable staples: corn, beans, squash, and gourds. The Illinois even

Rapids like these on the Tahquamenon River in Michigan meant the same thing everywhere in the Upper Country—portage, get out and carry the boat. Inset: a model birchbark war canoe made by an Ottawa chief, its six rowers depicting tribesmen of his day.

Chippewa warrior Strong Wind was portrayed in full regalia by George Catlin: face paint, earrings of wampum and bone, glass bead necklaces, a shell gorget, and two peace medals.

Below: The owner of this Menominee war bundle dreamed of the powerful "thunderers," painted on his deerskin mat (detailed are the Chief Thunderer and his helpers) to appear when the bundle was opened. Inset: a catlinite pipe bowl from a Miami war bundle.

At puberty every young woman knew she must begin retiring to the women's hut during her menstrual cycle. And every young man, after proper preparation, moved off to a secluded spot for fasting and prayer in hopes of receiving a vision that would become his guardian spirit for the rest of his life.

In the old days our people had no education. All their wisdom and knowledge came to them from dreams. They tested their dreams and in that way learned their own strength.
—*Ojibwa elder*

Religion permeated daily life in every realm. Although the languages differed, people throughout the region believed in a higher power, called the Master of Life or the Great Spirit or the Creator. Other spirits or beings were available to intercede with the higher power on behalf of earthly people. There was a spiritual essence in rocks, trees—everywhere

acquired foreign watermelon seeds. The Sauk and Huron raised thousands of bushels of surplus corn to use in trade. The spring and fall fish runs and the sap from the sugar maple were as important as a corn patch; dried blueberries would last through the winter. Wild rice was especially abundant along the Wisconsin-Minnesota border. The Dakota lived on fish and wild rice and traveled in birchbark canoes. To the north, where long winters discouraged farming, the people were mainly hunters, fishermen, and traders.

The people of the Upper Country loved children, and the villages teemed with them. Among the Algonquian groups, a child was born into the father's clan. The Huron, like other Iroquoian peoples, traced their descent through the mother's. In either case, clan affiliation remained a primary source of personal identity—though everyone had his or her own given name and sometimes several others acquired over a lifetime.

Pampered by their parents, indulged by a sprawling network of more distant relatives, children learned by storytelling and example rather than physical punishment. Grandparents were the principal teachers. Among the lessons of the elders was the value of generosity and sharing. Hoarding was deplored, and status was measured by how much a man gave away rather than how much he could accumulate.

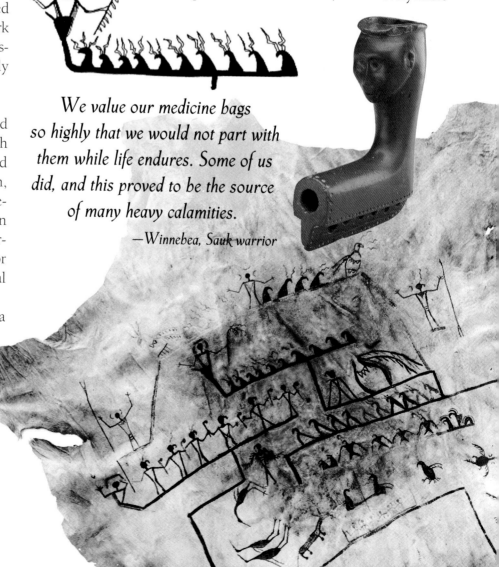

We value our medicine bags so highly that we would not part with them while life endures. Some of us did, and this proved to be the source of many heavy calamities.
—*Winnebea, Sauk warrior*

birchbark maps of the migration route with symbolic markings that indicated the songs and procedure for stages of the initiation rites. The Midewiwin promoted the knowledge of herbal medicine and advocated balance in all aspects of life.

Verily, the sky clears
When my Midé drum sounds for me.
Verily, the waters are smooth
When my Midé drum sounds for me.

—*Chippewa song of praise
for the Midewiwin*

The religion spread among other Great Lakes tribes: Potawatomi, Ottawa, Sauk, Winnebago, Fox, Kickapoo, and Shawnee. Great Lakes Indians, like others, developed an extensive knowledge of plant medicine. There were medicines to attract animals to traps and snares and to lure fish; love medicines, cures for respiratory problems and a whole catalog of human ailments, as well as contraceptive and abortion-inducing medications, insect repellents, and cures for poison ivy and snakebite.

Chiefs and Warriors

No great domains or chieftains controlled the Upper Country; each village was an independent community. A village leader was selected, usually by a council of elders, on merit alone. Proven ability in hunting and warfare, courage, stamina, and generosity—these were the valued traits. So, too, was skill as an orator. Since no village leader could force a path of action, he often needed to exhort, inspire, and cajole. Decisions were made

The Ojibwa holy man above, like other initiates, was entrusted with sacred Mide bark scrolls, drums used in healing rites, and (inset) inscribed wooden cases in which ceremonial eagle feathers were safely kept.

Carved figures called Manitoukanacs were placed on the path to an Ojibwa home to guard household members. People offered thanks by winding colorful cloth or ribbons around the silent sentries; the wooden specimen at right stands more than three feet high.

in the physical environment. All Great Lakes peoples (among others) told and retold the adventures of mythical figures who gave humans many valuable lessons.

There is not a lake or mountain that had not connected with it some story of delight or wonder, and nearly every beast and bird is the subject of some storyteller.... Night after night for weeks I have sat and eagerly listened. The days following, the characters would haunt me at every step, and every moving leaf would seem to be a voice of a spirit.

—*George Copway, Ojibwa*

The Ojibwa developed an institution of great importance called the Grand Medicine Society, or Midewiwin, and initiated members into the knowledge and rituals of the Mide (sometimes spelled Midé) religion. As part of the initiation ceremonies, a leader recounted stories of the origin of the people near the salt seas who had been guided west by a sacred shell. Mide priests kept

by consensus, with a highly formalized (and time-consuming) system of debate. On questions of war and peace, talks could consume days on end. A minority faction might move to another village or even join a different tribe.

Villages usually had a separate war leader, and joining a war party was a matter of choice. Even so, warfare was the bone and sinew of life in the region, deemed essential for sharpening the survival skills of the entire society. The ball games and running competitions of peacetime trained the young men of the village in attack and rapid retreat. Even small children were periodically deprived of food and water in order to inure them to the rigors of forced marches.

Having decided to go to battle, the warriors would set out after spring fishing or planting. They might be gone a few weeks or sometimes the entire summer, usually breaking up into war parties of six or ten—groups small enough to test their bravery and skill by penetrating enemy territory and returning unharmed. Most commonly, they attacked an enemy hunting party away from its village; captured warriors were subjected to ritual torture and death—although a very lucky captive might be saved for adoption. Alternately, the raiders might seize women and children out gathering wood and either adopt them or hold them for ransom. In either case, the number of victims was never large.

But one thing was essential: an enemy. Every tribal group had a traditional opponent. And since the motive for battle was usually revenge and retaliation, the bloodshed could perpetuate itself for generations.

❧

These are the words that were given to my great-grandfather by the Master of Life: "At some time there shall come among you a stranger, speaking a language you do not understand. He will try to buy the land from you, but do not sell it; keep it for an inheritance to your children."

—*Aseenewub, Red Lake Ojibwa*

Of Medicine and Memory

Said to be a gift from the Creator to the Ojibwa and their neighbors, the Midewiwin sought to combat illness through a knowledge of herbal cures and sacred ceremonies. The elements of each ritual were recorded in pictures on birchbark or wood, but only a select few learned to interpret them.

From a birchbark scroll of the Southern Ojibwa, this drawing depicts a sacred procession as it weaves around two cedar poles, or "trees of life."

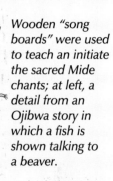

Wooden "song boards" were used to teach an initiate the sacred Mide chants; at left, a detail from an Ojibwa story in which a fish is shown talking to a beaver.

A healing chant is depicted on a bark record from Leech Lake, Minnesota. After the chant, water from the lake was mixed with tobacco to make a salve.

This rendering from an Ojibwa birchbark scroll shows a bear— one of the most powerful Mide spirits—behind a shield.

Images found on an Ojibwa comb case include a person with raised arms, suggesting spiritual power, and an otter spirit, perhaps the first to receive Mide initiation rites.

Four humanlike figures hold hands on a sacred scroll; horns traditionally were signs of supernatural abilities.

Plant images drawn on a Potawatomi prescription stick gave the "recipe" for an herbal compound.

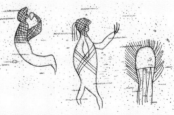

An Ojibwa scroll bears this picture of what may be a Mide medicine man (center), his heart visible, reaching out to higher powers, while the seated figure at left swallows a potion.

159

Strangers Among Us

The Man with a Hat that the old Ojibwa priest met on the St. Lawrence early in the 17th century was a French trader. There were perhaps a hundred Indian communities in the Great Lakes area then, when the coming of the Europeans introduced three new classes of humans: French traders, Jesuit missionaries, and in future decades an aggressive influx of English soldiers and settlers.

Of the three, the traders dealt best with the native people. What they wanted, of course, were furs—particularly quality beaver pelts from the north country, much in demand by European hat makers. Some were licensed merchants from Montreal, who usually hired seasoned *voyageurs* to paddle their wares into the fur-bearing areas. Many others were independent *coureurs de bois*, "runners of the woods"—unofficial, often illegal, and always tough. Able to live off the land, a coureur de bois could build a canoe, carry hundreds of pounds over a portage, or survive the bitter cold of a woodlands winter.

He rode the shifting currents of tribal loyalties and was the most adaptable of all the European colonials, adopting the customs and codes of behavior that brought understanding, respect, and profit in a foreign culture. Spreading throughout Indian settlements, these hardy opportunists learned the natives' languages, ate their food, wore their clothes, and married into their families, acquiring ties of kinship with the native population unparalleled in the 17th-century colonial world.

A French fur trapper (in an unmistakably European hat) canoes downriver with his native wife and children in "The Voyageurs," by Charles Deas. Left: the Fox preferred otter-pelt hats; cotton, silk, and glass beads decorate this one.

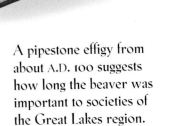

A pipestone effigy from about A.D. 100 suggests how long the beaver was important to societies of the Great Lakes region.

The Black Robes—Jesuits—also traded, but their real quarry was Indian souls for their God. In this they met with mixed success. Most Indians discovered the powers of these European shamans to be singularly ineffective. Fox warriors tried marking crosses on their clothing, but enemy arrows penetrated anyway. In the Ojibwa country, leaders considered the merits of Christianity with hours of thoughtful debate. They concluded that saying "the Prayer" might be suitable for the overseas people, but was not meant for them. Indeed, they decided that the Great Spirit had sent his Son to the overseas people because they were so wicked.

The Indians wanted not prayers and crosses but axes and knives, wool blankets, European-style shirts, fancy hats, and scores of other luxurious, exotic items. In return they offered furs. And the European appetite for fine animal furs seemed to have no limit. The best pelts came from the vast woodlands west and north of the Alleghenies, so the fur trade meant a complex network of supply reaching deep into the continent. The enormous profits also meant war.

The Beaver Wars

As the middle of the 17th century approached, the struggle for new fur sources prompted the Iroquois, who already dominated from the Hudson River to Lake Erie, to reach for more. Starting around 1640 and for the next six decades, Iroquois raiders struck and struck again, battling to take over the trade routes and rich trapping grounds around the Great Lakes. So began the spiral of bloodshed known as the Beaver Wars that would change forever the world of the Upper Country.

First to fall were the Huron and their allies north of the St. Lawrence. Acquiring guns and shot from the British—who hoped to break the French trade monopoly—the Iroquois began hitting outlying Huron villages. After a series of raids and truces, a surprise winter attack in 1649 by 1,000 Mohawk and Seneca warriors panicked the villagers east of Geor-

gian Bay. Thousands of Huron captives, mainly women and children, were absorbed into Iroquois towns. Other Hurons fled in small, scattered bands to seek refuge with tribes farther north and west. The heyday of Huron prosperity abruptly ended.

Iroquois war parties fanned out over the trade routes, spreading terror and chaos. In the next decade they crushed the Petun (also called the Tobacco Indians), then the would-be Neutral tribe north of Lake Erie: neutrality was no shield. Ranging farther west, members

SIR·JOS·JEBB.

of the Iroquois League attacked the Ottawa in 1660, then the Illinois and Miami, and for good measure they raided the Nipissing and the Potawatomi.

The north country seethed with desperate tribes on the move. Nipissings took refuge at Sault Ste. Marie, then spent decades in exile north of Lake Superior. The Potawatomi fled north to the Straits of Mackinac, where Lake Michigan flows into Lake Huron, then veered west to Green Bay. The Miami of Wabash River country pushed into southwestern Wisconsin, forming a loose coalition with the Fox, Kickapoo, and Mascouten.

Two Ottawa leaders from the fortified trading base at Michilimackinac wait for an audience with representatives of the king; their clothing is a measure of the pomp and decorum that surrounded such events.

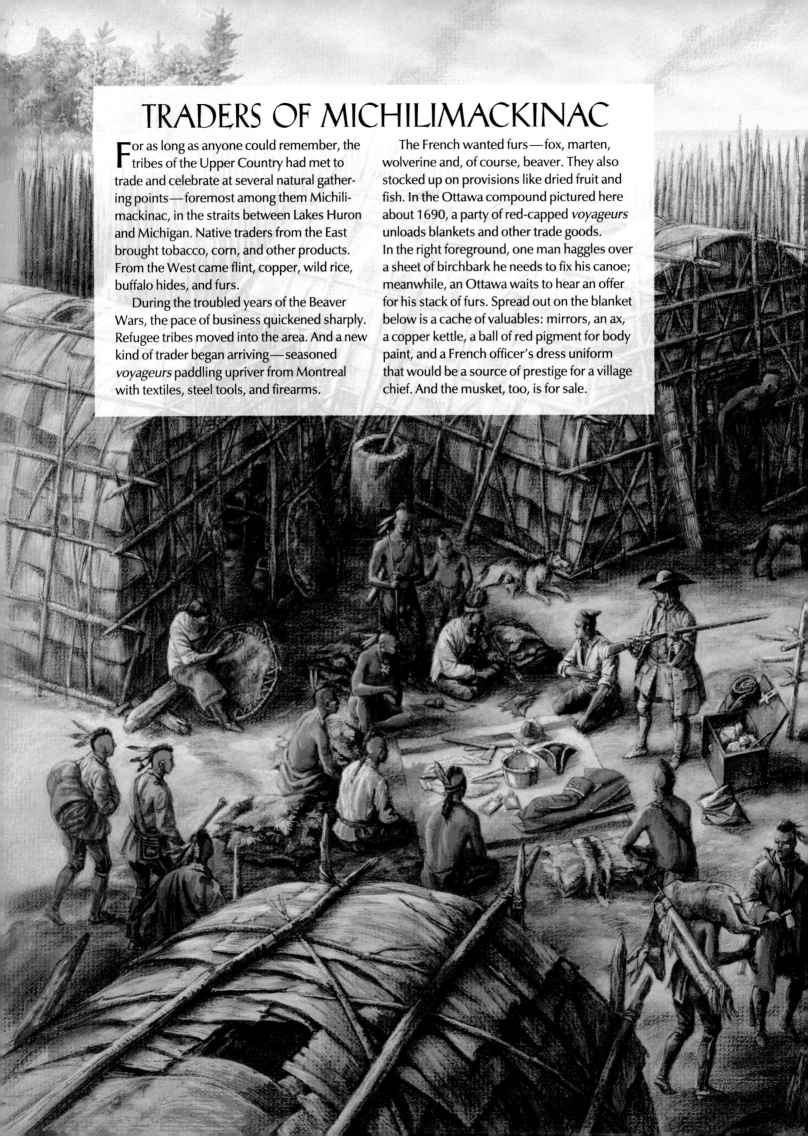

TRADERS OF MICHILIMACKINAC

For as long as anyone could remember, the tribes of the Upper Country had met to trade and celebrate at several natural gathering points—foremost among them Michilimackinac, in the straits between Lakes Huron and Michigan. Native traders from the East brought tobacco, corn, and other products. From the West came flint, copper, wild rice, buffalo hides, and furs.

During the troubled years of the Beaver Wars, the pace of business quickened sharply. Refugee tribes moved into the area. And a new kind of trader began arriving—seasoned *voyageurs* paddling upriver from Montreal with textiles, steel tools, and firearms.

The French wanted furs—fox, marten, wolverine and, of course, beaver. They also stocked up on provisions like dried fruit and fish. In the Ottawa compound pictured here about 1690, a party of red-capped *voyageurs* unloads blankets and other trade goods. In the right foreground, one man haggles over a sheet of birchbark he needs to fix his canoe; meanwhile, an Ottawa waits to hear an offer for his stack of furs. Spread out on the blanket below is a cache of valuables: mirrors, an ax, a copper kettle, a ball of red pigment for body paint, and a French officer's dress uniform that would be a source of prestige for a village chief. And the musket, too, is for sale.

Even after firearms were available, war clubs remained part of the native arsenal; long used to earn battle honors, they were still deadly in hand-to-hand combat. Below are two styles from the Great Lakes region: a traditional ball-headed club (with an otter figure at the top) and a newer version, adapted from a gunstock and fitted with an iron blade.

An Ojibwa victory over Iroquois invaders near Hudson Bay is remembered in a birch-bark drawing of an unlucky Mohawk at the mercy of two Ojibwa warriors.

The remaining Huron, meanwhile, began a decades-long odyssey. With their constant traveling companions, the Ottawa, they drifted first into Sioux country on the northern Mississippi. Driven from there, they moved in separate groups into Wisconsin, then north to Chequamegon Bay on western Lake Superior, where they set up a trading base.

For a time they seemed safe. A force of allied tribes demolished a large Iroquois war party near Sault Ste. Marie in 1665, thus permanently freeing the northern lakes from the Iroquois scourge. But safety still eluded them. Threatened by attack from the Sioux, the Huron and Ottawa retreated to the north shore of the Straits of Mackinac, at a spot called Michilimackinac. There, at the cutting edge of France's New World empire, they sought protection from the friendly forces of the French king.

Asylum with the French

Even as the tides of Indian warfare swirled about them, French traders and missionaries were pushing ever farther into the Upper Country. The explorer Jean Nicolet, first of a long line of newcomers, had paddled through the Straits of Mack-

inac as early as 1634. Nicolas Perrot, fur trader and backwoods diplomat, reached Green Bay in 1667, at the height of hostilities, in an effort to break up a long-standing Ottawa trade monopoly with the local Wisconsin tribes. Hard on his heels, Jesuit father Jacques Marquette arrived, seeking converts and founding missions at Sault Ste. Marie and Michilimackinac.

French military posts sprang up all across the region, from the forests north of Lake Superior, along Lake Michigan, to the rivers of central Illinois. Green Bay became a major trading post. The surrounding native population may have reached as high as 20,000 as refugee bands poured in from the eastern battlegrounds.

The focus of activity remained Michilimackinac, however. New native villages sprang up around the spires of Marquette's St. Ignace mission and under the ramparts of Fort de Baude. More than ever, the Straits became the place to gather, to swap news and barter trade goods, to celebrate festivals and organize war parties, to mingle with other tribes, drink brandy, and peddle furs.

As the tribes converged around the French installations, and the numbers of refugees in-

Exile and Return

And still the wars continued. The Iroquois war chiefs, turning their attention from the lakes region, struck deep into the Ohio Valley. They swept through the lands of the Shawnee in the 1670's, razing villages, destroying corn crops, and sending flotillas of refugee canoes down the Ohio and Mississippi rivers.

One contingent of Shawnee refugees moved west to the Illinois country, joining a huge intertribal community of 18,000 people that was gathering around newly established Fort St. Louis on the upper Illinois River, at present-day Peoria. They settled in among Miamis, Illinois, and a number of others, all prepared to defend themselves against any new assault. But most Shawnee groups kept moving, embarking on a diaspora throughout the southlands that lasted many generations. Not until the next century would they return to their Ohio Valley homelands.

Then, little by little, the balance began to shift. When Iroquois raiders thrust into Illinois in 1684, combined native forces from Fort St. Louis turned them back. In the Lake Huron area a French garrison at Fort St. Joseph, at the lake's southern tip, became a focal point for multitribal counterattacks against nearby Iroquois settlements. Across the river the Ontario peninsula was being reconquered by Ojibwa people from the north, who claimed it had belonged to their forefathers before the Iroquois came. The Miami and related tribes began returning to the Wabash River country, and the Potawatomi reoccupied ancestral sites in southern Michigan.

An uneasy peace began to take hold. The Iroquois still dominated vast areas—from Canada's Ottawa River in the north to the Cumberland River in Kentucky and east from

creased, so did the frictions between competing trade groups. The large band of Ottawa at Michilimackinac became the principal middlemen for the Ojibwa in supplying furs to the French. In Green Bay the Potawatomi distributed lavish gifts in hopes of achieving the same end. The Fox, deeply concerned that European rifles were being traded to their archenemy, the Sioux, joined forces with the Iroquois in order to disrupt that deadly flow of merchandise—and at the same time they hoped to obtain a larger share of beaver profits for themselves.

Armed with weapons reflecting the evolving technology of Great Lakes life— a bow with arrows, a gunstock club, and a rifle—Chief Peguis of the Lake Winnipeg Saulteaux was painted in the early 1800's by Peter Rindisbacher.

Created from a beaver pelt and decorated with porcupine quills, this Menominee medicine bag bears witness to the beaver's importance in spiritual as well as practical aspects of woodlands life.

Lake Erie. In the meantime, an aggressive new player had entered the scene. For nearly a century the English—patrons of the Iroquois—had been content to develop their colonies along the Eastern seaboard, growing tobacco and distilling rum. In the fur trade they dealt mostly through their Iroquois agents.

Now they began moving west. Already British merchants had set up trading posts in the far north, on Canada's St. James Bay. British arms and textiles—better and cheaper than the French—began filtering into the Upper Country. An English trader from Albany showed up at Michilimackinac in 1683, much to the dismay of the French. In 1690 fighting broke out in New York and New England between the forces of France and England. The two great powers made a show of patching up their differences. But the tensions remained, foreshadowing things to come.

Celebrating Peace: Montreal 1701

As the bloodshed abated in the Upper Country, the governors of New France took advantage of the lull to consolidate their position. Ambassadors went out from Montreal, inviting all the tribes to gather for a mass celebration of friendship and peace. Prisoners would be exchanged, and all remaining quarrels put to rest. Most of France's Indian allies readily agreed, and a large delegation of Great Lakes leaders met with the French governor general—"Onontio," they called him—to pledge their loyalty. But the French also made a particular effort to bring in the Iroquois, hoping to woo them from the British. The Iroquois councils deliberated in their unhurried, consensus-building manner for a full two years, weighing the pros and cons with their English patrons. Then they, too, decided to accept the proposed French accord.

Finally the day arrived. In midsummer of 1701 the canoes started landing on the beach at Montreal—Sauk, Fox, and Winnebago, Potawatomi and Miami, spiky-haired Huron and feathered Ojibwa, buckskin-clad Kickapoo, and Sioux in their eagle feathers and buffalo robes. In addition to these French-allied tribes came their former enemies, the Five Nations of the Iroquois League—Seneca, Cayuga, Onondaga, Oneida, Mohawk.

Close to 1,300 people attended, representing 39 separate tribes, and together they feasted and parleyed and smoked the calumet. The delegates worked out some last-minute details. The Iroquois received the right to hunt in Ontario country, and western Indians were given free access to trade in New York. Then on August 4 everyone assembled in a newly built courtyard just outside the city to hear the final orations and witness the signing of a

treaty that officially ended decades of intertribal war in the Upper Country.

But important issues remained unresolved. Some of the Great Lakes tribes complained they were running short of trade goods, the result of a French decision to vacate their far western trading posts. Intensive trapping had created a temporary oversupply of beaver pelts, and the French needed to cut costs. For the Indians, however, the measure hurt. A new French post, Fort Pontchartrain at Detroit, helped a bit. Then in 1715 the French reopened Fort Michilimackinac across the Straits of Mackinac from its old site, reestablishing trade in the northern lakes.

Far more difficult was the matter of the Fox. All through the peace negotiations the Fox protested bitterly that French traders were still supplying their Sioux enemies with guns. Already the arms deals had driven them into a

Hundreds of tribal leaders took part in the pageantry of the 1701 Montreal Peace Treaty illustrated here, and they arrayed themselves in appropriate finery. Two men who stood out even in this company were Onanguisse (front, center) of the Potawatomi, wearing the skin of a buffalo complete with horns, and the Fox delegate Miskousouath (right center), who delighted conferees with his powdered French wig. Presiding from a chair atop a platform for local dignitaries was Louis-Hector de Callières, governor-general of New France (far right). Standing impressively in a robe of beaver pelts, Chief Hassaki of the Kiskakon Ottawa opened the festivities with a speech and a display of one of the wampum belts exchanged by treaty signers; above, two belts thought to have been part of that exchange.

WAR DANCE OF THE SAUKS AND FOXES.

secret alliance with the Iroquois. Back in 1670, when Iroquois raiders attacked a Fox hunting camp in northeastern Illinois, the Fox elders made a decision not to retaliate. Instead, they sent a messenger suggesting that the Iroquois had surely mistaken the hunting party for someone else—Potawatomi, perhaps. Following this overture, the Fox ambassador returned with an Iroquois trading party, six canoe loads of merchandise, and an invitation to trade with the English in Albany.

Forced to play both sides in the high-stakes game of woodland power politics, the Fox did not take kindly to insult or neglect. French arms continued flowing to both the Sioux and the Ojibwa. And no matter how loudly the Fox objected, the French refused to listen.

A war dance of the Upper Country was documented in a 19th-century engraving that accurately illustrates the participants' head-dresses and other regalia and the highly individualistic designs of their war paint.

A bird's-eye view shows Fort Pontchartrain, built by the French at Detroit, as it appeared around 1750.

The Fox Strike Back

The disputants came to blows at the new French garrison at Detroit. Founded in 1701 by soldier and trader Antoine de la Mothe, sieur de Cadillac, Detroit was rapidly becoming a major center for soldiers, traders, and French *habitants,* whose graceful windmills and long, narrow cornfields lined the Detroit River. A large community of Huron and Ottawa refugees already lived in the area. Cadillac, ambitious to expand the fur trade, invited other tribes to come settle. More Huron moved in, and a sizable group of Potawatomi. Then in 1710 there arrived 1,000 Fox from Wisconsin—and with them, disaster.

The newcomers expected to be treated as guests and accorded proper privileges. But Cadillac had been assigned to another post, and the new French commandant showed little interest in welcoming them. Following a series of violent incidents in 1712, French troops laid siege to the Fox village. A truce was negotiated, but the French promptly broke it. Then, as the Fox families tried to escape under cover of a nighttime thunderstorm, the soldiers moved in and slaughtered most of them.

It was a betrayal the Fox never forgave. For the next quarter century Fox war parties staged lightning raids on key French outposts, crippling trade in the Upper Country. Nothing was safe. Isolated villages, canoe portage routes, even boats carrying corn from Detroit to Michilimackinac—Fox raiders hit them all.

The French tried to crush them—repeatedly—but the Fox always seemed to slip away. Superb military engineers, they fortified their villages with massive earthworks and oak-beam barricades. In one such compound, at Butte de Mort in Wisconsin, 500 Fox warriors withstood a siege by a French army sent from Montreal, which bombarded them with cannon ferried in by reinforced canoes.

Adroit Fox diplomacy enhanced their battlefield prowess. They made peace with the Ojibwa in 1724 and allied themselves in 1727 with their former enemies the Sioux. But the question of a new truce with the French opened a rift that could not be closed. Montreal enlisted its Indian allies, including most of the Great Lakes and Illinois tribes, and in 1728 sent a massive force into Fox country.

> You know well that chiefs like us, although well intentioned, are scarcely listened to.
> —Ouachala, Fox elder, on young warriors' refusal to compromise

The Fox by this time had split apart. One faction dispersed to continue waging war; the larger group headed east, hoping to find refuge with the Iroquois in New York. But in the prairies of central Illinois, they were seen by a band of Illinois hunters, who alerted the French. The Fox hastily fortified themselves in a village and soon came under attack. Among their opponents were the Sauk, who gave sanctuary to the Fox children, but of the adults remaining in the village, only 50 escaped death or capture. In the next decade, Fox survivors found refuge among the Sauk and negotiated another truce with the French—which the French again violated.

Enraged, they lashed out and killed as many Frenchmen as they could, including the commandants at Green Bay and Michilimackinac. The French in response had their prize Fox hostages, Chief Kiyala and his wife, sold as slaves in Martinique. Finally, in 1742 the Fox ended the cycle of violence and betrayal by sending emissaries to Montreal to promise "Onontio" that they would wage war no more.

West of the barrier to white expansion posed by the Appalachian Mountains lay the fertile soil and game-rich woods of the Ohio River valley. It was a tempting prize to land-hungry colonials—and an ancient homeland to the Shawnee, a gift from the Creator that must be defended at all costs.

White Battles, Red Blood

Even as the last of the Fox retired to their Wisconsin homeland, wandering bands of Shawnee began moving back to the Ohio Valley. Other groups were filtering in as well—Huron from the area around Detroit, Delaware refugees from the Eastern seaboard, Munsee from New Jersey, and even some Iroquois splinter groups known as Mingos. At the same time, the first English traders began to arrive.

Most came across the Appalachian Mountains from Pennsylvania. They made their base at Logstown, a multitribal village on the Ohio River several miles downstream from the

three-way fork where Pittsburgh stands today. With high-quality guns, knives, hatchets, and blankets—all offered at the best exchange rates—they threatened to displace the French as the region's prime supplier of trade goods. This, along with overlapping French and British land claims, triggered an escalating string of armed clashes.

> When the Frenchmen arrived at these falls, they came and kissed us. . . . They never mocked at our ceremonies, and they never molested the places of our dead. Seven generations of men have passed away, and we have not forgotten it.
>
> —*Chippewa chief*

One of the first was a French attack on a British trading post at Pickawillany, newly opened for business among the Miami in western Ohio. By reaching this far west, the British were, in effect, expanding their American empire into the realm of New France—and this the French could not allow. So in 1752 a force of Ottawa and Ojibwa warriors under French command swept down and

Portrait of a warrior: the Fox tribesman below, name unknown, was painted about 1731.

obliterated the post, killing a British trader and 13 Miami defenders. They seized the Miami leader, La Demoiselle, and—as the chronicle puts it—"made a broth" of him.

Thus rose the curtain on the so-called French and Indian War, the last colonial conflict in America between the great imperial powers. France threw up a chain of log-walled forts across the upper Ohio Valley and marshalled its Indian allies. By the time the fighting spilled across to Europe—where it was known as the Seven Years War (1756–63)—clashes had erupted in Ohio and Pennsylvania, north across the Great Lakes, and as far east as Nova Scotia. Indian leaders proclaimed their outrage, pointing out that Europeans should fight on their own soil, not theirs. But many of them took up arms for one side or the other.

The Ohio Valley remained the strategic crucible. A new British commander, General Edward Braddock, arrived in 1755 and immediately set out with 2,000 troops to capture Fort Duquesne, at the forks of the Ohio River. Less than ten miles from his goal, he ran

Gen. Edward Braddock and his British troops, approaching Fort Duquesne in 1755, were surprised by Indian forces allied with the French. As he falls from his horse (left) in this detail from "Braddock's Defeat," the horse's bridle is caught by Maj. George Washington.

A meeting in 1760 brought Ottawa chief Pontiac face to face with English major Robert Rogers, and on that occasion they smoked a calumet of peace. Three years later, Pontiac launched a multitribal uprising against British colonial authority.

into an ambush by a tribal coalition allied with the French. Braddock had four horses shot from under him and died of his wounds. Almost half his men died with him. One who survived was his aide-de-camp, a 23-year-old major named George Washington.

Braddock's defeat won all the tribes of the Upper Country to the French side. Even Britain's staunch allies, the Iroquois, wavered as western Indians swept the frontier in a series of devastating attacks. But within three years the tide had turned. Another British force took Fort Duquesne, renamed it Fort Pitt, and turned it into Britain's western headquarters. French military collapse soon followed and 1759 was marked by a succession of British victories culminating in the Battle of Quebec in September. The following year the French surrendered all of Canada.

Hostilities officially ended with the Treaty of Paris in 1763, which placed all lands east of the Mississippi in British hands. Garrisons of Redcoats took over the old French forts, and English-speaking settlers began crossing the Appalachians to carve out farms on the newly won frontier. But for the Indian people of the

Great Lakes and Ohio Valley—whom no one had bothered to consult—nothing was resolved. Far from feeling the sting of defeat, they considered themselves the winners.

Englishman, although you have conquered the French, you have not yet conquered us. We are not your slaves. These lakes, these woods and mountains were left us by our ancestors. We will part with them to no one.
    —Pontiac, Ottawa

Even before the ink was dry on the Treaty of Paris, seismic rumblings of discontent were vibrating through the Upper Country. The new British administrators seemed both arrogant and stingy. In years past, the French had followed a traditional path of frontier diplomacy, giving out food and trade goods in return for pledges of friendship and permission to use tribal lands. Most veteran British hands wanted to continue the practice. But to Lord Jeffrey Amherst, Britain's recently arrived governor general, handing gifts to Indians was mere bribery. "If they do not behave properly," he snorted, "they are to be punished."

Pontiac's Defiance

Even more troubling was the fear that England's victory would bring in a surge of white settlers. Resentment was already building against the white presence, fueled by a Delaware holy man, Neolin, who lived among the refugee villagers of the Muskingum Valley in Ohio. The Delaware Prophet, as he is more commonly known, delivered a scathing verbal assault on all whites, inflaming the tribes with a charismatic call for a return to the old ways—no more guns, no more trade goods, no more brandy or rum.

One of his listeners was an Ottawa chief named Pontiac, who had fought beside the French. A powerful orator in his own right, Pontiac traveled about the Upper Country, rising to speak persua-

The Delaware and Shawnee stopped fighting the British in late 1764, but peace was not formalized until July 1765. The treaty with the Delaware (above) was signed by Sir William Johnson; Shawnee chief Paytakootha, or Flying Clouds (inset above), negotiated a similar pact for his people. A symbol of Shawnee authority, the eagle feather headdress (above right) was on conspicuous display at such meetings.

sively at the camp fires and in councils. He envisioned an Indian confederation spanning the forests and valleys from the Great Lakes to the Mississippi. And summoning up the feelings of pan-Indian unity that had prevailed in the recent war, he called for the restoration of the French and renewal of the anti-British alliance.

Then in May of 1763, Pontiac made his move. Leading a multitribal force that included Ojibwa, Potawatomi, non-Christian Huron, and Menominee— as well as his own Ottawa—he laid siege to the British garrison at Detroit. Within a matter of weeks eleven frontier British forts had fallen to allied Indian warriors. The attacks came so swiftly that often the defenders had no idea a rebellion had begun. At Fort Sandusky, on Lake Erie, the raiders simply asked for a meeting with the commander, then seized control.

In taking Fort Michilimackinac, the Ojibwa and Sauk invaders staged a more elaborate ruse. They began with a lacrosse match held

just outside the main gate, ostensibly to honor the king's birthday. Suddenly one of the players lobbed the ball back into the stockade, and everyone rushed in after it. Dropping their lacrosse sticks, they picked up rifles that had been smuggled in earlier by the women.

By July only two besieged garrisons—Fort Pontchartrain at Detroit and Fort Pitt at the forks of the Ohio—still held out. To relieve Fort Pitt, Lord Amherst sent a task force of 450 veteran soldiers under Col. Henry Bouquet. Then, on his instructions, the fort commander invited the Delaware attackers to parley and presented them with a handkerchief and two blankets that had been infected with smallpox. Amherst's sinister experiment—perhaps the first use of germ warfare in American history—accomplished its goal. The epidemic spread through the Indian ranks and into their villages along the Ohio Valley. By autumn the siege had collapsed.

At Detroit the siege was also breaking up. An early freeze began driving its attackers to winter hunting camps, and the French, who up to now had been supplying Pontiac's forces with arms and encouragement, withdrew their support. Bowing to the inevitable, Pontiac called off his men.

But the rebellion had sent shock waves of alarm through Britain's Colonial administration. An estimated 2,000 British soldiers and settlers had lost their lives. Lord Amherst was recalled. Facing the prospect of extended off-and-on conflict in the west, the British began to build the same complex system of alliance and gift exchange that the French had maintained for a century and a half before them.

Royal Words

In addition, the British took a major step to calm Indian concerns about the threatened influx of white settlers. In October 1763, even before the fighting had ended, England's George III issued a proclamation limiting Colonial habitation to the region east of the Appalachian Mountains. Everything beyond the Proclamation Line, including most of the lakes and river valleys of the Upper Country, was officially designated as Indian territory.

Any hope that the Proclamation Line would stop anyone soon proved illusory. Settlers streamed west as though the ban had been an invitation. By the end of 1765, some 2,000 families, mostly squatters with no legal title to their holdings, had taken up residence along the forks of the Ohio River near Fort Pitt. Five years later there were 10,000 families. Farther south the frontiersman Daniel Boone hacked out the Wilderness Road through the Appalachians' Cumberland Gap to open a route into Kentucky and Tennessee. Boone's primitive trail would accommodate nothing larger than a pack mule, but it opened the way for an endless stream of settlers. (The Indians called them *chemokoman,* "Long Knives," because of their readiness to defend their newly claimed homesteads.)

The same headlong rush to settlement prevailed in the Great Lakes region, as land developers carved out territory in northern Ohio and New York. In an attempt to impose order, the Indian superintendent in the area, Sir William Johnson, cobbled together a series of land treaties. In the fall of 1768, Johnson orchestrated the largest treaty conference ever—gathering 3,400 Iroquois and other Eastern Indians, along with Shawnee and Delaware from the Ohio country, at Fort Stanwix in upstate New York. On the Colonial side were governors from Pennsylvania, New Jersey, and Virginia, along with land speculators, missionaries, and traders seeking compensation from losses during Pontiac's uprising.

The resulting agreement opened all the land east of the Ohio River to white settlement. As it happened, however, the only Indians who signed it were leaders of the Iroquois Confederacy, acting without the knowledge or consent of the others. When the Delaware and Shawnee got down to examining the treaty's fine points, they discovered that most of the lands being given up fell within their own hunting grounds—and that the Iroquois were being well paid for this betrayal.

The Americans' War

Conflicts over land continued to spin the plot in the border regions. Resentment built against the royal ban on westward settlement, adding to the litany of grievances felt by American colonists against British rule. Cries of independence echoed from the Eastern seaboard to the Western forests. And as the Revolutionary War drew rapidly nearer, it would envelop vast stretches of the Upper Country.

At first, most Indian leaders saw the Revolution as a family quarrel between whites, fought over issues of little interest to them. But they soon were drawn in anyway—into a struggle to hold on to their homelands. Even before the first rifle shots were fired at Concord and Lexington, Virginia militiamen were battling Shawnee villagers for control of the Ohio Valley. All across the borderland, this was the beginning of a new chapter.

Some tried to stay on the sidelines, but most were forced to choose. A faction of Delawares living near Fort Pitt signed an annual peace treaty with the Americans, who promised them a separate Delaware state at the war's end. But another Delaware group moved north to Sandusky, joining forces with the pro-British Huron. Indeed, the need to take sides sparked furious debate among many other groups, sometimes causing lasting rifts in the tribal councils. In the end most leaders decided their advantage lay with the British, who seemed more likely to respect the integrity of Indian lands.

My son, you are now flesh of our flesh and bone of our bone. By the ceremony performed this day, every drop of white blood was washed from your veins; you were taken into the Shawnee nation . . . you were adopted into a great family.

—Black Fish, Shawnee, recalling 1778 adoption of Daniel Boone into tribe

In the Shawnee settlements of the Ohio Valley, war chiefs mobilized for a full-scale campaign to evict the Americans. The warriors of Chief Black Fish, one of several Shawnee leaders, raged through the forest homesteads of Kentucky, repeatedly laying siege to the log-cabin village of Boonesborough, founded by Daniel Boone in 1775. By the February snows of 1777, scarcely one hundred whites able to bear arms remained in the Kentucky area.

One was Boone himself, who fought for the American side as a captain in the Kentucky militia. He took a flesh wound in the defense of Boonesborough, then led counterattacks against the Shawnee. During a salt-making expedition in 1778 to Blue Licks, on the Licking River, a band of 100 Shawnee warriors attacked his party and took him prisoner. Held three months in captivity, he was adopted into the tribe by Black Fish himself, who had lost his own son in the fighting. Finally Boone managed to escape, and returned to Boonesborough to defend it against yet another siege by Black Fish's men.

Long Knives and Hair Buyers

With desperate warriors pitted against the land-hungry American Long Knives, the Revolution in the west took on a vindictive savagery unknown in other sectors of the war. The main British headquarters on the frontier was Detroit; its commandant, Henry Hamilton, was also lieutenant governor of Canada. Hamilton supplied the Shawnee and pro-British Delawares with arms and ammunition, and as incentive to raid American settlements he reputedly paid a bounty for white scalps. Both the Indians and the Americans knew him contemptuously as "Hair Buyer."

His successor at Detroit was a half-Shawnee trader, Col. Alexander McKee, who pressed ahead with single-minded ruthlessness. In 1780 he led a force of British and Indian allies against Rundle's Station in

Kentucky, precipitating a massacre of 200 American men, women, and children.

No one aroused more wrath or controversy than McKee's deputy, Simon Girty, who as a child had been captured and raised by the Seneca. Fluent in native languages, skilled in wilderness survival—and thoroughly versed in traditional Indian methods for dealing with prisoners—he became the notorious "Great Renegade," roundly despised by frontier settlers. During a campaign in the Sandusky area, by one account—one of many stories in circulation—he ordered his Shawnee and Delaware followers to tie up a captured American colonel and burn him alive.

For tribes that backed the British, the American Revolution was an unalloyed disaster. As in the earlier conflicts between whites in America, the Indians had proved themselves to be formidable antagonists—masters of the swift attack, all but invisible in retreat, capable of inflicting severe casualties against huge odds. But in the end they were outnumbered and outgunned.

And in the end they were betrayed. For all their courage and skill in helping the British defend the trans-Appalachian frontier, they received barely a word of thanks. At the Treaty of Paris in 1783, which ended the Revolutionary War, no provision was made for them. On the contrary, as part of the peace agreement, Great Britain ceded all her western lands from the Great Lakes on down—virtually all of it Indian country—to the new United States. Even groups that had sided with the rebels ended up worse off than before. For a fledgling nation eager to show its mettle and expand its sphere, all Indians were a menace to future development.

The target of several earlier assaults, Boonesborough came under siege again in September 1778 by a combined force of British and Shawnee fighters, the latter led by Black Fish (large figure at upper right, in British officer's headgear). Addressing Daniel Boone (in broad-brimmed hat), the fort's founder—and his adoptive son—Black Fish demanded surrender. To no avail: convinced of the Americans' will, the attackers at length gave up. Boonesborough had survived again.

A triumphant participant in the 1791 rout of Gen. Arthur St. Clair's troops in Indiana prepares to take the scalp of a wounded officer. The battle, dubbed St. Clair's Shame, was the army's worst-ever defeat by native forces.

Little Turtle Fights On

Before the gun smoke had cleared from the last Revolutionary War battles, settlers were again streaming west across the mountains. By 1780 the forests of Kentucky and Tennessee re-sounded with the crash of falling trees as more than 50,000 Americans began clear-ing farmland and building towns. In Ohio, where few white people had lived before, land speculators were busy surveying tracts along the Musk-ingum River. More than 45,000 people would surge into Ohio over the next two decades; an-other 5,000 pushed on into Indiana. Not sur-prisingly, the onslaught provoked a reaction.

> I look to you as a good being. Order your people to be just. They are always trying to get our lands. They come on our lands, they hunt on them; kill our game and kill us. Keep them on one side of the line, and us on the other. Listen, my father, to what we say.
> —*Kaskaskia leader to George Washington*

Serious resistance was offered by a new coalition—militant factions of Ottawa, Wyandot, Shawnee, Potawatomi, Ojibwa, Mi-ami, and others who were determined to maintain control of their villages and hunting grounds. Indian raids between 1783 and 1790 took the lives of as many as 1,500 settlers.

The new American government could not tolerate these losses, and in 1790 President Washington ordered his commander in the Northwest Territory (as the Americans now

One of the chiefs who signed the 1795 peace treaty at Fort Greenville, ending Little Turtle's War, Shawnee leader Catahecassa (above, right) advocated friendship with the Americans. This pipe-tomahawk, with blade and pipe bowl com-bined, was presented as a peace token to an Ottawa chief who may also have attended.

called the region) to put a stop to them. So Gen. Josiah Harmer set out from Fort Washington, at present-day Cincinnati, with nearly 1,500 troops. Harmer had served with distinction during the Revolution, but in this campaign he managed to stumble disastrously.

His downfall was engineered by a brilliant Miami leader—Michikinikwa, or Little Turtle, principal chief of the tribal coalition. Little Turtle was careful to avoid direct confronta-tions, relying instead on surprise jabs and de-ceptive tactics. His warriors abandoned their villages and feigned retreat, luring Harmer's soldiers ever deeper into the forest. The Ameri-cans were soon weary, short of supplies—and ripe for the taking: in October 1790 Little Tur-tle caught them in a pair of ambushes that in-flicted 200 casualties and scattered the rest.

After this unexpected setback, Washington dispatched his army's highest-ranking soldier, Maj. Gen. Arthur St. Clair, to try again. St. Clair set out in the fall of 1791 with 2,300 men, many of them raw recruits. As they marched through Ohio in pursuit of the Mia-mi leader, he detached some of the troops to build new forts; others deserted. On November 3, with only about 1,400 men remaining, St. Clair made camp on a plateau overlooking the Wabash River in Indiana.

The position was dangerously exposed—and Little Turtle made the most of it. Early the next morning, 1,000 warriors rushed in on three sides and overwhelmed the sleep-dazed Americans. Many dropped their weapons and ran; some cowered in prayer. Few escaped. When the carnage was over, 650 Americans lay dead and nearly 300 more were wounded. In the annals of Indian warfare, "St. Clair's Shame" would take its place as the greatest loss ever suffered by American troops.

"A Chief Who Never Sleeps"

Furious at St. Clair's ineptitude and pressured by calls for help from desperate frontier settlements, Washington turned to Gen. Anthony Wayne—"Mad Anthony," his men called him—to do the job right. Determined to avoid the mistakes of his predecessors, Wayne recruited a 2,000-man force and spent a full year training it. He also added 1,000 mounted Kentucky sharpshooters and a detachment of Chickasaw and Choctaw scouts, traditional enemies of the Great Lakes tribes.

> We have beaten the enemy every time; we cannot expect the same good fortune always to attend us. The Americans are now led by a chief who never sleeps. In spite of the watchfulness of our braves, we have never been able to surprise him. There is something that whispers to me that it would be prudent to listen to offers of peace.
>
> —*Little Turtle, Miami*

On learning that the British were supplying the Indians with food and firearms, Wayne prepared to attack. Before he could move, a band of Ottawa fighters hit Fort Recovery in June 1774—only to be repulsed by heavy cannon fire.

It was the coalition's first defeat. In council meetings afterward, Little Turtle laid out the new realities. The American forces had grown so large, he said, that further resistance would be futile; better to withdraw and seek some sort of accommodation. With that, he handed overall leadership of the confederacy's 1,500 warriors to Shawnee chief Blue Jacket, his close ally in the campaign. From now on, Little Turtle would lead only his 250 Miamis.

Blue Jacket faded north into the rugged country west of Lake Erie, near the British garrison of Fort Miami. In a deep ravine on the Maumee River strewn with the trunks of trees uprooted by a recent tornado, he set up an ambush. His men performed the rites of fasting and prayer observed by Shawnee warriors before every battle. Then they waited. And they waited some more.

Wayne led his soldiers slowly up the trail in pursuit, intentionally delaying his arrival by three days. On August 20, 1794, as Blue Jacket's half-starved fighters began drifting off to hunt for food, Wayne attacked—sweeping in so quickly that he earned the Shawnee name Big Wind. The warriors fell back to Fort Miami, hoping for help from their British allies. It never came: the British commander, ordered to stay out of the fighting, bolted the door to the stockade. Hundreds were slaughtered.

So ended the Battle of Fallen Timbers, the last major clash of what history remembers as Little Turtle's War. The following summer, 1,130 chiefs and warriors assembled at Fort Greenville, Ohio, to make peace with the United States. The price they paid was bitterly high: the Ohio River borderland, so long coveted by Yankee land developers, would be opened up to white settlement.

Little Turtle, meanwhile, continued to advise cooperation. Lionized by the Americans whose armies he had twice vanquished, he traveled to Philadelphia to shake hands with President Washington and have his portrait painted by the illustrious Gilbert Stuart. Retiring on a government stipend, he lived out his days in a house on the Maumee River built for him by the governor of the Indiana Territory. Death came in 1812 from gout, usually considered a white man's disease.

> *The whole white race is a monster who is always hungry, and what he eats is land.*
>
> —*Chiksika, Shawnee*

The Shawnee Prophet and Tecumseh

Like other great events in the Upper Country, it began with a prophet's vision. Tenskwatawa, son of a Shawnee war chief who had died battling the whites, was mired in a life of alcohol and despair when, in 1805, he fell into a deep trance. Awakening, he began to preach a compelling message from the Great Spirit.

The ways of the white men, he proclaimed, were an evil that corrupted all they touched. Not only did whites continue to devour Indian lands—another 48 million acres had been ceded through bribery or coercion since the 1795 Treaty of Fort Greenville—but their very presence brought spiritual decay. Dependent on the white world's tools, enthralled by its trinkets, and poisoned by its whiskey, Indian people were losing their very soul.

Like the Delaware Prophet half a century earlier, Tenskwatawa called for a total rejection of white culture—its clothing and technology, its alcohol, and its religion. He also denounced the selling of land. No one really owned the land, he reminded his listeners, since by ancient tradition it belonged to everyone in common as a gift from the Great Spirit.

Along with this bracing message, the Shawnee Prophet echoed another powerful refrain: the vision of an intertribal confederacy that would embrace all Indians everywhere. The person who came closest to making it happen was the Prophet's brother, Tecumseh.

Tecumseh stood six feet tall and cast a shadow that reached across the nation. A spellbinding orator, regally handsome, wise in council and courageous in battle, he was perhaps the greatest native leader to step forward since the European invasion began in 1492. He led the Shawnee forces during Little Turtle's War, and he would not accept defeat: his signature is missing from the Greenville treaty. He was a man of learning—he studied the Bible and world history—and compassion. More than once he intervened to prevent the torture of prisoners, a common practice among both natives and whites.

More importantly, perhaps, Tecumseh thought of himself as an Indian first and a Shawnee second. Like his brother, he was inspired by a vision of Indian unity. The tribes must put aside their age-old feuds, he argued and join together in a great military confederacy—a single Indian nation embracing all of eastern North America, from Canada to the Gulf of Mexico.

> The whites are already nearly a match for us all united, and too strong for any one tribe alone to resist. Unless we support one another with our collective forces, they will soon conquer us, and we will be driven away from our native country and scattered as leaves before the wind.
>
> —*Tecumseh, Shawnee*

In pursuit of that vision, the two brothers set up headquarters in 1808 at the former Miami village of Tippecanoe in Indiana Territory. Intended as a place where native people could live free of white influence, it proved a powerful magnet for the Shawnee, Ottawa, Huron, Winnebago, Potawatomi, Ojibwa, and others. The place came to be called Prophet's Town.

The image of proud defiance, this striking portrait of Tecumseh—also called Shooting Star by his followers—was painted by an unknown artist. Tecumseh's crusade to forge a unified Indian nation won the respect even of his foes.

Tenskwatawa, in a portrait by George Catlin (opposite), holds a "medicine fire" in one hand and, in the other, a string of sacred beans used by his warriors in a ceremonial oath of courage before battle. He also carved the prayer stick at far right. Though blind in one eye, the Prophet saw far enough to predict an eclipse of the sun—convincing thousands of his spiritual powers.

Sell a country! Why not sell the air, the great sea, as well as the earth? Did not the Great Spirit make them all for the use of his children?

—Tecumseh, Shawnee

Meanwhile, Tecumseh traveled widely and tirelessly, from the Great Lakes woodlands to the wetlands of Florida, seeking out support for his new confederacy. Tribal leaders who balked at the proposal could expect a scathing reaction. "Your blood is white!" he railed at one Creek war chief who refused to join. "You have taken my talk, and the sticks, and the wampum and the hatchet, but you do not mean to fight!" Still, piece by piece, Tecumseh was bringing together the alliances that would make this coalition a serious military power.

Events elsewhere conspired against him, however. Back in Indiana, tensions between the residents of Prophet's Town and the territorial governor, William Henry Harrison, were growing worse by the day. Already trouble had erupted over a land deal that some Indians considered fraudulent, and Tecumseh had twice been forced to rein in his warriors. In warfare as in politics, he knew that timing is essential. It wasn't time yet.

Lift up your hatchets; raise your knives; sight your rifles! Have no fears—your lives are charmed! Stand up to the foe; he is a weakling and coward! Fall upon him! Leave him to the wolves and the buzzards!

—Tenskwatawa, Shawnee

Harrison, on the other hand, was eager for a showdown. Taking advantage of Tecumseh's absence, he advanced on Prophet's Town with 1,000 men on the pretext of looking for stolen horses. Tenskwatawa, temporarily in charge, was also looking for a confrontation. Urged on by Winnebago militants, who believed his sacred powers would protect them from harm, Tenskwatawa ordered a counterattack.

They struck before dawn, killing some 50 of Harrison's militiamen and taking probably an equal number of losses. But there was nothing equal about the result, for even one dead warrior meant that Tenskwatawa's vaunted medicine had lost its effect. He became an object of ridicule—a disastrous liability to his brother's cause. There were massive defections among the Delaware, Miami, and his own Shawnee. The alliance never fully recovered.

Harrison marched into Prophet's Town, now abandoned, and burned it to the ground along with the confederacy's stockpile of weapons and supplies. Later he would hold up the Battle of Tippecanoe as a great victory, and it helped him win the presidency in 1840.

Tecumseh, meanwhile, gathered his remaining forces and led a series of skirmishes against frontier settlements. Then destiny intervened in the form of a new conflict between the United States and Britain: the War of 1812. Much of the battle fever on the American side came from the Old Northwest, where the British continued to arm Indian war parties and encourage their raids against settlers.

WORDS OF FIRE IN THE SOUTHLANDS

All through the summer of 1811, Tecumseh journeyed among the tribes of the South to recruit warriors for a pan-Indian alliance strong enough to stop U.S. takeovers of native lands. Some responded readily, but opinions were mixed among the powerful Choctaw and Chickasaw. A large crowd gathered by the Tombigbee River in Mississippi to hear his long and impassioned message, portions of which follow. After others had spoken, Tecumseh strode slowly to the council fire:

❧ We meet tonight in solemn council—not to debate whether we have been wronged or injured, but to decide how to avenge ourselves. Have we not courage enough to defend our country and maintain our ancient independence?

Where today are the Pequot? Where are the Narragansett, the Mohawk, the Pocanet, and other powerful tribes of our people? They have vanished before the avarice and oppression of the white man, as snow before the summer sun. . . . So it will be with you! Soon your mighty forest trees will be cut down to fence in the land. Soon their broad roads will pass over the graves of your fathers. You, too, will be driven from your native land as leaves are driven before the winter storms.

Sleep no longer, O Choctaws and Chickasaws, in false security and delusive hopes! Before the white men came among us, we knew neither want nor oppression. How is it now? Are we not being stripped day by day of our ancient liberty? How long will it be before they tie us to a post and

Choctaw chief Pushmataha sought to protect his people through diplomacy with the Americans. He died during a trip to Washington in 1824, shortly after this portrait was painted. He was 60.

fire, a man renowned for his bravery and wisdom. He would be heard by this council. His name was Pushmataha:

⚡ I appear before you, my warriors and my people, not to contradict the many charges made against the Americans. The question before us now is not what wrongs they have inflicted upon us, but what measures are best for us to adopt. Reflect, I ask you, before you act hastily. . . .What you are contemplating is a war against a people whose territories are far greater than ours, and who are far better provided with all the implements of war, with men, guns, horses, wealth. . . . Let us not be deluded with the foolish hope that this war, if begun, will soon be over. It will be but the beginning of the end that terminates in the total destruction of our people.

Listen to the voice of prudence, O my countrymen, before you act rashly. But whatever you may do, know this—I shall join our friends, the Americans, in this war.

Tecumseh felt the tide turning against him and sprang to the fire: "All who will follow me in this war throw your tomahawks into the air!" he cried out—and the air was filled with tomahawks hurled overhead. Tecumseh cast a triumphant glance at Pushmataha, who promptly called for the same display of support. Again tomahawks filled the sky.

At length, the issue was put before an aged Choctaw seer; after more days of debate, ritual, and prayer, he spoke. His words foreshadowed the fate of Tecumseh's dream:

⚡ The Great Spirit tells me to warn you against the dark and evil designs of Tecumseh, and not to be deceived by his words; his schemes are unwise, and if entered into will bring sorrow and desolation upon you and your nations. Choctaws and Chickasaws, obey the words of the Great Spirit.

whip us, and make us work for them in their fields? Shall we wait for that moment, or shall we die fighting?

At this, some of the younger warriors leaped to their feet, shouting and flourishing their tomahawks in a frenzy of rage. Tecumseh raised his hand for quiet, then continued:

⚡ Shall we give up our homes, our country bequeathed to us by the Great Spirit, the graves of our dead, and everything that is dear and sacred to us without a struggle? I know you will cry with me: Never! Never! War or extermination is now our only choice. Which do you choose? I know your answer.

When Tecumseh finished, the throng remained silent. Several Choctaw and Chickasaw elders then rose to speak, most expressing support. Tecumseh was on the verge of triumph. Then another stood up and stepped gravely to the

181

Fighting hand to hand, Tecumseh's warriors clash with American troops at the Battle of the Thames in 1813. Pictured on horseback is Col. Richard Johnson, later a vice president of the United States, who launched his political career on the strength of his role in defeating the Shawnee leader.

Through White Eyes: Tecumseh Observed

If it were not for the vicinity of the United States, he would perhaps be the founder of an empire that would rival in glory Mexico or Peru. No difficulties deter him. For four years he has been in constant motion . . . and wherever he goes he makes an impression favorable to his purpose.
— *Brig. Gen. William Henry Harrison*

When Tecumseh rose to speak, as he cast his gaze over the vast multitude, he appeared one of the most dignified men I ever beheld. While he was speaking, the vast crowd preserved the most profound silence. From the confident manner in which he spoke of the Indians. . . he dispelled as if by magic the apprehensions of the whites.
— *Col. John McDonald, Ohio Militia*

He readily and cheerfully accommodated himself to all the novelties of the situation and seemed amused without being at all embarrassed by them.
— *British officer, on Tecumseh's demeanor at formal dinners for staff officers and their ladies*

I was near Tecumseh when he made his speech whereby the lives of hundreds of prisoners were saved, of whom I was one. . . . He was a truly great man and gallant warrior.
— *Capt. (later Gen.) Leslie Combs, survivor of Indian massacre of Americans near Detroit in August 1812*

The Americans were determined to push north and drive the remaining British garrisons from the area—and as the fighting broke out, Tecumseh was right in the middle.

Seeing the war as an opportunity to win back lost Indian territory, Tecumseh quickly joined the British side, and he led his men on a brilliant campaign through the Great Lakes region. A joint force of Indians and British took the American fort at Detroit. Potawatomi warriors under his command occupied Fort Dearborn. A war party of his Ojibwa and Ottawa fighters seized Fort Mackinac, overlooking the straits between Lake Michigan and Lake Huron. The British, recognizing a gift for frontier warfare unmatched in the era, commissioned Tecumseh as a brigadier general.

Other tribal leaders began flocking to his banner. He soon assembled a force of 2,000 warriors from 30 different Indian nations, including a contingent of Sioux from the edge of the Great Plains. Multitribal towns sprang up along the Illinois River in support of the war effort. The Potawatomi in southeastern Michigan grew corn crops at hidden locations to feed the massed warrior legions and their families. By the fall of 1812, virtually the entire

Great Lakes region had been brought under Indian control.

The initial triumph did not last. Unfortunately for the Indians, the British appointed a new general, Henry Procter, to command their western front. Indecisive and overly cautious, he frittered away the early British advantage. When an American naval victory on Lake Erie severed his supply routes in September 1813, Procter decided to retreat to Canada.

"A Sorrow in Our Heart"

Tecumseh tried to talk him into staying; he was wasting his breath. Deeply disappointed, and resigned to the loss of everything he had worked so hard to attain, he agreed to cover the withdrawal. The joint armies headed north, pursued by 3,500 Americans under Harrison. On the Thames River in Ontario, Tecumseh persuaded Procter to make a stand.

Before the battle, Tecumseh decided to exchange his red British officer's coat for tribal buckskin; perhaps he had a premonition of his own death, as some sources report. Whatever the reason, he was a warrior to the end. As Procter's forces broke and fled, Tecumseh held his ground against the advancing Americans, taking shot after shot. No one knows who fired the fatal bullet. Many took credit.

When an Indian is killed it is a great loss, which leaves a gap in our people and a sorrow in our heart.

—Chiksika, Shawnee, elder brother of Tecumseh

With the great Shawnee chief gone (his body, never found, was said to have been removed and buried in a secret location by his men), the dream of a grand alliance was shattered. Tribal leaders drifted away, taking their warriors with them. American forces followed in hot pursuit, inflicting damage as they went; raids by U.S. troops in Indiana late in 1813 left Delaware and Miami villages ruined.

A treaty signed in London in 1815 officially ended hostilities between Britain and the United States. On the frontier, peace was not so simple. Even a nominal truce in the western region took three years of council meetings and 17 treaties. For decades, Indians suffered through the ragged aftermath of fighting. In some parts of the Upper Country, Indian villages continued to fly the Union Jack, even as the Stars and Stripes fluttered from the ramparts of nearby American forts. As late as 1842, British officers at Fort Malden, opposite Detroit on the Canadian side, would distribute annual presents to their former Indian allies.

Inevitably, the march of westward settlement resumed and—inevitably, against all odds—the Indians tried to prevent it. American veterans of the War of 1812 were sometimes paid in land warrants instead of cash, and when land agents began buying up plots along the Wabash and Illinois rivers, the local Kickapoo fought back. In the 1820's a mining boom on the Galena River sparked a stampede into northwest Illinois, which in turn sparked a Winnebago uprising.

Honoring the Past: Black Hawk

Most of these attempts flared briefly, then failed. The story of one man, the Sauk leader Black Hawk, illustrates a rare kind of persistence in the face of continuous betrayal. Deceived into signing a treaty he did not understand—like so many others who were tricked or bribed or threatened—Black Hawk led his people west across the Mississippi to new territory. Then in 1831 he returned to his village, Saukenuk, to plant crops. What he found appalled him. Not only had white families arrived—some of them moving into the abandoned Sauk lodges—but they had fenced in the cornfields and they were plow-

Sauk chief Black Hawk, who led the last war of resistance in the Upper Country, poses with a hawk skin and a fan made of black hawk tail feathers in this portrait by George Catlin. After his capture in 1832 he was put on display in a tour of Eastern cities—where crowds reacted more enthusiastically to him than to President Andrew Jackson.

ing up his ancestors' graves. Black Hawk responded by settling in for the summer with 300 warriors and refusing to budge. The next year he returned, this time with 600 men.

This brazen defiance startled the federal government into sending out a large expeditionary force. It arrived at Saukenuk in May of 1832, and Black Hawk, duly noting the Americans' strength, decided to parley. His envoys approached the U.S. encampment under a flag of truce. The militiamen on guard, inexperienced and jittery, opened fire. Three Sauk men fell dead. The war had begun.

In the first large skirmish, 40 Sauk warriors repelled an attack by 275 militiamen under Isaiah Stillman and sent them fleeing (earning the episode its nickame: Stillman's Run). Over the next three months, several thousand federal and state troops chased Black Hawk and his people north across Illinois and Wisconsin. The Americans floundered through swamps, and fell ill with cholera, and still Black Hawk eluded them. The Sauk were traveling with their wives and children, moving fast with little food and no time to hunt; they suffered badly from hunger and fatigue.

On the first of August, the refugees halted at the Bad Axe River in Wisconsin to make canoes and rafts, plan-

An impoverished Pota-watomi family of the 1830's lingers by a road-side in this watercolor. In the following decades, most surviving tribe members were moved onto reservations west of the Mississippi; many had no means of supporting themselves there, yet they never received promised government aid.

ning to float downstream to the Mississippi and then on to safety. The next day a U.S. gunship steamed into sight, loaded with troops. Again Black Hawk raised a flag of truce. Again the Americans opened fire, killing 23 Indians.

The final blow came the following morning, when the main American force arrived. Some 1,300 troops swept through the Sauk encampment, firing indiscriminately at men, women, and children. The death toll in the Bad Axe River massacre (to the army it was a "battle") reached as high as 300. Black Hawk led a band of survivors north to seek refuge with the Winnebago—who betrayed him to white authorities in return for $100 and twenty horses. The war was over.

You have taken me prisoner with all my warriors. I am much grieved . . . I expected to hold out much longer and give you more trouble before I surrendered.

Black Hawk is now a prisoner of the white man. But he can stand torture, and he is not afraid of death. He is no coward. Black Hawk is an Indian.

—*Black Hawk, Sauk*

The Last Horizon

The reality of American settlement was felt unevenly across the region. Tribes to the south took the heaviest impact, as barges filled with Easterners floated down the Ohio River one after another, pushing the white population steadily higher. At the same time, frontiersmen from Virginia and Kentucky—the despised and dreaded Long Knives—moved north through Ohio and Indiana carrying a half-century of battle scars and pent-up animosity

My reason tells me that land cannot be sold—nothing can be sold but such things as can be carried away.

—*Black Hawk, Sauk*

toward Indians. The government had begun pressing tribes to resettle on reservations soon after the War of 1812, and the pressure rose dramatically during the 1820's and 1830's. By the eve of the Civil War, most of the societies that once called the broad Ohio Valley home had been splintered, absorbed by other tribes, or forced across the Mississippi onto reservations in the alien world of Indian Territory.

For native people of the Great Lakes, the experience was less traumatic. The opening of the Erie Canal in the 1830's produced a modest influx of newcomers, but the Americans arriving by that route—New Yorkers and New Englanders whom the Indians called Saganash (Englishmen) or Bostonais—proved relatively easy neighbors. Most important, American financiers were more interested in lumbering and mining around

the Great Lakes than in land development. The north country was too sandy, swampy, or rocky for prosperous farming, and so the Ojibwa, Ottawa, Menominee, and Winnebago, and many Potawatomi were left comparatively undisturbed until after the Civil War. Even then, despite some shifting around, Great Lakes groups managed to stay close to their traditional homelands.

Many remain there today. The region is hardly the same unspoiled, naturally balanced realm it was before the French explorers appeared four centuries ago. Yet through all the dark history that followed—the tragic violence and irretrievable losses—descendants of the Upper Country's first nations have preserved a living connection with those forebears from one generation to another, nourished by the conviction that they still belong to the land, and the land to them.

An aged Daniel Boone relaxes on the doorstep of his cabin on Great Osage Lake in Kentucky in an idealized scene by Thomas Cole (whose passion for landscape painting was born in frontier Ohio). In reality, by the time of Boone's death in 1820 more than a million Americans were living in the transmountain states of Ohio, Kentucky, Indiana, and Illinois—and native populations there had dwindled to a scattering of isolated villages.

We did not think of the great open plains, the beautiful rolling hills and winding streams with tangled growth as "wild." To us it was tame. Earth was bountiful and we were surrounded with the blessings of the Great Mystery.

— Luther Standing Bear,
Rosebud Sioux

6

LAND OF THE BUFFALO

THE GREAT PLAINS

In the spring of 1931, the famed Oglala Lakota holy man, Black Elk, walked some visitors to a hill he called Remembrance Butte on his personal allotment of land in the northwestern corner of the Pine Ridge Reservation in South Dakota. Now an old man of 78 winters, Black Elk wanted to pray where he could see the traditional lands of the Lakota— or Sioux, as his people had come to be called.

Some 20 miles to the south loomed the Paha Sapa, the Black Hills, sacred heart of the Great Plains, with the pointed crest of Harney Peak barely visible. The peak, he had been told by a spirit guide long ago, was the very center of the world. It was there—many lifetimes earlier, it seemed to Black Elk—that he had experienced a life-changing vision at the age of nine. In it he met the great powers of the world and received special abilities from them. But he could also see four generations into the future, and what he saw included adversities awaiting his people that he would have no power to change.

Black Elk gestured toward the grassless, broken-up landscape immediately surround-

ing his visitors. They knew this dry and craggy place as the Badlands, but his name for it was *mako sika,* "strange lands of the world." Then the old man swept his arm in the direction of what the Lakota called *awanka toyala,* "greenness of the world," the graceful rolling breadth of the shortgrass prairie.

He remembered the shallow, wooded ravines in that expanse—places where his people had gathered currants, plums, buffalo berries, coral berries, and the much-sought-after chokecherries that were collected by the hideful in late summer. In the springtime he had accompanied his family to look for the violet-colored blossoms on the exposed green flats that showed where sweet prairie turnips, called *tinpsila,* were ready to be uprooted with digging sticks. Eaten raw like carrots, they also were boiled to thicken buffalo stew and could feed a family through the winter if properly dried.

Finally, Black Elk looked to the east, to the flat, undulating tallgrass prairie known to his people as *oblayela,* "wideness of the world." The old holy man had been born at a time when his people felt themselves to be custodi-

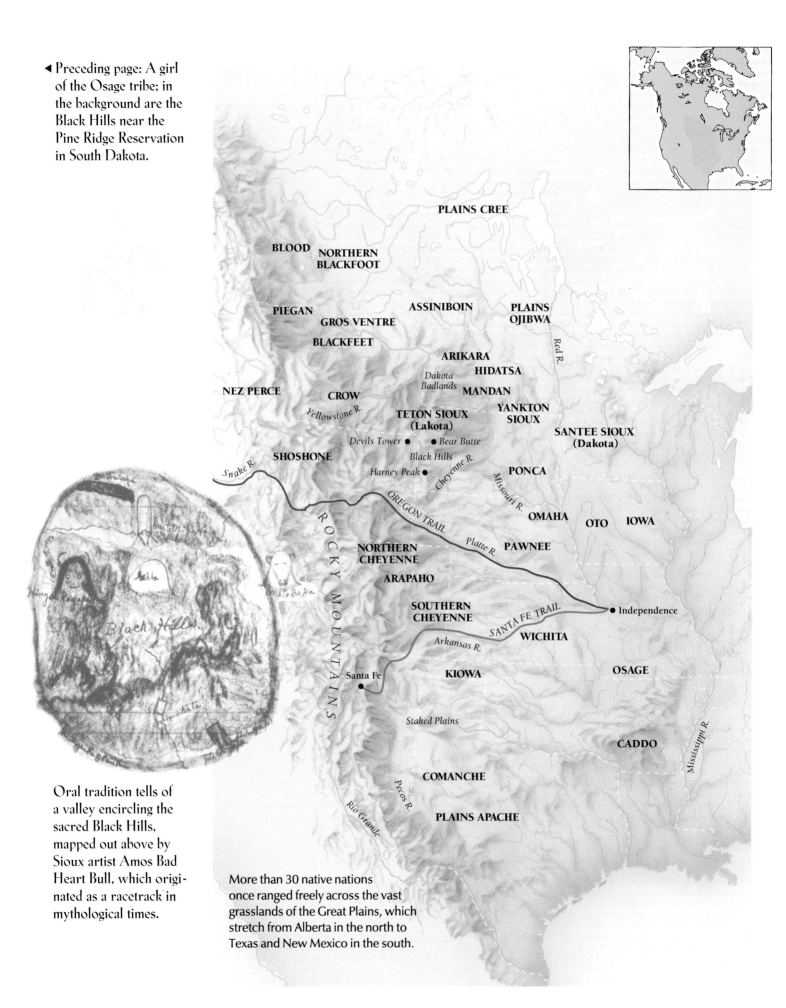

◄ Preceding page: A girl of the Osage tribe; in the background are the Black Hills near the Pine Ridge Reservation in South Dakota.

Oral tradition tells of a valley encircling the sacred Black Hills, mapped out above by Sioux artist Amos Bad Heart Bull, which originated as a racetrack in mythological times.

More than 30 native nations once ranged freely across the vast grasslands of the Great Plains, which stretch from Alberta in the north to Texas and New Mexico in the south.

PLAINS CREE

BLOOD   NORTHERN
         BLACKFOOT

PIEGAN   ASSINIBOIN   PLAINS
  GROS VENTRE   OJIBWA
  BLACKFEET
              ARIKARA
                  HIDATSA
              Dakota
NEZ PERCE   Badlands MANDAN
         CROW
                  Red R.
Yellowstone R. TETON SIOUX   YANKTON
              (Lakota)   SIOUX
         Devils Tower ● ● Bear Butte   SANTEE SIOUX
SHOSHONE   Black Hills   (Dakota)
Snake R.   Harney Peak ● Cheyenne R.
                              PONCA
                  Missouri R.
              OREGON TRAIL   OMAHA   OTO   IOWA
         NORTHERN   Platte R. PAWNEE
ROCKY   CHEYENNE
         ARAPAHO
MOUNTAINS
         SOUTHERN   ● Independence
         CHEYENNE   SANTA FE TRAIL   WICHITA
                  Arkansas R.
         Santa Fe ●   KIOWA   OSAGE
                                        Mississippi R.
              Staked Plains
                              CADDO

         Pecos R.   COMANCHE
    Rio Grande
              PLAINS APACHE

188

ans of this entire domain. Yet within the brief span of his own lifetime, everything had changed. Black Elk had witnessed the bitter end of the Sioux's terrible wars with U.S. troops and had seen his people reduced to impoverished isolation on four small reservations, a meager fraction of all that had once been theirs. As a descendant of renowned Lakota healers and medicine men, however, Black Elk still clung to a vision of his people's greatness, refusing to let it die.

Now with his visitors, looking over a landscape he knew like the back of his wrinkled hand, Black Elk prayed that his people might survive and might yet reclaim their ancient connections to this wide world with its many different spirits.

> Oh hear me, Grandfather, and help us, that our generation in the future will live and walk the good road with the flowering stick to success. Also, the pipe of peace, we will offer it as we walk the good road to success. Hear me, and hear our plea.

Sea of Grass, Land of Myth

Black Elk's names for the differing "lands" of the Plains aptly characterized this immense and wondrous region. Across more than 750,000 square miles, the heartland of the continent was a vast sea of grass, interrupted here and there by mountainous terrain and winding, forested river bottoms. The land continuously transformed itself as it extended south from Alberta, Canada, to the Llano Estacado, or Staked Plain, of western Texas and New Mexico. From the region's eastern boundary along the Mississippi River, a rider on horseback might travel for weeks before running up against the western wall of the Great Plains—the Rocky Mountains.

There was more to Plains ecology than its beauty and variety, however. Annual rainfall averaging 15 inches or less made the region

"An Indian Camp," by Hidatsa artist Bear's Arm, captures the scene after a successful buffalo hunt. Horses graze contentedly as buffalo hides are spread on the ground to be scraped; the meat has been sliced thin and hung out to dry. Prairie antelope (below) were also prized game animals.

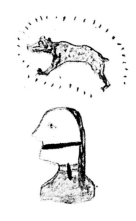

Signatures of a sort, Sioux name-glyphs (above) depict the animal spirits from which the men derived their names. Below, the land itself was viewed as the dwelling place of a multitude of spirit beings.

uninviting to early farmers. The Rockies created this condition, their towering peaks spilling the thunderheads that moved in from the west before they even had a chance to reach the Plains. From the earliest times, therefore, native hunters and farmers had made only limited use of the region—penetrating its river valleys to scout for the lairs and pastures of animals but never maintaining permanent settlements on the land.

When Black Elk was born in 1863, his people were among some 30 distinctive Native American nations known collectively as Plains Indians who called some portion of the open grasslands their home. For all the peoples of the Plains, the landscape itself had tales to tell.

According to tradition, an oval valley that rings the Black Hills came into being as a great racetrack, dug into the earth when all the world's creatures—two-legged, four-legged, and winged—ran in a race that established their various destinies, including the two-leggeds' right to hunt buffalo.

Just north of the Black Hills stands a dramatic monolith known to whites as Devils Tower. In a Kiowa tale this strange rock appeared long ago, when seven sisters were chased by a huge bear and sought refuge on a great tree stump. They escaped by rising to the sky, where they became the stars of the Big Dipper. The stump petrified, and to this day the deep gouges left by the claws of the angry bear can still be seen.

The most sacred place of all is *mato paha*, or Bear Butte, just northeast of the Black Hills racetrack. Here, in Mandan origin stories, their forebears found safety during the primordial flood. It was also here, say the Cheyenne, that their prophet Sweet Medicine was given the tribe's sacred icon of four arrows. And it was here that the Cheyenne, starving at the time, were given the gift of the Sun Dance so that they might yearly renew the world, its game, and its bountiful nature.

Sacred Origins

Scholars today seek to reconstruct the historical origins of the Plains tribes, but the people themselves narrated their own stories of origin. Instead of describing any early migrations from the east, for instance, one Hidatsa group told their children about the hero Charred

Body, who led the original 13 clans of the Hidatsa on a magical arrow that flew down from the world above to a site along today's Turtle Creek, not far from Mandan, North Dakota. Here Charred Body bested the local monsters so that his people could begin their existence as human beings.

The Kiowa's name for themselves, *kwuda,* can be translated as "coming out" and refers to a story about ancestors who ascended from the underworld by climbing through a hollow log. During that journey a pregnant woman got stuck in the log, preventing others from reaching the earth's surface—and explaining why the Kiowa were so few in number.

The Crow tell of a vision quest shared by two brothers. In the vision one received the gift of corn, and his people became sedentary villagers. The other was given sacred tobacco seeds and instructed to lead his people all around the Plains before settling in a promised land—the Bighorn country of present-day Montana. There they would flourish so long as they grew the sacred tobacco.

While part of what defined life on the Plains stemmed from a time beyond memory, much of it was of recent vintage—caused by

In the Realm of the Animal Spirits

All forms of animal life were revered by the peoples of the Plains as sources of supernatural power. The bear, for example, was associated with prowess in battle, and a warrior who had a dream or vision of one would in the process be infused with its valor. By depicting animals in art, Plains Indians believed they could attract and channel the particular power of each animal as a force for good in their lives.

The many powers of the elk included aiding in affairs of the heart.

The eagle's vision and courage are invoked by this image from a Crow war shield; above it is the morning star, sacred to many Plains warrior societies.

The buffalo lends protective force to the Lakota shield on which it appears.

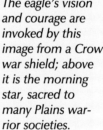

The panther is a common pictograph motif found in ancient canyon shelters.

A fanciful horse with buffalo horns graces a Lakota shield.

This porcupine, which appears on a Kiowa tepee grasping an arrow, safeguards the owner and his family.

A buffalo dancer joins in spirit with the bison to summon it for the hunt.

The bear claws depicted on a shield impart the animal's strength to the bearer.

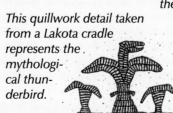

This quillwork detail taken from a Lakota cradle represents the mythological thunderbird.

This underwater creature painted on a Kiowa tepee may be the Zemoguani, a mythical horned fish.

the spread of European horses beginning in the late 1600's. Yet Black Elk's people knew that their ancestors had made good use of these lands long before that. From the earliest times they had forayed along the fringes of the Plains and ventured up the river valleys in search of deer, antelope, elk, and the greatest prize of all: the buffalo.

Ancient Hunters

Plains hunters, traveling on foot and armed with stone-tipped spears, could kill their swifter, stronger prey only with ingenuity and coordinated effort. They used two basic techniques. One method was to frighten animals out of the brush and ravines into wide channels created between two makeshift fences. Corralling the terrified prey into a circular enclosure at the end of this chute, they could then kill the animals at close range.

> The Dakota understood the meaning of self-sacrifice, perhaps because their legends taught them that the buffalo, on which their very life depended, gave itself voluntarily that they might live.
>
> — *Ella C. Deloria, Dakota*

Revered as the staff of life, the buffalo appeared in a variety of forms and images to serve many purposes. Above, a warrior emblazoned with buffalos is infused with and guided by their spirit in "La-Doo-Ke-A, The Buffalo Bull Grand Pawnee Warrior," by George Catlin. The quartzite effigy at right was probably used in calling-the-buffalo rituals that helped ensure a successful hunt. The painted buffalo tepee below conferred special power on its Kiowa owner, named Never Got Shot.

The other method was the "buffalo jump." According to Blackfeet and Crow storytellers, their forefathers successfully goaded buffalo to their deaths this way only when a gifted shaman oversaw the proceedings. At the start, hunt leaders would position women and children behind piles of stones arranged in a V-shape that narrowed to a point at the edge of a sheer cliff. The buffalo were enticed to enter the wedge by a slow-hobbling man disguised in a fur robe. Other people brought up the rear, yelling and flapping robes and waving the scented smoke of burning cedar in the air. This gave the impression of a terrifying forest fire, causing the great beasts to stampede over the edge of the cliff. Down below, a makeshift enclosure prevented wounded animals from escaping, while arrows and spears rained down from

all sides until the lifeless carcasses could be approached by butchering parties.

Nearby, on the flat prairie, there would be a campsite where women quartered and finally "flaked" the fresh meat, slicing very thin strips and drying them on pole racks. The dried meat was later prepared in various ways; a favorite and highly nutritious method was to pound it with granite pestles, blending in dried berries and buffalo tallow, and finally packing the mix into rawhide containers for later winter consumption.

For pack animals, these early Plains folk used domesticated dogs, whose narrow snouts and bushy tails suggested their probable kinship to coyotes. Short tepee poles were lashed to a harness over their haunches, creating a drag platform (French Canadian traders later termed it a *travois*) that the dogs pulled between campsites. In those days tepees were probably no more than ten feet high, pack loads were light, and the distance a hunting band might cover in a day was relatively short.

Even without horses, however, the geographical range of early Plains Indian commerce was astonishing. Brown flint, which made fine knife blades and arrow points, and soapstone, which was carved into sculptural pipe bowls, traveled from their sources in Montana to villages hundreds of miles away.

BOUNTY OF THE BISON

Of the two types of buffalo found in North America, the Plains variety may have numbered upwards of 60 million at the dawn of European arrival. Buffalo (or, more properly, bison) were the Plains Indian mainstay — their meat eaten at most meals, their different parts used for every domestic purpose imaginable. First came the edibles: the smoked tongue, considered the highest delicacy; the succulent semi-digested vegetal contents of the stomach and intestines; the tender liver, eaten warm and raw shortly after the kill; the hearty ribs, cracked and roasted over an open fire; and the leg meat and loins, which together with buffalo tallow and bone marrow were pounded into a high-energy pulp called pemmican for use on the war trail.

Hooves were boiled into all-purpose glue; sinew was dried and split for strong thread and bow-backing; horns were fashioned into cups and spoons. Long bones became tool handles, and ribs made fine sled runners in wintertime. Shoulder blades were transformed into hoe blades; the tail became a sweat-bath whip; the bladder served to store drinking water; and the stomach could be propped up on stakes, filled with water, and used as a kettle when hot rocks were placed inside. And, of course, there was the precious hide: thick-haired winter hides made the warmest sleeping robes; the inch-thick hump portion made shields that could deter arrows; and scraped summer hides were sewn together into tepee covers.

A common feature on Plains Indian altars was a painted buffalo skull, while from the sacred cottonwood center post of the Sun Dance Lodge, a buffalo head would look down upon the dancers. When Plains Indian life was in its tragic decline, these creatures were uppermost on the minds of the people. "I come to tell news," their visionaries would sing. "The buffalo are coming again."

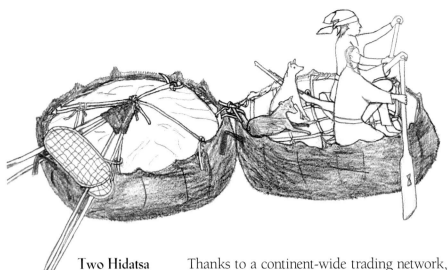

Two Hidatsa men, probably traders, paddle fully laden "bull boats" (so called for their coverings of male buffalo hide), with dogs and a travois for overland travel; the sketch is by Hidatsa artist Edward Goodbird.

A 19th-century Wichita village, below, was a model of versatility; the open-sided thatched structure at left was used for cooking, the adjacent grass house for sleeping, and the tepee frame for buffalo hunts. Corn was probably grown on the plot in the foreground.

Thanks to a continent-wide trading network, the people of the Plains also chipped arrow and spear points out of obsidian from the Yellowstone region of Wyoming and acquired copper from the Great Lakes, as well as shells and coral from the Pacific Northwest and the Gulf Coast.

Seeds of Agriculture

Around A.D. 850, some pioneering hunter-farmers began tilling the fertile floodplains of the Missouri River, establishing villages along a number of tributaries between present-day Nebraska and South Dakota. Occupied continuously during the summer growing season, the villages were used only part-time in the fall and winter, when hunting parties were away for long periods on buffalo hunts.

The prime location for a village was a bluff or high terrace overlooking a stream—the better to spy buffalo herds in the distance, to gauge the level of the spring runoff, or to see if women out berrying or fetching water were in

danger from bears or enemy tribesmen. Equally important, lookouts could watch for flocks of blackbirds that might threaten the life-sustaining gardens along the lower river terraces. There, using hoes made by lashing the shoulder blades of buffalo to wooden handles, women tended family gardens of corn, beans, squash, amaranth, and sunflowers.

Often in summer I rise at daybreak and steal out to the cornfields; and as I hoe the corn I sing to it, as we did when I was young. Sometimes at evening I sit, looking out on the big Missouri. In the shadows I seem again to see our Indian village, with smoke curling upward from the earth lodges.
— Buffalo Bird Woman, Hidatsa

To construct homes, a basic frame of heavy posts and beams cut from the towering stands of cottonwood along the river valley was roofed and walled with a tightly packed layer of smaller poles. A matting of buffalo grass followed, capped by a thick layer of sod or mud. The builders made these lodges snug for winter by excavating the floors slightly and insulating the entry tunnel with earth. Underneath their floors people dug deep, bottle-shaped cellars for storing the dried products of their fields during the howling winter months.

Women were in charge of the domestic arena as well as the garden plots. One or two fam-

ilies related through the female line lived in each lodge. Couples slept in booths ranged around the lodge perimeter, their babies safely bound in cushioned cradleboards. Common household goods included hardwood mortars and pestles for pounding corn, ceramic pots, and buffalo-horn utensils. Provisions and extra clothing were stored on drying racks and in storage nooks around the perimeter of the lodge. One corner might house a clan shrine —a small raised platform holding family icons—which children were taught to treat with respect. Smoke from a centrally placed fire blackened the ceiling but also inhibited insect infestation of the sod roof. Early chroniclers visiting earth-lodge villages commented favorably on their orderliness and cleanliness.

By about A.D. 1400 the population centers of these earth-lodge farmers were concentrated in two regions. In the central plains of Nebraska and Kansas lived the ancestors of the Pawnee, and along the upper Missouri River in North Dakota dwelled the forebears of the Mandan, who were soon joined by the early Hidatsa bands.

Round earth lodges encircle a central plaza in the Pawnee village seen in this hand-colored photograph from the 19th century. Some villagers sit atop one of the lodges to observe a ceremony in the plaza. The great Pawnee deity Tirawa was believed to enter each lodge through a smoke hole in the roof.

As these successful communities began crowding along the riverfront, struggles over available farmland followed, causing villagers to barricade themselves behind protective log palisades and dry moats. Within these walls ceremonial plazas opened up, and some buildings appear to have been devoted exclusively to ceremonial purposes.

Still farther south, near the great bend of the Arkansas River, there were other Caddoan speakers who farmed, but they dwelled in grass houses instead of earth lodges. These were Wichita tribespeople, and their beehive-shaped dwellings intrigued the conquistador Francisco de Coronado when he saw them in 1540. Along with raising squash and corn, the Wichita also crafted swirl-decorated blackware pottery and were noted for the intricate tattooing of their entire bodies.

While these peoples farmed along the prairie's rich bottomlands, other Plains tribes pursued a very different lifestyle. Far to the north, people who would become known as the Blackfeet survived by hunting and gathering in the wooded pockets and broad grasslands of southern Manitoba and western Saskatchewan. Along the borderlands of the western Great Lakes, the Dakota or Santee—the easternmost tribe of the Sioux—and the Ojibwa, largest of the Great Lakes woodland tribal groups, found themselves in bloody competition over the same inventory of natural resources. Both peoples harvested wild rice in the fall, hunted in the winter, made maple sugar in the spring, and farmed in midsummer. Their neighbors included Lakota tribes—branches of the great Siouan-speaking brotherhood—who preferred a buffalo-hunting way of life. Other early Plains people, including the Cheyenne, the Crow, the Hidatsa, and the Kiowa, would shift location more than once and consequently pursue several different Plains lifestyles.

It was along the southern rim of the Great Plains that Francisco Vasquez de Coronado became the first European to glimpse what would long be the popular image of the Plains Indian way of life. The stunted conical dwellings covered in tanned and sewn buffalo hides that his party visited near present-day Amarillo, Texas, in the spring of 1541 were almost certainly occupied by Plains Apaches. They "travel the plains with the cows," wrote Coronado, living in their tents "like Arabs."

Actually, these tribesmen were relatively recent occupants of the region and at that time of year were just settling by their gardens for the summer. It was common for Europeans to form a distorted view of a tribe's way of life depending on when they happened to observe it. Most Indians lived quite differently from season to season, depending on available foodstuffs, building materials, and climate.

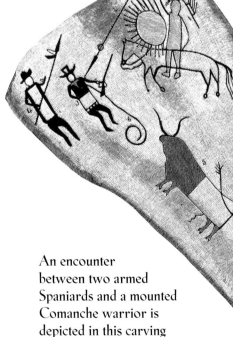

An encounter between two armed Spaniards and a mounted Comanche warrior is depicted in this carving made on a buffalo scapula.

Two decades after Coronado, another Spaniard, Don Juan de Oñate, first governor of Spain's New Mexico province, also ran into a Plains Apache camp, this one composed of some 50 tepees brightly painted in red and white and, he reported, "built skillfully as any house in Italy."

For another century or more after these armor-clad horsemen disappeared into the sunset, the Plains received no more visits by white men. But the absence of Europeans in the flesh did not prevent their culture from making its mark. Their legacy, in the form of the horse, was about to transform life on the Plains forever.

The Four-Legged Revolution

Well established in their colonial capital at Santa Fe in the early 17th century, the Spanish maintained a near monopoly on horse trading until 1680, when rebellious Pueblo Indians drove Spanish colonists and priests south out of New Mexico. Whole stables were suddenly unguarded; horses were there for the taking. Pueblo Indian traders and their Navajo allies wasted little time making these mounts available to the Comanche, who also became quite accomplished at stealing their own.

Over the next century there was growing evidence of the horse's steady spread: In 1682 a Catholic priest complained from El Paso about some Indians—probably Plains Apache—stealing a few hundred horses; as of 1690 every household of the Hasanai, a northern Texas tribe, owned at least four horses. By 1700 the Shoshone on the Snake River in southern Idaho had created a hub of horse trading; 20 years later horses were in the hands of the Nez Perce of the Idaho Plateau. By the 1770's the Santee Sioux of central Minnesota had become an equestrian people.

So was born the classic image of Plains Indians: the arrival of the horse gave rise to the war-bonneted, face-painted, mobile peoples

Displayed with obvious pride, the horse effigy is the foremost of this Blackfeet chief's many accoutrements. Such effigies were often used to honor specially trained warrior horses that had distinguished themselves in battle.

Oglala Sioux artist and medicine man Kills Two depicts members of the Horse Owners' Society on parade. Membership in this society was conferred on individuals who had dreamed "horse medicine" dreams, which granted them special prowess in capturing enemy horses.

whose way of life, at once spiritual and militaristic, captured the world's imagination.

In the oral traditions of many Plains peoples, however, the white man had little to do with their first introduction to horses. These four-legged creatures were such a marvelous gift, they could not have had such prosaic origins. Calling them mystery dogs, sky dogs, or elk dogs, many tribes told stories of how a vision seeker had acquired the great blessing of the horse through a supernatural encounter.

We had ponies long before we ever saw white people. The Great Spirit gave them to us. Our horses were swifter and more enduring, too, before they were mixed with the white man's horses.

— Smoholla, Wanapam shaman

Spreading northward from New Mexico, horses had reached Indian tribes in every corner of the Plains by the time of Albert Bierstadt's bucolic painting "View from the Wind River Mountains, Wyoming, 1860."

Crow Indian, you must watch your horses. A horse thief often am I.
— *Teton Sioux song*

The first view that the Comanche had of horses, according to their tradition, was with men on their backs. The Indians initially believed that horse and rider were a single animal—and when a Spanish-speaking man dismounted from one, they were astonished. Secretly they observed how the Spaniards watered the horses, let them roll on the grass before eating, used soft pads on their backs, and secured their legs with rawhide every night. Then the Comanche stole the horses and over the years returned for many more.

The Blackfeet told of an orphan boy, considered dim-witted, who sought this mysterious creature in a spirit lake. After undergoing a series of ordeals, he finally reached the lake and plunged into its waters. Underneath was a sacred landscape, where a spirit chief led him to galloping, lively *pono-kamita,* or "elk dogs." From the spirit chief the boy requested part of the elk dog herd. When he rode back into his home village, his people thought he was some half-man, half-animal monster. The boy turned the horses over to the people, saying, "Now we no longer need be humble footsloggers, because these animals will carry us swiftly everywhere we want to go. Now buffalo hunting will be easy. Now our tepees will be larger, our possessions will be greater, because an elk dog travois can carry a load ten times bigger than that of a dog."

Common Currency

Horses were stolen and traded from tribe to tribe by way of routes east and west of the Rockies. Before long there were herds of runaway horses, and eager tribesmen snagged their own wild mounts.

In the summer young Sioux horse catchers ventured into the Platte and Arkansas country, pursuing the herds in relays—riding one wild horse until it gave out, then hopping onto another, relentlessly driving the animals until they were utterly exhausted and easily lassoed. A second method took advantage of box canyons: relays of riders herded horses into narrow canyon passageways and then, tossing a loop attached to a stick, noosed them and tied them down.

Hunkpapa Sioux artist and warrior Swift Dog depicted himself capturing horses in this sketch; the circling footsteps indicate that he had sneaked into an enemy camp, where he captured three enemy horses tethered to their owners' tepee lodges — an admirable act of valor. The feathers attached to two of the horses' tails meant that they were prepared for war — a greater coup still for Swift Dog, for warrior horses were especially coveted.

The horse tracks engraved on this Osage quirt (right), made of elk antler and rawhide, provide a record of its owner's war deeds.

By the early 1700's, a common currency had entered the Plains in the form of the horse. Aspiring leaders won followers and status as their personal stables multiplied. Inevitably, as horses became the new index of wealth and warriors sought them by any possible means, the frequency of intertribal raids skyrocketed. Young men clamored to go out on these expeditions, often disobeying older chiefs to do so.

> By the time they came in close it was raining. They could see some Shoshones leading horses in to tie to stakes in front of their tepees. . . . Plenty Crows and Yellow Hair decided to find some really good horses, so they passed up seven or eight tepees. Then they found what they wanted and cut two horses loose, leading them to the center of the camp circle so their feet would not make noise close by the tepees.
>
> — *John Stands in Timber, Cheyenne, describing raid on Shoshone camp*

Stealing horses was even more exciting than capturing them wild. The seizure of enemy horses conferred honor comparable to that of killing an enemy. It offered the raiders a triumphant return to camp, past admiring women, galloping in with a string of snorting and whinnying trophies behind them.

Raiders prided themselves on their stealth, their ability to sneak into an enemy camp as silently as smoke. An old Indian fighter, Col. Richard Dodge, remembered how Comanches got away with his soldiers' horses. They crept into tents where a dozen men were sleeping, each with a horse tied to his wrist by a lariat. The Indians simply cut each rope within six feet of the sleeper and got away with the horses without waking a soul.

Horses transformed Plains Indian life by eliminating the uncertainties of food supply almost overnight. If buffalo could not be found nearby, hunters simply rode to wherever they were. Shooting at a thundering herd of buffalo from horseback was not only far less risky than running after them on foot and driving them off a cliff but also took less time and required fewer participants. Small

199

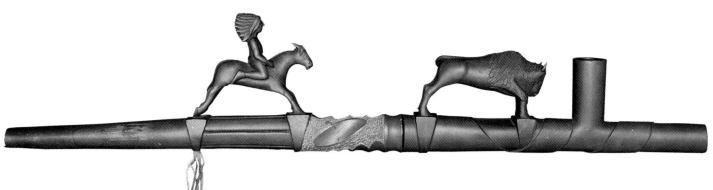

As the buffalo pipe (above) and the drawing by Sioux artist Sinte (below) both suggest, the adoption of the horse transformed buffalo hunting into a far more individualized pursuit.

bands or even individuals could locate a small herd and within a few hours slaughter enough to feed their people for months. It was then that true nomadism, a rarity in North America, began to flourish and tribal bands could come and go with few restraints.

While the horse enabled men to hunt independently, the women—whose role in forming the buffalo surrounds had previously been essential to the hunt—were now able to devote their time to processing the hides. After

every successful hunt there was now an excess of tanned buffalo skins, which translated into tradable goods and greater prosperity.

Trading Posts

Horses also gave Plains Indians easier access to trading posts, where they could exchange their surplus mounts and buffalo skins for European goods of all kinds. Since these new beasts of burden could drag far heavier loads than their dogs could bear in former times, Plains tribes were able to increase the quantity and variety of their household furnishings.

Tepees doubled in height, and in the Montana and Wyoming high country, the full 70- to 80-foot reach of arrow-straight lodgepole pines could be fully exploited for tepee poles. Indeed, Blackfeet women began sewing such large tepees that their hide covers had to be tailored in two halves, with store-bought brass buttons used to fasten them up the western side, while old-fashioned willow pins were used to lace them together on the eastern doorway side.

Among the much-sought-after products on the Plains were European-made glass trade beads in brilliant colors. These "pony" beads and, later, smaller "seed" beads replaced the more subtle, vegetable-dyed bird or porcupine quill decorations that Plains Indian women had traditionally used to embellish clothing and household items. Resplendent panels of beadwork began to appear on men's war shirts, leggings, moccasins, armbands and headbands, and on the pipe bags that they hung from their waistbands.

Initial trade contact with the English and French had occurred by the mid-1700's. The Mandan would come to call the white man "he who has everything," and they wanted what he had. By the early 1800's, axes, knives, awls, flint-and-steel kits, and brass kettles were becoming necessities of Plains Indian camp life.

TRADING ON THE SOUTHERN PLAINS

By the early 19th century, the Louisiana-Texas frontier had become the southern front of Anglo-American penetration into the West. Potential riches to be made from buffalo robes, silver ore — and, above all, wild mustangs — attracted increasing numbers of traders across the border to the Texas plains.

One such entrepreneur was Anthony Glass of Natchez, Mississippi, who in July 1808 set out from Natchitoches, Texas, for Taovaya-Wichita trading villages on the Red River. Blankets, cloth, beads, paints, tobacco, cookware, knives, hatchets, combs, mirrors, lead, gunpowder, and guns — all these and more were likely among the trade goods he brought with him.

Below are excerpts from his journal.

August 10th: WNW 18 miles . . . encamped about five Miles from the Panis [Taovaya-Wichita] Villages and according to custom dispatched a messenger to give notice of our approach.

August 11th: I then waited on the Great Chief and was received with every token of Friendship I informed him I would wait on him again the next day & informed him for what purpose we had come to his Country & returned to my tent we found our Camp filled with a quantity of green Corn, Beans, Water and Mus Melons.

August 12: I exhibited here some goods which I told them I had to exchange for horses several came and offered horses but were not satisfied with the offers made for them. A Chief man came up, and ordered the Indians all away; him and the principal chief spoke together some time and concluded that the fault was in my Interpreter and that it was him who made the difficulty; but they were mistaken. they demanded more for their horses than I could afford to give them two men went with me to my camp and were beginning to trade but before it was concluded the man who first made the difficulty came and ordered them all away.

The man I was endeavouring to trade with yesterday came over this morning and took the same for his horses I had offered him the day before. Several principal men came over and I bought about twenty horses without difficulty.

August 23rd: The Men who were out guarding the Horses came in this morning and reported that a party of Osages had stolen twenty nine of them, and the best we had.

Sept 6th: Met the Chiefs of the west side of the River in Council. some of the Company was displeased at the offer I had made him for his horse and said he would go and Inform the Spaniards that we were here — a Woman replied you may inform them but if they come here to interrupt our trading with these Americans I myself will kill their Captain — the other then said if that is your talk I don't go.

1839 pictorial calendar: a white trader conducts business in a tepee.

Sept 28th: A Party of Osages made their appearance on Horseback advancing directly to the village as though it was their intention to enter it, but it was soon discovered that their only object was to get between the Village and some of the Panie Horses so as to cut them off, which they effected and drove off a number. the Panis sallied out upon them and killed one of them and the Osages wounded a Pani so that he died the next day. . . . We were persuaded it was the same Party who stole our Horses on the 22nd of August — one of them was riding a remarkable Paint Horse that used to be my own riding Horse, which was stolen with those on the 22d of August—The Osage Indian that was killed was cut in pieces and distributed through the different Villages and all the men women and children danced for three days.

Oct 3rd: Satt off for an Hietan camp and had proceeded but a small distance . . . when the Panis found we were removing our goods a number came up to see us and began begging for something, the Wicheta Chief demanded a keg of Powder and said that if we refused to comply he said we should not travel on his side of the River. But he compromised for a small quantity.

White trappers and traders had penetrated the upper Plains via the Missouri River by the late 18th century. At right, a first encounter between the Cheyenne and white men on the river is portrayed by 19th-century Cheyenne artist Howling Wolf. European goods supplemented an already lively commerce among peoples of the Plains and the Southwest. Below, a white trader poses with a Navajo group — the men in European frock coats, the woman on the left with a Plains beaded bag prominently attached to her belt.

Extravagances such as pearl buttons and satiny ribbons were admired because they were pretty and colorful; ready-made trade woolens and calicoes not only were colorful but made life much easier for the women.

In Blackfeet country especially, some hunters turned from the open plains to the trading post as their source of supply. By 1780 the lucrative fur trade, chiefly controlled by the Canadian Hudson's Bay Company and the American North West Company, had expanded into the western Great Lakes region, and different breeds of the hairy newcomers the Blackfeet called *napikwans* ("old man persons") were penetrating their northern Plains stronghold. These so-called mountain men, who prowled the beaver streams of the Rocky Mountains to supply the vast European market for beaver-felt hats, were invariably followed by white traders.

Before long, the trading posts became hubs of commercial, social, and diplomatic interaction for many tribes. Here, in exchange for horses and buffalo meat, Indians could obtain

coveted firearms. Sugar, flour, coffee, and liquor entered the native diet. Throughout the Plains a growing dependence on these goods undermined traditional tribal cultures.

As elsewhere, alcohol had especially damaging effects. Liquor, diluted and cheapened, became known as Blackfeet rum. One trader to the Blackfeet commented in 1810, "That power for all evil, spirituous liquor, now seems to dominate them, and has taken such hold on them that they are no longer the quiet people they were."

Warrior Societies

The availability of horses brought an increase in male warrior societies that raided and hunted on horseback. When their bands camped in tepee circles, these societies kept the peace. When they traveled, with horses dragging their worldly possessions lashed on travois, the warrior societies rode flank, keeping an eye out for game, for grizzlies that could kill a man with one swipe of a paw, and for signs of enemies.

Warrior societies among the Assiniboin, Blackfeet, and Arapaho were "age-graded." Boys grew up through membership in an ad-

A Cheyenne man of status and power presents cloth to women of his tribe for their inspection in this drawing. The women seated in the foreground are wearing Navajo blankets, a popular trade item.

A buckskin shield cover painted by Big Bear, a Crow warrior, shows a bear emerging from its cave to charge a hail of bullets. Such an emblem (the bear traditionally symbolized valor in war) offered protection on the battlefield and, in most cases, was adopted after appearing to the warrior in a vision.

vancing series of societies, each with increased responsibilities. A few of the groups followed an extreme warrior code. The Cheyenne Bowstrings were also known as Contraries because they did everything backwards: when everyone else retreated in a hand-to-hand fight, they rushed forward. The Crazy-Dogs-Wishing-to-Die of the Crow staked their shoulder sashes to the ground with special spears, vowing to fight to the death unless released by a fellow warrior.

Warriors on horseback wielded small shields painted with powerful symbols such as medicine bears and birds to protect them from enemy fire. Bows were shortened and laminated for greater power, and clubs and short lances were crafted for close combat.

The use of firearms in warfare was not adopted throughout the Plains Indian world as readily as that of horses. Before the arrival of repeating rifles, warriors had to rely on smooth-bore muzzle-loaders, which were not very accurate and could not be fired as rapidly as arrows in the heat of battle. And to renew his gunpowder, lead shot, and spare parts, an Indian needed steady access to the white man's trading posts.

Highest honors were accorded the daring warrior who risked all to "count coups." A French word meaning "stroke" or "blow," *coup* could signify any sort of damage or humilia-

tion inflicted upon an enemy in war. Coups were the means by which a warrior gained status in his tribe, and they were scrupulously ranked—striking an enemy with a gun, bow, or riding quirt, for instance, might be considered a higher achievement than actually killing him. Other honors were granted for stealing horses, riding down an enemy, recovering his weapon, or scalping him.

Warriors proudly recollected their notable coups on formal occasions and recorded them with appropriate insignia, such as specially trimmed feathers, marks on their horses' flanks, beaded or quillwork strips on their

A buffalo-hide robe from the upper Missouri River records its owner's memorable coups by dividing the action into horizontal zones, each moving right to left, a format popular among Plains artists. Horse tracks and quirts indicate raids that the owner (who appears seven times, wearing a single feather and a black and red shirt) took part in.

war shirts, or pictographs painted on buffalo robes and tepee covers.

❧

When I was 16 years old, I accompanied a war party that fought with the soldiers. They retreated and we chased them. I was riding a steel-gray pony at the time, one of the fastest I have ever owned. I was ahead of the others. This was the first time I counted coup.

— *Chief White Bull, Teton Sioux*

❧

When following buffalo or enemies, Plains Indians might be led by daring, well-seasoned warriors who had struck many coups, so long

A young boy models warrior regalia, including a shell gorget and bear-claw necklace, in George Catlin's "Portrait of an Iowan Child."

pose. Later, when the westward-migrating Sioux took control of western Minnesota's quarries of brick-red pipestone, distinctive T-shaped stone pipe bowls gained acceptance as a badge of chiefly office throughout the Plains. Beaded pipe bags became an essential feature of male regalia, and the time-consuming etiquette that evolved around the ceremonial sharing of the pipe would often exasperate visiting white traders and diplomats.

Women's Guilds

As men became increasingly preoccupied with horse raiding and coup counting, the women of some Plains tribes were compelled to find new ways to assert their roles. Especially among the tribes that had formerly worked the land, the new nomadic lifestyle of increased warfare and year-round hunting eroded the women's traditional power base. As planters and harvesters of the village gardens in earlier times, they had enjoyed a relatively high position as providers and as guardians of domestic space.

Our native women gathered all the wild rice, roots, berries, and fruits which formed an important part of our food. Grandmother understood these matters perfectly, and it became a kind of instinct with her to know just where to look for each variety and at what season of the year. This sort of labor gave the Indian women every opportunity to observe and study nature . . . and in this Grandmother was more acute than most of the men.

— *Charles Eastman, Santee Sioux*

Now a woman's worth to her family and community increasingly came to rest upon her ability to manufacture and decorate a wide number of items not only for family use but also for trade. Throughout the Plains, women based their reputations upon the artistry they

as their power yielded ample game and no extreme losses in warfare. Staying in camp, however, called for more stable, chiefly leadership. Some tribes, notably the farming villagers, relied on their warrior societies to police the living areas and make sure that everyone was safely inside the log palisade by nightfall.

For the Cheyenne, the role of peace chief—charged with handling problems within the tribe—offered the highest degrees of prestige and responsibility. Men were chosen to join the "council of 44" peace chiefs for a 10-year term of office. During that time a chief was expected to be generous to the poor, to behave as a wise father to every tribal member, and to resolve disputes with a tenderhearted yet decisive manner.

Maintaining peace on an intertribal basis, however, called for more formalized rituals that centered on the use of tobacco. Adopted by all Plains tribes, ceremonial smoking established neutral ground among horseback tribes that found themselves in ever closer and more contentious proximity to one another. Animal-shaped or flat-disc pipe bowls carved from soapstone were originally used for the pur-

This Cheyenne baby carrier was probably produced in the late 19th century by a women's quilling society in Montana. European glass beads and brass tacks had by that time replaced porcupine quills as the primary decorative elements.

The portrait entitled "Chan Cha Uia Teuin, Teton Sioux Woman" by Karl Bodmer (above) shows a Lakota buffalo robe that exemplified Plains women's artistry at its best, using a complex vocabulary of abstract designs to represent the head, legs, torso, and internal organs of the buffalo.

brought to the making of pots, baskets, cradleboards, robes, moccasins, and beadwork. "Grandmother," one might address a venerated Blackfeet craftswoman, "we are happy to look upon one whose hands were always busy curing fine skins."

The burgeoning fur trade provided a ready market for the hides and pelts that women processed for export. Women's products were also coveted items on the intertribal trading network: 18th-century Europeans witnessed the Crow and Sioux trading decorated shirts, leggings, and animal-skin robes with the Mandan-Hidatsa for squash, corn, beans, tobacco, and guns.

Because the prosperity of the family—and of the community as a whole—was so closely tied to a woman's productivity, the Cheyenne considered a woman's creative accomplishments to be on a par with men's achievements in war. Special status was granted, for example, to a woman who had prepared 30 buffalo robes for trade.

Double Woman

Among the Cheyenne and other Plains tribes, artisan "guilds" controlled the production of all quillwork and beadwork. Members controlled the highly specialized knowledge needed for certain techniques, and instruction required payment. Those women who were fortunate enough to possess such knowledge were well paid for their creations. A quilled robe made by a member of a quilling society, for example, could easily be traded for a pony from the Arapaho or the Mandan-Hidatsa.

The quilling societies of the Sioux were organized by women who had dreamed of Double Woman, a supernatural figure who, according to legend, had first taught Lakota

women how to dye quills and perform intricate quillwork. Double Woman possessed two contrasting natures: one industrious and virtuous, the other idle and lascivious. She offered the dreamer a choice between the productive practice of special skills in craftwork and the ability to wreak havoc by stealing other women's men.

The quilling society was a force for stability, then, serving to prevent disruption before it occurred and providing the dreamer with a channel through which to direct her gifts for the benefit of the community.

If you are willing to remain in ignorance and not learn how to do the things a woman should know how to do, you will ask other women to cut your moccasins and fit them for you. You will go from bad to worse: you will leave your people, go into a strange tribe, fall into trouble, and die there friendless.

— Omaha elder

The Select Women sisterhood of the Kiowa and Southern Cheyenne came together regularly to pray, eat, and participate collectively on quillwork and, later, tepee making and beadwork. Their work might stem from a member's vow that she would sponsor a series of tepee-making sessions if someone close to her was cured of an illness or if a friend experienced easy childbirth or if a relative was about to be married.

The proceedings were initiated by special prayers and the burning of sweet-grass incense to bless the outcome of the work. An atmosphere of reverence was maintained as the tepee was cut to shape and sewn, and as its "dew cloth" liners were painted. Tepees accorded this loving attention were adorned with special tassels made of porcupine quills and dewclaws taken from deer. One member of a women's guild would recall that she was carefully instructed by her elders never to disclose any details of the tepee decorators' ceremony in the presence of men.

MANLY-HEARTED WOMEN

In most Plains tribes, women's duties centered on the home, while men were responsible for war and hunting. There were notable exceptions, however. A few women regularly participated in buffalo hunts, and some fought — and killed — alongside the men in battle.

Sometimes known as manly-hearted women, these female hunters and warriors displayed the same degree of courage and skill as their male counterparts. There are, for instance, accounts of Plains women charging their enemies in the thick of combat and counting coup on those killed. At least one such battle was named in honor of a woman's bravery.

Some of the best-known women warriors were members of the Cheyenne tribe. Perhaps the most illustrious of these was Buffalo Calf Woman, sister of the distinguished Cheyenne warrior Chief Comes In Sight. In the early summer of 1876, Buffalo Calf Woman rescued her wounded brother from a battlefield where he had fallen. Had it not been for her courage, Chief Comes in Sight almost certainly would have died that day. The high esteem in which the Cheyenne held her is evidenced by the fact that the fight became known as "Where the Girl Saved Her Brother."

Another Cheyenne woman who fought in battle was Island Woman, wife of White Frog. While taking part in an attack on the Pawnee, Island Woman was charged by a hatchet-wielding Pawnee warrior. She reputedly wrenched the hatchet from her assailant's hand, knocking the Pawnee from his horse.

Of all the Plains' manly-hearted women, the most ruthless may have been Ehyophsta, better known as Yellow-Haired Woman. The daughter of Cheyenne chief Stands in Timber and the niece of the old Bad Faced Bull, Ehyophsta fought not only in the battle of Beecher's Island in 1867 but also during the battle between the Cheyenne and the Shoshone the following year, when she counted coup on one enemy and killed another. One of the last of the Cheyenne fighting women, Yellow-Haired Woman died in 1915.

In addition to warfare, some Plains women excelled at hunting. The pictograph below is part of a dress that was owned by Pretty White Cow, niece of Sitting Bull, and shows two women hunters. One wears a long dress and chases an antelope on foot, while the other spears a bear from her horse. (On the opposite side of the dress, two women are depicted killing and butchering buffalo.) Pictured at right, the woman known only as "Betsy," from the Omaha tribe, was a widely renowned buffalo hunter.

WOMEN'S QUILLING SOCIETY

A meeting of a women's quilling society, held in a lodge in a Northern Cheyenne settlement in about 1820, has convened for a special occasion: the young woman seated on the left has invited members of the society to a feast celebrating the quilling of her first robe. The society offers graded memberships, based on the particular item that the woman has learned how to make. Ascending in order, there are membership divisions for moccasins; baby cradles; stars for ornamenting lodges; buffalo robes; and lodge linings, back rests, and parfleches.

With the help of an "old crier" who goes about the camp spreading news of the feast, the initiate has invited all members of the division she is about to join. Before the food is served, it is customary for each woman to tell of the robes she has quilled, just as warriors would recount their brave deeds. The initiate's instructor, seated beside her, leads off the tales by virtue of seniority. Afterward, the old crier may be asked to invite a tribal member — it could be a man or a woman, an honored leader or an elderly, infirm neighbor — to come and observe the initiate quill the robe. The guest, whoever it may be, will receive a handsome gift — perhaps a horse, a blanket, even the robe itself — and then depart. Finally, the ceremonies will conclude with an offering of prayers for the initiate and the serving of food to all those present.

MEANINGS OF THE MEDICINE WHEELS

While early belief systems on the Plains can only be speculated about, there are ovals of rock across the high country that undoubtedly are "fasting beds," special sites on buttes and promontories where vision questers sought spiritual empowerment.

More dramatic are the so-called medicine wheels — large spoked circles made of stones that range from Canada to Wyoming. The best-known wheel occupies a high flat area in the Big Horn Mountains of northern Wyoming. Its 28 stone alignments — or spokes — radiate to an outer circle marked by stone cairns. On the morning of the summer solstice, the rising point of the sun links an outer stone marker with one on the inside of the wheel. In addition, shortly before the solstice the wheel provides similar alignments for two very bright stars in the constellation Orion. Farther north, in the Saskatchewan plains occupied by the Blackfeet, other medicine wheels follow virtually identical plans. Were these forms of calendric markers set up so that priests might properly time the beginning of important ceremonies? The best answer is that there is no single answer. Many Plains tribes today make ancestral claims to these sites and have differing explanations for their original purpose. Some Crow people of Montana, for instance, say that the Wyoming medicine wheel was the prototype for their first Sun Dance Lodge, while others say with equal confidence that it was put there by the sun to show them how to make their tepees.

Powers of the Spirit World

Throughout the Plains, men and women alike sought spiritual power through dreams, visions, sacred objects, and songs that could impart special luck or the ability to alter events in their favor. The Oglala Sioux called this power *wakan*; to the Crow it was *maxpe*; in English it is usually translated as "medicine." A Lakota shaman named Sword described it this way: "Every object in the world has a spirit, and that spirit is *wakan*. Thus the spirit of the tree or things of that kind are also *wakan*. *Wakan* comes from the *wakan* beings. These *wakan*

The supernatural figure called Double Woman was commonly depicted as two women joined by a rope from which a doll or ball was suspended, as in this Sioux drawing. A woman who dreamed of her, the Lakota believed, was granted special prowess in quillwork.

beings are greater than mankind in the same way that mankind is greater than animals. They can do many things that mankind cannot do. Mankind can pray to the *wakan* beings for help."

To this end, at the time of puberty almost every Plains Indian boy set out on vision quests — periodic wilderness retreats in which the initiate hoped to receive guidance from the spirit world. Only with the aid of special power beings — such as the spirits of eagles, hawks, or bears — it was believed, could a person gain that extra jolt of supernatural assistance needed to succeed in war, curing, love, or tribal leadership.

After a purifying "sweat" in a bowl-shaped sweat bath framed with willows, shrouded with buffalo hides, and steam-heated with hot rocks splashed with water, the young quester shouldered his sleeping hide and trekked to a sacred butte. At the summit he fasted for four days, wept and prayed naked before the elements, and sometimes went so far as to cut off a finger to entice a spirit to grace him with an empowering vision.

After the quester returned to camp and again entered a purifying sweat bath, elders helped him assemble objects that his spirit guide had instructed him to collect. Wrapped

English (Witches) playing with
their Baby
Dakota (Wiwyan) Wakapika Wakriglula Wata

in a skin, these items were known as a medicine bundle and were a warrior's dearest possessions. They might be unwrapped prior to any perilous enterprise when a man needed the sacred protection that had been granted him during his original vision. Horses were often symbolized in these bundles. A Crow warrior might keep a red-winged blackbird stuffed with buffalo hair in his bundle because the bird was known to hover around tethered horses, and hence the bundle had the power to bring its owner and horses together.

Tribal Medicine

Most Plains tribes, in addition, had sacred objects that were unique to their history and as essential to their collective identity as their language. The Southern branch of the Cheyenne had four Sacred Arrows, and the Northern Cheyenne had a Sacred Buffalo Hat. The Sioux had a White Buffalo Calf Pipe; the Arapaho, a Flat Pipe; the Gros Ventres, a Feathered Pipe. The Kiowa kept a feathered effigy called the Tai-Me.

The Pawnee, who traced their origins to star deities, possessed a Morning Star bundle. The Crow had Tobacco Society bundles that carried the sacred tobacco seeds—seeds upon which the very survival of the Crow as a people was believed to depend. Clans or religious societies paid homage to these special medicine bundles, which they owned collectively, opening them in religious gatherings held during the first thunderstorm of spring or the first snowfall of autumn.

Women throughout the Plains played key religious roles in these community rituals. Some also undertook vision quests, became respected shamans, or used their special powers to excel in battle, but many more chose to channel their spiritual gifts through sacred women's societies. Among the Blackfeet, for example, buffalo-calling ceremonies were performed by members of the all-female *mutokaiks*, or Buffalo Bull Society. Women also participated in rites associated with tobacco planting and the lighting of the sacred Thunder Medicine Pipe.

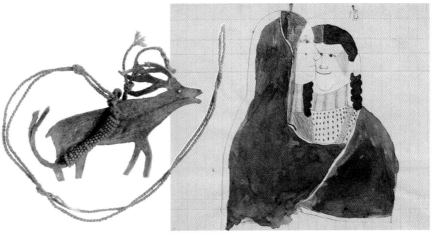

The Sun Dance

As the proliferation of horses allowed closer contact among various Plains tribes, many of them came to observe the same ritual, one of profound importance. It was the Sun Dance: a four-day religious festival in which singers, drummers, dancers, and spectators gathered to seek communally the sort of power that they sought as individuals in their private vision quests.

Some historians suggest that the Sun Dance appeared around 1700, possibly originating with the Cheyenne. To the Plains Indians, however, the ceremony was ageless—a divine gift from the supernatural world. In

A young warrior (top) is surrounded in a vision by wolves who initiate him in special wisdom. The spirit of the elk was thought to bring success in courtship; an amulet such as this Crow cutout of rawhide and glass beads (above left) may have aided the "Courting Couple" (above), by Cheyenne artist Old White Woman, to secure a happy ending.

any case, by 1750 virtually every Plains tribe practiced some variation of the Sun Dance.

To the Cheyenne it was known as the New Life Lodge; to the Ponca it was the Mystery Dance; to the Sioux it was the Gaze at the Sun Dance. Regardless of the name, all the tribes erected a central Sun Dance Medicine Lodge, which served as the sacred ceremonial space. Within a circular framework of poles constructed around a central sacred cottonwood tree, which was loosely walled with leafy boughs, young painted "pledgers" fasted and danced continuously.

Attended by tribal shamans, the youths prayed to their creator as the wind tossed banners hanging from the rafters of the lodge and rawhide effigies dangling from the center pole. Then the pledgers' skin was pierced with skewers, which were attached by rawhide thongs to the center pole. As the young men danced, they tore their flesh as a sacrificial expression of the sincerity of their prayers for a powerful vision—not only for their personal well-being but for the happiness and prosperity of their people as well.

Wakan' tanka, when I pray to him, hears me.
Whatever is good, he grants me.
—*Teton Sioux Sun Dance song*

Whatever similarities their Sun Dances may have shared, each tribe put its stamp of symbolism and interpretation on the ritual. For the Cheyenne it was a world-renewal ritual, and the altar featured elements that reminded them of their agricultural heritage. For the Crow it was unashamedly an opportunity to secure war-making power for successful revenge against enemies. For every group, however, these rituals served a deeply felt need on the part of the entire tribe to unite behind a common supernatural enterprise.

The Sun Dance camp was a huge circle of tepees, a symbolic universe that could reach more than a mile in circumference, as did this Blackfeet conclave in Montana. Each tribal clan, band, and other subgroup occupied the same sector of the circle year after year.

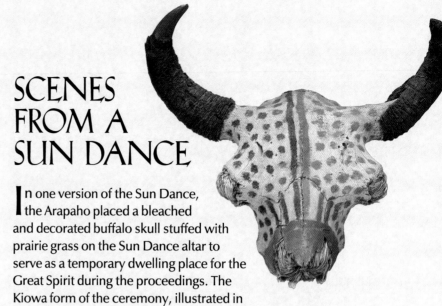

SCENES FROM A SUN DANCE

In one version of the Sun Dance, the Arapaho placed a bleached and decorated buffalo skull stuffed with prairie grass on the Sun Dance altar to serve as a temporary dwelling place for the Great Spirit during the proceedings. The Kiowa form of the ceremony, illustrated in five hide paintings by Kiowa artist Silverhorn, followed this sequence:

1. Two warriors (above center) return to camp from counting coup on a cottonwood tree selected to be the central pole for the Medicine Lodge, whose framework is already in place below the tree. The keeper of the Tai-Me (below right), the sacred image of the Kiowa, makes a smoke offering before the image is exposed in the ceremony.
2. Military society warriors stage a mock battle to capture the central pole, which is defended by women and other warriors.
3. The pole, with offerings attached, is raised within the camp circle.
4. The sides of the Medicine Lodge are filled in with leafy branches.
5. Sun Dance participants make use of ritual objects, including pipes, fans, whistles, rattles, a Tai-Me box, and an exposed Tai-Me. Also depicted (right) are peyote ceremonies, which were adopted in later times after the Sun Dance had been discontinued.

ARTFUL HOMES

Emblem of Plains life, the tepee (the word comes from a Siouan term meaning "used to dwell") reached the peak of its grandeur in the 19th century. Painted tepees were relatively rare and usually belonged to men. Such a shelter, with the considerable spiritual power and prestige that went with it, could be obtained as a gift from an ally, as war spoils, or through inheritance or outright purchase. A painted tepee could also be obtained through a direct supernatural encounter. According to tribal traditions, a guardian spirit — often an animal with special powers — would appear in a dream or vision and bestow upon the fortunate man his own "lodge," with instructions on how to paint the tepee cover and collect sacred material linked with the dwelling. The man could then paint his own tepee cover, prevail on friends for help, or employ an artist to do the work according to his visionary instructions.

Thereafter the tepee was part of a sacred package that included the narrative of the original owner's vision, the sacred objects (which were stored in a bundle on a tripod behind the tepee by day), and special songs associated with the dwelling.

The designs that appeared on painted tepees, such as these at Standing Rock Sioux Reservation (above), could be handed down over generations. The tepee in the foreground belonged to Old Bull, a nephew of Sitting Bull. Right and below: A Blackfeet four-pole tepee floor plan shows the doorway facing the rising sun. Its steeper rear side braces the tilted structure against prevailing westerly winds, allowing the fire to be directly below the smoke flaps.

Blackfeet women, sewing a tepee cover at left, could also paint abstract designs on the inside or outside of the tepee; more concrete images, however, such as the buffalo on the tepee in the foreground, were traditionally the province of men. Below (left to right) are some of the oldest Blackfeet symbols. The top of the snake tepee shows constellations of stars related to tribal legends about the origin of the snake tepee; the male snake is positioned on the southern side of the tepee and the female on the northern side, both facing the eastern doorway. The horse tepee uses the same traditional male-female positioning and has a similar pair of constellations at the top. On the buffalo tepee, the spiritual dimension inherent in the buffalo and all other creatures is made visible by the "heart line" extending from the animal's throat to its heart, both considered sites of supernatural power.

A Sioux warrior counts coup on a Crow enemy in the ledger book of Sioux artist Amos Bad Heart Bull. When trading posts made paper goods such as ledgers, calendars, and date books readily available, Plains Indians had a new medium in which to record autobiographical deeds or important tribal events.

The hands on this Mandan shirt from Fort Berthold, North Dakota, count its owner's coups, which may literally have been struck by hand or else by using an object like the Sioux coup stick (right). The human hair on the shirt may have come from friend or foe — as a gift of tribute from comrades its owner led in battle or as a war trophy from a vanquished enemy.

New Alliances

As horse-rich tribes staked out their favored roaming and hunting territories in the Plains, they forged military alliances based sometimes on shared cultural traditions and sometimes purely on the existence of common enemies. One early partnership arose between the Siouan-speaking Assiniboin people and the Algonquian-speaking Plains Cree. Opposing them was the mighty Blackfeet alliance, whose three constituent tribes—Piegan, Blood, and Northern Blackfeet (also called Siksika)—had long-standing bonds of language and custom. A third alliance, that of the earth-lodge communities along the middle Missouri River, was less a military than a self-protective and cultural coalition.

But there was a fourth great alliance that threatened all the others with aggressive militarism and overwhelming numbers: the "seven council fires" of the Sioux. Altogether they amounted to some 25,000 loosely affiliated tribesmen in the 1790's. The four Eastern groups were known collectively as the Dakota, or Santee Sioux. In the middle were the Yankton and Yanktonai, keepers of the sacred pipestone quarry. Fully 40 percent of the alliance belonged to the Teton, or Western, Sioux.

For good reason, then, the earth-lodge tribes—whose horses, dried squash, and corn the Sioux coveted—together with the Sioux's traditional enemy, the Crow, were constantly vigilant about survival. Once the Sioux bolstered their numbers with Cheyenne and Arapaho allies, they became the most formidable fighting force on the northern Plains.

Despite the sudden emphasis on warfare and the widespread abandonment of farming by many tribes, the earth-lodge villages of the Mandan and Hidatsa clung to their older, more sedentary way of life. Like still centers amid the whirling changes in Plains Indian life surrounding them, their towns continued to produce and dry much-desired vegetables for trade and to practice rituals that originated long before contact with the white man.

Their large, well-kept villages and their hospitable attitude toward outsiders were remarked on by white visitors. The French fur trader and explorer Pierre La Verendrye had visited one of their earlier villages near pre-sent-day Bismark in 1738 and commended the stout construction of its enclosing palisade and the spaciousness of the earth lodges. Another trader named David Thompson passed through in 1790 and measured one of the earth lodges at 90 feet in diameter. Nomadic Plains Indians were frequent visitors as well, bringing horses to trade for vegetables and tobacco.

The Sioux feast bowl above depicts the head of Eyah, god of gluttony, attached to a bloated stomach. With every feather signifying a coup counted in war, Crow chiefs (below) share a moment of noncombative repose at a feast in Montana.

Smallpox Winter

Another product of the white man's world began to spread across the Plains: disease. Pictorial calendar records, known as Winter Counts, kept by Missouri River villagers document six major epidemics between 1725 and 1802, with the first onslaught of smallpox striking the Plains Indians about 1780. If even a single member of a village returned from a visit to another tribe or a trading post with skin sores and high fever, the community was lucky if anyone was alive a few months later.

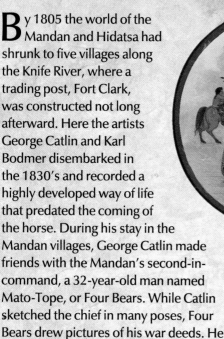

By 1805 the world of the Mandan and Hidatsa had shrunk to five villages along the Knife River, where a trading post, Fort Clark, was constructed not long afterward. Here the artists George Catlin and Karl Bodmer disembarked in the 1830's and recorded a highly developed way of life that predated the coming of the horse. During his stay in the Mandan villages, George Catlin made friends with the Mandan's second-in-command, a 32-year-old man named Mato-Tope, or Four Bears. While Catlin sketched the chief in many poses, Four Bears drew pictures of his war deeds. He had killed five enemy chiefs, as his own pictographic war shirt and painted buffalo robe vividly illustrated. The two men ate, talked, and smoked together in Four Bears' earth lodge.

George Catlin and Mato-Tope (Four Bears) had something in common: Both liked to portray their exploits. Above: Detail from a buffalo-skin robe painted by Mato-Tope, depicting one of his many acts of valor in battle. Left: "Catlin Painting the Four Bears," by George Catlin. Below: "Mato-Tope (Four Bears), Mandan Chief," by Karl Bodmer.

FOUR BEARS

No sooner had Catlin left for the East Coast than another artist, the Swiss watercolorist Karl Bodmer, arrived with an expedition led by Prince Maximilian du Weid. Again Four Bears had a painting partner and guest.

Four Bears became chief of the Mandan in 1837, but his tenure was tragically short-lived. An American Fur Company steamboat that tied up that summer near the Mandan villages had a smallpox-infected crewman aboard. Despite warnings from the captain, some Indians boarded the vessel. Four Bears' hospitality to outsiders was no protection against the scourge that now struck with a vengeance.

In just eight weeks, a population of 1,600 Mandans fell to 125. The disease spread to take half of the Hidatsas, who had just returned from their summer hunt, and many Arikaras, who had only recently come to live with the two tribes.

Four Bears — his entire family having perished before his eyes, his own face ravaged by the disease — is reported to have commanded his people: "It will be the last time you will hear me. Think of your wives, children, brothers, sisters, friends . . . all are dead, or dying, with their faces all rotten, caused by these dogs the whites. Think of that, my friends, and rise together and leave not one of them alive." He died that afternoon. Traumatized, the remnants of the tribe moved upstream, following an old Mandan prophecy that they must never descend the river to construct a new life.

Just after the turn of the 19th century, a major outbreak of smallpox and cholera struck again, nearly exterminating the Omaha, Ponca, Oto, and Iowa peoples. The vicious diseases spread north and south, heading up the Missouri River to decimate the Arikara, Gros Ventre, Mandan, Crow, and Sioux, and down the Mississippi to wreak havoc among the Kiowa, Pawnee, Wichita, and Caddo. The artist George Catlin was visiting the Omaha during this terrible period and witnessed the burial of a great chief, The Blackbird. The dead man was given his pipe and medicine bundle, plus flint and steel and tinder, wrote Catlin, "to light his way." And a tobacco pouch was filled to assist him to the "beautiful hunting grounds of the shades of his fathers."

꙳

If the Great Spirit sent the smallpox into our country to destroy us, it was to punish us for listening to the false promises of white men. It is a white man's disease, and no doubt it was sent amongst white people to punish *them* for their sins.

— *Neu-mon-ya, Paxoche*

꙳

In the Winter Count of the Kiowa, the time 1839–40 is remembered by a single pictograph: a man covered with red spots. The Mandan and Hidatsa were not the only ones to suffer from this "smallpox winter." It showed no favorites, killing perhaps 8,000 Blackfeet, 2,000 Pawnee, and 1,000 Crow. People committed suicide in vast numbers when the disease descended on their villages. All across the northern and southern Plains, the bodies piled up too quickly to be given decent burial. They were heaped in mass graves or thrown into the river.

There were other disturbing signs that the glory days of Plains Indian horsemen were on the wane. The 1804–06 expedition of Lewis and Clark to survey and document the landscapes, plants, animals, and Indian tribes of the West constituted a sort of scientific forerunner for the territorial takeover by the U.S. government that was soon to follow.

The next government probe into the Plains Indian world came in 1825. That year Brig. Gen. Henry Atkinson and Indian agent Benjamin O'Fallon sought out chiefs for negotiating treaties concerning trade and friendship. In early July, Atkinson's party intercepted the Cheyenne at their base camp near the Black Hills. An Atkinson aide described the 15 Cheyenne leaders who convened with the general as "decidedly the finest-looking Indians we have seen."

These 15 individuals willingly put their thumbprints to a document acknowledging U.S. political and commercial authority over their region. But they represented only one of the tribe's 10 bands; they were only 15 out of an estimated 3,000 Cheyenne. As would happen time and again in Indian-white frontier diplomacy, what U.S. officials considered a legally binding agreement, the great majority of Indians neither understood nor accepted.

The Gathering Storm

By the early 1830's southern Plains tribesmen began noticing long mule trains rumbling across their territory, loaded with cloth and store goods. They were bound for Santa Fe, where their merchandise could be traded for Mexican silver. Intrigued as well

Top: The Mandan placated O-kee-pa (the Evil Spirit) through special ceremonies, but neither ritual nor sweat bath — as sketched by George Catlin below — could keep smallpox at bay. The 1851 Oglala Winter Count (above), drawn by Oglala artist Shortman, recorded an epidemic that year.

*If I could
see this thing,
if I knew where it was,
I would go there
and kill it.*

— *Cheyenne warrior
dying of cholera,
1849*

as irritated, warriors of the Kiowa and Comanche, the Cheyenne and Arapaho soon stopped brawling among themselves and joined forces. The Cheyenne and the Arapaho made peace in 1840; the same year the Kiowa and the Comanche, who had stopped fighting each other in 1790, forged a potent alliance.

For the next quarter-century the swift horsemen and stealthy warriors of these southern tribes descended like hawks on the slow-moving pack trains along the Santa Fe Trail and also launched regular rustling forays against the cattle ranches that were proliferating in western Texas and eastern New Mexico.

At first these depredations brought new wealth into their tepee circles—silver to be beaten into ornaments, mirrors for dance regalia and silent signaling between war parties, and an occasional Mexican or fair-haired Anglo child as an adopted member of the family.

Farther north, however, similar traffic on what whites called the Oregon Trail was producing no fringe benefits for the native populations. By 1843 the road shoulders on both sides of the North Platte and Sweetwater sections of the Oregon Trail were virtually devoid of grass—and the wagon traffic west had

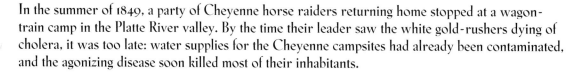

In the summer of 1849, a party of Cheyenne horse raiders returning home stopped at a wagon-train camp in the Platte River valley. By the time their leader saw the white gold-rushers dying of cholera, it was too late: water supplies for the Cheyenne campsites had already been contaminated, and the agonizing disease soon killed most of their inhabitants.

only just begun. In the summer of 1845, Col. Stephen Kearney ran into 460 wagons, 7,000 head of cattle, and more than 2,300 people on the same road. The buffalo were scared off, the meager stands of river-bottom timber were depleted, and streambeds were made muddy from cattle tracks.

At the same time Mormon wagon trains were lining up for Utah country in increasing numbers—nearly 800 wagons and 2,500 people arrived from Illinois in the summer of 1848 alone. With them came measles, scarlet fever, whooping cough, and other illnesses that would soon devastate the hunting and gathering bands of the Great Basin.

⁘

"I am unwilling for you to wander over this land," said the white man.

White Buffalo in the Distance said, "But we have wild animals, which are beyond our dwelling place, though they are on our land."

"Though you say so, the land is mine," said the white man.

— *Omaha hunter, recalling encounter with Mormon farmers in Iowa*

⁘

Many tribesmen also noticed disturbing changes in the populations and habits of the animals they depended on. Traders paid some Indians in liquor to hunt wholesale—a gruesome practice described in one case by George Catlin. Native hunters, Catlin reported in 1832, were wiping out a herd of 1,500 buffalo near Fort Pierre. Only the tongues were saved for transport to St. Louis; the meat and raw hides were left to the wolves. But with the demise of the beaver trade due to overtrapping in the 1830's, a new market for buffalo robes filled the vacuum in the late 1840's. At this time the Arapaho were complaining that the "white man was bad, that he ran the buffalo out of the country, and starved the Arapaho." An Indian agent foresaw that the buffalo would soon be hunted to extermination and that, in his words, "the Indians will have great difficulty in procuring sufficient for their own clothing and food."

The times were changing, and many Plains Indians read the signs with foreboding. One was a Southern Cheyenne war leader named Yellow Wolf. In August 1846 his buffalo-hide tepee was pitched beside William Bent's trading post, an important stopover on the Santa Fe Trail. Recuperating from an illness at the post was Lt. J.J. Abert of the U.S. Army, who was about to travel to Pueblo country for the government. Struck by the 60-year-old warrior's engaging intelligence, Abert recorded Yellow Wolf's thoughts in his private journal. The Indian observed that buffalo were harder to find and confided a deeper fear that unless his people adopted the white man's ways and found some alternative to their hunting way of life, they would disappear forever.

In fact, another 40 years of Indian rebellion still lay ahead—years of whole tribes removed and resettled, of pitched battles and pitiless massacres and violent deaths of many good-hearted Indians like Yellow Wolf, who fell at the age of 85. On all horizons of those Great Plains—the same vistas a somber Black Elk would point out to his visitors nearly a century later—there loomed the gathering storm-clouds of violent and irreversible change.

Heralds of a new epoch, wagon trains converge in 1870 at Red Buttes and the North Platte River in Wyoming, one of the key junctures for migrants on the Oregon Trail.

This 1820 entry in a Sioux winter count— a pictographic record of tribal history—was also a glimpse of the future. Its meaning, translated by a medicine man named Kills Two: "A white man built his house on Sioux lands without permission."

I recall all the memories
from those days . . . when all
meat was juicy and tender, and
no game too swift for a hunter.
When I was young, every
day was a beginning of some
new thing, and every evening
ended with the glow of the
next day's dawn.
—Ivaluarjuk Iglulik elder

7

NORTHERN WORLDS

THE ARCTIC, SUBARCTIC, AND NORTHWEST COAST

n a midsummer day in 1806, a white fur trader named Simon Fraser, leading an expedition deep into the mountain wilderness of British Columbia, landed his birchbark canoe on the edge of a forest lake. Stepping ashore, he squeezed off a musket shot to announce his arrival. Some local people—Dakelne, they called themselves—were standing by the tree line and, though the sky was clear, they thought lightning had struck. Terrified, they dropped to the ground. Fraser coaxed them into the open with an offer of tobacco, a leaf they had not seen before. Their leader, named Kwah, took a curious nibble but quickly spat it out: It was too bitter. Fraser then lit up his pipe, causing the Dakelne to gasp in astonishment. These strangers must come from the land of ghosts, someone said; they were blowing spirits into the air.

The confusions multiplied. Fraser offered bars of soap to the women, who took them to be cakes of bear fat and politely bit in. Foaming at the mouth, they hurried to the lake to wash out the taste. Familiar places acquired new names. The body of water where Fraser landed had always been called Nakal; Fraser decided it should henceforth be Stuart Lake, after one of his traveling companions. The river on which he traveled became the Fraser. The Dakelne themselves would soon be known to English speakers as the Carriers— because widows were expected to carry leather backpacks containing the ashes of their cremated husbands.

To the Dakelne, the customs of the whites seemed equally strange. When Fraser returned two years later to build a fur trading post at Stuart Lake, he celebrated its opening with a bagpipe concert. "A white witch doctor picked up what appeared to be a crane," a Dakelne elder told his listeners. "He put the bird over his shoulder. Then he blew, and made his fingers dance on the bird's bill. And what spooky sounds were made—a noise like the demons of the Mutche Manitou, that whistled all they way up the lake and whistled all the way back again."

Everywhere it was the same. Across the vast sweep of the North country—from the cool

WHITE MAN, RED MAN

When French explorer Jacques Cartier landed in Newfoundland in 1534, he came upon a band of hunters who called themselves Beothuk. "They wear their hair tied on top of their heads like a bunch of hay," he noted; "they paint themselves with a certain red color." Not only their bodies, but their caribou-skin clothing, bows and arrows, their birchbark canoes were all smeared with a mixture of red ocher and seal fat. Ever after, whites would think of Native Americans as "red men."

Cartier sailed on, but others (below) came to trade and colonize. Relations soon turned sour. Following an unwritten law of the region, that a hungry man takes what he needs, the Beothuk helped themselves to food belonging to the colonists—who in turn armed the nearby Micmac with muskets. The result was a war of extermination; by the early 1800's only a handful of Beothuks remained alive. Then three women were discovered, a mother and two daughters, all suffering from tuberculosis. The youngest, Shawanahdit (left), was adopted by a white family, who tried nursing her back to health. But in 1829 she, too, died—the last known Beothuk.

◄ Preceding page: Angokwazhuk, an Inupiat raised to be a hunter but hobbled by injury, discovered a talent for ivory carving that by the late 1800's made him the leading carver in Nome, known by his adopted name—Happy Jack.

Pacific rain forests to the muskeg swamps of Hudson Bay and north across the tundra to the Arctic ice pack—each new encounter between natives and whites seemed only to deepen the misunderstandings. Back in the 16th century, as English explorers sailed past Labrador, some fur-clad Inuit men had mistaken them for cannibals and jumped off cliffs to escape capture. At the western edge of the continent, when Captain James Cook sailed into Nootka Sound in 1778, a squadron of 50-foot war canoes approached his ship. A shaman threw handfuls of feathers and began a long harangue. Was it a greeting? A declaration of war? It turned out to be an invitation to trade, and Cook sailed off with a hold full of sea otter pelts—an event that would alter the course of history in the Pacific Northwest.

Even after years of contact, misapprehensions continued. Some years after Cook's departure, British Captain George Vancouver and Spanish Captain Bodega y Quadra met in Nootka Sound to settle their nations' conflicting land claims in the region. To honor their visit, Maquinna, powerful chief of the Nuuchal-nuth tribe (mistakenly named Nootka by the foreigners), prepared a feast that included great vats of fricasseed porpoise, whale, seal, and other rich and oily delicacies. The two Europeans, knowing from experience what the menu was likely to be, brought their own food and drink—and so delivered an insult that no native leader would soon forget.

At the time of the first encounters, the population of the North country was at least a third of a million and possibly much more, divided among more than 50 different tribal groups. The land they inhabited covered some 4 million square miles—larger than all the countries of western Europe combined. It reached from the fogbound Atlantic coast of Newfoundland to the windswept tip of the Aleutian Islands in the North Pacific, and from the dense evergreen forests that gird Subarctic Canada up through Arctic realms of pack ice and permafrost. The region's northern tier has a stark, desolate beauty unlike anywhere else on the continent. Winter cold dips to 60 degrees below zero in places, and winds howl relentlessly across the tundra. At higher latitudes the December sun becomes little more than a dim ghost on the southern horizon; the twilight lasts for months on end.

SIBERIA

ARCTIC OCEAN

Chukchi
Sea

Point
Hope
Point
Barrow
Bering Strait
awrence
Island
Cape Prince of Wales
INUPIAT
BROOKS RANGE

ivak
nd
INUPIAT
CENTRAL
YUPIK
ESKIMOS
KOYUKON
uskokwim R.
INGALIK
GWICH'IN
(Kutchin)
ALASKA RANGE
Yukon R.

TANAINA
HARE
Bloody Falls
Mackenzie R.
Great Bear Lake
Coppermine R.

KONIAG
Snag
YUKON
YELLOWKNIFE
COPPER
ESKIMO
Prince
William
Sound
TUTCHONE
DOGRIB
CARIBOU ESKIMO

Kodiak
Island

TLINGIT
Great Slave
Lake
Fort Resolution

TAHLTAN
SLAVEY

SEKANI
DUNNE-ZA
(Beaver)
Lake
Athabasca
CHIPEWYAN
Fort Prince
of Wales
Stuart Lake

HAIDA
DAKELNE
(Carrier)
WESTERN
WOODS CREE
Churchill R.

NUXALK
(Bella Coola)
WEST MAIN CREE

Nootka
Sound
NUU-CHAL-NUTH
(Nootka)

COAST
SALISH
Fraser R.
Columbia R.
ROCKY MOUNTAINS

NORTHWEST COAST
COAST MOUNTAINS

ARCTIC

SUBARCTIC

Ellesmere
Island
POLAR ESKIMO
Thule
Baffin Bay
Devon Island
Pond Inlet

IGLULIK

NETSILIK
BAFFINLAND
ESKIMO

QUEBEC
INUIT
Hudson Bay

LABRADOR ESKIMO
INNU
(Naskapi)
EAST CREE
INNU
(Montagnais)
BEOTHUK

MICMAC
Quebec
Montreal
St. Lawrence R.

GREENLAND ESKIMO

Fur Fever

Yet the same landscape enfolds pockets of natural wealth and cultural richness. Enormous herds of caribou once roamed seasonally between forest and tundra, offering a moveable feast for nomadic hunters of both the interior and the Arctic north slope. Sea mammals—whales, walrus, seals, sea lions—thrived in the frigid coastal waters, along with cod, halibut, herring, and Arctic char. In the milder ocean climate of the Pacific Northwest, food was wondrously plentiful; so huge were the salmon runs in the river estuaries of British Columbia and the Alaska panhandle that people there led lives of prodigal abundance. And cutting across the extremes of climate and terrain in the North country were seemingly endless numbers of fur-bearing animals: marten, muskrat, wildcat, wolverine, bear, fox, mink, otter, and beaver.

The lure of these furs is what attracted the first wave of Europeans. In the early 17th century, rival European traders hungry for profit and adventure pushed deep into the continent in search of beaver pelts and other marketable skins. The French set up posts at Quebec City and Montreal, then ventured inland along the St. Lawrence to the Great Lakes. A spirited breed of French wilderness traders, the *voyageurs*, stepped into canoes and paddled upriver, stopping at woodland villages to collect pelts harvested by native trappers. In return they offered knives, axes, wool blankets, firearms, and other goods. Many took Indian wives and raised Indian families.

The British, preempted by the French from the Great Lakes area, turned their attention northward. Stories reached England of unlim-

Peoples and cultures of three very different kinds found a home in the North country. Mobile hunter-gatherers roamed the vast evergreen forests of the Subarctic, its eastern half populated by Algonquian-speaking groups like the Cree and Innu and its western half by numerous Athabascan-speaking groups. The Arctic region held Eskimo-Aleut societies, including the Yupik and Inupiat of Alaska and various Canadian groups. The rainforests and warm currents of the Northwest Coast supported nearly 190,000 people, who spoke many languages but shared a common culture (see map, page 235).

Reports of beaver (top) and muskrat sparked a fur-trapping boom that transformed the entire North country. This brass coin, issued in 1820, was worth one prime beaver pelt.

ited populations of wildlife in the forests and marshes bordering Hudson Bay. In 1670 the British king, Charles II, gave a group of London merchants control of all territory around Hudson Bay—nearly 40 percent of present-day Canada. So was born the Hudson's Bay Company, an immensely powerful private government that came to dominate the entire breadth of the North country and forever changed the lives of the region's inhabitants.

The Subarctic Forests

In many ways life improved. For thousands of years the peoples of the Subarctic had survived by their hunting and fishing skills, spreading gradually eastward in pursuit of game. Scattered bands of Algonquian-speaking Cree, the largest tribal group, roamed the vast spruce and fir forests around Hudson Bay; other Algonquian peoples, like the Naskapi (or Innu, as they call themselves), pushed on toward the Atlantic.

They moved seasonally through the woodlands, usually in well-defined territories, tracking moose, bear, and caribou. Each summer they met at campgrounds by lakes or rivers to fish, gather herbs and berries, and socialize with fellow tribe members. The forest was their larder and tool kit. Bark from birch trees could be fashioned into tent covers, water pails, and the skins of canoes. White cedar poles, lashed together with spruce roots, served as frames for both canoes and toboggans. Spruce, birch, or willow branches could be bent into loops and, laced with leather webbing, transformed into snowshoes.

Survival meant constant struggle, however. Winter snows come early here, drifting deep and lingering far into spring. Tree limbs shatter with the intensity of cold. Caught in a blizzard without shelter, a Cree or Innu hunter ran serious risk of freezing to death. Starvation was never far away. Animal populations fluctuated from year to year, and when larger game grew scarce, hunters would turn to rabbit, muskrat, porcupine, even vermin. Sometimes in late winter these, too, were hard to come by. If no small animals found their way into a hunter's snare, he and his family might

A step-by-step guide to beaver trapping, set down in a numbered diagram by Hudson's Bay trader James Isham in 1743, includes a Cree trapper breaking into a beaver house (1-7); beavers in a stream where nets have been set (8-11); beavers felling trees (13-16); a graphic lesson on beaver anatomy (17-23); two more Cree hunters (10, 25); and various types of plants and wildlife.

be reduced to gnawing leather clothing or tent covers for nourishment.

Other creatures also shared the forest, no less real for being invisible. The most terrifying were the Windigos, superhuman beings with an insatiable appetite for human flesh. Thirty feet tall, with slavering lipless mouths and hearts of ice, Windigos began stalking the forest at the onset of winter, searching for human prey. If a hunter failed to return home, the inescapable fear was that he had been caught and eaten. No manmade weapon could destroy one of these monsters; only the secret rituals of a powerful shaman would lay him to rest. But come spring, the warm weather would send all Windigos fleeing north.

The conditions of life could also be harsh in the lands of the Athabascan-speaking groups that hunted in the territory west of Hudson Bay. Here the forests of spruce and fir stretch out across a marshy labyrinth of lakes, rivers, and muskeg swamp, past the huge Mackenzie River watershed, finally ascending the slopes of the snow-clad Shining Mountains (a native name for the Canadian Rockies) some 1,000 miles to the west. Winters are piercingly cold;

swarms of black flies and mosquitoes plague the hot, brief summers. To the north, the trees grow stunted and bent, then give way to the open tundra and scrub that whites called the Barren Lands. But not everyone saw this region with the same eyes.

You have told me that Paradise is very beautiful. Is it more beautiful than the land of the musk ox in summer, when sometimes the mist blows over the little lakes in the early morning . . . and the loons cry very often? Can I see the caribou roam where I look, and can I feel the wind?

— *Saltatha, Dogrib elder*

These far northern reaches were home to the Chipewyan, one of several Athabascan groups that tracked the region's great caribou herds. Each spring the caribou left the protective forest and moved to summer grazing grounds in the Barren Lands. In fall they re-

An Athabascan mother backpacks her baby as a landscape of Subarctic scrub and tundra rolls out behind her to the 20,000-foot-high peaks of the Alaska Range.

turned, their coats sleek, their bodies meaty. In good years the herds numbered in the tens of thousands. Chipewyan hunters gathered along the migration routes in both spring and fall and harvested enormous quantities.

Much like the buffalo on the Great Plains, the caribou provided virtually all of life's necessities in the Subarctic. Caribou hides became tunics, moccasins, tent covers; eight or more hides were needed to tailor a complete set of winter clothing for an adult. Strips of caribou leather were worked into snares for small game and webbing for fishnets and snowshoes. Caribou bones and antlers became ax handles, fishhooks, and other implements. For the Chipewyan, caribou meat was the culinary staple; much of the vegetable matter in the Chipewyan diet was the half-digested mass of lichens in caribou stomachs, which were roasted whole over a fire.

While their survival depended on the caribou, the Chipewyan believed they owed their very existence to another animal: the dog. In the days of the world's beginning, as the story goes, before there were caribou or men to hunt them, a primordial woman lived alone in a

A Cree marksman cradles a repeating rifle, obtained through trade and used to hunt the animals on this birchbark basket—beaver, bear, deer, and caribou. Below: A shaman of the western Subarctic wore this mask to enter the spirit world.

cave, subsisting on berries. One night a mysterious being in the shape of a dog crept in beside her. As the creature lay close, he began to change form: his limbs grew straight, his skin became smooth, his features were re-formed into those of a handsome youth. Nine months later a child was born: the first Chipewyan. Ever since, the Chipewyan have treated dogs with special respect.

Beyond the Chipewyan, on the forest's northern margin, lived the closely related Yellowknife—so called by Europeans because they fashioned ax heads and knife blades from copper nuggets found in riverbeds—and also the Dogrib and Hare. No group clung more precariously to existence than the Hare; living outside the main caribou migration routes, they relied on the flesh and skins of rabbits and other small game for food and clothing. Two groups to the west, the Slavey and the Beaver (Dunne-za), fished and hunted in the forest depths, taking moose, bear, and other game. They also hunted the woodland caribou, a more southern species that does not migrate to the tundra.

Farther on, more than a dozen different Athabascan groups inhabited the meadows, forests, and river basins nestled among the western mountains. No other Subarctic region contains such variety of local climate and terrain. The Gwich'in people, who followed the caribou between Alaska and the Yukon and whose hunting grounds reached above the Arctic Circle, endured some of the region's harshest extremes. The now-abandoned Tanana trading encampment at Snag, in the Yukon, holds a record for winter cold: minus 81 degrees Fahrenheit.

> Trap, fish, and dig ground root, and you will never starve.
>
> — *Kias Peter, Gwich'in*

Conditions were milder in the high country of British Columbia, the one-time home of the Tutchone, Tahltan, and Dakelne. Moose, bear, elk, and waterfowl thrived in the lush mountain valleys and river bottoms; mountain goats and Dall sheep grazed the alpine meadows. Berries, wild onions, rhubarb, and other edible plants grew in abundance. Pacific salmon fought their way upriver to spawn.

No clear division marked the boundaries between these various Athabascan groups. Through most of the Subarctic, local bands ranging anywhere from 10 to 75 members in size roamed from fishing camp to favorite hunting area, and one group blended almost imperceptibly into its neighbor. All spoke the same language, with minor variations. Bands with strong links to one another might form regional groups of up to several hundred people. No overall tribal structure unified them —except farther west, where groups like the Ingalik, Tanaina, and Tutchone were influenced by the more formalized societies of the Pacific Coast. Still, these regional groups usually provided the closest thing there was to a tribe or nation with which people could identify themselves. (The term Athabascan refers to a linguistic, not a tribal, grouping; it comes from the place-name for Lake Athabasca— "where there are reeds," in the Cree language. Those to whom it refers always thought of themselves simply as Diné: "The People.")

Koyukon hunters from central Alaska bring down a small caribou herd that has been driven into a corral (below). Another technique was to ambush the animals at river crossings. By the 1860's, when this scene was engraved, many of the Subarctic's people already carried rifles.

"Made Beavers"

Into this demanding world came the Hudson's Bay Company traders, and with them came opportunities. Not all native groups took up trading with equal enthusiasm. Some, finding the value of their furs going up, responded simply by supplying fewer of them. Some kept their distance, preferring to stay close to the animals and fish on which they had always depended. But the traders were welcomed by many others. The Cree were the first to profit. By the early 1700's, the Company had built some half-dozen trading posts on large rivers emptying into Hudson Bay, all in Cree territory. Cree trappers would paddle downstream from the interior, their canoes laden with a season's harvest of beaver pelts and other furs. Pitching their tents next to the fortresslike Company "factory," they would begin bartering for the trade goods inside.

The negotiations were part business, part celebration. The chief factor brought out helpings of food and a keg of rum, and the trading began. As the furs changed hands, the trappers acquired a rich store of new and useful marvels: steel tools, firearms, cooking pots, heavy wool blankets, tobacco, foodstuffs such as flour, sugar, tea, and lard. Prices were figured in "made beavers," a monetary unit pegged to the value of a prime-quality adult beaver pelt: three marten skins, for example, equaled one made beaver.

The Beaver does everything perfectly well; it makes kettles, hatchets, swords, knives, bread; in short, it makes everything well.
— *Eastern Algonquian*

For people accustomed to life in a very demanding environment, the fur trade brought the Cree material comforts never before imagined. Using a knife of hardened steel, a Cree woman could scrape a caribou hide in a fraction of the time it took with a flint or obsidian blade. She could cook a meal directly over the fire in an iron pot, rather than having to boil up water by dropping heated rocks into a container of birch bark or woven grass—which she first had to make herself.

Several Cree leaders seized the opportunity and switched from trapping to trading—and gained wealth and prestige as middlemen between the Company forts and native communities deeper in the forest. Cree warriors, armed with the firepower of English guns, pushed west into the hunting grounds of the Chipewyan, Slavey, and Dunne-za.

But as in most Indian-white exchanges, the Cree ended up losing. Hunters intent on harvesting pelts neglected the game that had been their traditional food supply. It takes different skills to trap marten and beaver than to track a moose or a caribou—animals that provided hides and meat, but which were of no use to Company fur buyers. Gradually the Cree began to loose their ability to support themselves in the way of their ancestors. Families became dependent on the trading posts for food, clothing, rifles, ammunition, and for the steel traps that were the basic tools of their new life.

This magnificent caribou coat from Quebec took its Innu creator months of effort—scraping and tanning the hides, stitching the seams with animal sinew, and painting the design with colors extracted from berries, bark, and other natural sources.

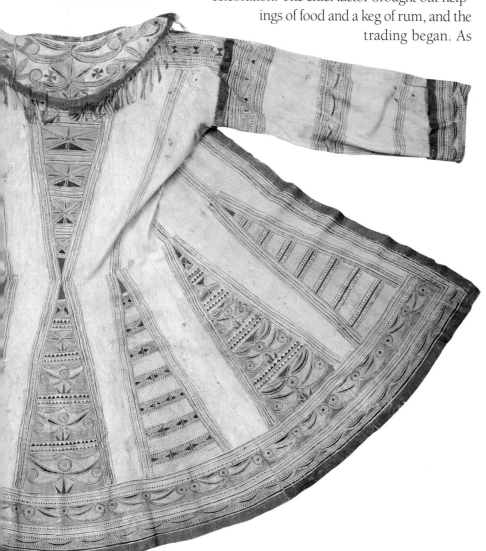

A Hudson's Bay trader carrying rifle and ax hauls home a sled laden with meat and skins. His Indian wife accompanies him, their child strapped to a cradleboard on her back.

A Gwich'in warrior clad in beaded caribou skins and carrying a traditional longbow strikes a commanding pose. Tattoos decorate his face, and in his nose he wears a dentalium trade shell from the Pacific Coast. The painting was made by fur trader Alexander Murray in the 1840's.

In time, intensive trapping in the lands around Hudson Bay reduced the number of fur-bearing animals, and the fortunes of the Cree slid into decline. The inevitable afflictions of white civilization came crowding in. Smallpox, whooping cough, and other European diseases swept through the region. The temptations of alcohol took their toll.

The Company Expands

As local fur sources began to dwindle, the Hudson's Bay Company extended its reach. By the mid-1700's it had opened Fort Prince of Wales at the mouth of the Churchill River, in the transition zone between the boreal forest and the Barren Lands of open tundra. During summer herds of caribou returned to graze, and beluga whales swam offshore. Hundreds of polar bears migrated through each autumn. This was the edge of Chipewyan country and the gateway to the Northwestern interior.

The Chipewyan showed little interest in trapping beaver, which had never been plentiful in their region. But they soon learned the short-term benefits of the fur business. Like the Cree, they found a profitable role as go-betweens, taking control of trade between the Company factors at Churchill and native groups to the west. So it was that an ambitious Chipewyan named Matonabbee rose to a position of prominence.

Over six feet tall, powerfully built, with a quick intelligence and dauntless will, Matonabbee worked as a guide for the Company. He made a lasting impression on one of its agents, Samuel Hearne, age 24 and equally ambitious. Together the two men spent 19 months trekking the Subarctic in search of a navigable route to the Pacific Ocean.

It was Hearne's third attempt. In 1769 he had turned back after just 200 miles when his native guide ran off with the expedition's ammunition and ice axes. A raid by tribal marauders cut short his second try. So in the dark of December 1770, Hearne set out from Churchill with Matonabbee as his guide and mentor. A band of Chipewyan hunters went with them, as well as a crew of women to haul supplies and set up camp. "Women were made for labor," Matonabbee explained. "One of them can carry . . . as much as two men." He himself had six wives and nine children.

Even with this support, the going was rough. Hiking as much as 20 miles a day across the muskeg, with game in short supply, the expedition ran low on food. During one two-day period they subsisted on nothing but tobacco and melted snow. Another lean stretch prompted Hearne to boil up an old pair of boots for dinner.

By summer they had reached the banks of the Coppermine River, which flows north into

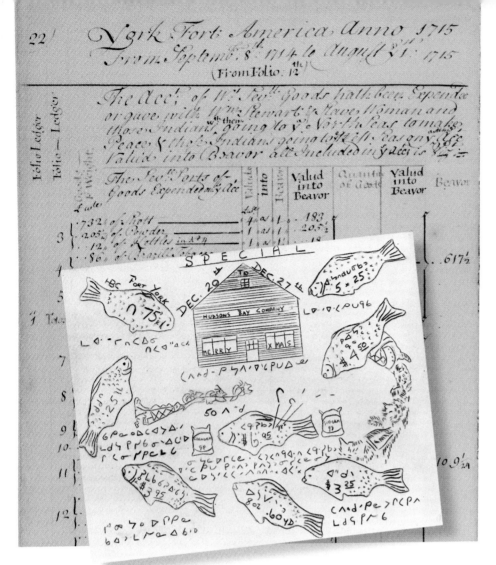

A Hudson's Bay Company ledger from 1715 (top) lists the prices of trade goods in numbers of beaver pelts: one pelt, for example, would purchase one pound of gunpowder. Two centuries later, the Company advertised Christmas specials on tea, flour, and other items priced in Canadian dollars. Their flier, written in phonetic Cree script, was distributed by dogsled.

the Arctic Ocean. They were now crossing a no-man's-land where Athabascan groups like the Chipewyan would occasionally come upon bands of Inuit, ancient enemies from the Far North. It happened now. Beside a small cataract, some Inuit families had set up a summer encampment. Spotting them in the distance, Hearne's Chipewyan companions underwent a sudden, terrifying transformation. Stripping to their loincloths, they tied back their hair and smeared their faces with red and black war paint.

That night, as the Inuit lay sleeping, Matonabbee's band attacked. Men, women, children—all felt his fury. An Inuit elder took 20 spear thrusts until, said the horrified Hearne, "his body was like a sieve." A woman had her eyes poked out. A young girl wrapped herself around Hearne's legs, begging for mercy as two Chipewyans stabbed her to death. Not one Inuit survived. The stranger had just learned a lesson about the power of blood feuds in this part of the world.

The expedition moved on, following the river, until it reached the ice-bound Arctic Ocean. Clearly, the route to the Pacific lay elsewhere. But Hearne's trip opened an unpredictable new era, and in his footsteps other

On the windswept barrens of northern Manitoba, Chipewyan traders pitch their tents outside Fort Prince of Wales, the first Hudson's Bay post in Athabascan country. In this early period, women—not dogs—usually hauled the birchwood toboggans.

Indian trappers, possibly Dogrib or Slavey, beach their canoes on Great Slave Lake, near the Hudson's Bay post at Fort Resolution.

white adventurers began thrusting their way into the hunting grounds of the Athabascans—one of them Simon Fraser, the ambitious trader who parleyed with the Dakelne at Stuart Lake.

Across the Shining Mountains

No such forays did more to open the western Subarctic to white expansion than the two journeys made by the Canadian explorer Alexander Mackenzie. He set off by canoe in 1789 from the North West Company post at Lake Athabasca, heading west. His native guide, nicknamed "English Chief," brought along two Indian wives. Like Hearne before him, Mackenzie hoped to find a navigable trade route to the Pacific. And like Hearne, he was disappointed. The river he followed—the continent's second mightiest, now called the Mackenzie—turned north across the tundra and emptied into Arctic Ocean. But along the way he made contact with the Dogrib, Slavey, and Gwich'in tribes and pioneered the way for future trade.

In 1793 Mackenzie set out again, paddling west up the Peace River, moving on through the lands of the Dunne-za and Sekani. As he climbed amid the dizzying crags and ledges of the Shining Mountains, the native inhabitants followed his progress with wary apprehension. Most bands had never seen a white man. Curiosity usually prevailed.

One Sekani warrior, his chest strung with a necklace of grizzly bear claws, handed Mackenzie his knife as a gesture of friendship—and an invitation to trade. Even in these remote mountain passes, the people wanted European goods. At a Dakelne camp in the high Rockies, where Mackenzie found a guide to lead him on toward the Pacific coast, the children wore earrings made from coins stamped "State of Massachusetts Bay."

Crossing the last high ridges, Mackenzie began his descent. The air grew warm and moist. Cedar trees towered overhead, their trunks so big that five grown men could barely reach around them. The explorer moved along an ancient trade route, where Dakelne hunters would transport pelts of beaver, lynx, marten, and bear to exchange with the coastal tribes for seashells, fish oil—and, increasingly, metal tools and weapons obtained from British or Yankee sea captains.

Everywhere he found signs of material prosperity. Instead of roving bands, there were settled villages. Some had elaborate clan systems and hereditary chiefs. In the lands of the Nuxalk (also called the Bella Coola), a village leader welcomed him with a lavish feast of roast salmon. An exchange of gifts ensued: a magnificent sea otter cloak for Mackenzie, a pair of scissors for the chief, to trim his beard. Mackenzie had stepped into the rich, distinctive world of the Northwest Coast.

I want the sea. That is my country.
—*Makah chief*

The Bountiful Northwest Coast

Carved spirit faces and a whale image, all centuries old, mark a seaside boulder at Ozette, site of an ancient Makah village. A more recent Kwakiutl dance mask (above) took the shape of a killer whale.

A two-thousand-mile ribbon of misty, forested seacoast runs along the continent's northwest margin, from the Gulf of Alaska to northern California, unfurling a landscape of astonishing beauty and abundance. A wall of snowcapped uplands — the Coast Mountains — rises abruptly on the landward side, its highest peaks cresting at more than 15,000 feet above sea level. Rivers cascade down the slopes, past majestic stands of cedar, hemlock, spruce, and fir. The climate is mild and moist; rainfall can measure more than 200 inches a year in the wettest sections. Deer, elk, mountain goats, and grizzly bear graze the high meadows.

To the west, deep ocean currents flood in from the Pacific, spilling past a

A wooden halibut hook (right), elegantly carved with the bound figure of a witch or slave, enticed the fish to impale itself on the sharp bone barb.

long chain of barrier islands into a labyrinth of bays, inlets, reefs, marshes, fiords, and estuaries and generating one of the richest concentrations of marine life anywhere in the world. Vast quantities of fish inhabit this coast, including flounder, cod, rockfish, 400-pound halibut, and enormous schools of herring and smelt. Seals, sea lions, and sea otters swim inshore to feed. Clams, mussels, crabs, and sea urchins litter the beaches, along with thousands of seabird eggs. A procession of whales and porpoises cruises offshore.

But from earliest times, the main resource was salmon in five different species. Beginning in late spring, the first huge runs would move inland, swarming over sandbars, battling river rapids, to spawn and die by the countless thousands. In just a few months, a Northwest Coast fisherman could spear or net enough salmon to sustain his family throughout the year. So massive was the influx, and so predictable, that some people

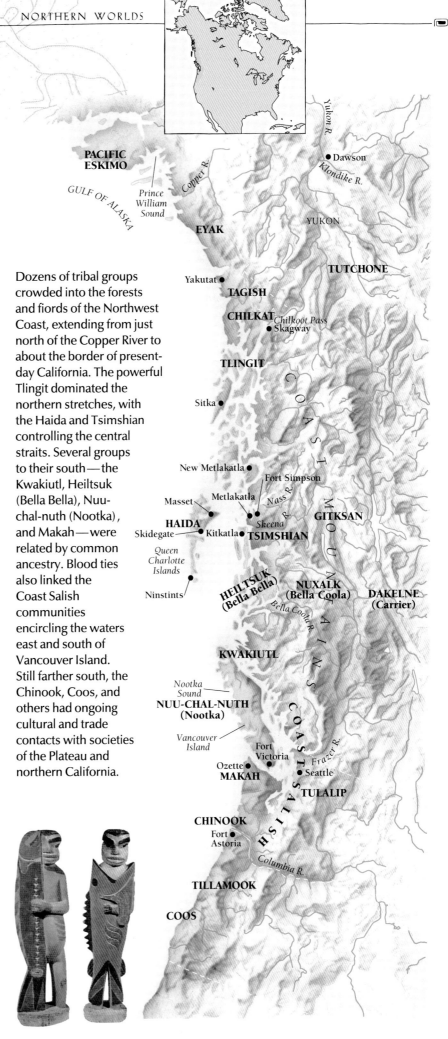

came to think salmon were immortal. According to legend, a tribe of salmon people spent the winter in houses beneath the sea. Then, when the season warmed, they changed into fish and swam upriver to offer their bodies for human consumption. Their souls, released from the flesh, would return to the ocean.

From the rain forest came the wood of the majestic red cedar—strong, aromatic, and resistant to rot. Massive cedar logs formed the framework of native houses, and split cedar planking sheathed their sides. The hull of each canoe began as a single cedar trunk, which the boat builders felled, scooped out with stone tools, then steamed to shape. Cedar boxes, intricately carved, served as storage space, household furniture, and containers for food and fish oil.

Clothing and blankets were woven from cedar bark, which Northwest Coast women softened by pounding, then cut into strips. Split cedar root (along with spruce root and grasses) became the raw material for the region's superb basketwork, with mesh so tight that the baskets held water. And a cedar-root raincoat kept the wearer dry in any weather.

This bounty of sea and forest gave rise to a way of life unique in all the Americas. Here such peoples as the Tlingit and Tsimshian, the Nuu-chal-nuth (long known as Nootka), Nuxalk (or Bella Coola), and Chinook fished, feasted, and vied among themselves for power and prestige. Some were ferocious warriors—like the Haida, whose 60-foot battle canoes sped south as far as present-day Vancouver to take booty and slaves from the more peaceable Coast Salish. Most, like the Tsimshian, were also shrewd traders. The Nuu-chal-nuth and Makah were renowned for their seamanship, venturing far into the ocean to harpoon the ultimate prey: whales. All of the region's people

Two Tlingit carvings show salmon metamorphosing into humans—a head emerging from a fish's mouth, a tail splitting into legs—both reflecting the ancient belief that salmon were a tribe of people who dwelled in the sea.

Dozens of tribal groups crowded into the forests and fiords of the Northwest Coast, extending from just north of the Copper River to about the border of present-day California. The powerful Tlingit dominated the northern stretches, with the Haida and Tsimshian controlling the central straits. Several groups to their south—the Kwakiutl, Heiltsuk (Bella Bella), Nuu-chal-nuth (Nootka), and Makah—were related by common ancestry. Blood ties also linked the Coast Salish communities encircling the waters east and south of Vancouver Island. Still farther south, the Chinook, Coos, and others had ongoing cultural and trade contacts with societies of the Plateau and northern California.

placed great importance on generosity, holding lavish ceremonies in which they gave out food, blankets, weapons, and other valuables.

A visitor approaching a coastal village anywhere north of Puget Sound would find a row of large cedar houses above the beach of a sheltered cove or riverbank. The village might include only three or four extended families, each in its own house. Or it might stretch a mile or more along the waterfront and contain as many as 800 or 900 people. On some houses the facades would be painted with intricate totem figures—semiabstract shapes of birds and animals that proclaimed the family's clan affiliation. Carved cedar totem poles marked the dwellings of the most important families. To the rear, behind the beachfront living quarters, were smokehouses, drying racks for fish, storage sheds, and the like.

Look at me, friend!
I come to ask for your dress
Since there is nothing you
cannot be used for.
I come to beg you for this,
Long-life maker.

— *Kwakiutl prayer*
to a cedar tree

In each community the social order was built on family status. Centuries ago, as the coast people's forebears settled in, certain families gained control of the best fishing grounds, berry patches, and cedar groves, thus appropriating most of the wealth. In time, as the rights to these assets passed from one generation to the next, a complex social hierarchy developed that contrasted sharply with most other cultures in native North America.

The great spirit Qautz created woman, whom he left alone in the dark forest. The woman lamented day and night, until Qautz took pity and appeared to her in a canoe of copper, in which many handsome young men were rowing. One of the rowers told her it was the great spirit who had supplied her with that companionship for which she sighed.

At these words she cried the more, and as the tears trickled down they fell to the sand. Qautz commanded her to look, and she saw with amazement a tiny child, a boy, entirely formed. Her firstborn son is the ancestor of the *taises,* while from her other sons the common people are descended.

— *Nuu-chal-nuth legend*

At the top stood a handful of aristocratic families—the *taises,* or chiefs of the wealthiest lineages and their close relatives. Some might be warriors, others powerful shamans, and still others trade chiefs who controlled the lines of commerce with other tribes or villages. Among the Nuu-chal-nuth and Makah, the captains of whaling canoes enjoyed the highest prestige.

Below these elite families were their more distant relatives—the *michimis,* or ordinary people. Unlike their rich cousins, who almost never soiled their hands in labor, the nonelite relatives did much of the community's physi-

A carved maple spindle whorl from Salish country depicts a man holding two otters. The towering red cedars behind were raw material for everything from rain coats to totem poles.

cal work. They felled the cedars, built the houses, hunted the game, repaired the fish weirs. On occasion, an artisan of unusual skill—a Kwakiutl woodworker famous for his carvings on canoes, for example—might rise above his normal station. But as a rule, rank was dictated by birth.

Except for the slaves. Up and down the coast, slavery was the bitter consequence of defeat in battle. Ambitious nobles would raid distant villages, looting valuables and seizing hostages. High-ranking prisoners might be sent home in exchange for a ransom payment, but all others remained the property of their captors. They were generally well treated. Slaves lived in the houses of their owners, ate the same food, and performed the same day-to-day tasks as other villagers. But their lives were always in jeopardy. When erecting a new family house, for example, some chiefs observed a custom of burying the body of a freshly killed slave under each corner post.

There was no mistaking who belonged where, particularly among the northernmost tribes. A high-ranking Tlingit spoke with grave authority, and he dressed in style. On

Spacious cedar houses line the beach at Kitkatla, a Tsimshian town of several hundred people. On a totem pole (right) from the facade of a Haida house, animal figures merge and mingle—from Thunderbird (near the top), through Sea Grizzly, down to Raven (embracing the oval entranceway in his wings).

ceremonial occasions he draped his body in a handsome fringed cloak of cedar bark and mountain goat hair, worked with intricate designs, and wore a broad-brimmed hat emblazoned with family insignia. Sometimes he wore a seashell or a ring in his nose.

What are you anyway? Do you have a labret as large as mine, or have you given as many gifts as I have? When you can come back with a labret as large as mine, I will accept you as an equal.
—*Tsimshian woman*

High-ranking women proclaimed their status by the size of their labret, a shelflike wooden plug inserted horizontally into the bottom lip. The labret forced the lip to protrude, and it

Shamans were revered for their close links to the spirit world and their ability to cure illness. This Tlingit holy man was photographed holding a carved bird whose wings would flap when he pulled a string.

power—and a craving for human flesh. In the Hamatsa Dance, these initiates would dash in from the forest, naked except for a few hemlock boughs, and in a frenzy of hunger lunge at bystanders, attempting to bite them. A struggle ensued in which the society's senior members seized the novices and forced them to control their hideous urges. Once pacified, they were inducted into the society.

Now I am going to eat.
My face is ghastly pale.
I shall eat what is given to me by
Cannibal-at-the-North-End of-the-World.
— *Song from Kwakiutl Hamatsa Ceremony*

When Europeans first witnessed these rites, they assumed that the Kwakiutl and others practiced cannibalism. That may once have been so, but by modern times it was mostly illusion—very realistic illusion. One observer in the 1890's noted that the dancers, instead of biting their victims, would lop off tiny chunks of skin with a hidden knife. Later in the ceremony, the skin would be returned (lest it be used for witchcraft) along with a formal apology and a handsome gift.

Other Kwakiutl winter ceremonies created their own dramatic effects. In the Warrior of the World Dance, the female ogre Toogwid came attended by ghostly puppets and a double-headed serpent, Sisiutl, who flew through the air (assistants pulled it with invisible strings between two rafters). Suddenly, a lieutenant drove a wooden spike into her skull. Blood spurted. Her eyes popped out of their sockets and dangled by thin threads.

This, too, was stagecraft. The "spike" was part of an ingenious wooden harness that fit over Toogwid's head, concealed by a wig. Its blunt end showed on one side, its point on the other; there was nothing in between. Bladders of seal blood provided the gore, and seal eyes suspended from the wig created the illusion that her own eyes had dropped out. After exposing her bloody corpse to the audience, Toogwid had the spike removed, and she stood reincarnated in all her former glory.

er, since the principal guest was honor bound to host a potlatch in return.)

Potlatches were generally held in winter, when the coastal people turned from hunting and fishing to a virtually nonstop round of festivals and ceremonies. It was the season of spirits and demons, of mythic beings from distant worlds who arrived in the villages to the accompaniment of rattles, drums, and eerie whistles, inspiring awe and terror among viewers. Secret dance societies marked the occasion with ancient and sacred rites.

No ceremonies were more renowned than those of the Hamatsa Society, or Cannibal Dancers. In Kwakiutl lore, a fearsome creature known as Cannibal-at-the-North-End-of-the-World would abduct certain high-born young men and women, imbuing them with spiritual

Reflections From the Spirit World

To the people of the North, humans and animals were caught in an endless cycle of transformation and rebirth. A bear might be a spirit in disguise—or a person who lived so long in the forest that he had grown fur and claws. When a hunter killed a deer or a seal, he returned the bones and bladder to nature, ensuring the survival of the creature's soul. All across the North country, drawings and petroglyphs honored the links between animal, spirit, and human.

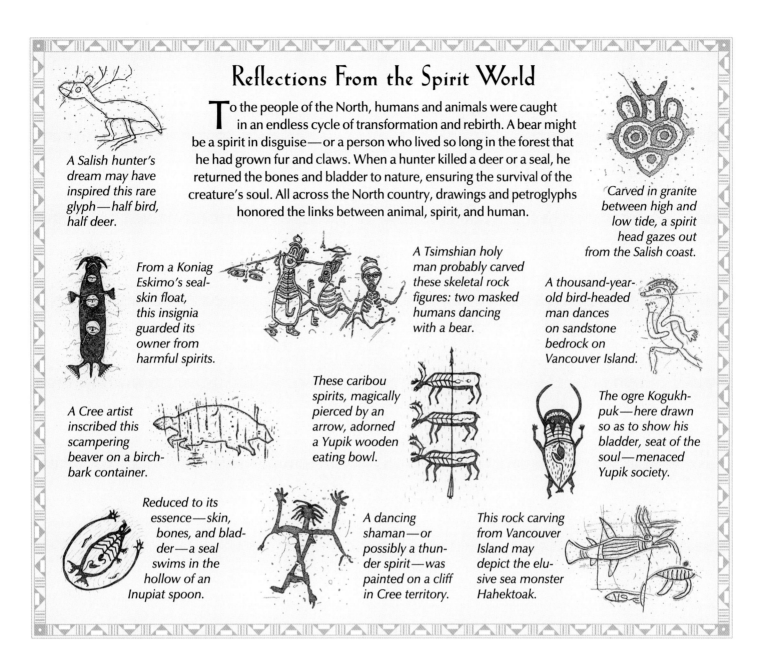

A Salish hunter's dream may have inspired this rare glyph—half bird, half deer.

From a Koniag Eskimo's seal-skin float, this insignia guarded its owner from harmful spirits.

A Tsimshian holy man probably carved these skeletal rock figures: two masked humans dancing with a bear.

Carved in granite between high and low tide, a spirit head gazes out from the Salish coast.

A thousand-year-old bird-headed man dances on sandstone bedrock on Vancouver Island.

A Cree artist inscribed this scampering beaver on a birch-bark container.

These caribou spirits, magically pierced by an arrow, adorned a Yupik wooden eating bowl.

The ogre Kogukh-puk—here drawn so as to show his bladder, seat of the soul—menaced Yupik society.

Reduced to its essence—skin, bones, and blad-der—a seal swims in the hollow of an Inupiat spoon.

A dancing shaman—or possibly a thun-der spirit—was painted on a cliff in Cree territory.

This rock carving from Vancouver Island may depict the elu-sive sea monster Hahektoak.

the Chinook and Coast Salish, a person's status depended in large part on individual merit. But among most coastal groups, family heritage was a matter of great consequence.

Festivals of Pride and Portent

The most dramatic celebration of family pride was the potlatch, an elaborate ritual of feasting, dancing, storytelling, and gift-giving that was a vital part of every Northwest Coast society. Whenever an important family moved into a new house, the occasion demanded a potlatch. So, too, did any dynastic event—a birth or a marriage, the death of a chief, the succession of an heir. Sometimes a clan leader would host a potlatch to repay a debt or erase a shame. No honors or titles were deemed valid until the recipient gave a potlatch "to make my name good," as the saying went.

The festivities could last for days or even weeks. There would be formal speeches recounting the family legends, dance performances, a display of heirlooms and family emblems—all certifying the right of the host to his titles and privileges. Finally, he would hand out presents, divesting himself of blankets, animal pelts, carved boxes, shell necklaces, cartons of fish oil, weapons, and—most valuable of all—engraved metal slabs called coppers. The more lavish his generosity, the more honor he gained for himself and his lineage. Some truly great chiefs were said to have distributed all they owned, then burned down their houses and executed their slaves. Such willful extravagance was the ultimate social gesture, worthy of enduring praise and esteem. (In practice, at least some of the wealth given out at potlatches came back to the own-

power—and a craving for human flesh. In the Hamatsa Dance, these initiates would dash in from the forest, naked except for a few hemlock boughs, and in a frenzy of hunger lunge at bystanders, attempting to bite them. A struggle ensued in which the society's senior members seized the novices and forced them to control their hideous urges. Once pacified, they were inducted into the society.

> Now I am going to eat.
> My face is ghastly pale.
> I shall eat what is given to me by
> Cannibal-at-the-North-End of-the-World.
> — *Song from Kwakiutl Hamatsa Ceremony*

When Europeans first witnessed these rites, they assumed that the Kwakiutl and others practiced cannibalism. That may once have been so, but by modern times it was mostly illusion—very realistic illusion. One observer in the 1890's noted that the dancers, instead of biting their victims, would lop off tiny chunks of skin with a hidden knife. Later in the ceremony, the skin would be returned (lest it be used for witchcraft) along with a formal apology and a handsome gift.

Other Kwakiutl winter ceremonies created their own dramatic effects. In the Warrior of the World Dance, the female ogre Toogwid came attended by ghostly puppets and a double-headed serpent, Sisiutl, who flew through the air (assistants pulled it with invisible strings between two rafters). Suddenly, a lieutenant drove a wooden spike into her skull. Blood spurted. Her eyes popped out of their sockets and dangled by thin threads.

This, too, was stagecraft. The "spike" was part of an ingenious wooden harness that fit over Toogwid's head, concealed by a wig. Its blunt end showed on one side, its point on the other; there was nothing in between. Bladders of seal blood provided the gore, and seal eyes suspended from the wig created the illusion that her own eyes had dropped out. After exposing her bloody corpse to the audience, Toogwid had the spike removed, and she stood reincarnated in all her former glory.

Shamans were revered for their close links to the spirit world and their ability to cure illness. This Tlingit holy man was photographed holding a carved bird whose wings would flap when he pulled a string.

er, since the principal guest was honor bound to host a potlatch in return.)

Potlatches were generally held in winter, when the coastal people turned from hunting and fishing to a virtually nonstop round of festivals and ceremonies. It was the season of spirits and demons, of mythic beings from distant worlds who arrived in the villages to the accompaniment of rattles, drums, and eerie whistles, inspiring awe and terror among viewers. Secret dance societies marked the occasion with ancient and sacred rites.

No ceremonies were more renowned than those of the Hamatsa Society, or Cannibal Dancers. In Kwakiutl lore, a fearsome creature known as Cannibal-at-the-North-End-of-the-World would abduct certain high-born young men and women, imbuing them with spiritual

cal work. They felled the cedars, built the houses, hunted the game, repaired the fish weirs. On occasion, an artisan of unusual skill—a Kwakiutl woodworker famous for his carvings on canoes, for example—might rise above his normal station. But as a rule, rank was dictated by birth.

Except for the slaves. Up and down the coast, slavery was the bitter consequence of defeat in battle. Ambitious nobles would raid distant villages, looting valuables and seizing hostages. High-ranking prisoners might be sent home in exchange for a ransom payment, but all others remained the property of their captors. They were generally well treated. Slaves lived in the houses of their owners, ate the same food, and performed the same day-to-day tasks as other villagers. But their lives were always in jeopardy. When erecting a new family house, for example, some chiefs observed a custom of burying the body of a freshly killed slave under each corner post.

There was no mistaking who belonged where, particularly among the northernmost tribes. A high-ranking Tlingit spoke with grave authority, and he dressed in style. On

Spacious cedar houses line the beach at Kitkatla, a Tsimshian town of several hundred people. On a totem pole (right) from the facade of a Haida house, animal figures merge and mingle—from Thunderbird (near the top), through Sea Grizzly, down to Raven (embracing the oval entranceway in his wings).

ceremonial occasions he draped his body in a handsome fringed cloak of cedar bark and mountain goat hair, worked with intricate designs, and wore a broad-brimmed hat emblazoned with family insignia. Sometimes he wore a seashell or a ring in his nose.

⌁

What are you anyway? Do you have a labret as large as mine, or have you given as many gifts as I have? When you can come back with a labret as large as mine, I will accept you as an equal.
— *Tsimshian woman*

⌁

High-ranking women proclaimed their status by the size of their labret, a shelflike wooden plug inserted horizontally into the bottom lip. The labret forced the lip to protrude, and it

Vividly depicting the Haida creation story, the ancestral Raven discovers the first tiny humans living in a clam shell as the primordial flood waters recede. The carved cedar sculpture is by contemporary Haida artist Bill Reid.

A Kwakiutl dance mask of the Eagle clan opens up to show a humanlike face, revealing the ancestral closeness between man and beast.

generated a flow of saliva—an effect that repelled the first European visitors. But to most people along the coast, the bigger the labret, the higher its wearer's status.

Within each village the more powerful lineages took precedence. But the chief of every household automatically held noble rank. He presided from a raised platform along the rear wall, opposite the door, where he lived with his wife and younger children; an elaborately carved screen often separated this private space from the rest of the building. Other families in the household, all related to the house chief, lived along the two side walls in order of rank. Slaves laid their blankets near the entrance.

Social standing told only half the story, however. Each household chief belonged to one of several hereditary clans—Owl, Whale, Sea Lion, Beaver, and others—in which everyone was presumably descended from a common ancestor. Additionally, communities were divided into two groups of roughly equal size. Every individual in a Haida village, for example, besides having a regular clan affiliation, also came into the world as either an Eagle or a Raven. By the same token, every Tlingit was a Raven or a Wolf.

The distinction between the two sides was as basic as the difference between day and night. All Ravens, no matter how distant their blood relationship, felt a sense of spiritual kinship and commonly addressed each other as "brother" or "sister." At the same time, neither side could get along without the other. When a Raven chief wanted to build a new house or erect a totem pole, he would appeal to his Eagle counterpart, who then sent workmen to do the job. The very survival of the tribe depended on such cooperation, since marriage could occur only across group lines: Ravens wed Eagles, never other Ravens.

In northern communities like the Tlingit and Haida, clan membership came down through the female line: the children of a Raven mother were Ravens. A Haida nobleman displayed the totems and heraldic crests of his mother's clan, and he reaped the benefits of her family's salmon river, hunting ground, berry patch, and other economic assets. He took his name from her and along with it inherited the rights to various family legends, guardian spirits, and ceremonial dances.

In later times white settlers caused no end of confusion by using their fathers' surnames. A daughter of Chief Edenshaw, a powerful Haida leader, was shocked when a missionary insisted on calling her Isabella Edenshaw. It seemed like sacrilege. "How can I take Eagle's name?" she asked, knowing herself to be a Raven on her mother's side.

Social structures tended to be more relaxed along the coast's southern reaches. A member of the Nuu-chal-nuth might choose the clan affiliation of either mother or father, and for

KWAKIUTL WINTER DANCES

Long ago, when spirits roamed the earth in human form, four hunters trekked deep into the forest in search of mountain goats. Pausing to rest in an abandoned hut, they heard an eerie whistling sound. Suddenly a giant strode in, the terrifying Cannibal-at-the-North-End-of-the-World, his red eyes gleaming hungrily. At his heels, with a great flapping of wings, came his flock of carnivorous birds: Hokhokw, who cracked open skulls to eat people's brains; Raven, who plucked out eyes; and Crooked Beak of Heaven, who drove men mad. Together they represented the darkest forces of uncontrolled human desire.

The hunters barely escaped with their lives. But in fleeing, they took with them the secrets of the cannibal's power, including his masks, whistles, cedarbark apron, dances, and sacred songs. Back in their village, they reenacted their ordeal — to the horror and delight of their countrymen. So began the annual rite of the Hamatsa Dance, the most venerated of Kwakiutl winter ceremonies.

Only the highest-ranking Kwakiutls joined the Hamatsa Society, but other dance groups played equally vital roles. The Grizzly Bears kept order at potlatches, enforcing protocol and punishing ceremonial lapses. So did the droopy-nosed Nutlamatls, or Fool Dancers — who also created their own special mayhem, darting about among the guests, upsetting furniture and tossing stones. Some figures embodied both good and evil. The two-headed serpent Sisiutl brought wealth and power to her favorites yet with a single glance could turn enemies to stone. Open-mouthed, wild-maned Dzonokwa ate babies but also made people rich. Each powerful being harked back to some ancestral myth, and as they danced the ancient rites, the untamed passions of man and nature came slowly under control.

Ceremonial props included Sisiutl (top) and masks of a Fool Dancer and shaggy-haired Dzonokwa, shown against a cedar-bark dance apron. Raven and Crooked Beak pose at left, and Hokhokw performs below.

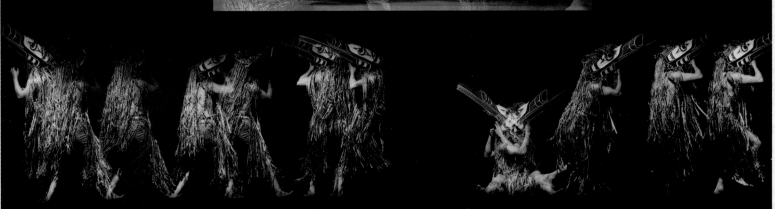

ATACKTED at JUAN, DE. FUCA, STRAIT'S.

As foreign traders invaded the coast, local residents sometimes challenged them (top) but more often wanted to bargain. By the mid-1800's, Haida craftsmen were turning out stone carvings (above) for sale to white visitors.

A living marine bonanza, the sea otter (right) grows fur so thick—an estimated 1,000 hairs per square inch—it has one of the richest pelts on earth.

Sailing Ships and Soft Gold

Like most events in this coastal land of plenty, the forces of change arrived by sea. One day in the 1780's, some Tlingit traders were paddling their canoes up the Alaska coast when two tall sailing ships rose into view. To the Tlingits they seemed like nothing so much as two enormous white-winged birds flying low across the water. On the terrible chance that one "bird" might be Raven, the great creator spirit, the Tlingits sped to shore and took cover. Looking directly at Raven could turn a person to stone, it was said, so they cautiously peered out through rolled-up skunk cabbage leaves. Then one of them, an old man who had seen much already—and knew that sometimes stories were exaggerated—paddled back out for a closer look.

And so the Tlingit elder met his first Europeans. They invited him aboard, showed him

around, and gave him food and a tin plate. In return, he presented them with his sea otter cloak. As it happened, sea otter furs were precisely what these strangers had come thousands of miles to get.

By the late 1700's European vessels were visiting the Northwest Coast in increasing numbers, drawn by the prospect of fabulous trading profits. The first had been the Danish navigator Vitus Bering, who sailed from Siberia in 1741 on a voyage of exploration for the tsar of Russia. Reaching land at Alaska's Prince William Sound, slightly to the west of Tlingit country, he found little of interest.

But on the return voyage, cruising past the 1,000-mile chain of the Aleutian Islands, the expedition discovered large rookeries of sea otters. No creature on earth grows a sleeker, softer, or more lustrous coat. Bering's crewmen collected a

number of pelts, and on reaching port, they sold them to Chinese merchants for enormous sums.

The promise of great wealth from sea otter fur—"soft gold," the foreigners called it—attracted other adventurers. The Russians moved in first, sweeping east through the Aleutians and onto the Alaska mainland, where they set up trading posts. To bring in pelts, the Russians enlisted the labor of the local Aleut population, often at gunpoint.

Farther south, a Spanish frigate heading north from Mexico in 1744 reached Haida Gwaii—the land of the Haida, known on today's maps as the Queen Charlotte Islands. The residents put out in canoes, sprinkling the waters with eagle down as a sign of welcome. The Spanish captain, Juan José Pérez, found them "cheerful, robust, with beautiful eyes," and offered them glass beads and other trade goods. Claiming the land for Spain, he sailed off with his purchases—bear, wolf, and sea otter pelts.

❧

When the first ship appeared, the people thought it was the spirit of the Pestilence and, dancing on the shore, they waved their palms toward the newcomers to turn back.

When the whites landed, the people sent down their old men, who had only a few years to live anyhow, expecting them to fall dead. But when the new arrivals began buying their furs, the younger ones went down too, trading for axes and iron the marten and otter skin cloaks they wore.

— *Haida narrative*

❧

Next came the British. The celebrated navigator James Cook sighted the coast at Vancouver Island in March 1778 and dropped anchor at a place he thought the inhabitants called Nootka. He heard wrong, in fact, since no local language contained this particular word. Even so, the place where Cook anchored continues to be called Nootka Sound, and its inhabitants, the Nuu-chal-nuth, became widely known as the Nootka.

A Makah sun mask includes a Yankee sea captain among its aura of resplendent rays. The tug of a string would make the rays pop up.

Cook stayed nearly a month, charting the waters and making friends. On first impression he thought the Nuu-chal-nuth people "mild and inoffensive"— until their trading savvy revealed itself. "These people got a greater medley and variety of things from us than any other," he noted. By the time Cook set sail, his ship had been stripped of virtually all surplus metal: copper kettles, tin tea canisters, brass candlesticks and bureau fittings, even the buttons off officers' uniforms. In return, Cook filled his hold with native artifacts—and a fortune in sea otter pelts.

The success of Cook's voyage ignited a worldwide frenzy of excitement. Ships from England, Spain, Portugal, France, and the soon-to-be-independent United States swarmed into the region. Profits were unbelievably high. One trader from New England arrived in 1785 and swapped some cheap metal items for 560 pelts, which commanded $20,000 in the China market. Four years later another Yankee captain, John Kendrick, took away 200 pelts in trade for an equal number of iron chisels. American ships alone gathered some 350,000 sea otter pelts altogether, for which native suppliers received an estimated $7 million worth of trade goods.

Inevitably, conflicts arose. As Kendrick's ship lay anchored at the Haida village of Ninstints, some local residents crept aboard and stole the Yankee captain's laundry, which was hanging out to dry. Kendrick, determined to prevent further pilfering, had his men seize the village chief, Koyah—whom he then had stripped naked, flogged, and shorn of his shoulder-length hair. No greater humiliation could have been imagined. To restore his status in the community, Koyah had to host an elaborate potlatch. Kendrick ultimately paid for this rough justice, since the Haida greeted his next visit with an all-out attack rather than the lucrative deal-making he had come for.

Open hostilities tended to be rare, however. What vexed the foreigners more was the talent of the coast's veteran traders for driving

A Nuxalk matron skewers eulachon, a type of smelt valued for its meat and oil, onto a drying rack. Both mother and daughter wear woolen dresses obtained in trade.

a hard bargain. They had been exchanging goods with each other for centuries, following old routes up and down the coast and across the mountains to the Athabascan tribes of the interior. The Nuxalk (Bella Coola) traded with the Dakelne—abalone shells, fish oil, and seaweed, among other goods, for dried berries, furs, and mountain-goat skins. The Nuu-chal-nuth specialized in whale products and highly valued dentalium shells.

One of the most sought-after trade items was the pungently aromatic oil of a smeltlike fish called eulachon, or candlefish—so named because its oil-saturated body, when dried, would burn like a torch. Eulachon oil was the region's universal condiment, used to flavor everything from dried salmon to mountain huckleberries. So much of it passed from the coast to the interior that the cross-mountain trade routes became known as grease trails. And the groups that supplied it, like the Tsimshian, were accustomed to exacting the highest prices they could get.

So when the Europeans brought their glass beads and cloth blankets, the local traders were well equipped to deal. Before long, the price of sea otter pelts began to soar. At the same time, village markets were becoming glutted with the cheap metals, like iron and brass, that at first had been so popular. As a result, visiting traders were increasingly hard pressed to come up with commodities that the local residents found acceptable.

Some found ingenious ways to profit, however. Joseph Ingraham, a skipper from Boston, arrived at Haida Gwaii in 1791 intending to exchange iron rods for pelts. The Haida, disdainful of iron pieces that by now were commonplace, refused to bargain. But Ingraham noticed that copper necklaces were held in high esteem, and he had an idea—have the ship's blacksmith twist the rods into neck rings of similar design. Several prominent chiefs purchased the new iron rings and they became great favorites, worn by the wealthy and coveted by all. Ingraham sold off his supply for three pelts each.

But the fashion soon passed—much to the dismay of traders who followed Ingraham. When a Captain Bartlett visited the Haida several years later, his cargo hold stocked with wrought-iron neck rings, he was informed that sheet copper—raw material for the shield-shaped "coppers" given out at potlatches—was now the only worthy trade item.

Native Trade Lords

In the end there was plenty for everyone, native and foreigner alike. Among the Haida, prominent families were amassing fortunes in coppers, blankets, firearms, and other valuable items. Down the coast it was the same. White traders coming into the region often preferred to deal with one or two powerful families, who became exceptionally wealthy as a result. Such was the case with the Nuu-chal-nuth chief, Maquinna.

By the late 1700's Maquinna had established himself as the most powerful figure in Nootka Sound. Playing host to visiting explorers like Cook and Vancouver, he became the principal middleman between the foreign sea captains and native fur hunters living in other sections of the island. And while most of his fortune came from trade, Maquinna did not ignore other opportunities. To avenge an insult from an American captain in 1803, he seized the ship and summarily killed nearly all of its crewmen. (Maquinna spared the blacksmith, John Jewett, and set him to work repairing guns and metal tools. Jewett's later account caused a sensation among readers back east.) In addition, the chief took possession of most of the vessel's cargo.

❧

Important occasions call for a potlatch— a wedding, a daughter's coming of age, the end of a year of mourning. . . . How much a chief is able to give away will affect his standing. His guests will be fed the best food, given the finest blankets, and the most handsome boxes. The chief knows that his gifts will be reciprocated with interest at future potlatches.

—*Marcia Parker Pascua, Makah*

❧

To celebrate his haul, Maquinna staged one of the grandest potlatches yet seen on that stretch of coast. Among the presents he was said to have given out were 200 muskets, 200 yards of cloth, 100 chemises, 100 mirrors, and seven barrels of gunpowder. After that, no one questioned his status as the paramount chief of the region.

Everywhere the riches from trade sparked an exuberant outpouring of native culture.

Houses became bigger, totem poles taller, potlatches more extravagant, ceremonial life more elaborate. Native wood carvers, trading their traditional stone implements for steel knives, turned out masks and boxes of increasing complexity and refinement, which they colored with bright new European paints. Where a village might once have displayed a single totem pole, it now sprouted dozens—carved interior house posts, lofty entrance posts, mortuary poles containing the remains of departed leaders, and poles erected simply to celebrate a particular family or event.

Nuu-chal-nuth trade chiefs swap rifles and sea otter pelts for strands of dentalium shells. The tooth-shaped shells, harvested off Vancouver Island, were used as money all along the Pacific coast. A spruce-root Nuu-chal-nuth hat (below, left) suggests another source of tribal wealth: whaling.

The Russian Wars

By the time of Maquinna's famous potlatch, trade along the coast had settled into a clearcut pattern. Independent sea captains—mostly "Boston Men" and "Men of King George," as people called Yankees and Britishers—plied the coast's lower reaches, making private deals with local chiefs. To the north, meanwhile, the Russian trade had been consolidated into a single government-chartered monopoly, the Russian-American Company, backed by the power of the tsar.

To anchor its position in the Alaska territory, the Russian company had established a series of permanent colonies. The first was at Kodiak Island, in Eskimo country, where administrators recruited workers by force. Then, in the 1790's, the company expanded down the coast, building forts at Yakutat Bay and at Archangel, near present-day Sitka. This was the land of the Tlingit, and there was trouble from the start.

No self-respecting Tlingit leader had any intention of working for the Russians or anyone else. Through trade with the British and Americans, they had acquired steel knives, rifles, and ammunition; already they were using them to defend their waters from poaching by Aleuts employed by the Russians. During a night raid into Prince William Sound, Tlingit warriors killed two Russians and nine Aleuts. A truce was patched together, with the Russians offering gifts in exchange for permission to hunt in Tlingit territory.

But tensions continued to simmer, and at the new Russ-

Armed for battle, a Tlingit warrior (right) wears cedar-slat body armor and a plumed wooden helmet and jaw guard. The scowling Tlingit helmet below protected its owner and inspired fear in his enemy's heart. Clan insignias mark the battle tunic at bottom, made of wood slats wrapped in sinew.

ian fort on Sitka they came to a boil. The Tlingit had leased the site for a respectable sum, but as they watched the stockade walls go up—and saw the Aleut boats return laden with sea otters—they had second thoughts. Chief Katlian, the local war leader, quietly gathered support from tribes down the coast. Haida canoes arrived with arms and ammunition from the British, who had their own reasons to contain the Russians. By June 1802 Katlian was ready.

More than 60 war canoes under his command approached by sea. Other forces moved in from land. On June 18 they attacked. Some 600 men wearing wood-slat armor and heavy wooden helmets charged through the settlement, shouting the war cries of their crest animals, firing rifles, and wielding knives with lethal skill. Only a handful of Russians were there to defend the fort. In a few minutes they all lay dead. Others had been out fishing and berry picking, and as they returned, the Tlingit overwhelmed them as well. In all, Katlian's men killed 20 Russians and 130 Aleuts, and they captured a group of women and children whom they sold back to the company for a large ransom.

The Tlingit attack sent shock waves through the Russian headquarters on Kodiak. It also aroused the ire of the company's manager, Alexander Baranov, the most powerful white man in Alaska. As the chief architect of Russian expansion, Baranov could not allow a Tlingit victory to go unpunished. So in 1804 four company-owned ships carrying 1,000 Russians and Aleuts set sail for Sitka, where they joined a government warship. The Russian guns methodically pounded Katlian's men into submission.

It did not end there. Tlingit warriors struck back in 1806, demolishing the Russian fort at Yakutat, and the next year they prepared for

another assault on Sitka. Gradually, however, the Russians established control. Trade pacts and gift exchanges helped to stabilize relations. Tlingit families began moving back to the villages they had evacuated during the conflict. A new economy developed in which native suppliers provided the Russian colony with fish, game, and even vegetables—which the Russians taught them to grow.

New Wealth From the Land

As it happened, peace was restored just as the region's original source of wealth—the sea otter—was declining. By the late 1820's, after decades of overhunting, this once plentiful mammal was close to extinction. To satisfy the demand for furs, traders switched their attention to the region's large population of land animals, such as marten, river otter, bear, and mink. At virtually the same moment, a powerful new entity—the Hudson's Bay Company—emerged from the deep Subarctic forests and planted itself on the coast.

Following in the track of explorers like Mackenzie and Frazer, the Anglo-Canadian fur giant had pushed its way west through the mountains, establishing trading forts as it went. In 1824 it merged with its main rival, the North West Company, picking up an important post in Chinook territory: Fort Astoria at the mouth of the Columbia River.

It then moved up the coast. The lure of special trading benefits drew scores of native families to the new Hudson's Bay forts. Nine separate Tsimshian groups—more than 2,000 people—switched their winter quarters to Fort Simpson, on the coast just south of the Alaska border.

That greatly enhanced the status of one already high-ranking tribal leader, Chief Legaic. By family inheritance Legaic held the right to trade with the Gitksan of the upper Skeena River, one of the region's richest fur sources. In addition, he had the good luck to marry his daughter to Fort Simpson's chief trader. So secure was his position that when the company tried to deal directly with the Gitksan, it had to pay Legaic for the privilege.

No other native leader at Fort Simpson could claim this kind of prominence—and therein lay a problem. While each noble family knew exactly where it stood within its own ancestral village, no mechanism in Tsimshian culture served to fix the status of families from

Hoping to found an empire, Alexander Baranov of the Russian-American Company (above, left) held control of the Alaska fur trade during the early 1800's. Resistance came from Tlingit war leader Katlian, shown above wearing a silver peace medal from the tsar. The Russian fort at Sitka is in the distance.

247

"TO MAKE MY NAME GOOD"

A high-ranking Tlingit leader has taken another name, and to celebrate the event—and validate his new title—he has invited the chiefs of neighboring villages to a potlatch. Now, after many months of preparation, the day is here. He waits on the beach at Sitka, his village, clad in his finest regalia: the inlaid staff with its fringe of human hair, the goat-hair blanket, the tall ringed potlatch hat with its ermine tassel and clan insignia, all confirming his status as an important member of the Ravens.

The guests arrive by water, their Wolf clan crests adorning the prows of their canoes. As the vessels drift close, the host delivers an elaborate speech of welcome, full of flowery metaphor. The visitors respond with songs and speeches. They step ashore. The potlatch begins in the host's new house. He presides from a platform at the rear, with the highest-ranking guest seated beside him.

The drums start beating, and Raven singers begin the opening chant. Masked dancers circle a central fire; the guests pound the floor in time to the music. A Raven speaker extols the virtues of the host, recounting the feats of his ancestors, the privileges of his house, and the reasons for his new honors. At the same time, by custom, he gently mocks the lineage of the guests. Food appears —a procession of dishes that will include, in the days ahead, dried salmon and fresh seal, roast venison, wild berries drenched in fish oil, fermented salmon roe, sweet cakes made from hemlock bark, and fish oil mixed with snow and beaten to a froth. The guests stuff themselves.

The festivities might last a week or more, with days and nights of feasting and storytelling. Wolf dancers and Raven dancers reenact clan legends. The host shows off his family treasures—carved totems, ceremonial bowls, wooden helmets, metal objects—and tells the history of each. Gifts are distributed: blankets for the lower-ranking guests and more valuable items—a canoe, a slave, perhaps even a copper shield—for the chiefs. Finally the guests depart, lavishly sated, and determined to reassert their ancestral honor with potlatches of their own.

different villages. So in order to establish their rank, newcomers to the fort resorted to a system of competitive potlatching. One after the other, Tsimshian leaders tried to outdo each other in the splendor of their entertainments, the number of guests, the quantity of food, and the extravagance of their gifts.

Besides showing off how much they could give away, the leaders found other ingenious

devices to flaunt their wealth—and humiliate their rivals. One powerful chief, Tsibasa, installed a set of trick stairs in his reception hall designed to unbalance an unsuspecting climber. Tsibasa's main target was his arch competitor—none other than Chief Legaic. Like a European monarch, Legaic typically arrived last in order to make a grand entrance. When he came late to a feast at Tsibasa's house, the steps "revolved" and threw him unceremoniously into the room, in full view of the delighted guests.

Legaic himself was not above using a bit of theater, and to demonstrate his power he once staged an impressive show of reincarnation. First he located a slave who closely resembled

Surrounded by family treasures, a favorite son beside him, a Tlingit host stands in his Chilkat River dwelling, known as the Whale House for the clan which he headed. The totem figures on the right-hand post (detailed in color) tell how Raven caught the King Salmon.

him. Dressing the slave in his own chiefly regalia, he went into hiding, thereby allowing the villagers to think the slave was Legaic. The slave was then killed and cremated. In a sensational performance that awed everyone who saw it or heard about it, Legaic arose from the box containing the slave's ashes, restored majestically to life.

While the land-based fur trade opened new opportunities for those who lived close to the inland forests—the Tsimshian and Kwakiutl most dramatically—it spelled disaster for some others. As sea captains stopped calling on the west coast of Vancouver Island, the Nuu-chal-nuth quietly declined. Another people in danger of lapsing into obscurity were the Haida, whose island home contained few fur-bearing animals.

The Haida had other assets, however, including a reputation as the best canoe makers in the Northwest. Expanding their activities, they began growing potatoes and shipping the harvest to the Hudson's Bay forts. Haida craftsmen carved wood and shale curios, which they sold to white traders. One beneficiary of the new trade climate was the village of Skidegate (named for its chief), strategically located on the main canoe trade route. To celebrate his good fortune, Chief Skidegate built himself an enormous house with towering totem poles and a ceremonial boardwalk leading up from the beach.

Another Haida town to benefit was Massett, on the north coast. A new chief, the rich and artful Wiah, had come to power, and he also erected a grandly imposing dwelling. Nearly 70 feet square, with nine totem poles (one of them 49 feet high), the structure could house nearly 100 inhabitants. People called it the Monster House.

The Whites Settle In

During the fur trade era, most whites came only briefly to Northwest Coast, conducting their business and then departing. Even in the trading posts of the giant fur companies, the permanent foreign population remained small. As a tiny minority dependent on the

Tlingits from Yakutat pose with their Raven clan regalia while attending a potlatch at Sitka in 1904. The gifts exchanged might have included an extremely valuable "copper" like the one above, with a crest design outlined in black pigment.

goodwill of their native hosts, the white traders tended to treat the local population with a certain respect. Bonds of genuine affection gradually took hold. Many of the whites took Indian wives.

Then, in scarcely more than a decade, everything changed.

The governments of Canada and the United States settled a long-standing boundary dispute in 1846, in effect opening the region to settlers. Before long, shiny yellow nuggets began showing up at the trading posts. There was a ripple of excitement over some gold deposits found in 1852 in the Queen Charlotte Islands. Then a true bonanza followed on the Fraser River in 1857.

White settlers poured in by the boatload: prospectors from England, the eastern United States, and California, then tradesmen, innkeepers, shipping agents, carpenters, farmers, bankers, brewers—all the supporting characters of a full-fledged gold rush. They stopped first at Fort Victoria, the Hudson's Bay headquarters at the southern tip of Vancouver Island. Fort Victoria in 1857 was a sleepy town of some 300 souls. Within a year it

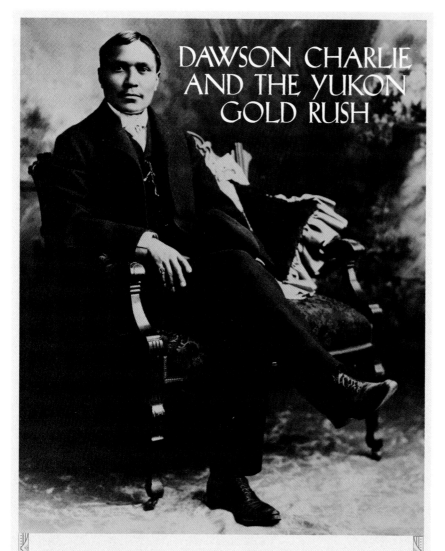

DAWSON CHARLIE AND THE YUKON GOLD RUSH

Just as the Fraser River gold fields were played out, a chance discovery deep in the Subarctic Yukon attracted a new swarm of fortune seekers. This time, at least one native resident, a Tagish hunter named Dawson Charlie (above), was able to profit.

In August of 1896, he was camping near the Yukon's Klondike River, famous for its salmon runs, with two companions — another Tagish, named Skookum Jim, and George Carmack, a white prospector. There had been several gold strikes in the Yukon in recent years, but none important enough to excite the world's attention. Suddenly that changed. A moose was feeding in the bush up a small side creek, and one of the friends went after it. Thirsty in the August heat, he cupped his hand into the creek's sparkling water — and pulled out a nugget as big as his thumb. All three promptly staked claims and hurried into town.

News of the Klondike gold strike swept the world like a midsummer tornado. Paddle steamers chugged up the mighty Yukon River to its junction with the Klondike, bringing a horde of prospectors. Others came overland from Skagway, in Tlingit country, heaving their gear up dizzying Chilkoot Pass and hiking on some 400 bone-wrenching, up-and-down miles to the mines.

By the century's turn, more than $48 million in nuggets and gold dust had been removed. Still, most prospectors left the Yukon with empty pockets. But the three pioneers — Cormack, Skookum Jim, and Dawson Charlie — took their winnings to splurge in Seattle, each one rich beyond his wildest dreams.

swelled to 3,000 permanent inhabitants, with another 6,000 transients camped nearby.

The effect was devastating. These new immigrants, unlike the whites of fur trade days, viewed the region's native inhabitants as "dirty, nasty-smelling creatures" with swarthy complexions and bodies that stank of fish oil. (Few settlers seemed to notice that most Indians bathed regularly in the ocean, and whites rarely.) Native customs were regarded with scorn; native art seemed "grossly obscene." A few years earlier, when a group of 500 Haida had paddled into Victoria, hoping to trade, they so alarmed the fledgling colony that Governor James Douglas (himself a former trader married to the granddaughter of a Cree chief) begged them to leave.

But still more Indians came, and the pressures multiplied. Most settled in squalid slums on the city's outskirts, elbow to elbow with white laborers and roustabouts. Alcohol flowed freely, and minor disputes exploded into ethnic violence. A cry went out for the Indians' removal. "How much longer are we to be inflicted with the intolerable nuisance of hideous, half-naked, drunken savages . . . reeling about and shouting?" demanded an angry letter to a Canadian newspaper in 1859.

Equally dismaying was the growing trade in female flesh. In the past, native chiefs had occasionally made village women available to European traders and explorers, with no taint of dishonor. The trade goods obtained in return would be handed out at the next potlatch. Now village women, usually slaves or commoners, would spend their nights "earning blankets" (as the saying went) at Victoria's brothels and dance halls. Returning home with their pay, some carried the deadly seeds of syphilis.

Other diseases also took a dreadful toll. Malaria, influenza, scarlet fever, whooping cough, and the like had struck periodically since the early days of the fur trade. Now came a smallpox epidemic that raged through the Victoria slums in 1862. In the crowded conditions of the native shantytowns, it spread like an invisible, poisonous fog. The authorities seized the opportunity to evict the inhabitants and burn their houses.

The refugees fled up the coast to their old villages, bearing the infection with them. Travelers reported seeing bodies festering along the shoreline, with canoes, blankets, and guns scattered nearby. The disease touched almost every village on Vancouver Island and on the mainland opposite. The death count among the Nuu-chal-nuth, Kwakiutl, and Coast Salish reached one in three. Among the Haida, so many died that entire communities ceased to function. In a few years only Skitegate and Massett remained. And still the contagion swept on. It scythed through the Tlingit, wiping out village after village. The one exception was Sitka, where the Russian authorities had

seen fit to vaccinate all residents, Tlingit and white alike. Elsewhere, down the length of the Northwest Coast, an estimated 20,000 native people died.

A Friend in the Church

Decimated by illness, reviled by white settlers, their community life disrupted by alcoholism and other social problems, native people increasingly found consolation in another alien intrusion: Christianity. The first converts were Aleuts and others in the Far North, who in the brutal early days of the fur trade found a sympathetic ally in the Russian Orthodox Church. Devout traders held impromptu prayer services, and they adopted Aleut godchildren, who in turn helped spread the faith. An Or-

At Newitti in Kwakiutl country, these villagers responded to changing times by turning their houses into trading posts to sell handicrafts to whites.

Anglican converts in their Sunday best line up on the church steps at Metlakatla, in Tsimshian country. The winged baptismal font, from a Methodist church at Fort Simpson, was carved in 1886 by Tsimshian artist Freddie Alexai.

thodox priest arrived in 1824—Ivan Veniaminov, who built a church, founded schools, and devised an Aleut alphabet. He then moved south to Sitka and began to minister to the Tlingit.

The Tlingit initially showed little interest; but Veniaminov persisted, and in time he began drawing in converts. Showing a wise tolerance for native customs—and a keen understanding of the Tlingit love for sumptuous display—he erected the imposing Cathedral of St. Michael, and when possible he endeavored to blend Christian belief with Tlingit ceremony. It was just the right strategy. Thousands of native Alaskans flocked to the Orthodox Church, which would remain a lasting legacy of the Russian colonial presence in North America.

To the south, Protestant missionaries arrived on the heels of the Hudson's Bay Company to convert the local population. None cut a wider swath than William Duncan, an Anglican lay preacher who came to Fort Simpson in 1857 to preach to the Tsimshian. Though impressed by the natives' intelligence and artistic skill, Duncan was appalled by just about everything else—the rites of the shamans, the extravagance of the pot-

latches, the cannibalistic dances at the Winter Festival, and the rising levels of drunkenness and prostitution. To save the Tsimshian from the dual temptations of "pagan" traditions and modern vice, Duncan saw only one remedy. He would isolate his congregation in a separate community built on principles of strict Christian virtue.

He picked Metlakatla, site of the abandoned Tsimshian winter camp. In May 1862 he moved in with just 58 converts; two days later the smallpox epidemic reached Fort Simpson, and hundreds more were suddenly inspired to join him. Metlakatla soon developed into a thriving Victorian town of more than 1,000 souls living in tidy rows of two-family frame houses. Self-contained and self-sufficient, Metlakatla had its own sawmill and blacksmith shop, plus a salmon cannery to provide employment. There was a town hall, a firehouse, a police force, and a large wooden church with gables, buttresses, and bell tower. No one drank and no one danced—though the town's brass band held frequent parades. Shamans and potlatches were banned.

So successful was Metlakatla that it became a model for other missionary endeavors. The community continued to flourish until 1887, when Duncan, following a dispute with the

Anglican bishop, left town and moved across the border to Alaska with 823 followers. Obtaining a land grant from the U.S. government, he promptly founded New Metlakatla, a close replica of the old, and propelled it to similar heights of virtue and prosperity.

Some people resisted the invasion of the missionaries, to be sure, and clung fast to their own traditions. Potlatches among the tribes of British Columbia became so lavish and wasteful—in the eyes of white authorities—that in 1885 the Canadian government outlawed the practice entirely. It continued in secret until the ban was finally lifted in 1951.

> We will dance when our laws command us to dance, we will feast when our hearts desire to feast. Do we ask the white man, "Do as the Indian does"? No, we do not. Why then do you ask us, "Do as the white man does"?
>
> — *Kwakiutl elder*

In some areas Christianity merged in surprising ways with native beliefs and ceremonial practices. Among the Salish tribes of the interior mountains, holy men in the late 1800's regularly borrowed from the sacraments of Roman Catholicism, urging their followers to observe the Sabbath and make the sign of the cross before meals. Then one day in 1881 a Coast Salish laborer named John Slocum, a Catholic convert, fell into a deep coma. As his grief-stricken family went off to buy a coffin, he felt his soul transported to the gates of Heaven. When it returned, Slocum awoke and began to preach a gospel of clean living and spiritual renewal. At first his message won few adherents. But again the miracle occurred: Slocum went into a trance, was left for dead, then arose to resume preaching.

During this second ordeal Slocum's wife, Mary, was seized with a fit of shaking, which everyone interpreted as yet another sign of divine visitation. So was born Tschadam, the Indian Shaker religion. Along with its Christian God—and stern prohibition of drinking, gambling, and other vices—it added the spirit power of certain traditional beliefs and the healing effects of a dancelike shaking ceremony. The religion spread from Seattle, where the Slocums built their first church, up and down the coast, from California to British Columbia, and there it survives to this day.

Spirit Dancers in the Puget Sound region celebrate a traditional Salish Winter Festival in this 1988 work by Tulalip artist Ron Hilbert Coy. "Our sacred practices are alive and will live through the ages," vows one modern believer.

Seasons of Life in the Arctic

Each spring, as the pack ice breaks up along the Alaska coast, herds of bowhead whales move north through the Bering Straits and into their summer feeding grounds in the Arctic Ocean. They are enormous creatures, the adults reaching more than 60 feet in length and providing up to 60 tons of meat and blubber. By April the whales reach Point Hope, an elbow of rock and tundra that juts into the ocean far above the Arctic Circle. It is a desolate-looking place, with little hint of the bounty swimming offshore.

Yet cut into the frozen ground are relics of a small city: the foundation pits of some 600 semisubterranean houses built by Stone Age whale hunters who made Point Hope their home. Navigating between ice floes in large, open sealskin boats called *umiaks,* they pursued the bowheads relentlessly. One kill would feed the entire community for months.

Some 500 miles north of the Arctic Circle, the cliffs of Devon Island rise from ice-flecked Baffin Bay, hunting grounds of the Canadian Iglulik. Half a continent to the west, the Inupiat whalers of northern Alaska wore carved wooden masks (above) to celebrate a successful season.

Of all the earth's regions, none seem more inhospitable to life than the northernmost expanses of the Arctic. Winter temperatures hover at 30 degrees below zero on average and can fall much lower in places. Gale-force winds howl across the snowfields; ice floes clog the oceans from Siberia to Greenland. On the islands of northern Canada, the sun drops below the horizon in October and remains there until early April.

In summer, when the sun returns, only the topsoil thaws. Pools of meltwater trapped in the soggy tundra are breeding grounds for swarms of mosquitoes and other biting insects. No trees grow here, and little vegetation of any kind. The only wood for building and toolmaking is driftwood gathered on beaches.

Yet it is possible to live and even thrive here. These are the hunting grounds of the continent's most recent native immigrants: the Eskimos, some of whom today use more specific names—Inuit, Inupiat, Yupik, and others, depending on where they live. The ancestors of all Eskimos arrived by sea from Siberia, long after the melting of the Ice Age glaciers had flooded the land bridge that linked Asia and North America.

The Yupik made the migration first, beginning around 3000 B.C., and settled into the damp, comparatively mild climate of Alaska's southwest coast, below the Arctic Circle. The Inuit, arriving later, paused in northern Alaska, then around A.D. 500 started moving again. Hauling their possessions by boat and dogsled, they crossed the continent's northern margin—across the Alaskan north slope, through northern Canada and down into Hudson Bay, then on past Labrador to the coast of Greenland, spreading themselves across some 5,000 miles. Along the way they carried the sustaining ingredients of Inuit life: kayaks and umiaks, ice picks and snow goggles, oil lamps, harpoons, fur-trimmed parkas, and the courage and skill to harvest the rich marine life of the Arctic seas.

> We Inupiat are meat eaters, not vegetarians. We live off the sea mammals. . . . The Bering Sea and the Chukchi Sea are our gardens.
>
> — *Jonah Tokienna, Inupiat*

Few pursuits are more hazardous than a whale hunt. The whale crews would converge on a spouting bowhead, usually six paddlers in each umiak, the *umialiks* (crew captains) steering from a seat astern. The lead umiak would draw alongside, and the harpooner, poised in the bow, would drive his stone-tipped shaft into a vulnerable spot, preferably

behind a fin. The harpoon point would remain embedded, and as the whale sounded, an attached line of seal or walrus skin would whir out behind him. Inflated sealskin floats would slow him down, bringing him back to the surface. Again and again the harpooners would strike, until the giant beast lay exhausted and could be killed with a lance thrust into a vital organ.

Every moment spelled danger. The flip of a bowhead's tail could toss an umiak's crew into the freezing water and to certain death. To pacify their prey, the crews wore sacred talismans and chanted special whale songs. Some coated the tips of their harpoons with the ashes of dead whalers. The umialik was thought to have shamanistic powers. His wife, ashore, lay still all during the hunt in hopes that the whale, following her example, would lie placidly on the ocean's surface.

Smaller whales like the beluga were easier and safer to catch—as were the seals, prime sources of meat and hides. Colonies of walrus inhabited the coasts, and with some adult males weighing up to a formidable 2,000 pounds, they could be dangerous when attacked. But walrus hide made a tough, waterproof covering for kayaks and umiaks, and carvers worked the ivory tusks into buttons, fishnet weights, harpoon toggles, and other objects of great beauty and utility. The blubber from whales, seals, and walruses, rendered into oil, heated the homes of Arctic natives, dried their clothing, and cooked their food.

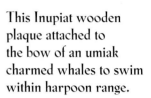

This Inupiat wooden plaque attached to the bow of an umiak charmed whales to swim within harpoon range.

The dreaded sea monster Palraiyuk chases whales and kayakers on this ivory Yupik pipe, carved from a walrus tusk. The graphite towline weight and whale-shaped box for harpoon blades were Inupiat whaling gear.

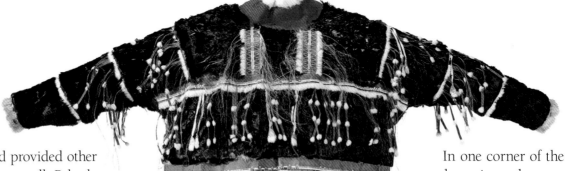

The land provided other staples as well. Polar bears roaming the ice floes were hunted for their meat and fur. Huge, shaggy musk oxen grazed the tundra grasses. Grizzly bear, wolf, wolverine, arctic fox, and arctic hare all crisscrossed the region. The approach of summer brought enormous flocks of ducks, geese and other waterfowl. At the same time, great herds of caribou moved into the tundra in the wake of the melting snow. Few natural materials afford the same combination of lightness and warmth as caribou skin; the hollow hairs trap a layer of insulating air, making the skins ideal for parkas, blankets, and mattresses.

As the Yupik and Inuit spread across the Arctic horizon, they discovered surprising variations of climate and terrain. Immense runs of salmon crowd into Alaska's Yukon and Kuskokwim rivers, and the Yupik took full advantage of them. The frigid waters of extreme northern Canada contain no salmon, so people there built stone weirs to trap the hardier Arctic char. Most groups made tools from stone, bone, and ivory; those living near the Coppermine River used metal, pounding knife blades and spear points from copper nuggets found in local streambeds.

> The caribou were hunted in kayaks at the crossing of rivers and lakes, being driven out into the water where they could be easily overtaken . . . but the rules were very strict about those places. To break them would be an insult to the souls of the caribou.
> —*Ivaluardjuk, Igluik*

Virtually every Eskimo group hunted caribou. One, the Caribou Eskimos west of Hudson Bay, made it their life's work, abandoning the sea entirely to press deep into the Canadian tundra in pursuit of land-based game.

A Koniag leader wore this bird-skin tunic, sewn from the shiny neck skins of hundreds of cormorants. The tassels are dyed animal gut.

Caribou Eskimos stalk their prey by kayak in a 1976 stonecut and stencil work by the Inuit artist Luke Anguhadluq.

In one corner of the Arctic, life took a unique, almost cosmopolitan turn. Along the coast of southern Alaska, from Prince William Sound to the tip of the Alaska Peninsula, conditions were remarkably temperate, with cool rainy summers, mild winters, and an absence of sea ice. This was the home of the Yupik-speaking Pacific Eskimos, who were kayakers and harpooners but who also bore a strong cultural resemblance to societies of the Northwest Coast. The Koniag of Kodiak Island, for example, lived in shoreline villages, held potlatches, and were ruled by a hereditary class of high-ranking families. Most Arctic societies, in contrast, were notably free of class distinctions. A stranger visiting the Labrador Inuit would be hard pressed to find a village headman—much less an aristocrat.

Another Arctic group resembling no other were the Aleut, distant cousins of the Yupik and Inuit, who inhabited the islands that arc 1,000 miles west from Alaska. They, too, lived in an ice-free world, but one surrounded by some of the foggiest, windiest seas on earth. To survive, the Aleut became superb kayakers. They also hunted birds, gathered roots and

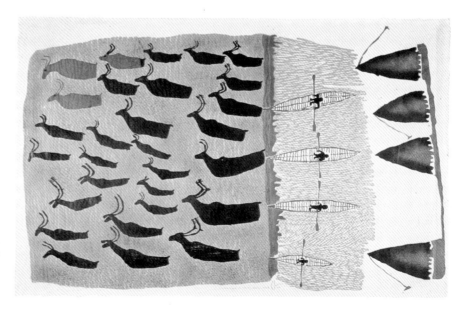

THE ALEUT: LORDS OF THE KAYAK

"Who can tell if the kayak is made for the Aleut, or the Aleut for the kayak?" So people said, for the two fit together like an otter in its skin. Snugged into the hatch with a waterproof drip skirt, a seal-gut parka nipped close at wrists and head, the Aleut was impervious to wet and cold. His craft was a masterpiece, its wooden ribs steamed to shape, notched together, and covered with sea-lion skins.

And the Aleut was a master at using it. Plying a double-bladed paddle, he could slip noiselessly through the water or dash ahead in quick bursts of speed to outpace any seal or sea otter. Once in range—about 40 yards—he hurled a four-foot harpoon with the aid of a wooden throwing stick.

Foul weather called for special skills. Setting out when the surf was up, he would carry his kayak to a rock shoulder, strap himself in, then have two companions heave him directly into the waves. If he overturned, a deft underwater paddle stroke would set him upright. At sea in a fog, he navigated by wind direction, the cries of gulls, the crash of surf, wave shapes, and shifts in water currents.

Out hunting, a kayaker invoked the spirit of the animals he pursued. Sometimes he wore a visored helmet made of steam-bent wood, painted with signs that would call the animals to him. Plumes of sea-lion whiskers each marked a successful catch, testifying to his hunting prowess.

berries, and wove beautiful watertight baskets from the tall grasses that grew on the beaches.

Depending on local circumstances, an Arctic family might build a house of sod, stone, wood, leather, or ice. In relatively populous areas of western Alaska, the Yupik lived in sod-house villages of a dozen families or more.

> The sod house is very warm . . . men and women wear almost nothing. Ladies are topless, but they wear beads around their neck. Most of them have tattoos on face, hands and arms. This makes them look beautiful and ladylike.
> —*St. Lawrence Island Yupik*

Typically, each house consisted of a single dome-shaped room dug partly into the ground, framed with driftwood or whalebone and roofed over with layers of turf. An opening in the roof, glazed over with seal intestine, let in light. Usually the only heat came from a saucer-shaped soapstone lamp that burned seal oil. Family and guests entered through a narrow, sunken corridor designed to keep heat from escaping.

Most other Eskimo groups lived in domed sod dwellings of similar design, at least in the winter months. Only the Inuit of central and eastern Canada lived in snow igloos, and then

Ivory kayak ornaments of the Bering Sea Yupik include (clockwise from top) float plugs depicting an owl and a human face; line fasteners (males smiled, females frowned); and spear guards with a "perforated hands" design.

This seal mask, carved from driftwood, may have been worn at a Yupik Bladder Festival. Such masks were normally created for a particular occasion, used once, then discarded.

only in the depths of winter. During warm weather virtually all Eskimos moved to caribou or sealskin tents. And everywhere in the North, communities swelled and diminished according to the season. Even the largely sedentary Yupik would leave their permanent riverside villages for hunting camps on the tundra. The more nomadic Inuit tended to roam their tundra hunting grounds in independent family bands, then come together for special occasions. Large schools of beluga swarmed into the shallow waters of the Mackenzie River estuary each summer to feed, and the Mackenzie Delta Inuit would swarm after them in kayaks, driving them onto shoals upstream where they were easily killed. The main staging area, the village of Kittigazuit, briefly hosted 1,000 people or more. A summer trade fair at Nigalik on Alaska's north slope attracted Eskimos from many regions; groups from the interior mountains would barter caribou hides and snowshoes for seal oil, ivory, and other marine products.

Winter was the period of communal life for the Inuit of central Canada. They were the "Es-

kimos" of popular imagination, people like the Netsilik and Iglulik, who built snow igloos, ate much of their meat raw, and lived at the outer reaches of human survival. They were never numerous—2,000 or 3,000 at most—but they met the rigors of Arctic life with deep reserves of stamina and ingenuity.

Strategies for Survival

As the sun sank low and the world iced over, Iglulik families would strike their caribou-skin tents, load up their dogsleds, and head out to sea. For the next several months they would live on the ice pack—now frozen to a depth of 6 feet or more—in small igloo villages of 50 to 60 people. Their purpose: hunting seals through holes in the ice.

Like all sea mammals, seals must come to the surface to breathe. As winter approaches and the ocean begins to freeze, a seal will return again and again to the same spot, breaking through the ice as it forms, thus opening a permanent breathing hole. The Inuit hunters used their sled dogs to sniff out the holes, then settled down to wait. The telltale fluttering of a piece of down placed inside a hole would announce a seal's arrival, and a quick harpoon thrust would kill it.

Inuit life changed dramatically with the seasons, as shown here by native artist Joe Tailrunili: summer meant skin tents and hunts by kayak for seal and walrus; winter brought snow igloos, dogsleds, and musk ox as game.

An Iglulik family from central Canada relaxes on skin-covered ice-block sleeping platforms in their 1903 winter home (left) while the evening meal simmers over seal-oil lamps. The caribou-headed ivory tool (above), made in western Alaska, was used to straighten arrow shafts.

At the end of the day, the hunters dragged the dead seals back to the igloos to be skinned and butchered. Every part was used or consumed. The meat might be simmered with blood and blubber over a seal-oil lamp, forming a thick broth. Some was left outside, to be eaten frozen. Internal organs were best consumed raw: in this land without vegetables, a slice of fresh, raw seal liver yielded generous amounts of vitamins A and C.

Even in the good years, survival was never certain. The story is told of an Inuit band that set out, some winters ago, to visit a Hudson's Bay trading post at Pond Inlet in Baffin Island. It was a journey of 400 miles. A sled was needed to haul gear and provisions, but wood to build one was scarce. So they improvised: for runners they used frozen rolled-up caribou hides glazed with ice; for crossbars, lengths of frozen salmon.

At the end of each day, the Inuit band built an igloo for shelter, and they secured the sled across the roof to keep it away from the dogs. But one night, about halfway along, a sudden thaw caused the igloo to sag. The dogs pulled down the sled and gobbled up the provisions, including the salmon crossbars. From then on, the travelers began to starve. Only one woman reached Pond Inlet alive.

Life on these precarious margins meant that every member of an Inuit band played an essential role. While her husband hunted, an Inuit wife spent much of her time making clothes—scraping hides, chewing the leather to soften it, and sewing the pieces with sinew. Every seam had to be windproof and watertight; a leaky boot could lead to crippling frostbite. Children and grandparents helped as they could—preparing food, packing sleds, harnessing dogs, setting up tents.

To improve their chances, families banded together in close alliances. Men shared each day's catch with one or more hunt partners, so that if anyone hit a streak of bad luck, the others would tide him over. Even closer was the bond between two song partners. While gathered in winter camps, Inuit families would meet for communal festivals of chanting and dancing, and song partners would perform as a team. The tie extended to most aspects of daily life. Song partners hunted to-

gether, traveled together, shared tools and labor—and, occasionally, spouses.

The worst disaster was a scarcity of game. The fate of an Inuit community lay in the hands of Sedna, a powerful goddess who lived under the ocean and controlled the movements of sea creatures. Sedna (known to some groups as Telliulik) had reason to mistrust human beings. As a young woman she was traveling with her father in an open umiak—fleeing an unhappy marriage to the Prince of Seagulls—when a terrible storm blew up. Huge waves came crashing over the side, threatening to swamp the fragile boat. So, to lighten the load, Sedna's father threw her overboard. When she tried to climb back in, her father chopped off her fingers. Still she held on, so he chopped again. Down she sank. Her finger joints became seals and walruses, and her hands turned into whales. Ever since then, Sedna has taken her revenge by withholding the beasts of the sea from any

A polar bear and a grizzly face off over a dead walrus as a distant hunter looks on; the painting is by James (Kivetoruk) Moses.

This shaman's mask may represent either a seal spirit or the Yupik moon god, Tunghak, keeper of game animals.

human hunter foolish enough to offend her.

Fortunately for the Eskimos of Alaska, the more benevolent Moon Man (sometimes called Tunghak) protected the sea mammals and other game in their region. But throughout the Arctic, hunters made every effort to treat the animals they sought, and their associated deities, with reverential dignity. North Alaska whalers donned new parkas at the start of each season, sang chants, and handled sacred talismans; before launching their harpoons, they politely greeted their quarry by name. When the Inuit set about butchering a seal, they first cleared the igloo of stored blubber and sprinkled the floor with clean snow, lest any untidiness cause offense. All slaughtered sea mammals were given a drink of fresh water in case their souls were thirsty.

Behind these courtly maneuvers lay a deep sense of unity in the natural order of things. Every living creature, from the

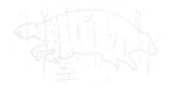

greatest whale down to the tiniest herring or tundra vole, was endowed with a share of the universal soul force. The Inuit called the force *inua* and saw it as the animating spirit within each individual being. To the Yupik it was a state of conscious awareness—alert to the world around it and subject to much the same needs and desires as the Yupik themselves. Sometimes it appeared in human form. But even inanimate objects possessed it.

> We felt that all things were like us people, down to small animals like the mouse, and the things like wood. The wood is glad to the person who is using it, and the person is glad to the wood for being there to be used.
> — *Joe Friday, Yupik*

Just as they shared the same essence, humans and animals were bound by an intricate network of mutual obligation. The Bering Sea Yupik hunted seals in spring and summer, harpooning them from kayaks. Whenever a seal was taken, its swim bladder was carefully preserved because it was thought to be the seat of the animal's soul.

At year's end the Yupik held a midwinter Bladder Festival to honor the spirits of the dead seals. The swim bladders of all the seals caught during the past season were inflated and hung at the back of the *kashim,* a house used by the men's society of a village, and they were regaled with songs, dancing, drumming, and lavish feasting. At the festival's climax, villagers took the bladders down to the ocean, deflated them, and pushed them through a hole in the ice—thus sending them back home to be born again as next year's seal crop.

Children of Thunder

Of all North America's original inhabitants, the people of the Arctic held longest to their traditional ways of life. Early contacts with European culture were brief and sporadic, leaving little impression on either side. Norsemen under Eric the Red set up a colony in Greenland around 985, and Norse sagas tell of fierce battles with the Skraelings (savages) who later moved into the area from the north. Apparently the Skraelings won: their Inuit descendants remained in Greenland, while the Norse moved out.

The ghost face peering out from the eye of this Yupik bear mask represents the bear's inua, its humanlike soul.

Dressed in preparation for a winter festival, Inupiat Wolf Dancers from Kauwerak, Alaska, wear furs, animal heads, and mittens adorned with birds' beaks. A shield-shaped box drum hangs behind them.

Symbol of tsarist power, the two-headed eagle marked Russia's land claims in Alaska.

Inuit archers of Baffin Island trade shots with Martin Frobisher's musketeers in a 1577 painting by John White, who sailed with the expedition. During the fight Frobisher suffered a flesh wound from a stone-tipped arrow.

European seafarers again reached the eastern Arctic in the 16th century. Portuguese fishermen plied the cod-filled waters off Labrador and Newfoundland. Adventurers like the Englishmen Martin Frobisher and John Davis braved the ice floes in search of a northwest passage to the Orient.

Most encounters were remarkably free of violence—except in the western Arctic. As Russian fur traders moved across from Siberia, first to the Aleutians and then on to the Alaska mainland, tensions built steadily. Some traders made an effort to deal fairly, but most simply took what they wanted. Armed gangs would move into a village, seize the women and children, and demand otter pelts as ransom. So the Aleut men would set out in their kayaks, forced to hunt for the Russians in order to rescue their families.

By 1763 the people of several islands in the eastern Aleutians had suffered enough. They waited until five Russian ships came within

striking distance; then they attacked—and in one stroke destroyed four Russian ships and killed most of the crew members. The Russian retaliation appeared in the person of a ruthless and determined navigator named Ivan Soloviev. Moving swiftly, Soloviev destroyed 18 villages on one island, every native dwelling on a second island, and several more on a third. Kayaks, harpoons, and other precious equipment were gathered into piles and burned. Prisoners faced terrible abuses. By one account, Soloviev, wondering how many bodies a musket ball could penetrate, tied a dozen Aleuts in a row, front to back, and fired a shot. The bullet stopped at the ninth man.

The Aleut put up little resistance after Soloviev was through. When the government-backed Russian-American Company took control of the Alaska fur trade, it used Aleut harpooners to bring in the furs and prepare them for market. In theory, the native hunters worked for half shares. But in fact they saw little profit, since the company charged them for tools, clothing, provisions, and a vague promise of "protection." As the Russians expanded east to Kodiak Island and beyond, they subjected the Pacific Eskimos to the same oppressive system.

White people are children of thunder. Everything they do and everything they have is accompanied with noise.
                    —Yupik shaman

Reports of atrocities eventually filtered to the outside world, and the Russian government ordered sweeping reforms. Soon the company was building schools and hospitals. Educated Aleuts and Yupiks rose to become civil servants, naval officers, even company managers. So many native Alaskans took holy orders that the Russian Orthodox Church came to be seen as a native institution. By the time Russia sold Alaska to the United States in 1867, all the region's inhabitants were being treated as free citizens of the Russian Empire.

Elsewhere in the Arctic, white influence arrived more slowly. But inevitably it came. A

growing demand for baleen—the flexible whalebone used to make corset stays in the mid-19th century—sent ship captains into the High Arctic in pursuit of the giant bowhead whales. The local Inuit found profitable jobs as guides, deckhands, and suppliers of fresh meat to the whale ships.

As Inuit bands moved into the whaling centers, the old foundations of Arctic life began to shift. Metal pots and kettles replaced the old containers of hide or stone; steel knives took over from bone; kerosene lamps, not dishes of seal blubber, lit Inuit dwellings; the explosive bark of the modern repeating rifle echoed across the hunting grounds.

If life seemed at first to look up, the improvement was often temporary. Armed with modern weapons, Inuit hunters began to deplete the stocks of caribou and seal. The numbers of caribou dropped so low in Alaska that people began to starve. Whiskey flowed freely along the whaling coasts, bringing its usual social disruptions. Diseases likewise took their alarming toll, particularly in the more densely populated villages of western Alaska.

In the wake of the explorers and whalers came the missionaries. Among the best known was Sheldon Jackson, a Presbyterian minister who in 1884 became the official U.S. Bureau of Education representative in Alaska. At Jackson's urging, various Protestant groups set up mission schools in the Arctic tundra—one sponsored by Episcopalians at Point Hope, another by Congregationalists at Cape Prince of Whales, and the third backed by Presbyterians at Point Barrow. All were determined "to lift up the white man's burden," as Jackson put it, on behalf of native Alaskans.

Jackson's energy and vision did much to help, in fact. But misunderstandings abounded. When pneumonia took 26 lives at Cape Prince of Whales, a village shaman attributed the deaths to evil powers released when children at the mission schoolhouse drew pictures on slate. Village hoodlums shot and killed the teacher, Harrison Thornton, closing down the school for several years.

Anchored to the ice in Baffin Bay, British explorers John Ross and William Parry exchange knives for narwhal tusks with Polar Inuit in 1818.

Offering skins and weapons, Yupik traders near the Bering Strait approach by umiak, ready to bargain.

To replace declining caribou herds, Alaska missionary Sheldon Jackson pursuaded the U.S. government to import 1,280 Siberian reindeer; these three at Cape Prince of Wales pulled sleds.

Four Beauties of Cape Prince of Wales, with Sled Reindeer of the American Missionary Association Herd.

Less heralded but also less trouble-ridden was the work of John Kilbuck, a Moravian brother who arrived in Alaska in 1885. The Moravian Church already had a history of success in the Arctic; its mission villages in Greenland and Labrador had thrived for nearly a century. Converts read the Bible in Eskimo and sang Eskimo versions of Moravian hymns, while continuing to trap, trade, and pursue other traditional activities. Key areas of Moravian teaching—injunctions to work hard, pray devoutly, and play an active role in village life—struck a deeply responsive chord.

In addition, Kilbuck was himself a full-blood (if thoroughly Anglicized) Delaware Indian with an innate sympathy for native concerns. "Somewhere in me there must be some of the old Injun left," he noted wryly after joining in one of the village's winter festivals, "for I was strangely moved." Fluent in Yupik, he settled happily into the Kuskokwim River area with his wife, Edith, and they remained there for more than 30 years. It was in no small measure a tribute to his efforts that the Moravian Church became an integral part of native life and culture in southwestern Alaska.

The human face of a Yupik caribou figure (right) reflects an enduring spiritual bond.

A Shaman's Vision

Yet even as Christianity took hold across the Arctic, traditions endured. No act of spiritual zeal rings out more clearly than the story of Kridlak, shaman of an isolated Inuit community on Baffin Island. From passing whalers, Kridlak learned of fellow Inuits who lived far to the north in a place called Greenland. A vision illuminated his mind, calling him to visit these distant brethren. So one day in the mid-1850's, he set out across the ice, accompanied by 38 men, women, and children. They trekked north from island to island, hunting seals and polar bears, pitching camp in the tundra when the summer thaw bogged down their dogsleds, moving on when the winter freeze reopened their passage over the ice.

A bitter dispute broke out after the second winter, and 24 members of the group, hungry and cold, turned back. But Kridlak, his vision still bright, pressed on with those who remained loyal. As he drove his dogsled through the Arctic night, his followers later reported, a white flame danced above his head.

They inched up the coast of Ellesmere Island, past pinnacles of rock and ice in the northernmost land on earth. After six years they reached the 30-mile stretch of frozen sea where Canada and Greenland almost touch. Hiking across the ice, they turned south. Finally they saw two sleds approaching, tiny in the distance.

If you remember on waking that you have dreamed about things at a great distance, it is because your eyes have actually been there while you were asleep.

— *Copper Inuit*

The Thule Inuit who greeted Kridlak were a sadly depleted people. An unknown illness had swept the region some 50 years earlier, carrying away the elders and the shamans and leaving only a few youngsters. With centuries of tradition erased, they had lost many essential arts of Inuit culture and survival.

Kridlak became their savior. He taught them to make kayaks, snow houses, and bows and arrows for hunting caribou; he also taught them ancient rites of celebration and belief. Kridlak's followers intermarried with the people of Thule, and today their descendants regard the Inuit of Canada and Greenland to be one people. In 1966 two men from Thule, honoring Kridlak's feat, trekked 400 miles by dogsled back to the settlement on Ellesmere Island. And the exchanges continue, celebrating the unity and persistence of Inuit tradition across the vastness of the Far North.

An Inuit encampment near the Coppermine River in northern Canada makes final preparations for a seal hunt. The photograph was taken in March 1944; the scene, with its snow houses, dog teams, and slanting spring light, remains timeless.

*My words are
tied in one with the
great mountains, with the
great rocks, with the
great trees, in one with my
body and my heart.
All of you see me, one
with this world.*

—*Yokuts prayer*

8

BETWEEN THE MOUNTAINS AND THE SEA

CALIFORNIA, THE GREAT BASIN, AND THE PLATEAU

An astonishing silhouette appeared on the Pacific horizon one morning in the summer of 1542. Two ships —Spanish, it turned out, under the command of Juan Rodríguez Cabrillo— sailed up the coast of California. The native Kumeyaay people were the first to see these amazing vessels with their billowing sails. No less amazing were the men on board, with their fair skin, beards, metal weapons, strange language, and even stranger clothing.

Fearful at first, the Kumeyaay tried to repel the Spaniards when they landed, wounding three of the sailors with arrows. Cabrillo's men then seized two Indian children and took them aboard their ship. After fruitless attempts to communicate, the Spaniards put the children ashore again, clad in new shirts. This gesture evidently convinced some Kumeyaay that the intruders meant no harm.

Because neither group understood the other's speech, they communicated with a makeshift sign language. In this halting and imprecise manner, the Kumeyaay told Cabrillo of other newcomers far to the East, men with beards who carried powerful weapons— swords and crossbows—invaders who had slain many people. This was probably the expedition of Francisco Vásquez de Coronado, who had indeed killed many during his expedition through New Mexico and Arizona.

Continuing north, Cabrillo's ships sailed past the inlet to San Francisco Bay in the late fall of 1542, then turned back. Along the way they encountered people from villages on both the mainland and the Channel Islands. Among them were the Chumash, who, unlike the Kumeyaay, welcomed the Spaniards warmly, offering them food and other provisions.

Cabrillo died as the result of an accident on San Miguel Island, one of the Channel Islands, in January 1543, and the Chumash soon watched the Spanish vessels depart their shores. This first European foray into California had left the inhabitants undisturbed. For two more centuries it would remain so.

The Chumash occupied a stretch of southern California from below present-day Ventu-

Chumash and other native women gathered acorns from the oak trees that grew in vast groves throughout California. The acorns were ground into flour, then washed to remove toxins and a bitter taste. The result was a nutrient-rich paste that could be dried and eaten raw, boiled as a porridge, or mixed with water and served as soup.

◀ Preceding page: Sarah Winnemucca, the Paiute activist, raised an early voice of protest against abuses of government power in dealings with American Indians.

Right: Obsidian, a glasslike volcanic rock ideal for knife blades and arrowheads, also had ritual uses and was linked symbolically with water. A Chumash man admiring an obsidian blade might say, "It shines just like water."

ra on the south to Morro Bay on the north, including the settlements on the Channel Islands that Cabrillo visited. Inland, Chumash territory extended beyond the Sierra Madre to the edge of the San Joaquin Valley.

Like other California peoples, the Chumash were hunters and gatherers of food rather than tillers of the soil. Roots, seeds, berries, and nuts made up a large part of their diet and were systematically collected by the women. The fall acorn crop for a single community, stored in granaries for use throughout the year, might run to hundreds of thousands of pounds. Chumash men hunted and fished, depending on the availability of game animals and proximity to water. Those living along the coast and on the Channel Islands were master seamen and boat builders. Designers of the only oceangoing plank canoes in North America, they harvested rich supplies of fish, mollusks, and sea mammals.

Blessed with such abundance, the land of the Chumash was truly an enviable inheritance. Indeed, so naturally beneficent was the entire California region, extending from the Colorado River northward to the realm of the giant redwoods, that it could support a

population of more than 350,000, making it the most densely settled region north of Mexico before the Europeans arrived.

The redwood trees are sacred. They are a special gift from the Great Creator to the human beings. . . . Destroy these trees and you destroy the Creator's love.
— *Minnie Reeves, Chilula*

California's inhabitants spoke more than 100 languages—an indication of the cultural, historical, and other differences separating them—but for the most part they lived peaceably with their neighbors. Rights to fishing, hunting, and gathering grounds were fiercely

defended, but when fighting broke out, disputes were usually settled by negotiation and payments to aggrieved parties.

An extensive and efficient trade network served the region's tribes with a dependable flow of surplus food, raw materials, and finished products. Inland groups typically exchanged acorns for dried fish from the coast. The Chumash, trading as far east as the Colorado River, had magnificent baskets to offer. Because they were not obliged to devote all their energy to the raw demands of survival, native Californians had time to achieve a level of craftsmanship that produced ceremonial objects like flawlessly wrought obsidian blades and decorative clothing.

Objects of Power

More than mere ornamentation, such regalia had strong spiritual connections. Among the Karuk people, for example, a scarlet woodpecker headdress was the embodiment of the spirit-being Paathkir. Regalia like the headdress did not just symbolize power but actually possessed it—and such objects not only had lives of their own but also desired to be seen and appreciated, especially in ceremonial dances. It was through them that the people joined with the great spirit-beings who had created their tribes.

Regalia also conferred prestige on their owner. It was understood that possession of regalia could come only to those who were steadfast, moderate, and fair in their dealings. Custom forbade using regalia as money, although they might be traded or given to others as presents. Regalia were an outward expression of religious traditions that could be found everywhere among the Indians of California. The Chumash, for example, revered earth, air, and water as sacred entities. Fire, wind, and rain were also sacred—but dangerous—spirits. Powerful shamans were the intermediaries between humans and such supernatural forces, good and bad. Some of the shamans were famous healers; others controlled weather, while still others could turn

Representing dramatic contrasts in geography, climate, and natural resources, California, the Great Basin, and the Plateau fostered equally striking differences in the ways their people lived. California's mild climate and abundance of food supported large, stable populations, peacefully linked by long-term trade networks. The vast, arid Great Basin, by contrast, was one of the most difficult environments on the continent; survival required an ability to reach scarce seasonal food sources quickly—something possible only for small, mobile bands, not settled communities. The extensive rivers and alpine landscapes of the Plateau yielded ample fish, game, and plant harvests; the terrain also provided natural barriers against attacks by enemies, native or white.

A YUROK PRICE LIST

The Yurok people of California had a highly developed monetary system based on the shell of the dentalium, a tube-shaped mollusk found in Pacific coastal waters. The Yurok strung these seashells into chains of dentalia 27 inches long, and that chain formed a basic unit of currency. Below are the prices or price ranges, in dentalia chains, of various goods and services, as well as the number of chains a perpetrator was required to pay in compensation for various offenses.

PURCHASES

Slave	1–2
Doctor's treatment	1–2
Large boat	2
Ordinary house	3
Redwood plank house	5
Wife (poor)	5 + 3 *plus boat*
Wife (wealthy)	5 + 5 *plus treasure*

PENALTIES

Uttering a dead man's name	2
Seduction and pregnancy	5
Adultery	5
Murdering a common man	5 + 5
Murdering a man of standing	5 + 5 + 5 *plus treasure*

When a canoe charm dreamer dies, his effigy canoes are buried with him. The little boats found in such a grave are no longer of value, for their owner is dead, and only he knows how to manipulate the charms.

—Fernando Librado,
Chumash elder

themselves into bears and then kill their rivals.

Like most native peoples, the Chumash paid close attention to the stars. Learned men linked the motions of the stars, sun, and moon to the changing tides and turning seasons. Each community had an open-air ceremonial enclosure with painted posts. Here the Chumash danced and worshipped the powers that the posts symbolized. Long after Spanish priests established missions in California, these rituals would continue to be practiced.

> The Chumash have a story.... It begins with a worm who is eaten by a bird. The bird is eaten by a cat whose self-satisfaction is disrupted by a mean-looking dog. After devouring the cat, the dog is killed by a grizzly bear. ...About that time comes a man who kills the bear and climbs a mountain to proclaim his superiority. He ran so hard up the mountain that he died at the top. Before long the worm crawled out of his body.
>
> — Kote Katah, Chumash

When the first Spaniards arrived in the region, they found nicely planned Chumash communities with as many as 2,000 people. A Spanish observer later described one of the Chumash towns: "They arrange their houses in groups. The houses are well constructed, round, like an oven, spacious and fairly comfortable; light enters from a hole in the roof. The beds are made on frames and they cover themselves with skins and shawls. The beds have divisions between them, like the cabins of a ship, so that if many people sleep in one house, they do not see one another. In the middle of the floor they make a fire for cooking seeds, fish, and other foods, for they eat everything boiled or roasted."

This carefully balanced world, however, was about to be turned upside down.

Miniature boats carved out of soapstone were used by Chumash fishermen as charms to ensure good luck.

THE HOUSE OF THE SEA

The coastal Chumash of California were a fishing and trading people, and for these purposes they had a remarkable craft, the *tomol,* or plank canoe. In the painting above, Chumash villagers watch as members of the Brotherhood of the Canoe launch a new boat, always a festive occasion. The tomol was made of driftwood (preferably redwood) split into planks, which were lashed together with cord made from milkweed fiber. The completed hull was caulked with *toy,* a mixture of tar and ground pine pitch, then painted with another sealant, red ocher paint, to make it more watertight.

Light and maneuverable, propelled with double-bladed paddles, this "house of the sea" generally carried a crew of two and a boy for bailing, although it could hold 15 or 20 people if necessary. Membership in the Brotherhood of the Canoe, composed of tomol crewmen, was eagerly sought, and those who belonged were among the richest, most powerful men in Chumash society.

An Army of Priests

In 1769 the Spanish government, alarmed by Russian land claims along the Pacific coast, decided to extend its American empire north from Mexico into what is now California. It was not the Spanish army, however, but the Catholic Church that had primary responsibility for accomplishing the task.

The missionary system elsewhere in the New World was well developed by this time. Depending on the amount of resistance expected from native populations, large or small detachments of Spanish soldiers would accompany the missionary group to its destination and there build a fort, or *presidio*, to defend it. The plan for the missionary compounds was preestablished, as was the practice of laying claim to large tracts of land and commandeering a native work force.

In charge of the new campaign in California was the Franciscan priest Junípero Serra. He set up his first mission at San Diego among the Kumeyaay Indians, who were fascinated by woven cloth and other Spanish goods but firmly resisted conversion to Christianity. Serra founded other missions to the north, where the Gabrielino, Costanoan, and Salina tribes were more receptive. During the next half century, Franciscans founded 21 missions from San Diego to Sonoma, north of San Francisco.

The Spanish Crown decreed that Indians should be converted to the Catholic faith. The missionaries brought an unquestioning fervor to their work, believing that the conversions reflected the will of God and were in the Indians' own best interests. Many natives did convert—perhaps because they were impressed by the priests' message of salvation and by the elaborate church ritual. Some may simply have wanted the food that the missionaries offered. Still others may have been attracted to Spanish tools and agricultural techniques.

In the mission, the Father is like a king. He has his pages, alcaldes, majordomos, musicians, soldiers, gardens, ranchos, livestock, horses by the thousand, cows, bulls by the thousand.

—*Pablo Tac, Luiseño*

Whatever their motivations, converts were drawn to the missions in considerable numbers—and those numbers were needed. Some mission farms and livestock *ranchos* covered tens of thousands of acres, requiring a large work force to operate them. The labor at first was provided entirely by neophytes, as new converts were called. But as was true in so many other places, European diseases took a

Architect of the mission system in California, Junípero Serra (above) is currently a candidate for sainthood—an idea vigorously supported by some native people but vehemently opposed by others, who cite the cruelty inflicted on many Indian converts. Mission Santa Barbara (top) was one of the flash points in a wave of dramatic uprisings that occurred in 1824.

workers by force from the general population.)

The lives of mission Indians were regimented to an extraordinary degree. Once baptized, neophytes were not permitted to leave the mission compound. The friars required them to learn the Spanish language, to dress according to Spanish custom, and to learn new trades such as farming, herding, and construction. Families could live together only if the parents remarried in the church. Unmarried adolescents were housed in sexually segregated barracks, an arrangement designed to protect the chastity of maidens. The women's quarters were kept locked at night in order to guard the residents from amorous neophyte youths—and also from roving Spanish soldiers and civilians. (Sexual assaults on Indian women by the Spaniards, wrote Father Serra, were a "plague of immorality" that would cause the Indians to "turn on us like tigers." His predictions were borne out time and again.) But barracks life was itself a hazard because concentrations of people in relatively small spaces increased the risk of disease.

Priests, soldiers, and Indian *alcaldes* (minor officials appointed by the priests) all imposed stern discipline on neophytes. Those who

One day they threw water on my head and gave me salt to eat, and with this the interpreter told me that now I was Christian.

—Janitin, Kamia

This scene at Mission San Gabriel of a tormented Jesus on the way to Calvary, painted on sailcloth in about 1800, is one of the first works of religious art by a native convert in California.

terrible toll. With no resistance to smallpox, measles, influenza, and other ills, converts and their families died by the thousands. The missionaries knew from experience that many would fall sick, but they believed that the spiritual good of conversion outweighed everything else. (The high mortality rate among neophytes, however, did create a labor shortage that had to be remedied, and the missionaries eventually resorted to conscripting

Native skills in basketry were put to use by the missionaries. The coiled Chumash basket below, made in 1822, carries a Spanish inscription and the royal coat of arms. In California and elsewhere, gambling was popular long before European contact. In a game played by the Yokuts, nutshell dice were tossed onto a woven tray (middle). The Pomo were famed for their feathered baskets (bottom), valued as gifts and often burned in ceremonial fires honoring the dead.

broke mission rules were subjected to harsh penalties, including whipping, imprisonment at hard labor, and the stocks. Indians who remained outside the missions were called gentiles. While rejecting the Spaniards' religion, some nevertheless accepted their crops, livestock, and other material goods. Occasionally gentiles worked for the missions, the army, or private *rancheros*. As a result, gentiles, too, fell victim to the virulent European germs.

When native healers proved incapable of curing the new diseases, some Indians saw it as evidence that the old ways had lost their power. If the sacred rites and incantations of the shamans could do nothing to save a victim of flu or smallpox, then the entire heritage of spiritual belief was threatened with collapse. The missionaries did their best to speed the process, equating the shamans' rituals with satanism and witchcraft.

Nevertheless, many Indians held tenaciously to old beliefs. Because the Spaniards seldom learned local languages and most Indians were given only rudimentary instruction in Spanish (since they were not considered to be worth training for positions of authority), neither group ever really understood the other. Long after embracing Christianity, the Chumash continued to celebrate the Hutash, a corn harvest festival, at Mission San Buenaventura. The friars evidently never suspected what was occurring.

But even such small, symbolic triumphs over Spanish authority were rare. The mission system entailed staggering changes in the lives of the California Indians. Neophytes experienced a loss of personal freedom, the banning of

their cultural and religious traditions, the exposure to deadly diseases, and the burden of following mystifying new rules uttered in an unfamiliar language. They were compelled to labor from morning till night. Resistance was difficult because the missionaries had soldiers to enforce their rules. Many neophytes chose the course of passive resistance—working as slowly or inefficiently as they dared.

Some converts, however, resorted to flight, a far more drastic step. Escapees had to fend for themselves in an increasingly barren landscape—vast tracts of hunting and fishing lands had been taken over by the missions— or find a tribe willing to give them shelter. Some returned to the mission of their own accord because they were unable to endure separation from family and friends, or because life at a mission from an early age had ill prepared them to survive on their own.

> The Indians at the missions were very severely treated by the padres, often punished by 50 lashes on the bare back. They were governed in the military style, having overseers who ... reported any disobedience or infraction of the rules, and then came the lash without mercy, the women the same as the men. ... We were always trembling with fear of the lash.
>
> —*Lorenzo Asisara, Santa Cruz neophyte*

But most had no intention of returning— while the Spanish had no intention of letting them remain at large. Fugitivism, as it was called, represented a threat to the authority of the mission and the strength of its work force, and troops were quickly sent out after defectors. When they were tracked down, the runaways were forcibly returned to the mission and severely punished. If fugitives were recaptured in a gentile village, its leader—or even the whole village—would likely be punished and perhaps drafted for forced labor.

Inevitably, the mission system pushed the Indians to violence. In

1775 an alliance of Christian Indians and un-converted Kumeyaays tried to destroy the San Diego mission. They were motivated in part by revenge for sexual assaults on native women. The Kumeyaays brutally slew a missionary, but Spanish reinforcements arrived to save the mission.

In February 1824 Chumash neophytes rose up at Mission Santa Inés and burned mission buildings. The revolt spread to the missions at La Purísima and Santa Bárbara. At La Purísima 400 angry Indians drove off the priests and soldiers and seized control of the mission compound. Mexican forces attacked La Purísima with artillery and forced the rebels to surrender.

At Mission Santa Bárbara a convert named Andrés assumed leadership and took a rebel force to the San Joaquin Valley. Mexican forces made two forays into the valley before some of the rebellious neophytes—including Andrés—agreed to return to the mission after Mexican authorities promised not to punish them further. Others, however, remained in the San Joaquin Valley.

A Legacy of Mixed Blessings

Ten years later the Mexican government, which had declared its independence from Spain, began to dismantle the missions. Secularization, as it was called, was meant to transfer mission property to private hands—especially to the neophytes. But corrupt officials betrayed the Indians, forcing them to become poorly paid workers rather than landowners.

In the meantime, gentile Indians regularly raided mission livestock herds, which they drove to the San Joaquin Valley. Sometimes they were joined in these forays by neophytes fed up with mission life, who stole the Spaniards' horses as they made their escape.

For Indian and Spaniard alike, herds of livestock were a valuable commodity, and horses were most precious of all. From the time the Spanish established permanent settlements in New Mexico in 1598, cattle, sheep, and horses were part of the coloniza-

Connections to the Cosmos

Through legend and ritual the peoples of California, the Great Basin, and the Plateau sought to understand their surroundings and ensure the continuity of their cultures. Guidance from the spirit world was sought frequently, and individuals' efforts to make contact with it were often recorded in pictographs—as were the dramatic visions that resulted.

Priestly Chumash astronomers incorporated geometric "sun crystals," feathered poles, and other ritual devices in their rock paintings.

This enigmatic figure with sunlike rays around its head, an elaborate costume, and feet like a bird's is only one of many carved in volcanic rock east of the Sierra Nevada in California.

A guardian spirit was sought during a vision quest in hopes of obtaining supernatural powers, represented here by rays emanating from the seeker's head.

A California cave was home to a Chumash gallery of multicolored Sky People who influenced many earthly events.

A Shoshone hunter aided by the medicine of a ceremonial horned hat takes aim at a bighorn sheep.

After a successful vision quest, members of the Salish or Kutenai tribes would paint stylized, highly personal images of their newfound spirit guides.

Found in a canyon in Oregon, this Wishram owl was said to be the husband of an ugly, child-stealing ogress.

A bowlegged character wearing chaps and holding what may be a riding crop suggests the white man's appearance in the Ute world after 1800.

Imposing twin figures, their heads radiating spiritual power, stand on either side of a small stick figure, who may be the dreamer during a vision quest.

The Ute villagers in Colorado who posed for this photograph in the late 1880's clearly considered it an occasion worth dressing up for. By that time, fast-growing trade across the Great Basin had made American, Mexican, Pueblo, and other styles of clothing available, along with decorative and practical goods of all kinds.

About 1846 an anonymous native artist recorded his impressions of the people and stock animals he had observed near Fort Benton on the upper Missouri River. It was a scene increasingly familiar across the West—domestic cattle crowding out the wildlife and men oddly dressed in European garb.

tion scheme. Gradually the surrounding Pueblo, Navajo, and Apache acquired horses, but the process accelerated explosively after the Pueblo Revolt of 1680 expelled the Spanish intruders from New Mexico. Before long, the horses that the Spaniards had tried to keep out of Indian hands were becoming readily available, passed along a network of trade routes to tribes in California, the Great Basin, and across the Great Plains.

Yet, coveted as they were, the horses and other livestock introduced by the Spanish created an environmental problem that has persisted in the West from that time to the present: overgrazing. As missionary herds expanded, cows, sheep, and horses consumed the plants that had long been part of the native diet. Farming practices imported from Europe also proved to have unforeseen consequences. The missionaries brought plants to California—wheat, barley, and oats, along with thistles and other weeds—that crowded out plant species on which the Indians had traditionally depended. As elsewhere in North America, the destruction of native flora and fauna, the overturning of their delicate natural balance, had far-reaching effects on the lives of California's peoples.

Peoples of the Great Basin

Hemmed in by mountains, the tribes of the Great Basin—Shoshone, Bannock, Paiute, and Ute—were among the most isolated in the American West. The Western Shoshone and Paiute inhabited the Great Basin's drier regions, where no more than a few inches of rain might fall in a year and summer temperatures of 110 degrees were common. But even in the driest zones, mountain ranges created small, scattered oases where plants and animals—and the humans who relied on them—could flourish.

The Ute and the Northern and Eastern Shoshone lived at higher, cooler elevations where there were 15 inches or more of rain per year. Compared with Paiute land, theirs was a rich world. The men hunted antelope and small game, especially rabbits from which they made robes for the cold winter months. Like the California tribes, the Basin peoples gathered plant foods, but instead of acorns, they had piñon nuts, mesquite beans, and agave plants. Limited food resources kept Great Basin populations in check—in all, they numbered perhaps 40,000. They lived in small groups, each with its own established foraging territory.

Great Basin Indians believed in a supreme being, as well as spirits who governed natural and human events. It was important to establish a personal relationship with a spirit who could bring success in hunting or other endeavors. As elsewhere, Great Basin shamans drew their healing powers from communion with the invisible world.

⟳

We do not call him a medicine man because he gives medicine to the sick, as your doctors do. Our medicine man cures the sick by the laying on of hands, and we have doctresses as well as doctors. We believe that our doctors can communicate with holy spirits from heaven. We call heaven the Spirit Land.

— *Sarah Winnemucca,*
Northern Paiute

⟳

Like many other societies across the continent, the Great Basin tribes saw their land as the center of the universe. The Southern Paiute, for example, believed that the Kaibab Plateau was the middle of the earth and that beyond the Pacific Ocean there rose a ring of high mountains (much like the ones that surrounded their own territory) upon whose peaks the sky rested.

Occupying a relatively harsh and inaccessible region, the Great Basin tribes were

Women of the Great Basin used sharp sticks to dig for roots— a practice that gave rise to the contempt-filled epithet "diggers," applied by ignorant whites to all Basin Indians.

among the last native people on the continent to lose their lands to permanent white settlers. But the Ute were probably among the first to come into possession of that most prized European import, the horse, by about 1700. The Shoshone and other Basin tribes quickly developed substantial horse herds as well, and the Basin became a highway for horse-mounted commerce in all directions.

Unlike the horse, however, another of the white man's innovations—the fur trade—posed a dire threat to the ways of the Great Basin peoples. As the fur trade became increasingly important throughout North America, Eastern tribes fought to obtain larger trapping grounds, pushing other tribes westward and extending the fur trade itself. In exchange for furs, traders offered manufactured goods, including metalware, textiles, iron tools, and guns.

Captive women and children also could be sold to white traders, who wanted wives and labor to keep house and dress furs. Slavery had long existed among Indians before the arrival of traders, but the new competitive pressures of the fur trade made slaves far more valuable commodities than in the past. Almost everywhere in the West, raiding and counter-raiding for horses and slaves disrupted relations among neighboring tribes.

The Travels of Sacagawea

In one such raid a girl named Sacagawea was captured. She had been born into a Northern Shoshone band in 1788 or 1789. When she was about 10, her family traveled to western Montana to hunt and harvest. A band of Hidatsa raiders swept down on their camp, causing the unarmed Shoshone men to take to their horses and flee. The women and children scattered, but in the melee Sacagawea was carried off and taken to the Hidatsa village on the Knife River in North Dakota. Sometime between 1800 and 1804, Toussaint Charbonneau, a fur trader, purchased the Shoshone girl. By the fall of 1804, the teenage Sacagawea was carrying Charbonneau's child.

Soon after Sacagawea gave birth, she helped shape the early course of U.S. history. In 1804 the United States had purchased the Louisiana Territory from France. President Thomas Jefferson sent Meriwether Lewis, William Clark, and a small detachment of soldiers to explore the headwaters of the Mis-

This painting on muslin depicts the annual Ute Sun Dance, the tribe's most sacred rite, being performed inside a lodge. More festive and social in character was their Bear Dance, the three scenes in the foreground.

A French traveler portrayed the beaver with more imagination than accuracy in a 1703 book. Europe's insatiable demand for pelts nearly killed off the entire beaver population.

souri River, then proceed westward to the Pacific. Jefferson wanted them to inform the Indians that they would profit more from trade with the now-independent United States than with the British. The Americans spent the winter of 1804–05 near the Mandan and Hidatsa villages, where they hired Charbonneau as a translator, guide, and sometime cook to accompany them up the Missouri. With them went Sacagawea and her young child.

She proved unexpectedly valuable. In the spring of 1805, Lewis and Clark needed horses, which the Shoshone were known to have. Sacagawea led the explorers to a Shoshone village, where she not only was recognized as one of their own, but found that the Shoshone chief, Cameahwait, was her brother. He readily agreed to supply the strangers with horses in exchange for gifts and a promise of guns in the future. Sacagawea continued on with Lewis and Clark, traveling all the way to the Pacific and back.

The expedition opened a new chapter in the fur trade. After it returned from Oregon, American trappers—the so-called mountain men—went to the headwaters of the Missouri and into the Rocky Mountains in pursuit of beaver pelts. Often mountain men lived among Indians and took native wives, so securing the trade advantages and tribal protection that kinship brought.

The traders paid for pelts with guns, powder, lead, blankets, knives, metalware of all kinds, and whiskey. Natives welcomed the goods, but they paid a heavy price for their involvement in the fur trade, becoming dependent on the system and too often succumbing to alcoholism, which broke up families and strained relations within the tribe.

In the end, the trapping of beavers was so intensive that they were wiped out over vast regions of the country. Traders and trappers ventured ever deeper into the mountains and deserts in pursuit of the beaver—and whatever else might afford them a living.

In 1826 Jedediah Strong Smith was driving a herd of California horses to the Rocky Mountains in the hope of making some lucrative trades when the Umpquah Indians of southern Oregon stole the herd and drove it to the Great Basin. Smith's venture failed, but other trappers followed his trail, realizing that trade in horses could be extremely profitable. They formed alliances with Yokuts and Miwok raiders of the San Joaquin Valley, who stole animals from missions and private ranchos to be sold in Eastern markets via the mountain men—prominent among them John "Pegleg" Smith, who earned a reputation for grit by amputating his own foot after being wounded. Smith at times teamed up with the charismatic Ute leader Walkara, a notorious figure in horse and slave trading from California to New Mexico.

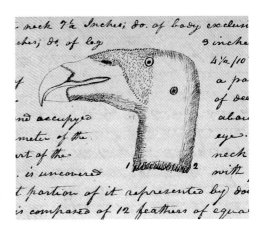

But Pegleg Smith, Walkara, and raiders like them were men whose time was already passing. The lawlessness that the fur traders had brought to the Great Basin would begin receding before the needs of white settlers intent on creating their own new worlds—on land that had been the Indians' forever.

The California condor, largest bird in North America and a figure revered by many native people, was duly noted (above) by Meriwether Lewis in his journal. It later joined other species endangered by the advance of white society.

Sacagawea was more than a guide and interpreter for the Lewis and Clark expedition. She was, in effect, a talisman. Seeing her, tribesmen assumed the mission to be a peaceful one—Indian war parties seldom included women and children. This encounter with Chinook canoes on the lower Columbia River was painted by Charles Russell a century after the fact, in 1905.

HAWK OF THE MOUNTAINS

During the 1700's and early 1800's, Mexican authorities conducted a thriving trade in Indian slaves — bartering arms, whiskey, and other goods for women and children destined for servitude in the homes of landowners and colonial officials. They encouraged native tribes to raid one another for slaves, assuring a lively commerce and fanning hostilities between tribes that might otherwise unite against them. No one was safe. Apaches, Utes, Comanches, and Navajos raided each other, as well as the more peaceable Pueblos, Pawnees, and Wichitas.

Walkara, son of a Ute chief, emerged as one of the premier slave traders in the Great Basin during the 1830's and 1840's. Over six feet tall, with enormous physical strength and stamina, he had angular features and penetrating eyes that earned him the nickname "Hawk of the Mountains." He was restless, vain, and cruel, a crack shot and an excellent negotiator, dealing with Mexican traders, Anglo mountain men, and Indian rivals in Spanish, English, and several native languages.

Walkara's band consisted of his four brothers, backed up by Paiute, Ute, and Shoshone followers handpicked for loyalty and toughness. He knew the key to their loyalty was a steady supply of good horses — and he stole enough of them to be dubbed "the greatest horse thief in history." When he learned that New Mexicans would trade one horse for a slave — or two per slave if the captive were delivered directly to Santa Fe (as shown here), Taos, or Abiquiu — he turned to slave trading with the same zeal he brought to horse stealing. He preyed especially on the docile, generally defenseless Paiute but was feared, with good reason, by all the tribes.

When the Mormons came, Walkara welcomed them as potential customers. But they were against slavery, and in 1851 Brigham Young declared that anyone caught selling Indian captives would be arrested and prosecuted. Most of the slavers took the hint and left the area; not Walkara, however. Angry but undeterred, he eluded the Mormons and continued trading humans for horses until his death in 1855.

Old Ways and New on the Plateau

Carved from elk antler with an image of two birds in flight, one holding a fish in its talons, this net gauge was used to make fishnets with the right mesh size for summer salmon runs on the Columbia River.

If your power is in feathers . . . and they fall down, then the power you had in the feathers is destroyed. Your prayer has been killed.

— Nez Perce man

Abundant, dramatically beautiful, and crisscrossed by large, isolated valleys that provided security from enemy attack, the Columbia River Plateau was home to a variety of peoples—the Nez Perce, Cayuse, Walla Walla, Flathead, Yakima, and others. Like most tribes of California and the Great Basin, they were generally hunters and gatherers, their seasonal travels dictated by food sources. Spring was the time for men to hunt rabbits and waterfowl and gather mussels from the rivers while women harvested roots. In summer the rivers filled with salmon, which the men netted or speared from platforms jutting over the rushing water. The scene shifted in fall to favorite bulb-digging grounds, where deer, elk, and other big game were also plentiful. By October it was time to return to winter villages with the stores of food for the cold months ahead, when women wove and repaired baskets while men played games and told stories that imparted sacred traditions and practical knowledge to the young.

In winter the Plateau Indians also held ceremonial dances to assure good harvests, promote social harmony, and give protection from evil forces. They believed that each individual had a guardian spirit that provided a unique identity and a special skill in hunting, perhaps, or healing or quilling. Care was needed to protect the power; if it resided in a medicine bag, for example, that object must be kept in a particular way. Allowing it to be mishandled, damaged, or touched by the wrong person could have disastrous results.

One malevolent force that could not be counteracted by traditional means was a new breed of disease. Geography had spared the Plateau from earlier white incursions, but contact was only a matter of time. When it occurred, the germs that swept through tribal populations caused not only terrible suffering

—between 1780 and 1810 European diseases killed more than half the native population of the northern Rockies—but also a crisis of belief. Shamans were powerless against these new afflictions, and people could not help but wonder if the wise men had lost their spiritual strength. As if to deepen people's fears, a huge volcanic eruption in the Cascade Mountains in the late 1700's had deposited a suffocating blanket of "dry snow"—volcanic ash—over large areas and convinced many that the world was literally coming to an end.

They beat drums and sang, and for a time held the praying dance almost day and night. They prayed to the dry snow, calling it Chief and Mystery, and asked it to explain itself and tell why it came.

— Nespelem elder

Over the next generation, the traditional winter dances of the Plateau were joined by a new ceremony, called the Prophet Dance for its connection to a mystical new breed of holy men whose voices carried a message of imminent and apocalyptic change. According to one prophetic vision, Chief, the supreme being who had created the world with Coyote's help, told the people: "Coyote and myself will not be seen again until the Earth-Woman is very old. Then we shall return to earth, for it will require a new change by that time." When he returned, all the spirits of the dead would come with him to dwell together with the living, and the Earth-Woman would regain her natural form and live as a mother among her children. On that day, Chief concluded, "things will be made right, and there will be much happiness."

Men From the Rising Sun

It was at this fateful juncture that Christians began to appear in the region and preach a new religious message. About 1820 a group of about two dozen Iroquois fur hunters—who several years earlier had left the Catholic mission at Caughnawaga south of Montreal on the St. Lawrence River and pushed westward over

MESSENGER FROM THE IROQUOIS

When Old Ignace (above, in white men's clothes) and his band of Iroquois settled among the Salish in Montana, he began to teach the Catholicism of his youth and extolled the powers of its priests—the Black Robes—so effectively that the Salish were soon convinced that this new religion was incomplete without Black Robes. In 1835 Ignace set off for St. Louis to urge church leaders to send out ordained missionaries. He was assured that it would soon be done, but no one had appeared by the spring of 1837. Again Old Ignace started for St. Louis, this time with four companions. They never arrived: all five died in an ambush by Sioux warriors. It would be another four years before his followers found their Black Robe: Father Pierre Jean DeSmet, one of the most inspired missionaries of the age. But DeSmet's success there might never have occurred without the work begun 20 years earlier by the gentle pioneer of his faith, Old Ignace.

Pio-pio-mox-mox, the astute chief of the Walla Walla, fought on the victorious American side in the war against Mexico—though with consequences no one could have foreseen. This portrait was painted by the Irish-Canadian artist Paul Kane, who traveled across the Columbia River Plateau in the late 1840's.

half a continent—arrived in Montana's Bitterroot Valley. There they were welcomed by the Salish and chose to stay. Educated by Jesuit missionaries, these Iroquois lost no time in sharing the teachings and rituals of the Catholic Church. Their leader, Old Ignace, spoke with deep reverence of the Catholic priests—Black Robes, he called them—who could show the way to heaven and eternal life.

Without realizing it, Old Ignace and his fellow Iroquois had wandered into a culture waiting almost breathlessly for strangers with a new religion that promised immortality.

> Soon there will come from the rising sun a different kind of man from any you have yet seen, who will bring with them a book and will teach you everything.
> — *Spokan Prophet*

With such highly charged expectations in the air, the appearance of Old Ignace and other missionaries fueled an astonishingly rapid and fervent acceptance of Christianity across the Plateau. Traveling through the region in 1805–06, the explorers Meriwether Lewis and William Clark had noticed no Christian practices among the native people there. By the 1830's many of the same tribes had become accustomed to making the sign of the cross and reciting the Lord's Prayer, which they

called the Great Prayer. They baptized their infants, placed crosses on the graves of their dead, never missed morning and evening prayers, and said grace at meals. They reserved Sunday for prayer and rest, choosing not to hunt, fish, trade, or travel on that day.

The adoption of so many Christian practices into daily life only seemed to whet the Plateau people's appetite for more. In 1829 two native men—one said to be the son of a Spokan chief, the other a Kutenai—began to make the rounds of villages along the Columbia River. Spokan Garry and Kutenai Pelly, as they were known, had been trained at a Protestant mission school recently built at the Red River Settlement in Canada. Greeted as great prophets, they added new evangelical passion to an already feverish climate.

Faith and Firepower

One of those reached by the Christian message was a young Nez Perce, Hol-lol-sote-tote, who heard Spokan Garry talk in the winter of 1830 and returned to his village brimming with excitement. His father was a village chief who had hosted Lewis and Clark in 1805 and never forgot their description of the benefits that would result from friendship between the Plateau people and the Americans. After discussions through the winter, the Nez Perce and their allies, the Flatheads, decided to send out a party of four men to seek the help of Christian holy men.

The potent medicine they hoped the missionaries could share with them would make the Nez Perce and Flathead people "immortal before the Great Spirit," as one of them put it. On a practical level, the strong medicine might include guns that would also make them indestructible before the Blackfeet, the Sioux, and other bitter enemies. The small band set off from Montana in the spring of 1831 and reached St. Louis only after a harrowing five-month, 1,500-mile journey by river and trail. Once there, however, the unusual delegation caught the fancy of the white press, sparking a flurry of activity as several missionary groups mounted new efforts west of the Rockies.

One of the first to reach the Plateau was a Canadian-born Methodist, Jason Lee, who worked among the Chinook and Kalapuya in Oregon's Willamette Valley. About the same time, a Presbyterian society in Boston sent the pious physician Marcus Whitman and his wife and fellow missionary, Narcissa, to Fort Walla Walla in southeastern Oregon. Farther east, in Montana, Pierre DeSmet set up his much-anticipated Catholic mission in the Flathead country primed for it by Old Ignace.

Before long, these and other Christian outposts were attracting white settlers in ever greater numbers—which caused apprehension and growing resentment among the native population. Ill feelings were already palpable when, in 1845, a party of Cayuse, Walla Walla, and Spokan traders set off for the Sacramento Valley. They were bound for Sutter's Fort, where the Mexican government (which still nominally controlled the territory) maintained a small garrison commanded by the Swiss-born adventurer and trader John Augustus Sutter. His job was to defend Mexico's interests in California against threats from hostile tribes—and from the growing ranks of Russians, British, and especially Americans.

The Cayuse party was led by Elijah Hedding, son of the renowned Walla Walla chief Pio-pio-mox-mox. On arriving at the fort, Hedding informed Sutter that their intention was to continue on to the San Joaquin Valley and recapture horses stolen by the Miwok Indians. This they did, but when Hedding's men drove the horses back to Sutter's Fort, a white man there claimed that he owned one of the animals. He argued with Hedding, then shot him dead. The rest of the Cayuse party fled.

Pio-pio-mox-mox was outraged when he learned of his son's murder and started for California the next summer with a band of warriors, determined to recover the horses for which Hedding had been killed. He did not know yet that he was riding directly into a war between the United States and Mexico.

Late in 1845 the U.S. president, James K. Polk, had sent an emissary to Mexico with in-

Many of the eastern Plateau tribes stayed out of the Yakima War at the urging of Father DeSmet and other Jesuits. At an 1859 conference at Fort Vancouver that ended the war, DeSmet (above) met with tribal chiefs. Front row: Victor, Kalispel; Alexander, Kalispel; Adolphe, Flathead; Andrew Seppline, Coeur d'Alene. Rear: Dennis, Colville; Bonaventure, Coeur d'Alene; DeSmet; Francis Xavier, Flathead.

FATHER PIERRE

Few white men have been so admired by Indians as the Catholic missionary Father Pierre Jean DeSmet. He was an extraordinary mixture of qualities. Short, heavyset, and agile, he had enormous stamina and strength. Added to his physical toughness were an adventuring spirit and almost boundless reserves of energy, good humor, optimism, and faith. At age 20, without his father's consent, he had left his home in East Flanders (now Belgium) for America, driven by a romantic's dream of becoming a Jesuit teacher among wild Indians. By 1839, after teaching for many years at an Indian school in frontier St. Louis, he moved on to work with the Potawatomi people resettled near Council Bluffs, Iowa. It was there that emissaries of the Flathead tribe found him and DeSmet made the momentous decision to go to their homeland on the Columbia River Plateau.

So elated were the Flathead and other Plateau tribes at the long-awaited appearance of a Black Robe that DeSmet was met everywhere with outpourings of reverence and affection. In 1841 he founded St. Mary's Mission, near present-day Stevensville, Montana, and from then until his death in 1873, DeSmet worked tirelessly to establish other outposts of his faith, from the Rockies to the Pacific and north into Canada. He hauled in supplies from as far away as Vancouver and St. Louis and raised funds not only in America but on many voyages to Europe.

This work often put DeSmet face to face with Indians who had little reason to love a white man, and his travels took him into territory controlled by hostile tribes such as the Sioux and Blackfeet, but never was he threatened or attacked. Of DeSmet's many qualities, perhaps the most remarkable was his ability to inspire and maintain trust. The Indians knew he did not covet their land, women, horses, or pelts, and did not sell whiskey or guns, but devoted himself solely to his God and to peace.

structions to purchase California and New Mexico. Mexico refused the deal, however, and the next spring U.S. troops clashed with Mexicans over disputed land along the Rio Grande.

The United States also sent forces to California, where Anglo-American settlers near Sutter's Fort were already in rebellion against the Mexican government. The Bear Flag rebels, as they called themselves, joined the U.S. troops and were preparing to move against Mexican forces when word came that Pio-pio-mox-mox's men were approaching.

Anxious and primed for combat, the Americans assumed that Pio-pio-mox-mox was marching south for vengeance. But he had not come to fight, and after some tense moments he was able to convince the Americans of his peaceful intentions. Sutter further calmed the situation by promising that Hedding's killer would be brought to justice.

So dramatically was mutual mistrust replaced by good feeling that Pio-pio-mox-mox's force—about a dozen men, mounted and well armed—agreed to fight for the American cause. Putting aside their recent bitterness, they even rode side by side with Miwok warriors against the Mexicans and together carried out devastating raids on Mexican horse herds.

But fresh tragedy lay just ahead. When Pio-pio-mox-mox and his men returned home from California, they carried the measles virus with them. Nearly half the native population around the Whitman mission died of the disease. Because tradition taught that illness was caused by spiritual transgressions, and because life had gone from bad to worse since the arrival of the Whitmans, the source of this latest calamity seemed clear. The Cayuse held Whitman and his wife responsible, and the missionaries paid with their lives. What followed was a three-year span of episodic bloodletting known as the Cayuse War.

The Cayuse sought to enlist other tribes in their fight but failed. In the meantime, white Oregonians formed a militia and pressured some of the Nez Perce to fight on their side. Several skirmishes were inconclusive, but Oregon authorities continued to demand that the Cayuse turn over the Whitman killers. Finally, in 1850, five Cayuse men were captured, tried, and hanged at Oregon City.

Mexican and Anglo rancheros who took over lands abandoned by the missions also acquired the services of mission neophytes— giving them a ready-made labor force when the California Gold Rush began.

The Gold Rush

On a cold January morning in 1848, what turned out to be a seemingly inexhaustible supply of gold was discovered at Sutter's Mill, on land John Sutter had been given by the Mexican government. There were then 100,000 or more Indians— Maidu, Miwok, Yokuts, and others—living in the area. For them the gold would better have been rattlesnake venom. The influx of gold-seekers from around the world swamped the native populations. For the first time, non-Indians would make up the majority of the population in California.

Indians were readily exploited as a source of cheap labor for the mines. In one sorry incident Anglo ranchers in the Coast Ranges took

> *Since the white man has made a road across our land, and has killed off our game, we are hungry. Our women and children cry for food and we have no food to give them.*
>
> —*Washakie, Shoshone*

100 Pomo Indians to a gold strike in Feather River country, where they mined for a summer. They returned for more the next summer, but malaria struck the party and all but three of the Indians died.

We mined a bag of gold as large as a man's arm but received only a pair of overalls, a hickory shirt, and a red handkerchief for a summer's work.

—*Augustin, Pomo miner*

When California was admitted to the union in 1850, its first governor promptly called on the state militia to attack Indians, whom he deemed to be a threat to miners and immigrants. But the rancheros still needed workers, so a state law was passed allowing courts to sentence Indians caught "loitering"—that is, Indians not already working for a white man—to work for farmers. This law, which remained in effect until 1863, also au-

thorized the indenture of native orphans or children whose parents gave their consent. For the sake of appearances, the measure outlawed the kidnapping and abuse of Indians, but this provision was widely disregarded. In northern California state militia units and marauding kidnappers roamed the countryside, killing parents and stealing their children for sale to farmers in the Central Valley.

Outside California the Gold Rush also took its toll. Wagon trains on the overland trails passed through tribal homelands where resources were sparse enough to begin with. Immigrants' livestock ate the forage that ordinarily fed Indian ponies. Hungry overlanders killed game at a rate that was fast depleting the supply and scavenged the countryside for firewood. Naturally enough, Shoshone and Paiute bands turned to stealing from the wagon trains that were impoverishing them—and inevitably turned against each other to fight for the remaining grazing lands.

From 1849 to 1860 some 200,000 immigrants took the overland trail through the Great Basin on their way to California; 42,000 more migrated to Mormon settlements in Utah. When silver was discovered in the Comstock Lode, new hordes flooded through the region.

"THE LAST WILD INDIAN"

When he was discovered in August 1911, crouching against the fence in the corral of a slaughterhouse, the man was naked except for a piece of canvas worn like a poncho. Taken into custody by a local sheriff, he could tell no one who he was or where he came from; no one understood his language. Newspapers seized upon this mysterious story of "the last wild Indian," and before long, two anthropologists at the University of California, Alfred L. Kroeber and T. T. Waterman, sent a telegram to the sheriff offering to take charge of him. As they suspected, he was a Yahi Yana —the last of his tribe—and gradually they learned his story.

Ishi, as he became known (*ishi* meant "man" in his language) expected to be put to death. After all, the whites had been killing off his tribe since before he was born around 1860. Between 1850 and 1872, his people had been reduced from about 2,000 to a mere handful. Ishi was among that small band of survivors. They had retreated into the hills, where they found just enough food to stay alive. Finally, only he and his mother were left. When she died, Ishi was filled with grief and loneliness. He walked south, not knowing or caring where he was going, until fatigue and hunger overcame him and he lay down to die in the corral.

For the next five years, Ishi lived at the university's museum of anthropology. He was intelligent and adaptable—and increasingly gregarious as he grew more familiar with his surroundings. He worked as a janitor at the museum and provided a wealth of information on Yahi Yana culture, including lessons in how to hunt with a bow and arrow, fish with a harpoon, make fire, and chip spear points, arrowheads, and knife blades. He died in 1916, mourned by all those who had come to know this truly brave, resourceful, and likable man.

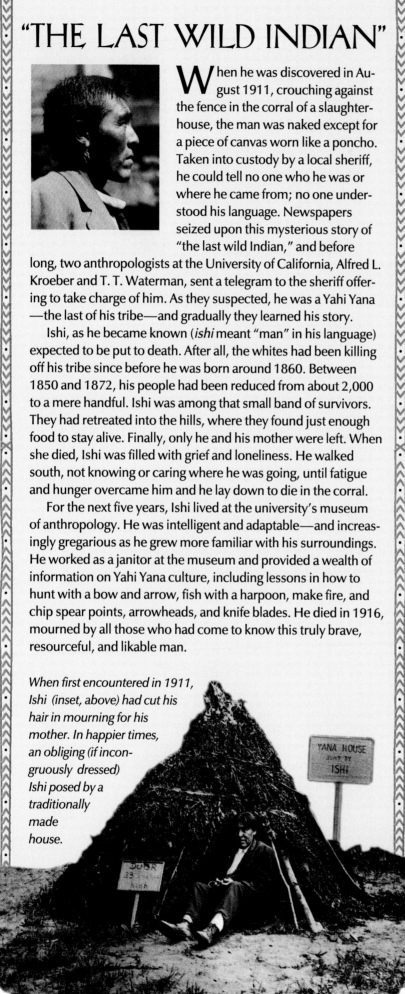

When first encountered in 1911, Ishi (inset, above) had cut his hair in mourning for his mother. In happier times, an obliging (if incongruously dressed) Ishi posed by a traditionally made house.

From Salt Lake to Bear River

In July 1847 Brigham Young led the first of his Mormon followers to the Great Salt Lake in the heart of Shoshone country. Indians occupied a special place in Mormon theology. They were viewed as descendants of Israel who should be converted to the Mormon faith—following which, it was believed, they would become white and "delightsome."

When the Shoshone offered to sell their land to the Mormons for powder and lead (so that they could better fight the Ute), Young rejected the idea. He feared the Ute and other tribes would claim payments as well. But Young recognized the needs of the Indians and announced that the Mormons would supply them with provisions—though not with guns and ammunition. His decision had a pragmatic as well as a moral side: it was, he reasoned, "manifestly more economical and less expensive to feed and clothe than to fight them."

Young's declarations were encouraging in principle, but in practice the Mormons (whose numbers burgeoned to more than 40,000 by 1860) did not provide the Indians with enough food to replace the resources that had been preempted. Much like the Utes and Paiutes displaced by California-bound wagon trains, hungry Shoshone bands and others raided stock from Mormon farms—triggering a familiar, increasingly vicious pattern of reprisals and counterreprisals.

The cycle reached a climax in the winter of 1862–63. Gen. Patrick Connor, head of the California troops, believed that Shoshones living on the Bear River in southern Idaho were responsible for an outbreak of thefts and killings. Even as the Shoshone chief Sanpitch was in Salt Lake City asking Brigham Young for help in establishing peace, Connor was preparing an attack on the Bear River village.

In the early-morning cold of January 29, 1863, the Californians marched on Bear River. Connor arrayed his troops before the Shoshone lodges, and the men came out to fight them. After four hours of terror and mayhem, 250 Shoshone villagers lay dead, among them many women and children who had fallen alongside their warriors. The following summer U.S. officials made treaties with the Shoshone, who had lost too many people to fight on. Reservation life was a bitter prospect—but the only alternative was more war, starvation, and suffering.

"They Will Not Be Alone"

During the same period an experiment of sorts was being conducted in California. Temporary reservations were set up on federally owned lands, with the understanding that they could be moved whenever white pressure demanded it. Such reserves served only a fraction of the native population at their peak, and by the early 1860's the government had abandoned most of them—leaving the reservation dwellers to fend for themselves. The scheme ended in an unmitigated disaster for the California tribes, forcing what had been the continent's largest native population onto mere patches of land.

> When the last red man shall have perished, and the memory of my tribe shall have become a myth among the white men, these shores will swarm with the invisible dead of my tribe . . . when your children's children think themselves alone in the field, the store, upon the highway, or in the silence of the pathless woods, they will not be alone.
>
> —*Chief Seattle, Dwamish, to Isaac Stevens*

On the Columbia Plateau the story was much the same. Settlers had taken most of the land west of the Cascades, and the young governor of Washington Territory, Isaac Stevens, was eager to rid the area of Indian land claims. In 1854–55 he pushed through a series of treaties creating reservations from Puget Sound to the headwaters of the Missouri.

Stevens's hastily made treaties and the reservations they established began to fall

Chief Seattle of the Dwamish tribe, a convert to Catholicism in the 1830's and long a voice for peace between whites and Indians, grew bitter toward white society and Christianity later in life. He felt it was inevitable that whites would push Indians aside and that eventually America's native peoples would disappear—though their spirits would remain part of the land.

apart almost at once. The Indians accused white negotiators of deceit and high-handed methods. To make matters worse, a gold discovery on the upper Columbia River brought a new stampede of miners to the Plateau, straining Indian forbearance to the breaking point.

In October 1855 the inevitable happened. Five hundred Yakima warriors attacked an army unit of 100 men, killing 5 and wounding 17 more. The commander decided to retreat, burning his supplies and burying a howitzer to keep it from falling into Indian hands. Other tribes joined the fight; even the missionary Spokan Garry, tired of broken promises and condescending talk from white officials, berated Stevens for looking down on his people.

> The difference between us and you Americans is in the clothing; the blood and body are the same. The Indians are proud, they are not poor. If you talk the truth to the Indians to make a peace, the Indians will do the same for you.
>
> —*Spokan Garry*

But it was too late for talk. The war dragged on until the fall of 1858, when the army defeated the Yakima at the battles of Four Lakes and Spokane Plains. Most of the survivors, beaten and exhausted, had no choice now but to face the grim reality of reservation life.

Your God is not our God. Your God loves your people and hates mine . . . he has forsaken his red children—if they really are his.

—*Chief Seattle, Dwamish*

Kintpuash, also known as Captain Jack, led his Modoc followers to temporary safety in the lava beds of northeastern California. There, for more than 5 months, a band of 60 Modoc fighters held off 1,000 U.S. Army regulars equipped with the latest in military hardware.

When President Ulysses S. Grant took office in 1869, a so-called Peace Policy was put in place with the goal of Christianizing and "civilizing" the Indians. Reservation life would be regulated so as to eradicate the last vestiges of tribalism; Indians would become God-fearing farmers and eventually would be accepted into the mainstream of white society.

> I will not; I do not need your help. We are free now; we can go where we please. Our fathers were born here. Here they lived, here they have died, here are their graves. We will never leave them.
>
> — *Old Joseph, Nez Perce*

Many native people had no desire to be white—but that was largely irrelevant to federal authorities. Indians were herded onto reservations, like it or not, and the army used force to round up any who strayed. For those most directly affected, it was hard to see what made the "peace" policy different from earlier policies. They had almost always ended in bloodshed; this would be no exception.

The Modoc Make a Stand

The Modoc, a small tribe on the California-Oregon border, were hunters and gatherers whose land, fortunately for them, contained no gold. But eventually livestock ranchers began moving into the rich grasslands near Lost River and Tule Lake. As a result, in 1864 the Modoc were pressured into signing a treaty by which they agreed to live with the Klamath Indians on a reservation 25 miles to the north.

But the 472 Klamath residents outnumbered and dominated the 300 Modocs. Led by Kintpuash, better known as Captain Jack, the Modoc returned to Lost River. When they asked the ranchers there to give them food as rent for the lands they had occupied, the ranchers demanded that the Modoc be evicted. A government agent named Alfred B. Meacham convinced the Modoc leader to return to the reservation, but in the spring of 1870, Kintpuash and about 150 followers returned again to Lost River and settled in.

Discussions with the Modoc brought no results. Then the U.S. Army and local volunteers tried to round up the resisters. At one point the Indians appeared to be surrendering, but after laying down his rifle, a Modoc named Scarfaced Charley refused to give up his pistol. Leveling a gun at Charley's chest, an officer fired; Charley fired at the same time. Improbably, neither man was hurt—but the first shots of the Modoc War had been fired.

The Modoc fled to an immense natural fortress of volcanic debris called the lava beds. Artillery could not breech the rock stronghold; soldiers could not overrun it. To the embarrassment of the army, with its superior forces, journalists described the stalemate in detail for national newspapers. Worse, they began to take the Indians' side, blaming federal agents and the army for the Modoc rebellion.

> I am very sad. I want peace quick, or else let the soldiers come. . . . Let everything be wiped out, washed out, and let there be no more blood. . . . I have given up now and want no more fuss. I have said yes and thrown away my country.
>
> — *Kintpuash, Modoc, note to army commander, 1873*

In February 1873, under a flag of truce, Kintpuash and other Modocs met with government emissaries to work out an agreement. As the talks dragged on, the Modoc ranks split. Some accused Kintpuash of cowardice. They demanded that he kill the white negotiators to force the setting up of a Lost River reservation. Some of the malcontents grabbed him and pushed a woman's hat on his head, then shoved him to the ground. "You coward! You squaw! You are not a Modoc. We disown you. Lie there, you fish-hearted woman!"

Kintpuash gave in to the pressure of his own men. On April 11, 1873, carrying concealed weapons, he and his compatriots killed the negotiators and another unarmed white. This treachery turned the tide of public opinion against the Modoc and hardened the army's resolve. Simultaneously, the Modoc lost their sense of unity and in small groups began to slip away from the lava beds.

The army ran them all down, one by one. A military commission sentenced Kintpuash

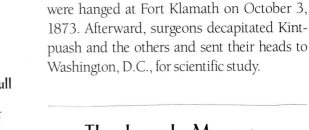

A Cayuse chief in full ceremonial regalia poses with an air of solemnity on his Appaloosa, a breed developed primarily by the Nez Perce and Cayuse. Inset: a beaded Nez Perce ornament worn on a horse's forehead.

and several of his confederates to death. They were hanged at Fort Klamath on October 3, 1873. Afterward, surgeons decapitated Kintpuash and the others and sent their heads to Washington, D.C., for scientific study.

Thunder in the Mountains: Chief Joseph and the Nez Perce

Not long after the Modoc War, the public's imagination was captured by another drama: the flight of the Nez Perce toward sanctuary in Canada. U.S. authorities, bowing to the demands of Oregon pioneers, had opened Nez Perce lands to white settlement and urged the Indians to move to a relatively large reservation in Idaho. Most of the Nez Perce agreed to settle there in 1855. But when gold was discovered on reservation land eight years later, they were forced out; under considerable duress, about 2,500 of them agreed to move to a much smaller reservation.

But 1,500 others refused to live on any reservation and instead settled along the lower Salmon River and in Oregon's Wallowa Valley. The leader of the Wallowa Nez Perce, Chief Joseph, insisted that his people had never agreed to give up the Wallowa country. Ultimately, however, he and his fellow chiefs saw the hard reality of the situation—right or wrong, they had no choice but to leave.

These young men have come from White Bird country, bringing horses with them. Horses belonging to a white settler they killed.... It will have to be war.

—*Two Moons, Nez Perce*

The Nez Perce were on their way to Idaho in mid-June of 1877 when three young warriors took the opportunity to settle some old scores against local whites. Joseph and the others, fearing the army would retaliate against any Nez Perces they could find, flew a white flag and sought to parley with a cavalry unit of about 100 men near White Bird Creek. The troopers ignored the flag and attacked. It was a disastrous mistake: the outnumbered Nez Perce killed 34 soldiers without losing one of their own men.

Now there was no alternative but to fight on the run. Heading northeast, the Nez Perce hoped to find refuge among their friends, the Crow, in Montana. Or perhaps they could reach Sitting Bull and his followers in Canada, where they had fled after the Battle of the Little Bighorn the previous year.

The fighting retreat of the Nez Perce, spanning 1,700 miles and nearly four months, was one of the most remarkable feats of arms in American history. Pursued across Idaho by Gen. Oliver O. Howard, territorial military commander, they outmaneuvered his troops at every turn. In a battle above Clearwater River in July, the Nez Perce kept 600 soldiers equipped with artillery pinned down for almost 36 hours while Chief Joseph led their old men, women, and children toward Montana and out of Howard's territory.

We traveled through the Bitterroot Valley slowly. No more fighting! We had left General Howard and his war in Idaho.

—*Yellow Wolf, Nez Perce*

White Feather, a Nez Perce woman who survived the Battle of Big Hole, said of the men, women, and children who died in the fighting, "They had done nothing wrong to be so killed. We had only asked to be left in our homes."

Joseph, leading a group of some 800 men, women, and children, desperately pushed up the tortuous Lolo Trail over the Bitterroot Mountains and, they thought, out of Howard's reach. But as they were resting at Big Hole, 200 soldiers from Fort Missoula in Montana attacked at dawn on August 9 and overran the camp before a ferocious counterattack drove them back. The Nez Perce suffered heavy casualties, but after two days they escaped again. Another column caught Joseph's people on September 13 and was beaten back, but the Nez Perce took little joy in this victory: Crow scouts, their former friends, rode with the soldiers. Now Canada was their only hope.

On September 30 the exhausted fugitives rested by Snake Creek on the northern edge of the Bear Paw Mountains, less than 40 miles from the border. There troops from eastern Montana led by Col. Nelson A Miles launched a sudden attack. Nez Perce riflemen were able to cut down 60 charging cavalrymen and forced Miles into a standoff. While the chiefs argued for five cold, miserable days about what to do, more than 200 Nez Perces slipped through the lines and made it to Canada. But 400 others were still trapped.

On October 5 Joseph rode into Miles's camp to surrender. There were bullet scratches on his forehead, wrist, and back, and bullet holes in his shirt sleeves and leggings.

I am tired of fighting....The old men are all dead....The little children are freezing to death. My people, some of them, have run away to the hills and have no blankets, no food. No one knows where they are....

Hear me, my chiefs! I am tired; my heart is sick and sad. From where the sun now stands, I will fight no more forever.

—*Chief Joseph, Nez Perce*

Miles assured Joseph that his people could return to the Idaho reservation, but Gen. William Tecumseh Sherman overruled Miles and ordered the Nez Perces to be imprisoned at Fort Leavenworth in

Kansas. After a brief stay they were sent to the Quapaw Agency in Indian Territory—later Oklahoma—and then to a hot, oppressively humid site on Salt Creek in the Cherokee Outlet, where many fell prey to disease.

After seven years in this alien place, Chief Joseph and his followers were relocated to the Colville Reservation in Washington. From there he tirelessly petitioned the U.S. government to allow his people to return to their reservation, pointedly citing Miles's pledge to him in 1877. In January 1879 Joseph made a trip to Washington, D.C., where he spoke with riveting eloquence before an audience of congressmen, cabinet members, and other dignitaries eager to meet the already legendary "Indian Napoleon."

> You might as well expect the rivers to run backward as that any man who was born free should be contented penned up and denied liberty....Let me be a free man—free to travel, free to stop, free to work, free to trade , where I choose . . . free to think and act and talk for myself.
> —*Chief Joseph, Nez Perce*

But it was no use. Not even personal intervention on Joseph's behalf by his old adversaries, Nelson Miles and Oliver Howard, succeeded in winning him the right to live where he chose: with his people in Idaho. Joseph was forced to remain on the Colville Reservation, and there he died in 1904.

Like other struggles by native peoples of the Plateau, the Great Basin, California, or elsewhere in the West to resist the juggernaut of American expansion, the Nez Perce's may have been doomed from the start. But in his life and deeds, Chief Joseph—whose tribal name, Hin-mah-too-yah-lat-kekht, meant Thunder Traveling to Loftier Heights—came to embody a larger spirit, a strength of will that might not guarantee victory but would not allow him to bow his head before any conqueror.

Words do not pay for my dead people.
They do not pay for my country,
now overrun by white men.
They do not protect my father's grave.
—*Chief Joseph, Nez Perce*

Not long after his surrender in 1877, Chief Joseph posed for this photograph by William H. Jackson, one of many that would accompany his growing fame. In the background, the Lolo Trail his people followed through the Bitterroot Range in Idaho—a place he would never see again.

I am a red man.
If the Great Spirit had desired
me to be a white man he would have
made me so in the first place.
Now we are poor but we are free.
No white man controls our
footsteps. If we must die we die
defending our rights.

—Sitting Bull,
Hunkpapa Sioux

9

PATHS OF WAR AND SURVIVAL

STRUGGLES FOR THE WEST

There may never have been a single day when the might and majesty of Plains Indian culture was more brilliantly displayed than on Monday, September 8, 1851. The sunrise that morning illuminated the greatest assemblage of Plains Indians ever seen in one place: the Great Indian Treaty Council, convened at Fort Laramie in Wyoming Territory along the banks of the North Platte River.

Indian families had been streaming in for weeks—their numbers reached an estimated 10,000—with tepee poles and hide bundles strapped to travois pulled behind their horses. Contributing to the general noise and commotion were hundreds of dogs, some of which would serve as prized delicacies in the feasting ahead. Everywhere people unpacked, kindled cooking fires, laid out bedding, displayed war shields on tripods in front of their tepees, picketed their horses near grassy areas, and watched their children splash and play in the nearby streams.

First to arrive were the proud Cheyenne and Arapaho and large bands of Oglala and Brule Sioux, who pitched their tepees along the Platte's northern bank. Next rode in the wary Shoshone—mortal enemies of the Cheyenne—led by Chief Washakie, who had been a staunch ally of the whites since the days of the fur trade in the 1830's. Soon they were joined by the Crow, looking glorious in their high-pommeled saddles on blankets made of whole mountain-lion skins.

In a sea of tepees that stretched to the horizon, these conferees represented nine different Plains Indian nations. A contingent of some 270 white soldiers watched in awe from the wooden walls of Fort Laramie, a 17-year-old trading center, as the assembled chiefs sat down to smoke the pipe of peace together and partake of nearly $100,000 worth of presents from the U.S. government.

This unique convocation was the brainchild of Thomas "Broken Hand" Fitzpatrick, a longtime mountain man and fur trapper who had guided the explorer John C. Frémont to California in the 1840's. Soon after that, Fitz-

patrick had been named Indian Agent for the newly created Upper Platte and Arkansas Agency, and he was now dealing on behalf of the U.S. government in treaty negotiations with the Plains Indians.

Fitzpatrick hoped to bring about a lasting intertribal peace by persuading the tribes to cease fighting and remain within fixed territorial boundaries. He also hoped to secure safe passage for the fleets of pioneer wagons on the Oregon Trail that were carrying ever-greater numbers of settlers from Independence, Missouri, to the Columbia River farming region in eastern Oregon and Washington.

The United States was now on the verge of its final burst of territorial expansion. The 1848 Treaty of Guadalupe Hidalgo with Mexico had placed the southern Plains, the Southwest, and California under U.S. dominion, opening up the continent for farming, ranching, mining and town building from sea to sea. For the Plains peoples caught in the path of this accelerating growth, there were ominous signs that their free-ranging way of life would not last much longer.

But worries over the future could be set aside for this occasion. The week at Fort Laramie was a rousing success, with grand tribal parades of Indians in full regalia astride horses painted with symbols of the battle hon-

A parade of splendidly attired warriors, like those in the painting above by Sioux artist Amos Bad Heart Bull, capped the festivities at the 1851 Fort Laramie peace talks.

◀ Preceding page: Yanozha, an Apache warrior, fought alongside his brother-in-law Geronimo in the final campaign of armed resistance, which did not end until Geronimo's surrender in 1886.

ors their riders had won. By day these sometime tribal foes vied in horse races and sought to outdo each other in displays of feathered war headdresses and beaded finery; by night their camps reverberated with the sound of drums, the celebrants singing and dancing until dawn.

Finally the long round of feasts, pageantry, and speeches about peace—along with the tougher talk of setting territorial boundaries for each tribe—drew to a close on September 17. Old enemies stood together in line to inscribe their marks on a document stating that they pledged to respect one another's boundaries, refrain from harassing settlers on the Oregon Trail, and allow new roads and military posts to be built on their lands. In return for this, the U.S. government would permit them to hunt and fish at will within their own territories. The tribes would also share a total of $50,000 worth of blankets, kettles, tobacco, and other goods disbursed by the government each year.

In 1853 Fitzpatrick arranged a similar gathering with southern Plains tribes at Fort Atkinson, on the Arkansas River near present-day Dodge City, Kansas. He met there with Comanche, Kiowa, and Plains Apache representatives, who had been leery of attending

The Shoshone chief Washakie was among the prominent tribal leaders who attended the conference at Fort Laramie, long a crossroads of trade in the northern Plains. A visit there nine years earlier by John C. Frémont's party was depicted in a contemporary lithograph.

the Fort Laramie session—because, as one delegate put it, "We have too many horses and mules to risk among such notorious horse thieves as the Sioux and Crow." The agreement they reached called for the tribes to give up buffalo hunting and take up ranching and farming on lands that the government would rent for them in the Leased District, an unsettled portion of Choctaw lands in Oklahoma that the tribe leased back to the government for the relocation of other Indians.

For all the lofty speeches urging intertribal amity at Fort Laramie and Fort Atkinson, this would be the last time that feuding Plains tribes would sit down together peacefully for years. Many of the delegates who signed the treaties were only headmen of individual clans, with no authority to speak for the widely dispersed and highly in-

dependent subgroups that were part of the same tribes. The government also failed to take into account how deeply the warrior ethic was ingrained in the Plains culture. Personal honor and tribal territory were prizes to be gained through combat—and such a legacy would not be removed by a few scratches of a white man's pen.

Some representatives, including the Sioux, were especially disgruntled at the notion of limiting their territories.

You have split my land and I don't like it. These lands once belonged to the Kiowa and the Crow, but we whipped these nations out of them and in this we did what the white men do when they want the lands of the Indians.

— *Oglala Sioux delegate*

Not surprisingly, the paperwork from Fort Laramie and Fort Atkinson had hardly made it back to Washington before the agreements began to unravel. From their domains in western Minnesota and the Dakotas, war-painted Sioux were pouring into Kansas territory to

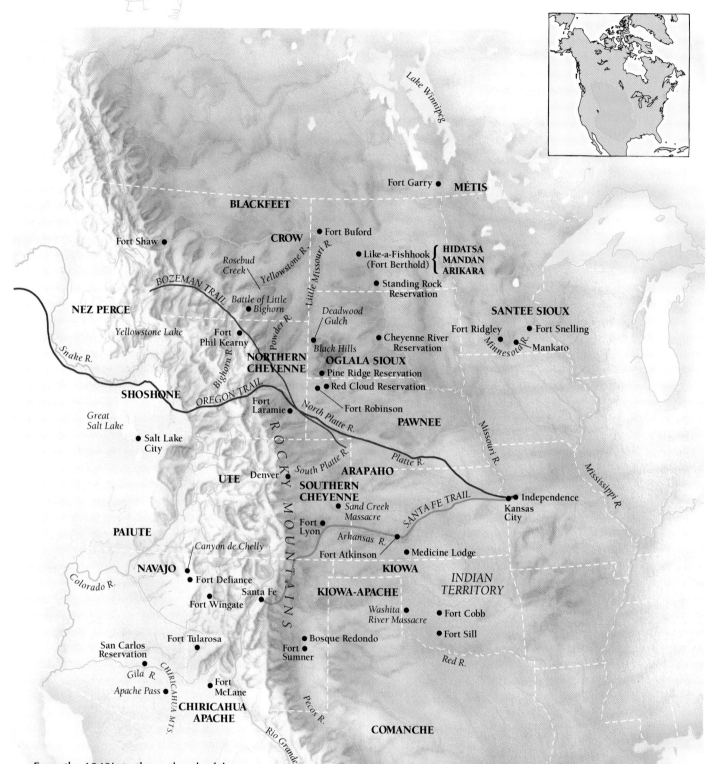

Fort Garry • **MÉTIS**

BLACKFEET

• Fort Shaw

CROW • Fort Buford

Rosebud Creek

BOZEMAN TRAIL

• Like-a-Fishhook (Fort Berthold) **HIDATSA MANDAN ARIKARA**

Yellowstone R.

Little Missouri R.

• Standing Rock Reservation

Battle of Little Bighorn

NEZ PERCE

Yellowstone Lake

Deadwood Gulch

SANTEE SIOUX

Fort Ridgley • • Fort Snelling

Fort Phil Kearny

Minnesota R.

• Mankato

• Cheyenne River Reservation

Black Hills

NORTHERN CHEYENNE

OGLALA SIOUX

• Pine Ridge Reservation

SHOSHONE

OREGON TRAIL

• Red Cloud Reservation

Snake R.

Fort Laramie •

North Platte R.

• Fort Robinson

PAWNEE

Great Salt Lake

• Salt Lake City

South Platte R.

Platte R.

Missouri R.

Mississippi R.

UTE Denver •

ARAPAHO

SOUTHERN CHEYENNE

• *Sand Creek Massacre*

SANTA FE TRAIL

• Independence Kansas City

PAIUTE

Canyon de Chelly

Fort Lyon •

Arkansas R.

Fort Atkinson •

• Medicine Lodge

NAVAJO

• Fort Defiance

KIOWA

Santa Fe •

KIOWA-APACHE

INDIAN TERRITORY

Fort Wingate •

Washita River Massacre • • Fort Cobb

Fort Tularosa •

• Bosque Redondo

• Fort Sill

San Carlos Reservation •

Fort Sumner

Red R.

Gila R.

Apache Pass

• Fort McLane

Pecos R.

CHIRICAHUA APACHE

COMANCHE

Rio Grande

From the 1840's to the outbreak of the Civil War, scores of military posts were built to protect white migrants using two major routes to the West. The Oregon Trail had its origins in the Lewis and Clark expedition of 1803–04, which opened the fertile Columbia River basin to settlers who journeyed from Independence, Missouri, to Oregon's Willamette Valley. The 1848 gold strike in California dramatically increased use of the trail (which branched south to the Sacramento goldfields) until

the first transcontinental railroad was completed in 1869. The Santa Fe Trail also originated in Independence, around 1821, and was used mainly by white traders bound for Santa Fe, where by 1855 some $5-million worth of goods were exchanged yearly. This trail, too, was eventually made obsolete by the completion of a railroad that connected Santa Fe to Independence in 1880.

Icons of Martial Prowess

Eagle feathers symbolized courage and vision; bears, ferocity; thunderbirds, divine power; while a slain enemy recalled personal triumph in combat. Plains warriors painted these and other images on their leather shields and ceremonial tunics to boast of past victories and summon up strength for future ones.

Two shields with sun symbols flank a masked Apache dancer.

Carved into sandstone, the markings on a warrior's shield carry untold spiritual force.

An Arapaho drew strength from this image of a captured enemy.

This potent image from a Sioux shield represents the owner's dream vision: a thunderbird.

A grizzly bear's spirit power deflects a hail of enemy bullets.

A Crow warrior's shield bore this dragonfly to make him quick and hard to see.

A bowman stripped for battle adorns the bone handle of an Osage horse whip.

The horse and shield of a slain Cheyenne represent a combat victory.

Shield raised, lance lowered, a feathered Mandan chief strides into battle.

Neither buffalo helmet nor feathered sash saved this adversary from a Mandan's arrow.

These signs on an Arapaho Ghost Dance tunic protected the wearer from harm.

---

strike at their old enemies, the Pawnee. Before long, the Crow of south-central Montana were vehemently protesting Sioux aggression and finally, in 1868, were given protection by U.S. troops on their own reservation.

In 1864 the Arikara in North Dakota had likewise demanded federal protection from Sioux attacks, bitterly pointing out that their chiefs who had taken part in the Fort Laramie accords were all dead now—cut down by Sioux arrows. The Hidatsa were even more virulent in their denunciations of the Sioux:

> They will not keep the peace until they are severely punished. Either keep them a year without gifts or provisions, or cut off some camp, killing all, and the rest will then listen.
> — Hidatsa leader

In the southern Plains, the Leased District in Oklahoma became a staging area for the relocated tribes to launch raids against Texas settlers and northern Mexico homesteads. The government was only temporarily successful in persuading the Southern Cheyenne and Arapaho to cease their raiding, while even a full-scale military campaign against the Kiowa and Comanche could not control their marauding along the Texas frontier.

By the outbreak of the Civil War in 1861, funding for Fitzpatrick's promised annual rations to the tribes had been cut back substantially. At the same time, the government was building a network of forts on the Oregon and Santa Fe trails, as well as along southern routes from Kansas and Missouri to the Rio Grande. A mere dozen years after the Fort Laramie accords, no fewer than 65 new army garrisons were protecting settlers and wagon trains pushing westward from the Mississippi. Everywhere the number of whites seemed to be multiplying; and wherever they appeared, trouble seemed to follow.

An anonymous Cheyenne artist portrayed a U.S. soldier (right) skirmishing with a Cheyenne warrior on the southern Plains. The revered Santee Sioux chief Little Crow (below) reluctantly accepted his people's call to lead the Sioux Uprising of 1862.

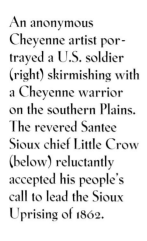

Count your fingers all day long and white men with guns in their hands will come faster than you can count. You will die like the rabbits when the hungry wolves hunt them. But Little Crow is not a coward. He will die with you.

— *Little Crow, Santee Sioux*

The Santee Sioux Uprising

In August 1862 four hungry young Santee Sioux men, hunters returning from another unsuccessful outing, stole some eggs from the homestead of a white farmer near the small community of Acton in the Minnesota River valley. For years, supplies pledged to the tribe by treaty in exchange for prime hunting lands had been systematically diverted—then sold to their rightful recipients by local merchants at exorbitant prices. The training and equipment that would make them self-sufficient farmers never materialized. Complaints of illegal liquor sales and outrages against Indian women by whites were ignored by authorities. The fall harvest of 1861 had been blighted by an infestation of cutworms, and the bitterly cold winter that followed left the Santee impoverished, half starved, and desperate.

Their 52-year-old chief, Little Crow, tried without success to get provisions from the local Indian agent or credit from local traders. "If they are hungry," said one storekeeper, "let them eat grass." The egg-stealing incident rapidly boiled up into a confrontation that left the farmer and four family members dead. With no more premeditation than a summer storm, the Sioux Uprising of 1862 had begun.

Tribal leaders hurriedly met with Little Crow, who agreed to lead them but harbored

no illusions whatever about their chances. In the next four weeks the Sioux lashed out against settlers in surprise skirmishes and large-scale battles up and down the Minnesota Valley. Hundreds of whites were killed and an estimated 30,000 others frantically sought refuge at Fort Ridgley. Little Crow, wounded in an attack on the fort, turned over his command to Chief Mankato. But then in the fierce battle of Wood Lake in late September, Mankato was killed by a cannonball—some said he refused to dodge it—and his warriors were routed by federal troops.

Some 1,700 captured Sioux were marched to Fort Snelling, where they were enclosed in a wooden stockade with scant food and little shelter against the approaching winter cold. Trials were held and more than 300 of the men were condemned to death. Back in Washington, President Lincoln was besieged by demands from his own military advisers—as well as an aroused national press—for quick executions. One lone voice of dissent was that of Henry Whipple, an Episcopal bishop and longtime advocate of the Sioux, who appealed to the president for clemency. Lincoln considered his plea and commuted the sentences of all but 39 of the prisoners, who were promptly separated from the rest to await their fate in Mankato, Minnesota.

THE MÉTIS REBELLION

After the tragic events of 1862, many Sioux decided they had seen enough bloodshed and worked to establish peaceable communities among their white neighbors. One group took refuge in Canada and sought help from the British, their former allies during the days of George III. Reluctantly, the Hudson's Bay Company provided land near Manitoba's Fort Garry for the impoverished exiles. Some Canadians feared a repeat of the violence in Minnesota, but the Sioux proved content to trap, hunt, and lead quiet lives as farmers and ranchers. They even remained neutral during the Métis Rebellion of 1869, an outburst with origins a century old.

By the mid-1700's a large population of mixed-bloods — descendants of European men and native women — had congregated around the Canadian Great Lakes. The term *métis* (French for "mixed") came to refer especially to those who were French-speaking and Catholic. The Métis enjoyed peaceful relations with their French and Scottish neighbors, hunting buffalo and providing furs to the North West Company, until the 1860's, when white settlers began carving up their ancestral lands along the Red River.

In 1869 a messianic Métis leader named Louis Riel and a band of armed followers seized Fort Garry, center of the Métis settlement on the Red River, and proclaimed a provisional government. Although Riel was forced to flee to the United States, the Canadian government appeared to meet the rebels' demands in the Manitoba Act of 1870, which established land grants to the Métis. The policy was never implemented, however, and further displacement of the Métis caused Riel to return from exile to lead a second uprising in Saskatchewan in 1885. This time his forces were quickly overrun, and Riel was sentenced to death. Maintaining to the end that his mission to establish a French Catholic state in northwestern Canada was divinely ordained, Riel wrote the note below shortly before he was hanged on November 16, 1885.

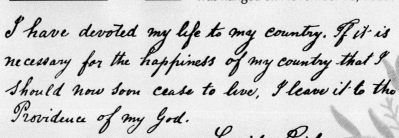

I have devoted my life to my country. If it is necessary for the happiness of my country that I should now soon cease to live, I leave it to the Providence of my God.

Louis Riel.

The formidable Mangas Coloradas led Apache resistance with his son-in-law, Cochise. In 1861 they closed off Apache Pass, in this part of Arizona's Chiricahua Mountains, until U.S. troops forcibly reopened it a year later.

As the sun rose on December 26, 1862, the prisoners began chanting their death songs, which they continued to sing as the scaffold was nailed together and white cowls were rolled down over their faces. When the trapdoor dropped beneath their feet, it was the largest mass execution ever to take place in American history. Little Crow was not among the victims, but six months later, while picking berries on a farm, he was shot to death by the owner. The state of Minnesota rewarded his killer with $500.

The Wrath of Cochise

In the Southwest—which the U.S. acquired from Mexico in the 1848 Treaty of Guadalupe Hidalgo and the 1853 Gadsden Purchase—widely dispersed bands of Apaches had been raiding ranches and pack trains for more than two centuries. Rigorously trained from childhood to endure hardship, to suck water from thorny cacti, to strike stealthily and disappear into the parched desert, Apache raiders swooped down like hawks on adobe-walled Mexican villages in search of horses, sheep, and clothing. They killed those in their way and occasionally made off with a child to adopt into their families and rear as their own. Freely they cut back and forth across the border, striking fast with little regard for the Federales—the Mexican troops usually in pursuit.

Confining their skirmishes to Mexico, the Apache for a time had few problems with the Americans. First a stagecoach line crossed the land, then miners in search of "yellow iron" in southwestern New Mexico. The Apache did not object, even allowing the stagecoach line to build a way station in Apache Pass and contracting to supply it with firewood.

The cooperation evaporated in 1861, when the Chiricahua Apache chief Cochise (who had granted the Americans use of Apache Pass in the first place) was falsely accused of stealing cattle and kidnapping a child. Almost six feet tall, with broad shoulders and a commanding air, Cochise was unmistakably a leader. Said one employee at the Apache Pass stagecoach station, "I don't recall that Cochise ever met his equal with a lance. I always recall the handsome picture he made as he stood out in front of the station with folded arms until the coach left."

Cochise arrived with his brother and two nephews at Apache Pass under a flag of truce to discuss the accusations against him with an army officer—who promptly tried to take

White children were sometimes seized in Apache raids on old Mexican homesteads, as was the case of young Santiago McKinn, photographed in a Chiricahua Apache camp in 1871.

them all prisoner. Cochise managed to escape and soon seized three civilian captives to exchange for his relatives, but the offer was refused, and Cochise, enraged, killed the hostages. The army in turn hanged his brother and nephews, triggering the furious vendetta known as the Cochise War. Before it was over, some 150 whites were dead, and the combined forces of Cochise and his father-in-law, Mangas Coloradas—"Red Sleeves," a six-foot-six-inch giant of a man—had brought all California-bound traffic through Apache Pass to a standstill.

By 1862 the Civil War had boiled over into the Southwest. Early on, Union soldiers from Colorado and California drove the Confederates out of New Mexico and Arizona. Then a new man, Gen. James H. Carleton, arrived from the Far West, vowing to reopen Apache Pass and bringing with him 3,000 California volunteers—Westerners who generally preferred killing Indians to talking with them—to replace the Union army regulars.

During a pitched battle in July 1862, an estimated 500 Apache fighters—perhaps the largest force their widely dispersed bands had ever mustered—engaged the Californians in ferocious combat until the enemy howitzers forced them to retreat. In a later skirmish Mangas, then in his seventies, was struck by a bullet in the chest. Surviving but in fragile health, Mangas sought to parley for peace. In

January 1863 he agreed to meet with an officer of the California militia—a trap, as it turned out. Mangas was locked up at Fort McLane, and when some soldiers began to taunt him one night with heated bayonets, he rose to protect himself and was shot dead—trying to escape, the official report said.

Now Cochise assumed leadership of the hostiles. From his stronghold in the Dragoon Mountains of southern Arizona, he and about 200 warriors renewed their attacks on white settlements. At this point another U.S. commander, Gen. George Crook, tried a strategy that proved more effective than any firearm—using Apache scouts as diplomats who traveled from band to band, cajoling their kinsmen to move onto federal reservations.

⤙⤚

I am alone in the world. I want to live in these mountains; I do not want to go to Tularosa. That is a long way off. The bad spirits live there. I have drunk of these waters and they have cooled me. I do not want to leave here.
— Cochise, Chiricahua Apache

⤙⤚

Reassured that his people would not be forced to relocate to the dreaded Fort Tularosa in western New Mexico, but instead could retain their ancestral lands on a reservation in the Chiricahua Mountains, Cochise and his followers relented in the fall of 1872.

You came into our country. You were well received. Your lives, your property, your animals were safe. We believed your assurances of friendship, and we trusted them.
— *Mangas Coloradas, Mimbreño Apache*

Exile and Return: The Navajo

Much like their Apache neighbors, with whom they shared a common ancestry, the Navajo (or Diné, as they called themselves) had a history of raiding both Mexican and Pueblo settlements across the Southwest. As Anglo-American settlers began trickling into the region in the 1840's, the Navajo considered them fair game as well. Losses of sheep, horses, mules, and cattle rose steadily, as did public clamor for the authorities to do something about it. The U.S. government tried to negotiate peace treaties in 1846 and 1849, but there was no possibility of coordinated talks among the far-flung Navajo —an estimated 12,000 people living in small, autonomous clans, herding sheep in canyons and mesas across the vast desert between the Rio Grande and the Grand Canyon.

The beauty of Canyon de Chelly in Arizona provided an incongruous backdrop for the bitter capitulation to U.S. troops there in January 1864 — and a focal point of longing and hope for the entire Navajo nation during four years of exile.

A more aggressive approach was signaled in 1851 by the construction of several military posts, including Fort Defiance about 30 miles southeast of Canyon de Chelly. Land that the Navajo had long used to graze their sheep was abruptly taken over for the soldiers' horses. The result was predictable: a long, increasingly bloody cycle of attacks and reprisals, climaxing in 1860 with an all-out attack by 1,000 warriors on Fort Defiance, which the army soon abandoned.

Any celebrations of this symbolic victory were cut short, however, by a punitive military campaign that cut across Navajo country, systematically destroying crops and confiscating livestock. Facing a threat of mass starvation, Navajo leaders signed a peace agreement early in 1861; its terms included a promise of government rations for the tribe, and later that year they were duly distributed at a fort in New Mexico. The atmosphere was festive, highlighted (as such gatherings often were) by horse racing and heavy betting by both sides. In the final race the army's rider was accused of cheating, but the judges—all soldiers—named him the winner. An uproar ensued and the troops hastily withdrew into the fort, whereupon their commander ordered them to open fire on the crowd. Within minutes more than 30 Navajos lay dead, a dozen women and children among them, and a brutal new round of vengeance seeking had begun.

Following the outbreak of the Civil War, General Carleton—who had so ruthlessly dealt with the Apache raiders in southern Arizona—turned his attention to the Navajo. In the summer of 1863, on Carleton's orders, Col. Christopher "Kit" Carson began a new campaign against the Navajo homesteads of northeastern Arizona, a larger version of the scorched-earth policy used three years earlier.

By January his forces were sweeping into Canyon de Chelley, the ancient and sacred stronghold of the Navajo. Families living in and around the canyon were rousted from their adobe-covered hogans, which were then burned—along with their saddles, clothing, and blankets. Their sheep, cattle, and horses were seized or slaughtered, their peach orchards were hacked down, and about 2 million pounds of Navajo corn went up in smoke. Families hiding in caves in the canyon walls were hunted down. Tribal accounts tell of some who chose to leap from the cliffs rather than leave their homeland. Before long, some 8,000 men, women, and children—most of the Navajo nation—were under armed guard.

After months of harsh internment at Fort Wingate and elsewhere, the prisoners were forced to make the infamous Long Walk, a grueling 300-mile forced march across most of New Mexico. Their destination was a narrow strip of land along the Pecos River in eastern New Mexico, a dry, desolate place known as Bosque Redondo. There, as General Carleton envisioned it, they would "acquire new habits, new ideas, new modes of life . . . and thus, little by little, they will become a happy and contented people."

The Navajo men were conscripted to mold adobes and construct Fort Sumner, while their families suffered terrible privations for nearly four years. The drinking water was bitter, the sterile land no good for growing corn. The fort used up all the available wood, so there was not enough fuel for fires to withstand the winter rains and cold winds. Illness was rife.

Most of the people got sick and had stomach trouble. The children also had stomach ache. The prisoners begged the Army for some corn, and the leaders also pleaded for it for their people. Finally they were given some — one ear of corn each.
— *Navajo survivor of Bosque Redondo*

One Navajo headman, a silversmith named Herrero, complained to Senate investigators in 1865 that his people were "dying as though they were shooting at them with a rifle. . . . There is a hospital here for us, but all who go in never come out." Starvation, prostitution, venereal disease, and sheer despair were wasting them away before his eyes.

Scenes of Kit Carson's 1863–64 campaign against the Navajo were recorded in a petroglyph on the walls of Largo Canyon, New Mexico. Many families had retreated to Canyon de Chelly in hopes of eluding Carson's troops. The soldiers, meanwhile, camped in their cornfields, burning the crops and killing sheep and other livestock.

Tough and resourceful, the Navajo leader Manuelito and a party of his followers managed to evade Carson's troops for a time. Eventually, though, most were relocated to Bosque Redondo. Below, the Long Walk across a harsh New Mexico landscape is remembered in the work of Navajo artist Raymond Johnson.

Initially a few bands of Navajo renegades evaded Carson's search-and-destroy campaign. Led by such men as Manuelito, a war chief of the Folded Arms People clan, and Barboncito—"The Orator"—a signatory of the ill-fated peace treaties of 1846 and 1849, they endured great hardships as they hid in canyons and caves. Most were eventually forced by hunger, thirst, or disease to surrender at Fort Sumner. At least one small band of Kayenta Navajo held out, however—having found freshwater springs in a hidden canyon behind the top of Navajo Mountain (called "Head of Earth Woman" in their language) that sustained them during the four years of the Fort Sumner captivity.

> My God and my mother live in the west and I will not leave them. I was born there. I shall remain there. I have nothing to lose but my life, and that they can come and take whenever they please. But I will not move.
> — *Manuelito, Navajo*

The crushing of the Navajo resistance and their Fort Sumner incarceration ultimately had its desired effect. "If we are taken back to our own country," one subdued tribal spokesman promised General Sherman, "we will call you our father and mother."

The treaty they finally signed in 1868 was in fact quite generous: the Navajo survivors retraced their Long Walk back to a new 3.5-million-acre reservation covering the old country they loved so much and virtually encircling the Hopi mesas, and the government let them keep 35,000 sheep and goats to give them a fresh start.

During the ordeal of 1864–68, the Navajo had lost about one-quarter of their population. No longer a threat to their white neighbors, they quietly set about rebuilding their shattered lives and replenishing their treasured herds of sheep and cattle. In the process their population began a steady recovery, from not much more than 10,000 in 1868 to an estimated 17,000 by 1890—a conspicuous exception to the fate awaiting so many other native nations during the same dark period.

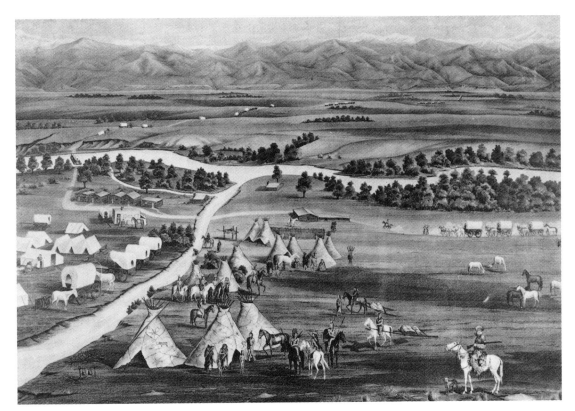

The city of Denver arose from mining camps that sprang up in 1858 with the discovery of gold in Cherry Creek. Although whites and Indians coexisted peacefully at first, they found themselves inexorably drawn into a cycle of conflict that culminated in the tragedy of the Sand Creek Massacre.

"Kill Them All, Big and Small"

Just as the exile at Bosque Redondo was beginning for the Navajo, an incident took place in Colorado that sent shock waves across the country. No sooner had gold turned up along Cherry Creek in 1858 than the city of Denver was born. The eastern flanks of the Colorado Rockies were soon dotted with mining camps, and within a few years prospectors for gold and silver had fanned out into Nevada and California and down the lower Colorado River. By 1864 the attraction of Montana's goldfields had expanded the territory's population by 30,000 new settlers. In the face of this rampant growth, it was only a matter of time before conflict erupted.

The pretext was supplied in Denver, where the slain bodies of a miner's family were laid out for public viewing as evidence of Indian savagery. It was unclear who had actually killed them—but no matter. A force of some 700 "Colorado militia," hastily recruited from local gambling halls and ranches, set out to teach the Indians a lesson. Just after sunrise on December 28, 1864, the ragtag troops, led by a former clergyman, Col. John M. Chivington, found a quiet encampment of Cheyenne and

Arapaho families along Sand Creek. Here they had set up their tepees as ordered by a post commander at Fort Lyon, to whom they had surrendered two months earlier. The leader at Sand Creek was the Cheyenne peace chief Black Kettle.

As soon as he saw the soldiers coming, Black Kettle called out to them and tried to talk, and raised an American Flag up on a pole and moved it back and forth hoping the soldiers would stop. But they did not.
— *John Stands in Timber,*
Northern Cheyenne

In a matter of minutes Chivington delivered his infamous battle cry—"Kill them all, big and small, nits make lice"—and his men attacked. Young and old, male and female, every Indian was fair game. A 70-year-old war chief named White Antelope sang his death song—*Nothing lives long, except the earth and the mountains*—before he crumpled under a hail of bullets.

"I saw the bodies of those lying there cut all to pieces," an eyewitness later testified, "worse mutilated than any I ever saw before, the women all cut to pieces . . . children two or three months old; all ages lying there, from sucking infants up to warriors." Of 123 dead, nearly 100 were women and children.

As reports from Sand Creek spread, they elicited the sort of contradictory responses that became more and more familiar in the coming years. "Colorado Soldiers Have Again Covered Themselves With Glory," headlined the *Denver News*. Indian scalps were proudly displayed at a local theater. The outcry came from settlers throughout the West to get tough on Indians, with most of the nation's military establishment in hearty agreement.

At the same time, calls for peace and compassion were heard from abolitionist groups, whose crusade against slavery had ended successfully. Liberal-minded citizens in the East—who, angry Westerners pointed out, were comfortably distant from the realities of frontier life—demanded an inquiry into the

ATTENTION! INDIAN FIGHTERS

Having been authorized by the Governor to raise a Company of 100 day

U. S. VOL CAVALRY!

For immediate service against hostile Indians. I call upon all who wish to engage in such service to call at my office and enroll their names immediately.

Pay and Rations the same as other U. S. Volunteer Cavalry.

Parties furnishing their own horses will receive 40c per day, and rations for the same, while in the service.
The Company will also be entitled to all horses and other plunder taken from the Indians.

Office first door East of Recorder's Office.
HAL SAYR.
Central City, Aug. 13, '64.

This 1864 recruiting poster for Indian fighters helped set the scene for the Sand Creek Massacre, depicted below. The American flag raised by Chief Black Kettle was a signal he had been told to use by army officers to identify his camp as peaceful.

events at Sand Creek. At length the government acted: In 1865 a congressional team headed by Sen. James Doolittle of Wisconsin was dispatched to interview Indians, traders, and missionaries across the West. Its goals were to establish who was to blame for Sand Creek and to determine why the populations on reservations such as Bosque Redondo were declining so rapidly.

The commission's final report recommended no action against Chivington or his men. It did cite such factors as disease, lawlessness by whites, corruption by Indian agents, and the loss of hunting grounds as causes of Indian depopulation—but offered no relief for the general "Indian problem," which, it concluded, "can never be remedied until the Indian race is civilized or shall entirely disappear."

Enraged at the Sand Creek slaughter, war chiefs of the Cheyenne, Arapaho, and Sioux had in the meantime held a council near the

Civil War. One especially keen observer was Red Cloud, a 44-year-old Oglala Sioux who had earned his chieftaincy on the strength of numerous honors won in battle. Red Cloud bitterly opposed the Bozeman Trail, which cut through the heart of the Sioux's Powder River hunting grounds and across treaty-protected lands, enabling miners to take a shortcut from the North Platte River in Wyoming to the goldfields of Montana.

In response to Indian attacks against travelers using the Bozeman, protective military posts were built along the trail. But Red Cloud, thanks largely to his military strategist Crazy Horse, consistently outmaneuvered the cavalry. Their greatest victory came on December 21, 1866, against Gen. William J. Fetterman (who had once boasted that "with 80 men I could ride through the Sioux Nation"). Staging a sham hit-and-run attack on Fort Phil Kearny in Wyoming Territory, they lured Fetterman and his troops out of the safety of the fort— and into a perfectly set ambush that left Fetterman and all 80 of his cavalrymen dead. In the face of this unexpectedly fierce resistance— and because a new railroad to the south would soon make the trail obsolete—the government reversed its position and offered to meet with Red Cloud to discuss a withdrawal from the "bloody Bozeman."

A member of Crazy Horse's band cuts a telegraph wire before a raid in "Silence," by Gregory Perillo. Oglala Sioux Chief Red Cloud (left) counted his greatest coup in 1868 when the U.S. Army abandoned its forts along the Bozeman Trail — ending the only Indian war in the West clearly won by native forces.

Republican River. Even as the Doolittle team was conducting its interviews, their warriors descended on stagecoaches and ranches, tore down telegraph lines, and raided with impunity from Colorado into the Dakotas.

> After the massacre, other Cheyennes came over to Sand Creek. My grandmother was with that party. None of them ever forgot what they saw. The Cheyennes were almost all in raids after that. When the chiefs tried to prevent it they would ask, "Do you want the white men to kill our people like that?"
>
> — *John Stands in Timber,*
> *Northern Cheyenne*

Yet their war parties could not stem the tide of freight caravans, stagecoaches, miners, and military reinforcements that was steadily filling up their countryside after the end of the

Medicine Lodge Creek

The last major peace treaty negotiations between the U.S. government and the Plains Indians were held a year after Fetterman's debacle. The first meeting took place in the valley of Medicine Lodge Creek in Kansas, where Kiowa, Comanche, Cheyenne, Arapaho, and Kiowa-Apache delegations convened once again with white peace commissioners on the full moon of October 1867. An unusual feature of this gathering was its extensive coverage by East Coast newspapermen, many of

Today is a good day to fight—today is a good day to die.

—Crazy Horse, Oglala Sioux

whom were seeing Indians in the flesh for the first time. Readers across the country were captivated by accounts of Indian personalities and engravings of the huge cottonwood arbors under which bedecked chiefs and uniformed generals sat down to negotiate.

In attendance were upwards of 5,000 Indians, led by a virtual roll call of the most celebrated southern Plains chiefs. Prominent among the Arapaho contingent was Little Raven, who had enthusiastically joined the Cheyenne in their earlier wars along the Kansas border but now was a leading spokesman for the nine peace chiefs of his tribe. Nevertheless, he insisted that the treaty be translated for him word for word. Two years earlier, he explained, a white negotiator "came and got them [the Indians] to sign a paper, but they did not know what it meant. The Cheyennes signed it first, then I; but we did not know what it was. That is why I want an interpreter, so that I can know what I sign."

From the Kiowa there was the dignified but resolute Satanta, or White Bear, who

Southern Cheyenne artist Howling Wolf attended the Medicine Lodge Creek peace talks of 1867 and portrayed that gathering in the painting above. Also present was Chief Satanta, below, who negotiated with steely determination on behalf of the Kiowa.

had grave misgivings about the treaty terms and expressed them bluntly. From the Kwahadi Comanche, the half-white Quanah Parker showed little interest in the proceedings and would remain a scourge of frontier towns and settlers for another seven years. But also in attendance was Ten Bears of the Yapparika Comanche, who pleaded for a lasting peace.

My heart is filled with joy when I see you here, as the brook fills with water in the spring. Two years ago I came upon this road, following the buffalo, that my wives and children might have their cheeks plump and their bodies warm. But the soldiers fired upon us, and since that time there has been a noise like that of a thunderstorm. Why do you ask us to leave the rivers and the sun, and live in houses?

— Ten Bears, Yapparika Comanche

Yet even the eloquence of Ten Bears could not prevent the tightening of the territorial noose around his people. The final Medicine Lodge Creek treaty created two large reservations in Indian Territory

—one for the Kiowa and Comanche in the Leased District, and one for the Cheyenne and Arapaho in the Cherokee Outlet—for the containment and pacification of these southern tribes. On paper, at least, the peace chiefs agreed to stop interfering with rail and wagon traffic across the Plains and to conform to the rules and routines of reservation life controlled by an Indian agency. This would include, among other things, compulsory church atttendance, white-run schooling for their children, periodic subsidies of flour and sugar and cattle—and, most alien of all, learning to till the soil for a living.

> We are on the mountains looking down on the soldiers and the forts. When we see the soldiers moving away and the forts abandoned, then I will come down and talk.
> — *Red Cloud, Oglala Sioux*

The second round of peace treaty negotiations with northern tribes took place the following spring of 1868, once again at Fort Laramie. With the immediate aim of ending Red Cloud's hostilities, the govenment agreed to abandon its military garrisons along the Bozeman Trail—effectively shutting the route down to white traffic. (As humiliated officers and their men filed out of Fort Phil Kearny, a triumphant Red Cloud rode through its gates and proceeded to burn it to the ground.)

The new Fort Laramie treaty also designated the Powder River country of Montana and Wyoming, plus all of today's South Dakota west of the Missouri, as the Great Sioux Reservation. Within these lands lay the Black Hills, held sacred by many tribes, including the Sioux, Cheyenne, Kiowa, and Crow.

But no treaty could assuage the deep, abiding hatred of white men that the Sand Creek Massacre had planted in the hearts of Cheyenne warriors like Medicine Water and Dull Knife, and Northern Arapaho fighters like Powder Face. Soon their tribesmen would join forces with the Sioux to outdo even the triumph over Fetterman and inflict the most stunning defeat on a white foe in all the years of the Indian wars in the West.

This building houses for us is all nonsense. You tell the Great Father that there is plenty of buffalo yet, and when the buffalo are all gone I will tell him.
—*Satanta, Kiowa*

To mark the occasion of the second Fort Laramie treaty talks in 1868, a Sioux chief named Old Man Afraid of His Horses smoked a ceremonial pipe.

OASIS ON THE PLAINS

While the Indian wars with white America dragged on across the West, a remarkable community was flourishing as a peaceful hub of commerce on the Upper Missouri River in North Dakota. In 1837, Hidatsa survivors of a devastating smallpox epidemic began moving upstream and by 1844 had rebuilt their old-style earth lodges on a bluff overlooking a sharp bend of the river called *mua-iduskupe-hises,* or "Like-a-Fishhook." Soon they were joined by about 250 Mandan survivors of the same epidemic, seeking shelter behind Like-a-Fishhook's protective stockade. In 1845 a fur company built a log trading post called Fort Berthold on the village's north side.

The location proved so advantageous for trading with Plains tribes that, by 1849, Like-a-Fishhook was said to have more inhabitants than any town in the new Minnesota Territory. In 1862 the Arikara, battered by constant Sioux attacks, joined the thriving community and for the next 20 years these three tribes—all with corn-growing, earth-lodge-building, highly ceremonial village traditions—kept alive a bygone era. Along the river, women continued to till the alluvial flood plain and observe rituals that kept the agricultural cycle on its proper course. The men built fish weirs, hunted deer and buffalo, and did business at the trading post.

The advent of land allotment in the 1880's brought an abrupt end to all this; villagers were soon scattered over a 50-mile span on individual homesteads, their earth lodges torn down lest anyone be tempted to return. The community has endured; they are known today as the Three Affiliated Tribes of the Fort Berthold Reservation. But the original village site lies hidden now beneath a lake created in 1954 by the Garrison Dam, built, over tribal protests, by the U.S. government.

Custer's First Stand

In the first 10 months following the l867 Medicine Lodge treaty, the southern Plains Indians continued to raid other tribes, even venturing so far as to attack Navajo camps along the Pecos River. Angry over the promised but undelivered cattle and blankets at their new Fort Cobb Agency, Kiowa and Comanche warriors raided the herds of their reservation neighbors to the east. A vast cultural gulf separated these frustrated Plains newcomers from the so-called Five Civilized Tribes, which had been removed to Indian Territory from the Southeast 30 years earlier. One spokesman, an irate Chickasaw governor demanding federal protection, wrote: "No less than 4,000 head of horses have been taken out of the country by these very naked fellows. . . . The wolf will respect a treaty as much as Mr. Wild Indian."

Adding to the rise in lawlessness was a powerful thirst for bootleg liquor. Some young Cheyennes, Arapahos, and others exchanged buffalo robes for so many whiskey kegs that entire villages degenerated into bloody brawling. In late summer of l868, the fragile southern Plains truce snapped in a chain reaction of outbreaks: Cheyenne war parties wreaked havoc on some 40 white communities over a two-month period, killing at least 79 settlers and kidnapping a number of children. In response, Gen. Philip Sheridan ordered an ambitious lieutenant colonel of the 7th Cavalry, George Armstrong Custer, to lead a surprise attack against a Cheyenne encampment on Oklahoma's Washita River.

The cottonwoods had just lost their yellow leaves when, on the morning of November 27, 1868, for the second time in his life, the peace chief Black Kettle noticed furious soldiers descending on his camp. He had survived Sand Creek; he did not survive Washita. Custer's take-no-prisoners policy resulted in l03 Cheyennes being shot to death—including Black Kettle and his wife, killed riding along the ice-encrusted river in a desperate attempt to flee. All the Cheyennes' horses were shot to inhibit the survivors' movements and to destroy their emergency food supply. Some

His brutal attack on a Cheyenne camp earned George Armstrong Custer the enmity of the Cheyenne people. They would win a measure of revenge eight years later at the Little Bighorn.

would later call the engagement Custer's First Stand. The Cheyenne never forgot it.

Sheridan waged a harsh campaign in the winter of l868–69 that drove most of the renegade Southern tribes back onto their reservations, although breakaway Comanche and Kiowa bands continued to harass Texas settlers along the Red River well into the l870's.

When Ulysses S. Grant assumed the presidency in l869, his new "peace policy" toward Indians sought to revise military and civilian roles on reservations. Military Indian agents, who had been notoriously prone to corruption, were to be replaced by emissaries from the Quaker Society of Friends and other religious organizations. Soldiers would be used only to pressure Indians onto reservations—and keep them there—while it would be the civilians' job to coax them into the "arts of civilization." In l870, Congress reflected the seriousness of Grant's policy by allocating $100,000 for the education of Indian youth and related purposes.

Yet a wide chasm separated the reformist attitudes in the East from the mind-set of most Westerners on the subject of Indian rights. The Sioux in particular were learning that the Fort Laramie accord Red Cloud had signed in l868 meant little to miners and settlers clamoring for access to their sacred Black Hills.

> In 1868 men came out and brought papers — we could not read them and they did not tell us truly what was in them. We thought the treaty was to remove the forts and that we should then cease from fighting. When I reached Washington, the Great Father showed me that the interpreters had deceived me. All I want is what is right and just.
> — Red Cloud to Ulysses S. Grant

Although the land was protected by treaty, in July 1874, Gen. William Tecumseh Sherman dispatched Custer to lead a survey expedition into these Sioux domains. A pack train accompanied by 1,200 troopers wound its way through this game-stocked preserve—

complete with guides, a photographer, a wagon master, a howitzer and three Gatling guns, 110 wagons, l,000 horses, and 300 cattle for meals along the way.

Once word leaked out that Custer's illegal 1,205-mile survey of the Black Hills had verified rumors of "gold from the grassroots down," mining in the area increased noticeably the following summer. In 1876, two years after the expedition, 6,000 newcomers had taken up residence in Custer City, South Dakota, and gold strikes in Deadwood Gulch predictably lured thousands more. Streams were clogged by sluice boxes, and timbering operations were already moving into the virgin forests of the Black Hills.

Not surprisingly, the Sioux were incensed that their sanctuary had been invaded in so flagrant a violation of the l868 treaty. Calls for resistance and revenge filled the air. When Senate negotiators came to Sioux territory in September l875 to try to work out a lease agreement to the Black Hills, a warrior clad in battle attire led a chant:

> Black Hills is my land and I love it —
> And whoever interferes will hear this gun.
> — *Little Big Man, Oglala Sioux*

When President Grant was told of the Indians' intransigence, he let it be known that from then on, government troops would not stop miners from invading the Black Hills. Moreover, the off-reservation Sioux who were roaming the Yellowstone and Powder River valleys in Montana would henceforth be considered threats to the general public.

In March l876, Gen. George Crook marshaled his troops for a campaign against the last remaining Plains Indian rebels. That month some troops struck a Cheyenne village, erroneously thinking it was Crazy Horse's camp. They came away with 600 Indian ponies, only to lose them to Cheyennes the same day. Meanwhile, the Cheyenne and Sioux were slipping away from their reservations, where food supplies had grown more

THE VANISHING BUFFALO

For Indians throughout the Plains, the disappearance of their main food source, the buffalo, inevitably meant the loss of their way of life. The herds were thinning out as early as 1854, but the problem increased a decade later when whites slaughtered buffalo by the thousands for robes and leather for Civil War soldiers. In the 1870's the market for thick-haired buffalo robe coats soared and buffalo tongue was considered a delicacy. Hunters using large-bore rifles that could load and fire eight times a minute camped by water holes and rivers where buffalo congregated, lit huge fires so that they could see their prey, and hunted around the clock.

The general slaughter was described by a Kiowa woman named Old Lady Horse: "Up and down the Plains those men ranged, shooting sometimes as many as a hundred buffalo a day. Behind them came the skinners with their wagons. They piled the hides and bones into the wagons until they were full, and then took their loads to the new railroad stations that were being built, to be shipped east to market. Sometimes there would be a pile of bones as high as a man, stretching a mile along the railroad track." The bones were shipped to the East to be pulverized into fertilizer. Most of the meat was left to rot, the stench drifting across the Plains as railroad cars creaked with the weight of buffalo hides.

Whites fully understood the critical link between free-ranging buffalo and Indian independence. "Kill every buffalo you can," an officer urged visiting hunters along the Platte River in 1867. "Every buffalo dead is an Indian gone." Buffalo hunters took up the challenge with a vengeance. An estimated 50 million bison still roamed the continent in 1870; by 1875 there were perhaps 1 million left.

The Sioux chief White Cloud knew a death sentence when he saw it: "Wherever the whites are established, the buffalo is gone, and the red hunters must die of hunger." Among the last to confront this fact were the Blackfeet, whose northern range was a refuge for stray herds. Over the infamous "starvation winter" of 1883–84, the Montana Blackfeet, already reduced to little more than 2,000 in all, were unable to locate any game — and helpless to prevent 600 of their tribe from freezing or starving to death.

Meditating upon the Deer Medicine Rocks in Rosebud Valley, Montana, Sitting Bull received a vision foretelling victory over Custer's forces.

We did not ask you white men to come here. We do not want your civilization—we would live as our fathers did and their fathers before them.

—Crazy Horse, Oglala Sioux

and more scarce, to join renegade bands along Rosebud Creek. Practically under the government's nose, thousands made camp on the Rosebud's banks in what proved to be the calm before the storm.

The Little Bighorn

On a ranch near the Northern Cheyenne town of Lame Deer in southern Montana stands a sandstone outcrop covered with incised designs. Across from these rocks on the other side of Rosebud Creek, tradition has it, the Sioux staged their annual Sun Dance. Seated near the rocks in June 1876, the great Hunkpapa Sioux chief Sitting Bull, then 42, sacrificed 100 pieces of skin, 50 from each arm, to bolster his prayers for a victory over the encroaching whites and their blue-coated soldiers. It was then that Sitting Bull fell into a trance and envisioned "dead soldiers without ears falling upside down into camp." They had no ears because the white man did not listen to what had been told him.

For his part, Gen. Philip Sheridan, who headed military operations that summer, proposed to confront the Indian hostiles—composed of Sioux, Cheyenne, and Arapaho—from three directions. His three army columns, amounting to about 2,500 men, would include Gen. Alfred Terry and Col.

George A. Custer coming in from the east, Gen. George Crook entering from the south, and Gen. John Gibbon striking from the west.

Coming upon the Indian camp at Rosebud Creek on June 17, Crook abruptly discovered that their numbers had been disastrously underestimated. For six hours his troops faced waves of attacks by well-armed warriors before he ordered a retreat. Meanwhile, other tribal groups were filtering into the area they knew as the Greasy Grass (and whites called the Little Bighorn River). More than 7,000 people in all camped in six great tepee circles, including 1,800 warriors hungry for more of the success they had tasted at Rosebud Creek.

Out of touch with Crook, Custer led a detachment of the 7th Calvary toward the Little Bighorn. Unaware that he was approaching the largest fighting force ever assembled on the Plains, Custer made an impulsive and fatal decision. Dividing his troops—about 210 men—into three attacking groups, he positioned them on a ridge above the camp.

A warrior named Wooden Leg remembered being awakened by the crack of gunfire. Stripping for the fight and leaping onto his favorite war pony, he and his friend Little Bird took off after a fleeing soldier.

We were lashing him with our pony whips. It seemed not brave to shoot him. He pointed back his revolver, though, and sent a bullet into Little Bird's thigh. As I was getting possession of his weapon, he fell to the ground. I do not know what became of him.
— *Wooden Leg, Cheyenne*

In the course of an hour, Custer and every one of his men perished; only a horse named Comanche, belonging to one of Custer's captains, was left alive. The victors promptly withdrew, most heading up the Little Bighorn Valley—where they held a great celebration below the mouth of Lodge Grass Creek.

It was a moment worth savoring. Not since the infamous defeat known to angry whites as St. Clair's Shame, inflicted by the Shawnee 85 years earlier in Ohio, had the U.S. Army suf-

fered so costly a humiliation at native hands.

And it did not take the army long to respond. In September 1876 a camp of Sioux trailing back to their reservations was attacked by troops at Slim Buttes in Dakota Territory and lost their leader, American Horse, in a hail of gunfire. At the Standing Rock and Cheyenne River Sioux reservations, veterans of the Little Bighorn and other hostiles were imprisoned. Witnessing his people's disintegration, Sitting Bull (who had not taken part in the battle) and a small group of followers fled to Canada in 1877. His appeals for aid to the Canadian government met with no success, and his people had trouble obtaining even minimal supplies. Faced with the prospect of starving in a foreign country, Sitting Bull and 187 others finally surrendered in July 1881 at Fort Buford in North Dakota.

The Cheyenne also faced reprisals. Only four months after the victory over Custer, a group of Northern Cheyennes led by Little Wolf and Dull Knife had their village destroyed and hundreds of their horses shot by U.S. troops. Accused of involvement at the Lit-

No photograph was ever taken of the Oglala Sioux warrior Crazy Horse, shown below astride a white horse in a depiction of the Battle of the Little Bighorn by Sioux artist Amos Bad Heart Bull.

tle Bighorn, they were deported by train to the Southern Cheyenne Agency in Indian Territory. But these lifelong inhabitants of the northern Plains hated this strange, oppressively humid place and waited for a chance to escape. In September 1878 about 300 of them began a 1,500-mile run for freedom.

For four months they managed to elude more than 10,000 pursuing troops, until at the Platte River a dispute over strategy led to a split up. Little Wolf's group surrendered soon afterward at the Little Missouri River and, ironically, was shortly hired as army scouts on the Tongue River Reservation. Dull Knife's followers did not fare so well. Captured near Nebraska's Red Cloud Agency, they were locked in an unheated brig at Fort Robinson in the dead of winter. When the desperate prisoners attempted a breakout, 64 were killed and 78 recaptured. But the 30 or so survivors who remained free were eventually allowed to return to the Rosebud Valley, where their descendants still live today.

After the Battle of the Little Bighorn, a group of Cheyenne women gathered on the battlefield to sing songs of mourning — "strongheart songs" — for their dead. Among them was Kate Bighead, who remembered the event in this illustration; her young nephew was one of about 50 warriors killed in the fighting.

San Carlos and the Apache Wars

In Arizona Territory the surrender of Cochise in 1872 had been followed by a peaceful interlude for the Apache that held until 1875, when the government sought to consolidate all the Apache bands on the San Carlos Reservation along the Gila River. Many independent-minded fighters among the Warm Springs and Chiricahua groups balked at the idea.

> Take stones and ashes and thorns, with some scorpions and rattlesnakes thrown in, dump the outfit on stones, heat the stones red hot, set the United States Army after the Apaches, and you have San Carlos.
> — *Warm Springs Apache*

Leading the Warm Springs renegades was a 40-year-old warrior named Victorio, who had once fought beside the great Mangas. Victorio fled from San Carlos in September 1877 with more than 300 followers. Recaptured a month later, he staged another breakout with 80 war-

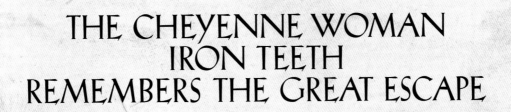

THE CHEYENNE WOMAN IRON TEETH REMEMBERS THE GREAT ESCAPE

This story was told by Iron Teeth, a Northern Cheyenne woman. Her people had been sent to a reservation in Oklahoma but found life there so hard that they insisted on returning to their Dakota homeland. She lived to recount the suffering endured in one of the landmark events in American Indian history.

In Dakota we Northern Cheyennes were told that we must go to Oklahoma to live there on a reservation with the Southern Cheyennes.

In Oklahoma we all got sick with chills and fever. When we were not sick, we were hungry. We had been promised food until we could plant corn and wait for it to grow, but much of the time we had no food. Our men asked for their guns to be given back to them so they might kill game, but the guns were kept from them. We had many deaths from both the fever sickness and starvation. We talked among ourselves about the good climate and the plentiful game food in our old northern country hunting lands.

After about a year, Little Wolf and Morning Star, our principal Old Man Chiefs, told the agent, "We are going back to the North." The agent replied, "Soldiers will follow and kill you."

The white soldiers chased us. But my older son kept saying we should go on toward the North unless we were killed, that it was better to be killed than to go back and die slowly.

We dodged the soldiers during most of our long journey. But always they were near us, trying to catch us. Our young men fought them off in seven different battles. At each fight some of our people were killed, women or children the same as men. I do not know how many of our grown-up people were killed. But I know that more than 60 of our children were gone when we got to the Dakota country.

Morning Star said we should be contented, now that we were on our own land. He took us to Fort Robinson, where we surrendered to the soldiers. They took from us all of our horses and whatever guns they could find among us. They said then that we must go back to the South, but our men told them it was better to die by bullets. After a few weeks of arguing, our men were put into a prison house. We women and children were told we might go to the agency. Some of them went there, but most of us went into the prison with the men. In the one room, about 30 feet square, were 43 men, 29 women, and 20 or 30 children. Eleven days we had no food except the few mouthfuls of dry meat some of the women had kept in their packs. Three days we had no water.

[We] decided to break out of this jail. I gave my son the six-shooter I had. He was my oldest child, then 22 years of age. After the night bugle sounded, my son smashed a window with the gun I had given him. Others broke the other window and tore down the door. We all jumped out. My son with the little girl on his back ran off in one direction, while the other daughter and I went in another direction.

I and the daughter with me found a cave and crawled into it. We could hear lots of shooting. We stayed in the cave seven nights and almost seven days. More snow kept falling, it was very cold, but we were afraid to build a fire. We ate snow for water. Finally a captain found our tracks [and he] and his soldiers then took us back to Fort Robinson.

I was afraid to ask anybody about my son and the little daughter, as my asking might inform the soldiers of them. But I kept watching for them among the Indians there. After a while the little girl came to me. I asked her about her brother. It appeared she did not hear me, so I asked again. This time she burst out crying. Then I knew he had been killed.

A day or two later all of us were again put into the prison house. Our number now was only about half what it had been. The soldier chief at the fort … asked if we were willing now to go back to Oklahoma, so that no more of us would be killed. But we were mourning for our dead and we had no ears for his words. Everybody said, "No, we will not go back there." We expected then that the soldiers would come at once into the prison and shoot all of us. Instead, a few days later we were taken to the Pine Ridge Agency [in South Dakota].

riors within a year. Victorio's swift-moving bands crossed the Rio Grande repeatedly— until a sharpshooter killed him in Chihuahua, Mexico, in October 1880.

Shortly after Victorio's death the appalling conditions on the San Carlos Reservation sparked a further series of Apache breakouts for old Mexico, where various bands joined forces and resumed freewheeling raids along the border. They even attacked the San Carlos Agency itself, killing four reservation police-man. Now a new leader emerged from among the Apache guerrillas, a seasoned fighter who had fought alongside Cochise and Victorio. He was named Goyathlay, or "One Who Yawns," but he was better known as Geronimo.

It was said that as a young man Geronimo had lost his mother, wife, and children to a surprise attack by Mexican soldiers, which gave rise to his pitiless campaigns of revenge on settlements south of the border. Now, in September 1881, Geronimo led about 70 Chiricahua warriors along with their families across the Rio Grande again and began strik-ing ranches throughout the state of Chi-huahua. But this time a regiment of Mexican troops managed to cut off most of the Apache

women and children and slaughtered them all.

By now General Crook, who had been called north in 1875 to deal with the Plains In-dians, was back in Arizona Territory. War-weary and losing followers, Geronimo managed to evade the paid Apache scouts Crook used to track him down until May 1883, when Crook located his base camp and took the women and children hostage. The last of Geronimo's band finally gave them-selves up in March 1884. As Geronimo and his warriors turned their energies to cattle ranch-ing back on the San Carlos Reservation, Ari-zona settlers and the army began to feel safe.

Yet Geronimo had one last fight in him. In May 1885 he and other leaders were caught consuming home-brewed corn beer, a violation of army rules. While the authorities debated his punishment, Geronimo cut their telegraph wires, killed a ranching family, and slipped back into his old haunts in Mexico's Sierra Madre with 134 warriors. Once again General Crook found himself in pursuit of America's last free enemy Indian chief.

In March 1886, Crook finally managed a two-day parley with Geronimo in Mexico's

Wanted by both U.S. and Mexican troops, Geronimo cut back and forth across the Rio Grande with apparent ease, evading capture on either side of the border for several years. The Chiricahua chief and his battle-hardened guerril-las obligingly posed for photographs in the Sierra Madre, where at length he negotiated a surrender to the Americans in 1886.

Cañon de los Embudos. Geronimo agreed to surrender and accept a two-year imprisonment at Fort Marion, 2,000 miles away in Florida. But along the way, while being led to Fort Bowie by Apache scouts, Geronimo and a handful of his followers broke free again.

When Usen created the Apaches, he also gave them their homes in the West. He gave them such grain, fruits, and game as they needed to eat . . . and all they needed for clothing and shelter was at hand.

Thus it was in the beginning: the Apaches and their homes, each created for the other. When they are taken from these homes they sicken and die.

— *Geronimo, Chiricahua Apache*

The army at this point replaced Crook with Gen. Nelson Miles, who committed 5,000 troops and 400 Apache scouts to the recapture of Geronimo. Even when confronted by a force of this magnitude—augmented by a civilian militia and Mexican military assistance—Geronimo's band of 38 men, women, and children still eluded their pursuers for six months. When Apache scouts finally talked Geronimo into laying down his gun in early September 1886, the surrender was bloodless and strangely anticlimactic. Recounted Geronimo's cousin Jason Betzinez: "Kayitah [an Apache scout] delivered General Miles's message. The general wanted them to give themselves up without any guarantees.

"The Indians seemed stunned. Finally Geronimo's half-brother, White Horse, spoke out. 'I am going to surrender. My wife and children have been captured. I love them, and want to be with them.' Then another brother said that if White Horse was going, he would go too. In a moment the third and youngest brother made a similar statement.

"Geronimo stood for a few moments without speaking. At length he said slowly, 'I don't know what to do. I have been depending heavily on you three men. You have been great fighters in battle. If you are going to surrender, there is no use in my going without you. I will give up with you.'"

Almost immediately General Miles had Geronimo's band taken into custody— along with the Apache scouts

Zotom, a Kiowa artist at Fort Marion, drew prisoners standing on the parapet (top), seemingly enthralled by their first view of the Atlantic Ocean. Cheyenne artist Cohoe sketched Fort Marion inmates dancing for tourists (above) in the mid-1870's to raise money for a prisoners' benefit fund.

who had tracked him down—and put on a train for Florida. Their destination was Fort Marion, the old Spanish fortress in St. Augustine where the army imprisoned its most dangerous Indians. There Geronimo would spend the next eight years.

Released from confinement in 1894, the old guerrilla accepted an offer from the Kiowa and Comanche to share their reservation in Indian Territory and spent his final years as a farmer outside Oklahoma's Fort Sill. He joined the Dutch Reformed Church, where he taught

Sunday school. Later, with government approval, Geronimo spent a year with a Wild West show and appeared in Omaha, Buffalo, New York, and at the St. Louis World's Fair, where he made money selling his photographs and bows and arrows. In 1905 President Theodore Roosevelt invited him to Washington, D.C., to ride in the inaugural parade. But to the day of his death in 1909, Arizona never considered Geronimo safe enough to let him set foot in his homeland again.

"All Happy and Forever Young"

One of Geronimo's outbreaks across the border, in 1881, had been sparked by the killing of a highly regarded medicine man on the San Carlos Reservation by U.S. soldiers. The doctrine espoused by this man—that dead Indians would return and a new world free of whites would soon dawn—apparently originated in the Walker Lake area, on the California-Nevada border, and had been circulating among different Western tribes for years.

When the Walker Lake Paiute staged their regular pine nut harvest festival in 1869, a man named Wodziwob, or "Fish Lake Joe," went into a trance. Afterward he told the others of his visit to their loved ones in the land of the dead and prophesied that they would soon return. This mystical promise inspired a new religious fervor in California, known as the Ghost Dance of 1870. Everywhere tribespeople awaited the coming flood or fire that would wipe the world clean of white people and their polluting culture.

Back in Nevada this doctrine of apocalyptic destruction and cultural renewal was taken up by Wodziwob's assistant, named Tavibo, a well-known shaman who was said to possess the power to affect the weather. But it would be Tavibo's son, the messianic figure Wovoka, who would inspire the Plains Indian version of the Ghost Dance, with its compelling message of tribal resurrection. Born around 1858 and known as Jack Wilson to the local ranchers for whom he worked, Wovoka had a mystical experience in Nevada during a solar eclipse that occurred on New Year's Day, 1889.

> I went up to heaven and saw God and all the people who had died a long time ago. God told me to come back and tell my people they must be good and love one another, and not fight, or steal, or lie. He gave me this dance to give my people.
> — *Wovoka, Paiute shaman*

After this he was said to have worked many wonders. By pointing his pipe at the sun, he brought heavy downpours to end a drought that year; he cured the many sick who flocked to see him; he could even withstand being shot at point-blank range.

Tribal emissaries came from far away to hear Wovoka's preaching and receive his blessing. During his vision Wovoka had seen those throngs of deceased Indians "engaged in their old-time sports and occupations, all happy and forever young." And the dance he had brought back to his people would make them happy too—and hasten the day when living and dead Indians would all be reunited in a native homeland in the West while the whites remained with their kind in the East.

Was it any wonder that a final glimmer of hope rose in the breasts of the Plains tribes when these accounts came in from Nevada country? They pondered the words of this great healer who had envisioned the ancestors returning, the buffalo once again teeming on the Plains, their Western land purged of the white man.

They would send more messengers to this man; they would clasp hands and dance the large circle dances he taught them; and they would induce their own visions in which they would see again the fathers and mothers who had died at Sand Creek and on the Washita River and at a hundred other tragic places.

Maybe the clock could be turned back and their people might once again be free to hunt and trade and fight and survive on their own.

Maybe there still was hope.

Short Bull, originally a Brule Sioux, visited Wovoka in Nevada as part of an Oglala Sioux delegation from the Pine Ridge Reservation. He returned as a priest of the visionary movement known across the Plains as the Ghost Dance.

*I will follow the white man's trail.
I will make him my friend, but I will not
bend my back to his burdens. I will
be cunning as a coyote. I will ask him
to help me understand his ways, then I will
prepare the way for my children.
Maybe they will outrun the white man
in his own shoes.*

— Many Horses, Oglala Sioux

10

THE RESERVATION YEARS

LIFE IN THE WHITE MAN'S WORLD

or bringing his demoralized band of exiles back from Canada in July 1881, Sitting Bull had been promised a pardon for his role in the Battle of the Little Bighorn five years earlier. Instead, he was summarily arrested and locked up at Fort Randall on the Missouri River in South Dakota. From there the Hunkpapa Sioux warrior could only watch as his tribe's lands were nibbled away by the U.S. government.

The next year, in exchange for 25,000 cows and 1,000 bulls, other Sioux chiefs were asked to sign a paper they could not read; it surrendered 14,000 square miles, about half the reservation lands guaranteed in the 1868 Fort Laramie Treaty. Suspecting the worst, a chief named Yellow Hair scooped up a handful of dirt and thrust it at the federal agent. "We have given up nearly all of our land," he said; "you had better take the balance now."

In August 1883 a commission led by Senator Henry L. Dawes of Massachusetts came to the Hunkpapa Sioux Agency at Standing Rock to investigate charges of an illegal land seizure.

Sitting Bull, only recently released from captivity, attended the conference but was at first ignored by the commissioners. When they finally asked for his opinion, he accused them of acting like "men who have been drinking whiskey" and led the chiefs in a walkout. Although professing loyalty to Sitting Bull, the other leaders were worried and persuaded him to apologize the next day. "The Great Father told me not to step aside from the white man's path, and I told him I would not, and I am doing my best to travel in that path," he told the commissioners.

They were not mollified. "The government feeds and clothes and educates your children now," one of them said, "and desires to teach you to become farmers, and to civilize you, and make you as white men."

The Bureau of Indian Affairs agent at Standing Rock, James McLaughlin, tried working with other Hunkpapa and Blackfeet Sioux chiefs. But Sitting Bull remained their favored leader—and, ironically, became a celebrity in the white world. At the driving of the last spike to link the Northern Pacific Railroad's transcontinental track in the summer of

◀ Preceding page: Holding the corn and pipe said to have been given their people at Creation, a Wichita Corn Dance leader stands with his wife, the cross of a new faith in her hand, on their Oklahoma reservation in 1893.

For the 1890 Plains Ghost Dance, traditional deerskin clothing was painted with stylized birds, stars, crescents, and other symbolic images — including, on this Arapaho shirt, a brilliant red dancer on the triangular neck flap. At top, Arapaho women sing and sway in the trancelike ritual.

1883, Sitting Bull was asked to deliver a speech drafted for him by a bilingual army officer. Ignoring the text, the renowned chief rose to announce in Sioux that he hated all white people. "You are thieves and liars," he told his uncomprehending audience. "You have taken away our lands and made us outcasts." The embarrassed officer read a few platitudinous sentences from the prepared speech in English, and the listeners sprang to their feet with applause for Sitting Bull.

The next year he made a government-sponsored tour of 15 cities and was so enthusiastically received that Buffalo Bill Cody asked him to join his Wild West Show in 1885. Sitting Bull agreed, but he declined Cody's subsequent offer of a trip to Europe: "I am needed here. There is more talk of taking our lands."

Indeed, the government tried in 1888 to carve up the Great Sioux Reservation (then comprising about half the present state of South Dakota, plus parts of Wyoming and Nebraska) into six smaller Indian reserves and purchase the remaining 9 million acres for 50 cents an acre. The Indians balked. A year later Gen. George Crook was sent to Sioux country with an offer of $1.50 per acre—and the implied threat that the land would be seized if the Indians did not agree to sell. Crook, dealing with the tribal leaders one by one, got nearly all to sign—with the notable exception of Sitting Bull. Asked how the Indians felt about surrendering so much land, Sitting Bull replied abruptly, "Indians! There are no Indians left but me!"

Revelation From the Desert

Having heard of the Paiute prophet Wovoka, several northern Plains tribes sent a delegation to Nevada late in 1889 to learn more about his prediction of a new age without white men. The emissaries returned the following spring to introduce the Ghost Dance religion to the Sioux and other tribes; by autumn of 1890 virtually all activities—trading, schooling, farming—came to a standstill as the people took up the frenzied ritual.

Understandably, perhaps, the whites grew alarmed; predictably, Sitting Bull was blamed for the unrest. "He is the chief mischief maker," James McLaughlin wrote from Standing Rock, "and if he were not here this craze so general among the Indians would never have

INDIANS ON EXHIBIT

When Sitting Bull agreed to go on tour in the fall of 1884, he was offering himself and the tribesmen who accompanied him as an animated museum exhibit. Indeed, the show opened at a wax museum in New York, where the Sioux living tableau featured natives in full dress smoking and cooking in front of a stage tepee. Six thousand people stormed the matinee and evening performances on opening day, and the show drew packed houses for two weeks before it was taken to the next stop, Philadelphia.

Joining Buffalo Bill Cody's Wild West Show the following year, Sitting Bull was paid $50 per week for the four-month tour, a bonus of $125 for signing, and the revenue from sales of his autograph and portrait. The Sioux medicine man and Cody became fast friends, and Sitting Bull made fellow trouper Annie Oakley—whom he called "Little Sure Shot"—an adopted daughter.

Even after Sitting Bull's death in 1890, Buffalo Bill made a point of keeping his image before the public.

Fairgoers at the 1893 Columbian Exposition in Chicago had a chance to see the "death cabin" from which Sitting Bull had been dragged and then shot, as well as the performing horse the Sioux warrior had ridden in Cody's traveling show eight years earlier.

The Indian Bureau relaxed its rules against the "primitive" activities of its wards by allowing some 500 tribesmen to participate in the Trans-Mississippi Exposition held at Omaha in 1898. Dressed in traditional costumes, the Indians could be observed weaving, making arrowheads and baskets, dancing, playing games, and even staging mock battles twice a week for the titillation of fairgoers. The Carlisle Indian School's Richard Pratt denounced it as "a Wild West show of the most degenerate sort." Indians also took part in the World's Fair at St. Louis in 1904 and the Panama-Pacific Exhibition at San Francisco 11 years later. A journalist described the natives as the "most interesting and the most pathetic" figures on display at the California fair.

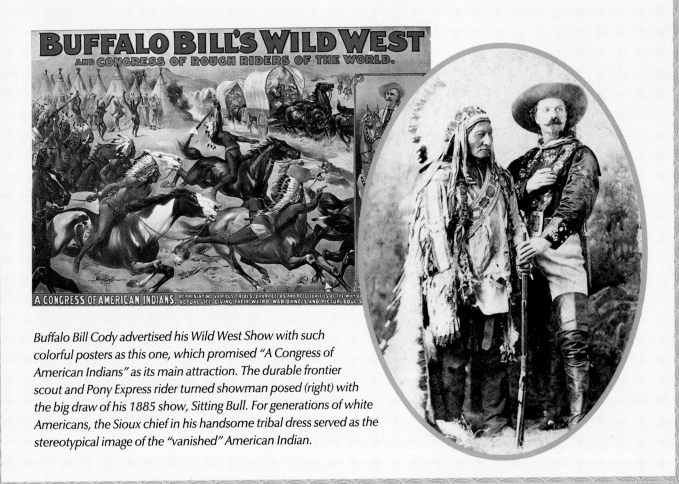

Buffalo Bill Cody advertised his Wild West Show with such colorful posters as this one, which promised "A Congress of American Indians" as its main attraction. The durable frontier scout and Pony Express rider turned showman posed (right) with the big draw of his 1885 show, Sitting Bull. For generations of white Americans, the Sioux chief in his handsome tribal dress served as the stereotypical image of the "vanished" American Indian.

The bullets will not go toward you. The prairie is large ... the bullets will not go toward you.

— *Yellow Bird, Miniconjou Sioux*

gotten a foothold at this agency." Barred from visiting other reservations in South Dakota, Sitting Bull led the Ghost Dance at Standing Rock, once gathering about 100 followers to dance for 200 spectators. By mid-December, McLaughlin had received orders to arrest him.

Let the soldiers come and take me away and kill me, wherever they like. I am not afraid. I was born a warrior. I have followed the war-path ever since I was able to draw a bow.

—*Sitting Bull, Hunkpapa Sioux*

The agency police who came to arrest Sitting Bull on December 15 were Native Americans themselves, as it happened—though a cavalry squadron was posted nearby in case of trouble. The chief put up no struggle, but one of his irate supporters shot the officer in charge, Lt. Bull Head. As he fell, Bull Head fired his revolver, wounding Sitting Bull in the chest. A second police officer, Sgt. Red Tomahawk, shot the prisoner in the back of the head. Sitting Bull fell dead to the ground.

A skirmish broke out between agency police and Sitting Bull's followers, then most of the Hunkpapas surrendered. A few fled south toward the Badlands to join the Miniconjou chief Big Foot, who had been leading Ghost Dancers on the Cheyenne River Reservation. On December 28 the cavalry caught up with Big Foot's band—106 warriors and about 250

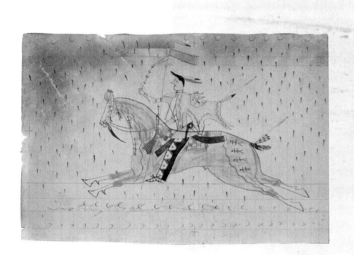

The frozen corpse of Big Foot was photographed at Wounded Knee on January 1, 1891, as workers removed bodies from the killing field. Inset: Protected by his Ghost Dance shirt, a warrior rides unharmed through a hail of bullets in this illustration from a ledger book found at Wounded Knee.

women and children—and persuaded the chief, who was grievously ill with pneumonia, to bring them to the Pine Ridge Reservation.

They were taken to a location on Wounded Knee Creek to be disarmed. Somewhere along that stream, according to tradition, was buried the heart of Crazy Horse, killed in captivity 13 years earlier. Big Foot's band included several veterans of the Little Bighorn. The cavalry, commanded by Col. James Forsyth, numbered about 500 and had four Hotchkiss guns—lethal, fast-firing small cannon. That night the officers broke out a keg of whiskey to celebrate Big Foot's capitulation.

On December 29, Colonel Forsyth distributed rations to the tribe. Then, summoning

the men to a council, he ordered them to surrender all their weapons. When only a few complied, Forsyth sent soldiers to search the tepees. They found 38 rifles. Forsyth next demanded that the men open the blankets in which they had wrapped themselves to show they had no hidden weapons.

An aged medicine man named Yellow Bird started chanting and swaying to a Ghost Dance song. Black Coyote, a young warrior who was reportedly deaf, raised his Winchester above his head and shouted that he would not give it up. When two soldiers tried to wrest it away from him, the gun went off. Taking the shot as a signal, other Indians threw aside their blankets and opened fire with previously concealed weapons. The troopers fired into the ranks of native warriors. Big Foot was among the first casualties.

E ven when most of the warriors lay dead, the shooting did not end. As women and children fled in terror, the rampaging soldiers followed, capturing and killing them in small, scattered groups as far as two miles away from Wounded Knee. By noon the guns were silent. About 300 Indians had been killed, most of them women and children; 31 soldiers had also died, some caught in their own crossfire.

Visiting the scene of the massacre later that day, the Oglala Sioux holy man Black Elk found dead and wounded women and children scattered all along a dry gulch where they had sought cover. Some lay in heaps where they had huddled together. An infant was trying to suck milk from its dead mother's breast. "When I saw this," Black Elk said in despair, "I wished that I had died too, but I was not sorry for the women and children. It was better for them to be happy in the other world."

The press hailed the killings as revenge for the Little Bighorn. "There is nothing to conceal

A nine-month-old girl found amid the carnage at Wounded Knee was adopted by Brig. Gen. Leonard W. Colby (above). One of the infant victims was said to have been wearing a beaded bonnet decorated with the American flag; this Lakota cap dates to about the same period as Wounded Knee.

We tried to run, but they shot us like we were buffalo.

— *Louise Weasel Bear, Wounded Knee survivor*

or apologize for in the Wounded Knee Battle," an army investigator concluded. "The Indians brought on their own destruction as surely as any people ever did. That they were under a strange religious hallucination is only an explanation, not an excuse." Eighteen of the troopers who took part in the killings were awarded the Congressional Medal of Honor.

The White Man's Road

Half a continent away, in Nevada, the prophet Wovoka went into mourning for the bloodshed brought on by his messianic religion. "My children, my children," he cried. "In days behind many times I called you to travel the hunting trail or to follow the war trail. Now those trails are choked with sand; they are covered with grass; the young men cannot find them. My children, today I call upon you to travel a new trail, the only trail now open—the White Man's Road." It was a road toward which Native Americans had been directed by the federal government with ever-increasing insistence in the quarter century since the end of the Civil War.

Peering westward in the aftermath of that great conflict, government officials in 1885 realized that the future of the newly reunited nation lay in developing the states and territories beyond the Mississippi. The recently passed Homestead Act was beckoning individual farmers. Texas ranchers were expanding the beef cattle industry north into Kansas and beyond. Gold miners, loggers, and others sought access to the land. But the path of expansion for some Americans ran straight through the domain of others. In order to develop the West, Indians had to be confined. If not already on reservations, they had to be put there

In the wake of Wounded Knee, the U.S. Army moved some 4,000 "hostiles" to the Pine Ridge encampment, photographed (top) late in January 1891. Inset: A Lakota woman at the Standing Rock Reservation.

—despite Gen. William T. Sherman's scathing appraisal of the typical reservation as "a parcel of land set aside for Indians, surrounded by thieves." Armed conflicts claimed many casualties in the years after the Civil War. There were also battles of a different kind—in some ways more devastating than any fought with guns—that echo through Indian country to the present day.

> As the hardy pioneer and adventurous miner advanced . . . in search of the precious metals, they found no rights possessed by Indians that they were bound to respect.
> — *Donehogawa (Ely Parker), Seneca*

Conventional wisdom of the period held that Indians would disappear. "All we can do is to smooth and make decent the pathway to the grave," a Massachusetts newspaper editor intoned. There was more than a little wishful thinking in this view. It would certainly have been more convenient for native people to vanish; then they would not hinder westward expansion and the government would no longer have open-ended responsibilities and expenses to worry about.

Nevertheless—despite centuries of disease, warfare, forced removals, and the destruction of whole societies—in 1865 there were still at least 300,000 Indians by official count living in the United States and its territories. The U.S. Indian Peace Commission, established in 1867, secured treaties with the Plains tribes and the Navajo in a period of feverish activity lasting through 1868.

"Feed 'Em and Fight 'Em"

The next year, as Ulysses S. Grant became president, Congress approved the creation of the Board of Indian Commissioners, which, with the secretary of the Interior, would be responsible for spending the funds earmarked for Indians. The board promptly called for the abolition of treaty making, and Congress approved the idea in 1871. Although many more negotiations would take place with Indian communities, they would now conclude in

KEEPER OF THE WESTERN DOOR

Although he achieved renown under his American name, Ely Samuel Parker was more correctly Donehogawa—the name given him when he was made a sachem of the Seneca in 1852 at the age of 24. It meant "Keeper of the Western Door," referring to his tribe's place in the Iroquois Longhouse, and it proved appropriate to the role he came to play in the white man's world.

Educated at the Baptist school on his upstate New York reservation and at two Indian high schools, Parker studied law but was denied admission to the bar because of his race. Learning that engineering was open to Indians, he trained at Rensselaer Polytechnic Institute and subsequently received United States government assignments— most notably one to Galena, Illinois, in 1860. There he met a former army captain, then a clerk in a harness store, Ulysses S. Grant.

At the outbreak of the Civil War the following year, Parker sought an army commission. Again he was rejected because of his race. In the summer of 1863, he turned to Grant, by then commanding the Union force besieging Vicksburg on the Mississippi, who pulled strings to get the valuable engineer commissioned and assigned to his staff. Parker followed Grant all the way to Appomattox Courthouse, where his patron asked him to transcribe the document ending the war. He was made a brigadier general as of that date, April 9, 1865. Four years later President Grant named Parker commissioner of Indian Affairs, the first Native American to hold that post. The Keeper of the Western Door now had to focus on the strife with the Plains Indians.

It was Parker who recommended to Grant what became known as the Peace Policy, naming agents nominated by religious groups in an effort to eliminate the corrupt officials who controlled the Bureau of Indian Affairs. He did not succeed, however, in getting any native members appointed to the independent Board of Indian Commissioners, which was to serve as the bureau's watchdog. What changes he did make brought Parker into conflict with the entrenched bureaucracy in Washington, which was able to delay appropriation of funds and, early in 1871, bring charges of misconduct against him. Although cleared of the charges, Parker resigned his post late in the summer. He later made and lost a small fortune on Wall Street.

Cartoonist Thomas Nast had a solution to the "Indian problem" (above)—send the whites back to Europe.

Government land allotment plans required tribal membership rolls, which were compiled at gatherings like this one in Dakota Territory.

"agreements"—rather than treaties, which accorded tribes the status of sovereign nations. Symbolically, Indians were being reduced in rank.

That movement accelerated during the Grant administration, when it was resolved that Indians must be confined on reservations, instructed about farming, and exposed to Christian men and women, who would have a positive, uplifting impact on their lives. Grant's program, labeled the Peace Policy, sparked conflict as well as coexistence. Because many tribes resisted attempts to reduce their traditional lands or relocate them to new ones, the 1860's and 1870's witnessed one war after another—from the Dakotas to New Mexico to Puget Sound. Cynical soldiers referred to the policy as "feed 'em in the winter and fight 'em in the summer."

As the 1870's progressed, native peoples increasingly found themselves confined to reservations. But even as they began adjusting

to this new world, Indians realized that it, too, might not last. Those intent on exploiting Indian lands, as well as reformers intent on altering Indian lifestyles, encouraged the idea of breaking up these islands of communally held land. Private property, after all, was part of the American way. How could American Indians become Indian Americans if they continued to hold land in common?

Subdivide and Conquer: Allotment

In 1879 Secretary of the Interior Carl Schurz outlined five central goals of the federal government: To help the Indians become self-supporting and to break them of their "savage" habits, he resolved to turn them into farmers. Education programs for the youth of both sexes would introduce the next generation to "civilized ideas, wants, and aspirations." Individuals would get title to their own farms, thus fostering "pride" of ownership rather than tribal "dependence," as had been the case when land was held in common. Once individual allotments had been made, the remaining tribal land would be leased or sold; the proceeds would go into a fund set aside to

meet Indian needs, thus reducing the government's obligation to pay for their support. Finally, when all this was done, Indians would be treated like all other inhabitants under the laws of the land. In short, they were to be assimilated.

A key element in Schurz's outline was the ticking time bomb of land allotment. It was embodied in the General Allotment Act of 1887, also called the Dawes Act for its sponsor, Senator Henry L. Dawes of Massachusetts. Assimilation had become the goal of federal Indian policy; allotment was the mechanism by which that goal would be achieved.

The Dawes Act dealt with the subject of individual versus tribal landholding in a blunt manner—by dividing reservations into parcels of 160 acres, a parcel for each head of a household. But not all tribal lands were immediately allotted, nor were all reservations equally affected. The Dawes Act was primarily applied to those most coveted by non-Indians, and so the northern Plains were hit especially hard. The Southwest, by contrast, although also pockmarked by allotment, did not feel so severe an impact.

They made us many promises, more than I can remember. They never kept but one — they promised to take our land, and they took it.

— *Red Cloud, Oglala Sioux*

What the Dawes Act initiated, subsequent laws and court decisions accelerated, making it far easier for those who sought Indian lands to obtain them through lease or purchase. The combination of such actions devastated Indian country. On reservation after reservation, Indians lost control of most or all of their land.

It was a brutal, one-sided process. For example, in *Lone Wolf* v. *Hitchcock,* the U.S. Supreme Court in 1903 denied the need of formal tribal approval for shrinking the tribal land base, as was customarily required in treaties and agreements. Congress, the Court decreed, could do what it wanted, when it wanted. If Congress wished to open part or all of a particular reserve, it could do so, the inhabitants' protests notwithstanding.

This process not only worked against the professed aims of creating independent, self-reliant farmers, but also permanently scarred many reservations and fashioned a pathetic legacy. By 1934 two-thirds of all Native Americans either had no land or else had so little that it scarcely counted. From 138 million acres in 1887, Indian landholdings had shrunk to 52 million—a reduction of more than 60 percent—and many reservations were left resembling checkerboards, with non-Indians owning or leasing more than half the total area.

Plains Indians recorded their history by means of a "winter count," an inwardly spiraling pictograph in which each image stood for the year's most important event. This Yanktonai Sioux winter count spans the years 1823 (top right corner) to 1911, during which the tribe moved from tepees to reservation log cabins at Devil's Lake, North Dakota. The circle with X's (second from right at bottom) records a meteor shower of November 1833, while the spotted figures fifth and sixth to its left represent smallpox outbreaks in 1837 and 1838.

THE HAND THAT FEEDS

Reformers urging the so-called Peace Policy on President Ulysses S. Grant envisioned the reservation as "a school of industry," not "a pen where a horde of savages are to be fed with flour and beef and supplied with blankets." Unfortunately, the latter image was too often the reality. Native people who had lived by buffalo hunting were herded onto lands not suitable for farming or much else. Then whites expressed dismay that they became dependent on government rations.

The dole was issued directly to individuals, not through their chiefs—another means of undermining tribal authority. Some Indians had to travel three days in each direction to receive the weekly handout; docile crowds such as those below at Pine Ridge, South Dakota, stood patiently in line at agency headquarters with their ration tickets (inset) for scarcely palatable food. The Crow Creek Sioux were fed from a six-foot-square vat in which beef heads and entrails, beans, flour, and pork had been boiled for up to 24 hours. Some succumbed to starvation after the nauseating mixture made them sick.

For the Arapaho at Wind River, Wyoming, a weekly ration in 1884 included 4 pounds of beef and 1.6 pounds of flour per person. But widespread corruption in the Bureau of Indian Affairs siphoned off a sizable amount of the money appropriated by Congress each year; by 1890 the ration at Wind River was down to 14 ounces of beef and 8 ounces of flour—and only about half the eligible people received even that.

An army colonel on frontier duty summed up the attitude of all too many whites: "Give to the Indians sugar and coffee, furnish them with plows and seeds, but let them at once and forever understand that the hand that feeds can, and if need be, will, strike."

Issue days were big times for all of us. The men who were to do the killing painted their faces and rode their fastest horses. For a few hours the Arapaho knew once more the excitement of the old buffalo hunt.... After 1896 the method of issuing beef was changed. To shorten the time and do away with the celebrating, live beeves were no longer given out. Instead, the cattle were slaughtered and issued from the block. Progress was catching up with us.

— Carl Sweezy, Arapaho

Catholic boarding schools on Montana's Crow Reservation helped discourage such "offenses" as the Sun Dance and polygamy. Here a Jesuit priest visits a Crow village in 1890.

Bibles, Not Bullets

In the meantime, native religious practices had come under attack across the continent in the name of assimilation. On the Great Plains, Indian agents in the 1880's had put a halt to the Sun Dance, a major yearly ritual for more than 20 different tribes, because it was considered "pagan." About the same time, the Canadian government outlawed the lavish potlatches that were at the heart of ceremonial life up and down the Northwest Coast.

Everywhere, Christian missionary groups, some of which were longtime rivals, divided up Indian country, so that one denomination had primary responsibility for one reservation—and access to a captive audience teeming with potential converts.

> This man was going to show the people how they could come back after they died. They thought he was some kind of medicine man. What he meant was that, if you led a good life, your soul would have eternal life.
>
> But the Indians thought that he could bring the dead back to life. Everybody started sending their children to that church.
> —*Jim Whitewolf, Kiowa-Apache*

"Bibles, and not bullets, are the proper instruments by which to reclaim savages and confer the blessings of civilization," proclaimed one undoubtedly well-meaning reformer. He spoke for countless other "friends of the Indian," progressive thinkers who did not want Indians to continue to live as Indians —but who believed that as God's children they had every right to live as white people.

Some Indians enthusiastically embraced Christianity—especially where the Bible was available in a native language, as it was for the Cherokee and Choctaw. Many were puzzled by the division between Catholics and Protestants and sometimes tried to play one off against the other. Others surreptitiously melded their own traditions into the adopted religion. So, for example, Christian camp meetings were held at harvest time and included features of the traditional Green Corn Ceremony.

An Apache woman in Oklahoma is called on by two Presbyterian missionaries in 1898.

I felt as if I were dead and traveling to the Spirit Land; for now all my old ideas were to give place to new ones, and my life was to be entirely different from that of the past.

— *Charles Eastman, Santee Sioux*

By 1910 this Crow family typified those who had adapted to the white man's lifestyle — no doubt proud as they posed at dinner in their tastefully appointed log-cabin home.

The High Cost of Education

In the same year that the Dawes Act gave land allotment the force of law, federal educational policy toward Indians was defined in terms of instruction in English: "This language, which is good enough for a white man and a black man," said Commissioner of Indian Affairs John D.C. Atkins, "ought to be good enough for the red man."

Schooling provided a crucial tool in changing not only the language but the culture of impressionable young people. In boarding schools students could be immersed in a 24-hour bath of assimilation. The founder of the Carlisle Indian Industrial School in Pennsylvania, Capt. Richard H. Pratt, observed in 1892 that "Carlisle has always planted treason to the tribe and loyalty to the nation at large." More crudely put, the Carlisle philosophy was "Kill the Indian to save the man."

A crusty veteran of the Indian wars, Pratt headed Carlisle from 1879 to 1904. During

The Onondaga moved to log cabins after settling on their upstate New York reservation in 1788; this one was photographed in 1905.

that quarter century, he and his school cast a long shadow over American Indian education. At Carlisle, Pratt instituted a quasi-military regimen, an approach that would be copied widely at other off-reservation boarding schools—Haskell in Kansas, Chilocco in Oklahoma, and Chemawa in Oregon, to name three of the most prominent—founded during the 1880's and the 1890's.

> Once there our belongings were taken from us, even the little medicine bags our mothers had given us to protect us from harm. Everything was placed in a heap and set afire. Next was the long hair, the pride of all the Indians. The boys, one by one, would break down and cry when they saw their braids thrown on the floor.
>
> — *Lone Wolf, Blackfeet*

Uniforms, strict regulations, marching in formation, and all the other trappings of the school were designed to create order and produce character so that students would be equipped for a life in the mainstream of white America. As another commissioner of Indian Affairs declared: "The Indian high school rightly conducted will be a gateway out from the desolation of the reservation into assimilation with our national life." In the service of

this goal, academic subjects took a back seat to vocational training: carpentry, masonry, and the like for boys; homemaking for girls.

These new institutions separated Indian children from their roots, transporting them halfway across the continent. The Sioux writer Luther Standing Bear remembered riding a speeding train across the Plains to a distant school in the East. Some of his friends were so frightened they began to sing the death songs of Sioux warriors approaching battle.

At the boarding schools children were forbidden to speak their native languages, forced to shed familiar clothing for white men's garments, and subjected to harsh discipline. Denied the teachings of tribal elders, the company of kin, the familiar foods, smells, and sights of home, students sometimes ran away from school or hid when it came time to leave in the first place. Youngsters who had seldom heard an unkind word spoken to them were all too often verbally and physically abused by their white teachers.

~

I remember my first test in this great educational system. A white man was pointing at a tub which was under a pump and he was saying something. I took it for granted that he wanted me to pump water and I nodded my head. He came over and pulled my ears and shook me. I stood there stunned, with my ears burning, wondering what he wanted.
— *Michael Wolf, Ojibwa*

~

For parents as well as students, the prospect of such long separations was a cause for deep anxiety. Many argued to keep their children at home, contending they were needed to work or to help out, or would miss necessary rituals, or were simply too young to go away. But they usually had little or no say in the matter. Children without parents and children from the poorest families constituted likely recruits; the food and clothing offered by the schools enticed some to enroll.

Carlisle required the longest journey for Indian students, but traveling to almost any

Memories of an Earlier Time

As Native Americans were uprooted and resettled on reservations, traditional ways of life were inevitably eroded by the products and practices of white society. One record of the old ways was preserved in another tradition—drawings people had made of their homes (or on them) since the earliest days.

The Mandan earth lodge was built with four poles supporting the roof, reflecting the four pillars holding up the dome of the sky.

Carved in the Puye Cliffs of New Mexico, this Anasazi figure hovers just above the doorway to a cave room.

The woman's role as home builder, recorded on a buffalo-hide tepee: Standing on pins at the bottom, she laces up the tepee with buffalo sinew.

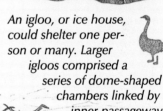

An igloo, or ice house, could shelter one person or many. Larger igloos comprised a series of dome-shaped chambers linked by inner passageways.

The "devouring mouth" framing the door of a Kwakiutl house warns that only worthy people may enter without harm.

In summer the Menominee built lightweight bark houses; this one has a bird on the roof and a rider on horseback beside it.

The detail above from a Sioux winter count for 1819–20 says, in pictographic form, "It is cold. The Crow people tried to look into the lodges for a place to stay."

The Apache dwellings called wikiups started with a light branch skeleton covered by thatch (or, later, canvas).

The image at right was found on an Iroquois carved stick, traditionally used to record events, stories, and prayers.

By the 1860's Plains Indians were beginning to preserve their stories on the pages of ledger books acquired from whites. Ink, pencils, and watercolors on paper were easier media than the stick and bone brushes on hide previously employed, and such traditional scenes as warriors on horseback were supplemented by more intimate ones like the courting couple below, rendered by a Lakota artist. Richard Wooden Leg (right), a Montana Cheyenne, is shown at his ledger book about 1928.

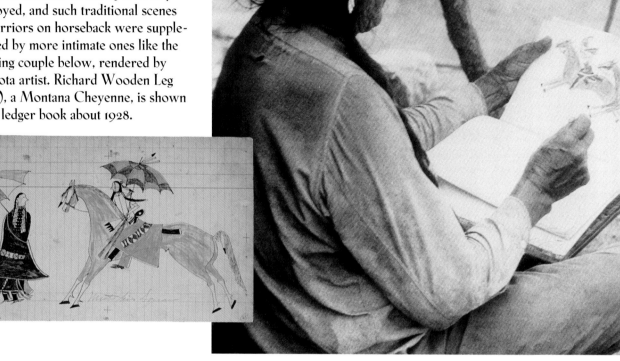

boarding school cut students off from their homes and communities. For Pueblo students who attended Santa Fe Indian School, for instance, the trip was not a long one geographically. But if you were a young girl from Taos Pueblo, you might as well have been going to Chicago or New York. As the train pulled away from Taos Junction to make its way south, one girl later recalled seeing the big mountain of her homeland vanish below the horizon: "The boys used to tell us, 'Look at the mountain for the last time, sisters!' And we started crying. We thought we were going some place that we would never come back."

And if you were a five-year-old girl from San Juan Pueblo, you would never forget the tears: "My mother was just crying her heart out, wiping her eyes with her sleeves as she put her best shawl on me. Pretty soon the train whistled around the bend near the Rio Grande. My grandpa was holding me on his lap, but when the train came, I got in. I saw the tears coming out of that brave man, my grandpa who was so brave and strong. I don't even know who was in the train because my mind was full of unhappiness."

But not everyone looked on the schools with despair. Some simply concluded that times had changed and knowing the whites' language and customs would be useful in the days ahead. A student at Carlisle described a visit to the school by some older, assimilated Indians. Writing in his school newspaper, he quoted one of them with obvious approval:

Boys, this was once all our country, but our fathers had not their eyes open as we have; our pale face brethren told us to move a little further and a little further, until now we are on our last stepping ground. Now, the only way to hold that even is to get educated ourselves.

— *Henry Jones, quoted by Ellis B. Childers, Creek*

Two thousand miles to the west, a Tohono O'odham (then called Papago) boy, James McCarthy, was enrolled at Santa Fe Indian School—and was pleasantly surprised to discover other Tohono O'odham students there. The schools had been expressly designed to mix students from different tribes, but tribal allegiances persisted, and having others of the same background nearby made an alien setting less intimidating.

McCarthy grew to like Santa Fe. As for many others, sports provided him with a vital outlet for his energy and competitive spirit. At the age of 18, as captain of the baseball team, he convinced one of the teachers to arrange a game with the Albuquerque Indian School, which "was beating everybody around the state." The Santa Fe team, mostly Tohono O'odham, took on the all-Navajo team of Albuquerque. The bigger and taller Navajos represented an ideal challenge, but Santa Fe won, 5-0. As his team returned home in triumph, said McCarthy, "We were the happiest boys."

Students at Riverside Indian School in Anadarko, Oklahoma, in 1901 were given such basic instruction as how to wash clothes.

Between the extremes of wholehearted acceptance or angry rebellion there were responses to the boarding schools that involved every imaginable mixture of emotions. Some youngsters, only half indoctrinated, became what the Stony Indians of Canada called their returned students—*aintsikn ustombe,* "the lost people." As a boy in New Mexico, Sun Elk recalled feeling that "I wanted to learn the white man's secrets. I thought he had better magic than the Indian." Willingly, then, he became the first from Taos Pueblo to make the long journey to Carlisle.

They told us that Indian ways were bad; they said we must get civilized. I remember that word. It means "be like the white man." I am willing to be like the white man, but I did not believe Indian ways were wrong.

But they kept teaching.... The books told how bad the Indians had been to the white man. We all wore white man's clothes and ate white man's food and went to white man's churches and spoke white man's talk.

And so after a while we also began to say Indians were bad. We laughed at our own people and their blankets and cooking pots.
— *Sun Elk, Taos Pueblo*

Sun Elk did not return to Taos for seven years. When he did, he was treated like an outsider by tribal elders and felt like one himself. Only after a harsh reentry ritual in the sacred kiva and a period during which he grew his hair long again, resumed wearing traditional clothes, and took a tribal bride could

Three Plains Indian girls were photographed (above) shortly after their arrival at Virginia's Hampton Institute late in the 19th century. Primly dressed, they posed at their checkerboard 14 months later (right) — perhaps less frightened but, from all appearances, no happier.

We thought windows were put in the walls so that we might look in to see how white people did their work and ate their meals.

— *Carl Sweezy, Arapaho*

Sun Elk say that he "became an Indian again."

A similar feeling of alienation, of being caught somewhere between two worlds and belonging to neither, was described by a Hopi man who had been taken away from his highly traditional community to be educated at a distant missionary school.

I could talk like a gentlemen, read, write, and cipher. I could name all the states of the Union, with their capitals, repeat the names of all the books of the Bible, quote a hundred verses of Scripture, sing more than two dozen Christian hymns and patriotic songs.

But I wanted to become a real Hopi again, to sing the good old kachina songs, and to feel free without the fear of sin or a rawhide.

— *Sun Chief, Hopi*

Even under the harsh discipline of boarding school education, many students were able to preserve tribal values. They shared food, learned from each other, and took delight in breaking school rules. And while all the schools were strict, some showed a remarkable—and refreshing—sympathy for native cultures and values.

At schools such as Albuquerque and the one at Fort Wingate, also in New Mexico, Navajo students learned traditional weaving. Pueblo painters worked with Santa Fe Indian School students to create murals of Indian life and Indian symbols on the walls of the cafeteria. The outstanding Navajo silversmith of his day, Ambrose Roanhorse, began to teach his art. Parents began to feel more welcome on the Santa Fe campus.

An unexpected outcome of intermixing children from diverse tribes was a special camaraderie that developed among them. Thrown together into these alien, scary environments, with only each other for support, young people from very different cultures discovered they had much in common by virtue of simply being Native Americans. When these students became adults, their

When Carlisle School founder Richard Pratt drew up the curriculum, he called on his experience teaching Indian prisoners at Fort Marion, Florida, where a Kiowa inmate made this sketch (above) of uniformed classmates in 1877. A quarter century later, classrooms at the Riverside Indian School in Oklahoma were said to be superior to most frontier schools for whites. The school had double desks, blackboards, gaslights—and at least one very large American flag.

MISSIONARY SCHOOL DAYS

For many Indian children, the missionary school was the gateway to an exciting, entirely different world from the one they had known in their tribal village. Such was certainly the case for Francis La Flesche, sent in the mid-1860's as a boy no older than six to the Presbyterian school for the Omaha Indians, situated some 80 miles north of Omaha, Nebraska. In his memoir, *The Middle Five*, originally published in 1900, La Flesche described his first day:

A bell rang, and from every direction came boys and girls crowding and pushing one another as they entered a large room. A big boy grasped me by the hand, fairly dragging me along as he said, "Come quick! We are going to eat." After considerable shuffling by the children, they suddenly became very still, everyone bowed his head, then a man with gray hair and whiskers, who sat at the end of one of the tables, spoke in a low tone. He finished speaking, then followed a deafening clatter of a hundred tin plates and cups. Young women carrying great pans of steaming food moved rapidly from table to table. One put a potato on my plate. "Give him two, he's hungry," whispered my new friend.

An older student consoles newly arrived Francis La Flesche.

La Flesche was allowed to keep the name of his grandfather, a French trader who had married an Omaha woman. Others had to change theirs.

All the boys in our school were given English names, because their Indian names were difficult to pronounce. Besides, the aboriginal names were considered by the missionaries as heathenish. And so, in the place of Tae-noo-ga-wa-zhe, came Philip Sheridan; in that of Wa-pah-dai, Ulysses S. Grant; and so on. Our sponsors went even further back in history, and thus we had our David and Jonathan, Gideon and Isaac, and, with the flood of these new names, came Noah.

Another newcomer faced a first-day ordeal:

A few boys were detailed to wash and dress the new arrival; so, with arms full of clothing and towels, the lad was taken up to the boys' dormitory. The first thing to be done was to cut his long hair, and soon the shears were singing a tune about his ears. He seemed to enjoy it, and laughed at the jokes made by the boys; but when by chance he caught sight of his scalp-lock lying on the floor like a little black snake, he put his fists into his eyes and cried.

Learning to speak and read a new language was the students' first and most important assignment:

"Third Reader," called Gray-beard [the children's name for their teacher], and some ten or twelve boys and girls marched to the place of recitation. The reading lesson was some verses on "Summer." The first boy called upon put his index finger on the line and slid it along as he read in a low, sing-song tone. "Read that over again," said Gray-beard. "Read it loud, as though you were out of doors at play." Bob read again, but in the same manner, and had hardly gone through half the line when the sharp crack of Gray-beard's ruler on the desk made us all jump. "That's not the way to read!" he exclaimed with some impatience and repeated the lines to show how they should be given. "Now, read as though you were wide awake."

History—white man's history—remained a vague blur:

"Who discovered America?" asked Gray-beard. Dozens of hands went up. "Abraham, you may answer."
Abraham put his weight on one foot and then another, the very picture of embarrassment. "Come," said Gray-beard, "we are waiting."
"George Washington," answered Abraham.

Chapel attendance was mandatory:

We sat in rows on Sunday mornings, afternoons, and evenings, ranged on long, high wooden benches without backs, our feet scarcely touching the floor, and listened to sermons which were remarkable for their length. I had many delightful dreams in the chapel, about Samson and his jaw-bone war club, the fight between David and Goliath, and the adventures of Joseph. Knowing my weakness, an older friend always secured a place back of mine to support me when I was in a slumberous mood.

Some native traditions could not be erased. A visitor asked the children to sing an Indian song:

There was some hesitancy, but suddenly a loud clear voice close to me broke into a Victory song; before a bar was sung another voice took up the song from the beginning. Then the whole school fell in, and we made the room ring. We felt, as we sang, the patriotic thrill of a victorious people who had vanquished their enemies.
The visitor shook his head. "That's savage!" he said. "They must be taught music."

friendships blossomed into marriages, inter-tribal visits, and political alliances. The phenomenon later called Pan-Indianism, a sense of shared Indian identity that transcended tribal boundaries, arose at least partly from these schools—the very institutions designed to erase the idea of "Indianness" from modern American life.

In time, the Indian boarding school—at least in some instances—achieved a vital transition. A history of Oklahoma's Chilocco School during the 1920's and 1930's concludes that Chilocco's Indian students had made the place their own. No longer could it be described as a school for Indians; on the contrary, says K. Tsianina Lomawaima, author of *They Called It Prairie Light,* "Chilocco was an Indian school."

Adversity and New Alliances

Even more than the schools, the reservations themselves evolved during these years. At first they were little more than prisons for most Native American communities. Administered in a heavy-handed manner by agents, many of whom lacked any qualifications for their assignments, reservations appeared to be nothing more than barren, isolated acreages to which unwilling groups of people had been banished.

The tribesmen on the northern Plains reservations seemed particularly bereft. The buffalo could no longer be hunted; wars could no longer offer glory and honor. Farming, an

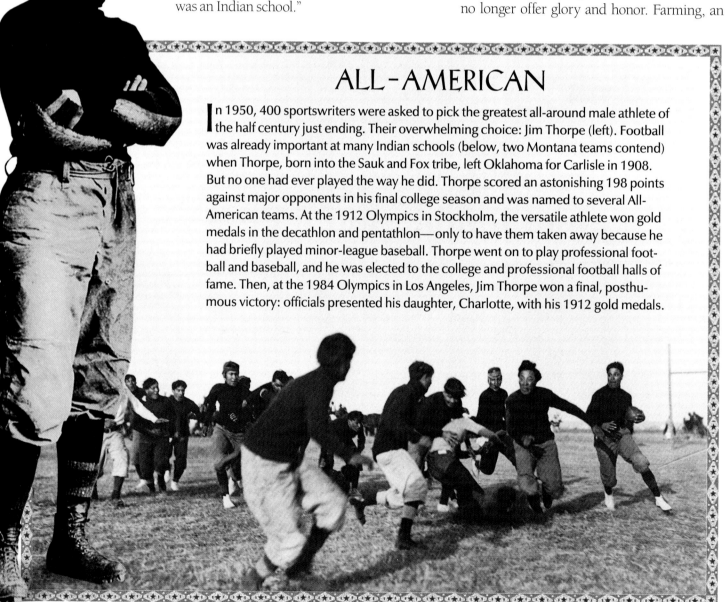

ALL-AMERICAN

In 1950, 400 sportswriters were asked to pick the greatest all-around male athlete of the half century just ending. Their overwhelming choice: Jim Thorpe (left). Football was already important at many Indian schools (below, two Montana teams contend) when Thorpe, born into the Sauk and Fox tribe, left Oklahoma for Carlisle in 1908. But no one had ever played the way he did. Thorpe scored an astonishing 198 points against major opponents in his final college season and was named to several All-American teams. At the 1912 Olympics in Stockholm, the versatile athlete won gold medals in the decathlon and pentathlon—only to have them taken away because he had briefly played minor-league baseball. Thorpe went on to play professional football and baseball, and he was elected to the college and professional football halls of fame. Then, at the 1984 Olympics in Los Angeles, Jim Thorpe won a final, posthumous victory: officials presented his daughter, Charlotte, with his 1912 gold medals.

W. Richard West, Southern Cheyenne artist, has documented his tribe's traditions in such paintings as this one of Cheyenne winter games. Here the entire community participates in a variety of activities—among them sledding, tobogganing, wrestling, arrow throwing, ice fishing, and gambling—some handed down but others picked up at Indian boarding schools.

occupation advocated by the government, was deemed unworthy work for a man. Cheyenne, Sioux, and other Plains Indian males no doubt shared the sentiment concisely expressed by the Shoshone leader Washakie: "God damn a potato!" Nonetheless, as early as 1886, the Indians at Wind River, Wyoming, were pooling their labor and sharing the produce of reservation hay fields and vegetable gardens.

In place of the gun, we must take the plow and live as white men do.

— *Simon Pokagon, Potawatomi*

Court decisions under the Dawes Act and related legislation wrenched millions of acres from Indian control. The carving up of the Great Sioux Reservation in the Dakotas was a bleak harbinger: as hordes of non-Indians swarming into vacated Sioux lands began to clamor for more, the new, smaller reserves— Standing Rock, Cheyenne River, Lower Brule, Crow Creek, Pine Ridge, Rosebud—seemed only temporary themselves.

Rosebud was one of the reservations opened to non-Indian settlement in the wake of the Supreme Court's *Lone Wolf* decision of 1903. Cheyenne River then caught the eyes of ranchers, farmers, speculators, and boosters.

In December 1907 a U.S. senator from South Dakota introduced a bill to chop off a piece of Cheyenne River to accommodate new homesteaders; not to be outdone, a local congressman introduced a bill in the House of Representatives calling for the entire unallotted portion of the reservation to be opened.

But at Cheyenne River, residents went on the offensive. Forming special reservation councils, they appealed to the Indian Rights Association, an influential group made up mostly of sympathetic whites. They sent a delegation to Washington, D.C., to lobby directly on their own behalf. Such united action represented a wave of larger changes taking place in Indian life.

Within a generation, a new sense of community was emerging at Cheyenne River through a process similar to the one in the boarding schools. The reservation brought together several previously distinct and fiercely independent bands of Teton Sioux: Miniconjou, Sans Arc, Blackfeet, and Two Kettle. While band affiliation remained important, the people soon began to see themselves as Cheyenne River Sioux. The ability to act together in a common cause would prove crucial to their survival.

Stampede to Statehood

Between 1830 and 1842, the Cherokee, Chickasaw, Choctaw, Creek, and Seminole had been forcibly removed from their homelands in the Southeastern United States and resettled in Indian Territory, part of what would become the state of Oklahoma. Overcoming that trauma—and the internal divisions it aroused—the exiles began to re-create their communities with remarkable speed and get on with their lives.

Before the deportations they had shown themselves willing, even eager, to embrace the trappings and values of white society. When whites referred to them as the Five Civilized Tribes, there was no hint of irony or sarcasm; it was a name that expressed respect. The theft of their lands in the Southeast did not rob the Five Tribes of their ambitions. They built substantial homes, re-established their own institutions and laws, printed newspapers and books in their own languages, opened schools based on the Christian principles they had embraced, and established themselves as successful farmers and ranchers.

One of the institutions they had adopted from whites proved a handicap, however: slavery. Many leading families among the Five Tribes were plantation-style slaveowners, and when the Civil War erupted in 1861, most threw in their lot with the Confederacy. At war's end the federal government demanded new treaties that opened their lands to railroads and to the relocation of other, less "civilized" Indians within their borders. Kiowa, Kiowa-Apache, Comanche, Cheyenne, and Arapaho were among the 60-odd tribes that eventually settled in beside the firstcomers.

The allotment system created by the Dawes Act of 1887 did not apply to the Five Tribes or to others in Indian Territory living on reservations created by earlier U.S. government treaties. But unrelenting pressure from non-Indian land seekers forced Congress to act. In 1889 it opened "Oklahoma Country"—an area of unassigned land in the center of the territory—to the first land rush by white settlers. Then in 1893 it opened the just-purchased Cherokee Outlet to an even larger wave of so-called boomers. Then, to clear the way for Oklahoma's eventual statehood, it established the Dawes Commission to negotiate terms and timetables with the Five Tribes and others for allotting their reservation lands and dissolving their tribal governments.

Egypt had its locusts, Asiatic countries their cholera, England its black plague. But it was left for unfortunate Indian Territory to be afflicted with the worst scourge of the 19th century, the Dawes Commission.

— *Oklahoma Creek*

The Five Tribes and more than a dozen others fought back by attempting to form their own separate state of Sequoyah. Congress responded with the Curtis Act of 1898, which abolished their tribal governments and effectively cut them off from the statehood process. When Oklahoma finally became a state in 1907, Indians throughout the area were soon swamped by a massive new influx of boomers. Native communities survived, but

their reservations were not preserved and the tribal land base disappeared almost completely. The impact was greatest on the Five Tribes—inevitably, since they had the most land to lose. Of their 19.5 million acres, 15.8 million were allotted, with much of the remaining land—nearly 4 million acres—sold off at public auction.

An exception was the case of the Osage tribe, which in 1870 had arranged with the government to sell its reservation in Kansas and relocate to the eastern part of the Cherokee Outlet, adjacent to the Cherokee Nation proper. In 1896, as the Dawes Commission's negotiations with various tribes were inching forward, oil was discovered on the Osage reservation—suddenly raising the stakes to an entirely new level. Talks slowed to a halt and remained deadlocked until an ingenious plan proposed by the Osage was accepted by Congress in 1906: the reservation's surface area would be allotted much as it was on other reservations, but mineral rights would continue to be owned communally, with proceeds to be shared by the 2,229 tribal members officially enrolled as of January 1907. Their foresight and shrewdness were well rewarded. The explosive demand for oil and natural gas in

The 1893 opening of Cherokee land in Indian Territory to white settlement triggered a stampede that left several would-be settlers dead. Seven such events added 14 million acres of "surplus" tribal lands to what became the state of Oklahoma.

Quanah Parker was dismissed from his post as a judge on a court dealing with Indian offenses—possibly because one of the court's responsibilities was to combat polygamy, and Quanah kept as many as five wives.

the 1920's produced so much money that until the Great Depression set in, the Osage were the wealthiest nation per capita in the world.

One unforeseen consequence of the Dawes Commission's work is that in Oklahoma today there are no Indian reservations such as exist in states to the north and west of it. Yet Oklahoma boasts the largest Native American population in the United States—more than 250,000. About 120,000 of those are Cherokee, which ranks not only as the largest tribe in Oklahoma but—with almost 310,000 people nationwide identifying themselves as Cherokee in the 1990 census—the largest in the United States and Canada.

Bureaucrats and Backroom Deals

Once they had been settled onto reservations, most Indian tribes would have preferred to be left alone—their outlook bleak, perhaps, but still within their own control. The Bureau of Indian Affairs, however, would never allow such independence. Determined to make the reservations economically self-sufficient, federal officals usually promoted farming as the solution. But in the arid climate of the West, before vast Indian lands could be made productive they had to be irrigated, and as more and more white settlers poured into the region, the competition for water resources grew increasingly severe.

A rare judicial victory regarding water rights was the 1908 Supreme Court decision in *Winters* v. *United States*. The case had reached the high court through the efforts of William Logan, the Indian agent at Montana's Fort Belknap Reservation. Logan testified on behalf of Gros Ventres and Assiniboins seeking to use water from the Milk River, which flowed through their lands but was being so heavily diverted by white farmers and ranchers upstream that what remained did not meet the reservation's needs.

The Supreme Court ruled that the Indians had never relinquished their claim to the water, but the victory proved largely symbolic: a

subsequent dam construction project to benefit the area's non-Indians sharply limited the amount of water arriving at Fort Belknap.

One activity that offered at least some hope of success was cattle ranching. Raising livestock at Fort Belknap and elsewhere in the West made sense for several reasons. It built on the native tradition of horsemanship and unfettered movement in the outdoors. It depended on cooperation among family members and offered ranchers an opportunity to show their generosity by giving cattle or beef to relatives and friends. And the grasslands on which most Western Indians had been settled were well suited for grazing.

On the northern Plains, the patterns of allotment, cession, and leasing often conspired against Indian cattle ranching. The federal government may have pressed the Indians to show economic initiative, but the activities of competing whites continually stymied it. Local moneymen conspired to lease reservation lands at cut-rate prices, and they colluded with all-too-willing government agents on other backroom deals. Even so, cattle ranching took hold on nearly all the reservations in this region, and it flourished—intermittently, at least—as the century progressed.

The Government issued a cow to each of us. It was no time when every one of us had a nice bunch of cattle. Every fall we used to ship a trainload of cattle to Chicago. We were happy; we had plenty; we had nothing to worry about. But this did not look good to the Indian Bureau. They leased our reservation to a big cattle company. In one year after that we were flat broke.

—*Martin Mitchell, Assiniboin*

In the southern Plains, Indian cattle ranchers faced comparable problems, but there were some who achieved at least temporary success. Quanah Parker, the famous Comanche leader, was one.

Texas cattlemen had discovered the grasses of Comanche country in the 1870's and promptly began to trespass on them. Quanah,

The people of Sandia Pueblo, New Mexico, graze cattle and grow wheat on their sandy plain east of the Rio Grande. Inset: A wheat harvest is featured in a 1910 issue of The Red Man magazine.

VOLUME 3, NUMBER 1   SEPTEMBER, 1910   ONE DOLLAR A YEAR

A Monthly Magazine by Indians

THE RED MAN

Formerly The Indian Craftsman

THE CARLISLE INDIAN PRESS
U. S. INDIAN SCHOOL, CARLISLE, PENNSYLVANIA

as he is more properly known (Parker was the name of his white mother, a captive of the Comanche), lobbied against such invasions but also knew an opportunity when he saw one. He obtained cattle from the local agent and from the Texas ranchers, and he put together mutually profitable leasing deals with them. Gradually enlarging his herd and his lands, Quanah became prominent in the newly established Native American Church, the controversial Indian religious organization whose rituals included the consumption of peyote.

There were others who found the ways and means to adjust advantageously to the changing circumstances of the period. A Ute man named Na-am-quitch—William Wash was his white name—raised cattle and alfalfa and sold hay to the troops at Fort Duchesne in Utah. Wash used his relative prosperity for some traditional goals, helping to feed less-well-off Utes and supporting the holding of the Sun Dance, even as federal officials tried to suppress the sacred ritual. Wash also joined the Native American Church, ridiculing claims that the peyote consumed in church rituals would kill practitioners: "Sometimes people die and no eat peyote. Horses die, cows die, sheep die. They no eat peyote. You can't stop them dying."

Overcoming the Odds

As the careers of Quanah and William Wash illustrated, Indians—surrounded though they were by bigotry and bureaucracy—did not have to be passive victims. They could survive and even prosper if they were willing to learn how the system worked. This was particularly true in Arizona, where the slow pace of white settlement meant an advantage for many native residents.

The Navajo had survived the agony of their Long Walk to exile and imprisonment at Bosque Redondo in eastern New Mexico in 1864, and by 1868 they had returned to a por-

In the 1877 drawing below, a young Kiowa artist named Wohaw envisioned his people's transition from buffalo hunting to cattle raising as a virtual tug-of-war between deeply conflicting cultures.

Using his "window technique," Shawnee artist Ernest Spybuck showed both interior and exterior of a peyote tepee in this 1938 watercolor. Below is the peyote button consumed in the Native American Church ceremony.

THE PEYOTE SACRAMENT

Although many Native Americans came to embrace Christianity, traditional beliefs survived as well and were often practiced in tandem with the new religion. One such was a peyote ceremony that gained a following in Oklahoma about 1890 and was soon adopted by northern Plains and Great Basin tribes.

A small, spineless cactus growing mainly in northern Mexico and southern Texas, peyote was used in Mexico as long as 10,000 years ago for both medicinal and ceremonial purposes. When eaten, its dried, buttonlike tops induce relaxation, euphoria, and psychedelic trances in which vivid visual images appear to the user.

The 19th-century ceremony was held in a tepee or brush enclosure with an opening to the east and typically began on a Saturday evening. Participants sat in a circle flanking the chief, who faced the entry; men and women were segregated, children sitting with their mothers. A central fire was kindled in front of a low mound of sand that served as an altar; nearby were a drum, a rattle, and a

whistle used to accompany singing as the peyote was distributed. With breaks at midnight and dawn, the ceremony lasted until full daylight on Sunday and was followed by a hearty breakfast.

Christian denominations and the Bureau of Indian Affairs moved quickly to suppress the practice, wrongly equating peyote with alcohol; tribal people in Oklahoma countered in 1918 by organizing the Native American Church. It celebrated Christianity through what it called the Peyote Sacrament and sought to teach its followers "morality, sobriety, industry, kindly charity and right living." The church found its ceremony outlawed in several states (though such laws did not apply to reservations), but Congress failed to pass a national ban and efforts by the Navajo tribal council to forbid peyote ran afoul of constitutional guarantees of religious freedom.

In 1944 a nationwide church organization was created; in 1955 it expanded to incorporate several affiliated Canadian groups, and today the church has perhaps 200,000 members.

tion of their homeland. The reservation established by the government initially consisted of a 3.5-million-acre rectangular tract situated on either side of what became the Arizona–New Mexico state line.

The rapid increase of the Navajo population and the need for additional territory for their livestock made an expansion of the reservation crucial. Congress had put an end to treaty making in 1871, but reservations could still be created or enlarged by executive order. By 1917 a total of nine such orders quadrupled the size of the Navajo estate.

Pathfinders of a New Age

The Navajo were not alone in sensing and seizing opportunities. Among those who saw promise in the days ahead were a number of forceful individuals whose words and work suggested what might await Native Americans. They hardly spoke with the same voice, but they shared a conviction that the Indian world had not come to an end but had merely entered a new chapter in its long history.

Charles Eastman, born in 1858 in a Santee Sioux community in Minnesota, fled to Canada with his grandmother and uncle in the wake of the Santee Uprising of 1862. Despite the uprooting, he was raised in the traditional world of Sioux culture. A decade later his father, who had been homesteading in Dakota Territory, came to take Charles back to the United States, determined that his son prepare himself for an existence that could only be gained through education.

Eastman probably surpassed his father's dreams, graduating from Dartmouth College and earning an M.D. from Boston University in 1890. He took up the physician's post at the Pine Ridge Reservation in South Dakota shortly before Wounded Knee. On the first day of 1891, fol-

lowing a blizzard that had prevented an earlier excursion, Eastman made the grim passage out to look for the wounded and bury the dead. He never forgot that scene—and he did not remain long at Pine Ridge. Moving to St. Paul, Minnesota, he began a career of writing and social work and helped establish a national native-rights organization, the Society of American Indians (SAI), in 1911.

From the Southwest came Carlos Montezuma, a Yavapai born around 1866 in central Arizona. Captured by Pimas as a young child, he was sold for $30 to a white man and later placed in the guardianship of a Baptist minister in Urbana, Illinois. He went to college and medical school, and by 1889, a year before Eastman, he, too, had become a doctor. Montezuma served as a physician on reservations in North Dakota, Nevada, and Washington before becoming the resident doctor at the Carlisle Indian School.

Although Montezuma had not grown up on a reservation, he had seen enough of them to form some strong opinions. He told a Chicago audience in 1898 that reservations were "a demoralized prison; a barrier against enlightenment, a promoter of idleness, beggary, gambling, pauperism, ruin, and death." The answer to the plight of the Indians, he declared, was the abolition of the Bureau of Indian Affairs—a campaign he later pursued through his own newsletter, *Wassaja*.

Edited by Wassaja (Dr. Montezuma's Indian name, meaning "Signaling") an Apache Indian.

Vol. 3, No. 2   ISSUED MONTHLY   May, 1918

Charles Eastman (top) was also known as Ohiyesa, "Winner." Gertrude Bonnin (above) published short stories of reservation life under the pen name Zitkala-sa, "Red Bird." Carlos Montezuma gave his native name, Wassaja, "Signaling," to his monthly magazine; the cartoon at left shows him directing a battering ram against the Indian Bureau.

Two veterans from the southern Plains—one in uniform, the other in tribal dress—stand proudly by the flag they helped defend in World War I. The Choctaw medal at right, commissioned to honor its World War I code talkers, is topped by the Choctaw Nation's seal, which displays a pipe hatchet, arrows, and an unstrung bow.

On a trip to Arizona around 1900, Montezuma met some of his relatives, and this began to complicate his view of Indian life. Returning for visits to the Yavapai Reservation at Fort McDowell, he recognized that despite everything, reservations were becoming homes for the people. His gradual appreciation of the reservation's role as a base for family and community life pointed Montezuma toward another crusade: protecting the rights of Indians who chose to remain there.

On the Cattaraugus Seneca Reservation in upstate New York, Arthur Caswell Parker was born in 1881 to a Seneca father, an accountant for the New York Central Railroad, and a white mother who taught school on the reservation. Because clan membership was inherited from the mother, Arthur had to be adopted into the tribal unit. Perhaps in part because of their son's mixed-blood status, the Parkers moved to White Plains, near New York City. An early interest in an-thropology led Parker to conduct field work at his home reservation, and although unable to finish college, he won a post as archaeologist at the New York State Museum in Albany. Parker became a key figure in the first decade of the SAI, working as editor of its journal, *The American Indian Magazine*, from 1911 to 1916.

We send our little Indian boys and girls to school, and when they come back talking English, they come back swearing. There is no swear word in the Indian languages, and I haven't yet learned to swear.

—*Gertrude S. Bonnin, Yankton Sioux*

Born in 1875 at Pine Ridge, Gertrude Simmons left home at age eight to attend a Quaker school in Wabash, Indiana. Her mother strongly opposed the idea: "Don't believe a word they say!" she admonished her departing daughter. Gertrude nonetheless went on to attend a Quaker college in Indiana, then taught at Carlisle before returning to South Dakota. In 1902 she married Raymond T. Bonnin, also a Sioux, and moved with him to the Uintah and Ouray Reservation in Utah, where she taught for more than 10 years—and came to appreciate her mother's hard-earned skepticism. She moved to Washington, D.C., in 1916 and for years championed the cause of Indian rights, as secretary of the SAI and later as founder of the National Council of American Indians.

Fighters for Uncle Sam

In 1917 Gertrude Bonnin was traveling to the annual meeting of the SAI, held that year in Pierre, South Dakota. A stranger noted her service pin. "You have a relative in the war?" he asked. "Yes, indeed," she said. "I have many cousins and nephews somewhere in France. This star I am wearing is for my husband, a member of the great Sioux Nation, who is a volunteer in Uncle Sam's Army." The countenance of the pale-faced stranger lit up. "Oh!

Yes! You are an Indian. Well, I knew when I first saw you that you must be a foreigner."

At the passage of the Selective Service Act in May 1917, many Native Americans had rushed to join the armed forces—though, as noncitizens, they could request deferment from the draft. By war's end, about 17,000 were in uniform—close to 30 percent of adult Indian males, double the national average.

Indians served in every branch, including the medical corps, military police, engineering corps, and—fittingly for a group of Oglala Sioux—the cavalry. Commanding General John J. Pershing authorized an Apache company of scouts; some of them were descendants of warriors Pershing himself had fought on the Southwestern frontier 30 years earlier.

"War is a terrible thing," a veteran from the Oklahoma Potawatomi summed up in December 1918, "but I'm glad I was in it. I feel I can look the whole world in the face now that I went and have come back."

All we ask is full citizenship. Why not? We offered our services and our money in this war, and more in proportion to our number and means than any other race or class of the population.

— *Charles Eastman, Santee Sioux*

Congress gave citizenship to honorably discharged Indian veterans in 1919, and that action helped the country move toward the ultimate goal of universal Indian citizenship —a goal finally realized in 1924. The legislation bestowing citizenship provided that "the right of any Indian to tribal or other property" was not to be impaired. It was drafted by Senator Charles Curtis of Kansas, a man of part Kansa and Osage descent, who later served as vice president under Herbert Hoover.

For Indians who had helped win the war, even with citizenship attained, there remained a sense of promises not kept and potential unfulfilled. The 1920's would witness a major campaign to change the course of federal policy—and with it the future of Native Americans in American society.

"WE SHALL LIVE AGAIN"

As early as the 1830's, it was widely assumed that Indians were facing extermination. The painter George Catlin dedicated himself to their rescue—not their lives but their culture, which he so faithfully recorded. "My heart bleeds," he wrote, "for the fate that awaits the remainder of their unlucky race." Only with the census of 1850 did the United States try to enumerate all Indians within its borders; the estimate was 400,000. Figures for the next four decades showed a gradual, seemingly inexorable downturn: from 339,000 in 1860 to 248,000 in 1890. "It took no prophet," concluded a Census Bureau report, "to proclaim the Indian's doom." In line with this belief, Joseph Kossuth Dixon called his famous photograph above "Sunset of a Dying Race."

But the predictions were wrong. Entering the 20th century, Indian numbers began to rise. The upturn was gradual at first, but by 1990 the survival of Native North Americans was indisputable. To the 1,960,000 (including Inuit and Aleut populations) in the U.S. Census for that year could be added some 740,000 native people in Canada and 30,000 in Greenland—for a total of nearly 2,750,000. This long, slow recovery, to some, seemed almost a fulfillment of the refrain in a century-old Comanche Ghost Dance song: *We shall live again; we shall live again.*

*I know how my father saw
the world, and his father before him.
That's how I see the world.*
—N. Scott Momaday,
Kiowa/Cherokee

11

PRIDE AND RENEWAL

CLOSING THE CIRCLE

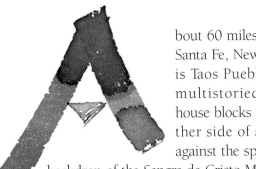bout 60 miles north of Santa Fe, New Mexico, is Taos Pueblo—two multistoried adobe house blocks set on either side of a stream against the spectacular backdrop of the Sangre de Cristo Mountains. Inhabited since A.D. 1350, the picturesque Indian village became a major tourist destination early in the 20th century. One visitor, a white social worker named John Collier, would have an enormous impact—for better or worse—on the course of Indian affairs in the United States.

A native of Georgia, Collier had labored for 12 years among European immigrants in New York City—an experience that showed him just how devastating forced assimilation could be to a group of outsiders. Frustrated by his work in New York, Collier departed for California to take a job directing the state's adult education program. He did not last long: an outspoken admirer of the 1917 Bolshevik Revolution and its promise to improve community life, he ruffled the feathers of conservative businessmen. Ready to leave for an extended trip to Mexico, he decided first to visit an old friend who had married a man of Taos Pueblo.

Arriving at Christmastime in 1920, Collier was transfixed by the beauty of the surroundings and transformed by a vision of the pueblo as a model for reinvigorating Indian life. Taos Pueblo's hardy blend of individualism and communal support and its respect for each stage of life pointed the way, Collier believed, to an alternative present and a brighter future for Native Americans. "They had what the world has lost," Collier said of the Taos people. "What the world has lost, the world must have again, lest it die."

But Collier also became aware of the pressures for change that could so alter native life as to destroy it—specifically, proposed federal legislation that put the burden of proving land ownership on the Pueblo Indians. The proposal amounted to a land grab, and in an effort to stop it, the 19 New Mexico pueblos met in council for the first time since 1680, when they had united to drive out the Spanish. Among their ardent supporters was Collier, who in May 1923 organized the American In-

◄Preceding page: Benjamin Marrowbone, an Oglala Sioux born in a tepee in 1883, poses here at age 102 with a great-great-grand-nephew. As a young man (below), he rode in Buffalo Bill's Wild West Show, went to Rome, and met the pope.

dian Defense Association, a small but influential pressure group that was partially successful in blocking the legislation. Soon Collier was embroiled in other Native American issues—writing, speaking out, and lobbying against what he considered misdirected federal policies and the incompetence of the Bureau of Indian Affairs (BIA).

> I knew an old Indian at this time who was being forced to leave his tent and go live in a new house. They told him that he would be more comfortable there and that they had to burn up his old tent because it was unsanitary. He looked thin and feeble, but he put up a terrific fight.
>
> —*John Fire Lame Deer, Oglala Sioux*

By 1926 Secretary of the Interior Hubert Work had heard enough of reformers' clamor to commission the independent Institute for Governmental Research to conduct a thorough study of contemporary Indian living conditions. Lewis Meriam of the University of Chicago headed the research, which included seven months of field work. The report, "The Problem of Indian Administration," was issued in February 1928.

"An overwhelming majority of the Indians

are poor, even extremely poor," the Meriam report concluded, "and they are not adjusted to the economic and social system of the dominant white civilization." Though restrained in tone, the report, with its litany of blunt, bleak facts—broken families, alcohol abuse, crowded boarding schools unable to prepare students for life either on or off the reservation, health care that produced appallingly high rates of disease—amounted to a sweeping indictment of the BIA. It called for more federal funds and better administration of the Bureau, but it raised no objection to a keystone of government policy—allotment, the distribution of tribal land to individual Indians in an attempt to make farmers of them. Indians, the report concluded, must still learn to adjust to "the dominant white civilization."

Collier, rejecting what he considered this endorsement of the status quo, urged Washington to recognize the intrinsic value of native cultures. Rather than merely imposing its own policies, he suggested, the government should involve the Indians themselves in the planning process. Collier outlined an ambitious program to enhance the status of all Indians, giving them responsibility for their own well-being and guaranteeing them the land essential to their survival.

Collier was not without foes—white farmers and ranchers who wanted free access to Indian land, missionaries opposed to tribal religions, even Indians who thought Collier wanted to preserve them as museum exhibits. One critic charged that his "schemes for reviving tribalism would wipe out most of the gains of the past 50 years." For once, however, a reformer had the chance to turn rhetoric into reality. At the start of Franklin D. Roosevelt's administration in 1933, the outsider became insider; John Collier, the outspoken critic, was named commissioner of Indian Affairs.

An Indian New Deal

Eager to launch a comprehensive reform program, Collier helped draft legislation that was signed into law as the Indian Reorganization Act (IRA) on June 18, 1934. Lengthy and ambitious, the act affected virtually every aspect of Indian life. It reversed the controversial land allotment policy, thus helping ensure the integrity of tribal lands, and it provided for the organization of tribal corporations and governments. One provision established a separate Indian version of the Civilian Conservation Corps, which put youth to work on public projects. Another set up a $10 million fund to promote economic enterprise, extend loans for vocational training, and provide special funding for Indian youth in public schools. The law spelled out programs to revive tribal languages and encourage native arts and crafts. Indians were to be given preference in filling BIA positions.

> The immediate impact of the IRA was not great, even though the Pueblos supported it. I suspect they did so because they regarded John Collier as a great and true friend.
>
> —*Alfonso Ortiz, San Juan Pueblo*

Writing laws was one thing; applying them, another. During congressional debates over the IRA, it became clear that the Oklahoma tribes, all without reservations since 1906—and most with members who had already made the transition into white culture—distrusted the "Indian New Deal." Collier, said one Oklahoma spokesman, was "seeking to frustrate the opportunity of the Indian to enter American life as a citizen."

The new commissioner also had trouble persuading other individual tribes to sign up with the IRA programs, as the legislation required. Between 1934 and 1936, 181 of the tribes or bands that held referendums accepted the IRA—but 77 others rejected it. As a result, less than 40 percent of the U.S. Indian population became eligible for IRA programs. Perhaps most galling for Collier was the decision of the Navajo to decline the offer. The nation's most populous tribe, the Navajo occupied the largest reservation, yet they narrowly rejected inclusion. So did another highly visible group, the Iroquois of New York State.

Still, Collier's work had some salutary results—most notably, stopping the allotment of land. Many tribes whose members were languishing without hope on remote reservations received vital aid: business loans, jobs, education, improved housing and health, and reorganized tribal governments that helped rekindle pride and a sense of worth. Apache leader Clarence Wosley, when asked about the Collier era, said that "the IRA was the best thing that ever happened to Indian tribes. It gave them the right to self-government." For many years, he remembered, the San Carlos Apache community held a celebration on June 18 to commemorate the signing of the act.

On the other hand, critics like Ramon Roubideaux, a Sioux, attacked the "socialistic" aspect of the IRA in setting Indian people "apart from the mainstream of American life." The IRA had the unhappy effect, Roubideaux said, of telling the Indian that "he was a problem from the very day he was born and, as he grew older, that he wasn't able to compete."

The advent of World War II dealt Collier's reforms a devastating blow. Congress, casting about for funds, slashed Indian appropriations. More than 800 regular BIA employees were drafted into military service or moved to other federal agencies directly tied to the war effort. Though Collier held his position until 1945—the longest tenure of any commissioner in history—his days as a reformer were effectively ended.

The Florida Seminole have taken the art of sewing patchwork designs on clothing and fabric to the highest levels of contemporary style.

THE UNBREAKABLE CODE

The U.S. Marine Corps had a secret weapon against Japan in World War II: the 420 Navajo code talkers who fought all the way from Guadalcanal to Okinawa. Using a blend of everyday Navajo speech and some 400 specially devised code words, they transmitted messages that completely baffled the enemy. Bombers were *jaysho* ("buzzards"); bombs, *ayeshi* ("eggs"); battleship was *lotso* ("whale"); destroyer, *calo* ("shark"); submarine, *beshlo* ("iron fish"). In a coded alphabet the Navajo word for "ant" was the letter *A*, the word for "bear" was *B*, and so on; thus, a place such as Bloody Ridge was spelled out with the Navajo words for Bear, Lamb, Onion, Dog, Yucca, Rabbit, Ice, Dog, Goat, and Elk. In keeping with a language that was rarely written, there was no code book. Until trained, even new Navajo recruits could not break encrypted messages.

Initially skeptical about the unconventional code, Marine officers finally had to acknowledge its effectiveness. "Without the Navajos," said one, "the Marines would never have taken Iwo Jima." In addition to the Navajo, there were Hopi (such as Private Floyd Dann, inset), Lakota, Sauk and Fox, Oneida, Chippewa, and Comanche code talkers in Europe and the Pacific.

Joining the War Effort

The Japanese air attack that surprised Pearl Harbor on Sunday morning, December 7, 1941, brought a swift response from the United States government: Congress declared war the next day. But some of the nation's citizens—Native Americans, as it happened—reacted even more quickly. In a rural area of northeastern Oklahoma, just hours after the radio reports about Pearl Harbor, war drums summoned members of the Osage tribe to repel the enemy. During the months and years that followed, the Osage saw many of their young people off to war and sought other ways to contribute to the defense effort.

Chief Fred Lookout presided over ceremonies at which warriors' names were bestowed on the tribe's men (and, in a departure from tradition, women) who entered the armed forces. By April 1943 there were 381 Osage in uniform, the most prominent among whom was Clarence L. Tinker. Before his combat death in 1942, Tinker had been made a major general in the Army Air Corps—the first Native American to achieve a general's rank since the Civil War, when Ely Parker, a Seneca, served as one of Ulysses S. Grant's closest aides and Stand Watie, a Cherokee, was the last Confederate general to surrender.

More than 200 Osage were employed in airplane factories located in Tulsa, the city nearest Osage County, where most of the tribespeople lived. Those who remained at home collected scrap metal, rolled bandages, and staged victory dances celebrating the exploits of tribal combatants. Using some of their remaining oil wealth from the 1920's, the Osage bought war bonds in quantity and added a distinctive flair to their defense effort by negotiating the purchase of a training airplane for the Army Air Corps.

Native Americans from tribes across the nation participated in the war effort with a similar spirit. Partially because of the previous generation's outstanding volunteer effort in World War I, Congress had granted U.S. citizenship to all Indians in 1924. As a result, native men between the ages of 21 and 35 were eligible for the draft and registered under the Selective Training and Service Act of September 16, 1940.

When the fighting stopped in 1945, about 25,000 Indian men had served, as had nearly

When I came back and went through the war deeds ceremony, lo and behold, I had completed the four requirements to become a chief.

— Joseph Medicine Crow, Crow veteran of World War II

1,000 Indian women. More than a third of all physically able Indian men between 18 and 50 saw duty, while the proportion reached 70 percent in some tribes.

⤳

> At the reception center I was thinking that I must be speaking the very worst broken English. But later when we were writing letters, one of the white men asked how you spell some easy word.... Then I realized that not every white man is well educated.
> — *Zuni veteran*

⤳

While thousands donned service uniforms, more than 46,000 Indians left their tribal homelands to engage in war-related work, often in nonagricultural jobs. At least 12,000 Indian women were employed in off-reservation jobs by 1943, and those who stayed at home took over traditional male tasks such as feeding livestock and driving trucks. Men and women alike often found life away from the reservation unsettling. It was the first time many of them had ever seen a city or experienced life as a member of a minority group.

For the scattered thousands, the exodus from their tribal homes usually meant learning better English and acquiring new skills, such as using a telephone and balancing a checkbook. But as more and more native people started buying cars, getting used to indoor plumbing, and shopping in supermarkets and department stores, the material drawbacks of reservation life became more and more obvious.

At war's end the veterans and home-front workers faced a painful choice—continue to live in mainstream America, with all its benefits and tensions, or return to the reservation. Many who decided to return discovered that conditions had grown even worse. Wartime shortages and reduced government spending

Navajo artist Quincy Tahoma captured the joy of a soldier coming home on furlough.

In protest of Nazi Germany's aggression in Europe, four Arizona tribes—Navajo, Apache, Papago (now Tohono O'odham), and Hopi—banned the swastika, an ancient native symbol, from their blanket and basket designs. Hopi Fred Kabotie (left) and Apache Miguel Flores signed the document proclaiming the ban in February 1940.

359

Badges of Pride and Protest

Colleges, charities, foundations, protest groups—Native Americans today proclaim their identity with many of the same signs and devices used by their ancestors centuries ago. Some figures—an artist's motif, a military shoulder patch—are direct transcriptions. Others freely adapt from ancient themes. Each conveys its own message for 20th-century America.

Two ant people evoking Anasazi figures hold hands on a ceramic seed pot made by K. Aragon of Acoma.

The emblem of Oglala Lakota College in South Dakota includes crossed peace pipes against a feathered shield.

Troops of the 45th Infantry Division proudly wore this thunderbird shoulder patch during World War II.

Among the graffiti left by militants at Alcatraz in 1969 was this powerful, enigmatic bird sign.

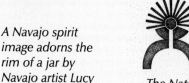

A logo worn by supporters of the American Indian Movement turns the feathered warbonnet on an Indian-head nickel into a V-for-Victory sign.

Acoma potter B. J. Cerno painted a Mimbres lizard figure on a 1981 polychrome jar.

A Navajo spirit image adorns the rim of a jar by Navajo artist Lucy Leuppe McKelvey.

The National Museum of the American Indian adopted a logo with a sunlike headdress resting solidly on Mother Earth, by Chippewa designer Larry DesJarlais.

An Ohio activist carried this weeping death's head insignia in a 1990 protest march.

The predominantly Mexican-American United Farm Workers Union features a thunderbird in its insignia.

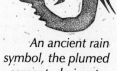

An ancient rain symbol, the plumed serpent, designates the New Mexico-based Archaeological Conservancy.

for Indian programs had both taken a toll. Large tracts of Indian land had been expropriated for military use, reducing the size of reservation holdings by about a million acres. At the same time, Indians in many places continued to face blatant racial discrimination. In New Mexico and Arizona, state law prevented them from voting. Returning veterans were denied GI loans. Prohibition, long since abandoned across the nation, was still imposed by federal decree on many reservations: "Look," said one former soldier, "I have a false eye, cheekbone, a silver plate in my head, but I can't buy liquor in a bar like any American."

An End to Guardianship

Something had to change. But just what, exactly—and how? As early as 1944, the House Committee on Indian Affairs was calling for repeal of the Collier-era initiatives and a rollback of New Deal federal programs. Everyone seemed to agree that the old trustee relationship between Native Americans and the federal government should come to an end—that "government should get out of the Indian business," as a slogan of the day put it.

A first step, hailed by Indian advocates and political conservatives alike, was the Indian Claims Commission, created in 1946 to settle outstanding grievances. These included treaty disputes, conflicts over Indian trust funds, unresolved land claims and the like, some dating back to colonial times.

> The earth was placed here for us…and we consider her our Mother. How much would you ask for if your Mother had been harmed? No amount of money can repay. Money cannot give birth to anything.
>
> —*Asa Bazhonoodah, Navajo*

The commission expected to finish work in five years' time; when it finally ceased operation in 1978, some of the hundreds of complex cases that had been filed were still unresolved. Furthermore, while the government handed out roughly $1 billion in payment for confiscated tribal lands, it gave back no lost territory. Thus, as late as 1994, Sioux tribes were refusing to accept the $100 million offered for their beloved Black Hills—holding out instead for restoration of the land.

Other tribes, bypassing the Indian Claims Commission, were more fortunate. Through litigation and congressional lobbying, Taos Pueblo in 1970 regained 48,000 acres, including its sacred Blue Lake, which had been incorporated into Carson National Forest in 1906. Maine's Passamaquoddy and Penobscot tribes received federal funds to buy 300,000 acres (in lieu of the two-thirds of the state they claimed); a $27 million trust fund helped them establish commercial farms and light industries. In Washington State, the Yakama (the original spelling of their name was formally restored in 1992) were awarded 21,000 acres adjacent to Mount Adams.

The strongest postwar advocate of severing the bonds between tribes and government was the new commissioner of Indian Affairs, Dil-

lon S. Myer. During the war Myer had been in charge of the mass detention of Japanese-Americans, and to him reservations were little better than concentration camps. He wanted to "free" the Indians from all forms of government patronage and control and blend them into the general population. Federal programs under the Indian Reorganization Act—including health, economic, and educational benefits—would be phased out. No longer wards of the state, the Indians would learn to fend for themselves. The buzzword for the new policy was "termination." The results were nothing short of disastrous.

"I make things out of memories," says Aleut painter Alvin Amason, who dedicated this 1985 oil to the memory of his father, a trapper, bear guide, and fisherman. Its title: "Papa Would Like You."

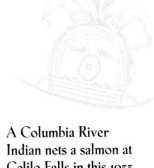

A Columbia River Indian nets a salmon at Celilo Falls in this 1955 photo. Two years later backwater from a massive dam flooded this prized fishing site. Fishermen from the Nez Perce, Yakama, and other area tribes each got $3,500 in damages—but the issue is still being hotly contested.

COME TO DENVER

THE CHANCE OF YOUR LIFETIME!

Good Jobs
Retail Trade
Manufacturing
Government-Federal, State, Local
Wholesale Trade
Construction of Buildings, Etc.

Happy Homes
Beautiful Houses
Many Churches
Exciting Community Life
Over Half of Homes Owned by Residents
Convenient Stores- Shopping Centers

Training
Vocational Training
Auto Mech., Beauty Shop, Drafting,
Nursing, Office Work, Watchmaking
Adult Education
Evening High School, Arts and Crafts
Job Improvement, Home- making

Beautiful Colorado
"Tallest" State, 48 Mt. Peaks Over 14,000 Ft.
350 Days Sunshine, Mild Winters
Zoos, Museums, Mountain Parks, Drives
Picnic Areas, Lakes, Amusement Parks
Big Game Hunting, Trout Fishing, Camping

With promotional leaflets such as this, the Bureau of Indian Affairs sought to lure Native Americans from their reservations to urban areas in the 1950's.

I nearly went crazy during the first two weeks. . . . No matter where I was, I always had to be somewhere else at a certain time. There was no rest.

— Crow Creek Sioux

Multiculturalism, nineties style: Hualapai photographer Randy Mike, age 10, took this cheerful shot on his Arizona reservation of friends who combine "Native" and "American" without even trying.

The extensive timber holdings of southern Oregon's Klamath Indians made them a prime candidate for termination. A tribally owned lumber mill earned the average family $4,000 annually—a respectable income in the mid-1950's. There was just one catch. Termination would officially end the Klamath's tribal status; their $100 million lumber enterprise would then be treated like any ordinary business corporation. Tribe members could continue to run it. Or they could sell it and split the proceeds

They voted to sell in return for a per-capita settlement of $43,000. "It was like throwing steak to the dogs," remembered one tribe member. With the cash soon spent, the people sank into unemployment and alcoholism. Although the tribe regained federal recognition in 1986, recent statistics show that 70 percent of Klamaths still live below the poverty level.

Termination of the Wisconsin Menominee tribe in 1961 proved equally traumatic. "No amount of explanation or imagination prior to termination could have prepared us for the shock of what these losses meant," one tribesman said as he saw the reservation hospital closing for lack of funds, desirable lakefront property being sold to whites, and young people abandoning their homeland for the cities. By 1968, 50 percent of the Menominee people who stayed behind were on welfare.

Along with termination came a policy of relocating native people to urban centers. The program was voluntary, and at first few stepped forward. Some of those who did made serious efforts to find jobs and get ahead, but most were simply curious about city life. What they found—crowds and telephones, elevators, checking accounts, even alarm clocks—was alien enough to send many back to the reservation. And there waited another culture shock. One newly returned Cherokee found himself waking in the middle of the night. "It puzzled me until I began to realize: It was quiet, that's what was wrong," he later recalled, "no fire engines or police sirens passing by, no street noises."

More than 100,000 Indians relocated to cities between 1952 and 1972, and nearly a third returned to their tribal homes. Others shuttled back and forth, unable to decide. A Crow Indian interviewed in 1974 had switched 10 times in 20 years between Long Beach, California, and his Montana reservation—lonely for his tribe, yet hungering for the comforts and excitement of the city. Children in San Francisco's Native American community, asked about life on the reservation, replied that it was a place where only Indians lived and where everyone was happy.

> Why is it so important that Indians be brought into the "mainstream of American life"? I would not know how to interpret the phrase to my people. The closest I would be able to come would be "a big, wide river." Am I then to tell my people that they will be thrown into the Big Wide River of the United States?
>
> — Earl Old Person,
> Blackfeet tribal chairman

Some critics of relocation, Indian and non-Indian alike, later defended the experience. "The relocation program was excellent for some people," declared Robert L. Bennett, an Oneida commissioner of Indian Affairs under President Lyndon Johnson. "The mistake was trying to make it successful for everybody."

More importantly, living together in cities helped usher in the next phase of development—a pan-Indian movement in which Native Americans rose above tribal differences to forge a common identity. Also, for the first time, they became aware that they shared concerns with other dispossessed and exiled groups, such as African-Americans. As Phileo Nash, President Kennedy's commissioner of Indian Affairs, put it: "Relocation created a generation of streetwise people. The Red Power movement, the confrontations on reservations, were direct outgrowths of the intimate contact that had developed between blacks and Indians in the cities."

SKYWALKERS

For generations, Mohawk ironworkers from eastern Canada and New York State have pieced together the struts and girders of today's suspension bridges and high-rise cityscapes. Their first job, in 1850, put a bridge across the St. Lawrence River at Montreal. Says Tom Diabo, whose grandfather worked on it:

> You know how Mohawks love to build things. So when the men from the town were watching the bridge being built, some of the younger guys just climbed right up to take a closer look. The Frenchmen were so scared they had to hold on to everything they could so they wouldn't fall off. But the guys from town just walked along the supports looking the job over, checking out how it was done. That is how we got into the construction trade.

Walking the high steel of Sault Ste. Marie Bridge in Michigan in 1888, the tribe's first casualty, Joe Diabo, plunged to his death. But the Mohawks went on, putting up the Empire State Building and thousands of other structures. Writer, curator, and former third-generation ironworker Richard Hill, writes in his book *Skywalkers*:

> You remember how windy it was, how the whole building shook in the wind. . . you hate that wind, you lean into it, then, suddenly, it's gone, and you're staring below.

But for Hill it was all in a day's work:

> The crane starts up with a big, smoky roar. The raising gang straps on their belts....Up you go. The impact wrenches hammer away on the bolts, turning the nuts, shaking the whole floor. They are already sending the next beam up. You steady yourself, hold the beam and guide it in place —slowly, slowly, there! You grab a bolt from your bag and make the connection. Here comes the next piece, and the next, up to 50 times a day. Tomorrow you will set even more....You'll show these guys what Ironworking is all about.

Richard Glazer-Danay, Mohawk artist, celebrated the skywalker spirit in this painted hard hat (1982).

Ready to Explode: Red Power

One of the earliest political action groups was the National Congress of American Indians, founded in the closing days of World War II. In June 1961 the NCAI gathered nearly 500 delegates from 90 separate communities, at the University of Chicago to ponder the direction of Indian affairs. After much deliberation the conferees produced a Declaration of Indian Purpose, which demanded an end to the government's termination policy and full native participation in the planning of all Indian-related programs.

For younger militants at the conference, this was not enough. Angered by the willingness of many tribal elders—"Uncle Tomahawks," they were called—to work within the system, the young bloods determined to move out on their own. Ten leaders met in Gallup, New Mexico, in 1961 to found the National Indian Youth Council (NIYC), and they selected a Paiute graduate student, Mel Thom, to be their principal spokesman. His message was simple and direct: confront the enemy.

The young militants could point to some tragic facts of life in Indian America: an average life expectancy of 40, the result of disease, alcoholism, and malnutrition; infant mortality rates twice the national average; unemployment 10 times higher than the rest of America; the worst teenage suicide rate in the country —the sad litany went on and on.

> As I look around at the Indian situation, it looks like one big seething cauldron ready to explode.
>
> —Robert K. Thomas, Cherokee

There were recent precedents for the NIYC's brand of activism. Mohawks from New York State's St. Regis Reservation publicly defied a court order during 1957 protests over government intrusions on tribal sovereignty. A year later a posse of Lumbee Indians of North Carolina—many of part African-American descent—stormed a Ku Klux Klan hate rally and sent members fleeing. This kind of aggressiveness tended to make tribal elders uncomfortable, but as protests intensified in the 1960's some of the early skeptics were swept up in the heady spirit of Red Power.

The Red Power movement announced itself loudly and clearly (above), inspired by such moments as the unfurling of a banner (top) seized by North Carolina Lumbee men at a 1958 Ku Klux Klan rally. Fueling the militancy was the sort of poverty visible in a Sioux home (right) in North Dakota—and everywhere else in Native America.

Their tactics were new, but the causes they took up had old roots. Despite more than 370 treaties and thousands of laws, rulings, and edicts meant to enforce them, Indians were still being treated as second-class citizens. Red Power advocates sought little in the way of new legislation—just enforcement of what was already on the books.

In the Pacific Northwest, for example, nearly all native lands had been ceded to the United States in the 19th century; at the same time, the treaties stipulated that tribal peoples

A canvas tepee set up on Alcatraz Island during the 1969 takeover overlooks Golden Gate Bridge, and a small Native American (above) shows where he stands on Indian rights.

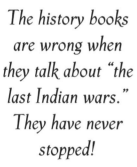

The history books are wrong when they talk about "the last Indian wars." They have never stopped!

—*Laura McCloud, Tulalip*

would retain fishing and hunting rights. Often these rights had been little exercised or even forgotten—but no more. Through the mid-1960's, Northwest Coast Indians clashed repeatedly with sportsmen and game wardens over the issue of fishing rights. "Fish-ins" to protest state-imposed limits on the tribes' annual catch led to pitched battles—Indian oars versus police clubs—on Washington's Nisqually River. The issue would take years to resolve, but the battle had begun.

> The scene that greeted the Alcatraz Indians seemed right out of a Keystone Kop movie. Ships, motor boats, sailing yachts, launches, dinghies, cutters—all heading toward them. . . .TV and radio bulletins had spread the word through the Bay Area and beyond. One bold headline proclaimed: "Indians Invade Alcatraz; U.S. Plans Counter-Attack."
> —*Adam Fortunate Eagle, Red Lake Chippewa*

The event that most galvanized public opinion was the takeover of Alcatraz Island in San Francisco Bay. Seventy-eight Indian activists made a predawn landing on November 20, 1969—claiming the former prison site

under the terms of an 1868 treaty that promised to return unused federal property to Indian control. The occupation lasted until June 1971 and drew worldwide attention.

Among the native groups that took part in the Alcatraz action was the American Indian Movement. AIM had started in 1968 with a program, modeled after the Black Panthers, to monitor police harassment of the urban Indian community in Minneapolis. It soon had chapters in San Francisco, Los Angeles, Denver, Chicago, and Cleveland.

Two men emerged as AIM's most visible leaders: Dennis Banks, an Anishinabe Ojibwa from Minneapolis, and Russell Means, an Oglala Lakota. Both had been born on reservations, and both had lived on the margins of white society—Banks serving time in jail for armed robbery, Means drifting in and out of schools and part-time jobs. Now, in their thirties, they found a new focus for their energies.

Well aware of the power of publicity, AIM militants seized the *Mayflower* replica at Plymouth, Massachusetts, on Thanksgiving Day 1970—and painted Plymouth Rock red for good measure. The following Fourth of July,

Means staged an AIM "countercelebration" atop the presidential faces carved on Mount Rushmore, demanding the return of Lakota lands in the Black Hills.

〜

I watched what they were doing, and I could see the pride in these young men and women....Then I looked at myself. I was making money and living in White suburbia....I started letting my hair grow long, and I stopped wearing a tie and started to sort of deprogram myself.

—*Vernon Bellecourt, Ojibwa*

〜

The actions continued. Demanding justice, Banks and Means led 1,300 followers from the Pine Ridge and Rosebud reservations to the town of Gordon, Nebraska, to force officials to jail the murderers of Raymond Yellow Thunder. In the dead of winter, the 51-year-old Sioux had been stripped of his pants and as-

Armed tribesmen at Wounded Knee stand watch outside the Episcopal church where a fellow defender in the bitter 1973 siege was fatally shot. History had come full circle: 83 years earlier nearly 250 Sioux had died here when fired on by the U.S. Army.

saulted by a group of drunken whites at the local American Legion hall; his frozen body was later found in a pickup truck.

On the eve of the 1972 presidential election, AIM joined eight other Indian organizations on the Trail of Broken Treaties, a massive cross-country march on Washington. Three automobile caravans set out from the West Coast, picking up Indian protesters on the way, and reached the nation's capital on November 1. Their goal was nothing less than sweeping reform of U.S. policy, including full sovereignty for all Indian tribes.

Denied meetings with high-level government officials, some 500 demonstrators seized the headquarters of the Bureau of Indian Affairs, renaming it Native American Embassy. For six days they occupied it, setting up barricades of furniture and equipment and rummaging through BIA files.

Wounded Knee II

Indian militancy reached its high point in 1973 at a fitting spot—near Wounded Knee Creek on the Pine Ridge Reservation in South Dakota, site of the 1890 massacre (still officially a "battle" in U.S. Army records) of almost 250 Sioux men, women, and children by Custer's old unit, the 7th Cavalry.

The new confrontation began as a dispute over local Sioux politics. When the conservative reservation chairman, Richard Wilson, banned all AIM activities from Pine Ridge, Russell Means began campaigning to remove him from office. Various tribal factions maneuvered for power. Eventually, on February 28, armed AIM members moved into the hamlet of Wounded Knee, took over the church and general store—and declared their independence from the United States.

During two months of occupation they were surrounded by the largest array of government forces to confront Native Americans in this century, and two Indians were killed in sporadic exchanges of gunfire. The conflict ended without further bloodshed—but not before the nation's long-buried history of injustice

Demonstrators carried banners, calumets, and bundles of purifying sage to mark the 10th anniversary of Wounded Knee II. "Ghost Dance I" (bottom), a mixed-media collage by Diosa Summers (Santa Clara Pueblo), recalls the death of Chief Big Foot at Wounded Knee.

toward its native people had been brought into the light. Whatever they thought of AIM's tactics, the vast majority of American Indians heralded what became known as Wounded Knee II for focusing attention on their cause.

> Anywhere Indians are standing up for themselves . . . that's where you'll find the American Indian Movement.
>
> —*Russell Means, Oglala Lakota*

Looking back, I really believed that the broken hoop was mended at Wounded Knee, and that the water was being given to the tree of life. Wounded Knee was an attempt to help an entire race survive.

—*Dennis Banks, Anishinabe Ojibwa*

367

A Hopi kachina imaged in silver and turquoise adorns a ring made by Navajo jeweler Philip Long in 1960.

YOUNGER THAN YESTERDAY: OLD ARTS, NEW HANDS

A pioneer of today's Native American artistic renaissance, Pueblo potter Maria Martinez cradles a magnificent example of her classic polished blackware.

Haida artist Robert Davidson created the wolf mask headdress shown above from red cedar, copper, shell, bark, and eagle feathers.

This 1986 ceramic piece by Lois Gutierrez de la Cruz of Santa Clara Pueblo is entitled "Tall Pot with Lady Bugs and Salamander."

At the end of the 19th century, it was widely believed that Native American art had long since reached its peak—destroyed by the arrival of Europeans and the confinement of scores of tribes on reservations. Condescendingly labeled as "primitive," it was usually relegated to museum displays showing how Indians once lived.

All this began to change in the 1920's and 1930's with the revival of traditional crafts by artisans on widely scattered tribal lands. Private collectors and museum curators discovered their works and put them on display. In the forefront were potters like Pueblos Maria and Julian Martinez and painters like Oscar Howe, a Sioux. Together they transformed tribal techniques and styles into vibrant new artistic statements.

Other traditional crafts—basketry, weaving, wood carving, jewelry making, beadwork—have likewise been revitalized. The basic materials have scarcely changed, but what native skills and imaginations have been producing in the second half of the 20th century measures up to the best work of any culture. "I get very upset when I hear people say that weaving is a dying art and that nobody is doing it," says Susan Billy, a leading Pomo basket weaver, "because I'm here, I'm doing it."

A Navajo pictorial rug designed by Nadine Nez and woven by Bruce T. Nez holds 82 birds and flowers, along with a cornstalk growing from a ceremonial basket.

Beaded tennis shoes by Teri Greeves (Kiowa/Cheyenne) are a cross-cultural extravaganza: the tepee is Sioux, the crossed boxes are Cheyenne, and the giant antlered jackalope is a Southwestern folk creature.

WHAT TO CELEBRATE?

The 500th anniversary of Christopher Columbus's 1492 landfall in America was meant to be a year-long festival of nonstop global merrymaking. Spain hosted Expo '92, the Dominican Republic built an enormous lighthouse, and a pair of $50 million movies retold the story. But as Columbus Day drew near, sounds of protest grew steadily louder; in bringing Europe to America, as historians now point out, the explorer caused the death of millions and destroyed entire cultures. Says Seneca educator Stephanie Betancourt: "For Native Americans, every Columbus Day is like salt in our wounds. These are days of mourning."

So the world took a second look. Instead of parades and fireworks, many communities held sit-ins and teach-ins. Indian rights groups staged countermarches (below). The city of Berkeley, California, declared Indigenous People's Day and premiered an opera, *Get Lost (Again), Columbus,* by White Cloud Wolfhawk. In schools the once-heroic navigator was recast as a villain. Everywhere his image changed. Tlingit artist Jesse Cooday imposed his own face on a traditional Columbus portrait (above). No longer was he the discoverer of America; as one student put it: "The Indians discovered the Spanish when they came in."

Sovereignty and Self-Reliance

The militant activism of the Red Power movement could only accomplish so much; real and lasting change would be harder to secure. One unexpected champion was President Richard Nixon, who in 1970 outlined a policy of Indian self-determination. "Indians will get better programs," the president said, "if the people who are most affected by these programs are responsible for operating them." Thus prompted, Congress passed legislation to repeal termination and strengthen tribal governments. Funds were set aside to prepare native leaders to administer programs formerly run by the Bureau of Indian Affairs and other agencies.

The new measures hardly solved all the problems of Native America, but they at least confirmed that the BIA's old paternalism was a relic of the past. "Sovereignty" became the watchword of the moment, a term that to Indians meant reasserting treaty-protected rights to determine their own futures. Some of the same energy that propelled the militancy of the 1960's and early 1970's was redirected into the quieter channels of the law. Across the country, tribal attorneys filed suits that resurrected old treaties—and in the process raised issues with far-reaching implications.

In 1979 a federal judge concluded from an analysis of old treaties that 25 tribes in Washington State were entitled to half of each year's salmon catch in Puget Sound. In Michigan, meanwhile, another judge's review of a 19th-century treaty upheld special privileges for Chippewa spear fishermen. And in one of the most watched claims cases, some 3,000 members of the Passamaquoddy and Penobscot tribes in Maine were awarded "aboriginal title" to almost two-thirds of the state. Ultimately, the lawsuit that began as an object of scorn (and a source of material for stand-up comedians) ended in a 1980 out-of-court settlement giving the tribes more than 300,000 acres and a $27 million trust fund.

Reclaiming a Heritage

He was an unlikely visitor to Manhattan, the aged Hopi priest who flew in from Arizona in 1989 for the opening of the gala Fall Antiques Show. But he was on a special mission. And he had the FBI with him.

Stopping at a museum exhibit that was part of the show, the old man peered intently at a mask on display: a 39-inch yucca-fiber disc covered by deerskin, painted with green, red, black, and white pigments and topped with a crown of braided cornhusks and feathers. He nodded to his FBI escort, confirming that this was what they had come for. Then he reached into a leather pouch at his neck. Pulling out a handful of coarsely ground corn, he sprinkled the white grains over the mask, symbolically feeding its spirit. "You have your God," he murmured in Hopi to the puzzled crowd that had gathered. "This is ours."

When he was done, the FBI agent confiscated the mask as evidence and served a museum official with a subpoena to appear before a grand jury in Phoenix. It soon was revealed that the mask, which represented a kachina, or sacred spirit, had been illegally removed from Old Oraibi village on the Hopi Reservation in Arizona. How or when it had been tak-

en was not known, but a Santa Fe dealer later sold it to a collector for $75,000, then borrowed it back for the museum exhibit.

> It's our stuff. We made it and we know best how to use it and care for it. And now we're going to get it back.
> —*John Pretty on Top, Crow*

The recovery of what the Hopi called their spirit friend was one episode in a growing nationwide movement among Native Americans to reclaim their cultural heritage—particularly to take back sacred objects seized by whites in the past and held in public collections. Their right to do so, established by earlier court rulings, was enlarged in 1990 by the Native American Graves Protection and Repatriation Act. It required some 5,000 federally

Hopi elder Mike Gashwazra (above) identified the stolen kachina after its return to Arizona. He had last seen it during a ceremony at Old Oraibi village (top) 60 years earlier.

I'm out here trying to pray for rain, but my praying is not doing any good with all these kachinas missing.
—*Mike Gashwazra, Hopi*

funded institutions and U.S. agencies to return Indian skeletons, funerary and religious objects, and other important artifacts to their rightful native owners. The very fact that such objects were ever in alien hands is painful for many people to contemplate. "What would America think," Curtis Zunigha, a Delaware/ Isleta Pueblo, asks rhetorically, "if Indian archeologists went to Arlington National Cemetery and dug up the graves of war heroes to study the clothing they wore?"

By early 1994 the funerary remains started going back home. Chicago's Field Museum sent the first 62 of its 2,000 exhumations; the Smithsonian Institution dispatched 2,000 of its 14,000 skeletons, with the rest to follow; the University of Tennessee repatriated 190 sets of Cherokee remains disinterred during a Tennessee Valley Authority dam construction; the University of Minnesota returned 150 bodies to the Devil's Lake Sioux.

At Busby, Montana, tribespeople turned out in force to reclaim and provide a proper burial for the skulls of 24 Cheyennes killed in 1878 while trying to escape from Fort Robinson, Nebraska. The skulls had rested for more than a century at three Eastern museums. Now, finally, they reached the destination the fugitives had been seeking.

> I look at these things as sacred objects. I don't look at them as just things—a legging, or shirt, or shield. It was a good feeling to know that I was able to see and touch something that some of our elders had touched long ago.
>
> —*Abe Conklin, Ponca/Osage*

And in October 1993 a ceremony at once solemn and joyful was held at Jemez Pueblo in New Mexico to mark the return of 86 religious and ceremonial objects from the National Mu-

We are united in urging Congress to support the treaty made in 1794 and refuse to give authority for the destruction of Indian homes.

—*Seneca Council*

Taking a final look, two Seneca elders walk tribal land about to be flooded by construction of the Kinzua Dam. The mid-1960's water project broke a 1794 treaty with the Seneca Nation, inundating 10,000 acres in Pennsylvania and New York; in return, the federal government paid $15 million.

seum of the American Indian in New York. "The Jemez people consider these objects to be living, breathing tribal members and not merely objects," said tribal archeologist William Whatley. "This is a homecoming of 86 tribal members."

Mixed Messages

Hard-won victories in treaty enforcement and repatriation of sacred objects were not always matched in cases concerning native spiritual practices and traditions. In 1978 Congress passed the American Indian Freedom of Religion Act, which allowed Indians to use the skins and feathers of protected wild animals in rituals and legalized the ceremonial use of peyote. It was also intended to preserve Indian sacred land for religious pilgrimages, burials, and vision quests.

The law was greeted by many as an encouraging step forward, one that would broadly apply the same principles that had brought about the return of Blue Lake to Taos Pueblo. Or so it seemed. In reality the law had no teeth to enforce those principles—a fact that became sorely obvious 10 years later, when the U.S. Supreme Court let the Forest Service run a road through the Yurok holy high country in northern California's Siskiyou Mountains.

The Yurok were not the only losers. After a series of battles in state and federal courts, the Navajo and Hopi were unable to block a ski development in their sacred San Francisco Peaks. The Sioux lost exclusive rights to their Black Hills fasting sites. And the Cherokee failed to stop a Tennessee dam that flooded their ancestral townsites—something that other native communities could identify with too well. In Indian country, the U.S. Army Corps of Engineers was second only to the BIA as a symbol of government callousness. The massive hydroelectric dams built by the Engineers represented progress to many Americans. To most Indian Americans they were monuments to the juggernaut of white civilization and its impact on the native world that was already there.

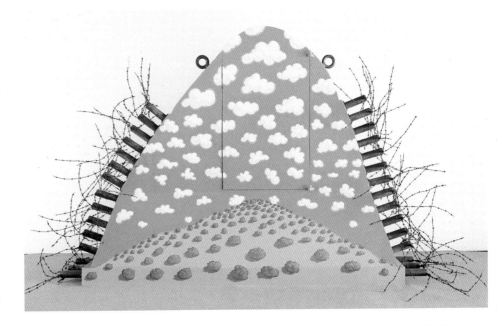

We were about the first to move out of that valley. We had no choice, I guess. Just like a gopher, you know, when they pour water in your house, you better get out or drown. That's how it was. It was very hard leaving the place.

— *Cora Baker, Hidatsa*

Time after time, Indian people across the continent had gone through the experience of being uprooted against their will. They had known the same grief of losing their homes, their sacred places, their ancestors' graves—

In "Border Crossing," a 7,000-pound painted steel construction made in 1991, the Chiricahua Apache/Navajo artist Bob Haozous delivers a complex view of cultural antagonisms—"the borders we create in our minds"—between natives and whites and within many of today's Indian communities.

their history. And they usually had something else in common: a treaty signed at some point in the past guaranteeing them possession of their land forever—"as long as the grass is green and the water runs," the phrase went.

Same Guys, Same Rock

But treaties with Indian tribes had a way of being brushed aside if they became inconvenient to someone influential, which they usually did sooner or later. So it was, as Associate Justice William J. Brennan wrote in his blistering dissent to the Supreme Court's 1988 Yurok decision, that for Native Americans, re-

Elders and friends at Taos, New Mexico, celebrate the return in 1971 of Blue Lake, their most sacred site, after 65 years in U.S. Forest Service hands. By Pueblo tradition, the lake (below) is the earth's navel, through which their ancestors emerged at the dawn of time.

ligious freedom ultimately meant "nothing more than the right to believe that their religion would be destroyed."

We should really be used to these broken promises, but it seems like each one never loses its punch. . . . Sociologists have concluded that when you impose a change on any group of people there are three consequences. One is hostility, one is apathy, and the other is self-destruction. These are good theories. They have all come to pass. I have witnessed these.

—Carl Whitman,
Hidatsa tribal chairman

A more down-to-earth perspective was offered by Sioux author and historian Vine Deloria, Jr., who likened the government's handling of Indian affairs to a grade-B western: "You can go to sleep and miss a long sequence of the action, but every time you look at the screen, it's the same group of guys chasing the other guys around the same rock."

We have no buildings there, no steeples. The lake is our church, the evergreen trees are our living saints. Blue Lake is the heart of our religion.
—*Taos Pueblo elder*

The Court, the Constitution, and "Big Bingo"

A Navajo story of the Creation tells of two groups of creatures vying to establish a world of either total darkness or constant light. To settle the issue they stage a game of hide-and-seek, betting on who will find a disc hidden in a moccasin. When neither side wins, they split the difference, dividing time into halves of daylight and darkness.

In a world that hinged on a bet, it hardly seems surprising that in 1994 the Navajo Nation voted to legalize gambling on its Arizona reservation. The greater surprise, perhaps, is that they took so long to join the ranks of Native American tribes turning to gaming as a source of income. More than a decade earlier, the Seminole of southern Florida had opened a bingo parlor; when state officials padlocked the building, a high-stakes legal battle began.

> We'd better call it Big Bingo these days because it's just not little bingo. It's in the thousands and millions of dollars.
>
> —*Donald L. Fixico, Creek/Seminole/ Shawnee/Sauk and Fox*

A series of court rulings barred states from interfering with bingo operations on tribal lands, and by the mid-1980's Big Bingo was living up to its name. Nationally, revenues were approaching $250 million a year—and because of laws stemming directly from the U.S. Constitution, the money was all tax-free. The next step raised the ante even higher.

In 1980 the Cabazon band of Mission Indians opened a casino on its reservation in Southern California. State officials challenged them, and the case ultimately led to a landmark 1987 Supreme Court ruling in favor of the Cabazon. Unless a state forbade all forms

WE THE PEOPLE: THE POWER OF NAMES

Since earliest times, most Native American tribes have gone by two different names: what they call themselves, and the name given them by outsiders. In most written accounts it is the alien—and often uncomplimentary—designation that has survived. But the people thus described know better. Some examples:

Apache, from a Zuni word meaning "enemy"; to themselves they are Nidé, "The People."

Arapaho, from Pawnee, "he buys or trades"; their self-designation is Hinonoeino, "Big Sky People."

Coeur d'Alene, a French phrase meaning "heart of an awl," referring to their sharpness in trade; originally they were Skitswish, "The People" or "The Discovered People."

Eskimo, from an Abnaki term meaning either "eaters of raw flesh" or, more probably, "snowshoe makers"; most Arctic groups use the local term for "The People"—Yupik in southwest Alaska, Inuit in most of Canada, and others.

Gros Ventre, meaning "big belly" in French; to each other they are Ah-ah-nee-nin, or "White Clay People."

Huron, from 17th-century French for "bristly," a reference to their distinctive headdress; to themselves they were the Wendat or Wyandot, "Island People."

Iroquois, Algonquian for "rattlesnakes"; their own name, Haudenosaunee, means "People of the Longhouse."

Ojibwa (also Ojibway, Ojibwe, Chippewa, and others), meaning "puckered up," from the stitching on a moccasin; originally they were Anishinabe, "Real People."

Papago, meaning "bean eater"; by majority vote and a 1986 revision of the tribal constitution, the proper legal name is now Tohono O'odham, "Desert People."

Sioux, short for the Ojibwa term *nadouessioux,* meaning "adders"; the oldest primary designations are Lakota and Dakota, variant words for "Allies."

Winnebago, from a Sauk and Fox phrase meaning "People of the Dirty Waters"; the tribe's Wisconsin band formally changed its name to Ho-Chunk, "People of the Big Voices," an Iowa term alluding to their oratorical prowess.

375

of gambling (including charity events like "Las Vegas nights"), it must allow recognized tribes to run gaming operations on their lands. With a federal law the next year setting some ground rules, a new era had begun.

> When I walk into that casino, I'm over-whelmed. I think, 'my people did all this.'
> . . . We had a chance to get out of being perpetual victims and we took it.
>
> —*Carol Cornelius, Wisconsin Oneida*

By the end of 1993 there were 124 Indian casinos scattered across 24 states, and in many cases the profits meant self-sufficiency, even prosperity, for tribes long dependent on government subsidies. In Minnesota the Mille Lacs band of Ojibwa had a 45 percent unemployment rate that fell to virtually zero after their casino opened. The Oneida Nation Casino near Green Bay became the largest minority-owned business in Wisconsin. The nearby Menominee used profits from their Wisconsin casino to establish a college so that the tribe's youth could get a higher education without leaving home. And the pioneering Cabazon built a power plant and almost 1,000 units of new housing with some of their profits.

But not all tribes see gaming as a panacea. Factional disputes among the Oneida of upstate New York (in contrast to the Wisconsin Oneida) have spawned bitter confrontations, as have plans made by the Seneca and Mohawk. And for tribes in remote areas there just weren't enough customers to make it work.

Colossus: The Saga of the Pequot

Whatever their opinions on the subject, tribal leaders are well aware of the wealth that reservation gaming can produce. They have only to look to the Mashantucket Pequot of Ledyard, Connecticut. In 1637 a savage assault on the main Pequot settlement by colonial militiamen seemed to accomplish its goal. "By the end of the following year," in the words of one history

Silhouetted against the winter sky, the palatial Foxwoods Casino earned the Mashantucket Pequot $775 million or more in 1994. Inset: a native employee at the Ojibwa's Grand Casino Mille Lacs in Minnesota calls a winning bingo number.

Revenues from Foxwoods support the Pequot Child Development Center (right) and built a new grade school (inset).

book, expressing the generally accepted version, "the Pequots had ceased to be a people."

Well, not quite. True, the once-mighty nation was nearly invisible, having dwindled by the 1970's to a few people living in trailers on a small tract of land. But all that changed in February 1992 with the opening of Foxwoods Resort and Casino. Climaxing a long campaign headed by tribal chairman Richard ("Skip") Heyward, the event triggered a gathering of scattered tribespeople—and a breathtaking influx of wealth. Within a year Foxwoods was bringing in an estimated $26 million a month, tax-free; by 1994 it was one of Connecticut's largest employers. It was also very likely the most profitable casino on earth, with revenues approaching $1 billion a year.

Inevitably there were critics. Foxwoods's non-Indian neighbors worried about a Pequot plan to annex 8,000 acres to the reservation,

property that would no longer be on local tax rolls. Some casino operators in Atlantic City, New Jersey, stung by the competition, questioned the authenticity of the Pequots on racial grounds—they didn't "look like Indians."

❧

Ours is a small tribe, but we have a keen sense of our own history. . . . We have survived, and we now flourish.
— *Richard A. Hayward, chairman Mashantucket Pequot Tribal Nation*

❧

But the state government was happy enough to accept $100 million a year from the

An old man demonstrates tribal traditions to the younger generation in Sioux Oscar Howe's painting "Dakota Teaching."

A lot of our tribes don't know their own traditions, teachings, or ways. And it's a shame . . . because someday your children and grandchildren will ask what their purpose is on Grandmother Earth.
—*Abe Conklin, Ponca/Osage*

In a swirl of color, dance contestants make their grand entry at a powwow held on the Chippewa/Cree Rocky Boy's Reservation in Montana.

I come to a powwow to be an Indian, to get a sense of myself. This is part of Indian spirituality, to help each other and to celebrate with each other. When I come to powwows, I gain strength to carry on with my life.
— *Rachel Snow, Assiniboin*

tribe in lieu of taxes on its slot machine income. And in October 1994 the Smithsonian Institution received a $10 million Pequot donation for the new National Museum of the American Indian, scheduled to open in Washington, D.C., in 2001. It was the largest cash gift in the Smithsonian's 148-year history.

Powwow: Symbol of Renewal

Watching Algonquian medicine men dance, Europeans of the colonial period mistook the name of the dancer, *pauwau,* for the name of the ceremony—and so, in time, the word "powwow" came to be used for any tribal gathering. In the latter part of this century, the powwow has become a dramatic public statement of a renewed Indian identity.

It has roots in a religious ceremony practiced by the Pawnee early in the 19th century and adopted by the Omaha and other tribes, who transformed it into a warrior ceremony and added speechmaking, gift giving, and a concluding feast. By the 1880's some 30 Plains tribes were holding powwows, bringing one-time foes together in peace to establish new friendships and celebrate shared traditions.

If you come to these celebrations, you'll see all our young boys and girls with their feathers on. They are proud . . . proud to be Indians . . . proud to be wearing the eagle feather. And to us, that is very sacred.
—*Hazel Blake, Hidatsa*

For decades powwows essentially remained tribal gatherings. But as they grew in size and number through the 1960's and 1970's, dance styles and costumes evolved

Let the spirits help you.
And they will help you—but you have to
have faith. They'll give you the understanding
and wisdom of your people.

—*Abe Conklin,*
Ponca/Osage

into truly pan-Indian forms, blending details and traditions drawn from numerous tribes. Today the dancers follow an expanding powwow circuit, traveling from Michigan to Texas, Connecticut to California, south Florida to Puget Sound.

One of the biggest powwows is the Red Earth Festival, held each June in Oklahoma City. Its dazzlingly attired contestants compete by age, gender, and style in Fancy, Shawl, Jingle, and other dance categories. The master of ceremonies calls for the audience to rise for the Grand Entry, a spectacle of sound and color that precedes the actual contests.

"We sing to the victories of our grandfathers, of our fathers," he shouts into his cordless microphone. "We sing to victory. We are still here!"

Pride in the Native American renaissance on the eve of a new century is personified by Boye Ladd, a Ho-Chunk (Winnebago) Fancy Dancer.

379

ONE THOUSAND YEARS

A CHRONOLOGY

c. 985–1014 Norsemen, including Eric the Red and Leif Ericson, set up outposts in North America and encounter Eskimos, Beothuks, and Micmacs.

c. 1200–1400 Ancestral Apache and Navajo bands separate from northern Athabascans and migrate to Southwest.

c. 1275 Drought and Athabascan raids lead to abandonment of Anasazi settlements in Southwest.

1492 Christopher Columbus, backed by Spain, reaches San Salvador (Guanahani to the natives), encountering Arawak and Taino people. Thinking he is in India, he calls them Indians.

1497–98 John and Sebastian Cabot explore east coast of North America for England. They kidnap three Micmac men.

c. 1500 European diseases begin killing native North Americans, who have no immunity to them.

1512 Spanish law gives Spanish land grantees the right to make slaves of Indians under the *encomienda* system.

1513–21 Juan Ponce de León of Spain reaches Florida and has extensive contact with Indians before Calusa war canoes drive his ships away. On an expedition in 1521, he is wounded by a Calusa arrow and later dies in Havana.

1523–24 Giovanni da Verrazano, sailing for France, explores the Atlantic coast, encountering Wampanoag, Narragansett, and Delaware Indians.

1534–41 Jacques Cartier of France explores the St. Lawrence River area in three voyages, making contact with Algonquian- and Iroquoian-speaking tribes. On one trip he reaches the Huron towns of Stadaconna and Hochelaga (now Quebec City and Montreal).

1539–43 Hernando de Soto claims Florida for Spain and explores the Southeast, encountering and alienating numerous tribes.

1540–42 Francisco Vásquez de Coronado of Spain explores the Southwest in search of Seven Cities of Cíbola.

1542 Juan Rodríguez Cabrillo and Bartolome Ferrelo explore the California and Oregon coasts.

1564–65 René de Laudonnière heads French colony on St. Johns River in Florida until expelled by Spanish. French artist Jacques le Moyne paints first known European depictions of Indians.

1565 Spanish under Pedro Menendez de Avilés found St. Augustine in Florida, the first permanent European settlement in North America.

Nuxalk (Bella Coola) carved sun mask from British Columbia.

1576–78 Martin Frobisher of England, seeking a Northwest Passage to the Pacific, encounters various Eskimo groups.

1585 Sir Walter Raleigh founds colony on Roanoke Island in what will become Virginia. In 1591 Gov. John White returns from a trip to England to find that the colonists have vanished.

1598 Juan de Oñate establishes first Spanish colony in New Mexico.

1598–99 Natives of Acoma Pueblo in New Mexico attack Spanish troops; a retaliatory force under Oñate kills as many as 800 Acomans.

1603–15 Samuel de Champlain's voyages in the Northeast lead to contacts with many Algonquian and Iroquoian tribes. In 1615 Champlain attacks Onondaga villages with the help of a Huron war party, thus turning the Iroquois League against the French.

1607 England establishes its first permanent settlement in North America at Jamestown, Virginia, under John Smith,

leading to extensive contact with the tribes of the Powhatan Confederacy.

1609–10 Henry Hudson, in service of the Netherlands, explores the river named for him. Manhattan Indians attack his ship; Mahican people make peaceful contact, and a lucrative fur trade begins.

1613 In response to gunfire aimed at them, the Beothuk of Newfoundland kill 37 French fishermen. The French retaliate by arming the Micmac, traditional enemies of the Beothuk, and offering bounties for scalps. The Beothuk are soon virtually exterminated.

1616–20 Smallpox epidemic strikes New England tribes between Narragansett Bay and the Penobscot River.

1620 Pilgrims from England arrive in Plymouth.

1624 Dutch settlers found Fort Orange (Albany, New York) in New Netherland.

1626 Canarsie Indians sell Manhattan Island to Peter Minuit, governor of New Netherland, for 60 guilders in trade goods. Dutch later have to pay Manhattan Indians, actual occupants of the island.

1629–33 Spanish found Catholic missions for Acoma, Hopi, and Zuni pueblos.

1633–35 New smallpox outbreaks among Indians of New England, New France, and New Netherland.

1636–37 Pequot War in New England: White colonists kill more than 600 people in surprise attack on main Pequot village.

1638 Sweden lays claim to land around Delaware Bay, maintaining trade outpost until 1655.

c. 1640 Beavers and otters nearly exterminated in Iroquois country. To expand territory, Iroquois launch decades-long "Beaver Wars" against Huron and other tribes. In 1650, 300 Huron survivors settle at Lorette under French protection.

1644 Second Powhatan Confederacy uprising against Jamestown; its leader, Opechancanough, dies in captivity.

IN NORTH AMERICA

1661 Spanish in Southwest raid sacred kivas of Pueblo towns and destroy hundreds of kachina masks in an effort to suppress native religion.

1664 England gains control of New Netherland from the Dutch and becomes ally and trade partner with the Iroquois.

1668–69 Pierre Esprit Radisson and Médard Chouart, sieur de Groseilliers, explore west of the St. Lawrence River as far as Lake Superior, plus the Hudson Bay region, for England.

1669–73 Louis Jolliet and Jacques Marquette of France explore the Great Lakes and the Mississippi River.

1670 Hudson's Bay Company is chartered by King Charles II of England.

1672 Colonial postal officials employ Indian couriers to carry mail between New York City and Albany; winter weather is too severe for white couriers.

1675–76 King Philip's War pits the Wampanoag, Narragansett, and Nipmuc against the New England Confederation of colonies. Metacom (King Philip) is killed in 1676.

1678–79 Daniel Greysolon Duluth of France explores Great Lakes and negotiates treaties between the warring Ojibwa and Sioux.

1680 Pueblo Indians rise up in rebellion against Spanish rule; the revolt, led by Popé, a Tewa medicine man, expels the occupiers. In 1689 the Spanish begin reconquest of the Pueblos.

1682 Robert Cavelier de la Salle claims the entire Mississippi Valley for France, naming the area Louisiana.

1682 William Penn's treaty with the Delaware begins a period of friendly relations between the Quakers and Indians.

1689 Nicolas Perrot formally claims upper Mississippi region for France.

1689–97 King William's War is the first in a series of colonial wars between England and France and their Indian allies, continuing to 1763. During these wars, the Iroquois League generally sides with the English, and the Algonquian tribes with the French.

1695 First Pima uprising against Spanish authorities in the Southwest; second uprising occurs in 1751.

1710 Three Mohawk chiefs and one Mahican are received in Queen Anne's court in England as the Four Kings of the New World.

1711–13 Tuscarora War on North Carolina frontier fought between British settlers and Tuscarora Indians. Remnants of this Iroquoian tribe migrate north; in 1722 the Tuscarora become the sixth tribe of the Iroquois Confederacy.

1712–34 Fox resistance against the French in the Great Lakes area.

1720–60 The Chickasaw fight the French and the Choctaw in the Southeast.

1729 French governor of Louisiana, wanting the site for a plantation, orders the Natchez to vacate their capital. The furious Natchez kill 200 Frenchmen at Fort Rosalie in response; the French answer by annihilating the Natchez.

1730 Seven Cherokee chiefs visit London and form an alliance, The Articles of Agreement, with King George II.

1738 Smallpox strikes the Cherokee in the Southeast, killing almost half the population. Smallpox also reaches tribes in western Canada.

1741 Vitus Bering, in service of Russia, reaches Alaska; Russians soon trade with natives for sea otter pelts.

1746 Typhoid fever epidemic breaks out among the Micmac of Nova Scotia.

1750 Moor's Indian Charity School is founded in Connecticut. It moves to New Hampshire in 1769; as Dartmouth College, it encourages enrollment of Indians.

1751 Benjamin Franklin cites Iroquois League as model for his Albany Plan of Union, later an influence on the U.S. Constitution.

1754–63 French and Indian War (the colonial phase of Europe's Seven Years War). In the Treaty of Paris, 1763, France cedes New France to England and Louisiana to Spain.

1755–75 William Johnson, British superintendent of Indian affairs in the northern colonies, persuades the Iroquois League to break its neutrality and side with England against France.

1760–61 Cherokee War on Carolina frontier flares up over continuing treaty violations by colonists.

1761–66 Aleut people revolt against Russian abuses in Alaska.

1763 Proclamation by King George III bans settlements west of the Appalachians and establishes a protected Indian Country there. White settlers ignore the boundary line.

1763 Indian raids in Pennsylvania lead to the Paxton Riots; peaceful Conestoga Mission Indians are massacred by settlers.

1763–64 Pontiac's Rebellion threatens British control of the Great Lakes region before being put down. Pontiac, an Ottawa chief, is killed in 1769 by a Kaskaskia Indian in Illinois.

1765 Reserve system in Canada begins with the provision of a tract of land for the Maliseet tribe.

1769 Gaspar de Portolá claims California for Spain and establishes mission system under Junípero Serra, a Franciscan priest.

1774 Lord Dunmore's War fought in Virginia between settlers and Shawnees.

1776–78 Capt. James Cook of England explores the Pacific Northwest.

Huron wampum belt believed to commemorate founding of mission near Quebec in 1600's.

1778 First treaty between the United States and an Indian nation is negotiated with the Delaware; they are offered the prospect of statehood.

1778 British and Iroquois forces attack and massacre American settlers in western New York and Pennsylvania. In 1779 a retaliatory U.S. campaign destroys Indian towns and crops, breaking the Iroquois League's power.

1780–1800 Smallpox and measles decimate Indians in Texas and New Mexico. In 1782–83 a smallpox epidemic hits the Sanpoil of Washington.

1781–89 The Articles of Confederation establish the principle that the central government, not the states, should regulate Indian affairs and trade.

1782 Christian Delaware Indians are massacred by Americans at Gnadenhutten in Ohio.

1783 Continental Congress proclamation bars white squatters on Indian lands.

1784 North West Company is chartered in Montreal to compete in fur trade with the Hudson's Bay Company. In 1821 the two companies merge.

1787 Northwest Ordinance calls for Indian rights, establishment of reservations, and sanctity of tribal lands; but it also sets guidelines for development of the Old Northwest that lead to increased white settlement.

1787–89 The new U.S. Constitution gives the federal government sole power to regulate commerce with Indian tribes.

1789–93 Alexander Mackenzie of Canada, seeking northern river route to the Pacific, travels to the Arctic Ocean; on second journey he crosses continent by land, making contact with many tribes.

1790 Spain signs the Nootka Convention, ceding the Pacific Northwest to England and the United States.

1790–91 Little Turtle's War: Shawnee, Miami, and other tribes win major battles against Americans in Ohio Valley, including defeat of Gen. Arthur St. Clair.

1794 Jay's Treaty restores trade between the United States and British colonies of Canada. It also guarantees Indians free movement across the border.

Tlingit-style brass hat with beads and sea-lion whiskers, made by Russians for presention to Tlingit Chief Michael of Sitka to celebrate peace agreement, ca. 1808.

1799 Handsome Lake, a Seneca chief, founds the Longhouse religion.

1799 Russian-American Fur Company chartered; launches aggressive policy in Aleutians and on Northwest Coast.

1802 Federal law prohibits the sale of liquor to Indians.

1802–1820's The Tlingit resist Russian incursions into their territory.

1803 Louisiana Purchase extends U.S. territorial control west of the Mississippi River; federal plans to resettle Eastern tribes beyond the Mississippi soon begin.

1804–06 Lewis and Clark Expedition opens the West to future white settlement.

1806 U.S. Office of Superintendent of Indian Trade is established to administer federal Indian trading houses.

1808 American Fur Company is chartered by John Jacob Astor to compete with Canadian fur trade.

1809 Treaty of Fort Wayne obtains 2.5 million acres from Indians for white settlers in Ohio and Indiana.

1809–11 Tecumseh, Shawnee chief, seeks to unite tribes of the Great Lakes, Ohio Valley, and Southeast against the United States. His brother Tenskwatawa, the Shawnee Prophet, is defeated at Tippecanoe in 1811.

1809–23 Sequoyah single-handedly creates a Cherokee syllabic alphabet so that his people's language can be written.

1812–15 War of 1812: Tecumseh, allied with the British, dies in 1813 at the Battle of the Thames in Canada.

1813–14 Creek War (also called Red Stick War) ends in treaty that strips Creeks of their land in Southeast.

1817–18 First Seminole War: Gen. Andrew Jackson invades Florida in punitive expedition against the Seminole.

1820–24 Kickapoo resistance to removal from Illinois Territory; Winnebago uprising in Wisconsin follows in 1827.

1824 U.S. Bureau of Indian Affairs (BIA) is created as part of the War Department.

1825 A separate Indian Country west of the Mississippi is first defined.

1827 The Cherokee adopt a constitution patterned on U.S. Constitution; it is nullified by the Georgia legislature.

1828–35 *The Cherokee Phoenix*, a bilingual weekly newspaper, is published, printing stories in Cherokee and English.

1830 Indian Removal Act passed by U.S. Congress, calling for relocation of Eastern tribes to an Indian Territory west of the Mississippi River. A Cherokee legal challenge produces an 1832 Supreme Court ruling in their favor, but President Andrew Jackson ignores it. From 1831 to 1839 the so-called Five Civilized Tribes (Cherokee, Chickasaw, Choctaw, Creek, Seminole) are forcibly moved from the Southeast to Indian Territory.

1830 Influenza epidemic strikes tribes of British Columbia. In 1830–33 there are multiple outbreaks of European diseases in California and Oregon.

1832 Black Hawk War in Illinois and Wisconsin waged by Sauk and Fox tribes under Black Hawk against U.S. forces.

1833–34 Missouri River expedition of German explorer Prince Maximilian and Swiss artist Karl Bodmer.

1835–42 Second Seminole War: Osceola, leader of resistance, dies in prison in 1838.

1837 Smallpox epidemic devastates the Mandan, Hidatsa, and Arikara of the upper Missouri. By 1870 four major smallpox epidemics strike Western tribes.

1843 Russian Orthodox Church founds first mission school for Eskimos in Alaska.

1846–48 U.S.-Mexican War begun by U.S. annexation of Texas (1845). The Treaty of Guadalupe Hidalgo (1848) cedes the Spanish Southwest, home of many Indian tribes, to the United States.

1847 U.S. Trade and Intercourse Act regulates commerce with Indian tribes and maintains peace on the frontiers.

1847 Outbreak of measles among the Cayuse of the Pacific Northwest.

1847–50 Cayuse War in Oregon.

1848 First white whalers reach Alaska.

1848–49 Gold discovered in California, starting the Gold Rush and escalating the pressures on California, Great Basin, and Plains Indians.

1849 Courthouse Rebellion in Canada launched by the Red River Métis.

1850–51 Mariposa War in California pits white miners against the Miwok and the Yokut; uprising by Yuma and Mariposa in California and Arizona.

1850–60 Cholera epidemic sweeps the Great Basin and southern Plains.

1851 Treaty of Fort Laramie marks turning point in U.S.-Indian relations on the northern Plains.

1853 Gadsden Purchase transfers Mexican lands in New Mexico, Arizona, and California to U.S. ownership.

1853–56 The United States acquires 174 million acres of Indian lands in a series of 52 treaties, all of which are subsequently broken by whites.

1854 U.S. Indian Affairs commissioner calls for end of Indian removal policy.

1855–56 Yakima War in Washington involves the Yakima, Walla Walla, Umatilla, and Cayuse tribes.

1855–58 Third Seminole War in Florida.

1858 Coeur d'Alene War (or Spokan War) waged in Washington by Coeur d'Alene, Spokan, Palouse, Yakima, and Northern Paiute coalition.

1861–63 Apache uprisings in Southwest led by Mangas Coloradas and Cochise.

1861–65 U.S. Civil War: Most Indian tribes remain neutral, but the Cherokee and others of the Five Civilized Tribes are induced to aid the South with promises to return tribal lands. After the war, the Five Tribes are forced to cede half of Indian Territory as punishment.

1862 Smallpox sweeps through Fort Victoria area and down the length of the Northwest Coast, killing an estimated 200,000 Indian people.

1862 William Duncan, an Anglican missionary on Northwest Coast, establishes village of Metlakatla with 50 Tsimshian followers, who adopt Christian faith and European lifestyles. By 1880 more than 1,000 converts live there.

1862–63 Santee Sioux uprising in Minnesota under Chief Little Crow ends with the hanging of 38 Santees on Dec. 26, 1863, the largest mass execution in U.S. history.

1863–66 Navajo War in New Mexico and Arizona. In 1864, 8,000 Navajo prisoners are forced on the Long Walk to Bosque Redondo. War chief Manuelito surrenders in 1866.

Carved ivory peg calendar thought to have been used by Aleut converts to keep track of Russian Orthodox feast days.

1864–65 Cheyenne-Arapaho War in Colorado and Kansas. On Nov. 29, 1864, Col. John M. Chivington's hastily assembled volunteers massacre more than 300 Indians camped at Sand Creek.

1864 Indians are declared competent witnesses under a new federal law and allowed to testify in trials against whites.

1866 U.S. Congress appropriates Indian lands as right-of-way for construction of transcontinental railroad.

1866–68 War for the Bozeman Trail in Wyoming and Montana pits Cheyenne, Sioux, and Arapaho forces led by Chief Red Cloud against the U.S. Army. It will remain the only full-scale "Indian war"

won by the Indians, a victory formalized in the 1868 Fort Laramie Treaty.

1867 U.S. purchase of Alaska from Russia adds Eskimo, Aleut, and Athabascan groups to the U.S. population.

1867 Hancock Campaign against the Cheyenne and Arapaho on the Plains.

1867 British North America Act creates the Dominion of Canada, which takes responsibility for native affairs.

1867 U.S. Peace Commission surveys Indian affairs and recommends that the existing treaty process be abolished; in 1871 Congress formally does so. Between 1778 and 1871 the U.S. Senate approves 372 treaties with Indian tribes.

1868 Fourteenth Amendment to the Constitution gives blacks the vote but specifically excludes Indians.

1868 U.S. Commissioner of Indian Affairs estimates that Indian Wars in the West are costing the government $1 million per Indian killed.

1868–69 Southern Plains War involves Cheyenne, Sioux, Arapaho, Kiowa, and Comanche forces.

1869 President Grant's Peace Policy is inaugurated and lasts until 1874. In 1870 Grant transfers control of Indian agencies from army officers to Christian missionary groups of various denominations.

1869 Brig. Gen. Ely Parker, a Seneca, becomes first Native American to head Bureau of Indian Affairs (BIA); he serves until 1871.

1869–70 Smallpox epidemic strikes Canadian Plains tribes, including Blackfeet, Piegan, and Blood.

1869 First Riel Rebellion in Canada launched by Red River Métis.

1869 Transcontinental railroad completed: the Union Pacific and Central Pacific join up at Promontory Point, Utah.

1871 Congress ratifies last of 372 treaties made with Indian tribes since 1778; later accords will not have treaty status, which recognizes tribes as sovereign nations.

1871 General Sheridan issues orders forbidding western Indians to leave reservations without permission.

Beadwork depiction on Oglala Sioux baby carrier of Chief Red Cloud and Col. John Smith, his escort during an 1871 trip to Washington, D.C..

1871 White hunters in United States begin wholesale killing of buffalo.

1872–73 Modoc War in California and Oregon. Modoc leader Kintpuash (Captain Jack) is hanged in 1873.

1874 Gold discovered in Black Hills of South Dakota, sacred to the Sioux. Treaties protecting them ignored by whites.

1874–75 Red River War on the southern Plains, involving the Comanche, Kiowa, and Cheyenne, is led by Quanah Parker, Satanta, and others.

1876 Canadian Indian Act gives individual natives the right to seek Canadian citizenship by renouncing their rights and privileges as Indians.

1876–77 Sioux War for the Black Hills waged by Sioux, Cheyenne, and Arapaho forces under Sitting Bull and Crazy Horse. On June 25, 1876, Custer's 7th Cavalry is crushed at Battle of the Little Bighorn. Sitting Bull and followers seek refuge in Canada; in 1877 Crazy Horse is killed while in custody.

1877 Blackfoot tribe cedes land to the Dominion of Canada.

1877 Flight of the Nez Perce under Chief Joseph in the Northwest.

1877–80 Apache resistance in the Southwest under Victorio.

1878 Bannock War in Idaho and Oregon involves the Bannock, Northern Paiute, and Cayuse.

1878 Congress votes funds for Indian police and in 1883 empowers tribal units to administer justice in all but major crimes. In 1885, federal courts are given jurisdiction over Indian cases involving major crimes on reservations.

1878–79 Flight of Northern Cheyenne under Dull Knife from Oklahoma to homeland in Dakota Territory.

1879 Carlisle Indian School founded in Pennsylvania, with the goal of assimilating Indians into white culture.

1879 In ruling on lawsuit filed by Ponca chief Standing Bear, U.S. federal court in Nebraska upholds right of Indians to sue

1881 Sitting Bull and 187 followers surrender to U.S. officials at Fort Buford, North Dakota.

1881 John Slocum, a Coast Salish laborer and Catholic convert, begins to preach a gospel of clean living and spiritual renewal. So is born Tschadam, the Indian Shaker religion.

1881–86 Apache resistance continues under Geronimo in the Southwest until Geronimo's surrender in 1886, which marks the end of the Indian Wars.

1884 Canadian Parliament passes the Indian Advancement Act, encouraging democratic election of chiefs. Mohawks at St. Regis, Ontario, resist the provision, preferring their traditional method of choosing leaders.

1884 Congress acknowledges the rights of Eskimos to Alaskan territorial lands.

1885 Canada outlaws the potlatch ceremony among Northwest Coast tribes. The law, often ignored, is repealed in 1951.

1885 The last great herd of buffalo in the United States is exterminated.

1885 Second Riel Rebellion is launched by Métis along the Saskatchewan River in Canada.

1886 Mohawk men of the Caughnawaga Reserve in Quebec are trained to help buik a bridge across the St. Lawrence River. So begins a tradition of high steel construction work among the Iroquois.

1887 Congress passes the General Allotment Act (the Dawes Act), which ends communal ownership of reservation

lands, distributing 160-acre "allotments" to individual Indians and disposing of the surplus. Tribes lose millions of acres.

1889 Two million acres of Indian Territory (later Oklahoma) are bought from Indians for distribution to white settlers; the first Land Run quickly follows.

1890 Ghost Dance movement led by the Paiute prophet Wovoka gains influence among Plains Indians. On Dec. 15, 1890, Sitting Bull is killed at Pine Ridge, South Dakota, increasing tensions there. On Dec. 28, U.S. troops massacre more than 200 Sioux preparing for a Ghost Dance at Wounded Knee.

1890–1910 U.S. Indian population reaches low point: less than 250,000.

1891 Congress authorizes the leasing by whites of allotted Indian lands.

1896–98 Klondike Gold Rush to the Yukon Territory and Alaska.

1898 Curtis Act seeks to extend allotment policy to "Five Civilized Tribes" by dissolving tribal governments, requiring abolished Indian nations to submit to allotment, and instituting civil government in Indian Territory.

1901 Snake uprising in Oklahoma Territory; Creek Indians under Chitto Harjo resist allotment.

1902 Entire Eskimo population of Southampton Island in Hudson Bay is wiped out by typhus.

1902 U.S. government offers first oil and gas leases on Indian lands in Oklahoma.

1902 Reclamation Act encourages settlement of the West by whites through subsidies for water development.

1906 Federal government seizes 50,000 acres of wilderness land, including Blue Lake in New Mexico, sacred to Taos Pueblo Indians, as part of a national park.

1907 Seventy high-steel workers of the Iroquois Caughnawaga Band killed while working on the Quebec Bridge.

1908 Supreme Court defines rights of the federal government to reserve water for the use of Indian tribes.

1909 Theodore Roosevelt, two days before leaving the presidency, issues eight executive orders transferring 2.5 million acres of timbered Indian reservation lands to national forests.

1910 Bureau of Indian Affairs (BIA) starts first regular Indian medical service.

1910 Federal government forbids the Sun Dance among Plains Indians, giving the use of self-torture as the reason.

1911 Society of American Indians, committed to Pan-Indianism and citizenship for Indians, is founded.

1912 Anti-allotment Cherokees, Creeks, Choctaws, and Chickasaws from the Four Mothers Society go to Washington to argue their case before Congress.

1912 Jim Thorpe, Sauk and Fox athlete of the Carlisle School, wins pentathlon and decathlon at Stockholm Olympic Games. In 1913 he is stripped of medals because he previously played semiprofessional baseball; they are reinstated in 1984.

1913 Federal government issues Indian Head nickel with composite portrait of three Indian chiefs—Cheyenne, Seneca, and Sioux—on one side and a buffalo on the reverse side.

1915 Congress authorizes Bureau of Indian Affairs to buy land for landless natives in California.

Charles Eastman (1858–1939), Santee Sioux physician, author, and advocate of Native American rights.

1917–18 World War I. Many American Indians enlist, fight, and die.

1917 U.S. government lifts restrictions on allotments, launching "Forced Patent" period, during which federal guardianship of many Indian lands ends and thousands of Indians lose their land to swindlers and corrupt officials.

1917 For first time in 15 years, American Indian birth rate exceeds death rate.

1917 Congress ends federal subsidies to religious groups for Indian education.

1917 Papago (Tohono O'odham) Indian Reservation in Arizona is the last to be established by executive order.

1918 Native American Church, with rites that include the sacramental use of peyote, is incorporated in Oklahoma by members of the Kiowa, Comanche, Cheyenne, Apache, Ponca, and Oto tribes.

1922 Rio Grande pueblos unite for first time since 1680, forming the All Pueblo Council to contest proposed legislation giving rights to white squatters on Indian lands. The legislation is defeated.

1922 Deskaheh, a Cayuga chief, travels to Switzerland to seek recognition of his tribe from the League of Nations.

1924 Congress bestows American citizenship on all native-born Indians who have not yet obtained it. This ruling results in part from gratitude for the Indian contribution to the American effort in World War I.

1926 National Council of American Indians is founded.

1928 Charles Curtis, a Kansa Indian and U.S. senator, is elected vice president under Herbert Hoover.

1928 The Meriam Report, after a two-year commission, deplores Indian living conditions and declares the allotment system a failure.

1930 Senate conducts a survey of Indian policy. One finding discloses the use of kidnapping by BIA school officials trying to educate Navajo children.

1930 Northern Cheyenne Reservation becomes last communally owned tract to be allotted.

1933 John Collier is named commissioner of Indian Affairs by President Roosevelt to administer the "Indian New Deal."

1934 U.S. Indian Reorganization Act (IRA) reverses U.S. policy of allotment, providing for tribal self-government and landholding and launching an Indian credit program. In 1936 Congress extends provisions of the IRA to Alaska natives.

1936 Congress passes the Oklahoma Indian Welfare Act for the organization of now tribeless Indians whose lands have been allotted.

1939 The Seneca of Tonawanda, New York, issue a Declaration of Independence from the state of New York.

1940 First Inter-American Conference on Indian life is held in Patzcuaro, Mexico.

1941–45 In World War II more than 25,000 Native Americans serve on active duty and thousands more in war-related industries. Navajo marines become famous for the use of their language as a battlefield code. Some Indians are jailed as draft resisters.

1943 Kateri Tekakwitha, a 17th-century Mohawk, is declared venerable by the Roman Catholic Church. In 1980 she is beatified, the last step before sainthood.

1944 National Congress of American Indians is organized in Denver, Colorado.

1946 U.S. Indian Claims Commission is created by Congress to settle tribal land claims against the United States and provide financial compensation.

1946 The policy of "termination," in which the government seeks to end special Indian trust status, goes into effect.

1948 Arizona is forced by court decree to give Indians the right to vote; a Tewa Indian had brought suit, claiming citizenship because he paid taxes on cigarettes.

1950 Dillon Myer becomes commissioner of Indian affairs; he supports termination and a program of relocation for reservation Indians, thus encouraging movement to cities and cultural assimilation.

1950 Navajo Rehabilitation Act calls for appropriations to benefit tribes.

1951 Canadian Indian Act gives native people the vote and generally applies same laws to them as to other Canadians.

1953 Congress repeals special Indian alcohol prohibition laws.

1953 With the Termination Resolution, Congress calls for the end of federal protections of many tribes. Congress also empowers some states to take over civil and criminal jurisdiction of Indian reservations without tribal consent.

1954 Indians in Maine, previously barred from voting on the grounds that they are not under federal jurisdiction, receive the right to vote.

1954–62 Congress strips 61 tribes, bands, and communities of federal services and protection. In 1973 the Menominee Restoration Act reinstates the tribe's trust status. In 1978 four Oklahoma tribes—Ottawa, Modoc, Wyandot, and Peoria—regain their trust status.

1957 Iroquois activism in New York State is marked by Seneca opposition to the building of the Kinzua Dam, Tuscarora challenges to the State Power Authority, and Mohawk reoccupation of lands taken by white squatters.

1958 The Miccosukee of Florida resist the Everglades Reclamation Project.

1958 Lumbee tribesmen drive off Ku Klux Klan members attempting to hold a rally in Robeson County, North Carolina.

1959 Alaska becomes a state, adding more than 42,000 to the native population of the United States.

1961 U.S. Department of the Interior changes federal land-sales policy to give Indian tribes first opportunity to purchase lands offered for sale by individual Indians, a partial reversal of its termination policy.

1961 Birth of modern Indian-rights movement, as the American Indian Charter Convention in Chicago and the National Indian Youth Conference in New Mexico meet to establish goals and new activist groups proliferate.

1961 Keeler Commission on Rights, Liberties, and Responsibilities of the American Indian recommends tribal self-determination and the development of tribal resources.

1961 U.S. Commission on Civil Rights reports on injustices in living conditions of American Indians.

1962 New Mexico forced by federal government to give Indians voting rights.

1964 Conference on Indian Poverty is held in Washington, D.C., with delegates reporting on poverty among their tribes. That same year, the Office of Economic Opportunity is created, with an Indian Desk that sponsors antipoverty programs.

1964 National Indian Youth Council sponsors "fish-ins" along the rivers of Washington State to support the fishing rights of Pacific Northwest tribes. Out of this action the Survival of American Indians Association is founded.

1964 U.S. Civil Rights Act prohibits discrimination for reasons of color, race, religion, or national origin.

Kwakiutl elder wearing a carved hat-mask associated with the approach of the Winter Ceremony.

1965 Voting Rights Act ensures equal voting rights.

1966 Alaska Federation of Natives is founded, representing Eskimos, Aleuts, and Indians of Alaska's Subarctic interior.

1967 At Expo '67 in Montreal, the National Indian Council plans the Canadian Indian Pavilion, using the opportunity to express long-standing grievances.

1968 Navajo Community College, the first accredited U.S. college controlled by Native Americans, is chartered in Arizona.

1968 President Johnson calls for establishment of a National Council on Indian Opportunity combining cross section of native leaders with heads of U.S. agencies involved with Indian programs; he also says that termination should be replaced by policy of self-determination.

1968 American Indian Civil Rights Act extends Bill of Rights protections to reservation Indians. It bars states from assuming law-and-order jurisdiction on reservations without tribal consent, and applies

same restrictions to tribal governments as to federal and state governments.

1968 American Indian Movement (AIM) is founded in Minneapolis to deal with problems faced by relocated urban Indians. It later becomes involved in struggles of reservation Indians as well.

1968 Mohawks of St. Regis, Ontario, attempt to block the St. Lawrence Seaway International Bridge to protest Canada's failure to honor the Jay Treaty of 1795, guaranteeing Mohawk rights to unrestricted travel between Canada and the United States. After this action, border-crossing rights are honored.

1969 An Indian Task Force of 36 tribes makes a statement opposing termination policy in response to Interior Department statements that Indians are overprotected by the trust status of reservations.

1969 N. Scott Momaday, a Kiowa, is awarded the Pulitzer Prize for fiction for his novel *The House Made of Dawn.*

1969 White Paper on Indian affairs issued in Canada calls for the repeal of the Indian Act and for termination of special Indian status and benefits as derived from treaties. Native groups reject the proposal, and it is never implemented.

1969 Red Power activists occupy Alcatraz Island in San Francisco Bay to call attention to the plight of contemporary Indians. The occupation lasts until 1971.

1970 The Blue Lake Wilderness Area in New Mexico, taken from Taos Pueblo in 1906, is returned to tribal control.

1971 Alaska Native Claims Settlement Act reaches a money-for-land settlement with Alaska natives.

1971 Model Urban Indian Center Program is created by the federal government to provide essential services for urban Indians.

1972 Trail of Broken Treaties Caravan, organized by AIM, issues position paper on the plight of Indians, then marches on Washington. Demonstrators occupy and destroy offices of the Bureau of Indian Affairs (BIA).

1972 White vigilantes beat Raymond Yellow Thunder to death in Gordon, Neb. A ruling of death by suicide causes protests by more than 1,000 Sioux from Pine

Ridge Reservation. Officials, forced to perform an autopsy, change their finding to manslaughter; two of the killers are subsequently tried and convicted.

1972 Yakima tribe is returned 21,000 acres in the state of Washington.

1973 Members of AIM and about 200 armed Oglala Sioux occupy site of the Wounded Knee Massacre on Pine Ridge Reservation in South Dakota for 71 days. A siege results, with outbreaks of gunfire and the killing of two Indians.

1974 In Minnesota, the first trial stemming from the occupation of Wounded Knee takes place. In 1975 AIM leaders Dennis Banks and Russell Means are convicted on assault and riot charges. In 1978 Gov. Jerry Brown gives Banks sanctuary in California.

1974 Navajo-Hopi Land Settlement Act seeks to resolve long-standing dispute between the two tribes.

1975 Shoot-out on Pine Ridge Reservation between AIM members and FBI agents results in the death of two agents. Leonard Peltier is later convicted, a verdict that remains controversial.

1975 Eighteen tribes receive 346,000 acres of land held by the U.S. government since the Submarginal Lands Act of 1933.

1978 Indian activists stage the Longest Walk, from California to Washington, D.C., to protest "new termination" laws under considerationn.

1978 Congress passes the American Indian Freedom of Religion Act, which states that Indian religions are protected by the First Amendment.

1978 Indian Claims Commission ends. In all, $800 million has been granted to Indian tribes since formation of commission in 1946, with tribes winning awards on 60 percent of their claims. The Court of Claims assumes the remaining cases.

1980 Federal Census reports that the Native American population in the U.S. exceeds the 1 million mark, at 1,418,195.

1980 Maine Indian Claims Settlement Act is reached; the Passamaquoddy and Penobscot tribes agree to abandon land claims in Maine in exchange for a $27 million federal trust fund and a $54 million federal land acquisition fund.

1981 Reagan administration initiates a policy of cutbacks of funds for Indian social programs. Eventually, as much as 40 percent of funding is cut.

1982 President Reagan vetoes $112 million congressional settlement of water-rights suit brought by Papago (Tohono O'odham) Indians against Arizona; a settlement is later reached, with the federal government to pay the tribe $40 million.

1983 President Reagan vetoes $900,000 congressional settlement of land-claim suit against Connecticut by Pequot tribe.

1983 Dennis Banks, the AIM leader, still under indictment in South Dakota for 1973 Wounded Knee occupation, takes refuge on the Onondaga Reservation in New York State. In 1984 Banks surrenders to officials in South Dakota; he is sentenced to three years in prison.

1984 Jim Thorpe Memorial Pow Wow and Games in Los Angeles honor the memory of the Indian athlete and 1912 Olympic gold medalist.

1985 National Tribal Chairman's Association votes to reject proposals of the Commission on Indian Reservation Economies, fearing new federal attempts to terminate tribal sovereignty and gain control of tribal resources.

1985 Wilma Mankiller becomes Principal Chief of the Cherokee Nation, the first woman in modern times to lead a major tribe.

1986 Smithsonian Institution's Museum of Natural History agrees to return Indian skeletal remains to tribal leaders for reburial. In 1991 the Smithsonian's Museum of the American Indian announces its policy for the repatriation of selected native artifacts.

1988 Congress passes Indian Gaming Regulatory Act, requiring that tribes wishing to operate casinos on reservations negotiate terms with states.

1990 Congress approves the Native American Graves Protection and Repatriation Act, which provides for the protection of American Indian grave sites and the repatriation of Indian remains and cultural artifacts to tribes.

1990 Centennial of the Wounded Knee Massacre is commemorated at the Pine Ridge Reservation.

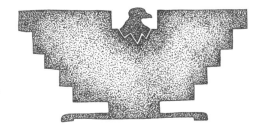

Eagle, traditional native symbol of spiritual power, as used by the United Farm Workers of America in their union insignia.

1991 U.S. Census reports 1,959,234 American Indians and Alaska natives living in the United States, an increase of almost 40 percent since 1980. Canadian natives number 1,002,675.

1992 Foxwoods Casino, built by the Mashantucket Pequot Tribe, opens in Ledyard, Connecticut. It becomes the most profitable casino in the Western Hemisphere.

1994 President Clinton invites leaders of all 547 federally recognized American Indian and Alaska native tribes to the White House, the first-ever meeting of its kind. Tribal leaders and U.S. officials identify issues for follow-up conferences.

2001 Scheduled opening of the National Museum of the American Indian in Washington, D.C. Native peoples of the Western Hemisphere are involved in all aspects of the museum.

FOR FURTHER READING

Arden, Harvey and Steve Wall. *Wisdomkeepers: Meetings With Native American Spiritual Elders.* Beyond Words Publishing, 1991.

Axtell, James. *Beyond 1492: Encounters in Colonial North America.* Oxford University Press, 1992.

Beck, Peggy V., and Anna L. Walters. *The Sacred: Ways of Knowledge, Sources of Life.* Navajo Community College Press, 1977.

Brown, Dee. *Bury My Heart at Wounded Knee.* Henry Holt & Company, Inc., 1991.

Bruchac, Joseph, ed. *New Voices from the Longhouse: An Anthology of Modern Iroquois Literature.* The Greenfield Review Press, 1988.

Champagne, Duane, ed. *Chronology of Native North American History: From Pre-Columbian Times to the Present.* Gale Research Inc., 1994.

Davis, Mary B., ed. *Native America in the Twentieth Century: An Encyclopedia.* Garland Publishing, 1994.

Debo, Angie. *A History of the Indians of the United States.* University of Oklahoma Press, 1984.

Deloria, Vine, Jr. *Custer Died for Your Sins: An Indian Manifesto.* University of Oklahoma Press, 1988.

Dickason, Olive P. *Canada's First Nations: A History of Founding Peoples from Earliest Times.* University of Oklahoma Press, 1992.

Edmunds, R. David. *Tecumseh and the Quest for Indian Leadership.* Harper Collins, 1987.

Erdoes, Richard, and Alfonso Ortiz, eds. *American Indian Myths & Legends.* Pantheon Books, 1985.

Fitzhugh, William W., and Aron Crowell, eds. *Crossroads of Continents: Cultures of Siberia and Alaska.* Smithsonian Institution Press, 1988.

Fowler, Loretta. *Arapahoe Politics, 1851-1978, Symbols in Crises of Authority.* University of Nebraska Press, 1982.

Gilman, Carolyn, and Mary J. Schneider. *The Way to Independence: Memories of a Hidatsa Indian Family, 1840-1920.* Minnesota Historical Society Press, 1987.

Hill, Richard W., Sr., and Tom Hill, eds. *Creation's Journey: Native American Identity & Belief.* Smithsonian Institution Press, 1994.

Hodge, Frederick W., ed. *Handbook of American Indians North of Mexico* (2 vols.). Rowman and Littlefield, 1975.

Hoxie, Frederick E., ed. *Indians in American History.* Harlan Davidson, 1988.

Hudson, Charles. *The Southeastern Indians.* University of Tennessee Press, 1976.

Jonaitis, Aldona. *From the Land of the Totem Poles: The Northwest Coast Indian Art Collection at the American Museum of Natural History.* Univ. of Washington, 1991.

Josephy, Alvin M., Jr. *The Indian Heritage of America.* Houghton Mifflin Company, 1991.

Kopper, Philip. *The Smithsonian Book of North American Indians: Before the Coming of the Europeans.* Smithsonian Books, 1986.

Limerick, Patricia N. *The Legacy of Conquest: The Unbroken Past of the American West.* W. W. Norton & Company, 1988.

McClellan, Catharine. *Part of the Land, Part of the Water: A History of the Yukon Indians.* Douglas & McIntyre, 1987.

McMillan, Alan D. *Native Peoples and Cultures of Canada.* Douglas & McIntyre, 1988.

Miller, Jay. *Earthmaker: Tribal Stories from Native North America.* Perigee/Berkley Publishing Group, 1992.

Nabokov, Peter, and Robert Easton. *Native American Architecture.* Oxford University Press, 1989.

Nabokov, Peter, ed. *Native American Testimony: A Chronicle of Indian-White Relations from Prophecy to the Present, 1492-1992.* Viking Penguin, 1992.

Penney, David W., and George C. Longfish. *Native American Art.* Hugh Lauter Levin Associates, 1994.

Perdue, Theda, ed. *Nations Remembered: An Oral History of the Five Civilized Tribes, 1865-1907.* Greenwood Press, 1980.

Ruoff, A. LaVonne Brown. *American Indian Literatures: An Introduction, Bibliographic Review, & Selected Bibliography.* Modern Language Association, 1990.

Sando, Joe S. *Pueblo Nations: Eight Centuries of Pueblo Indian History.* Clear Light Publishers, 1992.

Sturtevant, William C., gen. ed. *Handbook of North American Indians* (9 vols.). United States Government Printing Office, 1983-1990.

Swann, Brian. *Coming To Light: Contemporary Translations of the Native American Literatures of North America.* Random House, 1995.

Swanton, John R. *Indians of the Southeastern United States.* Greenwood Press, 1969.

Tanner, Helen H., ed. *Atlas of Great Lakes Indian History.* University of Oklahoma Press, 1987.

Wade, Edwin L., ed. *The Arts of the North American Indian: Native Traditions in Evolution.* Hudson Hills Press, New York, 1986.

Waldman, Carl. *Atlas of the North American Indian.* Facts on File, 1985.

Wallace, Anthony F.C. *The Death & Rebirth of the Seneca.* Random House, 1972.

White, Richard. *It's Your Misfortune and None of My Own: A History of the American West.* University of Oklahoma Press, 1993.

Winch, Terence, ed. *All Roads Are Good: Native Voices on Life and Culture.* Smithsonian Institution Press, 1994.

Wright, Ronald. *Stolen Continents: The "New World" Through Indian Eyes.* Houghton Mifflin Company, 1993.

CREDITS & ACKNOWLEDGMENTS

Commissioned Art

Robert Annesley	**70–71**
Francis Back	**133, 162–163, 166–167**
Betty Duke	**13, 32, 47, 96** (Maps)
Mick Ellison	**52, 80, 139**
H. Tom Hall	**48–49, 142–143, 180–181, 282–283,**
Greg Harlin	**98–99, 314–315** (Wood Ronsaville Harlin, Inc.)
Joe LeMonnier	**37, 79, 120, 154, 188, 225, 235, 271, 300** (Maps)
Roger Mignon	**126**
Sabra Moore	**11, 40, 81, 122, 159, 191, 239, 277, 301, 339, 360** (Pictographs)
Craig Nelson	**26**
Ray Skibinski	**39, 82**
John Stevens	**9, 35, 77, 117, 153, 187, 223, 269, 297, 327, 327, 355** (Calligraphy)
Dahl Taylor	**208–209, 220, 285**
Jan Timbrook.	**273**
Jack Unruh	**95**
Rob Wood	**30–31** (Wood Ronsaville Harlin, Inc.)

Text

Permission to excerpt or adapt material from the following works is gratefully acknowledged: *Atlas of the North American Indian,* by Carl Waldman, Copyright © 1985 Carl Waldman (Facts on File, Inc.). *From the Land of the Totem Poles,* by Aldona Jonaitis, Copyright © 1988 the American Museum of Natural History (Dept. of Library Services, American Museum of Natural History). *Indian Art of the Northwest Coast,* ed. by Bill Holm and Bill Reid, Copyright © 1975 Institute for the Arts, Rice University. *Land of the Spotted Eagle,* by Luther Standing Bear, Copyright © 1933 Luther Standing Bear, renewed © 1960 May Jones (University of Nebraska Press). *Native American Testimony,* ed. by Peter Nabokov. Expanded U.S. edition first published 1991 by Penguin Books, U.S.A., Inc. (Susan Bergholz Literary Services, NY). *Pictorial History of California,* by Paul C. Johnson, Copyright © 1970 Paul C. Johnson (Doubleday, div. of Bantam Doubleday Dell Publishing Group, Inc.). *Pueblo Nations,* by Joe S. Sando, Copyright © 1992 Joe S. Sando (Clear Light Publishers). *Skywalkers,* by Richard Hill, Copyright © 1987 Richard Hill. *Stolen Continents,* by Ronald Wright, Copyright © 1992 Ronald Wright (Houghton Mifflin Co. & Penguin Books Canada Ltd.). *Surviving Columbus: The Story of the Pueblo People,* Copyright © 1992 KNME-TV & Institute of American Indian Arts (KNME-TV & Institute of American Indian Arts). *They Came Here First,* by D'Arcy McNickle, Copyright © 1949 D'Arcy McNickle (HarperCollins Publishers, Inc.). *When the Rainbow Touches Down: The Artists and Stories Behind the Apache, Navajo, Rio Grande Pueblo and Hopi Paintings in the William and Leslie Van Ness Denman Collection,* by Tryntje Van Ness Seymour, Copyright © 1988 by Tryntje Van Ness Seymour, published by The Heard Museum, Phoenix, AZ, distributed by The University of Washington Press, Seattle, WA. Quotes appearing on pages 89 (left), 89 (right), 90, 92, 101, 107, 109, 110 (left), 110 (right), 112, and 115 are reprinted from *When the Rainbow Touches Down,* pages 139, 217, 226, 215, 133-134, 30, 35, 34, 41, 73, and 70, respectively, with permission of the author.

Special appreciation is extended to the following individuals and institutions for their generous assistance: Dan Agent, Office of Public Affairs, Smithsonian Institution; Judy Allen, Choctaw Nation of Oklahoma; Mr. Jack B. Baker, President, Goingsnake Heritage District Association; Valerie Bell, Saint Marie Among the Iroquois; Thomas Blumer, Historian, Catawba Nation, and Senior Editor, Law Library of Congress; David Burgevin, Still Picture Dept., Smithsonian Institution; Cabazon Band of Mission Indians; Rene Chartrand, Chief, National Collections, Canadian Heritage - Parks Canada National Historic Sites; Charles E. Cleland; Chester Conan, Oklahoma Historical Society; Ms. Katherine Creek, The Museum of Natural History Anthropological Archive; Mary Davis, Huntington Free Library, National Museum of the American Indian/Smithsonian Institution; Jennifer Diliberti, Milwaukee Public Museum; Bill Fox, Cultural Resource Manager, Parks Canada; Kenneth Funmaker, Cultural Coordinator, Ho-Chunk Language and Culture Program; Susan Gillis, Ft. Lauderdale Historical Society; Charles Grogan, Chief Cornplanter Council/Boy Scouts of America; Greg Harlin; Georgia Harris; Mr. Neil Hauck, The Museum of Natural History, Anthropological Archive; Violet Anderson Hilbert; Richard Hill; Mary Jane Hodges, Bill Holm; Rita James; G. Peter Jemison; Christine Kallenberger, The Philbrook Museum of Art; Gloria Lomahaftewa, Assistant to the Director For Native American Relations, The Heard Museum; John Lovett, Western History College, University of Oklahoma; Jeffrey M. Mitchem, Station Archeologist, Parkin Archeological State Park; Tom Mooney, Curator of Collections, Cherokee National Museum; Cynthia Nakamura, Denver Art Museum; Navajo Nation Library System; Richard Pearce-Moses, The Heard Museum; Rosella Woundedeye Rider; Prentice Robinson, Director of Education, Cherokee National Museum; Emory Sekaquaptewa, Bureau of Applied Research in Anthropology, Department of Anthropology, The University of Arizona; Vyrtis Thomas, The Museum of Natural History, Anthropological Archive; Jan Timbrook, Santa Barbara Museum of Art; Jake Thomas; Martha Vestecks-Miller, Nebraska State Historical Society; Rob Wood; Clarence Woodcock, Flathead Culture Committee.

Photographs

Abbreviations

AMNH	Department of Library Services, American Museum of Natural History
CMC	Canadian Museum of Civilization
DIA	The Detroit Institute of Arts
LC	Library of Congress
NGS	National Geographic Society
NMNH	National Museum of Natural History, Smithsonian Institution
NMAI	National Museum of the American Indian, Smithsonian Institution
NYPL	New York Public Library
RIPSA	Repin Institute of Painting, Sculpture and Architecture
SI	Smithsonian Institution
TGI	The Thomas Gilcrease Institute of American History and Art

2–3 Mathers Museum, Bloomington, Indiana. Photograph by Joseph Kossuth Dixon. **4** AMNH Neg.#317105, Photograph by J.K. Dixon. **5** *left column, from top* AMNH Neg.#316942. Photograph by J.K. Dixon; Eastern Washington State Historical Society, Spokane, Washington; SI, Neg.#56600; Special Collections, NYPL; SI, Neg.#2910–A–2; AMNH Neg.#317146; *right column, from top* Winter & Pond Collection, #PCA 87–. 297, Alaska State Library; AMNH Neg.#316637. Photograph by J.K. Dixon; LC; SI, Neg.#2412; AMNH Neg.#317144. Photograph by Rodman Wanamaker; LC. **6–7** *bottom* The State Historical Society of North Dakota. **8** *figure* Collection of St. Louis Museum of Science and Natural History. © Dirk Bakker, Photographer, DIA; *background* Fritz Prenzel/Bruce Coleman, Inc. **10** *top* Jim Zittgraff; *middle left* Ohio Historical Society. © Dirk Bakker, Photographer, DIA; *middle right* M.P.L.Fogden/Bruce Coleman, Inc; *bottom* Lynn Johnson/Black Star. **12** Arnold Jacobs. **14** *top* Tom Wolff; *bottom* Janet Foster/Masterfile. **16** Arctic Studies Center, SI. **17** *top* University Museum, Philadelphia; *bottom* Brenda Carter © NGS. **18** *top* L.L. Rue III/Bruce Coleman, Inc.; *bottom left* Kjell Sandved; *bottom right* Peabody Museum/Harvard University. Photograph by Hillel Burger. **19** Arizona State Museum, University of Arizona. **20** *top* Langdon Kihn © NGS; *bottom* Maximilien Bruggmann. **21** *top* Maximilien Bruggmann; *far left* NMAI #3958; *middle left, center, middle right, far right* John Bigelow Taylor. **22** *background* David Hiser © NGS; *inset* Michael A. Hampshire © NGS. **23** *inset* William Ferguson. **24** *top* Thomas Burke Memorial Washington State Museum. #2.5E603; *bottom* NMAI #3242. **25** *top* Santa Barbara Museum of Natural History. Photograph, Wm. B. Dewey; *bottom* National Archives of Canada. **27** Hot Springs National Park. **28** *top* Reprinted from "America's Ancient Treasures," University of New Mexico Press; *bottom* © DIA, The Gordon Hart Collection, Bluffton, Indiana. © Dirk Bakker, Photographer. **29** *top* George Gerster/Comstock; *bottom* Milwaukee Public Museum. **33** *top* Ohio Historical Society, Columbus. © Dirk Bakker, Photographer, DIA; *bottom* Richard Cooke. **34** Engraving by John Faber after a portrait by Willem Verelst SI. **36** *bottom* Steve Solum/Bruce Coleman. **37** *bottom right* British Library, London.The Bridgeman Art Library. **38** *top* Special Collections, USDA, National Agriculture Library, Beltsville, Maryland; *bottom* LC Engraving by Theodore DeBry. **39** *top* Philbrook Museum of Art, Tulsa, Oklahoma; *center* The Research Libraries, NYPL/William Henry Homes, "Art in Shell of the Ancient Americas," 1883. Second Annual Report of the Bureau of Ethnology. **41** *top right;* SI; *bottom* Royal Library, Copenhagen. **42** *top* University of Alabama Museum of Natural History, © Dirk Bakker, Photographer, DIA; *center* NYPL; *bottom* DeBry, America, 1590. Rare Book Division, NYPL; *bottom left* Temple Mound Museum, Fort Walton Beach, Florida, DIA, Photo by Dirk Bakker. **43** *right* AMNH Neg.. #299117. Photo Alex J. Rota. **44** *left* The University Museum, University of Pennsylvania. **44–45** *top* Wendell Metzen/Bruce Coleman. **45** *bottom* Drawing by Herman Trappman. **47** NMAI #4224; **50** *top left* Florida Museum of Natural History, Gainesville. Courtesy DIA Dirk Bakker, Photographer; *bottom center* Illinois State Museum, Springfield. Courtesy DIA Dirk Bakker, Photographer; *bottom right inset* Peabody Foundation, Andover. Courtesy DIA Dirk Bakker, Photographer. **50–51** *bottom* Richard Alexander Cooke III. **51** *top right* NMAI #3130. **53** *top* LC; *bottom center* The British Library, London; *bottom right* Ashmolean Museum, Oxford University, Oxford, England. **54** *top* NMAI #3106; *bottom* NMAI #3038. **55** *top* Architect of the Capitol, U.S.Capitol Building, Washington, D.C.; *bottom center* NYPL, Rare Books & Mss. Div.; *bottom right* Universitätsbibliothek, Erlangen-Nuremburg, Germany. Watercolor by Konrad von Gesner, "Historia Plantarum," ca. 1555. **56** *left* Florida Museum of Natural History. **57** *top* NYPL, Rare Books & Mss. Div., Arents Collection. Jacob Bigelow, "American Medical Botany" (1817–20), Boston; *bottom* Greenville County Museum of Art, Greenville, South Carolina. "Benjamin Hawkins and the Creek Indians," Artist unknown. **58** *top* Thomas J. Blumer and Georgia Harris; *bottom left & center* Georgia Harris, photos by Thomas J. Blumer. **59** *bottom* Burgerbibliothek, Bern, Switzerland. **60** *top* Peabody Museum of Archaeology and Ethnology, Harvard University. Photograph by Hillel Burger. **61** *bottom* AMNH. **62** *top left* SI; *top inset* SI Engraving by Le Page du Pratz. **63** *bottom* Peabody Museum of Archaeology and Ethnology, Harvard University. Watercolor by Alexandre de Batz. Photograph by Hillel Burger. **64** *bottom* NMAI #451. **65** *top left* AMNH Neg.. #123222, Photo by A.R.; *top right* AMNH Neg.. #48234, photo by Julian A. Dimock; *center* AMNH Neg. #123223. **66** *top left* Alabama Department of Archives and History. Painting attributed to Nathan Negus, Photo by Robert Fouts; *top right* Collection of Emil Edward Hurja; *center right* LC. **68** *top right* Lt. Henry Timberlake, "The Memoirs of Lt. Henry Timberlake," 1762. NYPL, Rare Books & Mss. Div., Arents Collection; *center* National Archives. **69** *center right* TGI. Engraving by McKenny & Hall; *bottom* TGI. "Eleanora C. Ross," Oil on canvas by John Mix Stanley, 1844. **72** *top left* NYPL, Special Collections. Oil portrait; Artist unknown; *center left* Archives & Manuscripts Division of the Oklahoma Historical Society. Photo from painting, O.H.S. Glass Plate Coll. **73** *top left* TGI. "Osceola, the Black Drink, a Warrior of Great Distinction," Oil on canvas by George Catlin; *top right* LC. **74** *top* TGI. "Trail of Tears," Black & White wash by Brummett Echohawk, 1957. **75** *top* LC; *bottom* Roy Blankenship, Photo by Frank Speck. **76** *figure* LC; *background* Stephen Trimble. **78** *top* Jerry Jacka; *bottom* Center for Great Plains Studies Art Collection, University of Nebraska-Lincoln. **81** *top* Roger Mignon. **82** *top* Dale Coker. **83** *top* Drawing by Charles Loloma, Hopi. Ancient City Press, from "Life in the Pueblos," by Ruth Underhill, (1991); *bottom* NMAI **84** *top* John Bigelow Taylor, N.Y.C. **85** *top* Jerry Jacka; *center* Native American Painting Reference Library; *bottom* Museum of Northern Arizona. Photo by Gene Balzer. **86** Maximilien Bruggmann. **87** *bottom left* Roy Anderson/NGS. **88** *top* Maximilien Bruggmann; *center left* Jerry Jacka; *center right* Maximilien Bruggmann; *bottom* Jerry Jacka. **90** *top left* NMAI; *center left* Courtesy of Museum of Northern Arizona Photo Archives Cat.#E8554/Neg.#83c.41. **91** *top inset* NMAI; *background* Binman Productions, Susanne Page, photographer; *bottom right* Museum of Northern Arizona, Photo by Gene Balzer. **92** *top* The Philbrook Art Museum, Tulsa, Oklahoma. **93** *bottom* LC. **94** *center bottom* Museum of Northern Arizona, Photo by Gene Balzer. **97** *bottom right* Tom Bean. **100** *top left* Bibliotheque Nationale, Paris. **101** *top right* The Rare Book Room, NYPL. **102–103** Courtesy of Indian Pueblo Cultural Center, Albuquerque, New Mexico. Drawings by Tommy Montoya **104** *top* Museum of New Mexico. Museum of Indian Arts and Culture. Photo by Blair Clark; *bottom* Seaver Center for Western History Research, Natural History Museum of Los Angeles County. Photo by A.C. Vroman. **106** *top* Philbrook Museum of Art, Tulsa, Oklahoma. **107** *center right* John Telford, Special Collections, University of Utah Library; *bottom center* Colter Bay Indian Arts Museum, Riddell Advertising & Design. Heidi A. Davis, Photographer. **108** *center left* Prints and Photographs Division, LC; *bottom* Edward S. Curtis photographer, SI. **109** *bottom* Museum of Northern Arizona. **110** *bottom left* NMAI. **111** *top* Museum of New Mexico. **112** *top* The Wheelwright Museum of the American Indian. **113** *bottom right* Photographer, Sam Winkler. **114** *top left* SI Photograph by Alexander Gardner. **115** *top* Museum of Northern Arizona; *bottom* Thomas A. Wiewandt. **116** Painting by J. Verelest/ The Bridgeman Art Library, London. **118** *both* Richard Alexander Cooke, III. **119** *top* Painting by Albert Bierdstadt, Capitol Building, Washington, D.C.; *center* Rochester Museum & Science Center, Rochester, N.Y. **121** *top* Painting by George de Forest Brush/ National Museum of American Art/ Art Resource, NY; *bottom* NMNH **123** *top left* Drawing by Seth Eastman; *top right* Cranbrook Institute of Science; CIS 1914. © Robert Hensleigh Photographer, DIA. **124** *top center* Arnold Jacobs, Photo by David Sharpe. **125** *bottom* Dick West/NMAI. **126–127** *top center* Bibliothèque Nationale, Paris. **127** *bottom right* Musée du Québec, Patrick Altman, Photographer. **128** *top center* LC; *bottom left* Collection of the New-York Historical Society. **129** *bottom left* AMNH Neg.#109083, Photo by H.S. Rice; *top right* John Underhill, "News From America," 1638/Rare Book Division, NYPL. **130** *top left* Shelburne Museum, Vermont. **130–131** *bottom* Onondaga Historical Association, Syracuse, NY. **132** *top left* National Life of Vermont, Montpelier, Vermont. **134–135** *top* Gary Meszaros/Bruce Coleman Inc. **134** *bottom* LC; *center* Superstock. **135** *center left* and *right* Charles Godfrey Leland, "The Algonquin Legend of New England," Boston Houghton Mifflin and Co., 1898. **136** *top center* Painting by Father Claude Chauchetière, SJ, ca 1680/St. Francis Xavier Mission, Kahnawake, Quebec; *bottom left* Ernest Smith/ Rochester Museum and Science Center. **137** *top* David Claus, "A Primer for the Use of Mohawk Children," 1786/Metropolitan Toronto Reference Library. **138** *top* Peabody Museum, Harvard University. Photograph by Hillel Burger; *center* AMNH Neg.#31931, Photo by Thomas Lunt; *bottom left* Peabody Museum, Harvard University. Photograph by Hillel Burger. **139** *bottom* Boltin Picture Library. **140** *bottom* Phil Degginger/Bruce Coleman Inc. **141** *top left* Painting by Gustavus Hesselius/The Historical Society of Pennsylvania; *top right* Giraudon/Art Resource, NY. Painting by Edward Hicks; *center right* The Historical Society of Pennsylvania; *center left* Culver Pictures. **144** *top* Painting by John Wollaston/Collection of the Albany Institute of History & Art; *bottom* Painting by E.L. Henry/Collection of the Albany Institute of History & Art; *center right* The American Numismatic Society, New York. **145** *bottom* Paul Revere, "The Boston Massacre," Rosenwald Collection, © 1994 Board of Trustees, National Gallery of Art, Washington, hand-colored engraving. **146** *top left* Copyright British Museum; *left* Painting by William von Moll Berczy/ National Gallery of Canada, Ottawa. **147** *bottom left* Painting by Ernest Smith/Rochester Museum & Science Center, Rochester, New York. **149** *top* Painting by John Mix Stanley/Buffalo and Erie County Historical Society; *center* Buffalo and Erie County Historical Society. **150** *bottom* Painting by F. Bartoli/Collection of the New-York Historical Society. **150–151** *top* Rochester Museum & Science Center, Rochester, New York. **152** *figure* SI, Neg.#646; *background* Carr Clifton/Minden Pictures. **155** *top* National Archives of Canada, Ottawa; *center* Photo by Mark Sexton/Peabody Essex Museum, Salem, MA. **156** *left* Mike Price/Bruce Coleman, Inc.; *bottom* CMC, Neg.#S92–4660. **157** *top* National Museum of American Art, Gift of Mrs. Joseph Harrison, Jr.; *middle and bottom* Neg.#33994, photo by J. Kirschner, AMNH; *middle right* DIA, 1995, Founders Society Purchase, Dirk Bakker, photographer. **158** *top left* Neg.#23351, AMNH; *top right* NMAI; *bottom* DIA, 1995, Founders Society.Purchase with funds from Flink Ink Corp., Robert Hensleigh, photographer. **160** *top* Painting by Charles Deas, The Rokeby Collection, on loan to The Metropolitan Museum of Art, NY; *middle* DIA, 1995, Founders Society, Purchase with funds from Flint Ink Corp., Dirk Bakker, photographer; *bottom* TGI. **161** *center* Sketch by Joshua Jebb, National Archives of Canada, Ottawa. **164** *left* Peabody Museum, Harvard University. Photograph by Hillel Burger; *bottom* Royal Ontario Museum. **165** *top* Manitoba Culture, Heritage and Citizenship Provincial Archives, Winnipeg; *bottom* Milwaukee Public Museum. **167** *both* Parks Canada. **168** *top* LC; *bottom* Burton Historical Coll., Detroit Public Library. **169** *bottom* Ian Adams. **170** *top* The State Historical Society of Wisconsin, painting by Edwin Willard Deming, 1903; *bottom* Bibliothèque Nationale, Paris. **171** *bottom* LC. **172** *background* NMAI; *foreground-left* LC; *foreground-right* NMAI. **174–5** *top* Drawing by Jack Unruh/NGS. **176** *top left* Anne S.K. Brown Military Collection, Brown University Library; *top right* LC; *middle* DIA, 1995, Founders Society Purchase with funds from Flint Ink Corp. Dirk Bakker, Photographer. **178** *top* The Field Museum, Neg.#A93851.1c, Chicago. **179** *middle* Art Resource; *right* Cranbrook Institute of Science, #CIS 2292, © Dirk Bakker, Photographer, DIA. **181** *right* The Warner Collection of Gulf States Paper Corporation, Tuscaloosa, Alabama. **182** *top* William l. Clements Library, University of Michigan. **183** *top* National Museum of American Art, Washington D.C./Art Resource. **184** *bottom* Tippecanoe County Historical Association. **185** *top* Mead Art Museum, Amherst College. Museum Purchase P1939.7. Painting by Thomas Cole. **186** *figure* SI; *background* Jim Brandenburg/ Minden Pictures. **188** "From A Pictograph History of the Oglala Sioux," by Amos Bad Heart Bull, text by Helen H. Blish, by permission of the University of Nebraska Press. Copyright © 1967. **189** *top* State Historical Society of North Dakota; *bottom* "Antelope Heads," Watercolor by Paul Kane, 1846. Stark Museum of Art, Orange, Texas. **190** *top left* AMNH Neg.#120548. **190–1** *bottom* Richard A. Cooke III. **192** *top* National Museum of American Art, Washington D.C./Art Resource; *middle* Glenbow Museum, Calgary, Alberta; *bottom* SI. **193** Jim Brandenburg/Minden Pictures. **194** *top* AMNH Drawing by Edwin Godbird; *bottom* SI. **195** Barney Burstein, based on a photo by William Henry Jackson, Peabody Museum, Harvard University. **196** *bottom* 1851–1857, Bureau of American Ethnology, SI. **197** *top* AMNH, Photo by Rodman Wanamaker; *bottom* The Beinecke Rare Book and Manuscript Library, Yale University. **198** Museum of Fine Arts, Boston. Gift of Mrs. Maxim Karolik for the Karolik Collection of American Paintings 1815–1865. **199** *top* Mark Lansburgh Collection, Santa Fe. Photo Warren Hanford; *middle* Collection of Buffalo Bill Historical Center, Cody WY #NA403.100 © Dirk Bakker, Photographer, DIA. **200** *top* Glenbow Museum,

Calgary; *bottom* AMNH Drawing by Sinte. Photo: Rota. **201** *top* Illustration by Ralph Shane used by permission from "The Big Missouri Wintercount" by Roberta Cheny, Naturegraph Publishers, Happy Camp, CA; *background* Denver Art Museum. **202** *top* "First White Men Seen by Cheyenne," Watercolor, Joslyn Art Museum, Omaha, Nebraska; *bottom* Culver Pictures, Inc. **203** *top* National Anthropological Archives, SI; *bottom* Collection of Buffalo Bill Historical Center, Cody, WY. DIA, © Dirk Bakker, Photographer. **204** NMNH. **205** *top* Collection, Musee de l'Homme; *bottom* DIA, © Dirk Bakker, Photographer. **206** Joslyn Art Museum, Omaha, NE. **207** *left bottom* State Historical Society of North Dakota; *right* State Historical Society of Wisconsin. **210** *bottom* DIA. **211** *top* Photograph © 1994 The Art Institute of Chicago, Gift of Richard A. Lent in honor of Mr and Mrs Lent 1977.576; *middle left* Peabody Museum, Harvard University. Photograph by Hillel Burger; *middle right* Jonathan Hollstein Collection. **212** *top right* NMAI. **212–213** *bottom* The Beinecke Rare Book and Manuscript Library, Yale University. Photo by Walter McClintock; *top all* SI. **214** *top* The State Historical Society of North Dakota; *bottom* From Nabokov, "Native American Architecture." **215** *top* Southwest Museum, Los Angeles. Photo by Walter McClintock; *bottom* Southern Plains Indian Museum and Crafts Center. **216** *top* From "A Pictographic History of the Oglala Sioux," by Amos Bad Heart Bull, text by Helen H. Blish, by permission of the University of Nebraska Press, copyright 1967 by the University of Nebraska Press; *middle left* Richard and Marion Pohrt collection, DIA. © Dirk Bakker, photographer; *middle right* DIA, © Dirk Bakker, Photographer. **217** *top* DIA, © Dirk Bakker, Photographer. *bottom* AMNH. Photo: Dixon. **218** *top* Bernisches Historisches Museum, Switzerland; *middle*. National Gallery of Art, Washington. Paul Mellon Collection; *bottom* Joslyn Art Museum, Omaha, Nebraska. **219** *top* Painting by George Catlin, The Beinecke Rare Book and Manuscript Library, Yale University; *middle* AMNH. Photo: Harold Walters; *bottom* AMNH, Drawing by George Catlin. Photo: Logan. **221** *top* Denver Public Library, Western History Department; *bottom* Illustration by Ralph Shane used by permission from "The Big Missouri Wintercount" by Roberta Cheny, Naturegraph Publishers, Happy Camp, CA. **222** *figure* Lomen Brothers, Nome, Alaska. Glenbow Archive, Calgary, Alberta; *background* Johnny Johnson/Earth Scenes. **224** *both* The Provincial Archives of Newfoundland & Labrador. Copy Print by Manfred Buchheit. **226** *top left* Academy of Natural Sciences of Philadelphia; *center left* Oregon Historical Society; *bottom* Hudson's Bay Company Archives, Provincial Archives of Manitoba. **227** *top* Cliff Riedinger/AlaskaStock Images; *center right* CMC. **228** *top left* Denver Art Museum, Photo Department; *top center right* Notman Photo, Provincial Archives of Manitoba; *bottom* NMNH 339831. Department of Anthropology, SI. **229** *bottom* From F. Whymper, "Voyages et Adventures dans la Colombie Anglaise, L'Ile Vancouver, le Territoire d'Alaska et la California." Paris, Librairie Hachette, 1880. NYPL. **230** *bottom left* Department of Ethnology, Royal Ontario Museum, Toronto, Canada. **231** *top* Hudson's Bay Company Archives, Provincial Archives of Manitoba; *bottom right* Hudson's Bay Archives. **232** *left top, both* Hudson's Bay Company Archives, Provincial Archives of Manitoba; *bottom* Photo by Ernest Brown, Provincial Archives of Alberta. **233** *top* W. Langdon Kihn, NGS. **234** *top* Lynn Johnson/Black Star; *center inset* Culin Collection. The Brooklyn Museum; *bottom* Peabody Museum, Harvard University. Photograph by Hillel Burger. Gift of the American Antiquarian Society. **235** *bottom* Phoebe A. Hearst Museum of Anthropology. **236** *left* Charles A Mauzy; *bottom* British Columbia Provincial Museum. **237** *top* Gordon Miller, Vancouver. *right* British Columbia Provincial Museum. **238** *top left* Bill Reid, Museum of Anthropology, University of British Columbia; *center left* and *bottom* AMNH. Photo, Lynton Gardiner. **240** *top* Winter & Pond, Alaska State Library. **241** *top* AMNH. Photo, Stephen S. Myers; *center top* AMNH. Photo, Craig Chesek; *center left* AMNH. Photo, Stephen S. Myers; *center* Theo Westenberger; *center right* AMNH. Photo, Stephen S. Myers; *bottom* Photo by Eberhard Otto. Dance by Tony Hunt. **242** *top* Oregon Historical Society; *left center* Peabody Museum-Harvard University, Photograph by Hillel Burger; *bottom* Oregon Historical Society. **243** *top center* The Field Museum of Natural History with permission from Makah Cultural and Research Center. **244** *top* Museum of Anthropology, Vancouver, BC. **245** *bottom left* Peabody Museum of Archeology and Ethnology, Harvard University; *bottom right* Greg Harlin, NGS. **246** *left center* NMNH; *bottom left* Museum of Anthropology and Ethnography, Leningrad 2454.8; *top center* Beinecke Rare Book & Manuscript Library, Yale University Library. **247** *top left* and *top right* RIPSA Leningrad. **248–9** Bill Holm. **250** *top center* AMNH; *bottom* Winter & Pond, Alaska State Library. **251** *top right* AMNH; *center right* Royal Ontario Museum. **252** *top left* Yukon Archives, McBride Museum Collection. **253** *bottom* AMNH Photo by Edward Dossetter. **254** *center left* Museum of Anthropology, British Columbia; *bottom* AMNH. Photo by Edward Dossetter, 1881. **255** *top* "Spirit Dancing: The Practice of Our Ancestral Religion," by Ron Hilbert Coy/The Thomas Burke Memorial Washington State Museum, #1988–101/1. **256** *top* Janet Foster/Masterfile; *center* NMNH. **257** *top right* Addison Doty; *bottom* Phoebe Hearst Museum of Anthropology; *bottom right* NMNH. **258** *top center* NMNH; *bottom* "Hunting Caribou from Kayaks," by Luke Anguhadluq/CMC. **259** *top* Bill Holm; *bottom right* NMNH. **260** *top left* Kjell Sandved, NMNH; *bottom* Joe Tailrunnili, Inuit Art Section, Department of Indian and Northern Art, Ottawa, Canada. **261** *top* National Archives of Canada; *top right* The British Museum, London. **262** *top* J. (Kive Toruk) Moses, Nome, Alaska. Collection, Barbara and Milton Lipton. Photo by Geoffrey Clements; *bottom* Kjell Sandved/NMNH. **263** *center right* NMNH; *bottom* Glenbow Archives, Calgary, Alberta. **264** *top left* NMNH Photo-Arctic Studies Center; *bottom left* The British Museum, London/The Bridgeman Art Library. **265** *top* Scott Polar Research Institute, University of Cambridge, England; *bottom* The Beinecke Rare Book and Manuscript Library, Yale University. **266** *top* Culver Pictures, Inc.; *bottom* NMNH. **267** T.H. Manning/NGS. **268** *figure* Nevada Historical Society; *background* Bill Ross/Westlight. **270** *top left* National Geographic Magazine, Jan.1945/NGS, Painting by W. Langdon Kihn; *center* The Bettmann Archive; *bottom right* Kjell B. Sandved. **272** *top left* Gift of Florence O.R. Lang, Montclair Art Museum, Montclair, NJ.; *bottom* Santa Barbara Museum of Natural History. **274** *center left* The Granger Collection. **274–275** *top* Huntington Library, San Marino, CA. **275** *bottom* San Gabriel Mission Parish, "Stations of the Cross," Artist unknown. Photograph by Henry Groskinsky. **276** *center left* Phoebe Hearst Museum of Anthropology; *bottom left* The University Museum, University of Pennsylvania; *bottom center* NMNH, Photograph by Kjell B. Sandved. **278** *bottom left* Collection of Jerry Grossmann/Photo by James McInnis. **278–279** *top* Denver Public Library, Western History Department. Photo by Thomas McKee. **279** *center* National Park Service, Nez Perce National Historic Park, Spalding, Idaho. **280** *top* Denver Museum of Natural History; *bottom* NYPL, Rare Book & Mss. Div. **281** *top* American Philosophical Society; *bottom* Amon Carter Museum. **284** *center left* Thomas Burke Memorial Washington State Museum. Photo by Eduardo Calderon. **285** *bottom* The Snite Museum of Art, University of Notre Dame. **286** *left* Royal Ontario Museum, Ethnology Department. **287** *top* Jesuit Missouri Province Archives-DeSmetiana Collection. **288** *bottom left* The Bettmann Archive. **289** *top* Oregon Historical Society. **290** *both* Phoebe Hearst Museum of Anthropology. **291** *top* Suquamish Museum, Suquamish Tribal Archives. **292** *top left and right* SI. **293** *center* Nez Perce National Historic Park & Museum, Spaulding, Idaho; *bottom right* SI. **294** *bottom* Montana Historical Society, Helena. **295** *right* David Muench; *center* SI, Bureau of American Ethnology Collection. Photograph by Charles Milton Bell. **296** *figure* SI, National Anthropological Archives; *background* Tom Bean. **298** *top* From "A Pictographic History of the Oglala Sioux" by Amos Bad Heart Bull, text by Helen H. Blish, 1967, by permission of the University of Nebraska Press. **299** *center* Wyoming State Museum; *bottom* The Granger Collection. **302** *top* SI; *bottom* Drawing by Frank B. Mayer/National Archives. **303** *center bottom* Royal Canadian Military Police Museum; *bottom* Glenbow Museum. **304** *lower left* The Granger Collection; *bottom* Mannfred Gottschalk/Tom Stack & Associates. **305** *top* LC. **306** *top* and **307** *bottom right* David Muench. **308** *top left* The Bettmann Archive; *bottom* "Long Walk" by Raymond Johnson/Navajo Comm. Coll. Press. **309** *top* Colorado Historical Society. **310** *top center* Colorado Historical Society; *bottom* "Sand Creek Massacre" by Robert Lindneux. Colorado Historical Society. **311** *left top* SI; *top right* Gregory Perillo/The Perillo Museum of Western Art. **312** *top* Courtesy New York State Library, Albany. Photo: J.S. Meyer; *bottom center* SI. **313** *bottom* SI. **316** *center* The Bettmann Archive. **317** *top right* The Granger Collection. **318** *top* Michael Sample; *top right* Royal Canadian Military Police Museum. **319, 320** From "A Pictographic History of the Oglala Sioux" by Amos Bad Heart Bull, text by Helen H. Blish, 1967, by permission of the University of Nebraska Press. **322–323** *bottom* SI **323** *right bottom*. SI/National Anthropological Archives. **324** *top* The Beinecke Rare Book and Manuscript Library, Yale University; *center left* From "A Cheyenne Sketchbook" by Cohoe/Commentary by E. Adamson Hoebel and Karen Daniels Petersen, Copyright © 1964 by the University of Oklahoma Press. **325** Hamburgisches Museum für Völkerkunde. Photo by Frederick Weygold. **326** *Figures* SI, National Anthropological Archives; *background* Grant Heilman/Grant Heilman Photography. **328** *top* SI; *center* Buffalo Bill Historical Center, Cody, WY. Chandler-Pohrt Collection, Gift of the Searle Family Trust and Paul Stock Foundation. **329** *lower left* The Granger Collection; *lower right* Ed Vebell. **330** *left center* Milwaukee Public Museum. **330–331** *center* SI. **331** *top right* Western History Department, Denver Public Library; *center right* America Hurrah, NYC. **332** *top* LC; *center* Photo by David F. Barry, State Historical Society of North Dakota. **333** *center right* SI. **334** *top left* Culver Pictures; *bottom* Library Company of Philadelphia. **335** *top* DIA, Gift of Richard and Marion Pohrt, © Dirk Bakker, Photographer. **336** *center* Western History Collection, Denver Public Library; *center left* North Dakota State Historical Society. **337** *top* Western History Collections, University of Oklahoma Library; *bottom right* Western History Collections, University of Oklahoma Library. **338** *top right* St. Marie Among the Iroquois, Onondaga Co. Department of Parks, Liverpool, NY. *bottom left* SI. **340** *top right* Photo by Thomas Marquis, *ca.*1928, from "The Warrior Who Fought Custer," 1931, University of Nebraska Press; *center left* Milwaukee Public Museum. **341** *top right* Western History Collections, University of Oklahoma Library; *center left* and *bottom* Peabody Museum, Harvard University. Photographer unknown. *ca.* 1880's. **342** *center left* "A Class of Indians in Fort Marion, Florida with teacher (Mrs. Gibbs)" by Zo-Torn, Kiowa artist, 1877, from "1899 Plains Indians Sketchbooks of Zo-Torn and Howling Wolf"; *bottom* Western History Collections, University of Oklahoma Library. **343** *center* Francis LaFleche. **344** *left* The Granger Collection; *bottom* Montana Historical Society. **345** *top* Philbrook Museum of Art. **346** *top* Western History Collections, Denver Public Library. **347** *bottom* Culver Pictures Inc. **348** *bottom left* SI. **349** *top* Brown Brothers; *right* The Newberry Library; *bottom* "Indian Between Two Cultures," 1882.18.32. Wo-Haw Drawing. Department of Photographs and Prints, Missouri Historical Society. **350** *top* The Heard Museum; *bottom* Chihuahuan Desert Research Institute. **351** *top right* SI; *center right* E. DeLoria Collection, University of South Dakota; *bottom* The Newberry Library. **352** *left bottom* Nebraska State Historical Society; *center* Choctaw Nation of Oklahoma. Photo by James McInnis. **353** "Sunset of a Dying Race," Photograph by Joseph Kossuth Dixon, *ca.* 1913. SI. **354** Dmitri Kasterine. **356** *top left* UPI/Bettmann News photos; *bottom* Private Collection. **357** *right top* M. Timothy O'Keefe/Bruce Coleman, Inc; *right center* James McInnis. **358** *top* UPI/Bettmann. **359** *top* The Heard Museum; *bottom* The Lundoff Collection. **361** *top* "Papa Would Like You" by Alvin Eli Amason; *bottom* Ray Atkeson. **362** *top left* National Archives; *bottom* Randy Mike, courtesy of Jim Hubbard/Shooting Back, Inc. **363** *top* Peter S. Mecca/Black Star; *bottom* "My Dog Spot," 1982, by Richard Glazer-Danay. **364** *top left* Wide World; *center left* Dan Budnik/ Woodfin Camp & Associates; *bottom* Martin J Dain/Magnum Photos. **365** *top left* Dan Budnik/Woodfin Camp & Associates; *top right* UPI/Bettmann. **366** *top* UPI/Bettmann. **367** *center right* Kevin Barry McKiernan/Magnum Photos; *bottom left* Diosa Summers/Photo by Judy Ware. **368** *top left* Eagle of Dawn Artist Limited; *top right* Philip Long/School of American Research, Santa Fe; *center right*; Jerry Jacka; *bottom* Lois Gutierrez de la Cruz/Photo by Jerry Jacka. **369** *top* Photo by Jerry Jacka; *bottom* Teri Greeves/Photo by Mark Nohl. **370** *top* (detail) "Clear Cut Columbus," 1993, by Jesse Cooday. Mixed Media; *bottom* Joel Gordon. **371** *top* Dan Budnik/Woodfin Camp & Associates; *center right* Dan Budnik/Woodfin Camp & Associates. **372** *bottom* AP/Wide World Photos. **373** *right top* and *center* Bob Haozous, Courtesy of David Retting Fine Art, Santa Fe. **374** *top* Marcia Keegan; *bottom* Dan Budnik/Woodfin Camp & Associates. **376** *top* Bob Sacha; *center inset* Grand Casino Mille Lacs. **377** *top* Philbrook Museum of Art; *center* Thomas Hoepker/Magnum Photos; *bottom* Bob Sacha. **378–379** *top* David Alan Harvey/Magnum Photos. **379** *right* C. Roberts. **380** *center* AMNH Neg.#2104. **381** *bottom* McCord Museum of Canadian History. **382** *top* AMNH Neg.#K16468. **383** *center* AMNH. Neg.#326748. **384** *top* AMNH Neg.#4639. **385** *bottom* Courtesy Dartmouth College Library, Hanover, NH. **386** *center* Special Collections, NYPL. Photograph by Edward L. Curtis. **Dust Jacket: front** Satank (Sitting Bear) Kiowa/Sarcee, SI. **back** *clockwise from top left*: "Mató-Topé (Four Bears) Mandan Chief," painting by Karl Bodmer, Joslyn Art Museum; Ah-En-Leith, Zuni, LC; Redwing Nez, Navajo, photograph by John Running; Sitting Bull, George W. Scott, Collection of Kurt Koegler, New York; "Eleanora C. Ross," painting by John Mix Stanley, Thomas Gilcrease Institute, Tulsa; Navajo woman, LC; Kwakiutls in ceremonial dress, SI, National Anthropological Archives; Natchez man, SI, Ethnology Department; "Peo-Peo-Mox-Mox," painting by Paul Kane, Royal Ontario Museum.

READER'S DIGEST COMPUTER GENERATED ART

Maps: **23, 93** Susan Welt. *Decorations*: **11, 15, 21, 27, 85, 105, 113, 201, 207, 210, 218, 224, 252, 303, 321, 329, 358, 368–69** Susan Welt; **39, 54, 129, 148, 272, 285, 287, 336, 343, 344, 350** Georgina Sculco. *Illustration*: **131** Wendy Wong.

INDEX

Page numbers in bold type refer to illustrations and maps.

D

E

F

READER'S DIGEST PRODUCTION

Assistant Production Supervisor: Mike Gallo
Prepress Specialist: Karen Goldsmith
Quality Control Manager: Ann Kennedy Harris
Production Supervisor: Mary S. Nemeth

Book Production Director: Ken Gillett
Prepress Manager: Garry Hansen
Book Production Manager: Patricia M. Heinz
U.S. Prepress Manager: Mark P. Merritt

Engraver: Lanman Progressive
Printer: R. R. Donnelley & Sons
Willard Manufacturing Division